HEAVEN

— A History —

HEAVEN

— A History —

Colleen McDannell and Bernhard Lang

YALE UNIVERSITY PRESS
NEW HAVEN AND LONDON 1988

For our friend
John F. Hurdle

Set in Linotron Goudy Old Style by Best-set Typesetters Ltd, Hong Kong; printed and bound by Murray Printing Corporation, U.S.A.

Library of Congress Cataloging-in-Publication Data

McDannell, Colleen.
  Heaven: a history.

  Bibliography: p.
  Includes index.
    1.   Heaven – History of doctrines.   2. Future life –
History of doctrines.   I. Lang, Bernhard, 1946–
II. Title.
BT846.2.M37   1988   236′.24′09   88-10765
ISBN 0-300-04346-5

CONTENTS

Preface   x

1   The Dawn of Heaven   1
The Semitic Background: Communicating with the Dead   2
Yahweh Alone: No Promise for the Dead   7
Apocalypticism: The Promise of Resurrection   11
Hellenistic Judaism: The Promise of Heaven   14
Jewish Views of the Afterlife in the First Century   19

2   Jesus and the Christian Promise   23
Jesus: No Marriage in Heaven   24
Paul: Spiritual Bodies   32
Revelation to John: The Heavenly Liturgy   37
The Christian Promise   44

3   Irenaeus and Augustine on our Heavenly Bodies   47
A Compensation for Martyrs: The Glorified Material World   48
The Ascetic Promise: A Heaven for Souls   54
The Ecclesiastical Promise: Physical Beauty Eternalized   59
The Varieties of the Patristic Paradise   67

4   Medieval Promises   69
Paradise Garden and Heavenly City   70
The Empyrean Heaven as a Place of Light   80
Everlasting Contemplation of the Divine   88
The Promise of Love   94
Medieval Heavens   108

5   The Pleasures of Renaissance Paradise   111
The Pleasures of a Paradise Garden   112
Meeting Again in Heaven: Lovers and Saints   123
The Geography of Heaven   142

6   God at the Center: Protestant and Catholic Reformers   145
Protestant Reformers: Luther and Calvin   146
The Catholic Reformers   156
The Pious and Ascetic Middle Class   167
Theocentric Heaven   177

7   Swedenborg and the Emergence of a Modern Heaven   181
The Immediacy of Life after Death   184
The Material Character of Heaven   190
Matter in Motion   199
Society, Friendship, and Love   209
Modern Heaven   224

8   Love in the Heavenly Realm   228
Pre-Romantic Precursors: Milton and Swedenborg   229
Heaven as Union of Lovers   233
Love and Marriage   257
Life in the Heavenly Home   264
The Triumph of Human Love   273

9   Eternal Motion: Progress in the Other World   276
Kinetic Revolution in Heaven   277
Persisting Theocentric Traditions   287
Spiritualism: A Thick Description of Heaven   292
Anthropocentric Heaven   303

10   Heaven in Contemporary Christianity   307
Modern Heavens: A Wish...   309
...and a Theology   313
The Decline of the Modern Heaven   322
The Symbolist Compromise   326
Realized Eschatology: Heaven on Earth   332
Theocentric Minimalism   335
Theology without Promise   345
What Happened to Heaven?   349

Paradise Found: Themes and Variations   353

Notes   359
Author Index   398
Subject Index   402

ILLUSTRATIONS

Figures

1	The universe as seen by the ancient Semites	4
2	The ritual universe of the ancient Semites	4
3	The ritual universe of early Judaism	8
4	The Heavenly Liturgy in the book of Revelation	42
5	The universe of Dante, c. 1300 (*Mark Musa*)	86
6	The Spiritual universe of Swedenborg	192
7	*God's Outline of History (Harvest House Publishers)*	341

Plates

1   A Roman lady enters the Elysian Fields, 4th century   16

2   Life in Elysium, 4th century (*Bayerische Staatsbibliothek, Munich*)   17

3   The New Earth as Paradise Restored, 12th century (*Warburg Institute*)   71

4   The Heavenly Jerusalem as a city, c. 1275 (*University Library
of Ghent, Belgium*)   75

5   The universe as seen by Cosmas Indicopleustes, 6th century   81

6   Rose Window above front entrance of Reims Cathedral, France,
late 13th century (*Giraudon, Paris*)   87

7   Redeemed couple holding hands, c. 1210–20. Central portal of
Notre Dame Cathedral, Paris (*Roger-Viollet, Paris*)   99

8   The soul as a queen, enthroned with Christ, 12th century
(*Bayerische Staatsbibliothek, Munich*)   104

9   Christ and Mary enthroned as lover and beloved, 12th century
(*Alinari, Florence*)   105

10   Giotto, *The Last Judgment*, 1306 (*Alinari, Florence*)   113

11   Nardo and Andrea di Cione Orcagna, *The Glory of Paradise*,
1350s (*Alinari, Florence*)   114

12   The Blessed beholding their Savior/Paradise, Cathedral of Torcello,
c. 1200 (*Alinari, Florence*)   116

13   Paradise. Detail of *Last Judgment*, c. 1420–30 (*Bibliotheca
Hertziana, Rome*)   117

14   Hieronymus Cock, *Paradise*, 16th century (*Rijksmuseum, Amsterdam*)   120

15   Giovanni di Paolo, *Souls and the Trinity*, c. 1438–44 (*British Library*)   124
16   Giovanni di Paolo, *Souls in Paradise*, c. 1438–44 (*British Library*)   124
17   Giovanni di Paolo, *The Blessed Virgin in Paradise*, c. 1438–44
(*British Library*)   124
18   Lucas Cranach, *The Golden Age*, 1530 (*Alte Pinakothek, Munich*)   122
19   Fra Angelico, *The Last Judgment*, c. 1431 (*Alinari, Florence*)   129
20   Fra Angelico, *In Paradise*, detail of *Last Judgment*, c. 1431   130
21   Fra Angelico, *The Dance of the Blessed*, detail from *Last Judgment*
(*Alinari, Florence*)   131
22   Giovanni di Paolo, *Paradise*, c. 1445 (*Metropolitan Museum of Art,
New York*)   132
23   Dieric Bouts, *Paradise*, 15th century (*Giraudon, Paris*)   135
24   Luca Signorelli, *The Coronation of the Elect*, 1499/1502 (*Alinari,
Florence*)   138
25   Luca Signorelli, detail from *Coronation of the Elect*, 1499/1502
(*Alinari, Florence*)   139
26   Jean Bellegambe, *Paradise*, c. 1526–30 (*Staatliche Museen, East
Berlin*)   141
27   Life Everlasting, 1554   149
28   The Blessed in adoration of the Trinity, 1569 (*Staatliche
Kunstsammlungen, Kassel*)   158
29   'Le paradis', Louys Richeome, S.J., 1607 (*British Library*)   159
30   The Blessed Virgin in heaven, Antonino Polti, O.P., 1575
(*New York Public Library*)   161
31   A Marian vision of life everlasting, Peter Canisius, S. J., 1560   162
32   Jean Fouquet, *The Blessed Virgin and the Trinity*, 15th century
(*Giraudon, Paris*)   164
33   Peter Paul Rubens, *The Last Judgment*, 1615–17
(*Alte Pinakothek, Munich*)   179
34   John Flaxman, *The Sea Shall Give up the Dead*, 1784
(*Walwins, Gloucester*)   187
35   William Sharp after Benjamin West, *Female and male angel*, 1779
(*British Library*)   220
36   Emanuel Swedenborg, *Cities in the Spirit World*, 18th century   190
37   Emanuel Swedenborg, *Cities in the Spirit World*, 1889   191
38   G. Köler, *The Heavenly Jerusalem*, 1630   195
39   Johann Baptist Zimmermann, Mary in the Glory of Heaven, 1733
(*W.C. von der Mülbe, Dachau*)   197
40   Nicolas de Mathonier, *Life Everlasting*, 1611 (*Helmut Knirim
Münster*)   214
41   Reginald Knowles, *Children in the Other World*, 1938   222
42   William Blake, *The Last Judgment*, 1806 (*Stirling Maxwell Collection,
Glasgow Museums and Art Galleries*)   237
43   William Blake, *Vision of the Last Judgment*, 1808 (*A.C. Cooper
for The National Trust, London*)   238
44   William Blake, *Vision of the Last Judgment*, 1808 (*Courtauld
Institute of Art, London*)   244
45   William Blake, *Satan Watching the Endearments of Adam and Eve*,

ILLUSTRATIONS

1808 (*Museum of Fine Arts, Boston*)   240

46   William Blake, *The Reunion of the Soul and the Body*, 1808   241

47   William Blake, *The Meeting of a Family in Heaven*, 1808   242

48   William Blake, *The Day of Judgment*, 1808   243

49   William Blake, *Epitome of Hervey's "Meditations among the Tombs,"* c. 1820–25 (*Tate Gallery, London*)   245

50   Dante Gabriel Rossetti, *The Blessed Damozel*, 1879 (*Fogg Art Museum*)   254

51   Dante Gabriel Rossetti, *Lovers, newly met*, 1876 (*Fogg Art Museum*)   255

52   John Byam Shaw, *The Blessed Damozel*, 1895 (*Godfrey New Photographics for Guildhall Art Gallery, London*)   256

53   Charles Kingsley, *Charles and Fanny as Amor and Psyche*, c. 1840 (*Angela Covey-Crump*)   263

54   Charles Kingsley, *"Of such is the kingdom of heaven"*, 19th century (*Angela Covey-Crump/British Library*)   264

55   Frederika Bodmer, *Crossing the River*, c. 1880 (*Mary Evans Picture Library, London*)   267

56   *"I'll See You in Heaven, Honey!"*, 1977 (*Chick Publications*)   310

57   Grave marker with couple (*C. McDannell*)   311

58   The ideal family – here and hereafter (*C. McDannell*)   312

59   Lee G. Richards, *Family Reunion in the Other World*, 1949 (*President of the Church of Jesus Christ of Latter-day Saints*)   319

60   *The Descent of the Modernists*, 1924   337

61   Charles Anderson, *The Rapture*, 1974 (*Leon Bates*)   339

62   Georg Meistermann, *Apocalypse*, 1963 (*Urbschat, Berlin*)   344

PREFACE

When we first began to discuss our research with friends and colleagues
we were frequently met with surprised reactions. How could anyone write
a history of heaven? Have you been there? Doesn't everyone know that
heaven is just God and a few people who fly around like angels? Once
initial astonishment was registered, almost immediately another flood of
comments followed. Have you read this? Have you seen that painting?
You must not forget this particular group or that author. We faced two
reactions simultaneously: one told us that eternal life is just what it says
– eternal. It does not change. The other response was to overwhelm us
with suggestions about where to look for new images, descriptions, or
portrayals. Heaven was everywhere – in theology, in literature, in art, in
preaching, at the movies. On second thought, we were told, perhaps you
can write a history of heaven.

We have not written a history of heaven. We have written a history of
the images Christians use to describe what happens after death, when
time ceases and everlasting eternity begins. Typically, Christians believe
in two lives. One spans the time between birth and death and the second
reaches out beyond death. This second existence has a beginning but no
end. It is characterized by unsurpassable happiness in a place commonly
termed "paradise" or "heaven." Whether heaven commences immediately at death, or following a period of purging, or at the end of human
history, eventually the righteous hope to be rewarded with eternal life.
This book assembles and interprets the ways in which Christians have
understood everlasting life – life beyond death, after the millennium, in
the final state.

For many Christians throughout history, their entire existence from
birth to death is a preparation for eternal life. In the hope of reaching
heaven and its rewards, people have endured poverty and exploitation,
trials, and sufferings, even persecution and martyrdom. For heavenly
reward, people made – and continue to make – substantial donations to
ministers and priests, churches, and monasteries. The issue of life beyond
death is central to the Christian experience. But what is it that will be
experienced at the end of Christian lives? What will an eternity in
heaven be like?

If our research has proven conclusive about anything, it is that Christians have struggled with those questions for centuries, arriving at a variety of answers. In learned tomes of theology, in sermons, letters of consolation, poetry, the visual arts, and countless unrecorded conversations, possible solutions are given. For the most part, those solutions are not weak generalizations or flimsy explanations but strikingly detailed presentations. Visionaries claim to have travelled to the beyond; philosophers present their reasoned speculations; artists paint their inner visions. Their descriptions show a remarkable variety. For some, life everlasting will be spent on a "glorified" earth. Others think of heaven as a realm outside of the universe as we know it. There are those who predict an eternal life focused exclusively on God. Still others describe individual friendship and marriage. Eternal rest vies with eternal service. The Christian creed asks its adherents to believe in "life everlasting" but not in the details of heavenly existence. There is no basic Christian teaching but an unlimited amount of speculation.

For the theologian, the lack of agreement on what goes on in heaven may be disappointing. For the philosopher, the idea that heavenly doctrines provide no fixed ontological structures can be frustrating. For the historian, however, such change and variety is a delight. Rather than taking the diversity of views on heaven as evidence of its chaotic and unpredictable nature, we have struggled to find order and meaning within the confusion. *Heaven: A History* is an attempt to extricate from the wealth of beliefs and images those elements which show greater persistence over the centuries. Although at times we discuss the images of death, the millennial heaven on earth, the religious lifestyle needed to attain heaven, and the philosophical debates over immortality, these are not our main concern. We have assembled the major images used by Christians to describe paradise and heavenly activities, placed those ideas in a social and religious context, and assessed their long-term cultural implications.

The construction of our chapters reveals what we see as the most critical periods and personalities in the development of ideas of heaven. At times, we have focused on representative individuals – Augustine, Swedenborg – and at others, on standard historical periods – the Middle Ages, the Renaissance, our contemporary world. In both, we have looked for metaphors, analogies, assumptions, and symbols which structure the understanding of eternal life. We have provided an in-depth analysis of some sources and authors and have assembled a large number of diverse documents to substantiate general themes and trends. As historians, we are interested in how older images are reformulated and criticized in the light of new ideas, experiences, or social events. We wondered how the cultural climate of the period affects, and is affected by, constructions of eternity. We tried to sort out and systematize available images and ideas while presenting to the reader a sense of their richness and diversity. Although often looking like the play of unbridled fantasy, concepts of heaven have their own logic, history, and meaning.

This book is specifically a "social and cultural history" of heaven. This means that we have taken as a starting point the traditional understanding of heaven as a *community* of saints. This community could be as large as everyone who has ever lived or as small as one soul and the divine. We wanted to investigate what that community does for eternity: how do the saints behave? How do they interact with one another and how does God relate to them? By asking these questions we entered into a mostly unknown world of heavenly employments, progress, marriage, and societies. Although many Christians have been satisfied with Teresa of Avila's dictum that "God alone suffices," others have imagined a world busy with human activities. Whether heaven is composed of only the gaze of the beloved (God or a human companion) or the complex interactions of countless souls meeting, teaching, working and playing with one another, it has a social structure.

Social interaction cannot take place without utilizing a set of symbols and meaning systems. Heaven — perceived as a culture itself — has its own set of assumptions, beliefs, expressions, and values. The saints do not only interact with God or with each other. Their interactions are productive of ritualized activities, institutions, and ideologies. Heavenly culture consists variously of eternal worship, intimate lovemaking with Christ, playing in the fountain of life, or singing 'Holy, Holy, Holy.' We found that some saints are naked, some sport business suits, and others wear the finest silks. In some accounts they stand motionless in front of the divine presence, and in others they play pianos, attend wedding ceremonies, and visit earthbound friends. In each of the heavens we studied, there exists a set of ideas which control the behavior of the blessed.

In order to decipher the society and culture of heaven — or rather the societies and cultures of heavens — we freely chose from a great variety of European and American sources. In doing so we broke the academic rule of sorting sources into popular and elite literatures and dealing with each separately. We found that the distinction between upper-class 'beliefs' and lower-class 'superstitions' must be used with great caution. While medieval scholastics and numerous twentieth-century theologians look down at "vulgar" concepts of heaven, such two-tiered opinions have not always existed. In the nineteenth century, for instance, most erudite theologians and ministers believed in the same qualities of heaven as did popular writers and spiritualists. Although we certainly were open to the idea that the canon of Christian thinkers — Augustine, Aquinas, Dante, Luther, Kant, Tillich — would dominate the understanding of life after death, we found the contrary to be true. The most creative insights into the beyond often came from those seldom spoken of in scholarly circles: Mechthild of Madgeburg, Emanuel Swedenborg, Elizabeth Stuart Phelps. Frequently, those who made the most sense of heaven had no schooling in theological discourse at all. Poets, painters, novelists, epitaph-writers have attacked the issue of life after death with a boldness which puts most educated clergy to shame. Consequently, Dante Alighieri receives no greater honor than Dante Gabriel Rossetti, Aquinas shares a chapter with Gerardesca of Pisa, and both Paul Tillich and Hal Lindsey are presented as contemporary theologians with equal insights on the beyond. Our eclectic collection of sources not only helps in understanding how Christians imagine heaven, but also serves as a reminder that Christianity is a diverse set of symbols, beliefs, rituals, and images. No one group or set of authors dominates.

One of the privileges of writing a preface is to tell the reader what one's book is not. We must confess that while we give readers the impression of comprehensiveness by starting with the origins of heaven in ancient Judaism and ending with contemporary Christianity, this is in no way an all-inclusive study. We have with great pain and trepidation omitted many heavenly visions, refused to add one more illustration, or place one more writer in an endnote. This book cannot be read without the feeling that "they left out the most important source." We hope that our research will spur others to search their own special fields of interest and competence for more definitive answers to the question, "what next?" *Heaven: A History* is a starting-point.

Finally, we must admit that the future life is of interest to us only as it explains the mystery of this life. Our book is not a map of the beyond. We are not theologians, visionaries, or spiritualists presenting our own other-worldly reflections. We study heaven because it reflects a deep and profound longing in Christianity to move beyond this life and to experience more fully the divine. The ways in which people imagine heaven tell us how they understand themselves, their families, their society, and their God. They give us insight into both the private and public dimensions of Western culture. Changing ideas about love, friendship, work, God, and spiritual growth in the other life can serve as guidelines for understanding cultural ideas and ideals of this life. Heaven is not merely a collection of idle fantasies, a projection of human hopes, or a reflection of religious doctrine. We would go a step beyond Ludwig Feuerbach's admission that heaven is the key to the deepest mysteries of religion and venture that heaven can be used as a key to our Western culture.

* * * *

It is not always the case that two heads are better than one. When two set out to work together they find that they need twice as many libraries, friends, and advisors. Our studies have taken us to a variety of libraries around the world. To all accommodating librarians we give thanks as we do to individuals and institutions which have loaned illustrations acknowledged in the 'List of Illustrations.' There are a few specialized collections that are not accessible to the public, which were particularly gracious in allowing us to use their treasures: the Bibliotheca Hertziana (Max Planck Institut) in Rome, Italy, and the "Institut für Grenzgebiete der Psychologie und Psychohygiene" in Freiburg, Germany. The reference librarians at the USAREUR Library and Resource Center in Heidelberg patiently ordered inter-loan books on the most unusual topics without complaint. Thank you.

The advice of specialists and friends has proved to be invaluable. We can credit them with helping us locate sources and avoid some, but not all, mistakes in both fact and interpretation. On both sides of the Atlantic we thank: Peter Brown, Charles Trinkaus, Margaret Marsh, Jane Brown, Morton D. Paley, Charles Lohr, Mary Boyce, Allen F. Davis, Horst G. Schwebel, and Peter Dinzelbacher. For their help with inter-loan books, xeroxes, diagrams, photography and editing, we are much obliged to Robert Baldock, Eberhard Bauer, Helga Bender, Edeltrud Büchler, Bernhard Dachner, John W. Dickason, Marilyn Fraser, Deanna Thompson, and Elisabeth Wacker. Absolutely indispensable was the cooperation of John F. Hurdle. John created several computer-generated diagrams, supervised the word-processing, and served as a wise arbitrator between the authors. His sense of humor and justice prevented many oncoming quarrels between two equally strong-willed and stubborn writers. To him and to all who helped with this seemingly everlasting project, thank you.

──── CHAPTER ONE ────

The Dawn of Heaven

In the ancient world, belief in life after death was widespread, considered normal, and not generally weakened by skepticism. Death ended the visible form of our life on earth, but did not extinguish existence altogether. While the images provided by tradition and learned speculation may not have promised an idealized or "better" life, the complete denial of an afterlife remained the exception rather than the rule. The majority of ancient authors, in spite of periods of doubt, assumed that some form of life existed after death.

If we are to understand the Christian concept of heaven, we must begin by clarifying the speculations on the afterlife by the ancient Jews. Living in the mountains and valleys between the Jordan river and the Mediterranean, the Jews struggled to maintain their religious outlook and culture in the face of vassalage and colonization by powerful foreign overlords. The Hebrew Bible and other writings not included in this collection developed in the colonial period which began in the ninth century BCE and did not end until the second century CE when the Romans virtually destroyed all sizeable Jewish existence in Palestine. Israel's written legacy thus was formed during a period of foreign domination, although it preserves the traditions and vague memories of the semi-nomadic patriarchs, Moses the liberator, and the glorious age of King Solomon.

Conflicting responses to foreign rule, Israel's exposure to a variety of cultural influences, and certain enduring basic human needs all functioned to create a multi-layered response to the question of life after death. These ancient Jewish responses to the afterlife may be simplified into four major perspectives. The first layer of tradition, which originated in the Semitic world in which the Jews lived, pictures the cosmos in three levels – earth, heaven, and netherworld. The dead reside in the lower realms where they can be placated by their earth-bound relatives. At the highest level sit the sky gods, separated both from the gods of the dead and from the earth. Those who live on the earth – between the upper and lower worlds – may call on the residents of either level to help them with their earthly problems.

The second layer of ancient Jewish tradition rejects communication with the dead. The belief in life after death is minimized and Jews are asked not to venerate their dead ancestors. Even speculation about the fate of the dead is avoided. Only Yahweh, Israel's national God, may be worshipped. As a God of the living, and not of the dead, Yahweh alone can provide for the defeat of foreign rulers. The gods of the netherworld and the sky are no longer recognized as significant actors in the cosmic drama. The Jews are left alone with a god who demands total obedience and dedication.

The third perspective moves beyond the insistence that the dead have no importance and instead includes them in the fate of the kingdom of Israel. This viewpoint is decidedly political and ties the dead to a renewed Jewish community. After the destruction of the colonial empires, Israel's God will resurrect the faithful among the dead and permit them to join the living in an earthly kingdom. All the hardships which the dead and living have undergone will be erased and a full life will be lived on earth. Both the dead and the living eventually will share in the glory of a new era of Jewish supremacy.

The final current turns away from national and political concerns and focuses on the individual's quest for justice in a world of adversity. While the second view considers the dead to be powerless and places them in the netherworld, and the third has them resurrected to a life on earth, the fourth perspective elaborates a philosophical and mystical concept of the soul's ascent to heaven. The nation may languish under colonial rule, but good souls look forward to being with the God in whom they trust. The ascent of the immortal soul to heaven allows for the continuation of the individual, if not the nation.

These ancient Jewish concepts of life after death provide the backdrop for understanding New Testament attitudes toward the afterlife. Each was present in first-century Palestine and had an impact on how later Christians would understand heaven. The Sadducees, Pharisees, and Essenes – Jewish groups contemporary to Jesus – expressed views of the afterlife consistent with earlier outlooks. By understanding those earlier viewpoints, and by speculating on how they were seen by first-century Jews, we can gain a better insight into the environment in which Christian concepts of heavenly life grew and developed.

The Semitic Background: Communicating with the Dead

The ancient Near East incorporated a vast diversity of peoples who, for the most part, have left only archeological ruins and brief texts in cryptic languages to help scholars understand their cultures. We know of the Assyrians, Babylonians, Canaanites, and Phoenicians, as well as the Hebrews, from biblical references, excavations of their cities, and modern translations of their various written records. During the eighteenth century, scholars created the word "Semitic" as a shorthand term to refer to this group of people who shared similarities in language and culture. Not all peoples of the ancient Near East were a part of this Semitic world. The Sumerians and the Egyptians, the Hittities and the Persians were important ancient cultures whose languages were quite different from those of the Semites. Although later biblical writers condemned the influence of other cultures on emerging Judaism, the Semitic basis of Israelite culture cannot be denied. It was the Semitic understanding of the afterlife which later Hebrew writers rejected or at least hoped to modify.

The ancient Semites pictured the world as a big house with a three-tiered structure: an upper realm of the gods (heaven), a middle human world given to us by those gods (earth), and a lower part consisting of a great cave situated deep below the surface of the earth (the netherworld or Sheol) (Fig. 1). In contrast to the upper world of the gods, Sheol housed the dead and the infernal deities. Although ancient people pictured Sheol as a dark and silent place, we must not think of it as hell. A deity called Mot, "Death," ruled over the dead and the infernal gods. Since human beings lived between heaven and Sheol, they could expect to be influenced by both the upper and lower worlds.

Human communication with the divine world of the upper layers and the gods of the lower world was of paramount importance. The inhabitants of the earth might be rich ladies, wealthy landlords or merchants, proud warriors, aristocrats or princes; yet they felt essentially weak and dependent on the gods. Only by establishing temples, sponsoring priests and temple choirs, offering lavish sacrifices, chanting elaborate prayers, and listening to wizards and prophets could the people be assured of divine blessing and benevolence. Fertile flocks, abundant harvests, victories in battle, and everything belonging to success, prosperity, and peace depended on the graciousness of the gods residing in either heaven or Sheol.

Consequently, ancient Near-Eastern ritual was complicated and manifold. Only the priests, thoroughly trained in private and public ritual and lore, knew the intricacies of communication with the upper and lower worlds. To achieve earthly benefits, rituals either appealed to the dead and the gods of the netherworld, or addressed the powers of heaven (Fig. 2). To appeal to the dead meant basically to call upon lost relatives residing in Sheol to aid the living. Ancestor worship, carried out by or on behalf of genealogically related individuals, venerated dead forefathers and perhaps foremothers. From these dead relatives the living

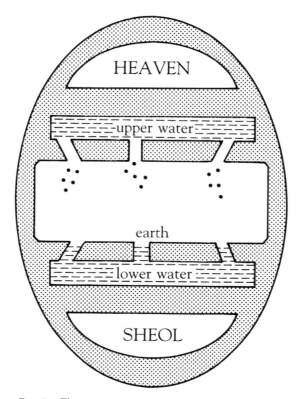

Fig. 1. The universe as seen by the ancient Semites.
[Devised by B. Lang and J.F. Hurdle]

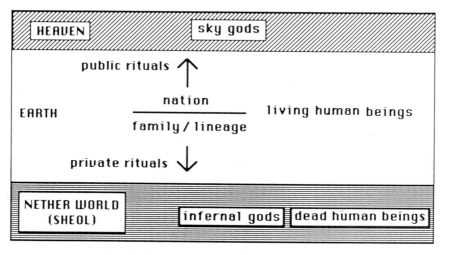

Fig. 2. The ritual universe of the ancient Semites.
[Drawing by B. Lang and J.F. Hurdle]

expected personal protection and, more importantly, numerous off-spring. The veneration of ancestors assumed organized ritual forms. In one such ritual, the participants consumed large quantities of wine and poured out wine for the dead. During this rite everybody present got drunk, including the dead. A simpler ritual consisted in placing offerings of water and food near the family tomb.[1]

Since ancestor worship did not involve the community at large, we will call it a private ritual. Small groups of family members in private worship venerated their ancestors without the participation or inter-ference of the larger political or ethnic group. However, when the gods of heaven rather than the dead were invoked, the whole community became involved. Regular sacrifices on behalf of the king, and through him the whole society, were offered in state temples by priests. These were public rituals which went beyond the confines of an individual family or clan. Important public liturgies celebrated the cycle of the agricultural year: the sowing and reaping of grain, picking fruit, and eating the first fruits of the season. They connected the people not with their dead relatives, but with the gods of the sky who were responsible for rain and the rainy season. Without this communion with the sky gods, they believed, no vegetation could grow in the arid zones of the Near East.

Both kinds of ritual — the public one addressed to the celestial gods and the private one appealing to the ancestors in the netherworld — existed at the same time and were practiced by the same people. The people decided which of the two to perform according not to what they hoped to gain from the gods, but for whom the gain was intended. If a family member would benefit, then a private ritual was performed. If the community as a whole benefited, a public liturgy was conducted.

To die meant to change one's place in the ritual universe. This change did not occur immediately at the onset of death, because the process of bringing another inhabitant into the netherworld was a slow one. First the family had to bury the body, thus removing it from the sight of the celestial gods. Burial usually took place in an underground vault or simply by covering the body with earth. Removing the body from the surface of the earth brought it into contact with a new and lower realm of being. While the flesh decayed and the bones dried, a shadowy replica of the deceased appeared and descended into a vast underground mausoleum.[2]

What was life like there? The Semites, unfortunately for scholars, specialized in establishing ritual contact with the world of the dead, not with speculating about life in Sheol. We know they believed that in the netherworld the dead met and joined the ancestors, prompting the bibli-cal expression that a dead person "goes to his fathers [ancestors]" or is "gathered to his people [kin]." The shadowy life of the dead was permanent and did not fade away. The different degrees of life in the netherworld depended on one's past earthly existence and on the regularity with which one's offspring engaged in certain rituals. Someone who died at a ripe old age and who received regular offerings of water and food placed near the tomb by faithful descendants achieved the best fate. Residing in the upper and perhaps somewhat lighter part of Sheol, that ancestor could help his or her descendants by bestowing powerful blessings. Ancestors might also get angry, withhold their blessings, and eventually do harm. The ancestors thus became "gods" who could affect the lives of the living in dramatic ways.[3]

If living relatives neglected their veneration or interrupted their ancestor-offerings, the fate of the dead worsened. Rather than residing in the lighter regions, they would be relegated to the lowest and rather unpleasant areas of the netherworld. People who died the death of criminals or on the battlefield, without having their bodies properly buried, populated the lower regions. In an Israelite mock-dirge, a king who tyrannized his vassals ended up in the depths of the abyss. After his death in a battle, he descended into Sheol where he lay in mud and filth, covered with worms. His arrival, duly noted by kings who preceded him, confirmed their suspicion that now "you are as weak as we are." They too led a shadowy life of their own, with dreamy pomp and ceremonial. With hardly visible forms, sitting on thrones, they greeted their distinguished new arrival with only a flicker of interest and emotion.[4]

The living contacted the dead not only through ancestor worship but also through mediums and wizards who had access to the netherworld. In one necromantic session described in the Bible, King Saul attempts to learn the outcome of an imminent battle. Finding that his normal channels of communication with the divine realm – dreams, priestly manipulation of lots, the advice of prophets – have failed, he turns to other means. Out of desperation Saul resorts to a necromancer. In a night-time consultation, Saul's medium digs a hole in the crust of the earth so that the world of the living may be joined to the realm of the dead. Eventually the witch announces that a deceased prophet has ascended for questioning. Only she can see the "old man, wrapped in a robe," and only she can actually communicate with the spirit and pass on the messages received. The consultation ends with the spirit's clear announcement that Saul will lose his life in battle the very next day. The dead expect him soon in the other world. Then the fading spirit returns to the darkness and silence of Sheol. Saul, of course, dies as foretold during the consultation.[5]

The story presents us with a glimpse of an afterlife in which the dead, although apparently deprived of material substance, retain such personality characteristics as form, consciousness, memory, and even knowledge of what happens on the other side. While life in the netherworld is less than appealing, the dead have the power to aid or do harm to the living. Such power permits them to function as gods. Private rituals, conducted by kin, emphasized the bonds between the residents of the earth and the netherworld. These private rituals contrasted with public liturgies whose focus centered on the concerns of the larger community. Although our knowledge of this early stratum of Semitic thought is sketchy, we can see a shadowy afterlife where the status of the dead depends on the veneration of the living, and the state of the living may be influenced by the inhabitants of the netherworld.

Yahweh Alone: No Promise for the Dead

Institutions such as ancestor worship and necromancy were condemned by later biblical writers as inherently pagan and not a legitimate part of Israel's religion. By the eighth century, the political pressure on Israel exercised by the powerful Assyrian empire had become more and more intolerable. As small vassal kingdoms, the Israelite states of nothern Israel and southern Judah paid heavy tribute and survived under military supervision. Their overlords noted any delay of payment and attempts at rebellion were crushed immediately. In this situation of permanent crisis, a prophetic movement advocated the exclusive worship of one god, Yahweh. The worship of all other gods and goddesses was to be abandoned.[6]

The prophetic movement expected that Israel's God, the only one with real power, would eventually intervene and alter the political scene in favor of his people. This party, which scholars term the "Yahweh-alone movement," not only banned the worship of the sky gods but also insisted on outlawing the cult of the dead. The Yahweh-alonists forbade ancestor worship because they perceived it as a magical deviation from true worship. Magic, according to sociologists Hubert and Mauss, "is not part of an organized [communal] worship, but private, secret, mysterious" and is often prohibited by the controlling group. The Yahweh-alonists believed that ancestor worship, which gave preference to kin concerns, slighted national interests. For them, national and public matters assumed clear priority over private and family affairs.[7]

After the Assyrian destruction of the northern Israelite kingdom in 722 BCE, the Yahweh-alonists became even more convinced of their cause. They attributed the military disaster to the neglect of the one God whose exclusive worship they advocated. In the now truncated Israel (the small southern kingdom of Judah), King Hezekiah (728–699 BCE) attempted a cultic and legal reform. A description of his efforts survives in the book

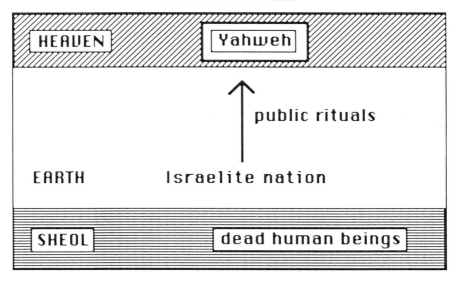

Fig. 3.   The ritual universe of early Judaism.
[Drawing by B. Lang and J. F. Hurdle]

of Exodus. According to the king's legislation, first-born sons must be "given" to Yahweh. By urging people to perform this symbolic dedication of their sons to the national God, the new law redefined the meaning of an ancient ceremony. In earlier times, the first-born son was expected not only to care for his aged parents but also to bury them properly and venerate them as gods. In the Semitic world, the first-born directed his concerns to his parents – living or dead. Now, this ceremony had been transformed and the first-born was not to address the ancestors or some deity of the netherworld, but Yahweh the state God. The divine claim, "you shall be men consecrated to me," stated the aim of the reform: Israelites now belonged to the national God rather than to a family deity or divinized ancestors (Fig. 3).[8]

Possibly, King Hezekiah's reforms failed or remained unimplemented. Almost a century was to pass before the Yahweh-alone movement became the decisive factor in official Judean policy. The reform accomplished its goal when, in 623 BCE, King Josiah proclaimed Yahweh the only god to be worshipped. The biblical report explained that "Josiah got rid of all who called up ghosts and spirits [of the dead], of all household gods and idols, and all the loathsome objects." By taking the decisive step toward monotheism, the reform drastically reduced private worship, especially ritual activities relating to the dead. While the Yahweh-alonists still tolerated the placing of food near or in the tomb as a funerary offering, they stripped it of its cosmological significance. What used to be a real sacrifice to the gods of the underworld was reduced to a simple gesture of convention or tradition. The dead might be fed and thereby kept alive, but the reformers condemned any other contact. Denied the exercise of influence over the living, the ancestors faded into the distance, into the eternal darkness of Sheol.[9]

In order to keep the dead and the living apart, the new law placed stricter taboos on dead bodies. Those new taboos intensified the separation between the living and the dead. Traditionally, a human corpse was polluted and could pollute others for only a short period of time. This period could be as short as the actual time of mourning during which the flesh decomposed and the spirit journeyed to Sheol. Once the body decayed into a pile of dry bones, the remains no longer endangered the living. The new orthodox believers prolonged the pollution period by declaring that although the dead themselves were powerless, the bones could harm the living. Nothing could be more unclean, and therefore be more dangerous, than dead bodies. We hear of this fear of contacting impurity in a New Testament passage. Hypocrites, according to Jesus, are like whitewashed tombs "full of dead people's bones and all uncleanness." Rather than acting as a source of aid or even a means of predicting the future, the dead and their remains were to be avoided.[10]

King Josiah's reform outlawed certain traditional practices concerning the dead but did not create new beliefs to replace earlier traditions. A more philosophical examination of the meaning of death and the afterlife appears in the book of Job, which dates from the fifth century BCE. The book of Job also devalues the role of the dead, continuing in the trend begun with King Hezekiah. It insists that the dead have no knowledge of the living and cannot influence those on earth. Even the fate of their descendants remains a mystery to them. Referring to a dead householder, the book asserted that "his sons may rise to honor, and he sees nothing of it; they may sink into obscurity, and he knows it not." The traffic between ancestor and offspring, so vital in polytheistic thought and ritual practice, disappeared. The living and the dead must be eternally separated.[11]

Job and his contempories agreed with the older pessimistic traditions of the Semitic world that the fate of the dead was a deplorable one. Who wants to exist in "a land of gloom and chaos, where light is as darkness"? Such remarks remind us of the Babylonian epic of Gilgamesh which portrays the netherworld as "the house wherein the dwellers are bereft of light, where dust is their fare and clay their food." In spite of this gloomy view of the land of the dead, however, death may have its benefits. As Job pointed out in a skilful eulogy, death does place us outside our earthly misery. Death resolves the problem of social inequality by releasing us from servitude. Since the dead no longer can help the living, they are freed from being involved in human troubles. Sheol, if not a place of happiness, at least can be appreciated as a place free from the trials of earth.[12]

For the devout worshippers of the God of Israel, however, even such rest might be undesirable. The book of Sirach (Ecclesiasticus) explained that upon death, fellowship with Yahweh ceased. "Who will praise the Most High in Sheol," it queried, "in place of the living who give him thanks? When a man is dead and ceases to be, his gratitude dies with him." It is when "he is alive and well," emphasized the writer, "that he praises the Lord." Just as the exiles living in Babylonia could not sing the Lord's song on foreign soil, so the dead were not able to offer praises in a polluted cave. In Sheol they would have to venerate a deity of the netherworld, rather than a god of the sky and the inhabited land of Israel. As a sky god, Yahweh remembered the dead no more, "for they are cut off from [his] hand." Whoever withdrew from life, also withdrew from the Lord of life.[13]

Consequently, there could be no relationship or reciprocity between Yahweh and the dead. From the Semitic world-view we already know that the dead had no contact with the celestial gods. When the dead descended to the netherworld they praised the infernal gods. The new reform, however, commanded the Jews, even those in Sheol, not to worship any other god but Yahweh. The Yahweh-alonists reached into the afterlife and robbed the dead of their infernal gods. These two taboos – that of not relating to any deity but Yahweh and the prohibition of the sky gods in the netherworld – condemned the dead to a meaningless existence in weakness. The dead had neither the care of Yahweh nor the protection of the gods of the underworld.

The dead, existing in a "godless" environment which rendered them powerless, also could not ask for consolation from the living. Since the realms of the living and the dead were completely separated, no communication could take place between them. The residual veneration in the form of funerary offerings notwithstanding, the dead expected nothing from their descendants. Those on earth in turn no longer waited for their ancestors' help. Consequently, the living looked solely to Yahweh. "You are the sons of Yahweh your God," reminded the new legislation, "you shall not cut yourselves or make any baldness on your foreheads for the dead." As the major representative of the public religion of Yahweh, the high priest especially avoided any ritual connection with the dead. Priests were even asked to stay away from their own parents' funeral. A public figure was not to be defiled by private pollution.[14]

From the time of King Josiah onward, orthodox Israelites no longer defined themselves in relation to their ancestors but exclusively in relation to their national God. Since only Yahweh should be honored, the reformers condemned ancestor worship and replaced it with veneration of the patriarchs and Jewish martyrs. As public rather than private heroes, the martyrs "vindicated their race, looking to God and enduring torments even to death." When Jesus Sirach praised Israel's ancestors as men of renown whose "wealth remains in their families," he carefully pointed out that only "through God's covenant with them" did their families endure. Ancestral blessings did not contribute to their prosperity. National and communal rituals and orientation replaced more private, family-oriented forms of worship.[15]

In contrast to the Semitic ritual universe, King Josiah's reform sealed off the netherworld. Israelites simply excluded the dead from ritual consideration. Far from being the powerful and influential ancestors, the deceased became weak shadows of negligible vitality. By not being able to praise the only God, they were doomed to a meaningless existence in the eternal darkness of Sheol. Israelite theology focused on the practices of a this-worldly religion rather than on futile speculations about the life of the dead. The pious who met with unfortunate circumstances on earth had to be promised redress in this life. Job, faced with a miserable earthly existence, was not promised rewards after death. Whatever other messages his story presented, the implication of its last page is clear. God rewarded Job for his patience and devotion with health, wealth, and family. Job received his blessing, "twice as much as he had before," on earth and not in the afterlife. The Judaism of King Josiah's reform held no promise for the dead.[16]

Apocalypticism: The Promise of Resurrection

In the summer of 586 BCE the Babylonian army abruptly brought the Judean monarchy to an end. Home rule status, granted at first by the Babylonian authorities, quickly collapsed. Now the Babylonians integrated their former tribute-paying vassal into their system of provinces. Israel no longer existed on the political map of the Middle East. Those who felt that Yahweh promised the Jews a special place in history could not accept the demise of the political state of Judah. The dream of an independent Israel restored by divine intervention continued. Frequently, in times of political upheavals and turmoil, the fire of independence flared. Whenever one superpower vanished, giving way to new rulers – the Babylonians to the Persians, these to the Greeks, and eventually the Greeks to the Romans – the hope for a shift in political status swelled.

Many Jews, recognizing the difficulty of achieving independence, merely sought to make better political arrangements with their alien rulers. Others had greater expectations and hoped that the new rulers would leave Israel a niche to exist as an independent state. The most extreme version of this hope assumed not only that Yahweh intended to restore Israel's statehood but that he would also permit the dead to live in the new Jewish commonwealth. The belief in a "bodily resurrection" held that the dead must not be deprived of the blessings of a new age. Restored to full bodily life, they would live for many years in a new world, enjoying a renewed life.

The concept of a bodily resurrection and life in a restored world had nothing in common with the views of the afterlife contained in King Josiah's reform. Indeed, Jewish writers borrowed the notion from the ancient Iranians. The idea of bodily resurrection first appeared in the teachings of the Iranian prophet Zoroaster (ca. 1400 BCE). Zoroaster's firm convictions about the soul's fate after death included the belief that after mortal life the soul would be individually judged and either rewarded in heaven or punished in a less pleasant place, hell. Complete happiness, as Zoroaster understood it, required more than just the eternal existence of the soul. It rested upon the reunion of body and soul, not in a heavenly paradise, but here on earth. Zoroaster expected a general resurrection of the dead, a universal divine judgment, and an eventual cleansing of the earth. Restored to its original perfection and beauty, the world would then serve as the true and eternal kingdom of Ahura Mazda, the Creator. In this new world men and women would live forever.[17]

In the sixth century BCE, Jews living in Babylonia and other areas in the orbit of Iranian influence became aware of the similarity between certain Zoroastrian beliefs and their own hopes of liberation. Iranian religion helped Jewish theologians shape their own tradition by serving as a catalyst, causing Judaism to define itself by contrast as well as by imitation. In the process of encounter, debate, and stimulation by outside philosophies, Jewish theologians adapted new doctrines, such as a con-cept of resurrection, to their speculations on the fate of the dead.

The first Jew to use the Iranian idea of a bodily resurrection was Ezekiel, a prophet active in the Babylonian exile. Between 585 and 568 BCE he delivered a series of oracles of hope, which included visions of a gloriously rebuilt Jerusalem with a magnificent temple. In one of his visions Ezekiel recognized a vast plain covered with dry human bones, bleached by the sun. Such a plain recalls a Zoroastrian funeral ground, since worshippers of Ahura Mazda never buried their dead. They let the bodies lie for a year under the sun so that rain might fall upon the carrion and birds devour the flesh. Zoroastrian doctrine insisted that the Creator, who made each human being, reassembled the scattered parts of the body at the general resurrection. Ezekiel, after being shown the plain strewn with human bones, was commanded to prophesy to the bones and announce their resurrection. Immediately, the skeletons were reas-sembled and bodies were formed. Again, God asked Ezekiel to speak and to order the winds to breathe on the bodies. The bodies then came back to life, and the resurrected people returned from Babylonian exile to their homeland in Palestine. The vision, with its marked similarities to Zoroastrian belief, may have been inspired by ideas easily available to this sixth-century prophet living close to areas of mixed Elamite and Persian population.[18]

The Jewish prophets obviously redefined and adapted the Zoroastrian concept of resurrection to fit their religious and political outlook. While the original Iranian doctrine implied the end of human history, as well as the end of death, the prophet took it to refer to a miracle that inaugurated a new era in Israel's national life. Ezekiel linked the idea of resurrection to national concerns, rather than to universal, cosmological expectations. Ezekiel expected not a new universe, but a renewed Jewish commonwealth free from foreign oppression.[19]

By the third and second centuries BCE, the weight of heavy taxes claimed by Greek rulers and the Jewish persecution in 167–164 BCE rekindled the fire of national pride, resistance, and expectation of a better future. Political rebels and religious radicals, receptive to martyrdom, heard the Zoroastrian teaching once again. The book of Daniel, which dates from these days of persecution, expected that "of those who lie sleeping in the dust of the earth many will awake." One Jewish martyr is reported to have declared, "It was from Heaven that I received these [limbs]; for the sake of His laws I disdain them; from Him I hope to receive them again." Denied a chance for political independence and prosperity during the present time, martyrs and heroes looked to a future time when God would return his people to their proper place in the universe.[20]

While the kingdom God created would be never-ending and eternal, the lifespan of the resurrected was limited. According to the book of Enoch, for instance, they would live "five hundred years" or "a long life on earth as [their] fathers lived." Their "fathers" were not their immediate ancestors, but rather the biblical patriarchs who, according to Genesis, lived to such ripe ages as 895 and 930. After a long, peaceful life which made up for their difficulties on earth, they would eventually die.[21]

The expectation of resurrection and the establishment of a divine kingdom provided one answer to the question of why God did not intervene on behalf of his people. Far from being indifferent to Israel's political fate, God was simply waiting for the special day that he in his wisdom had chosen. Only then would the faithful be resurrected, restored to bodily life, and established in their universal kingdom on earth. From this apocalyptic perspective, God would release the dead from Sheol so that they could appreciate a renewed earth. No longer would his people be condemned to a meaningless existence either in this world or in the netherworld. Those who suffered on earth would eventually die again, but only after an extended period living a full life in God's new kingdom.

Hellenistic Judaism: The Promise of Heaven

Not all the Jews living after the political disaster of 586 BCE, the end of the Judean monarchy, were nationalists espousing an apocalyptic hope. Many made their peace with their various overlords and accepted foreign rule. As long as the overlords granted free exercise of Jewish ritual, they saw no reason to be dissatisfied. Jews who took such a stance, especially those with a more philosophical outlook, explored the fate of the dead in a way vastly different from that of the nationalists. The idea of a glorious communal future with a restored Israelite nation faded into the background, giving way to speculations about the *post-mortem* future of individuals. When considering whether an afterlife in eternal darkness was all that could be reasonably expected, some concluded that there must be more to life everlasting than Jewish tradition assumed. Would not God rescue his friends from the darkness of Sheol?

The earliest effort to put forth a more philosophical, individualistic response to life after death occurred in two psalms. The poet-author of Psalm 73 begins by recounting how he envies the lot of the wicked. "I saw how they prosper," he recalls, "no pain, no suffering is theirs." Tempted to conclude that his own virtues remain unrewarded, he checks himself with the realization that such ideas would betray the order of society. Instead he turns to the thought that the prosperity of the wicked is fleeting. All their good fortune will become as insubstantial as a dream when it is past, because God's judgment will bring swift destruction. Yet this still does not satisfy the psalmist. Pondering the problem further, he asks: what does he possess that the wicked do not? He has his misfortune, but he also has God. "Yet I am always with thee," he cries, "thou holdest my right hand; thou dost guide me by thy counsel, and afterwards wilt receive me with glory." He concludes his prayer by asking rhetorically, "Whom have I in heaven but thee?"[22]

Psalm 49 discusses the same theme even more explicitly. The rich, boastful, and arrogant wicked will be unable to bargain with God. Their fate is to perish and be sent to the abyss of Sheol. In Sheol they will survive without their riches, denied any glimpse of light. The righteous, on the other hand, can be confident: "But God will ransom my life,/ He will take me from the power of Sheol." The psalmist appears quite aware that this is a new doctrine. He presents the new insight as the solution of a difficult "riddle" and enthusiastically asks "all who inhabit this world" to hear his teaching.[23]

Both poets belonged to well-known families of Jerusalem temple singers, the Sons of Asaph and the Sons of Korah. Being employed by the Temple, they thought of themselves as friends of God who enjoyed his permanent and, indeed, everlasting fellowship. Their songs demonstrated a strong element of personal concern and sentiment. The strong "I" of the compositions, primarily referring to the singer himself, only by implication concerned the rest of the community. The singer revealed his personal convictions and professed his own belief. While an individual, everlasting life with God might have only been intended for the privileged Temple singer, the psalms were used to promise a hopeful future for all.

By saying that God would eventually "receive" them after their deaths, the psalmists boldly reused vocabulary traditionally associated with figures like Enoch and Elijah. These two pious men had not died; God had bodily assumed them into heaven. From the psalmists' point of view, what was possible for them could be possible for others as well. Thus the concept of heavenly assumption was redefined in less extraordinary terms. God "received" his faithful *after* death, without having to resort to the miraculous procedure of taking them away while still alive. Searching the Scriptures, the psalmists found the ancient story of heavenly assumption and creatively expanded it. They translated the myth of heaven, once only possible for the special few like Enoch and Elijah, into a hope and expectation for the many.[24]

The psalmists, however, failed to give any description of this heavenly realm. They did not present any intimation of a future existence which surpassed anything we know in this life. The poets instead spoke of a continuing fellowship with God and only vaguely referred to future glory. Speaking during a time which lacked a firm and acknowledged doctrine of an afterlife in heaven, the psalmists offered only inconclusive speculations. Their reflections were "but jets of religious feeling, spasmodic upleapings of the flame of love of existence," explains theologian Andrew B. Davidson. Theirs was a "love of God, which flickers most wildly and convulsively just when it is about altogether to expire." Convinced of God's love for the righteous, the psalmists made the bold conclusion that God recognizes the goodness of his creatures and has the power to place them in a celestial realm.[25]

The psalmists' conviction that God can confer the privilege of residence in heaven (instead of Sheol), combined with the ethical argument that righteousness must be rewarded, was eventually supplemented by a third idea. Wherever diaspora Jews met Greek intellectuals, the idea of an immortal soul surfaced. The Homeric concept of surviving death as weak, emaciated shades was not the only Greek idea of the afterlife.

According to other mythical speculations, the entire person existed after death. It was up to the gods either to punish or to reward the dead. The rewards could be quite enticing.[26]

In a second-century BCE relief decorating a Greek philosopher's tomb, two figures recline in an other-worldly meadow while a winged character pushes a wicked person out of the Fields of the Blest. While the tomb relief is too faded to reproduce here, later paintings reveal a similar focus on relaxation and pleasure. A pagan fresco in a fourth-century CE catacomb in Rome pictures an angelic figure introducing Vibia, an elderly lady, to the other world. The mural portrays her sitting among men and women at a refreshing meal (Pl. 1). In a fourth-century manuscript we find another glimpse of an enjoyable afterlife. The illumination narrates a passage of Virgil's *Aeneid* in which some of the dead are said to "train on grassy rings, others compete in field games, others grapple on the sand; feet moving to a rhythmic beat, the dancers move in formation as they sing!" (Pl. 2). The classical world called this privileged area of relaxed enjoyment the Elysian Fields or the Isles of the Blest and the dead entered it symbolically through a gate.[27]

Ancient writers like Plato (428–347 BCE) and Cicero (106–43 BCE) located the Isles of the Blest in a heaven above the stars. The rationale which moved the Elysian Fields upwards centered on Plato's reasoning that the soul contained the most vital aspects of the person. Once released from its imprisonment in the body, the spirit became not weaker but actually stronger and more powerful. Plato assumed that, as with all that is refined and godlike, the soul rose upward. Rather than sink down

Pl. 1.   A Roman lady enters the Elysian Fields. 4th century CE pagan catacomb of Vincentius, Rome, Italy. Johannes Leipoldt, *Die Religionen der Umwelt des Urchristentums* (Leipzig: Deichert, 1926), no. 166

16

Pl. 2.   Life in Elysium. Late 4th century CE. Engraving after an illumination in the Vatican. Virgil
manuscript Vat. lat. 3225, fol. 52, recto. Angelo Mai, *Virgilii picturae antiquae ex codicibus
Vaticanis* (Rome: n.p., 1835), pl. 49

into the netherworld, the righteous soul ascended. Thus, the individual
spirit not only survived death, it found its ultimate home in the transcendent, celestial realm of the Platonic ideas. It made no sense for the
Elysian Fields to remain in a lower position. Thus philosophers rejected
the earlier Homeric tradition and established a precedence for Jewish
thinkers.[28]

Greek doctrines about the soul made a lasting impression on Jewish
and eventually Christian beliefs. Both the biblical book of Wisdom (first
century BCE) and the work of Philo of Alexandria (ca. 20 BCE–45CE)
reflect a concern with the nature of the soul. While the book of Wisdom
accepted the soul's immortality as a simple fact, Philo developed and
explained the Greek idea. By creating a unique synthesis of Platonic
philosophy and biblical tradition, Philo paved the way for later Christian
thinkers. For him, death restores the soul to its original, pre-birth state.
Since the soul belongs to the spiritual world, life in the body becomes
nothing but a brief, often unfortunate, episode. While many human
souls lose their way in the labyrinth of the material world, the true
philosopher's soul survives bodily death and assumes "a higher existence
immortal and incorporeal." In addition to being immortal and immaterial, it seems to be asexual – neither male nor female.[29]

In heaven the soul joins the incorporeal inhabitants of the divine
world, the angels. In certain cases it advances even higher and lives in
the world of ideas. If it moves even higher it can live with the deity

17

itself. Whereas Enoch, according to Philo, resides among the pure ideas, only the soul of Moses has entered the highest realm to live with God. Another possibility for the soul would be not to ascend further, but to descend again into the material world. By adopting the Platonic view that "some, longing for the familiar and accustomed ways of mortal life, again retrace their steps," Philo conceded the possibility of reincarnation. Far from living a static, shadowy life in Sheol, the dead now possessed a variety of options.[30]

Like Philo of Alexandria, Hellenistic Jews showed no interest in recreating a Jewish national state. They considered Judaism to be a philosophy, a system of belief, rather than the ideology of a state. The individual embraced the Jewish faith and preferred a contemplative and private life to an active and political one. Ideally, the Jew should be a philosopher who like Philo led the retired life of a thinker preparing the soul for its celestial ascent. Preparation for death served as a basis for meditation, rather than for getting ready for a resurrected society.

Unlike the earlier Jewish monotheists, the Hellenistic Jews believed in the immortality of the individual human soul. For those Jews influenced by Greek ideas, at death angels approached and greeted the soul and invited it to mount a chariot which traveled to a far-off place. The body remained behind to be buried a few days later. The virtuous soul lived on the Isles of the Blest of Greek mythology or in the transcendent realms of Plato's eternal ideas. There the soul spent its everlasting days in the company of other souls, angels, and ultimately God. Although the imagery remains vague, we see a heaven of philosophers contemplating abstract ideas and ideal forms without being distracted by other people or the necessities of human life. Scholars might continue their research, which would be easier after the soul's release from the body. The body no longer hampered and distracted the spirit. While Philo's views imply that there must be a heavenly community of souls and angels, his philosophical method prevented him from commenting on celestial social life. He held his imagination under the firm control of reason and did not speculate on matters beyond it.[31]

The philosophical contemplations of Hellenistic Jews deepened the musings of the poets of Psalms 73 and 49. While they sang of the mercy and justice of a God whose power saved them from a meaningless existence in Sheol, they failed to articulate how this would occur. Platonic thought provided the system for transforming the weakened shade trapped in Sheol into an immortal soul destined for the highest realms of existence. For some Hellenistic Jews who turned away from the idea of overthrowing the seemingly endless stream of colonial rulers, an individual heaven appeared more rational than the promise of a renewed kingdom of Israel where people lived to be nine hundred years old. They rejected both the Yahweh-alonist idea of the futility of the afterlife and the nationalists' hope for a restored communal existence. Instead, they answered their questions about life after death by insisting that the individual soul, freed from bodily confines, would achieve immortality.

Jewish Views of the Afterlife in the First Century

By the first century CE, when Christianity first appeared, three Jewish views of the afterlife were prevalent. Out of those three perspectives on what happened after death a fourth one, the Christian response, emerged. The teachings of first-century Sadducees, Pharisees, and Essenes were not unique but extensions of the Yahweh-alonist, apocalyptic, and philosophical views of the afterlife. This variety furnished Jewish sages, lay people, sectarians, and philosophers with material for debate and speculation. Although the ancient sources are sketchy in describing fully these three responses, we can reconstruct them tentatively. More particularly, we can speculate on the people to whom they appealed. New Testament Christianity derived much of its understanding of eternal life from the sectarian disputes which provided for a vigorous religious life in Roman-ruled Palestine.[32]

The Yahweh-alonists' lack of interest in life after death appeared in the first century with the philosophy of the Sadducees. The Sadducees were probably upper-class Jews who promoted strict adherence to the Scriptures and voiced a conservative opinion on questions of ritual and belief. Unfortunately, no works of the Sadducees have been preserved and we have only brief mention of them in the writings of the Jewish historian Josephus (37–100 CE), the New Testament, and their philosophical opponents. Since virtually all ancient sources on the Sadducees are unsympathetic to them, and do not attempt to understand their perspective on death, we can only offer a provisional and somewhat speculative evaluation of why they believed that life ended at death.

According to Josephus, the Sadducees held that "the soul perishes with the body." While other Jews argued for some type of survival, the Sadducees held that Scripture contained no such assurance. A possible clue to the Sadducean this-worldly spirit and denial of an afterlife might be their participation in the wealthy priestly aristocracy. Tradition attributed to the Sadducees a this-worldly attitude, reporting that they "use vessels of silver and gold all their lives" and do not "afflict themselves in this world" as did ascetic-minded Jews. According to Paul they found satisfaction with the slogan, "let us eat and drink, for tomorrow we die." Given such a background, we can postulate that they lived a comfortable life and expected no further compensation for hardship in a future one. Like the Yahweh-alonist reformers, they insisted that proper religious sentiments must be directed toward earthly existence. Their own social position in Palestine did not lead them to think that a better life could be experienced after death.[33]

If the Sadducees were involved in priestly activities or associated with the priests, then they most likely had a heightened sense of the meaning of religious rituals. To perform the Temple ritual allowed the priests to function in God's presence. Enjoying the presence of God in the Temple, in spite of the difficulties inflicted upon the general Jewish society, meant experiencing the fullness of the divine in this world. Their ritual activities allowed them to feel that they were closer to God than other Jews. Such a life on earth required no compensation after death since "a day in thy court [temple] is better than a thousand elsewhere." Being able to be close to God while living on earth meant they did not have to look forward to death bringing them into contact with the divine. Modern theology calls this type of speculation "realized eschatology" because it assumes that the promise of a full, heavenly existence can occur within one's own lifespan. Consequently, not only would the Sadducees have a prosperous material life – thus making a blessed afterlife superfluous – but they could also fully experience the presence of God here on earth. The Sadducees, carrying on the tradition of the Yahweh-alonists, believed that God was a God of the living and that at death the soul withered away.[34]

While the Sadducees expressed their skepticism on the soul's fate after death, the Pharisees asserted their belief in survival. This popular movement sought to reconstruct Judaism as a culture whose identity was shaped by meticulous observance of religious law, especially regulations concerning purity. They formed small urban groups whose strict observance of the law was meant to be a model for others to emulate. Believing that the ritual purity of the Temple priests should be achieved by all Jews, they sought to limit contact with non-Pharisees.[35]

We can only speculate about how the Pharisees viewed the possibility of life after death. Since they were primarily concerned with the ritual dimension of Judaism, only fleeting indications of their beliefs can be found in ancient sources. Presumably, the Pharisees shared the view of those prophets who predicted the glorious re-establishment of a renewed state of Israel and the destruction of her enemies. Accordig to Josephus, they assumed the imperishable nature of the soul with the important qualification that "the soul of the good alone passes into another body." From an early Christian account, in the Acts of the Apostles, we learn that the Pharisees accepted the resurrection of the dead. Paul, a Pharisee "born and bred," must have already developed a perspective on the resurrection before becoming a Christian. Could the doctrine of the resurrection have added to the Pharisaic expectation of a completely regenerated Jewish nation?[36]

If the Pharisees hoped to renew Judaism through the application of rigorous purity laws, then perhaps they assumed that at some point in the future God would take over that process of purification. Eventually, the faithful among the dead would participate in a renewed society, a society in which one could be a Jew without having to compromise. At the resurrection of the dead and the re-establishment of the Jewish nation, all would be able to share in the purified fellowship which had been so difficult to achieve under pagan rule. Like Ezekiel, the Pharisees might have hoped that the dry bones of a conquered Israel would rise up and claim their place on a renewed earth. The apocalyptic expectation of a purified Judaism connects the Pharisees with the writers of the book of Daniel.

While the Sadducees denied the resurrection of the dead and the Pharisees upheld it, a third Jewish movement adopted a more individualistic perspective on the afterlife. The philosophical view that at death the immortal soul ascended to heaven appealed not only to cosmopolitian Hellenistic Jews like Philo of Alexandria. Some evidence indicates that the Essenes also hoped for freedom from bodily constraints and eventual rest in a heavenly kingdom. Unlike Philo, the Essenes seem to have speculated about a new Jewish state under the leadership of a messianic king. Yet they withdrew from active anti-colonial politics and led their lives in secluded communities such as that in Qumran, an isolated place in the Judean desert near the Dead Sea. The Essenes rejected the skepticism of the Sadducees as well as the crude materialistic notions implied in the belief in a future resurrection. Placing the spiritual over the material, they preferred lifestyles that separated them from too much involvement with the world.

At least some of the Essenes were celibate. Josephus not only comments on their celibacy, the communal ownership of goods, and their simple lifestyle, but also their concept of life after death. According to Josephus, the Essenes held that "the body is corruptible" while the soul is "immortal and imperishable." Like Philo, they believed that at death souls were released "from the prisonhouse of the body...and are borne aloft." For the virtuous, "there is reserved an abode beyond the ocean, a place which is not oppressed by rain or snow or heat but is refreshed by the ever-gentle breath of the west wind coming in from the ocean." Like the philosophers, the Essenes looked forward to a calm and comfortable hereafter. Their idea of the afterlife, given the limitation of the sources available to scholars, appeared to be a pleasant environment, free from the burdens of desert life, where the individual soul could contemplate God. Unlike the Sadducees who were happy with their lives on earth, or the Pharisees who expected the re-establishment of a Jewish community, the Essenes looked forward to an eternity in a land not unlike the Isles of the Blest.[37]

The ancient Jewish attitude toward the afterlife reflects the complicated relationship between individual, family, and national concerns, as well as theological concepts. Far from being static, belief in the nature of Sheol and eventually heaven changed considerably during the pre-Christian period. As religious reform movements found new meanings in the nature of God, coped with the demise of Israel as a state, and tried to survive under non-Jewish governments, they formed new ideas about life after death. These ideas consequently shaped how the Jews understood the relationship between God and humankind. Innovations in belief and ritual, however, never totally eliminated older concepts of the hereafter. By the first century, the environment of Palestine provided a fertile soil for the development of Christian notions of heaven.

CHAPTER TWO

Jesus and the Christian Promise

Emerging first-century Christianity drew from a wealth of Jewish teachings about life after death. In spite of Sadducean skepticism, most Jews and their pagan neighbors assumed that the dead did not just vanish into the dust. The dead were not mere memories but active participants in the universe. Contacting the netherworld for advice or providing offerings for the well-being of its residents, although condemned by reformist movements, still persisted in ancient Jewish and gentile society. The assumption that God rewarded the good — either on a renewed earth or in a blessed heaven — helped ease the individual and cultural alienation brought about by colonization, religious persecution, and existential anxieties. Life in the next world would no longer mean the darkness of Sheol but the light of God earned by faith and steadfastness. Innovations in the Jewish mythic structure, such as the idea of an immortal soul which God can assume upward, described a method for arriving in heaven. The vast storehouse of apocalyptic teaching, including the belief in the resurrection of the dead, God's final judgment, and the establishment of an everlasting divine kingdom, gave an immediacy and graphic quality to eternal life. Given the environment of the ancient world, early Christianity could not help finding the question of what happens after death to be a pressing one.

The early Christian image of eternal life was distinctive and different from that of both the Pharisees and the Essenes. The chief architect of the new image of heaven was of course Jesus, but important expansions and modifications were made by Paul and the author of the book of Revelation. In all three cases, Jewish philosophical and metaphysical arguments for an afterlife held less importance than the intense experience of the divine which promised everlasting blessedness. While earlier writers saw life after death in terms of the re-establishment of the Jewish state or as a special reward for the virtuous, the New Testament heaven eliminated the notion of compensation. Heaven was not the place or time when an elect group who lacked something would find fulfillment, but rather the promise that Christians would be permitted to experience the divine fully. Caught up in religious excitement and enthusiasm, followers of Jesus rejected the world and focused their eyes on a future with God alone.

Jesus: No Marriage in Heaven

In the first century CE Judaism was mainly an urban religion. Before the destruction of the Temple (70), believers from all over the Roman Empire made their pilgrimages to the Jewish city *par excellence*, Jerusalem. There they offered sacrifices in the Temple. Jews also went to synagogues and listened to experts in biblical law and lore who taught how to lead an existence separate from pagan society. The variety of sectarian groups – Pharisees, Sadducees, Essenes, Zealots – provided a rich and controversial Jewish life under the watchful eye of Roman rule. Certain rural districts of Palestine remained at a distance from the priestly religion of the Temple and the learning of the rabbis. It would be from these outlying areas that a new form of Judaism, and eventually a new religious tradition, would emerge.

Biblical scholars point to Galilee, the home of Jesus, as one of those areas where priestly and rabbinical Judaism had not taken much root. Located in the northernmost part of Palestine, Galilee was a densely populated rural district with some two hundred villages. While the Galileans were by no means wicked unbelievers or people perverted by pagan culture, they showed little interest in temple ritual and religious learning. According to a note in the Jewish code of law, the Galileans knew nothing (or refused to know) about the "half-shekel" – the annual amount to be paid by each adult Jewish male to support the Jerusalem Temple. Galileans were also said to "hate the Torah," since they had little respect for the law as taught in the books of the Hebrew Bible and explained by the teachers. On the periphery of Jewish Palestinian life, Galileans cultivated their own kind of Judaism.[1]

The villagers of Galilee participated in a Judaism brought to them by local holy men and miracle-workers like Haninah ben Dosa and Jesus of Nazareth. By performing miracles in the name of Israel's God, these men mediated between the divine presence and the rural population. Healing miracles emphasized the intervention of God in desperate situations. More importantly, however, miracles were signals that God and the holy men participated in something extraordinary, something which tran-scended the normal course of everyday events. Just as the holy man himself, preoccupied with preaching a message of divine love, did not participate in normal occupational life, so God also transcended the concerns of the peasant and the fisherman. Galilean Judaism had a tinge of other-worldliness – God's kingdom was not of this earth.[2]

The most famous Galilean, Jesus of Nazareth, did not furnish his followers with a written legacy. If we want to reconstruct his original teaching, we must rely on the gospels that are now generally believed to be written by second- or third-generation Christians who had no personal knowledge of Jesus himself. Composed to meet the needs of the early community rather than to satisfy historical curiosity, the gospels' reliability is not above suspicion. Far from being simple biographies, the gospels contain legendary accretions. Their wish to give guidance to their contemporaries shaped – and perhaps distorted – the original tradition. Although we must not become too discouraged, it is important to recognize the limits of the sources available to us. A careful examination of early Christian literature allows for the reconstruction of a conjectural but plausible outline of Jesus' own teaching on the afterlife.

The most revealing gospel passage concerning heaven – and one which will be debated throughout Christian history – makes clear that Jesus did not avoid contemporary arguments about life after death. A group of people, we are told in several gospels, came to Jesus and presented the following case: if a man's brother dies, leaving a wife but no children, Jewish law requires him to marry the widow and raise their children for his dead brother. Now there were seven brothers; the first married a wife and died without having children. Then the second brother married her and died, and then the third brother and so on until all seven brothers had married her, died, and left no children. Eventually, the woman also died. At the resurrection, the group asked, whose wife will the woman be? In Luke's version Jesus answered that "the children [literally: sons] of this age marry and are given in marriage, but those judged worthy...of resurrection from the dead neither marry nor are given in marriage. They become like angels and are no longer liable to death. Children [sons] of the resurrection, they are children [sons] of God." The woman, then, will not be the wife of any one of the seven brothers at the resurrection of the dead.[3]

Three views can be distinguished in this story: Sadducean, apocalyptic, and Christian. Each represents a different opinion circulating in first-century Palestine. According to the gospels, it was a Sadducee who asked Jesus the question about the woman and her seven husbands. The Sadducees, as disbelievers in the resurrection, held that the worship of God had little to do with the fate of the dead in Sheol. In their theological conservatism, these priestly aristocrats rejected any philosophical or apocalyptic speculation about life beyond the grave. The case presented to Jesus was not an honest inquiry, but an effort meant to ridicule the views developed in apocalyptic circles. The story of the wife with seven husbands, from the Sadducean perspective, was a polemical joke.

The position at which the Sadducees hoped to poke fun was the second view, that of the apocalyptic movement. Apocalypticists expected the bodily resurrection of the righteous who would live in a blissful divine kingdom on earth, enjoy married life, and have numerous progeny. People would die after a long life and then live on in some higher, spiritual world. It was this earthly millennium that the Sadducees caricatured in the gospel passages. The excessive loyalty to the Mosaic law lightheartedly opposed the possibility that all the seven brothers would want to have sex with the same woman in the next world. The Sadducees assumed that all who heard the question would be familiar with apocalyptic beliefs (especially those held by the Pharisees) and that the audience would be amused at their cleverness in disarming their opponents.

Unfortunately, the New Testament does not supply the authentic legal answer, if there was one. We do not know how the Pharisees or other apocalyptic Jews would have countered the ridicule of a rival perspective. We can reasonably suspect, however, that the widow would be married only to the first of the brothers, her original husband, and have children only from him. Apocalyptic Jews looked forward to a fertile and rich society, but one also ruled by the law of Moses. The earthly kingdom of God would be a world of divine order, not of confusion.[4]

The response of Jesus presents us with a third perspective. Although siding with the Pharisaic school in its insistence that there was life after death, it radically questioned the apocalyptic image of marriage and family life in the next world. Against the apocalyptic perspective Jesus explained that there would be no marriage in the resurrected life. Given the ancient association of marriage with reproduction, by implication we can assume there also would be no sexual relationships. Men and women would be angel-like, asexual beings. Jesus calls them "sons of God," probably referring to an Old Testament passage which reports that angels or "sons of God" left heaven because of their lust for human women. In heavenly existence, such lust will not exist any longer. Death, too, can no more threaten the never-ending life of the resurrected. By rejecting the existence of both marriage and reproduction, as well as the possibility of a death after a long fertile life, Jesus departed from current apocalyptic speculation.[5]

Jesus imagined the new life not only as spiritual and immortal, but also as contemporaneous with this one. He supported this idea by using a scriptural proof which seems cryptic to those of us who are unacquainted with rabbinical learning and logic: "Moses in the passage about the bush," the gospel of Luke reports, "showed that the dead rise again when he called the Lord the God of Abraham, and the God of Isaac, and the God of Jacob. God is not the God of the dead, but of the living. All are alive for him." Jews listening to this response in first-century Palestine might have asked: How could God be the God of the three dead patriarchs and at the same time be called the God of the living? Is it not true that those who have died have no access to God? The two statements seem to contradict one another.[6]

The conflicting scriptural statements can only be reconciled on the assumption that the patriarchs are dead only to us, but not to God. Rather than languishing in Sheol, Jesus asserted that the dead have risen up to God. They now live in his presence in heaven. From this conclusion it is further inferred that many men and women must also be with God in the same way. The dead do not have to wait to inherit a renewed earth, as the proponents of the apocalyptic perspective would have it, but can participate immediately in a heavenly world. From the rabbinical point of view, the logic of Jesus was impeccable and was justly acclaimed by some who were present at the debate with the Sadducees.[7]

Jesus' answer to the Saducean question ignored the traditional reception of the dead into the community of their ancestors and other deceased persons. While the Sadducees were interested in whom the wife would *really* be married to, Jesus found this concern to be irrelevant. In his new perspective, the dead are related to God as well as to Abraham, Isaac, and Jacob. As religious figures these patriarchs replace both the dead man's spouse and his more immediate ancestors and kinsmen. In the New Testament period, the dead were no longer "gathered to their people [kin]," but "carried by the angels to Abraham's bosom." Close relatives were replaced by religious heroes.[8]

Resurrection, as Jesus understood it, referred to the individual's post-mortem exaltation to heaven. He challenged both the Sadducean rejection of the afterlife and the apocalyptic expectation of a long life on earth. His response indicated that a new alternative was being constructed. In heaven, according to Jesus' answer, one related to religious figures – God and Abraham – rather than to kinsfolk and spouse. Family networks, so crucial to the economic and political structure of the ancient world, ceased to exist. Both the dead and the living were asked to concentrate on God and religious notables.[9]

The same anti-family, pro-God bias can be observed in one of Jesus' parables, the story of "The Rich Man and Lazarus." There once was a rich man who dressed in purple and in the finest linen. He feasted in great magnificence every day. At his gate lay Lazarus, covered with sores, a poor man who would have been glad to satisfy his hunger with the scraps from the rich man's table. When Lazarus died, he was carried away by angels to be with Abraham. The rich man also died and was buried, but his soul entered a place of fire and torment. Looking up he saw, far away, Abraham with Lazarus sitting beside him. He pleaded with Abraham to send Lazarus to dip the tip of his finger in water and cool his tongue. This is impossible, said Abraham, for "there is a great chasm fixed between us; no one from our side who wants to reach you can cross it, and none may pass from your side to us." Abraham also was unable to send someone to warn the rich man's unsuspecting brothers of their impending fate thus making them listen to God's commandments. Jesus told those listening to the parable that the brothers should not wait for a doubtful message from beyond the grave. The dead cannot speak to the living. What the living must do is listen to "Moses and the prophets"; that is, to the voice of Scripture.[10]

The lesson to be learned was clear: a rich person who is ungodly and does not give alms to the poor must ultimately become wretched. A poor person will, after a life of misery, enter a region of everlasting joy. Heaven is for the poor and hell for the rich. Jesus had expanded the ideas developed by the psalmists who assured their listeners that God would eventually receive them in glory. The rich, boastful, and arrogant wicked would be unable to bargain with God and would perish in Sheol. Although some critics have disputed the authenticity of this parable, which has close parallels in ancient literature, the unconditional promise of heaven to the poor and needy seems to echo the original and characteristic teaching of Jesus. The poor man's desire to be fed with what falls from the rich man's table is frustrated in this life, but in the other world he will not suffer any more. The kingdom of heaven is for the poor and reverses their fate.[11]

Even though the parable does not give us a detailed account of life after death, a general outline emerges. At death the soul will pass into another world, while the body remains in the grave. No bodily resurrection is mentioned or expected, and the happiness of the poor man seems to be perfect and final. He is granted eternal bliss in heaven. The rich man, on the other hand, is immediately punished in hell. There is no mention of a final, renewed earth which the poor man inherits. Thus, we can safely infer that heaven and hell coexist with human history.

However we feel about the authentic or apocryphal nature of this parable, its view of the other life is in remarkable agreement with Jesus' answer to the Sadducees. It teaches the same message: in both texts Abraham has already passed to the other side and is joined there by those permitted to enter into God's heavenly kingdom. They also share an anti-familial bias: in heaven, Lazarus joins Abraham rather than his ancestors and kinsfolk, and the rich man is denied the right to send a message to his brothers. Communicating such a message would make sense in a world in which contacting dead relatives was an institution. In orthodox Judaism, such practices had long been outlawed. Dead relatives were not a source of religious knowledge. Only "Moses and the prophets" could help the living.

Jesus himself did not have the least doubt about joining the celestial community after his own death. Apart from Abraham and the patriarchs, this community included Old Testament saints like Elijah and Moses, the two figures to whom Jesus is reported to have spoken when caught up in mystical rapture. From other passages we learn that heaven also consisted of common men like Lazarus of the parable, the widow of the Sadducean question, and the repenting thief crucified next to Jesus. In agony, Jesus promised to this thief that "today" he would be with him in paradise. Jesus also assured his followers, especially his disciples, of places in heaven. In a farewell speech addressed to them, Jesus told them that he went to prepare a place for them, for "there are many rooms in my [divine] Father's house." These "rooms" or "dwelling places" (the "mansions" of the King James Bible) are not given any domestic flavor. Although the dead would have company in heaven, Jesus underscored the spiritual nature of the other world: the saints would share the angelic form which excluded marriage and reproduction, the foundation of domesticity in the ancient world.[12]

Jesus' view on life after death did not include a concern for what happened to the dead body. While his miracles of healing and feeding presuppose regard for the living human body, Jesus took no interest in corpses. "Follow me," he said to one he met on the road; "leave the dead to bury their dead." Since the dead body was not the eternal part of the personality, Jesus could comfort those of his followers who suffered persecution and enmity by saying that the enemies can "kill the body but cannot kill the soul." The body, although obviously essential for earthly life, was not important for eternal life. The kingdom of God or heaven, as announced and proclaimed by Jesus, was a reality one would normally experience after death. At death, the individual soul would be judged, and those worthy granted eternal life in God's heavenly kingdom.[13]

Although Jesus assumed that at death the righteous immediately went to God and the patriarchs in heaven, he did not break with the apocalyptic hope for an end of Israel's suffering. As did many of his contemporaries, he shared the belief in the imminent close of human history. That ending would be a dramatic event inaugurated by the coming of God or perhaps some mythical figure. The righteous were then expected to be admitted even as living people into the divine kingdom. Jesus insisted, however, that there was no difference between the two ways of entering heaven. The contemporaries surviving the dramatic end of history would have no advantage over the dead, and vice versa. The kingdom was the same for all who were received into it.[14]

Whatever we can ascertain from the New Testament about the original message of Jesus, and however divergent the views of modern scholars may be, all agree on the God-centered, "purely religious" outlook of Jesus. Here was a man living entirely in the presence of the divine: the searching and penetrating gaze of God which beckoned and overwhelmed the soul. The message of Jesus issued directly from being possessed by a definite experience of God and a notion of the divine will. "To Jesus the whole meaning of life is religious," wrote Ernst Troeltsch, "his life and his teaching are wholly determined by his thought of God." While the teaching of Jesus certainly contained admonishments on proper social relationships, we cannot overestimate the importance of God as the center of the Christian message.[15]

Religious virtuosi, such as Jesus, often expected that divine judgment would be imminent. From their perspective, God's sovereign majesty was so overwhelming that the world had no choice but to sink into nothingness quickly. When everything was drawn to God, the judgment must be close at hand. Confronted with its creator, the world would be consumed in the flames of his terrible majesty. The more the individual was drawn to God, the more the world shrank in comparison. Life as we normally experience it could not compete with the intensity of life with God. Fully imbued with the spirit of the divine, Jesus showed little interest in speculating about what humans would find in restored paradisal conditions. What counted was God alone and his restored rulership over his creatures.

What Jesus experienced of God he summed up in one word, *abba*, the Aramaic term for father. Although *abba* can refer to God as an exalted father figure, it also suggests intimacy and trust. It was the word people used when speaking about or addressing their human fathers. Jesus considered this intimacy as something unique which he did not share with other people. He could, however, serve as an intermediary between the divine Father and others. "All things have been delivered to me by my Father," he preached, "and no one knows the Father except the Son and any one to whom the Son chooses to reveal him." For Jesus, experiencing the Father comprised the central force of his message. Heaven could not be a place of mere material reward, as the apocalyptic movement predicted, but must consist of the most important reward – the experience of the divine.[16]

The revelation Jesus brought from the heavenly Father was not a theoretical doctrine but the practical advice to throw away cares, to rely on the loving Father, and thus to find rest. "Come to me, all who labor and are heavy laden," Jesus called, "and I will give you rest. Take my yoke upon you, and learn from me; for I am gentle and lowly in heart, and you will find rest for your souls." For some members of the movement, to be drawn to God meant to leave everything behind. They followed Jesus on his wanderings through Palestine, devaluing wealth, occupational life, and family. God would provide for all the necessities of life, just as he provided for the birds of the air and the lilies of the field. To rest in God, first on earth and then in heaven, meant not to focus on worldly cares but to concentrate on preserving an intimate relationship with the divine and the religious community.[17]

It would not be easy for everyday people to give up their hopes for a fruitful earthly life and embrace a theocentric heavenly orientation. Jesus' ministry, however, "was characterized by a power and authority which was neither learned in any school nor bestowed by any human agency but which came to him in a direct and spontaneous manner." His closeness with God gave Jesus a type of authority that sociologist Max Weber called "charismatic." Charisma is an extraordinary talent, understood as a divine gift that gives the bearer influence over others. Charismatic leaders are able to motivate people to change their lifestyle and beliefs radically. Charismatic figures are also free from any institutional legitimation. They assert their independence by standing above normal occupational and family life. Jesus' God-oriented heaven was only part of his perspective on life. In order to be fully present in God, the soul must have no interest in non-godly concerns: family, society, or wealth.[18]

Devoting his existence to the one cause by which he is obsessed, the charismatic leader cannot fully engage in the normal range of commitments. Although this non-involvement has several dimensions, it is epitomized by celibacy and the denial of family duties. Significantly, Jesus departed from the Jewish wish of having many children. He remained unmarried and childless as well as alien to an ideal of family and domesticity. Jesus called his disciples and followers out of their families and united them into a community in which marriage formed no structural element. Far from being a stabilizing factor in society, charisma tends to disrupt marriages and families. Thus Jesus claimed to "have come to set a man against his father, and a daughter against her mother." The ideal Christian remained unmarried and at a distance to his or her family.[19]

Ernest Renan, in his *Life of Jesus*, pointed out that the founder of Christianity neither grew up in an idyllic home nor as an adult promoted a family ideology. He was harsh to his relatives; they did not love him. His tenuous relationship to them contributed to the rise of the story that Jesus had no human father and was born from a virgin – which would drastically reduce the number of his kin. While most children are visibly tied into the fabric of a family, Jesus rebelled against parental authority even in his early years. Family relationships with their petty loyalties meant little to him. He preferred an unsettled life which allowed for mobility and left him free to follow his idea of creating new spiritual relationships among his growing group of followers. "Jesus, like all men exclusively preoccupied by an idea," explained Renan, "came to think little of the ties of blood. The bond of thought is the only one that natures of his kind recognize." Jesus engaged in a "bold revolt against nature... trampling under foot everything that is human – blood, love, and country." He was possessed by the idea of God.[20]

The early Christian community must have included many who gave "up home, or wife, brothers, parents, or children, for the sake of the kingdom of God." The true saints were those who surrendered their lives to the new group, becoming father and mother, brother and sister, son and daughter to all believers, rather than to their own clan. Jesus ignored his family even in the ritual sphere by not celebrating Passover with them as required by the Scriptures. Celebrating it with his disciples, who substituted for family and kin, Jesus dramatized a new law. Religion must replace family as the primary focus of life.[21]

Given this background to Jesus' world-view we can see why his heaven included God and excluded almost everything else. Denying the existence of marriage in heaven had nothing to do with a disdain for sexuality, but was a more general rejection of family ties and concerns. At death, the decreased person passed into a different realm which was either heaven or hell. In heaven – also called the kingdom of heaven or the kingdom of God – the fate of those who had an unfortunate life was reversed. Like contemporary Jewish philosophers, Jesus was not concerned about the fate of dead bodies. What survived after death had spiritual qualities and could be termed a soul. The intense experience which Jesus felt toward the divine would be duplicated in the next life. Earthly concerns of sexuality, family, or compensation for lost wealth would be of no importance.

Paul: Spiritual Bodies

The Jesus movement quickly developed into an enthusiastic religious community. "Enthusiasm," often used to mean extravagance in religion, more specifically refers to a level of religious experience and commitment beyond the societal norm. Enthusiasm prevails in a community where high surges of devotion and excitement are commonplace, and the divine is frequently experienced in visions, inspired utterances, and miracles. The enthusiastic community, moreover, spurns organized life, giving preference to spontaneous charismatic leadership. A member of such a community typically belongs to the lower classes, and women often figure prominently.[22]

As early as the first generation after Jesus, Christianity moved beyond its original Palestinian setting. Within several months of the death of Jesus, Paul, a Greek-speaking Jew of Tarsus in Asia Minor, joined the community. An indefatigable traveller and missionary, he brought the new faith from rural Palestine to cities like Corinth and Philippi in Greece, and Tavium and Ancyra in the Roman province of Galatia.

Paul's letters, which survive in the New Testament, reveal his pre-occupation with God and Christ. He shared Jesus' intense religious experience. Everything Paul did and wrote was for the glory of God and the lordship of Jesus Christ. The letters also leave no doubt about his strong sense of personal authority, which he exercised in the communities he founded. Like Jesus, Paul was a charismatic leader who never compromised in matters of authority: "What I am writing to you is a command of the Lord. If any one does not recognize this, he is not recognized."[23]

As a charismatic leader Paul also was free and independent, keeping his involvement with the world at a minimum. Himself unmarried, he recommended this ideal to others and gave it a religious meaning. "The unmarried man is anxious about the affairs of the Lord, how to please the Lord," he wrote, "but the married man is anxious about worldly affairs." Affairs of the Lord or worldly affairs — these were the alternatives and the only categories in which Paul could think. In order to ensure his financial independence, Paul engaged in a marginal occupational life, though he also relied on the generosity of many women and men who supported his cause.[24]

Paul considered Christianity as a religion in its own right, based on a new revelation and separate from traditional Judaism. This does not mean that the new movement shed its enthusiastic origins and quickly developed into an ordered, institutional church. Christianity remained sectarian and enthusiastic. According to the Acts of the Apostles and the letters of Paul, the sensation of divine power still manifested itself in miraculous healings, visions, prophecy, and "speaking with tongues." The community still depended on such immediate experiences for their worship and devotion. Any believer might see a vision or prophesy as a part of healing or evangelism. Organized, regular authority had barely developed. "The earliest Christian community," summarized James Dunn, "was essentially charismatic and enthusiastic in nature, in every aspect of its common life and worship, its development and mission." First-century Christianity remained loyal to its original inspiration.[25]

As a Pharisee-turned-Christian, Paul drew from a set of basic concepts concerning life after death. Along with many first-century Jews, Paul accepted the idea that at death the person "sleeps," presumably in the netherworld. Also following Jewish custom, he forbade even the Gentile converts to engage in any form of ancestor worship; only one dead person was to be revered — the resurrected Christ. Unlike Jesus, who told parables and made brief statements about the righteous joining God immediately after death, Paul followed the Pharisaic tradition which delayed reunion with the divine. At an appointed time in the future, a resurrection of the dead to bodily life would occur. Then a kingdom would be created where God himself ruled. Although Paul boasted of having been "caught up – whether still in the body or out of the body, I do not know; God knows – right up into the third heaven," his discussion of eternal life was oriented to the future, not the present.[26]

Paul gave Jewish apocalyptic concepts new meaning by infusing them with Christian ideas. The coming of the Messiah, he believed, would be the second coming of Jesus Christ. It would not be the virtuous Jews who would rise, but the dead Christians. Paul particularly echoed the Christian position when he eliminated the apocalyptic notion that the resurrected dead would have real, fertile bodies. In sharp contrast, he argued that the resurrected body was "spiritual." A spiritual body would not be occupied with producing numerous offspring and enjoying those earthly activities denied by colonial rulers. For Paul, there would be no earthly kingdom of the Messiah. Paul's view of the body reflected the innovation of Jesus who asked his followers not to be concerned with the things of the earth but to focus their attention on the divine.[27]

The resurrected bodies of Pauline thought are not material but "spiritual." The bodies of those Christians who happen to be alive at the time of the resurrection will be changed "in a twinkling of an eye" into spiritual beings that are immortal. Transformed people – those having "spiritual bodies" – do not remain on earth, but are caught up into heaven. After "meeting the Lord in the air," they are probably scrutinized, judged by Jesus Christ, and given their due rewards. Paul refers only to the good Christians; he does not elaborate on what happens to pagans and other damned ones. At that point, Jesus hands the rulership over to his father. The redeemed will always be in heaven, in the presence of Christ and God.[28]

But what of the messianic kingdom? Here we have the boldest reinterpretation of Jewish apocalyptic tradition. The Messiah's rulership, for Paul, will not be a post-resurrection event, but is a present reality. The Messiah is Jesus Christ, and he rules here-and-now in the enthusiastic communities. As a life-giving spirit, Christ manifests himself wherever there is speaking with tongues, prophecy, healing, or charismatic leadership. Sometimes a person is so totally possessed by Christ's spirit that he or she can say, "I live no longer I, but Christ lives in me." The intensity of the religious experience replaces the human personality with the life-giving spirit of Christ.[29]

Paul was of course aware that even spirit-filled individuals grow old and eventually die. "Though our outer nature is wasting away, our inner nature is being renewed every day," wrote Paul of his own situation. The body grows old and becomes weak, although still refreshed by the divine spirit. For the believer, God has given a "guarantee" or "pledge" of eternal spiritual existence. "He who has prepared us for this very thing [life everlasting in a spiritual body] is God," Paul assured his followers, "who has given us the Spirit as a guarantee." Life after death continued what had already been begun in this life: existence under the impact and guidance of the divine.[30]

Unfortunately, much of the Pauline view as we have presented it must be conjectured. Paul never explained himself fully in his letters, probably because his readership already had a good grasp of these elementary teachings. The only detail Paul described more fully, though with less explicitness than we might wish, was the nature of the resurrected body.

The physical body (in contrast to the resurrected body) may be compared to a tent or garment where the *ego*, or soul, lives. According to Paul, God will prepare another home or garment for the soul after the death of the body. To move from one garment into the other necessitates a perilous journey, literally a death. Like any other human being, even Jesus was not spared death. He left his physical body (the "old garment") in the grave and assumed a new and imperishable one. His unique privilege was that the transformation occurred in only two days. He did not have to wait until the end of the world. Like Jesus, dead Christians also leave their physical bodies in the dust. God will eventually provide the dead with a new and imperishable "spiritual" body. Paul's language does not imply the restoration of the physical human body. He probably was not familiar with the legendary reports of the empty tomb of Jesus. The physical body, Paul assumed, remained in the grave.[31]

Paul did not define what he meant by the "spiritual" quality of the new body, but we can form a reasonably coherent picture of what he might have had in mind. According to the biblical view, a human being is made of two components: one material and earthly; the other spiritual and divine. At the first creation God formed a human-shaped clay model which was material and earthly. This model had no life. Then God gave his breath or spirit to the matter he created and it came alive. At the resurrection, however, a new creation would emerge which required no material elements. The new men and women would be fully spiritual and entirely under the control of God. Christians during their lifetime had experienced only the fragmentary or perhaps temporary control of Christ. Now that control would be complete. The body could lie in the grave because it was of no more importance. God's rulership over the new creation would be perfect and perpetual.

The new body over which God would rule needed a special or new design. Paul hinted that the spiritual body would not have the anatomy or physiology of the earthly body, because God would destroy both the stomach and the food in it. Perhaps we can think of it as an airy, human-shaped entity which shares the essential qualities of God – spirituality and immortality. It may consist, according to one biblical scholar, of "the fine celestial substance of light as it is native to the stars."[32]

The spiritual body, which will be the resurrected body, can be more clearly understood when set in the context of Paul's understanding of the earthly body. For Paul, we are involved in a permanent inner struggle between flesh and spirit: "The desires of the flesh are against the spirit, and the desires of the spirit are against the flesh, for these are opposed to each other." The "flesh" or "body" (with the connotation of sinful urge) must be placed under the control of the spirit. "Spirit" here stands not just for the human spirit, but for the innermost being renewed and "possessed" by the divine spirit. The divine spirit bestowed upon the initiate serves as a transforming, life-giving force. The transformation ensures that worldly, material, and sinful concerns – called the "deeds of the body" – no longer dominate the lives of Christians. The fleshly person behaves like unbelievers, who do not have the spirit. Vices (non-physical as well as physical) are the works of the flesh. Virtues are the fruit of the spirit. The gift of the spirit focuses the believer entirely on God. True, the spirit leads to virtue in everyday life, but "the proper act of the Spirit is prayer."[33]

Paul's theology of body and spirit reflects his view of social values. The relationship between individual and the community is often expressed in terms of spirit and body. Individualists and enthusiasts who look for freedom from social constraints typically advocate the higher value of the spirit. The charismatic mind, by giving religion priority over everyday social concerns, tends to emphasize the distinction between body and spirit, matter and mind. It is through the body that we are related to "the world" – to the family, economic life, and politics. The spirit, on the other hand, links us to religion, the community of believers, and ultimately to God who is spirit. Emphasis or over-emphasis on the spirit necessarily alienates us from the present order of things. Conversely, whoever is disinterested in ordinary social life is likely to set the material world against that of the spirit and to lack concern for "the body." Those who think of themselves as beings of primarily spiritual nature, also tend to emphasize individuality which may not be swallowed up by the claims of the family or business concerns.[34]

In Paul's theology, every Christian (not only spiritual leaders and missionaries like himself) must be independent from social constraints and filled with the divine spirit. The Christian initiation ritual of baptism dramatized the replacement of the life of the flesh by the life of the spirit. To be immersed in water symbolized death, the death of the baptized person's past life and identity. Baptism then substituted natural kinship ties by a religious kinship system. Christians gave up earthly family ties in order to be adopted as God's children. Ritually, this was expressed in the initiate's invocation of God as *abba* (father), a clear echo of Jesus' own way of addressing the divine. That the fellow Christians were brothers and sisters was obviously implied, but not made explicit by Paul. For the charismatic Paul, the adoption into divine sonship or daughtership was more important.[35]

Divine adoption enabled the Christian to receive from God the special spiritual gift called charisma. The divine spirit, according to Paul, empowered some believers for extraordinary tasks. One brother might stand up in the assembly and pronounce an address that strengthened others in their faith. Another sister might fall into a trance or ecstasy and praise the Lord; a third might have the charisma of leadership. Early Christians took such manifestations of the divine spirit as the "exhibition before the world of the believer's separation from the world." Believers are different from non-believers because the spirit makes the difference. Charisma, the spiritual gift, operates strictly in a religious setting and serves for the "common good" and "edification of the church." It does not promote personal interests in secular life. In fact, it may actually work against normal life, disrupt marriages, and cause some to embrace celibacy.[36]

The Christian community was based on the devaluation of family and marriage. Baptismal and eucharistic rites established new social bonds which took clear precedence over kinship ties. Christians shared sacred meals that united them in the spirit, not beds that united them in the flesh. They were a community of the spirit. Paul's notion of the spirit was not only central for his concept of Christian life in this world; it also shaped his view of life everlasting. Likewise, he turned away from the Pharisaic hope for a renewed earthly life at the end of time and promised instead an eternal life of the spirit. Just as the true Christian left the confines of family and everyday life and entered into a deep relationship with Christ, resurrected Christians would continue this intensity in eternity. Everlasting life for Paul meant everlasting possession by the divine spirit. The religious community, both in the Christian centers established by Paul and in heaven at the end of time, would be primary in importance. Heaven implied the final defeat of fleshly concerns and the total acceptance of life with God. Paul, following in the steps of Jesus, understood heaven to be a place for those willing to live entirely in the presence of God. There could be no other option.

Revelation to John: The Heavenly Liturgy

With the book of Revelation we are in the second generation after Jesus, when Christianity was firmly established outside Palestine. Still a minority religion, it was threatened by Jews who considered it a dangerous heresy. Pagans, who frowned upon both Jews and the new Jewish sect, were even more threatening. Another danger for Christians came from their own ranks: the danger of compromising with the pagan world. The author of the book of Revelation, who continued the trend begun by Jesus and developed by Paul, assured that heaven could only be a place radically separate from this world. Heaven was fulfillment in God.

The book of Revelation gives us only an occasional glimpse into the biography of its author. His background was Jewish and his interest in ritual matters suggests priestly descent. He may have left Palestine during the Jewish war against Rome (66–70 CE) in order to settle in western Anatolia. Possibly following Paul's advice to care only for the Lord's affairs, he remained celibate. As a master prophet he sent revelatory messages to various Christian communities under his – real or assumed – jurisdiction. The book of Revelation presents him as a member of a prophetic movement or "order" within the churches of Asia Minor. Whatever his relation with these communities may have been, he addresses them with the authority of a charismatic leader. He tells us that his name is John and that he is a servant of the Lord.[37]

John was shocked by the thriving imperial cult which involved worship of the emperor, notably Domitian (81–96 CE). He was even more shocked by Christian participation in that cult. The excuse probably given, that the Roman emperor was only honored as God's servant, was unacceptable to him. For the true religious charismatic, even the "normal" measure of human readiness to compromise had to be condemned as inspired by demonic powers. Everyone who does not live up to the standards of heroic religion is in the claws of Satan. John thus fought against any accommodation to pagan cult and culture which, for him, was satanic. His uncompromising stance brought him into conflict not only with his fellow Christians but also with Roman authorities. John's eventual exile to the island of Patmos in the Mediterranean, and the Martyrdom of one of his friends, prompted his critical attitude. On Patmos John composed the book of Revelation as a call for an end to accommodating to the surrounding culture.[38]

Much of John's writing deals with Christian involvement in a universal conflict between God and the powers of Satan, the latter being represented by the Roman empire. Eventually, he argues, God will overthrow the pagan political system and establish a new and everlasting order. His account of the battle is carefully framed by two visions of heaven. The book opens with a vision of the heavenly liturgy at which the seer is allowed to be present. It ends with another liturgy – that of the new and eternal Jerusalem in which heaven and earth coincide. The splendor and dignity of the heavenly worship serves as a powerful contrast to the terrible world of persecution, bloodshed, war, and idolatry.

According to his report, John was permitted to see "a door open in heaven" while an angel told him to "come up here." Entering the door the seer finds himself in a vast chamber where he sees the divine throne and God himself in human form. The throne and the one enthroned are so dazzling that their glorious appearance can be described only in terms of precious gems. The splendor of the one enthroned is like that of jasper and carnelian. The throne itself casts a glow comparable to that of an emerald rainbow which acts as a halo and frames the scene. Immediately around the throne are grouped four strange animal-shaped spirits – each with six wings, multiple eyes, and various animal faces. These seem to be the spirits who guard the throne. Beside them on either side of the throne are twelve lesser thrones occupied by twenty-four elders wearing white garments and golden crowns, apparently throne attendants or the court council. Behind them appear the host of angels filling the background. In the foreground, illuminating the scene, are seven lamps, a sea of glass, and a mighty angel who utters a proclamation with a great voice.[39]

The circle of rainbow-colored light, flashes of lightning, peals of thunder, loud voices, and the winged spirits' never-ending song of "Holy, holy, holy is the Lord God Almighty; he was, he is, and he is to come" add up to a powerful and awe-inspiring scene. While God occupies the throne in immoveable majesty, the spirits wave their wings and the elders prostrate themselves. Movement and stillness, colors and light, animals, men and angels are carefully arranged to underscore the divine majesty who "looked like a diamond and a ruby."

Like other visionaries John felt the impulse to write down what he saw. Although his vision seems quite fantastic to us, what he saw was largely based in tradition. He relived and re-experienced the vision of an Old Testament prophet who had lived seven hundred years earlier. When Ezekiel encountered the divine majesty he saw a person of a fiery nature, sitting on a throne surrounded by four animal-shaped, winged spirits. There is, however, one essential difference between the conventional representation of God and the way John saw him. While earlier visionaries beheld God surrounded by angels or spirits, John and his contemporaries also recognized human beings next to the divine throne.

Without losing its awe-inspiring celestial dignity, heaven has become more human. Twenty-four elders with white robes and golden crowns surround and attend to God's throne. Robes, crowns, and the number twenty-four – the traditional number of Jewish priestly families – identify them as priests. Soon, there is more movement in the scene as God is joined by the Christ – "a lamb that seemed to have been sacrificed." The elders are joined successively by numerous angels, by 144,000 people of all the tribes of Israel, as well as "a huge number, impossible to count, of people from every nation, race, tribe, and language." All of these angels and people join the elders in worshipping God by playing harps, swinging palm-leaves, singing, shouting, and burning incense on an altar which stands in front of the throne. From time to time the heavenly liturgy is interrupted by an awed silence which lasts, we are informed, for about half an hour. Then the liturgy is resumed.[40]

One of the heavenly elders initiates a conversation with the visionary and tells him who these people are, and why they are there:

> These are they who have passed through the great ordeal; they have washed their robes and made them white in the blood of the Lamb. That is why they stand before the throne of God and minister to him day and night in his temple; and he who sits on the throne will dwell with them. They shall never again feel hunger or thirst, the sun shall not beat on them nor any scorching heat, because the lamb who is at the heart of the throne will be their shepherd and will guide them to the springs of the water of life; and God will wipe all tears from their eyes.

In other words, all these people – probably including the elders – are martyrs who died for their Christian belief. Speaking of the "great ordeal" or the "great persecution," John used an expression that must have been current among the early Christians, perhaps referring to the persecution under Emperor Nero in 64 CE. The underlying idea is that martyrdom ensured instantaneous bliss as well as a place close to the divine throne.[41]

In another passage the "souls" of the dead lie under the altar of the heavenly temple. These seem to be Jewish martyrs. They stay below the altar, but are given white robes. How they relate to the elders and the Christian martyrs is not explained. Again another text reports how two men as Christian prophets preach repentance on earth, but are finally killed as martyrs. After three and a half days they rise, apparently bodily, and ascend to heaven – most probably in order to join in the celestial liturgy. John's heaven is a heaven peopled with martyrs who are considered the saints *par excellence*.[42]

Whereas the heavenly liturgy seems to be the exclusive occupation of the saints, the angels enjoy a greater variety of activities. Michael with his angels fights against Satan and his host. Other angels blow trumpets, pour out bowls full of plagues over the earth, make announcements, or guide the seer on his heavenly journey. The static activities of the saints as they worship contrast sharply with the involvement of the angels in celestial and terrestrial affairs. Most of the book of Revelation is devoted to picturing the final drama of human history – the overthrow of the Roman Empire and its spiritual basis, the influence of Satan and his evil angels. The forces of darkness will be conquered by those of the light, and God will establish his eternal kingdom.

What John describes as happening at the heavenly court seems to be a mixture of Hellenistic-Roman court ceremonial and early Christian worship. In John's vision we see the granting of permission to enter the throne chamber, the prostration of the twenty-four elders before the throne, and their praise of the one enthroned. A mighty angel requests for one worthy to read from a scroll, and after the reading takes place the elders praise the one who has read. Finally all present prostrate themselves before the one enthroned. John presents to his readers a courtroom scene. The herald announces the permission to come into the royal presence. The emperor's decrees are read; then follow the petitions of those who have been admitted into the imperial presence. Finally, all prostate themselves in acceptance of royal authority. God is worshipped in a court ceremony like a human emperor.[43]

The laudations and hymns connected with reading from a scroll also suggest a liturgical pattern. The service begins with an invitation to partake of its blessings. It continues with the singing of a trishagion ("Holy, holy, holy is the Lord God Almighty") followed by a brief praise of God as Creator, sung by the choir. The congregation prostrates itself before the altar (i.e. the throne), and the major portion of the service is then taken up with the reading of the Scripture and the recitation of prayers, including a psalm of praise to Christ the Slain Lamb. After the psalm is sung, the congregation responds with an appropriate versicle. Finally, the service closes with congregational singing of a doxology to God and Christ, concluding with a choral Amen.[44]

Just as the celestial liturgy described by John replicates Christian worship or imperial court life, heaven as a sacred space resembles first-century ritual architecture. We must not be misled by John's use of the word "temple." The Jerusalem Temple was a house for God, not a hall for solemn assemblies which John saw in his vision. What John experiences is a heaven laid out like a big synagogue (Fig. 4). The center is God himself, sitting on his throne (rather than God's word, present in the *torah* shrine). He is surrounded by angels who sit or stand behind the divine throne, while the blessed are in the nave. One also thinks of an ancient Roman basilica, a hall in which the emperor held court or received delegations. Both the Jewish synagogue and the Greco-Roman basilica were appropriate models for understanding the place of heavenly worship. The early Christian meeting-place in members' homes did not provide a grand enough space for such a celestial liturgy.

John presents the establishment of God's kingdom in two phases. In the first phase, the angels will not entirely annihilate the evil forces, but have Satan and his following locked away in some subterranean dungeon where they can no longer do harm. Human history will continue, but humankind will spend one thousand years under the reign of the returned Christ and the resurrected martyrs who will not die again. After this period the satanic forces will be unchained and allowed to make their final, though futile, attack against the established order of things. Satan

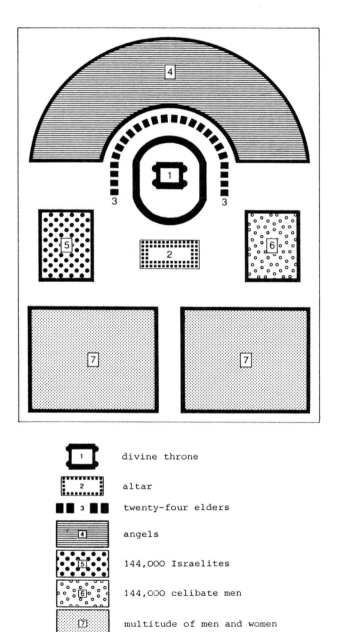

Fig. 4.   The Heavenly Liturgy in the book of Revelation. Adapted from Theodor Bogler, ed., *Tod und Leben* (Maria Laach: Abtei, 1959), 120.

[*Drawing by B. Dachner*]

will deceive all the nations of the earth with the exception of "the camp of the saints which is the city that God loves" – that is, Jerusalem. Satan's armies will come swarming over the entire world and besiege the city, "but fire will come down from heaven and consume them." The devilish armies will be annihilated, and their leader will be thrown into a lake of fire and sulphur to be tortured for all eternity.[45]

In the second phase, after the general resurrection of the dead, the Last Judgment will ensure that anybody whose name cannot be found written in the Book of Life will be thrown into the burning lake. The others will be granted eternal life on a renewed earth. The center of this world will be the new and eternal Jerusalem which the visionary sees descend from heaven and situate itself on the earth.

The city of God described by John was not actually a city with build-ings, walls, towers, and open space. Instead it resembled a gigantic hall in the form of a cube with sides measuring about 1,500 miles. The new building would dwarf the sanctuary of the old Jerusalem Temple with its sides of thirty-five feet. The construction which John saw was made of the most precious materials he could conceive. Twelve gates gave access to the structure whose center was occupied by a double throne of God and Christ. The divine center radiated so much light that there was no need for windows to let in the light of the sun or the moon. A river and plants called the "river of life" and "trees of life" were incorporated into it. While "river of life" and "tree of life" in the Semitic idiom may simply refer to a river that always carries water and a plant that would never wither, the latter at least had supernatural qualities. The trees of life served as a "cure for the nations [pagans]," probably by giving them spiritual refreshment.[46]

Since our seer was preoccupied with the precious building materials, he only briefly mentioned what actually happened in this miraculous structure. The innermost part of the old Jerusalem Temple, the holy of holies, was "unapproachable" and "invisible to all." Even the high priest rarely entered it. The Jerusalem Temple's counterpart in the new world, however, would be the visible center of the universe. John reported that its open gates and broad avenues seemed to be thronged with pilgrims who devoutly approached the divine throne in order to offer their prayers and presents. Although everyone could approach God and Christ, only a particular group called "God's servants" attended to the throne and saw God face to face. Though it is not indicated in the next, these men could be the twenty-four elders of the earlier chapters of Revelation. They led the never-ending heavenly liturgy which was now brought down to earth and accessible to everyone, especially to those who had kept their faith in times of adversity and persecution.[47]

As with the predictions of Jesus and Paul, John's visions reveal a decidedly theocentric heaven. God and Christ sit at the center of a magnificent structure radiating so much light that the natural sun or moon are no longer needed. Rivers and trees provide spiritual and not physical nourishment. Even the precious gems decorating the new temple are far superior to anything found on earth. Closest to the divine center are those who have sacrificed the most for Christ. Celibates have given up the earthly concerns of marriage and family. Martyrs have even offered the flesh itself. The world, which John saw as full of persecution, bloodshed, war, and idolatry will be replaced with a never-ending repetition of divine praise. In the face of both external and internal threats to Christian enthusiasm, John reasserted the primary Christian promise. John's new Jerusalem was not an ordinary city designed for the accommodation of the blessed; essentially a temple, it served as the final place for their full and total communion with God.

The Christian Promise

Jesus and the early Christians knew the opinions held by their contemporaries about life after death. An important New Testament tradition indicates that Jesus actually engaged in a debate and discussion with the Sadducees over what life in the resurrection would be like. The Christian promise, however, was not merely a duplication of Jewish or Hellenistic beliefs. Jesus and his followers Paul and John of Patmos completely remodelled the received versions of heaven. Their new perspective on eternal life was shaped by two main ideas found throughout their teachings: the priority of orientation toward God with direct experience of the divine, and the rejection of ordinary society structured by kinship, marriage, and the concomitant family concerns.

The first emphasis – orientation toward the divine – was represented by Jesus, Paul, and John of Patmos with equal clarity. The Sadducees were told that in heaven men and women would be "children of God" and thus similar to the angels. Their entire existence would be focused on the divine. This was the view of Jesus who experienced an intimate connection to God. In the same vein, Paul defined heavenly existence as "being with Christ." For him, this also meant being with the divine, because Paul often used God and Christ interchangeably. With "spiritual bodies," the blessed would no longer be detracted from the divine. They would taste God's presence in permanent, not just occasional, ecstasy. More graphically, the book of Revelation placed the redeemed around the heavenly throne occupied by God and Christ. John envisaged the next life as everlasting worship whose splendor the visionary never tired of extolling.

The distance from ordinary society – the second emphasis – was a consequence of giving priority to the divine. Jesus' charismatic denial of family ties and the marriage bond was reflected in his heaven where the blessed "neither marry nor are given in marriage." Paul's depreciation of "the flesh" and the "deeds of the body" implied a heroic renouncement of nature, which was seen as prone to sin. It also mirrored his rejection of the unbelieving world from which he was alienated. In Revelation, John expressed that alienation mainly in political terms: the Roman imperial system was declared satanic. The cult of the emperor eventually had to give way to the only acceptable liturgy: God and Christ eternally adored in heaven.

The New Testament heaven depended on a particular understanding of the Christian's role in society. As a religion with enthusiastic followers, early Christianity left little room for those who wanted to be both in the spiritual community and in the world. People could attain immortality only when they belonged to the community of believers who were in the flesh but not of the flesh. Just as the present world of persecution and sin would pass away, so the human body, as a part of that world, must die. "Flesh and blood can never possess the kingdom of God," Paul wrote, "and the perishable cannot possess immortality." The spiritual character of God and the theistic and asexual nature of the hereafter were closely connected to the early Christian disdain for established society.[48]

From the New Testament perspective, as long as we live in the flesh and put up with the vagaries of earthly existence, we can never be fully involved with the divine. Compromises with the world – living itself – limit our commitment to God. After death, however, we are freed from physical and social constraints and thus can meet all the requirements of charismatic participation in the divine. The early Christian began life with God by symbolically putting off the old garment in baptism and accepting a new life in Christ. Kin, sexuality, and political concerns were exchanged for participation in the Christian fictive family. Total renewal, however, could only occur once the old garment, the physical body, had been replaced with a resurrected, spiritual body in heaven or at the end of time. The New Testament promise of eternal life aims at leaving the limitations of this life and experiencing fully the presence of God.

The commitment of Jesus, Paul, and John of Patmos – indeed that of any charismatic leader – is difficult to duplicate. To forsake social position, economic security, and sexual intimacy by rejecting the family cannot be accomplished by all. As the end of time seemed less and less imminent, living an enthusiastic life in a Christian community became more difficult. While the decline of the Roman empire and the influence of Platonic philosophies gave some Christians fuel for their disgust with worldly matters, others found the demands of spiritual life to be excessive. The eventual social acceptance of Christianity and its establishment as the religion of the empire ensured that a re-evaluation of the world would take place.

CHAPTER THREE

Irenaeus and Augustine on our Heavenly Bodies

Between the second and the fifth centuries, Christianity developed from a provincial Jewish fringe cult to the official religion of the late Roman Empire. While the Christianity of the New Testament was based largely on charismatic, inner effervescence, later theology often developed as a response to social conditions imposed from the outside. Merchants, emigrants, and missionaries succeeded in establishing Christian communities almost everywhere in the ancient world, and those communities faced external persecution and internal loss of religious enthusiasm. The early years of Christianity were difficult ones, but by the fourth century the Roman threat had ended and the new religion faced the task of becoming the church of the empire. During these formative years of Christianity, the God-centered heaven of the New Testament underwent important modifications.

The will to survive in a hostile civilization despite persecution and martyrdom led to an understanding of heaven as the compensation for lost earthly privileges. One Christian writer, Irenaeus of Lyons, looked to the next world for compensation for the loss of productive life on earth. The church of the martyrs, which Irenaeus represented, did not reject the world. It resented the fact that Roman persecution had made it impossible for Christians to enjoy God's good gift to humanity fully. As a glorified material world, Irenaeus's heaven would offset earthly limitations. Other early Christians perceived the situation quite differently. Inspired partly by fashionable Greek world-renouncing philosophies, ascetic Christians despised pagan life and wanted to withdraw from it. The young Augustine not only looked upon Roman society with suspicion; he extended this attitude to the entire material universe. Alienated from everything pertaining to "this world," ascetic Christians such as Augustine espoused the dualistic philosophies of Gnosticism or Neoplatonism. They rejected the compensational heaven of Irenaeus and predicted that life after death would entail the continuation of their ascetic, spiritual lifestyle. As spirit was superior to matter on earth, so it would be in heaven.

In the fourth century, Christianity became first a recognized religion

(313), then the official religion of the later Roman Empire (381). Christians were now no longer rejected, but became respected members and eventually the leading class of society. As Christianity settled into its new role as state religion, the philosophies of alienation gradually declined in appeal. In his later years, Augustine tempered his ascetic values and no longer expressed total disenchantment with the political and social world. As the cult became a church, heaven became an ecclesiastical community. The saint in heaven, while still quite spiritual, became more material, more sensual, more open to communication – in short, more human. All three images of heaven – the compensatory paradise of Irenaeus, the ascetic afterlife of the early Augustine, and the ecclesiastical model – were to reappear in various guises throughout Christian history.

A Compensation for Martyrs: The Glorified Material World

The periodic eruptions of violence directed at Christians in the second and third centuries forced them to consider seriously their relationship to Roman society. The church of the martyrs appreciated the world as something good but felt that it was "occupied" by the enemy, that is, the pagans. Typically these Christians lived in or around the urban centers of the Roman Empire where they engaged in trade or business. They were not isolated from pagan society but depended on the non-Christian world for their physical survival. As urban Christians, they interacted continually with a non-believing society which caused them both psychological and physical difficulties. Pagan culture, as they experienced it, often denied them their God-given right to enjoy the material blessings of creation.[1]

The problems faced by urban Christians in the second century can be illustrated by examining the career and writings of Irenaeus, bishop of Lyons (c. 140–200). Irenaeus was born in Asia Minor, educated in Smyrna and possibly Rome. Settling in the West, he became a presbyter active in Vienne and Lyons. With an estimated 200,000 inhabitants, Lyons was not only the capital of Gaul, but also the greatest city in Europe after Rome. Lyons must have been a paradise for traders. A great clearing-house for the commerce in corn, wine, oil, and lumber, it served as a manufacturing and distribution center for most of the articles consumed by Gaul, Germany, and Britain. Those who profited from the trade and related financial activities were mostly foreigners who did not attain local citizenship. Like Irenaeus, the Christians living in Lyons

48

were mainly immigrant merchants coming from western Asia Minor. These urban Christians, like their pagan neighbors, were professional people possessing slaves.[2]

In 175–177 tensions between pagans and Christians of Lyons led to bloody persecutions. They were begun by a mob, but the Roman governor and his soldiers eventually took an active part. After the bishop of Lyons died during the persecutions, Irenaeus became his successor. Irenaeus seems to have saved his own life by hiding during these years. When the persecutions subsided, a member of the neighboring Christian community of Vienne wrote a report detailing their past afflictions. The author, who might well have been Irenaeus himself, glorified the achievements of the martyrs.[3]

Taking his inspiration from the legends of Jewish martyrs found in the second and fourth book of the Maccabees, the writer of the report praised the martyrs in biblical style. As parts of the Septuagint Bible these books were well known in the early church although now they are no longer in the Protestant canon. One story described how a Jewish mother was martyred together with her seven sons. Refusing to eat pork in violation of the Jewish law, one family member after another was brutally tortured and killed. All of them died in the hope of getting back their bodies and being reunited in another life here on earth. They accepted martyrdom "that they might rise again to a better life." In one version, the mother referred to Ezekiel's vision of the resurrection as a scriptural warrant for this hope. One of the sons offered his limbs to his torturer saying, "It was from Heaven that I received these; for the sake of His laws I disdain them; from Him I hope to receive them again." This is not a death-wish of someone tired of life, but the triumphant belief in a material life, even beyond death.[4]

The same ardent belief in bodily resurrection formed the center of the Christian creed as professed by the martyrs of Lyons. This was well understood by their persecutors, who burnt their victims' mutilated bodies "in order that they may not even hope of a resurrection." After having thrown the ashes into the Rhone river, the persecutors remarked, "Now let us see if they will rise again, and if their god can help them." The Christian reports of the tortures and deaths of martyrs followed the Jewish tradition. The pagans could brutally persecute the mortal bodies of the faithful, but could not prevent those loyal to Christ from regaining life in a future world. From the Christian perspective, even dumping the ashes in the river would not stop the body from resurrecting and gaining back all it had lost.[5]

Another contemporary document, the *Martyrdom of Polycarp*, included the same message. When bishop Polycarp, the teacher of Irenaeus, was persecuted, he did not seek martyrdom. He left Smyrna in order to hide in the country. Eventually, however, he was spotted, arrested, and burnt at the stake (155 or 166). In his last prayer before dying, the aged bishop asserted his firm belief in "the resurrection of eternal life of both soul and body, made incorruptible by the Holy Spirit." Polycarp did not march bravely to his death because he hated the world and wanted to flee into the next. He tried to preserve his life, but when the reality of martyrdom was upon him he took comfort in knowing that his body and soul would be resurrected. Contrary to our assumption that those who die for Christ despise this world, Christian martyrs accepted the goodness of their natural lives. They expected that after martyrdom they would experience an improved earthly existence. They wanted to enjoy *this* world, not some imaginary heavenly realm. This belief was shared by their theologian, Irenaeus.[6]

Irenaeus's theology, set forth in his treatise *Against the Heresies*, distinguished three successive periods of human history: the present era of persecution, the Kingdom of the Messiah, and the Kingdom of God the Father. These three periods follow one after the other. They are historical phases in God's plan for all Christians and not stages in the fate of the individual human soul. History, for Irenaeus, occurs in this world and includes a world governed successively by the pagans, the Messiah, and eventually God the Father. The compensation martyrs receive is not that of their souls moving upwards through various levels of the universe, but rather their earthly life back again.

For Irenaeus, the present era of persecution was characterized by a basic tension between the goodness of creation and pagan hostility. Irenaeus wrote extensively against Gnostic Christians who felt that the present world was intrinsically bad and probably the work of an evil god. Against this "heresy" he affirmed the goodness of creation. God gave humanity not only scriptural guidance to earn salvation, but also the blessings of nature. The highest blessing was the incarnation, when God's son in the figure of Christ became human. The very fact that the divine took on human nature ensured that the human could become divine.

Despite persecution by state authorities, Irenaeus did not take a negative view of the Roman Empire as such. The world created by God was not essentially evil, nor were its people – even the Romans. When discussing the secret name of the Antichrist in the book of Revelation, Irenaeus considered that perhaps "Lateinos" was suitable. "The Latins are they who at present bear rule," he commented; "I will not, however, make any boast of this [coincidence]." Thus he dismissed the identification, rejecting the idea that the Antichrist's empire was that of the Romans. Elsewhere, Irenaeus was more explicit. "The world enjoys peace through [the Romans]," he insisted, "and we can travel by land and sea wherever we want without fear." Unmolested travel was of course essential for a community of merchants. Irenaeus, involved in the commercial life of Lyons, respected the Romans for creating a safe environment for business.[7]

Irenaeus's acceptance of the natural world and his hope of living in harmony with pagan society also shaped his polemic against the heresy he detested, Gnosticism. The radical dualism of a bad material world and a superior spiritual existence allowed Gnostics to distance themselves from all social conventions and all established authorities. Theirs was a mentality prone to subversion. Why bow to the social customs of this world if everything not spiritual was fundamentally evil? From Irenaeus's perspective, the reputation of the whole Christian church was at stake. True Christians must dissociate themselves from those radicals who assembled in unauthorized meetings, like regular congregations. At a time when the general society was still suspicious and not quite ready to welcome Christians as reliable partners in social and business life, the Gnostics were a continual threat. The Gnostic movement, as Irenaeus perceived it, disturbed societal peace and order and thus undermined the respectability of good Christians. In a community where trade was a major concern, social stability was essential.[8]

Irenaeus appreciated the secure Roman Empire as well as the civilized urban life it produced. The Gnostic heretics, however, ignored "the necessities of our mode of life." The bishop warned his followers against behaving like a mad Gnostic who "glories in his own wisdom, separates from the company of the Gentiles, and possesses nothing [derived from] other people's goods, but is literally naked and barefoot, and dwells homeless among the mountains as any of those animals that feed on grass." Unlike the Gnostic, whom Irenaeus saw as rejecting the world, the true Christian valued life. Yet, a dilemma plagued the community at Lyons. Pagan leadership could be so total that the authorities could, and sometimes did, claim the lives of Christians. The deaths of the martyrs prevented Christians from enjoying the goodness of creation and from fully participating in the blessings brought to them by Christ.[9]

The first period of history, then, was marred by persecution. Although the world was seen as good and intended for Christian use, pagan society kept peace and prosperity from occurring. Irenaeus resolved this dilemma by predicting a second period of human history, the Kingdom of the Messiah. God would begin this kingdom by resurrecting the righteous among the dead and restoring their bodies to full material life. The new life would not take place in some distant heavenly realm, but on earth. "For it is just that in the very creation in which they toiled or were afflicted," Irenaeus wrote, "being proved in every way of suffering, they should receive the reward of their suffering. In the creation in which they were slain because of their love to God, in that they should be revived again." God has not created the world as a dungeon in which the righteous should be tortured and martyred, but as a place for truly living and enjoying material blessings. In the messianic kingdom the martyrs will reclaim the world as the possession which was denied to them by their persecutors. In the creation in which they endured servitude, they will eventually reign.[10]

Ever since the Old Testament book of Daniel and the New Testament book of Revelation, a connection had existed between the situation of martyrdom and millenarian views. Among the oppressed and martyrs of today we find a similar inclination to adopt millenarian hopes. According to the notes of a contemporary traveller, the poor peasants of Brazil entertain the hope of bodily resurrection and the return of the dead in a way not preached to them by the Catholic church. With crude letters a peasant wrote on the wall of his hut: "And I will lay sinews upon you, and will cause flesh to come upon you, and cover you with skin, and put breath in you, and you shall live." This biblical passage from Ezekiel 37 announces God's resurrection of the dead. In a similar vein, a widow, whose husband had been killed by the agents of a big landowner, wrote to a priest: "Even if they kill us, we will surely return, and then we will be millions." Oppressed and martyred Christians believe in a God who cannot ultimately deny life to them.[11]

Irenaeus brought millennial views from Asia Minor to the West where they gained new relevance during the persecution in southern France. Using numerous references from the Old and New Testaments, as well as apocryphal writings, he strove to paint an image of the new world he expected: restored to life, the human body will be placed in an ideal environment. There the body will be immensely fertile, and women will give birth to numerous children. Nature itself will provide wine and grain in abundance so people will no longer tire their bodies by working. The Lord himself will prepare a table for the righteous, supplying them with all kinds of delicacies. There are of course no enemies in the new world. Not even the beasts can be counted as foes because they are subject to human rule. In the new world, no one will ever grow old and die.

Again and again Irenaeus assured his readers that whatever could be inferred from the Bible and other sources about the coming bountiful age must be understood literally. "Nothing is capable of being allegorized, but all things are steadfast and true and substantial, having been made by God for the enjoyment of the righteous." Creation was "steadfast and true and substantial," and no divine promise must be spiritualized. Just as the persecutions of the pagans were real, so would be the restoration of a prosperous life in the future. In the Kingdom of the Messiah the saints "wax stronger by the sight of the Lord," thus preparing themselves for the next stage of universal history.[12]

Millennial visions of the future were not accepted by later theologians, but sometimes their polemical summaries can serve as a guide to understanding these doctrines. "Being fond of his body (*philosomatos*) and very carnal," wrote Eusebius (264–340), an alleged heretic "dreamt of a future according to his own desires, given up to the indulgence of the flesh, that is, eating and drinking and marrying." By the fourth century, millenarian views would be outlawed, but in the second century there was nothing unusual about imagining a future kingdom of Christ where the human body would be given its due.[13]

After one thousand years the Kingdom of the Messiah would be succeeded by the Kingdom of God the Father. While this kingdom was to last forever, Irenaeus described it only allusively. In one passage he stated simply that God the Father will "subsequently [i.e. after the millennium] bestow in a paternal manner those things which neither the eye has seen, nor the ear has heard, nor has thought concerning them arisen within the heart of man." Elsewhere Irenaeus spoke of "communion with the holy angels, and union with spiritual beings." After predicting a fruitful and rich existence in the Kingdom of the Messiah, Ireneus seemed unsure of what the Kingdom of God the Father would bring.[14]

For Irenaeus, the spiritual Kingdom of God the Father, to be established after the millennium, was not as important as the Kingdom of the Messiah. Irenaeus's mind was full of colorful images and inspiring expectations of a life which followed the one we have here and now. He struggled to understand the resurrection of the righteous who would enjoy a real life in a material world. Here they would be compensated for whatever was denied to them by a hostile pagan environment. Men and women who had set their hope in Christ could only temporarily, but not forever, be excluded from the full enjoyment of God's creation. What happened after experiencing those joys for a thousand years under the guidance of Christ was of little concern. Once Irenaeus assured his fellow Christians that their unhappy lives would be given back to them in greater glory, the question of what followed was superfluous.

For urban Christians like Irenaeus, the next life must be a continuation and completion of the present existence – an existence often endangered and cruelly cut off by martyrdom. The tortured body of the saint would be restored to its wholeness and integrity. In the fertile environment of the life to come, Christians would bear and raise children. Passing references to an ensuing Spiritual Kingdom of God the Father represented Irenaeus's attempt to find a place for the New Testament teaching of no marriages in heaven. The doctrine of the Spiritual Kingdom only underscores the realistic, material nature of the millennium in which Irenaeus believed. For Christians who wanted to live in the world, carry on business, and raise families, compensation in a glorified material world was God's great promise. Their loyalty to Christ had already been tested by torture and humiliation; now they were ready to experience a full life on earth.

The Ascetic Promise: A Heaven for Souls

By the fourth century, martyrs were figures of the past venerated as saints. The days of testing one's loyalty to Christ by enduring physical suffering imposed by pagan authorities were over. Christians now looked for another model of saintliness and perfection. They found it in asceticism. The Christian ascetic, like the martyr, proved his or her loyalty to Christ by heroically accepting pain, rejecting the comforts of family life, and striving for total commitment to the life of the spirit. With the ending of the period of persecution, asceticism became the highest goal. Asceticism made sense as a powerful solution to the main problem of religion: how to bridge the gap between the human and the divine. By participating both in this world (through the body) and in the realm of God (by leading the angels' virginal life), the ascetic provided the missing link. To follow the historical shift from the world of the martyrs to that of the ascetics we turn from Irenaeus to the young Augustine. We also move from France to North Africa and Italy. In that environment steeped in Greco-Roman thought, Augustine developed his ascetic and mystical theology, a spirituality that was far removed from the down-to-earth millennialism of Irenaeus.

In an environment dominated by ascetic ideals, traditional images of a this-worldly millennium were too materialistic, too carnal, to be compatible with the new spirit. The expected end of the world could no longer be thought of as the prelude to just another phase of human history. The blessings of the millennium – living long on a fertile earth and having many children – held no attraction for them. Christians now longed for spiritual rest and enjoyment of God's presence. Since the entire world had been absorbed into the Roman political system, people were prepared to take the decline of the later Roman Empire as a sign of the end of all human history. When the political crisis culminated in the sack of Rome by the Goths (410), one could no longer ignore the signs of the times. For Augustine and many of his contemporaries, God's everlasting spiritual kingdom seemed close. Eternal life would commence without a millennial period.

As is well known, Augustine (354–430) did not start his life as a saint. In his *Confessions*, he retrospectively admitted all the sins of his youth. A successful student in law and rhetoric in Carthage, North Africa, he had time to attend the theater and enjoy the company of women. "It was a sweet thing to me both to love and to be loved," he reported, "and more sweet still when I was able to enjoy the body of my lover. And so I muddied the clear spring of friendship with the dirt of physical desire and clouded over its brightness with the dark hell of lust." Augustine took a concubine with whom he had a son. He also spent much time with a student gang known as the Subverters, "a savage and diabolical name" which the fashionable group chose for itself. He spurned the Christian faith of his widowed mother who supported him financially. An unbelieving youth, Augustine had a rousing good time. Only later would be reflect that he "was brought down to the depths of hell."[15]

Gradually, however, Augustine discovered the world beyond the senses of the body. At first, he was attracted to pagan philosophy, but soon he discovered religion in the stern, puritan beliefs of Manichaeism. Then an important brand of Christianity, Manichaeism emphasized the malefic nature of matter in general and flesh in particular. For Manichaeans, everything carnal was sinful and sin culminated in the sexual act. Here began the story of Augustine's inner struggles that were only resolved more than a decade later when he bacame a celibate priest not of the Manichaean sect, but of the Catholic church. Echoes, however, of the endless conflict between the lust of the flesh and the calling to continence and purity can be heard even in Augustine's latest writings.

According to the *Confessions*, the chief agent in bringing Augustine to the right faith and in instilling in him the ideal of continence was his mother, Monica. She prayed for him, shed tears, followed him to Italy, persisted in admonishing him, and eventually succeeded in changing her son's life. In 386, she made him send away his concubine in hope of making way for a legitimate marriage with a woman of status. The repudiation of his companion became the first step toward Augustine's celibate life. A year later he had a conversion experience. Reading on an impulse Paul's letter to the Romans, the words struck home: "[Let us walk] not in rioting and drunkenness, not in chambering and impurities, not in contention and envy; but put ye on the Lord Jesus Christ, and make not provision for the flesh, to fulfill the lust thereof." This experience in a garden in Milan, within hearing distance of his mother, marked Augustine's conversion to the Catholic faith. His baptism followed and, more importantly, another garden experience.[16]

The year was 387. In the leisurely, quiet atmosphere of a villa in Ostia, Italy, the newly baptized Augustine and Monica "were alone and talking together and very sweet our talk was." Leaning out of a window which looked onto the garden, they mused about heaven, attempting to discover "what the eternal life of the saints could be like." In his *Confessions* Augustine reported how they advanced step by step through all bodily things up to the sky. Advancing still further, the pair touched divinity itself, and together the young Augustine and his mother experienced an ecstatic rapture. Augustine later recalled that "the greatest possible delights of our bodily senses, radiant as they might be with the brightest of corporeal light, could not be compared with the joys of that [eternal] life." Although touching the deity "just lightly," they were overwhelmed with joy and happiness. They became silent, "and we sighed."[17]

Augustine had prepared and purified his soul for this moment. He also received support from the presence of Monica. According to one historian, "the mere presence of a woman gives the vision of Ostia a touching character." The mystical episode in the garden underscores Monica's role in her son's spiritual life. She funtioned as a companion, a spiritual guide, and an intercessor between her son and God. In Augustine's view, her constant prayer and sacrifices offered up to God served to procure for him the special grace which led to his salvation. It was a testimony to the mutual love between mother and son that they were able to foretaste the beatific vision together. Yet their closeness did not lead to a shared encounter with the divine. Linked to God individually, each soul enjoyed the vision alone. The ascetic heaven they experienced was God-centered and left no room for communication among the blessed.[18]

After the rapture in the garden of Ostia had faded, Monica expressed a wish to her son which exemplified the ascetic nature of her ecstasy. "My son, as to me, I no longer find any pleasure in this life," she remarked. "What more I have to do here, and why I am still here I do not know." The loving intimacy which Augustine and Monica shared could not be compared with the delights of the divine. Lovers want to stay together, but mystics yearn for parting and being with the Lord. Monica no longer cared that she would be buried beside her husband in her native soil. The mystical experience had severed her from worldly attachments as well as loosening her soul from her body. Within a fortnight, Monica was dead.[19]

The heaven of which Augustine had a foretaste in the garden of Ostia was the hereafter of platonizing Greek philosophy. This philosophy was adopted by numerous Christian intellectuals who considered the Greek-speaking world as possessing the most sophisticated culture of the time. Augustine and many of his contemporaries venerated the work of Plotinus (205–70), a Neoplatonist who in his later years served as court philosopher to the Roman emperor Gallienus. Plotinus's teaching strongly recommended the renunciation of the world and the adoption of an ascetic lifestyle. In order not to become entangled with the material world, he claimed that we must renounce power, office, and rulership. We should also not fall prey to the snares of "flawless skin and beautiful bodies."[20]

Plotinus believed that all of these worldly delights detract and alienate us from our real concern, which should be the contemplation of true beauty. That beauty could only be found in the transcendent world of eternal, immaterial ideas. In that realm absolute beauty was uncontaminated by flesh and body. The aim of philosophy was to loosen the soul from the body, to strengthen its spiritual power, and to prepare it for its eventual heavenly ascent after the death of the body. Through meditation and contemplation one could attain "deliverance from the things of this world. . .escape in solitude to the Solitary." Fleeing to the Alone or One, the detached, lonely soul rose upward and glimpsed the eternal and truly beautiful.[21]

In less abstract terms, the same philosophy can be found in a pagan treatise called *Poimandres*, probably dating from Plotinus's lifetime. This book describes how at death the well-prepared soul of the ascetic philosopher leaves behind everything mortal and corruptible. Rising through the seven spheres of heaven, the soul travels to the deity. There it joins other spirits who spend eternity "singing with sweet voice to God." The God of *Poimandres* is the supreme deity acknowledged by many ancient philosophers. Both Plotinus and the *Poimandres* assumed that through solitary concentration on the divine, the soul would loosen its connection with matter and ascend to its true home.[22]

When the young Augustine left his native Thagaste in North Africa to study in Carthage and Rome, he was exposed to such philosophies. What he eventually adopted was a blend of Platonism and Christianity. In his *Confessions* he admitted that he struggled to gain access to a mystical experience of the higher reality. Inspired by his reading of philosophy, he concentrated on his soul's heavenly ascent. The first results he had in Milan in 386 were disappointing. The vision of the divine was fleeting and could not be attained as something permanent and abiding. A lack of sufficient moral strength and mental purity, he thought, prevented him from sustaining union with the divine.

It was then that he decided that a mental, spiritual union with God meant the ultimate human happiness − a decision of momentous consequence for Christian history. In his *Confessions* Augustine not only reports on his various mystical raptures, but also explains how to advance "step by step" to ever higher realms. Leaving the material world behind, the mind focuses on the soul. Moving always inward toward the soul's interior, the Christian arrives at a point when, "in the flash of a trembling glance," the deity can be reached. In such moments, Augustine experienced "a kind of sweet delight." To remain in that state permanently "would be something not of this world, not of this life," but of the life to come. If such ecstasy went on forever it would be indistinguishable from the joys of heaven.[23]

Along with this mysticism, Augustine adopted the ascetic lifestyle recommended by Neoplatonism and firmly established in monasticism. Anecdotes and sayings current among the early monks echoed the Neoplatonic "escape in solitude to the Solitary." "Unless a man shall say in his heart, 'I alone and God are in this world,' he shall not find quiet," summarized one dictum. A similar opinion was expressed by "an old man" who was asked what kind of person a monk should be. He answered: "As far as I am concerned, a loner to the Alone (*solus ad solum*)." Inspired by this attitude, Augustine's conversion led him to reject his sexual appetite and to lead a sternly celibate life which he never abandoned.[24]

Augustine exchanged the marriage bed for the Bible: "May your scriptures be my chaste delight," he prayed in the *Confessions*. Reading the word of God afforded more pleasure than making love. Accordingly, he extolled celibacy as the "life of the angels" which actually anticipated heavenly existence. Virginal integrity and freedom from all carnal relations served as a foretaste of eternal life. "Let all conjugal chastity bow to this," he insisted. Although he acknowledged the virtues of conjugal life, Augustine gave clear preference to the angelic mode of existence. It is not difficult to see Plotinus's spirit in this attitude. Fleeing from the delights of the senses to the pleasures of reading, the religious intellectual would be uncontaminated by worldly matters. As the bishop of Hippo in North Africa, Augustine still thought and lived the ascetic paradigm taught by the philosopher.[25]

The influence of Plotinus was also evident in Augustine's biblical exegesis. In a treatise called *On Faith and the Creed* (393) Augustine struggled with St. Paul's assertion that in eternal life we will have "spiritual *bodies*." What will be the bodily dimension of heavenly existence? Augustine took great care to reconcile the Pauline expression with Neoplatonic philosophy by liberating the term "body" (*corpus*) from all its material connotations. After the resurrection, there will be an "angelic change" in which our bodies lose their material quality. There will be "no more flesh and blood, but only body." A celestial body cannot have "celestial flesh," Augustine carefully pointed out. There can be no fleshly dimension to the next life. Everything must be spiritual. Thus Augustine "began his career as a Christian priest and author with an idea of immortality of the soul which excludes resurrection of the body."[26]

While the young Augustine could call his dead parents his "fellow citizens in the eternal [heavenly] Jerusalem," this touching thought remained unexplored as well as unrelated to his basic philosophy. This is not to say that Augustine was unaware of social joys. His love of friendship was evidence to the contrary. Yet Augustine insisted on the irrelevance of any social joys for true happiness. "Whoever knows you [God]," he decided, "and others besides, is not happier for knowing them, but is happy for knowing you alone." The pursuit of happiness was a fundamental human appetite, but one that could only be satisfied by God himself. For the ascetic Augustine, human community provided solace in this world, but God would provide all happiness in the next.[27]

Ascetic Christians not only rejected the remnants of pagan culture but looked upon the entire material universe with suspicion. The world served as the domain, if not the creation, of the devil. The dualist approach of both Gnosticism and Neoplatonism stressed the value of spirit over matter. Moderate adherents of this spirituality, like Augustine, lived in the city and sought the companionship of like-minded intellectuals. There they debated and studied in order to nourish their spiritual life. Others left the city, retiring to the desert where they lived as monks or nuns. By preferring celibate lifestyles, ascetics of both city and desert eliminated the sensuality of sexual intercourse and the distracting ties of the family. Like charismatic New Testament Christians, they could try to live fully in the spirit of God.

Augustine's spiritual heaven was the continuation of an ascetic retired life. It was a world of immaterial, fleshless souls finding rest and pleasure in God. This notion made sense to monks, hermits, and philosophers who all preferred the life of the spirit to that of the flesh. It would not make sense to those urban Christians, like Irenaeus, who hoped for compensation for their earthly trials. Although Augustine was a celibate priest, he did not lead the contemplative life of a hermit. Appointed bishop in 396, he found himself responsible for a large number of people who lived in "the world." These fourth- and fifth-century believers were the heirs of those second-century Christians who had experienced the goodness of the world. Thus Augustine came to be closely related to the world of business, politics, families, and ambition. Toward the end of his life, Augustine revised his view of heaven.

The Ecclesiastical Promise: Physical Beauty Eternalized

According to Augustine's monumental *City of God* (413–27), eternal bliss consisted of the supreme enjoyment of "seeing God." Later doctrine called this the "beatific vision," because in heaven "we shall have eternal leisure to see that He is God." Seeing the deity was related to loving and praising God. Augustine, in unsurpassed rhetoric, reported: "There we shall rest and see, see and love, love and praise. This is what shall be in the end without end." Or elsewhere, "He [God] shall be the end of our desires who shall be seen without end, loved without cloy, praised without weariness." In a sermon, Augustine imagined someone asking about human activities in eternal life: "What will I do? There will be no work for our limbs; what, then, will I do?" The bishop answered simply: "Is this no activity: to stand, to see, to love, to praise [God]?"[28]

Read in isolation, this looks very much like the heaven the young

Augustine had experienced in the garden of Ostia, the only difference being that his language had become more biblical. The bishop of Hippo, however, shifted his ascetic, theocentric views with a new assessment of the community of the blessed. This assessment went far beyond his earlier assertion that his dead parents would be "fellow citizens in the eternal Jerusalem." From a letter of consolation written in 408 a first glimpse of the bishop's revised view of the other life emerges. "You should not grieve as the heathen do who have no hope," he wrote to Italica, a Roman lady of rank who had lost her husband. "We have not lost our dear ones who have departed from this life, but have merely sent them ahead of us, so we also shall depart and shall come to that life where they will be more than ever dear as they will be better known to us, and where we shall love them without fear of parting." Existence in heaven, as Augustine now saw it, no longer consisted merely in the ecstasies of individual souls linked to God. The expectation of reuniting with friends and family gave heaven a new, social dimension. The bishop did not hesitate to extend the notion of community to the angels. They, too, "see each other, enjoying their company in God." Communication would be a universal feature of eternal existence.[29]

Instead of echoing the ascetic wisdom of Plotinus, Augustine now followed what was "the most popular classical belief about what happened in Hades." Family reunions, where the long-established dead greeted new arrivals in the netherworld, retained its place in pagan descriptions of life after death. This originally Greek belief spread to the Latin-speaking West where it was popularized by Cicero, in his dialogue *On Old Age* and especially in *Scipio's Dream.* Cicero intended in *Scipio's Dream* to encourage young Romans to participate in republican politics and administration. Both the dialogue and the dream culminated in the promise of eternal life in heaven for those who dedicated their lives to the welfare of others. The Roman statesman Scipio – the dreamer – met several citizens of heaven including his own father whom he embraced and kissed with tears of joy.[30]

Both bishop Ambrose of Milan (340?–397) and his student Augustine knew these famous texts. When Ambrose wrote a book of consolation after the death of his brother, he expressed in words borrowed from Cicero his hope to be reunited with his family after death. The bishop of Milan also used Cicero's meeting-again motif in his well-publicized funeral orations for two Roman emperors, Valentinian (died 392) and Theodosius (died 395). Ambrose imagined the heavenly happiness of Theodosius "when he receives Gratian and Pulcheria, his sweetest children, whom he had lost here; when his [wife] Flacilla, a soul faithful to God, embraces him; when he rejoices that his father has been restored to him; and when he embraces [the emperor] Constantine." The

Christian promise of Ambrose was no different from that of the Roman hope of Cicero.[31]

Meeting family in heaven sounded convincing to fourth- and fifth-century Christians. Had not St. Paul, in his heavenly vision, met the Virgin Mary, Old Testament patriarchs, and several of the prophets? This heavenly reunion could be read about in an apocryphal text dating from around 388. In that year, Paul's "original" and hitherto unpublished description of his ecstatic vision was allegedly found in his house in Tarsus. Entitled the *Vision of Paul*, it enjoyed wide circulation and was known – and not taken too seriously – by Augustine. Searching for more serious religious literature, the bishop found a passage on heavenly reunion in Cyprian's book *On Mortality*. The text's Ciceronian flavor may have attracted Augustine, and he quoted the passage with approval. "Why do we not hasten and run," Cyprian asked, "that we may see our [heavenly] fatherland, that we may hail our relatives? A great number of those who are dear to us are expecting us there. A dense and abundant crowd of parents, brothers, and sons are longing for us." What may have sounded daring in the days of Cyprian of Carthage (died c. 258), now had a new and convincing ring.[32]

Although Augustine never elaborated on the meeting-again motif, he did in his later years discuss in greater depth the meaning of the spiritual bodies promised to Christians. In the blessed state, he maintained, human beings will have bodies – beautiful, fleshly, tangible bodies by which they communicate. The elderly Augustine allowed the blessed to have more substance than he had granted them earlier. In his *Retractations* (427) he explicitly modified the notion of heavenly bodies as explained in *On Faith and the Creed* written over thirty years earlier. He now maintained that the spiritual body would be like the resurrected body of Christ – made of flesh and bones, seen with all its parts, and touchable by others.[33]

"Take away death, the last enemy," preached the bishop in a sermon of 417, "and my own flesh will be my dear friend throughout eternity." Even "the substance of flesh will exist in the kingdom of God." Augustine no longer saw any difficulty in introducing "the flesh" into heaven. "Our faith," he exclaimed, "instructed by God, praises the [human] body." The blessed also may eat and drink – just for pleasure, of course, not for satisfying hunger or quenching thirst. Even the vision of God can be spoken of in bodily terms. Our bodily eyes will be able to see God, although he is pure spirit. Augustine offered this speculation despite the lack of a scriptural warrant. The bishop could no longer be accused of being an enemy of the flesh.[34]

This was not to say, however, that there would be no spiritual element in our heavenly personalities. In fact, the spirit will dominate and guide the flesh, and the flesh will not be rebellious any more. "When the flesh serves the spirit," explained Augustine, "it will justly be called spiritual." The glorified human body, although spiritual, will not be a spirit. Augustine did not have to repudiate his earlier rejection of the flesh. Instead what he did was to acknowledge that once the flesh was redeemed and led by the spirit it could participate in the glory of God.[35]

With his characteristic preference for the divine nature of beauty, Augustine envisioned a heaven populated with men and women reflecting his aesthetic ideals. In life eternal all bodily blemishes that mar human beauty will be removed. "Where there is no proportion," Augustine asserted, "the eye is offended." The body, he contended, "shall be of that size which it either had attained or should have attained in the flower of its youth, and shall enjoy the beauty that arises from preserving symmetry and proportion in all its members." Therefore, "overgrown and emaciated persons need not fear that they shall be in heaven of such a figure as they would not be even in this world if they could help it." Equally, "a certain agreeableness of color" will not be overlooked in our heavenly bodies. There will not only be bodies in heaven, they also will be unspeakably lovely.[36]

The persistence of the scars of the martyrs is the only exception to the perfection of the spiritual body. The scars will not only remain visible but actually enhance the appeal of the saints' bodies. "The love we bear to the blessed martyrs causes us, I know not how, to desire to see in the heavenly kingdom the marks of the wounds which they received for the name of Christ; and possibly," Augustine concluded, "we shall see them." Such a desire was hitherto unknown among the martyrs who wanted their bodies restored to full health and perfection. Scars were intriguing only as a theological paradox — that of the presence of marks of violence on perfectly beautiful bodies. For Augustine, the wounds of the martyrs had become as mythical as martyrdom itself.[37]

In heaven, beauty reigns. Discussing the functional and aesthetic aspects of the human body, the bishop noted that bodily functions will have a limited meaning, for "need is bound to pass away, and the time will come when we shall enjoy nothing but one another's beauty, without any lust." Despite the exclusion of lust, some form of erotic appeal can be discerned in his view of heavenly beauty. Augustine pondered the question of whether or not resurrected women will be deprived of the features of their sex:

> Both sexes will rise. For there will be no lust there, which is the cause of shame. For before they sinned they were naked, and the man and woman were not ashamed. So all defects will be taken away from those bodies, but their natural state will be preserved. The female sex is not a defect, but a natural state, which will then know no intercourse or child-birth. There will be female parts, not suited to their old use, but to a new beauty, and this will

not arouse the lust of the beholder, for there will be no lust, but it will inspire praise of the wisdom and goodness of God, who both created what was not, and freed from corruption what he made.

Thus in heaven men and women will be able to appreciate the perfect beauty of bodies that are restored to the nakedness of paradise. And yet this erotic appeal is not bound up with the desire and possessiveness characteristic of this life. In the other life, there will be no temptation of sexual intimacy, because there will be no temptation at all.[38]

Sexual intimacy is conspicuously absent in Augustine's heaven, even though the aged bishop allowed Adam and Eve to enjoy a certain amount of physical delight in paradise. Paradise restored, apparently, will be somewhat less attractive than the original design. The aesthetic appreciation of physical human beauty, however, will remain. Augustine did not miss the opportunity to endow heavenly beauty with a theocentric twist. The new female appearance will not be enjoyed purely for its own sake, but will "inspire praise of the wisdom and goodness of God." If on earth feminine beauty drew men away from God, in heaven it will bring them toward God. Augustine's heaven is a place of true love (caritas), not of lust (cupiditas). In his paradise no love will exist "without reference to God." All human relationships will have a theocentric orientation.[39]

For Augustine, true human relationships even in this life must have the same theocentric quality. They have to be formed on the basis of belief in and love of God. "All of us who enjoy God are also enjoying each other in Him." Augustine borrowed the theocentric clause "in Him" from the New Testament. He explained the clause by saying that "when you enjoy a human person in God then you are actually enjoying God more than the human person."[40]

Modern readers of Augustine have not always approved of his idea of loving someone "in God." We feel uneasy with a philosophy that thinks of people as means for loving God rather than as ends in themselves. "Although Augustine succeeds in subordinating lesser loves to the one considered most important," argues critic Irving Singer, "his doctrine falsifies the love of persons. It even commits a disrespect toward the works of God. If everything is but a means to an ultimate object of love, nothing can be cherished or fully appreciated except that ultimate. As a mere instrumentality, no person, thing, or institution could be loved in itself." Must men and women be a mere accessory used as a means to love God? Do not human beings merit love in themselves?[41]

While it must be admitted that Augustine's language was not always felicitous, and lends itself to such questions, critics like Singer have failed to understand what the bishop really meant. Augustine's philosophy of love culminates in identifying love of God with the love of other humans. The love of God is not abstract as in Neoplatonism, but concrete and, in a way, social as well as worldly. Although some Christians, we are told by Augustine, were disturbed by the question of "how much love we ought to spend upon our brother, and how much upon God," the bishop stated that an alternative did not exist. "We love God and our neighbor from one and the same love," and the one act of loving touches on our fellow humans and God at the same time. We cannot attain God without loving our neighbor.[42]

Augustine carefully protected this statement against misunderstanding. For the bishop, God cannot be reduced to human size since he always remains greater than any creature. Consequently, God is always more loved than creatures. On the other hand, when our love reaches beyond the merely human, this does not falsify its truly human quality. True love always respects the needs of our neighbor. "We should not love human beings as things to be consumed," Augustine cautioned; "friendship consists in benevolence, leading us to do things for the benefit of those we love." Or again: "Our love must not be feigned but sincere, seeking the happiness of our sisters and brothers, and expecting no other profit than their happiness." While having a strong theological dimension, Augustine's love retains its human integrity. People are not to be mere conduits for transmitting messages of love to God. [43]

Augustine's view of the fellowship of the saints in heaven reflects his understanding of the divine nature of love. In heaven, earthly relationships – "friends, household, children, and wife" – will be replaced by "the society of the angels and the heavenly community [civitas coelestis]." In the heavenly community, the individualized relationships of earth are dissolved. Friendship, marriage bonds, and the household have no place. In spite of Augustine's promotion of the cult of friendship, he did not allow dyadic or small-group affection to continue in the other world. Sharing Cicero's high esteem for friendship, Augustine agreed with the Roman statesman that the bonds of affection "always unite two persons only, or, at most, a few." In heaven, there will be no exclusive emotional attachments or the intimacy of shared thoughts between individuals.[44]

Since in the city of God there will be no special friendships, there will be no strangers. All special attachments will be absorbed into one comprehensive and undifferentiated community of love. With this theory, Augustine resolved a problem that must have plagued him throughout his whole life. Human fellowship, from simple acquaintance to deep friendship, must remain incomplete and unsatisfactory in this world. Our separation from God also results in our separation from our fellow human beings. The burden of sin is loneliness. "In this sojourning life all carry their own hearts," Augustine observed, "and every heart to every other heart is shut." Even the husband is "better known to himself" than to his wife. Closed hearts and mutual ignorance, in Augustine's view, create endless suspicions which make human division seemingly insurmountable. "Most of the evils of humankind," he suggested, "have no other cause but false suspicions." The result is confusion: we often hate our friends, while trusting our enemies. Could we but *know* one another, we should be less tempted to say to ourselves, "I alone am good."[45]

But in the eternal city of heaven, "the hearts of all will be transparent, manifest, luminous in the perfection of love." Gone will be the suspicions and confusions. There will be no darkness, no obscurity in heaven, and hence no divisions among its citizens. God's light will shine upon the hidden, and in that light each to each will be "the better known, the better beloved." When obscurity, the basis of division, no longer exists, there must be true and eternal fellowship between *all* the blessed. Nothing will be hidden between ourselves and others, "for none will be strangers." Augustine had no notion of romantic intimacy and shared secrets. His concern was with universal fellowship based on complete openness of mind and heart. The universalized love of heaven permits no exclusive, restricted circles of friends. In the heavenly community, friendship will be replaced by love.[46]

The bishop not only lacked the notion of shared secrets and romantic intimacy; he was also unable to appreciate the variety of human personalities. On earth people cannot be fully united because of their diverse wills, judgments, opinions, and customs. A threat to social peace and harmony, diversity can always ignite into dispute and fighting. In heaven, however, all differences will be gone, for people will be united "fully and perfectly." In the presence of God all diversity will vanish.[47]

Augustine's new theology of heaven must be seen in the context of his biography. As a young convert, Augustine had been a stern world-renouncer whose Christian spirituality was in keeping with the Neo-platonic "flight from the world." By the middle of his life, the harshness of the young man had mellowed. Historian Peter Brown detected that as Augustine aged, he became "far more open to the reality of the bonds that unite men to the world around them." When Augustine came to think of Catholicism as a universal religion, rather than the privilege of a small sect of ascetics striving for perfection, he could no longer de-preciate the world or exclude sexuality. The belief that sexuality could be abandoned reflected the faith that society could be stepped out of – a belief the old bishop no longer entertained. He came to believe in the essential goodness of created things, including the human body and marital sexuality. "According to each part," he wrote in *On Continence* (414–16), "both soul and body, the human being was made good by a good God." Revising his earlier views, Augustine now appreciated "conjugal embraces" as both "enjoyable" and "legitimate." As the "original good" contrasts with the "original evil" of sin, human fertility belongs to the great blessings God has bestowed upon humankind. Propagation, therefore, cannot be sinful even in this fallen state.[48]

Augustine's reorientation brought him closer to the realities of both church and state. In the *City of God* he spoke of the church as the institution through which Christ exercises his millennial reign. That reign extends over the world, not in some distant future, but *here and now*. In his controversies with other theologies, the bishop successfully used the help of state authorities to condemn rival Christian systems. "For all his intellectual distaste for Rome," explained William Frend, "he became increasingly a Roman official in outlook as he grew older." As Augustine moved closer to the world, he came to a fresh assessment of human relationships. The human community was now seen to continue in the other world, with the body taking on more material qualities than his earlier philosophy had allowed.[49]

A crucial step in the movement toward his appreciation of this-worldly realities was the new way in which Augustine defined the relationship of spirit and matter. In his later writings he no longer separated mind and matter with the hope of escaping into a world of pure, uncontaminated spirit. Instead, he consistently pointed out how spirit or spiritual values operate *within*, rather than above and beyond, material and social structures. The spirit is not separate from the realm of matter, but the former should dominate the latter. The integration of spirit and matter, with spirit ruling over matter, can be traced in all levels of Augustine's thought.

When a human individual is fashioned, for example, God connects "in some wonderful fashion the spiritual and corporeal natures, the one to command, the other to obey, and by mating and joining them makes a living creature." While this relationship of command and obedience remains imperfect in this life, it will be perfect in the next. Then, Augustine predicted, the spirit will dominate and guide the flesh. The flesh will serve the spirit, and there will be no alienation between the two. What the bishop affirmed on the individual level was also true for the body politic. Political life replicates the relationship of spirit and flesh. Just as the flesh should serve the spirit, so — in the language of Psalm 2 — the kings of the world must serve the Lord. The state must serve the church and accept its guiding role. The bishop's new philosophy fell more in line with the realities of a church involved in society and politics. What Augustine presented was not an *ad hoc* argument to support the claims of the church, but a full-blown ideology based on a comprehensive theory of mind and matter. It was this theory which led the bishop to form new ideas about heavenly bodies.[50]

The Varieties of the Patristic Paradise

The three images found in patristic writings correlate with three types of early Christian spirituality. Irenaeus, an author reflecting the urban Christianity of the martyrs, thought of *heaven as the glorified material world*. This heaven on earth included enhanced fertility in a worldly kingdom reigned by Christ. According to his millennial view, the world will some day be freed from the ungodly pagan control and placed into the hands of the righteous, who will then live for a thousand years and enjoy life in their material, fertile, and childbearing bodies. The characteristics of eternity after the thousand-year reign held little importance. The new life after death compensated persecuted Christians for sacrificing their bodies for Christ. All else was superfluous.

With the early Augustine, ascetic values were extended into the beyond. He expected a *purely spiritual heaven*, a world of "fleshless" souls that found rest and pleasure in seeing God. Spirit replaced matter in the celestial kingdom. Like the life of a celibate philosopher, life in heaven would be devoid of human interaction and family concerns. The older Augustine revised his earlier view by introducing the community of the blessed into the next world. Although still giving clear priority to the vision and praise of God, he spoke of meeting other saints and the mutual appreciation of their beautiful bodies. There still would be no family life or even friendship, since God would be the aim of all love. In this *semi-spiritual heaven* the soul united with the flesh in such a way that spirit dominated matter.

What Irenaeus and the "two Augustines" reported about our heavenly existence replicated, on a symbolic level, how they saw earthly realities. Irenaeus's expectation of a fertile and childbearing body corresponded to an appreciation of the human body as well as creation in general. The early Augustine's "fleshless" soul is understandable in the context of a negative attitude toward the human body generated by ascetic non-involvement with the world. The late Augustine's heavenly body, in which the flesh is completely at the will of the spirit, paralleled the bishop's understanding of life in this world. The body should be under the control of the spirit in the same way as the world should be under ecclesiastical guidance. Moreover, transformed, or nearly transformed, human bodies existed already in this life – among virgins and celibate monks and priests.

Celibacy in an ecclesiastical context acquired new meaning. In early Christianity the ascetic stepped out of the world in order to indicate the proper direction of human life: away from the world and toward God. The celibate person bridged the enormous metaphysical gap between the human and the divine. By the time of the later Augustine, the ascetic still performed this function but he or she was seen in a different manner. Now the ascetic, standing between the world and the deity, became a channel of divine grace for society. Just as heavenly bodies combined spirit and flesh – with spirit controlling and glorifying matter – the celibate invigorated the world. Virginity and the rejection of family imitated eternal life and reflected the descent of the Holy Spirit into the earthly realm. Thus the celibate priest, in whose body the Spirit resides, would be the ideal advisor or leader even in worldly affairs. The virgin who dedicated his or her life to God did not necessarily seek isolation from the political or social order, but acted in the community as an inspired guide. Just as the saint in heaven possesses and rules over a glorified and beautiful spiritual body, so the celibate clergy exerts divine control over the world of matter.

While the compensatory as well as the ascetic view of the next life were occasionally revived in later Christian speculation, the elderly bishop of Hippo defined a heaven which functioned as the leading theological model for more than a thousand years. Compared with the New Testament and ascetic conceptions, the heaven of *The City of God* was more mundane, more human, and less theocentric. The new human being, while still called spiritual, was more material, more sensual, more open to communication, and more like ourselves. At the same time, however, Augustine insisted that the Fall of Adam and Eve, resulting from their attempt to be independent of their Creator, had perverted the human will. Fallen humankind was proud and self-centered, with a will necessarily directed toward evil. Only the intervention of God could heal the individual human will and restore its original orientation toward the good and the divine. According to Augustine, therefore, humility and dependence upon the divine must shape Christian identity in this life and the next.[51]

In order for this utter dependence on God to change, human self-confidence and self-reliance had to be built up. This was not possible during the decline of the Roman Empire and the subsequent years of cultural stagnation. It would only become possible in the flourishing European communities of the Middle Ages – in monasteries, cities, and universities. Mystics redefined the abstract vision of God in terms of a more personalized relationship of love between Christ and the individual soul. Eventually, Renaissance and modern theologians even dared to focus on individual love among the glorified saints in heavenly paradise – at the expense of the beatific vision. The humanizing element which Augustine introduced could not sprout in the fifth century, but later religious thinkers, artists, and poets were to exploit his speculations to the fullest.

CHAPTER FOUR

Medieval Promises

From cities of the ancient Roman Empire – Lyons in Gaul and Hippo in North Africa – we now move to a complex network of monasteries, urban centers, and universities covering most of Europe. Seven hundred years have also passed, in which theology flourished but without creating new styles. In the twelfth and thirteenth centuries, major cultural change led to new theologies and to a thriving culture resting on a solid economic basis. For the first time, Europe had not only a rich feudal aristocracy but also a well-to-do class of merchants and artisans. The wealthy believed in the church and in supporting monks and monasteries, cathedrals and crusaders, scholars and preachers. They acknowledged that religion was as important as, if not nobler than, wealth and worldly power.

Most Europeans felt themselves to be members of a single community in the religious, social, and economic activities of which they enthusiastically participated. An optimistic spirit prevailed, and the people felt that God was with them. Christ, in the mass, came to Christians under the guise of bread. The newly recovered Aristotelian philosophy helped theologians develop the doctrine of transubstantiation to understand how the sacred could be so vividly present in the world. As the repository for the Eucharist and holy relics, churches radiated divine blessing. God was neither separated nor estranged from the human world. During the Middle Ages, heaven lost the abstractness of Augustine's descriptions. Medieval theologians, artists, poets, and visionaries made the afterlife more visible and accessible – at least to reason and imagination. Heaven became a part of the general world view.

Three new cultural concepts gave heaven its medieval shape: the city, the intellect, and love. An *urban revival* throughout Europe inspired religious writers to describe heaven no longer as a paradise garden but as a city, as the new Jerusalem. The paradise garden – a weak version of outlawed millenarian views – was made into a pleasant plain surrounding the heavenly city. While the city inspired the monastic mind, the *discovery of the intellect* challenged scholastic theologians. These pressed Augustine's often elusive speculations on heaven into a rigorous systematic structure, bringing the "vision of God" into sharp focus. The search for religious knowledge by theologians accompanied the *discovery of love* by poets and mystics. A new culture of male-female relationships in courtly life gave rise to the wish expressed by some poets of being reunited to the beloved in the next world. More characteristic of the Middle Ages, however, was the theocentric love of the mystics. In ecstatic rapture, mystics – often women – experienced in their lives what they expected as their eternal destiny: a passionate union with Christ. Medieval piety provided fertile ground for diverse and rich speculations on heavenly life.

Paradise Garden and Heavenly City

In the early Middle Ages monasteries were typically built in obscure out-of-the-way places. Often settling in the middle of an impenetrable forest or uncultivated land in uninhabited frontier regions, the monks devoted themselves to contemplation and agriculture. They followed St. Benedict's rule of *ora et labora* – pray and work. By tilling the soil, growing and harvesting crops, waiting for sufficient rain, and fearing the constant threat of bad harvest, they experienced the hardships and labors of traditional peasant life. Although many monasteries eventually grew rich and their members no longer did agricultural work themselves, the monasteries still depended on the land for their survival. Even wealthy abbeys could be paralyzed by drought or cattle plague.

The agrarian lifestyle of monastic communities made their members particularly responsive to the biblical story of paradise in Genesis. The educated read the story in the Latin Bible, and everyone heard it in sermons. Explaining humankind's fall from a nobler state, it described how the original pleasant life of Adam and Eve in a luxuriant garden changed into the miserable existence of peasants. Expelled from paradise, Adam struggled with the thorns and thistles of the cursed soil, while Eve was condemned to suffer pain in pregnancy and childbearing (Gen. 3). The Old Testament story aptly summarized the hard life of medieval society.

Someday, however, God would reverse the Fall and restore the original paradisal condition. At the end of time God would create a new earth and release the monks and all the righteous from their toils. "There, lilies and roses always bloom for you, smell sweet and never wither," promised Otfrid of Weissenburg, a German ninth-century monk and poet, "their fragrance never ceases to breathe eternal bliss into the soul." The implied symbolism suggests the new paradise as the

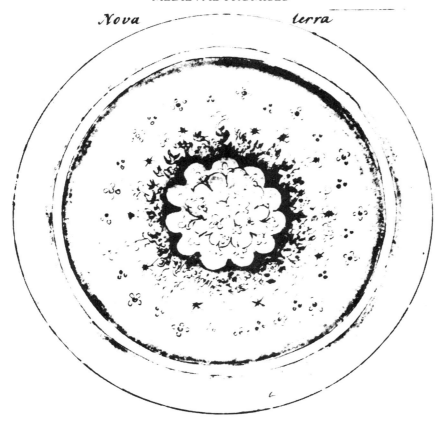

Nova — — *terra*

Pl. 3. The New Earth as Paradise Restored. 12th century. Herrad of Hohenbourg, *Hortus Deliciarum: Reconstruction*, ed. Rosalie Green et al. (London: Warburg Institute, 1979), pl. 140

appropriate home for martyrs ("roses") and celibate monks, saints, and virgins ("lilies"). The *Elucidation*, a widely used monastic manual of theology, concurred; the world will not always mirror our first parents' sin. Compiled in Latin around 1100, possibly in a Bavarian monastery, the book was frequently copied and printed throughout the Middle Ages. Vernacular translations and adaptations exist in German, Dutch, French, and English. The *Elucidation* described the new earth in much the same way as the Alsatian monk Otfrid, but supplied more detail.[1]

According to the *Elucidation*, after the Last Judgment God will remove all the consequences of the Fall: "The punishment for sin: that is, coldness, heat, hail, storm, lightning, thunder, and other inconveniences will utterly disappear." The new creation will be a fragrant, pleasant garden. The earth "in whose bosom the body of the Lord lay, will be like Paradise in its entirety and, because of having been irrigated

71

with the blood of the saints, it will be decorated eternally with sweet-smelling flowers, lilies, roses, and violets that will never fade." In a twelfth-century manuscript which quotes the *Elucidation* on the renewed earth, the passage is illustrated with a sphere representing the new earth (Pl. 3). The mass of flowers decorating the sphere reflects the paradisal beauty of the new creation. Once cursed and covered with thorns, the earth will "then be blessed forever by the Lord. There will be no more toil or pain." No medieval reader missed the absence of thorns as an indication that God will take back the punishment inflicted on Adam and Eve. The peasant world will entirely disappear in order to be replaced by something very much like the pleasure-garden of a monastery.[2]

In paradise the blessed will be restored to nakedness. "They will be nude," explained the *Elucidation*, "but excel in modesty, and will not blush because of any parts of their body more than they do now because of having beautiful eyes." Just as Adam and Eve did not feel ashamed with their naked bodies before the Fall, so the saints living on a renewed earth will regain the innocence of Eden. The blessed will return to a state of natural simplicity where even clothes, a mark of cultured life, will be superfluous. When the monastic teacher of the *Elucidation* finishes explaining such matters pertaining to eternal life, the student cannot hide his enthusiasm: "As a thirsty peasant is refreshed by a sweet well, so is my soul refreshed by the honey dripping from your mouth." The very language used by both *discipulus* and *magister* betrays the rural orientation of the manual.[3]

Whenever we have the rare chance of hearing about the common people of the period, similar images crop up. A popular Cathar story, found in an Inquisition document, describes the "beautiful groves with singing birds" in the next life. The blessed can look forward to living in an ideal climate where "neither thirst nor hunger, or cold or heat, but most moderate temperatures" will occur. Bishop Otto of Freising in the twelfth and William of Auvergne (bishop of Paris) in the thirteenth century both acknowledged that the paradisal image of the next life belonged to the popular preaching of monks. They were not pleased that this was the case, but they recognized the widespread acceptance of rural images of heaven.[4]

We must not, however, assume that all popular medieval heavens were depictions of perfected nature. In the twelfth and thirteenth centuries most of Europe saw an urban revival. While rural life still dominated the countryside, between 1150 and 1250 the number of towns in central Europe increased from about 200 to 1500. The emerging urban culture never embraced more than five per cent of the population, but it had a far greater impact on society at large than the small figure would imply. The flourishing cities with their strong, high walls, their towers and cathedrals, busy marketplaces, workshops, and rich living quarters inspired a new mentality and new religious ideas. Money and piety blended to vitalize Christian culture. Money built the cathedrals, supported the crusades, financed the charities, and gave life and substance to the magnificent religious life of the thirteenth century: money and of course an ardent faith. Townspeople, apart from the poorest, exhibited a more vibrant and intense piety than that of the peasants and the aristocracy. In the new cities, Christianity acquired an emotional quality not often experienced in villages and manor houses.[5]

The spiritual needs of the urban populace had to be met, and this was done by the new mendicant orders. These orders allowed their members to lead a life of chastity, poverty, and obedience in accordance with monastic tradition. At the same time, they worked in the world, thus contributing to the welfare of urban society. This principle of serving society while simultaneously pursuing the ascetic life characterized the Franciscan and Dominican friars. The ascetics no longer withdrew from society but thronged into the cities. While criticizing excessive luxury and inculcating the duty of charity, at least some of the preachers promoted a spirituality acceptable to the upper bourgeoisie. For them, urban wealth did not hinder virtue but helped it. The good life and an orderly society, according to mendicant preachers, depended upon private property and trade (which smacked of usury).[6]

The friars also promoted a more urban concept of heaven, one that gave prominence to culture over nature. Turning from the first pages of the Bible to the last ones – from paradise to the heavenly Jerusalem – spiritual writers found biblical warrant for their new ideas. The book of Revelation provided a rich repertoire of urban imagery. The holy city with its gates, walls, and streets sparkled in supernatural splendor. Its construction materials of jasper, gold, and pearls dazzled all viewers (Rev. 21). Gone was the natural simplicity of the Garden of Eden and in its place was the drama and majesty of the celestial city. The urban friars pushed all unpolished peasant fantasies into the background. In popular preaching the heavenly Jerusalem formed the abode of both the newly dead and all the blessed after the end of time.[7]

The idea of an urban hereafter echoed in the liturgy of the church. "May the angels lead you to paradise," sang the priests, "may the martyrs welcome you when you arrive, and may they guide you to the holy city of Jerusalem." Ever since the ninth century some form of this text had been chanted. It suggested that the soul entered first a garden and then the holy city. In the eleventh century even a hermit like Peter Damiani (1006–72), who hated the city, began to appreciate the urban imagery of the book of Revelation. What was bad for the world was not necessarily bad for heaven. Peter Abelard (1079–1142) and Joachim of Fiore (1132–1202) wove bucolic and urban themes together to create poetic views of the world to come. Gottschalk of Holstein (1190), a

German visionary, described the straight avenues and regularly arranged houses of his heavenly Jerusalem. For visionaries and poets the next world was a well-planned city-state situated in the midst of a paradise-like garden with rivers and rich vegetation.[8]

Giacomino of Verona (late thirteenth century) was a Franciscan friar who composed a poem, "On the Heavenly Jerusalem," in elegant Italian rhymes. When speaking of the roads, squares, and avenues of the lovely celestial city, he simply followed the imagery provided by the book of Revelation. Giacomino, however, moved beyond the biblical imagery in his description of the individual dwelling-places of the blessed. Ironically, it is just here that he claims to have the (unavailable) support of Scripture:

> The Holy Writ and all its clauses testify
> That every dwelling-place and mansion there on high
> Is such a work of art, he surely tells a lie
> Who says such wonders might be found beneath the sky.

> Of fine rare marble all its even blocks appear,
> Whiter than ermine, bright as glass, most pure and clear;
> Chambers and chimneys, in the front and rear,
> Are painted with the blue and gold of waves not near.

Denying that "such wonders might be found beneath the sky," the poet insists on the superior, unheard-of splendor of the heavenly city and its buildings. By doing so, he betrayed his own knowledge and appreciation of urban architecture. He may well have thought of the splendid Romanesque buildings in Verona. One senses here the enthusiasm of a penniless country lad who left his farm in order to go to town, join the friars, and work as a musician and choirmaster.[9]

Gerardesca (1210–1269), a woman tertiary of the Camaldolese order, presented a more detailed description of an urban heaven. Although she lived as a recluse in Pisa, her visions led her to detail heaven as a city-state with a vast park-like territory. Gerardesca distinguished three areas in which the blessed live: the city itself (the heavenly Jerusalem), seven castles built on mountains encircling the city, and numerous minor fortresses in the vicinity. The city proper is the abode of the Trinity, the Virgin Mary (the foremost of the saints), and the choirs of angels and the holiest saints. In the seven castles live those of the blessed whose merit is less, but still distinguished. These castles are visited three times a year by the entire heavenly court. The minor fortresses are given to the rest of the blessed, all of whom have free access to the Holy City. The land surrounding the city is unpeopled because there are no peasants. Everyone in heaven is a citizen in the literal sense of the term: an inhabitant of the city. We know of Gerardesca's vision from an anonymous biography now printed in the *Acta Sanctorum*:

Pl. 4.   The Heavenly Jerusalem as a city. C. 1200. *Liber floridus*: manuscript 92, fol. 95 recto.
Ghent University Library

She saw a vast plain called the territory of the Holy City of Jerusalem. There were castles in amazing numbers and very beautiful pleasure-gardens. All the streets of the city-state of Jerusalem were of the purest gold and the most precious stones. An avenue was formed by golden trees whose branches were resplendent with gold. Their blossoms remained rich and luxuriant according to their kind, and they were more delightful and charming than anything we can see in earthly pleasure-gardens. In the middle of this territory lay Jerusalem – holy, sublime, very beautiful and ornate. Nobody lived in the territory, only the city was peopled.

The city was surrounded by seven charming castles with arms bearing the glorious Virgin's name. Situated on steep mountains of precious stones, they had stairs leading up and down, made of even more precious gems. . . The castles were furnished with the richest decoration and had banners of victory hoisted, showing the picture of the Blessed Virgin Mary. In the castles were precious chairs, shining with holy radiance, for our Savior and the glorious Virgin, for the angels and archangels, the apostles and and prophets, confessors and virgins, and all the saints. All of them were arranged according to their rank. Visited three times a year by the entire celestial court, these castles are filled with ineffable jubilation and incomparable glory.

What Gerardesca saw was not unknown in her time. She experienced the new Jerusalem of the book of Revelation as a city-state of thirteenth-century upper Italy. Heaven is a city in a vast territory (contado) surrounded by castles. We may think of the Swiss-Italian city of Bellinzona as it can still be seen, with its citadels on the mountains. Gerardesca's assertion that nobody has to live outside the city gives us a glimpse into the longings of medieval men and women. For them the city held the good life. There one could escape the oppression of hunger, cold, and darkness. The city promised urban security, if not prosperity. In heaven no one would be condemned to a precarious, hardworking peasant existence beyond the city gates.[10]

Gerardesca's vision also reflects the relationship between the city and the castles which often surrounded it. Like the city, the castle was considered a privileged place of power and security. By the eleventh century, the castles and the men who controlled them dominated large areas of the European countryside. The castellans were a tumultuous group, constantly feuding with the lords above them or with one another. Over time, many of the greater lords were able to impose order and loyalty upon the castellans. The city, not the castle, eventually mastered medieval space. The feudal lords struggled to create an integrated and stable urban setting utilizing the protective capability of the castles. In Gerardesca's heaven, the warring castellans do not exist. Only the ideal of harmony and stability between city and castle reigns.[11]

In Gerardesca's eternal city-state, the fabric of medieval society with its kinship networks and complicated social structure of nobility, estates, and clergy is strikingly absent. Yet the blessed are not equal. At feasts a strict seating arrangement is observed, whereby they are placed "according to their rank" (*secundum ordinem suum*). A preoccupation with heavenly rank and hierarchy, while acknowledging the relative equality of the blessed, is a common theme in medieval texts. On the one hand, the nobility of descent will be replaced by a new, spiritual nobility of reward accessible to all. The saint need not be born into a landed and wealthy family in order to assume a high place in heaven. "There everyone is paid alike. . .for the Lord is no niggard," explained a middle-English poem called the *Pearl* (fourteenth century). The *Pearl* understood Christ's parable in which every laborer is paid the same amount, irrespective of the nature of the actual work, to refer to the equality of heavenly rewards. On the other hand, the new spiritual aristocracy will not be chaotic and unstructured. There are the virgins, the martyrs, the apostles, the patriarchs, the doctors and so on, each of whom forms a group or "choir" of its own. Gerardesca revealed that each group is arranged in accordance with their heavenly rank. Rank itself is not eliminated, but spiritual qualifications replace birth as the criteria shaping the hierarchy.[12]

The paradox of equality and hierarchy is elegantly resolved in a fourteenth-century satirical poem, *The Vision of Piers Plowman*. The poem describes the state of the penitent thief who is promised paradise by the crucified Christ. Although the thief of the Gospel enters heaven, he enjoys a lesser degree of bliss than those who have led more virtuous lives. At the Lord's banquet he gets as much delicious food as the others, but he is served on the floor like a beggar. "He sits neither with St. John, St. Simon, or St. Jude, nor with the virgins, the martyrs, or the holy widows," the poem insists, "but by himself all alone, and is served on the earth." Simple, undifferentiated equality did not satisfy the medieval poets' sense of justice. Rank in heaven involved reward to those who followed a life not of pride and conquest, but of spiritual purity. The thief may have been promised glory, but that did not mean he merited the same as the virtuous saints.[13]

By the end of the twelfth century, readers of the *Elucidation* were puzzled by its suggestion that the saints would be naked. One manuscript included a marginal gloss attributing the thought to Augustine. Without citing an outstanding authority, such a strange opinion would not have been acceptable to medieval Christians, who assumed that when the citizens of heaven enjoyed elaborate banquets they wore rich robes. The higher the heavenly rank, explained the fourteenth-century English poem, *Purity*, the costlier and better the clothes. The poem pointed out that "always the best and brightest attired" sat at the front. The noblest, "who were the most beautifully dressed" sat at a slightly lower position and after them came "lower down, a goodly number of [ordinary] people." In another English poem, a monk praised Mary, Queen of

Heaven, for furnishing her heavenly devotees with "royal robes, brace-lets, and gold rings." Everyone in the Virgin's celestial household is "clothed with white brocade." German abbess Hildegard of Bingen (1098–1178) described the saints in the celestial castle as "clad in garments of silk and wearing white shoes." The wearing of rich clothes and shoes not only underscored the cultured life of heaven, it also symbolized heavenly rank. Just as in medieval society, only a few were permitted – and could afford – to wear the silks and finery of nobility.[14]

The popular medieval image of heaven included an urban and courtly leisured class preoccupied with splendor, from beautiful clothes to magnificent architecture to splendid festivities. Worldly splendor was enhanced, glorified, and made permanent. We must, however, not mis-understand the medieval mind. Heaven was not a place of human self-indulgence. All celestial pleasure had a decidedly theocentric flavor. For all its urban and courtly qualities, heavenly life focused on the divine and retained the liturgical pattern of the book of Revelation. The saints living in Giacomino of Verona's urban heaven, "have no other thought or care/Save that of blessing Him," who sits on a royal throne in their midst. For Giacomino, the idea of blessing the Lord through heavenly song and music belonged to standard medieval rhetoric and no doubt came easily to this Franciscan choirmaster. Moreover, a city without a lord or a court without a prince would make no sense. Whether the saints' residences were visited by the divine court, as in Gerardesca's vision, or the blessed were invited to a dance in the divine palace, as in a French poem, the structure remained the same. Heaven for the medieval popular mind must be a place dominated by religious concerns.[15]

It was not only medieval literature that considered heaven to be a city-state with a court organized around a divine Lord. The urban heaven found its most impressive realization in the Gothic cathedral located at the center of many medieval towns. Even before the Middle Ages, Christian liturgy and speculation identified the church building with the heavenly Jerusalem. The hymn *Urbs Hierusalem beata*, sung on the feast of the church's dedication, compared the earthly building to "the city of Jerusalem, the blessed," whose "streets and walls of purest gold are fashioned," and whose "gates shine with pearls." At the original ded-ication, the priests read the biblical text on the new Jerusalem which descends from heaven "prepared as a bride." The Benedictines of Cluny in France especially linked the church to the heavenly Jerusalem. In the eleventh century Cluny saw the creation of a solemn and elaborate liturgy whose splendor was enhanced by impressive architecture, beauti-ful vestments, and the use of precious vessels. The urban church, not the Jewish synagogue or Greco-Roman basilica of John of Patmos, now served as the model for the heavenly Jerusalem.[16]

In the mid-twelfth century, the renewed interest in liturgical splendor culminated in the creation of the Gothic style. Large stained-glass windows made the stone walls almost disappear, replacing them with glass, color, and light. In the urban cathedral heaven was not only invoked symbolically but actually brought down to earth. When the faithful entered the cathedral they felt transported into "heaven on earth" through the beauty and magnificence of the sacred space. The splendid liturgies celebrated on feast days enhanced this impression. In the liturgy the earthly Christians joined with the citizens of the heavenly church. The liturgy itself, for ecclesiastical author William Durandus (1230–1296), became celestial. Writing about the clergy's solemn procession into the sanctuary, he could not avoid a lyrical digression: "When entering the church while we sing," he reported, "we arrive with great joy in our [heavenly] fatherland. . .the chanters or clerics in their white robes are the rejoicing angels." In an immediate, sensual way both clergy and laity participated in the celestial which became tangible in the weightlessness of the building, the supernatural light, and the divine singing.[17]

From the perspective of Abbot Suger (1080–1151), who renovated the abbey chuch of Saint-Denis near Paris, the house of God must be more impressive than any other structure. This church, a pilgrimage center and burial place of kings, would become the French national sanctuary and an early example of the Gothic style. The abbot's account of Saint-Denis's renovation stressed not only architectural improvements, but also the importance of including magnificent furnishings of gold and jewels in the church. Gems were bought in large quantities and used to embellish a huge cross placed in the center of the edifice. Suger was pleased to hear from travellers that his cathedral displayed more valuables than the Hagia Sophia in Constantinople. Gothic churches like Saint-Denis used and displayed precious materials wherever possible: in crucifixes, reliquiaries, lamps, tabernacles, and chalices the craftsmanship of which could not but arouse admiration. The cathedral treasures evoked the splendor of the heavenly Jerusalem, where the blessed would be dressed in silks and gold jewelry. Thus it celebrated the urban idea of the world to come.[18]

Medieval laity and clergy alike frequently felt transported from the cathedral to heaven, from the material to the spiritual. Every gem reflecting natural light reminded them of the True Light which is Christ. Literary images also led readers to higher, spiritual realities. The materialism of John's heavenly city could easily be transcended and treated as an allegory of the splendor of the Church Triumphant because Jerusalem is built of "Living stones" (1 Peter 2:5). Yet a preference for the spiritual and allegorical never obliterated the material, tangible reality of objects. For all their enthusiasm for the divine and invisible, medieval men and women never lost contact with the world. The literal quality of the heavenly city captured the attention of most medieval Christians.

Scholastic theologians, however, were not satisfied with biblical literalism, playful allegories, or visionary explorations. Critical theological inquiry required a different heaven.[19]

The Empyrean Heaven as a Place of Light

The twelfth and thirteenth centuries saw not only the revival of the city, but also the rebirth of the intellect. For the first time since antiquity, western society was able to encourage and support an intellectual class. In theology, the comfortable traditionalism of the monastery and cathedral schools was pushed to the periphery. Dissatisfied with the lack of precision and method in monastic teaching, a new generation of scholars developed more rigorous approaches to theology. The writings of Peter Abelard, Peter Lombard, and Thomas Aquinas led to the "school theology" or scholasticism which came to dominate medieval thought. With the creation of universities in Italy (Parma, Bologna, Salerno), France (Paris, Toulouse), and England (Cambridge, Oxford) the scholastics found both a place to conduct their thinking and a group of students to teach. The rediscovery of Aristotle's work also opened new intellectual vistas and spawned numerous brilliant controversies. Academic life flourished. In this atmosphere of innovation, the scholastics substantially revised the traditional theology of heaven.

In the ancient world, there were two views of the physical universe, one popular and the other scientific. For many people, the universe was made up of a flat earth surrounded by the sea and vaulted over by the dome of heaven. Cosmas Indicopleustes, an Egyptian monk of the sixth century, devoted an entire book to describing the flat earth. In his *Christian Topography* he defined the popular world view as the only one compatible with Scripture (Pl. 5). For him, the earth was flat, not a sphere, and the universe was shaped like a huge box. Inside this box were two superimposed levels: the earth and heaven. In the present age, the earthly realm is inhabited by human beings and angels. Heaven is the dwelling-place of God and Christ. In the age to come, men, women, and angels will be admitted to heaven and share the deity's abode. Once humans leave the earth to dwell with God, the earth will no longer bring forth fruit. As a desolate place it will serve as hell, the place where the damned must lead their miserable existence.[20]

The scientific view developed by Aristotle (384–322 BCE) and Ptolemy (85–160 CE) rejected the flat-earth theory. They considered the earth to be a sphere that formed the center of several concentric spheres. These spheres were thought of as the transparent carriers of the heavenly

Pl. 5.   The universe as seen by Cosmas Indicopleustes. 6th century. Manuscript Plut. 9.28, fol. 95
verso (10th century), Biblioteca Medicea Laurenziana, Florence, Italy. Reproduced from *The
Christian Topography of Cosmas*, trans. J.W. McCrindle (London: Hakluyt Society, 1897), pl. 1:2

bodies – the moon, the sun, and the other planets. The outermost
sphere encompassed the entire universe and carried the stars.

Augustine was acquainted with both popular and scientific conceptions. He discussed them in a tantalizingly brief passage in his *Literal
Commentary on Genesis*. While the biblical evidence seemed to favor the
popular view, the relevant texts could also be understood in terms of the
scientific model. Augustine refrained from making any further commitment. He professed his disinterest in cosmology: "Statements about the
heavens and the stars and the movements of the sun and moon" do not
form "an integral part of religious doctrine." Discouraging the study of
astronomy, he advised Christians to use their time for more profitable
pursuits. Augustine made no attempt to explain the spatial dimension of
eternal life or to localize heaven within the structure of the universe. All
of this was theologically irrelevant.[21]

By the twelfth century, theologians had discarded both Augustine's
disinterest in cosmology and Cosmas's support of the primitive world
view. Continuing a long tradition of western interest in Aristotle's
physics of the universe, scholastic theology adopted the geocentric
system. Scholars now read Aristotle's work in translation. They also used
modern, updated versions like John Sacrobosco's *Sphere* or al-Bitruji's
Principles of Astronomy. While medieval astronomers were chiefly concerned with the movements of the heavenly bodies, the interest of

theologians lay elsewhere. Theologians speculated about where heaven and hell might be located. They also developed theories about the fate of the earth after the Last Judgment.

Scholastic theologians agreed with Aristotle that the universe was made of concentric spheres and levels. The innermost region – hell inside the earth – consisted of coarse and unrefined material. The higher one moved up through the various planet-carrying spheres, the lighter, more luminous, and more perfect became the heavenly bodies. The outermost sphere comprised the firmament, a spherical shell that enclosed the material universe. Beyond the firmament was God's own world, organized on two levels. The first one, called the "spiritual heaven" or the "empyrean" was the abode of the blessed and the angels. Among them God presided. Theologians insisted, however, that the empyrean was only God's "exterior dwelling-place." The Trinity itself resided above this realm on another level, the "heaven of heavens." Also called the Heaven of the Trinity, it was reserved for God alone. Here neither angels nor saints – not even the Blessed Virgin – could enter. This heaven was identical with the deity itself.[22]

While scholastic theologians refrained from further speculation about the properties of God's abode in the heaven of heavens, they took more interest in the lower abode of the angels and saints, the empyrean. When looked at from the earth, the empyrean appeared as the highest heaven, because it was situated above all the planet-carrying heavenly spheres. John Ruusbroec (1293–1381) reflected that

> God created the empyrean or highest heaven as a pure and simple radiance encircling and enclosing all the heavens and every corporeal and material thing which he ever created. It is the exterior dwelling-place and kingdom of God and of his saints and is filled with glory and eternal joy. Because this heaven is eternally resplendent and free of all admixture, there is within it neither movement nor change, for it is securely established in a changeless state above all things.

Although "glory and joy" are mentioned, the descriptions of Ruusbroec and other theolgians remain abstract. Scholastic authors and their followers avoided any reference to the more graphic and tangible, a city or a paradise garden. They never asserted anything more than that light was present in the celestial realm.[23]

Literally, the empyrean is the "fiery place," but theologians understood the term to refer to its luminosity and splendor, rather than to the heat of a region outside the physical universe. Medieval authors assumed that such a luminous place could not be made of the four elements they knew: earth, water, air, and fire. The empyrean must be made of a fifth and nobler element, the quintessence, which must be something like pure light. While the various heavenly spheres were resplendent with light, the region below the moon comprised fallen nature. Alexander of Hales (1185–1245) speculated that this part of the universe was not superfluous. God created the complete and ordered universe "to show the supreme power, wisdom, and clemency in the complete series of bodies with a middle between the well-defined extremes." For Alexander, "the extremes are the luminous at the one end and the opaque at the other." The luminous at the one end was the empyrean heaven; the opaque was the earth. The earthly world was grossly material, dark, and sinful. Here reigned change: growth and decay, birth and death.[24]

The empyrean heaven served as the home of the blessed souls following death. After the Last Judgment, it would function as the eternal dwelling-place of the blessed with their new glorified bodies. "When the bodies of the saints arise from the earth," wrote Thomas Aquinas (1225–74), "they will ascend to the empyrean." Alexander of Hales explained that the empyrean, itself of bodily quality, could contain both spiritual and non-spiritual substances. The glorified body of Christ and the spiritual bodies of the citizens, while still essentially of matter, could enter the heavenly fatherland.[25]

Medieval cosmology cannot be spoken of without reference to light. According to Neoplatonic philosophy, light is not something material like the four elements but a force that shapes and gives form to things. Sometimes it was said to be something divine – an emanation from God. Brilliance is not a property of objects but something they possess because they participate in God, the divine light. In precious materials like gold, gems, glass, and everything with a shiny surface, light has begun to conquer the coarseness of the grossly material. Pervaded by light, these objects are of a transcendent, other-worldly beauty. More than other objects, they demonstrate their divine origin.[26]

Thomas Aquinas endowed the glorified human body with the supernatural splendor of light. "The bodies of the blessed," he wrote, "will shine seven times brighter than the sun." Aquinas admitted that there was no scriptural warrant for this assertion. For the general idea, however, he referred to the New Testament with its impressive symbolism of light. "The righteous will shine like the sun in the kingdom of their father," said Jesus (Matt. 13:43). Another biblical text refers to an angel whose "appearance was like lightning, and his raiment white as snow" (Matt. 28:3). Will we not be like angels in the next life? Will we not be like Jesus when he was transfigured and spoke to Moses and Elijah in the presence of his disciples when "his face shone like the sun, and his garments became white as light" (Matt. 17:2)? Not all the blessed will be equally luminous. "The saints," argued Albertus Magnus (1200–80), "will receive different degrees of clarity according to their different degrees of merit." A virtuous saint will radiate more light than someone who needs to be purified in purgatory before being admitted to the final state of glory.[27]

Not only the glorified human body will be endowed with supernatural brilliance or "clarity" (*claritas*). The world below the empyrean – the stars, sun, planets, moon, and earth – will be made into a house of light. According to Aquinas, the universe before the sin of Adam and Eve was full of light. At the Fall, God reduced the luminosity of the heavenly bodies. When God renews the universe at the end of time, the original luminosity will be established again, only more intensely. The elements, too, will be infused with light. The earth will no longer be dark and dull but will have a shiny surface like glass, and be semi-transparent. Water will be like crystal and probably solid. Air will be luminous like the cloudless sky, and fire will be lustrous like the stars. Light will finally conquer the material. In hell, however, utter darkness reigns. Dante called it "a place where every light is muted." According to bishop Otto of Freising the fire of hell lacks all power to give light, although it burns with great heat. The little gloomy light that Aquinas permitted will function only to increase the pains of the damned who can thus see the scenes of horror around them. For the blessed, on the other hand, "the excess of light is delightful."[28]

According to Aquinas, neither plants nor animals will have a place in this world of light. Heavenly bodies will cease to move, because their movement indicates and indeed promotes both growth and decay. Upon the cessation of celestial motion the "mixed" entities (things made of more than one of the four elements) will dissolve into their constituent parts so that organic material no longer exists. What once was a plant will again become air, water, and earth. The universe will stand still, like a big machine whose parts are polished to shining brightness but no longer move. The world below the empyrean will not be the space in which the blessed live but something to be contemplated. It will remain empty or nearly so. If it were not for the interior of the earth functioning as a dungeon where the damned are tortured eternally, the universe could be annihilated.[29]

Far from being only the esoteric teaching of scholastic manuals, the doctrine of heaven as pure light attracted the attention of educated poets and artists. Dante's *Divine Comedy* and the Gothic cathedrals are the supreme examples of artistic renderings of a luminous heaven. They have also outlived the world view from which they derive.

In the *Divine Comedy*, finished shortly before Dante's death in 1321, the poet travels through hell and purgatory, and is eventually granted permission to ascend through the various heavens all the way up to the empyrean. His guide through the heavenly spheres is Beatrice, a noble Florentine lady whom Dante adored but who died in 1290. Upon arrival in the empyrean heaven of pure light (*ciel ch'è pura luce*), Beatrice leaves him. She joins the blessed who are seated in a vast rose-shaped amphitheater below the angels and the Trinity. The poet sees the nine orders of angels in the form of nine circles of light spinning around the brilliant point of God's light at the center (Fig. 5). Sitting in the rose, Beatrice smiles at the poet briefly and then returns her gaze to God. Dante then finds himself standing before his Creator in utter loneliness, absorbed into the light of divine glory.

> *Within Its depthless clarity of substance*
> *I saw the Great Light shine into three circles*
> *In three clear colors bound in one same space.*

Within the divine light, Dante perceives the features of a man, that is, Christ. He also feels an impulse of love – of that love "that moves the sun and the other stars." The divine and the human love meet and merge: the human desire to be united with God and the divine charity that descends toward the human. With the pilgrim having arrived at his final goal, the experience of the divine in light and love, the poem ends. "When the Source or the First, which is God, has been found," the poet explained, "there is nothing to be sought beyond."[30]

The concentric circles of light, with light standing for the divine and the circle for perfection, were not an invention of Dante. When Abbot Suger replaced the heavy Carolingian apse of Saint-Denis by a more spacious choir, he surrounded the chancel with a circle of small chapels. The stained-glass windows lit up the resulting hall-like space. The light filled the space with an intricate play of rays and endless degrees of shadow. The abbot reported that "the whole church would shine with the wonderful and uninterrupted light of most luminous windows, pervading the interior beauty." By the age of Dante, the huge circular windows of Gothic cathedrals united the light of divinity and the circle of perfection. The large circular "rose window" perforated their facades high above the front entrance (Pl. 6). Whatever other meanings this window received through its stained-glass narratives, it also served as a symbol of God's presence. While the *Divine Comedy* ends in a vision of intangible light, architects and builders made that light accessible and tangible.[31]

Art historians point out that Suger did not simply play with the aesthetical possibilities of twelfth-century architecture and craftsmanship. He was steeped in theology and especially attracted to the medieval philosophy of light. According to an inscription he placed in the church, noble works of art should "brighten the minds, so that they may travel, through the true lights, to the True Light," that is, to Christ in heaven. For Suger, and any educated person who shared his theology, the cathedral was a celebration of the empyrean heaven. This earthly heaven

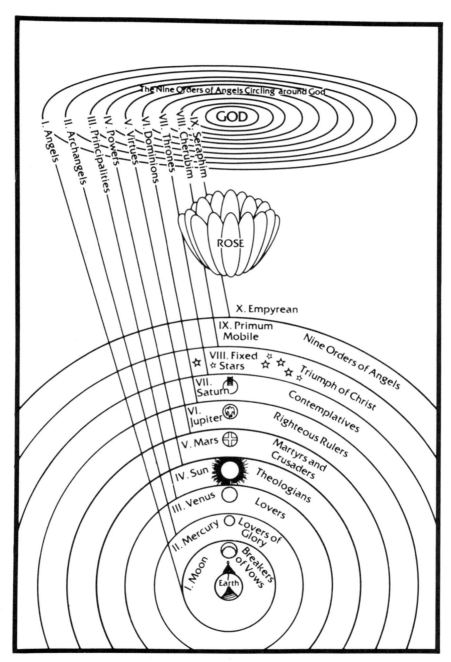

The Nine Orders of Angels Circling around God

GOD

I. Angels
II. Archangels
III. Principalities
IV. Powers
V. Virtues
VI. Dominions
VII. Thrones
VIII. Cherubim
IX. Seraphim

ROSE

X. Empyrean

IX. Primum Mobile

VIII. Fixed Stars

VII. Saturn

VI. Jupiter

V. Mars

IV. Sun

III. Venus

II. Mercury

I. Moon

Earth

Nine Orders of Angels

Triumph of Christ

Contemplatives

Righteous Rulers

Martyrs and Crusaders

Theologians

Lovers

Lovers of Glory

Breakers of Vows

Fig. 5.   The universe of Dante. C. 1300. Dante Alighieri, *The Divine Comedy. Vol. III: Paradise,*
trans. M. Musa (Harmondsworth: Penguin, 1986), 25

Pl. 6.   Rose Window above front entrance of Reims Cathedral, France. Late 13th century

represented weightlessness and light: weightlessness despite stone and luminosity despite a completely closed space, the windows of which did not permit an outside view. The huge windows served as delicate filters that left the world outside, a world with its medieval connotations of sin and transitoriness. Only light, the divine element present in the world, could penetrate the timelessness of sacred space. Refracting the divine light, the stained glass bathed the beholders in a myriad of miraculous colors, giving them a foretaste of heaven.[32]

Everlasting Contemplation of the Divine

The thirteenth century was not only an age of innovation, but also a time of summing up, an era characterized by an almost compulsive urge to collect and systematize all forms of knowledge. Accordingly, much effort went into constructing systematic compendia for all fields of thought. While it has become the standard practice of historians to hail the comprehensive thirteenth-century textbooks as embodying the unique "medieval synthesis," recent authors are less enthusiastic. They point out how the scholastic writers' wish to reconcile divergent opinions aborted what could have become a truly scientific revolution. Inquiry and debate were sacrificed at the altar of harmony and synthesis.[33]

In theology, the most famous systematic presentation was written by Thomas Aquinas. When he died in 1274, he left the *Summa against the Gentiles* in complete form, while the more comprehensive and more ambitious *Summa theologica* remained unfinished. These compendia discussed what the author, and with him all scholastic writers, considered to be both the aim of the human intellect and the everlasting occupation of the blessed: the knowledge and contemplation of God. Although Aquinas repeated many of Augustine's arguments, his presentation was more systematic and often more detailed. Aquinas aimed not for innovation; he intended to state the true doctrine as precisely as possible and prove it from Scripture, philosophy, and theological tradition. While philosophy, for Aquinas, meant Aristotle, his main theological authority was Augustine.

A Dominican friar, Thomas Aquinas followed the "evangelical counsels" of poverty, celibacy, and obedience, leading the contemplative rather than the active life. This did not mean that he retired from all activities, devoting his life to the silent contemplation of the divine. Aquinas pursued an academic career of studying, teaching, and writing. Even though contemplation, for Aquinas, meant "to ponder an intelligible [religious] truth interiorly and take delight in the consideration and love of it," he acknowledged that the academic activities of reading, studying, and teaching also belonged to it. Although teaching was not a necessary dimension of the contemplative life, it was an extremely valuable means by which to acquire merit. Aquinas considered the teacher, the virgin, and the martyr as the three most outstanding models of sainthood. For these three, heaven held special rewards.[34]

In heaven, according to Aquinas, there will be no more active life; only contemplation will continue. Contemplation, in this world a fragmentary and imperfect endeavor, will then be perfect. In heaven it will involve an unsurpassable knowledge of God. "We will see Him as He is," was the scriptural basis for this assertion (1 John 3:2). Following the biblical tradition and Augustine, Aquinas spoke of the "vision" of the divine. "Intellectual cognition is called vision," he explained, adding that sight is nobler and more spiritual and therefore closer to the intellect than other senses. For scholasticism, the highest vision implied the highest bliss; hence the term "beatific vision" used by later authors. Beatific vision can be more precisely translated as the beatific knowledge of God; to have this knowledge meant to enjoy eternal bliss. To be left in ignorance meant unhappiness; hell served as the place of ignorance and obscurity. To heaven belonged knowledge and light.[35]

Aquinas developed his notion of beatific knowledge from the human quest for happiness. He agreed with Aristotle and Augustine that this was the most fundamental of all human quests. Happiness, for Aquinas, consisted in an operation of the intellect, and he contended that the highest happiness could only be derived from the highest operation of the intellect. This he identified as the contemplation of divine things and ultimately of God himself. Contemplative happiness transcended the philosopher as a human being and immortalized him.[36]

Aquinas also argued that to know God must be the final end of all human activity. According to Aristotle, "every agent acts for an end," and that end must be a "good," because "good is the object of every appetite." The human being, dominated by the intellect, acts for intellectual ends. The knowledge of God must be the final goal of our intellectual quest. In the present life, our knowledge of God is imperfect because it depends upon the perceptual system of our senses. In the life to come, Aquinas observed, the senses will have no part in knowledge. We will know God through the immediate contact of the human and the divine spirit. When knowledge is perfect, happiness is also complete. Aquinas insisted that as a state of the human spirit, happiness does "not depend on the senses." The ultimate end of human activity is not sensual happiness, but the happiness of direct knowledge of God.[37]

The abstract nature of his argument and the emphasis on the intellect cannot be overlooked. Aquinas, even when using more personal language, gave priority to the intellect. He could speak of our end as "a perfect union of the soul with God, insofar as it enjoys him perfectly, seeing him and loving him in perfection." Nothing, however, can be enjoyed and loved without being known. "Love results from knowledge...for nothing is loved except it be first known." As a scholar, Aquinas placed knowledge above all else. The blessed achieve this knowledge not through debate or scientific inquiry, but through contemplation. "The ultimate and perfect happiness, which we will await in the life to come, consists entirely in contemplation." According to Aquinas, the blessed will do nothing else but contemplate. Liberated from the many necessities of earthly existence, the blessed no longer will have to interrupt this quiet activity. They will be able to concentrate fully on *one* thing – the study of God. A variety of activities would not afford pleasure, but detract from what is most pleasing. Moreover, "nothing that is contemplated with wonder can be tiresome."[38]

In his theological work Aquinas again and again explored the ramifications and implications of the beatific knowledge. He discussed, for instance, whether a created, finite being can actually acquire knowledge of the uncreated, infinite deity. He answered in the negative. In order for that knowledge to be possible, we have to be aided or strengthened by God. This enhancement of the intellect is called "illumination." Aquinas was also interested in determining the extent of the knowledge of God. Will the blessed, in their ultimate knowledge of the divine, also know all the thoughts of God? Some theologians seemed to assert this; but the scholastic master was less sure. Aquinas refrained from attributing too much thought-reading to created spirits. Even in eternal life, the blessed cannot transcend the limits implied in their createdness.[39]

Will beatific knowledge be the same for all the blessed? Aquinas again answered in the negative. In an intricate system, he linked the degrees of merit, the degrees of love of God, and the degrees of worthiness with eternal beatitude and beatific knowledge. "The more love [of God] someone will have [in heaven], the more perfectly one will see God, and the more blessed will one be." Aquinas explicitly referred to "degrees" (*gradus*) of the beatific vision: "All the blessed see the Highest Truth [i.e. God], but they do so in various degrees." The measure of the beatific knowledge depends on how much one loved God in one's earthly life and how much merit one has acquired. Those who possess the greatest merit receive the greatest rewards. In heaven no more merit can be won and therefore one's knowledge of God and the concomitant beatitude can neither grow nor decrease. Lowest on the scale are the children who died in infancy before being baptized. They are not granted the beatific vision proper but have to be content with a natural knowledge of God. They enjoy a simple, natural, and perhaps animal-like happiness which is somewhat imperfect because it lacks the supernatural dimension.

Aquinas insisted, however, on the completeness of their beatitude, because any deficiency will forever remain unknown to them.[40]

Despite this gradation, the blessed experience complete happiness. Nothing imperfect, incomplete, or awaiting fulfillment survives. On his heavenly journey, Dante asked one of the blessed:

> But tell me: all you souls so happy here,
> Do you yearn for a higher post in Heaven,
> To see more, to become more loved by Him?

No, the saint answered. The inhabitants of heaven enjoy conforming to God's will. To move up would simply be against God's plan. The famous phrase, e 'n la sua voluntade è nostra pace (in his will is our peace), summed up the answer for Dante. There can be no progress in heaven to a higher happiness because this would mean that the earlier stage was imperfect. Equally, there can be no regression. In the static heaven of Aquinas, the blessed enjoy "beatific immobility."[41]

Aquinas was intrigued by the visual metaphor preferred by Paul when he spoke of seeing God "face to face." Should this be understood literally? Will the blessed see God with their bodily eyes? Aquinas based his answer on a typically scholastic distinction, contending that there are three different ways of seeing supernatural realities. When the Babylonian king Belshazzar saw a hand – perhaps God's hand – writing mysterious words on the wall of his palace, that must be classified as a corporeal vision, seen with bodily eyes. In Scripture, another kind of vision appears more frequently, that of "interior seeing." John, for instance, saw the new Jerusalem of the book of Revelation not with his bodily eyes, but inside himself. A third type of vision is devoid of any visual qualities, even seeing inside oneself. This will be the way the saints see God in heaven. "God can in no way be seen with our corporeal eyes or with any other [physical] sense, neither here, nor in the [heavenly] fatherland," summarized Aquinas. Our eyes will be able to perceive the Christ, however, because the human form of the second person of the Trinity persists in the other world. In this sense we will physically see God. Moreover, all the other glorified realities, especially the human body, will reflect the divine glory. Consequently, God's presence will be always felt.[42]

Are there any other sources of eternal happiness besides God? Aquinas explored two possibilities: the body restored to the soul in glorified form and the community of the blessed. Upon death, the truly righteous enjoy the beatific vision immediately. They are souls though, purely spiritual beings. At the Last Judgment, the saints will receive their glorified bodies. This will add to their bliss "because their happiness will be not only in the soul, but also in the body." All in the body that hampered the full perfection of the soul will be removed. The reunion of body and soul will contribute a certain perfection even to the soul:

> Now the more perfect a thing is in being, the more perfectly is it able to operate. Therefore, the operation of the soul united to such a [glorified] body will be more perfect than the operation of the separated soul. But the glorified body will be...altogether subject to the spirit. Hence, since happiness consists in an operation [of the spirit], the soul's happiness after its reunion with the body will be more perfect than before.

The glorified body, though important, will always be dominated by the spirit. The domination will be so thorough that spiritual bodies will not depend on eating and drinking. According to medieval polemicists, only Muslims imagined a heaven involving physical consumption and therefore needed to invent ridiculous theories about the absence of excrement.[43]

While Aquinas appreciated the contribution of the body to the individual's eternal bliss, he was unwilling to acknowledge any social joys among the saints. From the book of Revelation the scholastic theologian knew that eternal life will not be spent in eternal solitude with God, but in the company of the blessed and the angels. He also knew – and endorsed – Aristotle's appreciation of social life which culminates in friendship. The philosopher praised friendship as one of the major conditions of human happiness. "It would be strange," Aristotle wrote, "to make the blessed person a solitary; for none would choose to possess all good things on condition of being alone. The human person is a political being and one whose nature is to live with others." While this was true for the natural order of this life (which alone Aristotle had in mind), it posed a problem in the description of the supernatural situation of heaven. For Aquinas, God must be the exclusive source of eternal beatitude. No creature can really contribute to the felicity of a blessed human being. While in the present life we cannot be happy without the company of friends, this must be different in the next. "If we speak of perfect happiness which will be in our heavenly fatherland," Aquinas reasoned, "fellowship of friends is not essential to happiness, since the human being has the entire fullness of perfection in God." Aquinas did not hesitate to add that "if there were but one soul enjoying God, it would be [perfectly] happy, though having no neighbor to love." In a note, he mitigated this stern view by admitting the purely theoretical nature of his statement. The saints' happiness, he conceded, is also supported "by the fact that they see one another and rejoice at their fellowship in God."[44]

With the last two words – "in God" – Aquinas made sure that all understood the primacy of the divine. Although softening his harshest expression, he made no real concessions. Horrified by the Islamic heaven of sexual joys, which he condemned as a grave error, Aquinas felt justified in maintaining his theocentric view. The glorified body could be accepted as a source of bliss but not of heavenly social life. Without the body only the soul would be able to participate in the beatific vision. Once the body united with the soul, it too could participate in the glory of heaven. Consequently, while friendship between the blessed could conflict with the worship of God, existence of the body only increased the enjoyment of the divine. Preoccupied with God and the human individual, Aquinas saw the fellowship of the blessed as a possible detraction from the deity. A saint's friend must not rival the divine.[45]

Giles of Rome (1247–1316), a student of Aquinas, dared to disagree with his master in his speculations on a heavenly society. Giles predicted that the saints form a *societas perfecta*. In heaven, the blessed lead a harmonious, enjoyable, and indeed perfect social life based on communication. Giles presented his idea in an intricate rhetoric that transcended the dryness of standard scholastic discourse:

> When indeed it is argued that society depends upon language, then we have to say that in a state in which society is not abolished but made perfect, language, too, is not abolished but also made perfect. In a society, and the brotherhood of the saints is a real brotherhood and a real society...language cannot disappear. It will be the saints' social solace in both thinking and verbal expression. To be able to speak is not a sign of imperfection, but of perfection – and everything perfect must be said of the saints. Therefore I assert that in heaven the saints will use a real, audible language. The gift of language is given to us not only for overcoming ignorance and acquiring knowledge, but also, as said before, as a social solace. In this way, those who love each other take pleasure in talking together. Just talking to the beloved affords great pleasure, and is done without the intention to learn anything.

Heavenly men and women, according to Giles, retain their mental and social faculties, including speech, in order to lead nothing less than a perfect social life.[46]

The Franciscan theologian Bonaventure (1221–74) also displayed a more positive attitude toward the social joys of heavenly existence, and seemed unconcerned about Aquinas's exclusion of human sources of eternal bliss. Bonaventure explained that the love among the blessed will be so complete "that whoever seems to be remote [now], will be in the [heavenly] fatherland the dearest friend. Love will then be extended to all the saints in a way which was possible only toward one single dearest friend." True friendship will be universal. While theologians like Bonaventure recognized the importance of the community of saints, they rejected any idea of individualized friendship in the beyond. Like Augustine, they understood love between the saints to be general and non-exclusive. Their elimination of special friendships would bother

other medieval Christians who hoped to find more personalized love in the beyond.[47]

The Promise of Love

Scholastic writers refrained from developing or exploring the idea of a perfect social life any further. The mere statement of fact was sufficient. The vision of the divine remained more important than the vision of another social world. Scholastic authors were interested in conceptual clarity, not in detailed speculation. Intellectual concepts, however, could satisfy the critical scholastic mind, but not the heart of many medieval men and women. For them, the theological discourse on the love of God and love among the blessed in the heavenly fatherland appeared too abstract. Intellectual, distant, and bloodless, the love of the schoolmen lacked one essential and most human quality – passion. Here poets and mystics moved beyond the teaching of scholastic manuals. "The heart's life is love," mused Hugh of St. Victor (died 1141); "hence it is wholly impossible that there be a heart wishing to live without love."[48]

The twelfth century abounds in treatises on the complex stirrings and movements of the human heart, and these writings focus naturally on love. Poets, mystics, clerics, and musicians studied love in all its aspects, from carnal appetite to the spiritual friendship of God. More conspicuous than learned writings was the unprecedented proliferation of love poetry in which knights and troubadours celebrated their ladies. "If the Middle Ages can be credited with anything new in sensibility," suggests Jacques Le Goff, "it is courtly love." Marriage, commonly understood as the means for procreating legitimate offspring, was caught up in a binding network of kinship relations, economic necessities, and hierarchical structures. Not only were two persons united in marriage, but two fortunes, two properties, two families. Within marriage, love had a limited meaning. Love must never disturb the delicate balance of medieval familial, social, and religious alliances. The new fashion of courtly love allowed for a stable, loving relationship to exist beyond the marriage bonds. Never without an erotic dimension, but in its purest form without a sexual one, courtly love existed free from institutional expectations.[49]

The purely theocentric heaven of the theologians could not satisfy those who promoted the idea of courtly love. One knight reportedly told his lady of a twofold hereafter: one for women who responded either too quickly or not quickly enough to the overtures of their knightly lovers and the other for women who abided by the courtly code. He described the paradise of the good women (which he claimed to have seen) as a place where "numerous couches [*tori*: bridal beds] were laid, adorned in wondrous fashion, for they were strewn with silken coverlets all round and crimson trappings." There the fine ladies reclined while "the knights chose seats for themselves at their own discretion. Human tongue could not recount to you the extent of their happiness and splendor. For the whole area of the Pleasance [paradise] was devoted to the pleasures of the ladies." According to medievalist Betsy Bowden, the knight "leaves no question as to what eternal bliss consists of: Each blessed woman has a *torus* [bridal bed] prepared especially for her, then each soldier of love chooses his lady."[50]

The story of the heaven of ladies was told by an imaginary character in *On Love*, a manual of courtly love compiled by Andreas the Chaplain, a cleric who was associated with the court of one of the French king's daughters. Written around 1180, the book is believed either to portray life at the French courts or to satirize it. Whatever the real intention of its author, the book presents us with the boldest example of the medieval version of a heaven of lovers. Most likely the text depended on Celtic sources, as its heaven of erotic lovers had no precedence in Christian theology. In this other world God is markedly absent, and the inhabitants are ruled by a queen and king of love. By drawing from a pagan tradition, the author avoids the issue of how to integrate the love of God with passion for the opposite sex.[51]

Another medieval lover also faced the tension between love of God and love of the lady. Aucassin, the hero of a light-hearted French song-story (*chantefable*) written shortly after 1200, boasted that "I do not seek to win Paradise." Heaven was not a desirable abode but a rather dull place. "Your old priests and your old cripples, and the halt and maimed, who are down on their knees day and night, before altars and in old crypts...such are they who go to Paradise." He preferred hell, "for to hell go the fine churchmen and the fine knights... With them I will go, so I have Nicolette my most sweet friend with me." A somewhat milder protest than Aucassin's can be heard in a sonnet by Giacomo da Lentini (died 1246):

> *Without my lady, though, I would not go [to Paradise]*
> *The one with golden hair and limpid eyes;*
> *Because my bliss without her cannot grow*
> *If distant from my love my spirit lies.*

To this the poet added an excuse: "but these my words are said innocently, and not that I by them to sin be driven." He seemed well aware of the boldness of his desire.[52]

Giacomo's poem must be seen in the context of a new awareness of love between the sexes, first expressed by the Provençal troubadours in the early twelfth century. The troubadours – poets working for a courtly audience – were caught in a dilemma. The medieval church made them well aware of the vanity of earthly existence, the conflict between the flesh and the spirit, and the sinfulness of folly. At the same time, their devotion to love made them feel the tension between personal happiness and social convention, between love for the lady and love of God. Whenever a poet's pursuit of love verged on idolatry, he feared a divine charge like the one imagined by Guido Guinizelli of Bologna (1230–76): "God will say to me when my soul is standing before him, 'How dare you! You travelled beyond the sky and come to me, only to regard me as a parallel for your worldly love. Praise is for me and for the queen of the worthy realm where all dissimulation ends.'" In God's presence, religion told him, the courtly love relationship must cease to exist. At best, the troubadour might transfer his veneration of his beloved to the Blessed Virgin. Worship of the lady and love of the divine seemed incompatible.[53]

At least one troubadour who flourished around 1200 escaped from this dilemma by reconciling the two loves. Arnaut Daniel advocated that a man's love must be purified from the attachments of family and kin. Worthy of true love is not one's family, but one's lady and God. The veneration of a lady in courtly love can actually lead to heaven. Arnaut expected to enjoy in the next world the double bliss of his lady's and his Lord's presence. "I love her more than I do cousin or uncle," he sang; "hence in Paradise will my soul have *twofold* joy, if ever a man through fine loving therein enters."[54]

More than a century later we can perceive a faint echo of Arnaut's two-fold solution in Dante's *Vita Nuova* and in Boccaccio's (1313–75) *Life of Dante*. At the end of his powerful love poems, Dante expressed the hope "that my soul may go to see the glory of my lady, that is of the Blessed Beatrice, who now in glory beholds the face of Him who is blessed for ever." In speaking of Dante's death Boccaccio suggested that the poet's soul was indeed received into the arms of his friend. There Dante lived joyously with her and before God, "in the sight of Him who is his supreme good." Although the divine and the human existed in harmony, the two Italian poets made sure to give the divine the first place, if only to conform to pious rhetoric. Even the most ardent lover must recognize God as the supreme good.[55]

The "two-fold joy" of Arnaut's heaven survived outside the poetic tradition in an unexpected context. Friar Jordan of Saxony served as master general of the Dominicans for fifteen years (1222–37). He not only promoted the establishment of nuns' convents; he was also deeply attached to the religious women. In his surviving thirty-seven letters to Diana of Andalò he never attempted to conceal his love for the noble nun who lived in a convent in Bologna, Italy. An indefatigable traveller between Dominican establishments in Germany, Italy, and France, Jordan visited Diana infrequently. "O Diana," he sighed in one letter,

> what a wretched state of affairs this is, which we have to endure! Our love for each other here is never free from pain and anxiety. You are upset and hurt because you are not permitted to see me the whole time, and I am upset because your presence is so rarely granted me. I wish we could be brought into the fortified city, the city of the Lord of Hosts. . .where we shall no longer be stranded from Him or from each other.

For Friar Jordan, his love of God and his spiritual passion for Diana could only be fulfilled in the "fortified city," the heavenly Jerusalem.[56]

Few shared Arnaut's and Jordan's balance of human love and spiritual desire. It must have been their personal solution, arrived at with considerable reflection and spiritual struggle. In the case of Arnaut it is uncertain whether he maintained the belief in a "twofold joy" throughout his lifetime. According to one medieval tradition, he gave up both poetry and "fine loving" and died a monk. Although published and available, Arnaut's heavenly compromise never became commonplace.[57]

One would not expect Petrarch (1304–74), the father of Renaissance humanism and admirer and imitator of Arnaut, to be involved in the conflict between love of God and human passion. But in many ways he still remained a medieval figure, unable to shed the burden of tradition. After his beloved Laura's death, no solution came to Petrarch. When he imagined his dead friend's (poetic) invitation to be with her in the other world, he defended the idea as "a holy and unsullied speech." Against his own doubts as well as possible outside criticism, Petrarch defended a theocentric heaven. In another poem, though, he felt brave enough to repeat Arnaut's synthesis, saying he longed to see both Christ and Laura – "my Lord and my lady" (*veggia il mio Signore e la mia donna*). In Petrarch's anguished mind, a simple and convincing harmony in heaven between the human and the divine seemed impossible.[58]

Throughout his poetic career, Petrarch could not escape from the conflict between the two loves, indeed between "humanist confidence and Catholic guilt." When the poet suggested that Laura in all her purity had improved his character and ennobled his spirit, guiding him to God, he felt the contradicting weight of the scholastic tradition, voiced by Augustine, his imaginary interlocutor. "She has detached your mind from the love of heavenly things," commented Augustine, "and has inclined your heart to love the creature more than the Creator. And that one path alone leads, sooner than any other, to death." According to Augustine, a clear hierarchy of love prevailed. The love of God comes first and any other loves must be derivative and secondary. Divine love and human desire must not be confused. To assume an eventual transformation of human passion and desire into the pure love of God is a deception. In his writing, if not in reality, Petrarch submitted to the authority of his imaginary spiritual director.[59]

Solutions to such conflicts often come through art. The tympanum above the central portal of Notre Dame Cathedral in Paris is filled by a relief of the Last Judgment (Pl. 7). There male and female saints are clad in long robes and wearing crowns. Just having passed the archangel's test, they are absorbed in the contemplation of their Savior enthroned above them. One female saint divides her attention between the Lord and her beloved. While gazing upwards, she affectionately holds her husband's (or lover's?) hand. A century later, Dante allowed Beatrice a brief glance and smile at the poet before she returned her gaze to the divine light. While the loving glance and the holding of a hand may have satisfied the requirements of scholastic speculation, would it have quenched Aucassin's passion and Petrarch's desire?

Religious authors like Bernard of Clairvaux (1090–1153) attempted to appropriate the new sense of love sung by the troubadours for a totally different end. Rather than insisting with the scholastic theologians that knowledge led to the divine, Bernard argued that only love full of passion and desire directed the soul to God. Finding scriptural warrant in the Song of Songs, Bernard gave its eroticism a spiritual meaning. The young lovers of the Song, identified as the soul and God, acted as a model for understanding and developing religious experience. Bernard's *Sermons on the Song of Songs* infused medieval Christianity with an emotional dimension and inspired generations of mystics.

The love mysticism preached by Bernard of Clairvaux found vivid expression in the visions of medieval women. In the high Middle Ages numerous nunneries and béguine houses were founded and attracted an ever-growing number of women. Unlike earlier seers, the thirteenth-century female mystics were not interested in heaven as a physical place, the parklike or urban quality of which they could report to an eager audience. Although their heaven was certainly material and tangible, later mystics focused on the Lord of heaven with whom they longed to be united. "You can see," reported Jacques de Vitry (1180–1254), "some of these women dissolved with such a particular and marvelous love toward God, that they languish with desire, and for years have rarely been able to rise from their cots." These human brides of Christ "have no other infirmity save that their souls are melted with desire of Him. Sweetly resting with the Lord, they are comforted in spirit as much as they are weakened in the body." Jacques de Virtry spoke with reverence of these saintly women and their contact with the other world.[60]

In their raptures, some of the mystics felt that the Lord visited their soul. Others reported that their soul left the body, ascended to heaven and met Christ, whom they adored as bridegroom or lover. Christ as the lover responded with similar passion, and the human and the divine met

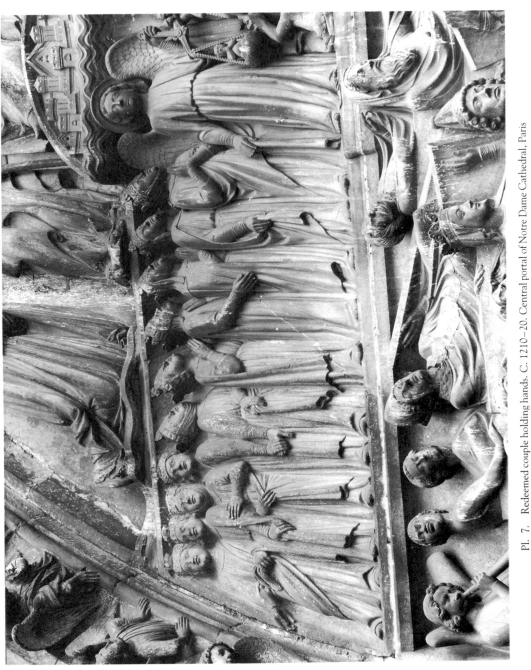

Pl. 7. Redeemed couple holding hands. C. 1210–20. Central portal of Notre Dame Cathedral, Paris

in real partnership. This partnership controlled the life of Mechthild (c. 1207–82), a German mystic. In her early twenties, Mechthild fled to a béguinage in Magdeburg, where she spent more than three decades. Béguines were women, often of noble descent, who left their families in order to retire to small independent communities. A typical béguine community functioned in a city, elected a mistress, and divided its time between prayer and work. Béguines kept vows of chastity and obedience as long as they remained in the sisterhood, but could leave when they wished and marry without disgrace. In the béguinage Mechthild had her visions and wrote them down in low German vernacular. Often in highly poetic form, her writings betray her courtly education.

Mechthild described heaven and Christ's place in it in the *Flowing Light of the Godhead*. Heaven appears in Mechthild's visions not as undifferentiated space but as a series of distinct locations each with its own characteristics. In a normally inaccessible place somewhere on earth is the *earthly paradise*, the lowest part of heaven. By special privilege Mechthild's soul met two Old Testament figures, Enoch and Elijah, in the earthly paradise. There they walked through a lovely garden with trees, sweet-smelling air, and gently flowing rivers. Above the earthly paradise rises its heavenly counterpart. Mechthild laconically reported that the souls who are neither sent to purgatory nor deemed worthy of entering heaven proper live there.[61]

If this middle ground may be called the *first heaven*, then the *second heaven* stretches out above the first. The second heaven comprises an immense dome of ten levels or "choirs." Each level is smaller than the one below, and provides space for fewer and fewer angels or saints. Originally angels occupied all the levels, but because a rebellion occurred in heaven, forcing Lucifer and his host to be expelled, vacant spaces exist. After the Last Judgment, the blessed will fill up all the empty places according to their merit. Children who died at an early age and therefore have not been able to acquire merit populate the lower ranks. Unlike the other blessed, they do not wear crowns and can thus be recognized by Mechthild. Not having lived, they cannot gain the crown of life. Not having fought, they cannot receive the crown of victory. God reserves the three uppermost rungs of the second heaven for the martyrs (the eighth level), the apostles (the ninth), and the holy women (the tenth). This latter choir, formerly belonging to the leaders of the fallen angels, is set aside for virgins like Mechthild and of course Mary, the Most Blessed Virgin.[62]

In one of her visions Mechthild viewed the reception of souls into heaven from purgatory. All the newcomers were given crowns, some of them by God himself. Thus God literally fulfilled the biblical promise, "Be faithful unto death, and I will give you the crown of life." The blessed sang and danced in adoration of the Trinity, and their song was answered with a flood of light issuing from the deity. Their heavenly liturgy comprised a dramatized form of the beatific vision.[63]

On yet a higher level that may be called the *third heaven*, a more intense liturgy takes place. God resides in the third heaven with his divine throne, a palace, and Christ's bridal chamber. "Above the throne of God," Mechthild reported, "is nothing but God, God, God, infinite, great God." Normally the saints do not enter this highest realm. For those holy women, however, who occupy the tenth and uppermost rank in the celestial hierarchy, an intimate union with Christ can occur in his bridal chamber. During one of Mechthild's visits to heaven, she too was admitted into the "secret chamber" saved for the virgins of the tenth choir. According to one report, she approached Christ as he sat on his throne: "She knelt down, thanking him for his favor. She took her crown from her head and placed it onto the rose-colored scars of his feet and wished that she could come closer to him. He took her into his divine arms, placed his paternal hand unto her breast and beheld her face. And in a kiss she was elevated above all the angelic choirs." For the purest of virgins, Christ prepared an ultimate and unexcelled delight.[64]

The courtly motif of a clandestine lovers' rendezvous occurs in another vision of heavenly intimacy. In heaven, Mechthild's soul appeared as a noble lady who has long refused the love declarations of a "beautiful youth" who pursues her. Now, though, she lets him know she is yielding. Hearing that the duke – this youth – approaches, her chamberlains adorn her and send her out to a wood where nightingales and other birds sing. After a dance the lady wearies and longs for union with the beloved. Meeting at midday in the shade near a brook, they go to a palace. "The beloved [Mechthild] goes to the most beautiful youth [Christ] and enters the chamber of the invisible deity. There she finds the bed of love." Here the Lord speaks to her sweetly, saying, "Put away [the garments of] fear and shame and all outward virtue. Keep, in eternity, only those virtues that are inside yourself by nature. They are your noble lust and your ardent desire; to these I will respond eternally in my boundless tenderness."[65]

Mechthild answers, at first reluctantly and timidly: "O Lord, now I am a naked soul and you a God most glorious." Love eventually casts out her fear and lifts her soul to equality with the divine lover. Having regained her confidence, she reflects: "Our union is eternal life without death." In an equally confident manner she tells her readers: "Thus comes to pass what both of them desire: he gives himself to her, and she herself to him." Mechthild knows that the blissful union, celebrated in secret, cannot last forever. After a brief meeting they part, but their hearts can nevermore be separated.[66]

In heaven, from Mechthild's perspective, there are two levels on which to enjoy God. The simple beatific vision exists for all the blessed, with the martyrs and apostles having the opportunity to be closest to the divine throne. The beatific *union* with Christ, however, is reserved only for the privileged and the purest of virgins. Holy women join with Christ in an unsurpassable union. The other saints simply "see him in a sweet manner," enjoying his presence in the beatific vision. Female virginity, according to Mechthild's vision, receives the highest and most intimate of heavenly rewards.[67]

The consummation of the soul's desire has nothing to do with illicit erotic contact – a blasphemous thought. Nor does it even concern rightful marriage. Mechthild and Christ are not wife and husband, but lovers who follow the rules of courtly love. In "pure love," explained one medieval treatise, "the final consolation is avoided, for this practice is not permitted for those who wish to love chastely." The code of courtly love permitted the lovers to see each other, engage in sweet conversation, and indulge in the physical delights of kissing, embracing, and judicious contact in the nude. When Mechthild and her divine lover meet, however, they follow the dictates of courtly love only up to a certain point. Mystical union granted to Christ and the soul what chaste courtly love denied human lovers.[68]

Mechthild spent the last decade of her life in the Cistercian convent of Helfta in Saxony, not far from Eisleben where Martin Luther was to be born three centuries later. In the days of Mechthild other mystics lived in the Helfta convent, most notably Gertrude (1256–1302), who became a saint of the Catholic church. Gertrude relied on Mechthild's spiritual guidance, although her surviving mystical diary, the *Herald of Divine Love*, reveals a character quite different from Mechthild. While Mechthild entered the béguine community in her early twenties, Gertrude grew up in the monastery and received a thorough theological education. Unlike Mechthild, she could read and write Latin. She often quoted her favorite authors Augustine and Bernard of Clairvaux.

Gertrude of Helfta understood the mystical bridal relationship very literally, and when she referred to her intimate union with Christ there were hardly any overtones of courtly love. In her visions Christ appeared to her in the form of "a handsome youth of sixteen years, beautiful and amiable, attracting my heart and my outward eyes." The friendship of this companion sweetened her monastic solitude. Preferring the erotic imagery of the Song of Songs, she addressed Jesus as her lover and spouse:

> *You are the delicate taste*
> *Of intimate sweetness.*
> *O most delicate caresser,*
> *Gentlest passion,*
> *Most ardent lover,*
> *Sweetest spouse,*
> *Most pure pursuer.*

Jesus, on his part, showed no less ardor in his declaration of love. "I am so closely united to you by love," he confided to her, "that I would not willingly enjoy beatitude without you. . . I could not bear that we should be separated from each other." Gertrude reported that on one occasion Jesus sang a song of love to her, and declared to her that had his union to her been the sole fruit of his labors, sorrows, and passion, he would have been fully satisfied. Can a lover do more for his beloved than die?[69]

While Mechthild described the free and easy union of lovers in the style of courtly love, Gertrude employs the nuptial imagery of Bernard of Clairvaux. According to one report, "The Lord took her into his arms, holding her fast in his embraces and caressing her tenderly. . . He covered her eyes, ears, mouth, heart, hands, and feet with kisses." Gertrude protested, of course, that her love was chaste: "When I love him, I am chaste; when I touch him, I am pure; when I possess him, I am a virgin." Elsewhere Gertrude insisted on being a queen who shared both throne and bed with the heavenly king. To her the Lord declared, "I cannot be hindered from exalting you with myself. Who shares the king's bed is rightly called a queen and is therefore an object of respect."[70]

Twelfth-century illustrations give graphic clarity to what Gertrude had in mind. In a Bavarian manuscript the blessed soul (also understood as the church) sits enthroned at the side of Christ (Pl. 8). She is embraced by him and wears a crown. In a better-known mosaic from Santa Maria in Trastevere in Rome, Christ places his arm around his mother – his spouse and queen (Pl. 9). Whether the woman is identified as the Virgin Mary or the human soul makes no difference because they both share the same fate, union with Christ. Medieval priests preached the same sentiment: "The King of Heaven," Stephan Langton (1150–1228) promised, "embraces you with loving arms and bestows upon you the kiss of salvation."[71]

Gertrude expected at death to be finally united to her Spouse. In an elaborate spiritual exercise designed to prepare her for death, she prayed in unambiguous terms: "In conjugal love and nuptial embraces show me your greatness. . . in a kiss of your holy mouth take me as your possession into the bridal chamber of your beautiful love." Death, for her, would be a heavenly assumption very much like that of the Blessed Virgin. According to the liturgical poetry of the feast of the Assumption (15 August), "the Virgin Mary was taken up to the heavenly bridal chamber where the King of Kings sits upon His starry throne." Another antiphon, recited on the same occasion, stated that "today, the Virgin Mary ascended to the heavens. Rejoice, for she reigns with Christ in eternity." Gertrude applied these ideas to herself. Was she not a virgin like Mary?[72]

When Gertrude spoke of herself as a spouse of Christ, she did so at the risk of an apparent paradox. She was not the only spouse of the Lord; all devoted virgins are spouses of the same Lord. In spite of all the special privileges they enjoyed in ecstatic rapture, neither Gertrude nor

Pl. 8. The soul as a queen, enthroned with Christ. 12th century. Manuscript lat. 4450,
fol. 1 verso. Bavarian State Library, Munich

Pl. 9. Christ and Mary enthroned as lover and beloved. Mosaic, 12th century. Santa Maria in Trastevere, Rome, Italy

Mechthild considered themselves as individuals with unique experiences that could not be shared by others. They never stood apart from, let alone above, the community. To the contrary, their experiences functioned as models to be imitated and emulated by others. Since there were many virgins, there could be many spouses, and nuptial ecstasies were possible for all of them. Gertrude's *Spiritual Exercises*, her second book, actually includes a communal liturgy in which virgins (i.e., nuns) celebrate their conjugal union with Christ. When the prayer-leader pronounces the seemingly individualistic "In a kiss of your holy mouth take me as your possession into the bridal chamber of your beautiful love," the community answers in liturgical unison, "We beseech Thee to hear us" (*te rogamus audi nos*). Medieval mystics did not seek individual self-fulfillment in a unique relationship to Christ; rather, they promoted the sense of belonging to a group and defined the role of "spouse" as a new pattern for religious experience.[73]

Accordingly, Gertrude spoke not only of her own eternal fate, but also of that of her fellow nuns. They, too, will ascend to heaven to be united with the Spouse. Gertrude, concerned about every death that occurred in the convent, sometimes caught a glimpse in a vision of someone's post-mortem state. At the death of one fellow nun, Gertrude saw how angels escorted her soul to heaven. The deceased nun came before the divine throne where "Jesus, the spouse of virgins, turned toward her with great love and said, 'You are my glory.' Then he rose to crown her as a queen, and enthroned her on the throne of glory." Before her own death, Gertrude fell into one trance after another, and her mind was haunted by visions. She heard Jesus explain that upon death she would be guided to a celestial palace where she would be attended with all honor until the nuptial day. Then the king would come to her himself and conduct her to his imperial throne. When she prepared to die, she beheld herself in the form of a young woman reposing in the arms of the Lord.[74]

Both Gertrude and Mechthild saw themselves as women responding to a male Jesus. Mechthild used a courtly model for defining the mystical relationship. She was the lady and Christ acted in the role of the lover. Gertrude departed from Mechthild's model in defining the relationship between herself and Christ as that of spouses. Gertrude applied the bridal imagery in a radical way. While Bernard of Clairvaux considered every sainted soul to be the spouse of Christ, Gertrude restricted divine intimacy to virgins like herself. According to her, only women can be true brides of Christ. Like Mechthild, she also tacitly distinguished between the beatific vision and the beatific lovemaking. The beatific vision is general, objective, and accessible to all the blessed, including the angels. Admission to the celestial bridal chamber is higher, more individual, and restricted to a small group of perfect virgins. Such doctrine would have shocked the professional theologians. They believed that no creature could ever enter the *coelum Trinitatis*, the highest level of heaven and abode of the deity. The heaven of Aquinas was shaped by the powers of reason and intellect rather than by erotic emotion and sentiment. The scholastic intellect separated the human and the divine, but mystical emotion joined them in unsurpassable intimacy.[75]

The idea that a nun or béguine was a real spouse of the Lord was not unique to mystical visions but also surfaced in liturgy and sermons. Abbess Hildegard of Bingen dressed her nuns on feast days in white bridal gowns, complete with crowns, Christ's heraldic animal (a lamb) and rings. Medievalist Caroline Bynum imagined the nuns to be thus dressed to receive communion, a foretaste of being united to their divine spouse. The concept of the nun as the bride of Christ remained a vital image in Catholicism; in some orders women religious still wear wedding gowns and are given rings when making their vows.[76]

In the *Ancrene Riwle* (Anchoresses' Rule) women are instructed by their priestly advisor to pray to the Blessed Virgin as follows: "O Lady, St. Mary...grant that I may see in heaven thy blessed face, and at least look upon the glory of those who are virgins, even if I am not worthy to be blessed in their company." To behold the holy virgins belongs to the highest enjoyments heaven has in store. In a vernacular English sermon also dating from around 1200, a priest speaks of patriarchs and prophets, apostles, martyrs, confessors, and maidens in the other world. He gives a little gloss on each of these, but when he comes to the last group, his rhetoric becomes enthusiastic and lyrical. "The beauty of their features, the sweetness of their song," he imagines, "no tongue may tell." Female virgins surpass all the other blessed, and their charm never fails to impress their fellow saints, nor even God himself. All heavenly residents are entranced by the sweetness of the holy maidens' scent which fills the air wherever they are. God, who normally sits on his throne when listening to prayers and petitions, rises in their honor when the women approach him. This kind of enthusiasm was no doubt known among béguines and nuns, and some of them, like Mechthild and Gertrude, used it as a starting-point for their own private theology.[77]

The ample use of marriage or erotic imagery drawn from the biblical Song of Songs and from courtly poetry gave the mystics' accounts a distinctive emotional quality. Courtly manners and attitudes toward love gave the traditional Christian preference for virginity a new meaning. Now the virgin could also be a lover. In the Bible, love of the divine had to be commanded and lacked spontaneity and ardor. Love was often a juridical concept which implied submission, loyalty, service, and obedience of the nation, rather than emotional involvement of the individual. Mystical experience transcended these categories, and God or Christ could be loved individually, with passion, personal attachment, and sublime eroticism.[78]

Medieval Heavens

Heaven in the Middle Ages came to mean the promise of an eternal city, the promise of the knowledge of God, and the promise of love, especially the love of Christ. The new developments of the city, the intellect, and love did not create a unified view of the other world, but three new and distinct concepts. Medieval thought was complex and rich, a mirror of heterogeneous social groups. Artists and poets, educated theologians, and women mystics each presented a perspective on heaven which contained its own intrinsic logic and meaning. After a long period of cultural stagnation, their visions challenged the ascetic heaven of the New Testament and broadened the insights of Augustine.

Monks and friars, depending on whether they felt more at home in the countryside or in the city, preached a heaven defined primarily in terms of environment. Heaven contained the verdant land, temperate climate, and sweet-smelling flowers of Eden. Men and women would be naked and innocent. While this image was important in some early medieval tracts, it would not fully emerge until the Renaissance. What caught the imagination during the Middle Ages was the rediscovery of the city. Heaven became a city – the biblical city of the new Jerusalem, the earthly magnificence of the Gothic cathedral, or the visionary experience of celestial castles. Accounts of the other world resonate with descriptions of golden streets, jewelled buildings, and richly dressed residents. In spite of (or perhaps because of) the reality of medieval urban life, with its narrow and darkened streets, drafty castles, and coarsely dressed inhabitants, the celestial city assumed its place in Christian notions of heaven.

For medieval theologians, who saw themselves as an intellectual and privileged elite, the speculations of monks and friars served only to amuse the people. Heavenly environments held no interest for those who placed knowledge above all else. Bishop Otto of Freising (1112–58) concluded his manual of universal history with a preview of eternal life, making sure not to promote unwarranted expectations. The new Jerusalem will not be a literal city on earth, of real stones, with streets of gold and pearly gates. Likewise the blessed will *not* be "refreshed and affected by flowering and verdant meadows, by pleasant places, by the singing of birds, by fragrant things such as cinnamon and balsam." "These things," explained the learned bishop, "are frequently set down by certain teachers that the simple may thus be directed through the visible to the understanding of the invisible." The educated theologian expected a heaven which conformed to scholastic ideas of light, harmony, and contemplation. Heaven was the empyrean heaven, and heavenly life was knowledge of the divine. The visions of monks and mystics, from the theological perspective, only reflected the unsophisticated belief of simple minds.[79]

If the scholastic theologian sought God through the intellect and hoped for ultimate knowledge of the divine, then the mystic sought God through love and hoped for ultimate union. Thinkers such as Aquinas prepared systematic explorations and summaries of what they perceived to be the truth concerning heavenly existence. With the advent of courtly love and the flourishing of medieval mysticism, heaven achieved a more personalized character. The poet, troubled by his love for God and his lady, found in heaven only a tentative resolution of the conflict. A hand held in a Last Judgment relief, a smile of the beloved before she turned back to the beatific vision – these were all the medieval lover could expect. The woman mystic who renounced earthly ties could look forward to more intense experiences of heavenly love. Drawing from both courtly love and the nuptial imagery of the Song of Songs, the consecrated virgin envisioned a passionate union with Christ her bridegroom. During the Middle Ages the enthusiasm which marked the New Testament community was transformed into mystical experience. The mystical experience did not deny the intensity of sexual union but instead translated it into the love of the divine for the soul. The carnal lust, which Augustine feared would draw the Christian away from the clear spring of friendship, was replaced by a heavenly passion as sensual as it was pure.

While the visions of medieval mystics such as Mechthild and Gertrude are provocative and enchanting, they never became a part of the canon of Christian teaching. Their visions, unlike the theology of Thomas Aquinas, remained basically a private form of spirituality. Later writers within the mystical tradition, however, would use similar themes to discuss the intimate relationship between God and the soul in heaven. The clarity and abstract nature of Aquinas's thought on celestial matters would become standard in Catholic theology, but the emotion-filled richness of afterlife visions would invigorate each generation of heavenly speculations. Although at times there would be tension between the intellectual, abstract heaven of the theologians and the emotional, colorful heaven of the mystics, for the most part these two perspectives would coexist peacefully. The theological heaven would be voiced in the public space of the university, seminary, and pulpit, and the mystical heaven in the private space of the diary, cloister, confessional, and chapel.

The idea of heaven as paradise restored and the issue of human companionship in the next world made only tentative entrance in religious thought and in the arts. The paradisal image, available in the monastic *Elucidation*, diminished as the ideal of the city challenged any romanticizing of nature. The longing for human love and companionship beyond death could be heard in the declarations of poets, but was never allowed to shape the teaching on the next life. Scholastics were more interested in the knowledge of God and mystics in the love of the divine. When in the fourteenth and fifteenth centuries Italian Renaissance writers and artists redefined the cultural and theological landscape of Europe, these neglected traditions came to the foreground in the new intellectual climate.

CHAPTER FIVE

The Pleasures of Renaissance Paradise

In his *Most Ridiculous Dialogue* the Italian playwright Ruzzante (1502–42) has a dead man report that there are two paradises in the other world. One heaven contains those who have led a virtuous active life; the other, the world-renouncers. The inhabitants of the first paradise continue to "eat and drink, and do whatever they like." In the other paradise, however, the saints "do not eat and drink, since they are satisfied as before with fasting and abstinence and not tasting any food. They do not cease to contemplate God, and in this consists all their bliss." For all its frivolity, Ruzzante's joke reveals the basic structure of the Renaissance paradise. Heaven ceased to be acknowledged as the exclusive domain of God, as the scholastic doctors taught. In the fifteenth and sixteenth century, heaven was split into two levels, one human and one divine. Artists, theologians, and visionaries all tended to give both heavens their due.[1]

While medieval culture continued to thrive throughout Europe, fifteenth-century Italian cities developed a new cultural, intellectual, and political style – the Renaissance. The other-worldly orientation of the Middle Ages, which considered the contemplative life in the monastery to be better preparation for eternity than the busy life "in the world," began to fade. Scholars and merchants, poets and prelates considered life "in the world" to be at least as pure and valuable as that in the monk's retreat. Rather than renouncing the world, they said, we should shape and enjoy it. By the mid-fifteenth century, the magistrate, the noble lady, and the soldier might hold their heads up: the celibate no longer monopolized virtue. Originating in cities like Florence, Siena, and Venice, Renaissance culture spread throughout Italy and eventually the rest of Europe. By the early sixteenth century Michelangelo, Machiavelli, Rodrigo Borgia (alias Pope Alexander VI), and Erasmus of Rotterdam symbolized the Renaissance interest in art and architecture, books and building, women and worldly power.[2]

Philosophical discussion supported the idea that the action-oriented human will, rather than the contemplation-oriented intellect, acted as the noblest human faculty. While medieval schoolmen invoked the authority of Aristotle to defend their contemplative ideals, Renaissance

111

writers preferred Cicero, the active statesman and orator. The "age of Aristotle" – the thirteenth and fourteenth centuries – gave way to the "age of Cicero," the fifteenth and sixteenth centuries. Renaissance theology insisted that as noble beings we are invited to enjoy rather than renounce the world. The first chapter of Genesis sanctioned the new ideal of an active life (*operosità*), detailing how creative humankind reflects the image of God the Creator. By loving, enjoying, and participating in God's world, Christians display their love of God.[3]

The new cultural climate of the Renaissance reshaped earlier ideas of eternal life. Since God and humans were seen as being in harmony rather than competing as rivals, the human side of heaven gained more prominence. Theologians, and especially poets and artists, no longer considered God the exclusive source of eternal bliss. Friends, too, became an important ingredient of paradise. In its boldest form, the new theology envisioned heaven as a place of erotic human love in the bucolic setting of a comfortable natural landscape. Within or above that paradise stood the holy city in which God would be eternally praised by his angelic hosts. Key concepts inherited from the Middle Ages: the restored paradise garden, the new Jerusalem, and heavenly love were redefined and brought into a new configuration. Without losing its divine center, heaven became more worldly, more human.

The Pleasures of a Paradise Garden

In Giotto's *Last Judgment* of 1306, a wall fresco in the Arena chapel of Padua, Italy, the figure of Christ separates (with the help of his angelic hosts) the righteous from the sinners (Pl. 10). The saints are sent to heaven, while the sinners fall prey to the powers of hell. As with other medieval depictions, heaven is placed in the upper part of the painting. There the saints sit with their faces pointed toward the divine center. Once admitted to heaven, the blessed are taken out of the judgment drama and stand or sit in eternal immobility. Likewise, in the Strozzi di Mantova chapel in Santa Maria Novella, Florence, the figures in the paradise fresco of Nardo and Andrea di Cione Orcagna hold static poses (Pl. 11). Built between 1340 and 1350 in the honor of Thomas Aquinas, the chapel contains one wall of the righteous in paradise and another of the damned descending to hell. The saints in several horizontal rows surround the throne of Christ the King and Mary his Queen. Most of the blessed stare entranced at the divine couple and two angels, but a few break the pattern of the beatific vision and look at each other. Breaking concentration on the divine only tends to emphasize the static quality of

Pl. 10. Giotto, *The Last Judgment*. 1306. Arena Chapel, Padua, Italy.

Pl. 11. Nardo and Andrea di Cione Orcagna, *The Glory of Paradise*. 1350s. Santa Maria Novella, Florence, Italy

Pl. 12. The Blessed beholding their Savior/Paradise. C. 1200. Detail of *Last Judgment* mosaic, Cathedral of Torcello, Italy

the fresco. As in Dante's celestial rose, the blessed are seated according to their spiritual rank; they remain in their places in everlasting immobility.

The Byzantine artistic tradition, however, brought an addition to the linear heaven of western Christianity. The other world included not only the place where the blessed see and praise the divine judge, as in the Padua and Florence frescos, but also a place where the blessed exist by themselves. According to a pattern book for painters, the damned "look over a long way to those who are in Abraham's bosom in Paradise, and who rejoice with all the saints. Paradise is surrounded outside by a wall of crystal and pure gold with precious stones all over it. About it grow richly adorned trees with various birds." From this perspective, heaven comprises both the city of crystal and gold *and* the renewed earth of plants and animals.[4]

The West was familiar with this tradition at least from the eleventh century, when builders like Abbot Desiderius of Monte Cassino — who later became Pope Victor III (1086/7) — imported craftsmen from Constantinople. These men were hired to carry out mosaic decorations as well as instruct others in their techniques and skills. In the lagoons near Venice, the twelfth-century cathedral of Torcello contains one such mosaic of the Last Judgment which fills an entire wall (Pl. 12). In the upper register, the blessed, praying with outstretched hands, look upward to Christ. The lower scene lacks such orientation toward the divine; it shows the blessed in two juxtaposed scenes. In the lower mosaic, paradise includes a field with flowers and big palm trees. An angel and St. Peter — the man with the key — point to the gate of the garden, guarded by a cherub angel. Through that gate, in the lovely garden, are several figures known from the Bible. The man in the loincloth holding a cross is the thief to whom Jesus promised paradise at the crucifixion. The female saint with her hands in a gesture of prayer is the Blessed Virgin. The third person, a saint sitting and holding a smaller figure in his lap, is Abraham with Lazarus in his bosom. Souls in the form of children stand by Abraham's feet on both sides.[5]

In the overall plan of the Torcello Last Judgement mosaic, the paradise scene stands isolated. The characters in it look outward at the viewer, not upward at the divine. It is the only scene uninvolved with the judgment drama. The artists of the Middle Ages did not readily adopt the paradise motif hinted at by Byzantine artists. Renaissance artists, however, developed this inconspicuous theme, making it a major expression of their view of the beyond. Heaven was divided into two realms: the place of the beatific vision and the place of palms and flowers.

When an anonymous painter around 1420 decorated the church wall of Santa Maria in Piano, located in the Abruzzi town of Loreto Aprutino, he expanded the Byzantine motif (Pl. 13). The theme of the Last

Pl. 13.   Paradise. Detail of *Last Judgment.* C. 1420–30. Santa Maria in Piano,
Loreto Aprutino, Italy

Judgment was conventional enough, but the way in which the artist
handled the paradise scene departed from Medieval prototypes. The
blessed, once they have crossed a bridge, are not yet in paradise. They
are brought naked before an elaborately dressed angel holding a pair of
scales. The angel weighs and ranks the newcomers according to their
merit. Two kinds of reward are then given: admission to the paradise
garden or admission to the new Jerusalem. Nine naked saints in the
paradise garden climb the palm trees and joyfully wave palm leaves while
looking at the new Jerusalem. The heavenly city is represented by a two-

117

storied square tower with terraces – a fine example of Renaissance architecture. A male figure, who must be St. Peter, stands in the entrance door. On the lower terrace an angel dresses the newcomers in robes. The upper terrace reveals the ecstatic joy of the citizens of the new Jerusalem. All of them wear their new garments. Some dance, lost in their ecstasy. Others look over to the grove of palms and seem to exchange joyful greetings with the denizens of paradise. There is no intimation of any disharmony between the two realms, the garden and the castle. Although their rewards are graded (palms of victory indicating the lower rank), all the blessed share in the same fullness of bliss. The paradise garden is not purgatory. No one suffers or anxiously awaits promotion to a higher place.[6]

For the anonymous artist, departing from the established way of representing the Last Judgment did not imply a departure from traditional doctrine. This is still a medieval heaven, but not one taken from the textbooks of scholastic theology. Aquinas and Bonaventure insisted that neither plants nor animals exist in heaven. The painting in Santa Maria in Piano reflects not the scholastic tradition but the earlier monastic concept of paradise restored. This is the heaven of the *Elucidation*, a garden full of "sweet-smelling flowers, lilies, roses, and violets." The painting also shows the influence of popular medieval legends. According to the *Golden Legend*, compiled by the Italian archbishop James of Voragine in the thirteenth century, an angel brought a palm branch to the Blessed Virgin when he announced to her that she would die. It was believed that palm branches, as symbols of victory, would be awarded to all after this life's battle. In another legend, a knight on his heavenly journey negotiated a narrow bridge, under which a river of sulphur and fire gurgled. Safely crossing to the other side, the knight arrived in a pleasant meadow which was paradise. The anonymous artist's reliance on such legendary motifs and traditional monastic teaching emphasizes that there are no new ideas in the painting: minor trends in medieval art and theology are being revitalized.[7]

The collapsing together of the medieval images of paradise restored and the abode of God occurred in the visions of Mechthild, where a hidden earthly garden comprised the lowest heaven. Mechthild, however, preferred to speak of the higher levels that included the heavenly bridal chamber, and showed less interest in the paradise garden. By the fifteenth century, though, religious writers were spending equal time describing each environment. In the *Compendium of Revelations* (1495) of the Dominican friar Savonarola (1452–98) of Florence, both celestial worlds appear with clarity. Savonarola situated his heaven above a very high wall of precious stones encircling the universe. Beyond this firmament was paradise. Once the soul accustomed its senses to the dazzling light of that realm, it distinguished a variety of levels.　•

The lowest level Savonarola portrayed as "a very broad field, covered with delicious flowers of Paradise. Live crystal streams flowed everywhere with a quiet murmur." A large number of "mild animals" (sheep, ermines, rabbits), all whiter than snow, played among the flowers and grass alongside the flowing waters. "There were leafy trees of various kinds decorated with flowers and fruits," the Dominican recounted, "in whose branches a crowd of varicolored birds flying here and there in a wonderful way sang a sweet melody." Although Savonarola's order followed the teaching of Aquinas, he departed from the scholastic theologian. His heaven was not an intellectual world of pure light but a garden of vegetation and animals.[8]

On a level above the paradise garden were the nine ranks of the angelic hierarchy, the throne of Mary, and the "wondrous light of the three faces," the Trinity. Savonarola travelled all the way up to the Blessed Virgin, approaching her as the patroness of Florence. Mary's presence made heaven human and accessible; this was not only the heaven of Christ the judge. The saints rested in their places among the angelic hierarchies or journeyed down to paradise. Mary also reigned in the paradise garden from another throne. Everyone enjoyed total freedom and mobility in heaven. A huge ladder conveniently connected the two realms – the paradise garden and the levels above it. Savonarola indicated that he as a visitor from earth needed this ladder, while the blessed could move up and down without such help. Having shed all material heaviness, their glorified bodies floated without effort. Unlike the medieval saints who sat in rigid immobility, the blessed of the Renaissance moved freely between garden and city. While they retained their seats in the heavenly hierarchy, they were no longer confined to that place. The two heavens existed simultaneously for the benefit of the saints.[9]

The separation of the heavenly residence from the garden paradise appears more explicitly in a painting of Hieronymus Bosch (1450–1516) than in the work of earlier artists (Pl. 14). Unfortunately, all that remains of Bosch's paradise is a fragment of a part of the Last Judgment dating from approximately 1505–10. While the original composition is lost, a mid-sixteenth-century etching based on the painting can be taken as our guide to Bosch's twofold vision of heaven. The etching divides in half, with a formal garden situated on the seashore and an architectural heaven over it, above the clouds. The impermanent and movable structures of paradise – tent and ship – provide a sharp contrast to the eternal, immobile church-like abode of God, complete with fine Gothic spires and arches.[10]

The separation of paradise (as abode of the blessed) and heaven (as the residence of the Trinity) corresponds to the distinction between nature and culture. Paradise, however, is not exclusively Edenic or pastoral.

IVSTORVM ANIMAE IN MANV DEI SVNT, NEC
ATTINGIT ILLOS CRVCIATVS.

Pl. 14. Hieronymus Cock,
Paradise. After Hieronymus
Bosch. 16th century.
Detail of *Last Judgment*

Redeemed nature cannot be the same as before the Fall; it must surpass the original creation. Consequently, elements of culture invade Eden. A boat, a fountain, and a tent are placed in the painting. These furnishings never overwhelm the natural surroundings; culture does not compromise nature. As a carefully cultivated park, paradise avoids the disadvantages of both wilderness and city. A balance is preserved between the cultured heaven of the Trinity and the natural paradise of the blessed.

The engraving based on the Bosch painting is not only a summary of traditional biblical imagery – the Garden of Eden and the heavenly Jerusalem. Renaissance artists, theologians, and poets rediscovered the classical writers and integrated the concept of the Golden Age and the Isles of the Blest into their understanding of heaven. According to classical mythology, the first era of human history was free from war and toil. Following that age came ever less noble and comfortable periods. According to the ancient author Hesiod, the Golden Age continues only on the Isles of the Blest, a post-mortem haven reserved for heroes and heroines. Cronos, the god who once ruled over the Golden Age, now rules over the Isles of the Blest or Elysian Fields. Classical mythology provided a rich repertoire of ideas and images for Renaissance art, poetry, and speculation.[11]

Following the classical tradition that denied houses and homes to the inhabitants of the Elysian Fields, Bosch placed the blessed in tents. "None of us has one fixed home. We walk in shady groves," explained one of Virgil's blessed pagans; "and bed on riverbanks, and occupy green meadows with fresh streams." These same images appear in Bosch's Christian paradise. The fountain which the saints enjoy blends the biblical "fountain of life," the mythical "fountain of love," and the Renaissance fountain beginning to appear in architecture and land-scaping. According to the *Roman de la Rose*, contact with the fountain of love makes men and women the prisoners of Cupid, the son of Venus. Hence they must love. "Because of the seed that was sown" to attract people like birds to a trap, explains the *Roman*, "this fountain has rightly been called the Fountain of Love, about which several have spoken in many places in books and in romances." In an enthusiastic letter of 1543, an Italian humanist related a visit to a garden with a fountain, in which he bathed in the "charming and courtly company of several gentle-men." He enjoyed the chance "to see, hear, bathe myself, and taste the wonderful water, which was so clean and pure that it truly seemed virginal, as it is named." The biblical fountain of life easily merged with, or was transformed into, the fountain of love. The existence of real fountains cemented the idea in the Renaissance imagination.[12]

For all their interest in cities and civic life, Renaissance men and women also appreciated the country. They loved to be outdoors, outside the city which was a world of stone. There were no gardens in the

Renaissance city, no green plots where one's eye could rest. People longed for the fresh verdure of the fields and the quietness of the rural life, which they praised with great eloquence. A country villa at Vaucluse near Avignon was Petrarch's (died 1374) refuge, while his friend Boccaccio (died 1375) preferred rural Certaldo to noisy Florence. Only when seeing "fields, hills, trees, all clothed with green leaves and variegated flowers" could Boccaccio "enjoy and feel something of eternal happiness." In the *Decameron* (1353, first published 1470), the young company enjoy idyllic gardens and parks. The sight of one place complete with flowers, trees, lawns, birds, and a fountain, "gave so much pleasure to each of the ladies and the three young men that they all began to maintain that if Paradise were constructed on earth, it was inconceivable that it could take any other form than this garden." The paradise garden no longer referred only to the Garden of Eden. With the rediscovery of classical images and the interest in the quiet of the countryside, heaven increasingly assumed a pastoral quality.[13]

The changing character of heaven can be summarized by examining how one Renaissance artist interpreted the heaven of Dante. Sometime around 1440, Giovanni di Paolo (1403–83) illuminated a manuscript of Dante's *Paradiso*. In two illustrations of Canto 30, he painted the blessed free from clothes. In the one case naked saints float above or dive into a field of flowers (Pl. 15). Dante's river of light is restyled as a meadow. In the other case they sit on the stone benches of an amphitheater (Pl. 16). Giovanni transforms Dante's heavenly thrones into benches on which naked figures bath their youthful, relaxed bodies in warm light. In his illustration of Canto 31, Beatrice shows to the heavenly pilgrim the Virgin in a lovely garden (Pl. 17). Neither nakedness nor plants have a clear warrant in Dante's text. Dante felt comfortable with Aquinas's theocentric heaven of piercing light. Giovanni took the liberty of making the empyrean into a garden – an Elysium with flowers and bathing nudes. He preferred to indulge in Renaissance fantasy rather than produce a literal rendering of the *Paradiso*.[14]

It is not merely the shady groves and riverbanks that remind us of the classical heritage of the Golden Age and the Isles of the Blest. The saints enjoying the pleasures of Bosch's paradise appear to be unconcerned with the sacred drama going on above them. They play with one another, listen to angels strum on their instruments, splash in the water, and feed the birds. The winged angels, who mark the engraving as particularly Christian, are no longer busy as members of God's choir, praising his glory. Instead, as musicians, they serenade the couples as they sit or walk at leisure, enveloping their sweet talk in fine melodies. Even God does not intrude on the scene. In spite of the angels and the deity, Bosch's saints act like the shepherds and shepherdesses celebrated in Virgil's

Pl. 15.   Giovanni di Paolo, *Souls and the Trintiy*. C. 1438–44. Manuscript Yates Thompson 36, fol. 183 recto

Pl. 16.   Giovanni di Paolo, *Souls in Paradise*. C. 1438–44. Manuscript Yates Thompson 36, fol. 184 recto

Pl. 17.   Giovanni di Paolo, *The Blessed Virgin in Paradise*. C. 1438–44. Manuscript Yates Thompson 36, fol. 186 recto

Eclogues. The ideal life was not merely a pastoral landscape filled with meadows, shady groves and rivulets with gently gurgling water. The Renaissance also inherited the classical tradition that the righteous enjoy each other's company after death.[15]

Meeting Again in Heaven: Lovers and Saints

In *On Old Age* and *Scipio's Dream*, the classical Roman orator Cicero supplied his Renaissance readership with an attractive set of ideas about the other life. Cicero's ideal candidate for heaven was not the ascetic who renounced the active life, but the statesman and public benefactor. Although they had lived generations before his time, Cicero recommended the protagonists of these books, Cato and Scipio, as archetypes of republican courage and virtue. As with Cato and Scipio, Cicero believed that anyone displaying dedication to the state would eventually ascend to heaven and meet political figures as well as ancestors and relatives. Favorite books of the humanists, and present in any Renaissance library, *Scipio's Dream* and *On Old Age* never failed to impress their readers.[16]

Early mention of Cicero's influence on images of the Renaissance afterlife can be found in the writings of Petrarch. "Marcus Tullius [Cicero], however, whose paganism is as famous as it is to be regretted, was not of this opinion" – that there was no life after death – wrote Petrarch in a letter of consolation. Cicero "believed in the immortality of the soul and that some celestial abode awaits the honorable souls after this life." Petrarch also explained how Cicero, in his book *On Old Age*, has Marcus Cato frankly discuss his heavenly nostalgia. Cato, the elder statesman, not only longs to join old friends who have died and whose company he misses. He also wants to meet people about whom he has only heard or read in books. At the other end of the Renaissance, Petrarch's Ciceronian eschatology was shared by Erasmus (1466–1536). In one of his *Familiar Colloquies* he quotes a passage on "heavenly reunion," which had earlier impressed Petrarch, and has one of his fictional characters exclaim, "Can a Christian say anything more pious?" Renaissance reflection on life after death begins and ends with the same quotation from Cicero.[17]

Classical poets like Tibullus (c. 54–19 BCE) insisted that lovemaking in the Golden Age was uninhibited and free. "They had love always wherever they were," reported Tibullus; "to those on whom Love's God breathed kindly did gentle Venus bring open pleasures in the shady vales. No watchers were there, nor doors to close against the vanquished." The Renaissance shared with Tibullus the nostalgia for the Golden Age as the

Pl. 18.   Lucas Cranach, *The Golden Age*. 1530. Alte Pinakothek, Munich, Germany

age of Venus, for the time in which free love "was not a matter of evil tongues." Illustrations of the Golden Age often showed naked couples dancing, playing or reclining at ease in a meadow (Pl. 18). Following that pattern, life in paradise meant leisure and loving in a natural setting. Men and women were naked. Generally paired, they spent their time relaxing in the grass, bathing and swimming, or simply strolling about for Tibullus, the Golden Age was not just a reality of the distant past. It survived in the beyond in the Elysian Fields, the land of the dead:

> But me, for I have been ever pliable to gentle Love, shall Venus' self escort to the Elysian Fields. There never flags the dance and song. The birds fly here and there, fluting sweet carols from their slender throats. Untilled the field bears cassia, and through all the land with scented roses blooms the kindly earth. Troops of young men meet in sport with gentle maidens, and Love never lets his warfare cease. There are all on whom Death swooped because of love; on their hair are myrtle garlands for all to see.

Both Cicero's philosophy of the beyond and the poetic vision of Tibullus fuelled the Renaissance imagination. Christian writers, theologians, and artists strove to integrate classical imagery with that of their own tradition.[18]

Dominican humanist Francesco Colonna (1433–1527) invented a

125

daring vision which, like Tibullus, emphasized love in the world beyond our own. In his book *Hypnerotomachia: The Strife of Love in a Dream*, the protagonist was granted entry into the world of nymphs and their lovers. He met them as they played in a picturesque place with fountains, delightful meadows, fresh streams, hills with laurel trees, and shady groves. There a great company of delicate maidens and their young beardless lovers frolicked. Some reclined, teasing and playing with each other. Others sang "amorous sonnets and verses of love," while others "feigned that they were forsaken" and ran after one another with girlish laughter. There were also lovers who "with great courtesy were putting rose leaves one after another into their [friends'] laced breasts, adding after them sweet kisses." While the Dominican's tale of flirtations in the other world remained unrelated to Christian notions of the beyond, sixteenth-century poets remedied this defect. For them, heaven became a half-pagan, half-Christian land of lovers.[19]

Pierre de Ronsard (1524–1585), the founder of modern French poetry, perhaps best exemplifies the Renaissance poets' view on love after death. In his ode "O pucelle plus tendre", the poet clings to his beloved lady and in a mutual embrace the lovers articipate death:

> Bound together, kissing, we will go
> And cross the muddy lake below.
> Passing through where raging Pluto reigns
> We will arrive on scented plains,
> On fields that were decreed by gods of yore
> To be the fortunate lovers' shore.

The fields decreed for fortunate lovers are of course the Elysian Fields of classical mythology. In another poem, Ronsard's dream is even more explicit. The Elysian Fields are the place of endless love:

> Sitting daily where the myrtle grows
> (After having died because of love)
> Let us join the ancient heroes.
> These their heroines embrace
> And speak of love in every place.

In this dreamy world the newcomers are welcomed by "la troupe sainte autrefois amoureuse," the saintly band of ancient lovers. The saints of Ronsard's heaven are lovers.[20]

When Madame Louise of Savoy – the mother of the French king – died in 1531, an elegy was written which echoed sentiments similar to those of Ronsard. Clément Marot (1469–1544) assured his readers that Madame Louise "has been received in the Elysian Fields:"

Thère, where she is, nothing has lost its bloom; never do the day and its pleasures die there; never dies the richly colored green... Every ambrosial fragrance flourishes there, and they have neither two nor three seasons, but only spring, and never do they mourn for loss of friends. . . There she eats fruit of inestimable price; there she drinks that which appeases every thirst; there she will know a thousand noble souls. Every pleasant animal is found there, and a thousand birds give immortal joy.

The medieval popular concept of heaven as paradise restored is enriched with the rhetoric of Elysium.[21]

Poets and artists were not the only ones captivated by the classical idea of love in the next world. Renaissance theologians at times also utilized classical themes. This is especially true of Lorenzo Valla (1405–57), who ended his dialogue *On Pleasure* (1431) with a scene of paradisal bliss. One of the foremost Italian humanists, Valla knew Cicero's view of meeting one's relatives and famous people in the afterlife. However, he was far from simply endorsing what the Roman statesman had written in *Scipio's Dream* and *On Old Age*. With his characteristic zeal for surpassing Cicero, Valla strove to make the classical heaven pale in the light of the Christian paradise.

Valla's imaginary interlocutor Antonio gives a full description. Upon death, angels guide the righteous soul up through the various heavenly spheres. When the blessed person arrives, heaven resounds with solemn music as if "the bells of all the churches ring to show the city's joy." Relatives and friends come and cordially greet, kiss, and embrace the newly arrived soul. A flock of saints, too, come to greet him, and the Mother of God "will clasp you to her virginal breast on which she suckled God; and she will kiss you." Then the saints escort him to the new Jerusalem where they present him to God. Upon arrival in heaven, the newcomer is not only welcomed by saints. Valla's Antonio hopes to meet his father and mother, his two boys and his beloved daughters, as well as his brother and sister who died before him. The theme of meeting again weighed so much on Valla's mind that he had Antonio insert a personal note, granting us a glimpse of his tormented soul: "As for me, I am oppressed and consumed by my daily desire to see again a number of people but especially my good father, my brother and sister, for whom there were such great expectations, and whom I looked upon as my children because they were so much younger than I. When they died I wept myself nearly blind on their beds and on their graves. Oh, when shall I see them?"[22]

Valla's heavenly reception already went beyond all Cicero and other classical authors had written, but the humanist continued. A life of leisure awaits us – a life in which all our senses will be gratified in unspeakable ways. Our bodies will be infused with a sweetness "that thrills you to the marrow, so that no venery can be compared to it." Upon a moment's reflection he added, apologizing, "perhaps I am using here language that is too obscene for the dignity of the subject." A true humanist, Valla looked forward to knowing all the world's languages and mastering all learning and every art, "without error, doubt, or ambiguity." He also speculated about meeting angels – spirits whose beauty "does not inflame but extinguishes lust, and infuses a most sanctified religious awe." Having bodies that can move wherever we want with unencumbered swiftness, we will play with our winged companions in the sky, upon mountains, in valleys, or at the seaside. Perhaps we will even be able to dive into the sea, spending time under water like fish.[23]

An attempt to give Valla's ideas graphic expression has been seen in a sculpture made by Donatello in 1440 for the singing-gallery of the Florence cathedral. But it is not quite certain whether the Roman-style putti racing back and forth behind a line of columns are in fact human souls enjoying the pleasures of heaven. The speculations of Valla found little outlet in an art still dominated by traditional notions of heaven. New developments can be traced with greater assurance in the iconography of the Last Judgment. In the fifteenth century, artists began to include in their Last Judgments a paradise garden where the saints would meet. Giovanni da Fiesole, better known as Fra Angelico (1400–55), departed from the medieval canon when he painted a *Last Judgment* panel (c. 1431) in Florence (Pl. 19). Following established convention, on the right side of the panel the damned who have risen from their graves run away from the judging Christ and toward a hell of torture. At the top center, Christ and the saints sit in majesty. This is the heaven of the scholastic writings described by Fra Angelico's fellow Dominican, Thomas Aquinas. Angelico, however, does not leave the panel with only two alternatives – heaven of bliss or hell of torment. He must have sensed that without a glimpse of paradise the scene is incomplete.[24]

Angelico's paradise fills all the space available on the left side of the painting. The setting is a garden, a fresh meadow with trees. Angelico, whom art historians acknowledge as the first painter of an identifiable landscape, took great care to give realistic detail to the garden. While many of the blessed still look up to their judge, others are led by angels to this garden. Here the blessed dance gracefully hand-in-hand in a round in which saints and angels alternate. The sentimental and human quality of the scene is certainly intended. In the lower right corner of the garden, a friar and an angel embrace (Pl. 20). "Here we see a monk," the art historian Herbert Stützer maintains, "who during all of his life had renounced contact with the other sex, but now is tenderly embraced by a female angel. Thus pious Fra Angelico transfers worldly bliss to heaven." While Stützer exaggerates the angel's female features, the artist clearly moved beyond the scholastic view that angels have no gender. Angelico displays none of the classical enthusiasm for love which we saw with

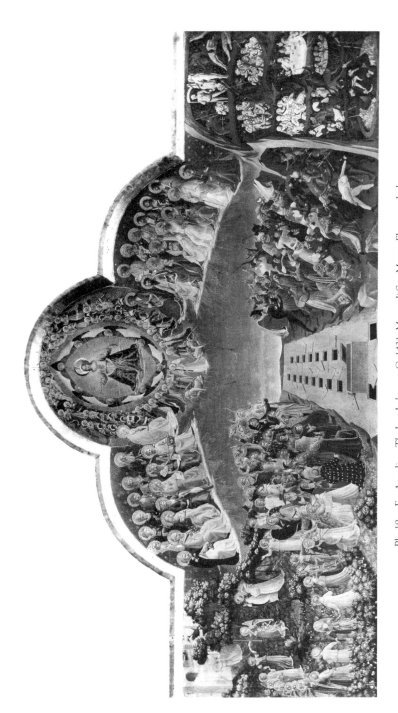

Pl. 19. Fra Angelico, *The Last Judgment*. C. 1431. Museo di San Marco, Florence, Italy

Pl. 20.   Fra Angelico, *In Paradise*, detail of *Last Judgment*. C. 1431. Museo di San Marco,
Florence, Italy

Francesco Colonna and Ronsard, but the affection which the angels and
saints show for one another is unmistakable.[25]

Above the paradise garden, almost out of the painting, is a city gate
streaming with golden light. Two saints make their way toward the light.
The city is the new Jerusalem, the high golden walls, wide-open gates,
and radiating light of which are all referred to in the Bible. The saints
float above the ground, suggesting that they can move without effort.
The contrast stresses the radical difference between the old and the new
body. In the world people endure the hardship of walking barefoot on
dirty and rough roads. In the heavenly state they move effortlessly. For a
community of preaching monks who travelled extensively, effortless
motion in heaven must have seemed a very special gift.

Fra Angelico's addition of paradise divides heaven into two sections.
While the luminous city seems to be for the eternal worship of God
(according to the book of Revelation), the garden outside the city
functions as a space in which the saints and the angels meet, talk, and
dance at leisure (Pl. 21). The graceful gestures and regular movements of

the dancers contrast effectively both with the chaotic movements of the damned (right side) and with the immobility of the heavenly hosts sitting in the empyrean (above, Pl. 19). Keeping well within the bounds of Christian purity and love, the saints and angels touch and express affection. Angelico has placed movement, sentiment, expectation, and humanity in paradise.

The round dance dramatizes not only ordered motion stimulated by intense joy, but also the feeling of security. In Angelico's heaven, the blessed do not appear to be concerned that they dance outside the gates of the city. In heaven, they feel as secure outside the new Jerusalem as they would feel inside. Consequently, the ramparts of the celestial castle have lost their function of defense. The inclusion of the heavenly gates must therefore be explained in aesthetic terms. The golden walls serve to mark off the garden from the city: the two heavens remain distinct and separate environments. At the same time the city walls which close off the light of heaven provide a stark contrast to the open caves of hell with its various torture chambers. In heaven the blessed are received into the fellowship of loving saints – in garden and city – while the damned are left with the emptiness of agony.

Apparently imitating the great Angelico, the Sienese artist Giovanni

Pl. 21.   Fra Angelico, *The Dance of the Blessed*, detail of *Last Judgment*. C. 1431. Museo di San Marco, Florence, Italy

di Paolo painted a *Paradise* for a 1445 altar panel (Pl. 22). This *Paradise* was part of an otherwise lost series of five small paintings forming the predella or bottom piece of a large altar panel. The paintings, each representing a separate scene, apparently consisted of Creation, Paradise, Last Judgment, Hell, and Deluge. As with Angelico, paradise is a garden with carefully selected features – a meadow perfumed with small flowers and fruit-bearing trees. Monks, prelates, nuns, and lay people are received by angels who affectionately embrace or engage them in pleasant conversation. The artist arranges the blessed in pairs, thus giving due

Pl. 22. Giovanni di Paolo, *Paradise*. C. 1445. Metropolitan Museum of Art, New York

132

emphasis to the personal and individual, rather than Angelico's communal enjoyment of eternal bliss.

The art critic John Pope-Hennessy detects another feature that indicates Giovanni's attempt to depart from Angelico's model. The faces of Fra Angelico's saints are "infused with a single vacant serenity, which leaves the most enchanting of his compositions unrevealing and impersonal." In Giovanni's version of paradise, however, "each figure expresses distinct and individual reactions – humility, surprise, affection and contentment, which have a particularly affecting quality." These reactions are all the more human when we consider that Giovanni's *Paradise*, as a whole, has an independent existence without relationship to Christ or God.[26]

Neither in Angelico's nor in Giovanni's paintings would a search of the list of saints identify the people in the paradise gardens. The paradise of the artists was not a place where only the famous, canonized saints met, leaving the less dignified citizens of heaven to live elsewhere. Renaissance artistic expression avoided giving prominence to the theological, dogmatic assumption of a graded heaven where reward corresponds to virtue. The common medieval notion of the various heavenly "classes" (the apostles, virgins, martyrs, etc.) is also absent. Irrespective of spiritual merit and state, the blessed of Angelico and Giovanni di Paolo mix freely in the relaxed atmosphere of a garden. Why should not a doctor talk to a virgin or a martyr to a holy widow? In a later version of his *Paradise*, Giovanni allows even the Holy Innocents – naked children whose martyrdom is indicated by a delicate red spot – to play and frolic among the other saints. Thus the artists depicted a single paradise where the ordinary person, irrespective of his or her rank, might live. "Patently many of its inhabitants would have been monks, friars, or nuns," explains Pope-Hennessy, "but in principle it was a communist unit." Paradise was for *all* the righteous.[27]

The idea of a single heaven or paradise for all the righteous is clearer in Giovanni's work than it is in Angelico's. The very position of Giovanni's painting between Creation and Last Judgment suggests that he thought of the heavenly garden as paradise restored. Therefore it makes sense that he should omit the new Jerusalem. The righteous live in a garden, as did Adam and Eve, not in a city. Significantly, Giovanni also introduced animals – playful litle rabbits – into the garden. Paradise again is complete with all the creatures which Aquinas banned from eternal life. Heaven contains a renewed earth where humanity can enjoy all good living things.

The visions of the artists are echoed in mystical experience. The heavenly visions of Dominican Osanna of Mantua (1449–1505) are full of affection, kisses, embraces, and sweet talk among saints. In one of her raptures, two saintly men – Paul and Simeon – meet the nun, greet her lovingly, and take her by the hand to the divine throne. God himself talks to her affectionately, calling her his most beloved daughter. As if to insist that heaven is not for God alone, Osanna lists the other saints she sees after having spoken to God: Thomas Aquinas, Mary Magdalene, and her favorite saint, Catherine of Siena. On the feast day of St. Dominic, Osanna is again transported to paradise where she meets the founder of her order. As is to be expected, he speaks to her with fatherly benevolence and tenderness. To her disappointment she saw neither Catherine of Siena nor her friend, the late Columba (1476–1501), founder of a Dominican nunnery in Perugia. She knew that her friend was in heaven, because she had actually seen Columba at the hour of her death in far-away Perugia ascend into the celestial realm. In another vision, Osanna would later meet her friend, finding that she could hardly free herself from Columba's embraces.[28]

Erasmus of Rotterdam, the prince of the humanists, presented a more restrained but equally emotional meeting in heaven. When his friend John Reuchlin died in 1522, Erasmus imagined Reuchlin meeting numerous angels and one special saint in a delightful meadow. That saint, the church father Jerome, greets and honors the new arrival with a joyful embrace. He gives him a beautiful robe in three colors, symbolizing his expertise in Hebrew, Greek, and Latin. Reuchlin and Jerome as Hebrew scholars form a perfect pair. Jerome then guides the newly robed saint to an elevation at the center of the meadow. As they stand there embracing each other, heaven opens. In a channel of divine light linking heaven and paradise, they ascend to the accompaniment of angelic music.[29]

Erasmus did not invent the ascension from the paradise garden to God's abode; he placed his characters Reuchlin and Jerome in a supernatural landscape familiar to Renaissance contemporaries. Dieric Bouts's *Paradise* of c. 1470, painted for the town hall of Leuven in Belgium, illustrates the scene quite well (Pl. 23). Angels meet the blessed in a garden near an elaborate fountain with a Gothic steeple; they then guide them to an elevation, above which heaven opens to receive the ascending saints into a realm of light.

At least one theological treatise echoed the Renaissance dream of meeting and loving others in the heavenly world. In a book entitled *Pleasing Explanation of the Sensuous Pleasures of Paradise* (1504) we can read of the beauty of the glorified human body, its enhanced ability to see and hear, and to sing praises to God far superior to any song produced in this life. We will be able to smell, taste, and touch. From the gospel passage reporting that Jesus embraced little children, it is boldly inferred that the saints in heaven can touch each other and will also be embraced by Christ. "Thus we will embrace our fathers, brothers and sisters," the book explains, "the saints, especially, will embrace Christ who in turn

Pl. 23.   Dieric Bouts, *Paradise*. 15th century. Musée des Beaux-Arts, Lille, France

will embrace them. See Mark 9 where he embraced little children."
The saints who hug each other simply follow the example set by Christ
himself.[30]

The spiritual nature of our bodies, however, will not diminish the
pleasure derived from such embraces. Kissing will also be a part of the
state of glory. We will kiss Christ and he will kiss us. "The same can be
done to our beloved ones and to whatever male and female saint we want
to kiss." The author proves this by quoting sermons, published by
acknowledged authorities (Pseudo-Augustine and Bernard of Clairvaux),
on the Assumption of the Blessed Virgin. When Mary entered heaven,
Jesus welcomed his mother with a real, "bodily" kiss. This was possible because both Jesus and Mary had already received their glorified
bodies. Saints, therefore, must also be able to kiss and receive kisses.
What is more, kisses can also be exchanged at any distance, when
the beloved partner happens to be elsewhere in paradise. "Thousand
thousands of miles" are no obstacle, and kissing at a distance affords the
same pleasure as when the lips actually meet. No longer constrained
by physical separation, lovers can always establish close contact, immediately as well as intimately. References to the sweet fragrance
connected with kissing underscore its "physical" rather than purely
spiritual character.[31]

The author of the treatise was a celibate monk, Celso Maffei (1425–
1508), re-elected seven times by his fellow monks to be the general of
their order, the Canon Regulars of the Lateran. Dedicated to Pope Julius
II (1443–1513), the work describes a paradise based on a hierarchy of
pleasure. "According to a rough estimate," Maffei claims, "the body of
the lowest saint will taste fifty times better than honey, sugar, or some
natural or artificial food and drink of this world; another saint will taste a
hundred times sweeter, and a third one more than a thousand times
better – and so on." At the end of the learned treatise, however, Maffei
sounds a note of both triumph and apology. The pleasures of the senses
constitute *human* happiness, we are told. Lacking bodies, the angels are
not capable of such felicity; they do not enjoy the kisses of heaven. The
pleasures which the saints, not the angels, enjoy will be superior to any
earthly experience. Without violating chastity or virginity, all our
corporeal senses will be satisfied. His brief apology – "without violating
chastity" – sounds like the echo of an ascetic ideal no longer entertained
by Renaissance Christianity. After reading the treatise one wonders
whether the monk actually led the celibate life he was expected to
lead.[32]

The sensuality of Maffei's saints does not appear in the chaste and
delicate art of Fra Angelico or Giovanni di Paolo but in the striking
compositions of Luca Signorelli (1441–1523) (Pl. 24). Commissioned
to decorate one of the chapels in the cathedral of Orvieto, Italy, Signor-

elli finished the project begun a generation before by Fra Angelico. Unlike Angelico he preferred the gravity of monumental design and painted the huge walls of the chapel in the years 1499–1502. At Orvieto Signorelli charted the drama of the Last Judgment as a series of individual acts, each represented in a painting of its own: the Resurrection at the blowing of the trumpets, the torments of the damned, the coronation of the blessed, and finally the ascent to heaven.

Signorelli dedicated one complete wall of the chapel to the theme of the *Coronation of the Blessed*. He crowded the lower half of the painting with men and women, some with draped loins and others quite naked. They gaze upwards and receive the golden crowns which the angels place on their heads. Above, seated on clouds, are other "female" angels draped in many-folded robes, playing musical instruments and singing. In the center of the fresco float two more angels who gracefully throw flowers. All the men and women have strong, youthful, and flawless bodies (Pl. 25). "There is not an ounce of extra fat on any of them," observes one art historian. "Their skin is like a transparent sheet of rubber stretched over the muscles. Their poses are calm and relaxed." Unlike earlier painters of the Last Judgment, Signorelli makes no distinctions as to state or age among the blessed, the only exception being the monk's tonsure.[33]

The bodies of the saints are not the glorified, luminous bodies described by Aquinas. These bodies remind us of the later Augustine who, ignoring his earlier denial of the existence of "celestial flesh," argued for the beauty of the heavenly body. Signorelli's saints like Augustine's are in the flower of their youth and freed from any physical limitation. Stretching their arms, they flaunt their bodies' symmetry and proportion. Men and women stand together, displaying no bashfulness, since they enjoy one another's beauty without any lust. Women, who on earth were accused of leading men into sin and away from the divine, receive their crowns on equal terms with the men.

While it makes sense that in a Resurrection fresco everyone should emerge naked out of the grave, Signorelli's insistence on nudity in the crowning scene holds special meaning. One would expect the crowning of the saints to be preceded by their investment with robes. This, for instance, is the sequence followed in the British coronation service: first the robe, then the crown. Signorelli omitted the investment with robes, assuming that in paradise restored the blessed need no garments. He adhered to the Renaissance celebration of the human body while at the same time exploiting the theological sentiments contained in medieval theology and popular imagination. Recall the *Elucidation*'s prediction that the blessed "will be nude, but excel in modesty and never blush because of any parts of their body any more than they do now because of having beautiful eyes." Signorelli celebrated the naked human body as

Pl. 24. Luca Signorelli, *The Coronation of the Elect*. 1499/1502. Cathedral of Orvieto, Italy

Pl. 25.   Luca Signorelli, *The Coronation of the Elect*, detail, 1499–1502.
Cathedral of Orvieto, Italy

the hallmark of paradise restored. One art historian suspects that some of
the loincloths were added to make the fresco meet the requirements of
later, prudish taste. Be this as it may – Signorelli clearly delighted in the
resurrected body in all its vigor and youthful freshness. It is no surprise to
see Michelangelo develop this theme in his unrivalled *Resurrection* fresco
in the Sistine Chapel.[34]

At first sight Signorelli's crowd of men and women seem unstructured.
Everybody waits to be crowned and then, in the following scene, to float
up to heaven in his or her muscular (yet weightless) body. There is,
however, at least one important structural element ordering the company
of saints: the couple. In the foreground three couples can be recognized:
one standing at the far left, another in the middle, and a third at the far
right. According to Signorelli, heaven is not free from the male-female
relationship. If God created paradise with humanity ordered in pairs,
then paradise restored must also include this fundamental unit. The
communion of saints does not need to be an undifferentiated mass of
people arranged by spiritual rank. In Renaissance art and theology,
special relationships defined by the saints themselves can exist in the
next world. God no longer has the sole authority over who sits next to
whom.

· Renaissance artists and theologians shared the conviction that pleasure and happiness are the goals of human life in general and Christian life in particular. For them both Christian and Epicurean philosophy asserted that virtue was only a means to achieve happiness, and certainly not an end in itself. Happiness was nobler than virtue. Happiness, moreover, presupposed human company. Humanist Bartolomeo Facio (died 1457) celebrated "the concourse of citizens" as one of the supreme joys of the other life. "For it seems," Facio explained, "that the solitary life detracts not a little from happiness." This idea, mild as it may appear, departed from standard scholastic theology. Aquinas, in his *Summa theologica*, not only insisted on the irrelevance of human friendship; he emphasized the "spiritual" nature of heavenly pleasures in contrast to the views of Jews, Muslims, and millenarian heretics. From the Renaissance perspective, it could no longer be argued that friendship with other people was irrelevant for those who enjoyed the eternal love of God.[35]

Around 1526–30 the Dutch artist Jean Bellegambe painted a triptych for the altar of a church (Pl. 26). Within the painting, Bellegambe brashly presents the major elements of the Renaissance heaven. The two layers of heaven are clearly delineated. On the lower level naked saints greet one another, play in the grass, and converse with the angels. In the center of the painting is the fountain – of the biblical, classical, and Renaissance traditions. The sheer number of naked bodies reminds the viewer of the classical Golden Age or Isles of the Blest. This is not merely a paradise restored with a few saints symbolizing the primordial couple, Adam and Eve. The paradise of Bellegambe is filled with a community of frolicking saints enjoying their relationships with one another. They appear unconcerned about the heavenly city protruding from the sky, or the crowning and robing in progress in front of them. Traditional Christian themes – the celestial city and the finely dressed angels – are in no way minimized, but set in balance with the more "pagan" elements of play, conversation, and touching.

Renaissance men and women looked forward to meeting their friends in paradise without risking their orthodoxy. Petrarch could now meet his divine Lord and his human lady. That Dante, after his death, "was no doubt received into the arms of his most noble Beatrice" and "now lives with her in the sight of Him, who is his supreme good," was no longer the bold suggestion of a fourteenth-century outsider like Boccaccio. By blending the Isles of the Blest with paradise restored and adding a selected dose of scriptural warrant and visionary description, both God and humanity could enjoy beauty and harmony in heaven. Heaven was no longer imagined as a place where God received the praise of the saints with no concern for their creaturely happiness. The glorified bodies of the blessed were taut with muscles which radiated their specifically human nature. The Augustinian and scholastic problem of the two loves

Pl. 26. Jean Bellegambe,
Paradise. C. 1526–30 Part
of *The Last Judgment* panel.
Staatliche Museen, East
Berlin

– true love of God and the derived love of creatures – no longer existed. The rivalry between commitment to God and fascination with the beloved did not need to impinge on heaven. The divine and the human could both be satisfied.

The Geography of Heaven

The new dignity of "worldly" occupations and the Ciceronian hope of meeting friends reshaped the traditional Christian views of eternal life. Renaissance authors and artists found medieval views of heaven un-congenial to the mentality of their day and thus unsatisfactory. Given its emphasis on the beatific vision, scholastic teaching did not allow for the development of the human side of heaven. Renaissance theologians and artists made up for these deficiencies by envisaging a twofold heaven, one that would take account of God's majestic presence and also give the redeemed their due as creatures with independent dignity. God's holy city and the saints' paradise combined to satisfy theological requirements as well as the human dream of loving company in a pastoral setting.

The geography of the Renaissance heaven reflected the division of the celestial city from the restored paradise garden. Marked by brilliant light and shining Gothic architecture, the abode of God blended images from the book of Revelation with Renaissance ideas. John of Patmos in the New Testament described a new Jerusalem as basically a huge temple. While it had the dimensions of a city, it functioned only as a center for worship. As a temple it left little room for non-liturgical activities. The heavenly city in Renaissance art displays its gate and walls, but not much of its interior structure. We are not shown what goes on inside. The Gothic designs utilized by the artists, however, evoke an ecclesi-astical image. This heavenly environment is constructed primarily as a residence for God and not as a residence for the saints. Just as God's earthly home is the church, his heavenly home is the celestial city. The saints enter God's city not to live but to worship.

The blessed in heaven, just like the people on earth, do not live where God presides. Although the saints and angels travel up into the divine light, they appear to live in a more human environment. The area within the golden gates may be visited to praise God, but the realm of the saints is paradise restored. The paradise garden of heaven is a different, but no less dignified part of heaven. It contains all those elements forbidden in Aquinas's empyrean heaven. Trees, birds, flowers, and meadows flourish. It is not wild nature which survives, but nature suited for human interests and needs. Heavenly nature is domesticated; there are no spectacular vistas or dramatic scenery. Fountains, tents, boats, and gates do not break the pastoral harmony, but are unintrusive props for the saints. People touch, play, listen to music, and pass eternity in pleasure. Angels, once spoken of only in terms of the divine, serenade the saintly couples, crown them with flowers, and embrace them with heavenly welcome. In Renaissance art, even the angels appear more human – taking on decidedly feminine characteristics in some paintings.

No artistic, literary, or theological evidence supports the idea that the space of the Renaissance heaven is portioned out by merit. The scholastic heaven depicted in medieval art lined the saints up in a rigid order depending on their level of spiritual attainment. Thomas Aquinas argued that the amount of merit a person earned on earth would fix the relationship between the soul and the divine center. The more spiritual the individual, the closer he or she would be to God. The closer to God, the greater the knowledge of the divine available. We can imagine the medieval heaven shaped like a huge cone, becoming smaller and smaller as one goes upward. Mystics like Mechthild assumed that female virgins would be on the top rung. More conventional writers placed the apostles, martyrs, and the Blessed Virgin closer to God.

The Renaissance heaven – both the place of light and the paradise – does not display spatial gradation. The rigidity, motionlessness, and hierarchy of the medieval heaven is gone. Those in paradise express no sadness that they are enjoying the fountains and meeting friends. They are not waiting anxiously to move into a more refined state. Nor do those freed from clothes or other encumbrances appear to be less holy than other saints. Their nakedness emphasizes their equality and similarity before God. Only a few marks of social differentiation – the monk's bald head being the most frequent – persist. While God might give the blessed different rewards in heaven to suit their earned merit, the relationship between the saints does not reflect that difference. Martyrs can chat with virgins, teachers sing to merchants, and couples stroll hand-in-hand. The creators of the Renaissance heaven were not interested in the fine distinctions of the medieval heaven; they looked to Cicero and classical mythology for models of a human-oriented afterlife.

If the heaven of the Middle Ages is essentially a cone with God at the top, then the Renaissance heaven is a box with divine worship going on at the top and a paradise garden at the bottom. The two realms are not isolated from one another, but divine characters can move between the two. Savonarola saw a ladder connecting the place of God and the saints' paradise. The fountain of life also links the abode of God with the home of the saints. The fountain of life (and of love) symbolizes the abiding presence of divine blessing. Even the upward sweep of the tents and mast in Bosch's paradise seems to serve as an *axis mundi*, a mythical pole connecting the two realms. When Erasmus imagines Jerome and Reuchlin engaging in everlasting pleasant conversation, he implies their permanent access to the garden where they first met. The heavenly ascension of the blessed does not remove them from the meadow as from a cursed place to which they would not wish to return. Even Mary, according to Savonarola, has a throne in the area of paradise restored.

The paradise garden allows for movement which is virtually absent from the theocentric heaven. Like Aristotle, Aquinas felt ambiguous about the "agility," the effortless movement, of the blessed. He asserted that "movement is the act of an imperfect being." Therefore, "that which shares the divine goodness without movement shares it more excellently than that which shares it with movement." Will the saints eventually participate in God's immobile perfection? Aquinas knew that this could not be the case; only God is omnipresent and therefore never has to overcome distance by movement. For creatures, the absence of omnipresence is a "defect" that will remain in heaven. Hence movement must be possible for the blessed. But will they actually move? Despite the imperfection implied in motion, Aquinas thought it "likely" (verisimile) that the blessed "will sometimes [aliquando] move as it pleases them. . . so that their vision may be refreshed by the beauty of the variety of creatures." The blessed enjoy the variety of created things because in these "God's wisdom will shine forth with great evidence." By the fifteenth century, the argument of Aquinas had lost much of its force. As people who loved to travel to distant cities or countries, Renaissance thinkers were no longer satisfied with the rare and brief "movements" possible for the saints of Aquinas's heaven. No longer a mark of imperfection, movement could now invade and shape paradisal existence. Fra Angelico's blessed dance with joy, and Bosch even has them sailing in a boat. When Valla imagines the saints flying like birds and playing in mid-air or diving into the sea like fish, he may exaggerate Renaissance dreams; yet he gives expression to a common sentiment. If Paradise is to be human, then it cannot be a place of inactivity and immobility.[36]

The Renaissance celebration of a sensuous paradise had little time to flourish. It subsided as the Reformation put new facts onto the agenda of intellectual Europe. By the end of the sixteenth century it was virtually forgotten. Only one idea survived: the idea of heavenly reunion. The theme of meeting again in the other world, however, rarely received the prominence it had had in authors such as Lorenzo Valla. Reformers and Counter-Reformers rejected such unscriptural speculation. The bitter controversies sparked by the Reformation and the Catholic reform destroyed the theology of the humanists. Putting God, rather than the dignity of human self-expression, at the center, these movements constructed new patterns of this life and new images of the next.

CHAPTER SIX

God at the Center: Protestant and Catholic Reformers

The sixteenth, seventeenth, and eighteenth centuries brought religious turmoil to Europe. Doctrinal debates engaged more people than during the Middle Ages and led to excommunication, persecution, and even war. Dissenters established new churches and reform movements sprang up within the existing ones. No longer could all divergent theologies be seen as attempts to grasp the same essential truth. By rejecting celibacy, papal authority, and scholastic theology, the two reformers Luther and Calvin created new churches with different organization and teachings. From the Catholic point of view, this meant that heresy succeeded in asserting itself, thus destroying the unity of the Christian world. The seamless garment of Christ was rent. For Protestants, the true gospel teaching had now freed itself from distortion, superstition, and abuse. Biblical purity was restored. Protestants and Catholics were redrawing the religious map of the western world.

The realignment of religious Europe provoked a readjustment in the Christian understanding of heaven. With the challenge to traditional ways of religious thought, new models of heavenly life were presented by both Protestants and Catholics. Luther and Calvin combined traditional views of eternal life with their own new perspectives on the nature of God and humankind. For these reformers the righteous soul could look forward to everlasting communion with the divine. Catholic thinkers also revitalized their conception of eternal life. In response to the Reformation, they built on late-medieval mysticism and initiated a devotional revolution which also restructured the traditional perspective on the afterlife. Typical of the new Catholic spirituality was the promotion of mystical inwardness and its propagation of modified monastic values among devout lay people. God's intimacy with the soul and the prominence of the Virgin Mary overshadowed the heavenly humanism of the Renaissance.

When the effervescence and enthusiasm of both the Reformation and the Catholic reform subsided, new movements sprang up hoping to keep alive the original ferment of renewal. Catholic Jansenists, as well as Protestant Puritans and Methodists, no longer shared the worldly optimism of the sixteenth-century reformers. These new movements advocated withdrawal from the world and the practice of sometimes excessive austerity. Catholic asceticism still meant retreat into the monastery. Protestants promoted a worldly asceticism, a stern morality, and introspective meditation in order to transcend earthly transitoriness. These attitudes resulted in an image of heaven that reflected the disdain for worldly concerns and the insistence on the exclusive dominance of God.

All of these three groups – Protestant reformers, Catholic counter-reformers, and the new ascetics – created their own distinctive images of eternal life. These images, however, shared one essential feature: the focus on the divine. Once God was placed at the center of the Christian life, it was only reasonable to assume that a righteous life must culminate in an eternity with the divine. While others during the seventeenth and eighteenth centuries described a more human-oriented heaven, the reformers' heaven became the orthodox Christian perspective. Even though religious enthusiasm waned, the theocentric model of heaven continued. Pious Christians were reluctant to give up the straightforward and clear image of a God-dominated heaven.

Protestant Reformers: Luther and Calvin

The century preceding the Reformation saw a marked increase of religious fervor among the people of central and northern Europe. Popular devotions flourished, new brotherhoods were created, pilgrims travelled to distant lands, and an ever-growing readership devoured religious books. Christian spirituality and devotion, once considered the domain of priest, monk, and nun, became a lay concern. As religious intensity grew, both laity and religious became estranged from the pope, bishops, and secular clergy. Voices for reform criticized the established church's prevailing interest in money and political power. Friars like Savonarola in Florence and mystics like Thomas à Kempis (1380–1471), author of *The Imitation of Christ*, provided a more powerful spiritual leadership than that offered by the established clergy and bishops. Such charismatic figures tried to present a God-oriented, theocentric religion. For them, popular interest in pilgrimages or buying indulgences lacked the support of Scripture and tended to lead souls away from true Christianity. The true religious quest must focus on God. "When shall my mind be fixed on you, O Lord," queried Thomas à Kempis, "on you alone?" Radical God-centeredness formed the basis of the new spirituality.[1]

The most radical – and certainly the most successful – critics of religious life and ecclesiastical doctrine were the Augustinian friar Martin Luther (1483–1546) and the Swiss layman John Calvin (1509–64). In their theology, the two reformers stressed the absolute superiority and majesty of God. The Catholic sacraments, pilgrimages, indulgences, and pious works of charity offered to the laity as means of securing salvation were only distractions from total faith in God. In their ethics, Luther and Calvin promoted a new openness to the secular world and its values. The pious Christian no longer had to renounce the world and enter monastic life. This world, while sinful, had meaning and value. These two elements of Reformation thought – emphasis on God and openness to the world – shaped the character of heaven in fundamental ways by balancing its theocentric character with the doctrine of a renewed earth.

Luther held one of the most God-centered theologies in the history of Christianity. "He saw God as embracing all things, controlling all things, and pervading all things," reads a modern appreciation of the reformer's creed. The vastness and inconceivable greatness of God directed Luther's entire thinking. Never tired of insisting on the absolute priority of the divine, Luther wrote that someone who "does not sufficiently promote Christ and the grace of God," could not be his friend. "Human things carry more weight with him than divine things," was the reformer's critical verdict on Erasmus of Rotterdam. For Luther, the Renaissance idea that humanity might achieve an almost divine status perverted true Christian doctrine. From the Reformation point of view, individuals could only appear as sinners and beggars for divine grace and mercy. Men and women no longer served as God's adequate partners. "We are beggars, this is true," Luther reportedly wrote as his last sentence before dying. Only the compassionate Lord himself could take the initiative needed to save humanity from eternal damnation; a damnation it actually deserved. According to Luther, to try to save ourselves by presenting our own "works" to God was useless.[2]

John Calvin's perspective on the primacy of the divine varied little from Luther's. "Our very being," Calvin wrote, "is nothing but subsistence in the one God." The true Christian life, therefore, must be entirely focused on the divine. "There is no part in our life and no action so minute that it ought not to be directed to the glory of God"; so for this reason "we should endeavor to promote it even in our eating and drinking." In his catechism, Calvin taught that "nothing worse can happen to the human being than not to live for God." Calvin, like Luther, never left any doubt about his theocentric perspective. God, as the source of all good, demanded the absolute attention and love of his human creatures. The Christian life should be a God-centered life.[3]

The theocentric emphasis in Reformation theology emerged from a variety of sources. We can discern the incalculable, majestic God arising out of nominalist philosophy. Mystical meditation emphasized the God who called for undivided love. The all-powerful deity of the biblical psalms of petition and penance, and the God of Paul who cleanses all sins, were particularly powerful images for the reformers. We might even include the enlarged image of Luther's repressive father as a source for a powerful God who controlled the lives of his children. Whatever the source, the reformers promoted their view of God with charismatic zeal. In Luther and Calvin, a powerful God found uncompromising advocates.

In keeping with their theocentric outlook, the reformers saw eternal life primarily as the individual's unsurpassed communion with God. Luther admitted in one of his table talks that he often mused about what eternal life will be like – a life without change, without eating and drinking, without anything to do. "But I think," he suggested, "we will have enough to do with God. Accordingly [the apostle] Philip put it well when he said, 'Lord, show us the Father, and we shall be satisfied.' This will be our very dear preoccupation." When Luther died, his friend Philipp Melanchthon (1497–1560) took the funeral oration as an occasion to depict the theocentric nature of the Reformation heaven. "Let us rejoice," he invited his audience, "that he now holds that familiar and delightful conversation with God, His Son, our Lord Jesus Christ, with the prophets and apostles, which by faith in the Son of God he always sought and expected." Delivered from the mortal body, the deceased "has entered that vastly higher school, where he can contemplate the essence of God, the two natures joined in Christ, and the whole purpose set forth in founding and redeeming the Church." Seeing the Savior "now face to face, he rejoices with unspeakable joy; and with his whole soul he ardently pours forth thanks to God for His great goodness." Melanchthon made it clear that a God-centered Christian life, such as the one which Luther had lived, could only be fulfilled in an equally theocentric heaven.[4]

Luther's and Melanchthon's emphasis on the divine as center of both this life and eternal life concurred with the outlook of Calvin. "Wholly intent on beholding God," Calvin explained, the saints "have nothing better to which they can turn their eyes or direct their desire." In seeing God, the blessed are passive while God is fully active. "He will reveal to us His glory, so that we may behold it face to face," the reformer of Geneva predicted. The Lord will "give himself to be enjoyed" by the elect "and what is more excellent, will somehow make them to become one with himself." In order to safeguard the distance between Creator and creature, Calvin insisted that even in heaven "our glory will not be as perfect as to allow our vision to comprehend the Lord completely... there will be a wide distance between Him and ourselves." Awe and fascination, distance and closeness – the major dimensions in the experience of the divine – will be present in heaven as they are on earth.[5]

Early Reformation artists shared Calvin's concern for the primacy of

God by placing the divine majesty in the center of their illustrations. In 1549 Melanchthon published a picture-catechism which included a depiction of the Apostles' Creed (Pl. 27). For the last article of the creed, "and life everlasting. Amen," the artist chose to present a Last Judgment scene rather than a vision of heavenly life. The figure of Christ dominates the woodcut. By insisting on the majesty of the Christ-judge any illusion of sentimental closeness to the deity is prevented. There are no saints or patriarchs present to mitigate divine wrath or humanize eternal life. The angels cannot perform these functions. Rather than interceding on behalf of sinners, they execute divine judgment. Thus the artist creates an extremely stern judgment scene, devoid of medieval inti-

Pl. 27. Life Everlasting. From Melanchthon's Protestant Catechism. Wittenberg, Germany, 1554. Ferdinand Cohrs, ed., *Philipp Melanchthons Schriften zur praktischen Theologie* (Leipzig: Haupt, 1915), I, 466

mations of mercy and glory. Christ has already divided the dead into the blessed and the condemned, and the angels awaken all from their graves. The artist gives us no indication of what kind of life awaits the righteous. In keeping with Melanchthon's religious perspective, the emphasis is not on the final creedal promise of eternal life but on the expectation of a judgment at the end of time. Heaven is the domain of a judging God.

When the reformers created their first doctrinal platform in the Augsburg Confession of 1530, it included no discussion of heaven. The doctrine of "life everlasting and eternal delights" stayed outside the controversy, explained Luther's friend Melanchthon. In the sixteenth century, western Christianity divided not over the image of heaven but over getting there. Declaring the vision of God as the chief content of life everlasting, the reformers simply repeated standard scholastic teaching. In a more subtle way, however, they redefined the relationship between God and the Elect. According to scholastic theology, merit achieved during one's earthly existence made the soul worthy of God. After death that accrued merit permitted the soul to come closer to the divine center. God preferred the worthy ones to those less deserving. Although all the blessed saw the Trinity, "yet according to the diversity of merits, some [see it] more perfectly than others." For the reformers, this variation in the beatific vision was impossible. Reformation theology held that human creatures could never invade heaven, approach God as a friend, and expect different degrees of intimacy. Even in eternity the soul retained the status of an unworthy being, merely permitted to meet the Savior. In heaven, God would give himself to the blessed in an intimate way, but without giving particular preference to any one. All saints were equal in relation to God. Calvin reminded his readers that God acted like the biblical landowner who gave equal reward for unequal work; paying his laborers the same amount for either a whole day or just an hour's labor.[6]

This was not to say that there would be no individual rewards in the other life. Although the reformers were reluctant to contradict the clarity of the biblical text which spoke of different rewards in eternity – the gospel's hundredfold, sixtyfold and thirtyfold fruit – they sought to weaken the scholastic heavenly hierarchy. Since such special rewards had nothing to do with the beatific vision, they could only be secondary and negligible. "We will be equal," preached Luther, "to St Paul, St Peter, our beloved Lady, and all the saints in their honor and glory." In other writings, however, Luther spoke of the saints receiving various rewards. Peter, for instance, would have a reward different from that of Paul, since Christ had assigned them different earthly tasks. Luther himself expected to be "close to God and placed with Jeremiah, since both of them had a hard life...which they endured with divine help." Rejecting the scholastic doctrine of the different degrees of intensity in the vision of God, Luther returned to the opinion of Augustine: there are different degrees of merit and reward, but heaven itself must be the same for all. Calvin also intimated that the concept of heavenly reward can be misleading. In this world, he explained, the Lord does not bestow the same gifts on every Christian; in the other world he will not change this system. God might prefer some saints to others, but this does not bring them closer to the divine. In any case, this decision is totally up to God. Humankind cannot alter the divine relationship through earthly activities. Calvin thought in terms of the sovereignty of the divine will: what God does needs no explanation, let alone justification. Consequently, Luther and Calvin both minimized the concept of reward and gave it no more than a marginal place in their theological system.[7]

The Protestant reformers balanced the God-centered nature of their theology with a new appreciation of the world and its affairs. Although God commanded the attention of his chosen on earth and in heaven, this did not necessitate the avoidance of non-religious activities. Luther's rejection of his monastic life and his marriage to a former nun marked a new pattern of spirituality. A new theology acknowledged the importance of worldly concerns and no longer tolerated celibacy and the contemplative life, once valued as the superior path to God. For Luther, "we are not made for fleeing human company but for living in society and sharing good and evil." The reformers rejected the distinction between two classes of Christians, the contemplative religious and those who lived "in the world." The world and its activities assumed a new respectability.[8]

As the Reformation became a political issue for magistrates and princes, Luther and Calvin worked out the practical implications of their teaching more fully. It is impossible "to rule a country, let alone the entire world, by the gospel," Luther insisted. Since worldly affairs can be successfully conducted by reason and experience, they can be autonomous and independent from religious involvement. "God has placed human civil life under the dominion of natural reason which has ability enough to rule physical things," the reformer noted; "we need not look to Scripture for advice" in such temporal matters. Even the heathen are blessed with reason and thus are able to live their daily lives. Luther accepted the world. Although he never claimed sacramental dignity for mundane matters, he came to appreciate the married state, householding, and professional life more than the standard Catholic theology of his day allowed.[9]

What Luther acknowledged in blessing everyday life were essentially the rural and small-town values of his family background. A man of the city, Calvin ventured further into the world. He based his social ethics on a recognition of capital, credit, banking, large-scale commerce, finance, and the other practical necessities of urban business life. Since that life risked losing its connection with religion, Calvin insisted on its spiritual qualities. Christians must seek the glorification of God not by prayer only, but by action – sanctification of the world by strife and labor. Sanctification through work was the Calvinist's permanent thanksgiving for the gift of eternal life. Blessed with success, people "receive already some fruit of their integrity" which they read as signs of election for a blessed eternity. Conversely, the poor and those with no luck in their economic efforts appeared damned by God and therefore unworthy of alms. Unperturbed by remorse or generosity, the rich continued to accumulate and invest capital. The incentive to succeed and the devaluation of poverty – once the hallmarks of Christian perfection – fostered worldly optimism.[10]

Because of their appreciation of the world, the reformers tempered their theocentric heaven with an eternal life that recognized the importance of the earth. Speculation about the distant empyrean heaven of scholasticism, which had no need for a renewed earth, was replaced by a concern for nature and the universe. Continuing the medieval tradition of seeing the earth as the static, immobile center of the universe, the reformers simply ignored or merely dismissed the new astronomy advocated by their contemporary, Nicolaus Copernicus. His heliocentric theories held no place in their perception of the heavens. Luther believed, along with medieval writers, that the earth was the center of a universe with exceedingly pure upper regions. As one moved downwards, the spheres became increasingly impure. At the end of time, at the Last Judgment, God would purify the earth positioned in the lower spheres. Acting like an alchemist who in his furnace "extracts and separates from a substance the other portions, carrying upward the spirit, the life, the strength," God would force all "the unclean matter, the dregs, to remain at the bottom." Thus, after the Last Judgment, God would purify the world by fire and banish everything unclean and ungodly into hell at the center of the earth. By doing this, all the world (except the bowels of earth) would eventually be as pure as the upper regions of the medieval universe.[11]

God would show his concern for the existing universe by purifying it and preparing it for the saints. Once the lower spheres achieved the same purity as the upper, the saints would no longer be confined to the highest regions, but restored to the earth. The whole universe would also be available to them because "all heaven [sky] and earth will be a new paradise." Perhaps Luther felt that heaven will be united with the earth, enclosing it, with the boundaries removed between the two realms. The blessed then would have an expanded home and could "play with heaven [sky] and earth, the sun and all creatures." Rather than predicting the elimination of the universe, Luther imagined its renovation.[12]

The earth itself would also be renewed and refashioned. "The flowers, leaves and grass will be as beautiful, pleasant, and delightful as an emerald, and all creatures most beautiful." Asked whether there will be animals in paradise, Luther quickly answered: "You must not think that heaven and earth will be made of nothing but air and sand, but there will be whatever belongs to it – sheep, oxen, beasts, fish, without which the earth and sky or air cannot be." He also referred to insects: "Ants, bugs and all unpleasant, stinking creatures will be most delightful and have a wonderful fragrance." Since everything will be as it was in Eden, every man will be like Adam who "was stronger than the lions and the bears, whose strength is very great. He handled them the way we handle puppies." Nature, moreover, will fulfill all our wishes. The Elbe river will flow with pearls and precious stones, the sky will be able to send a shower of coins, and trees may have silver leaves, golden apples, and pears.[13]

Children were allowed their own heavenly fantasies. Luther's daughter Magdalene spoke of paradise as a place where she could get "lots of apples, pears, sugar, plums, and so on." Her father did not object to such "cheerful speculation"; he supported it. To his little boy Hans he described heaven as "a pretty, beautiful and delightful garden where there are many children wearing little golden coats. They pick up fine apples, pears, cherries, and yellow and blue plums under the trees. They sing, jump, and are merry. They also have nice ponies." While we can admire the facility with which Luther entered the world of his children, it should be clear that he presented a different view to the adults. As a good teacher, he provided milk for the young and solid food for those advanced in learning. Children were permitted childish views, but adults were expected to possess more theologically correct images of heaven.[14]

In eternal life, the adults were told, we will neither eat and drink nor sleep. Only heathen fools would want to have a body producing feces and urine, Luther protested, no doubt thinking of Muslim tradition. Our glorified bodies will no longer depend on food. Floating through space and playing with "the sun and all creatures," they will "forget about eating and drinking." The universe will not be eliminated, but it must not be seen as the ultimate home of the righteous. Only the vision of God could be the true home for the saints. While the earth "will be delightful to look at," Luther reiterated his theocentric conviction that the "body and soul will be sustained by God himself who will be all in all, and to see him will give more life, joy and delight than all creatures." God, who will be "all in all," will be the saints' food and drink, garment, house and home. Although Luther respected the natural creation of God, he assumed that the blessed will be sustained spiritually.[15]

Calvin also agreed the renewed earth must not detract from the magnificence of God. Scripture indicated the location of paradise quite clearly. Christians could read in the Sermon on the Mount that "blessed are the meek, for they shall inherit the earth." Along with Luther, Calvin conceded the existence of plants and animals as well as the absence of "dross and other corruptions in metals." Animals and plants would be "perfect," but what that perfection meant and whether it implied immortality, he admitted he did not know. In keeping with scholastic thought, Calvin did not predict that the blessed would live on the renewed earth. There would be a certain distance of the saints from the new earth. The new earth's purpose was for contemplation, not for use. "In the very sight of [the renewed earth]," explained Calvin, "there will be such pleasantness, such sweetness in the knowledge of it alone, without the use of it, that this happiness will far surpass all the amenities that we now enjoy." The saints will enjoy the new world, but they will not enter into another earthly existence.[16]

Both Luther and Calvin argued that God would renew the earth and purify the universe. Animals and plants would continue for eternity in their newly perfected state. An intrinsic part of God's plan, the world would not be destroyed. Although there would be a new earth, the reformers refused to allow that the blessed would live an earthly life in it. For Luther, the saints might visit the new earth, but it would not be their home. For Calvin, they would not even desire to know the new world. God rehabilitated the world only to make it a part of the vision of the divine. Once the Last Judgment occurred and time ended, earthly existence would stop. Even a life on a perfected planet could be only secondary to the eternal vision of God. Eternal life, existence in a truly God-centered universe, had to be qualitatively different.

One aspect of this difference between earthly and heavenly life concerned the society of the blessed. What will the community of saints look like? According to Luther, although the blessed will retain their gender, they will lose their identities of rank and profession. Luther and Calvin agreed that there will be no princes or peasants, magistrates or preachers, for all will be equal. The hierarchical organization of society, so characteristic of the present state, will cease to exist: "As the world will have an end, so also will government, magistry, laws, the distinction of ranks, the different orders of dignity, and everything of that nature. There will be no more any distinction between servant and master, king and peasant, magistrate and private citizen." There could be no purpose for continuing earthly concepts of status and position. Since God will be the only authority and all the saints will be focused on his presence, there will be no need for one saint to rule over another. For Calvin, this also meant the end of the "ministries and superiorities of the Church." Bishops, teachers, and prophets will all have to resign from their office, as will the angels. Because all men and women are equal before their Creator and Savior, no one can claim leadership because of a preferred religious state like that of the ascetic and world-renouncer, or because of special theological knowledge. When God reigns, he will not share his rulership with others.[17]

The assumption that authority structures ceased to exist in heaven also meant that the family unit did not survive death. For the sixteenth-century reformers, the household could only function when lines of authority were maintained. Husband ruled over wife, parents over children, and master over servant. Since marriage implied rule and submission, and in heaven there could be no differences in rank, there could be no marriage in eternal life. Men and women in this world united in marriage "will be torn apart from each other," asserted Calvin. Likewise, since children needed figures of authority, there could be no children. While Luther had no doubts that he and his dying father would "shortly see each other again in the presence of Christ," this did not mean their household would be re-established. Meeting one's kin did not imply the renewal of submission and obedience. Therefore, according to Luther, only a fool can say, "If my wife is in heaven, I do not want to go there."[18]

The reformers inherited the theme of heavenly reunion from the Renaissance not via theological texts but through the writings of the classical author Cicero. Although the reformers did not take great interest in classical learning, Cicero's writings received a permanent place in Protestant education. *On Old Age* became a standard textbook in the Latin courses at the university, and so students read of the old Cato's heavenly wish for meeting the old friends he missed. Humanist and reformer Melanchthon wrote to a far-away friend that "in the heavenly community I will embrace you again and then we will cheerfully talk about the sources of wisdom." The Swiss reformer Zwingli (1484–1531) included a passage on meeting again in his *Exposition of the Faith.* Hoping to lure the French king François I to the Protestant cause, Zwingli promised him eternal felicity in the company of his own pious ancestors as well as biblical figures. With a splendid humanist flourish, he added that characters like Hercules, Socrates, the Catos and Scipios would also await the king in heaven. The Catos and Scipios were of course included as a combined reference to *On Old Age* and *Scipio's Dream.* Apparently, Zwingli's skillful allusion to Cicero did not impress the king of France. François and his country remained Catholic. Although Luther chided Zwingli for including "pagans" in his list, in an unguarded moment he himself expressed a *hope* that Cicero would be among the blessed.[19]

The motif of meeting again figured prominently in the minds of educated sixteenth-century Protestants. Only Calvin, the sternest of the reformers, could deny its relevance altogether. "To be in Paradise and live with God," he insisted, "is not to speak to each other, and to be heard by each other, but is only to enjoy God, to feel his good will, and rest in him." Since denying heavenly reunion seemed too harsh, preachers like Johannes Mathesius (1504–65) – Luther's student and first biographer – strove to give it a theocentric thrust. Mathesius, who started his career as the headmaster of a Latin school, was well-versed in Cicero. In one of his sermons he actually referred to *Scipio's Dream* – with a note of caution that patriotism alone does not lead to heaven. But in another sermon he presented his list of those pagans whom he expected to be in paradise: Alexander the Great, Scipio, Lucretius, Aristides, and so on. Although Mathesius repeatedly preached about the heavenly reunion of spouses and of children with their parents, it was not his dominant note. He made sure to place his heavenly citizens close to God or Christ, or at least in the company of the patriarchs, apostles, or their respective wives. Meeting one's spouse and kin was less important than beholding the angels and conversing with biblical figures. For all his humanism, Mathesius preferred a biblical and theocentric emphasis. Likewise, Melanchthon in his funeral oration for Luther imagined that once the prophets see the great reformer they "hail him gladly as a companion." These religious companions and not Luther's family, greet the newly arrived soul. Luther, according to Melanchton, "now embraces them and rejoices to hear them speak, and to speak to them in turn." Family reunions were insignificant when compared to meeting the patriarchs and prophets.[20]

The early Reformation view of eternal life combined the features of a renewed world with the absolute rule of God. Luther and Calvin continued the scholastic perspective on the heavenly empyrean, but they softened it by introducing animals and plants into a perfected earth. They permitted the fantasies of children (though not of adults) and speculated on the possibility of reunions of family and friends. Such human elements, it must be emphasized, never clouded the primary focus of their heaven – that God ruled. Catholic reformers, and those who hoped to counter the influence of the Protestant Reformation, ignored the interest in a renewed world at the end of time. Their concern lay not with the end of history but with the individual's heavenly life after his or her death.

The Catholic Reformers

The Protestant Reformation was not the only movement to promote religious renewal in the sixteenth century. Catholic reform, the spirit of which went back at least a hundred years, is hard to delineate. Informal and often inarticulate, this spirit can be recognized in early sources as disparate as the *Imitation of Christ* (c. 1420) and the passionate sermons of Savonarola, who was hanged an excommunicated heretic in 1498.

The renewal of Christian life came in a hundred different ways and different places. It came not only through the Council of Trent (1545–63), but also through religious orders, theologians, mystics, and individual cardinals and bishops. What Catholic reform shared in common with the Protestant Reformation was a combination of theocentric mysticism, a zeal to teach others how to live a truly Christian life, and an effort to renew the structure of the church. Even the scholastic heaven of the Middle Ages came under the reformers' eyes.

Cardinal Pierre de Bérulle (1575–1629) perhaps best expressed the theocentric emphasis of the new Catholic mentality. By the seventeenth century, heliocentric astronomy with the sun as the immobile center of the universe and the earth as a revolving planet had become quite well known. According to Bérulle, while this new opinion might or might not be viable in astronomy it was useful "in the science of salvation." "Jesus, in his grandness," postulated Bérulle, "is the immobile sun which makes all things move." Sitting at the right hand of God the Father, Jesus shares "his immobility and makes all things move. Jesus is the true center of the world, and the world must always move toward him. Jesus is the sun of our souls; from him they are influenced, receiving all grace and illumination." As astronomy *might* be heliocentric, so *must* religious life be theocentric, with the soul moving around the deity as its center. In the words of the Spanish mystic Teresa of Avila (1515–82), "God alone suffices" (*Sólo Dios basta*).[21]

When writers of the Catholic reform era imagined what eternal life would be like, they endorsed the teaching of the *Catechism of the Council of Trent* (1566) that the happiness of the blessed "consists in the vision of God and enjoyment of His beauty who is the source and principle of all goodness and perfection." When Catholic artists portrayed heaven, they also emphasized the divine center. In an etching after Maarten van Heemskerck (1498–1574), the heavenly hosts encircle the divine center like the planets orbit the sun (Pl. 28). All eyes are turned to the vision of the deity. Although the musculature of the saints reminds us of Signorelli, van Heemskerck has eliminated any sense that the righteous take pleasure from their bodies. Whereas Signorelli's blessed stretch and greet the crowning angels with a human enthusiasm, van Heemskerck's saints are fixated by the controlling Trinity. The number of bodies lacking individual characteristics underscores the belief that in heaven all attention will be on God. There will be no need for human personalities to emerge. Even the feet, dangling from the upper part of the engraving, give us the sense that every eye in the vast heavens is turned toward God.[22]

The sparsely clothed saints in van Heemskerck's engraving reflect the assumption that at death the righteous souls need only God. Although the more virtuous might take their place on one of the concentric circles

Pl. 28.   The blessed in adoration of the Trinity. 1569. After Maerten van Heemskerck. Staatliche
Kunstsammlungen, Kassel

closer to the divine, all marks of earthly status disappear. In a Jesuit catechism dedicated to the French dauphin on the occasion of his baptism, even the prince comes to heaven without royal attire (Pl. 29). On the page opposite the illustration, the dauphin is given an elementary lesson of restraint: "Who aspires to the goods of heaven must despise all the gifts the world has to offer" (*Qui d'un bon clin les biens du ciel advise/Tous les presens de la terre il méprise*). There is no room for royal splendor in Paradise. Before the deity, even a dauphin is naked.[23]

Protestants and Catholics stressed the divine heavenly center in both their theology and their art. Catholics, however, continued to populate heaven with saints committed to the ideals of virginity and the contemplative life. Italian Dominican friar Antonino Polti, in his book *On the Supreme Felicity of Heaven* (1575), described an empyrean paradise

Pl. 29. "Le paradis." Louys Richeome, S.J., *Catechisme royal* (Lyon: Pillehotte, 1607)

filled with innumerable angels and Catholic saints. His list of fifty-eight names included not only figures like John the Baptist, Augustine, and Jerome (who can also find a place in a Protestant paradise), but also Pope Gregory the Great and the founders of the foremost religious orders: St. Benedict, St. Dominic, and St. Francis. Polti's heaven was a paradise of virgins, martyrs, monks, and friars, without, of course, a single Protestant or pagan. A Dominican friar and theologian of unquestionable Catholic orthodoxy, he refrained from naming any member of the heavenly community not found in the official calendar of canonized saints.[24]

The most important figure among Polti's saints was the Blessed Virgin, "the most serene Empress of Heaven, Queen of the Angels, and Mother of all the Elect". Her presence in heaven meant a "most conspicuous enhancement of the glory of all the blessed." Mary was "exalted above all the angelic choirs, adorned with all heavenly and earthly beauty." Taking more delight in the physical beauty of the Virgin than in her spiritual qualities, he extolled her as "the greatest enhancement of the glory of paradise by way of her bodily beauty and her divine presence." Polti, who also published a separate treatise on the Virgin's *bellezza corporale*, continued an already venerable tradition in his praise of the sensual beauty of the mother of Christ.[25]

The reference to the Virgin's "divine presence" was more than pious rhetoric. For Polti, Mary represented the divine center of heaven. The Dominican friar invoked the biblical sentence, "to see your face is like seeing the countenance of God," spoken by Jacob to his brother Esau, to explain what the blessed feel when seeing her. Polti included in his book an etching showing Mary surrounded by the heavenly host (Pl. 30). The etching underscored the feminine, Marian center of his paradise. As the Queen of Heaven, Mary presided over all the other saints. The crowned Virgin participated in the royal splendor and power of Christ, just as human queens shared in the authority of their spouses.[26]

Polti was not the only theologian to present the beatific vision – or something very close to it – in Marian terms. An early edition of the often-printed catechism of the Jesuit Peter Canisius (1521–97) illustrates the last article of the Creed – life everlasting – in a similar way (Pl. 31). The people who kneel in adoration of the Blessed Virgin represent both those who are in heaven and those who are on the way there. The artist presents Mary as the Mother of Mercy whom the faithful invoked in the *Salve Regina* as "our advocate." For the late medieval Catholic, Mary was *advocata nostra*, the supreme intercessor at the hour of death and the Last Judgment. In Last Judgment paintings she was frequently placed near the Christ-judge to mitigate his sentence. Priests and lay people alike recited the *Ave Maria* (the angelic greeting of the Virgin), to which they added: "Holy Mary, Mother of God, pray for us

VIRGO PARES, ORDO AGELICVS RVTILÁT IÁ MEBRA
SÁCTOS, STVX ETÍA. ET CVTA CRFATA BEÁT

Pl. 30. The Blessed Virgin in heaven. 1575. Antonino Polti, O.P., *Della felicità suprema del cielo*
(Perugia: Rastelli, 1575)

Pl. 31.   A Marian vision of life everlasting. 1560. Peter Canisius, S.J., *Kurtzer Unterricht vom Catholischen Glauben* (Dillingen, 1560). Friedrich Streicher, *S. Petri Canisii Catechismi* (Rome: Universitas Gregoriana, 1933), II, 32

sinners, now and at the hour of our death." While Melanchthon's cate-chism illustrated "life everlasing" with the Christ-judge to underscore divine justice, Canisius included the Mother of Mercy to emphasize divine benevolence.[27]

Mary, however, is not only the intercessor; she is also a heavenly being in her own right. Despite its iconographic simplicity, the woodcut blends the image of Mother of Mercy with the Queen of Heaven in a subtle and appealing way. Surrounded by cherub angels, who normally encircle God or the Trinity, Mary represents the deity itself. Daring as this picture may seem, it is founded on solid Catholic tradition. The Council of Trent required that all religious art be attuned to Catholic dogma and supervised by the bishops. Catholic artists had to submit their heavenly visions to theological scrutiny. No orthodox Catholic questioned that Mary would be a prominent figure in the other world. "A great portent appeared in heaven," wrote John in the book of Revelation, "a woman clothed with the sun, with the moon under her feet, and on her head a crown of twelve stars." Tradition identified this woman as the Blessed Virgin.[28]

Mary's prominent position in heaven enjoyed long tradition in Catholic thought. According to the medieval theologian Bonaventure, among "other almost countless wonders [of heaven] there is one that brings joy to the mind of every blessed spirit, and fills every holy creature with a happiness beyond words: the vision of the heavenly Queen's divine radiance." Jean Fouquet's fifteenth-century illustration of the beatific vision places the Virgin on a throne next to the Trinity, fully encircled by divine light (Pl. 32). In one of his heavenly visions, Savonarola was so dazzled by this light that he almost took her for the deity. "Had one not seen that supreme brightness [of the Trinity]," he explained, "one would doubtless have thought that the Virgin is God." In his massive treatise *On Mary the Incomparable Virgin and Most Holy Mother of God* (1577), Peter Canisius made even stronger connections between Mary and the Trinity. In heaven, not only was God acknowledged day and night with singing (Rev. 4:8), but Mary was as well. The choir of angels surrounding the Virgin (as depicted in the catechism) sang the "Hail Mary" in praise of her. Canisius specified that Mary was honored with song "by the three hierarchies of the angels with a loud and beautiful voice." For the Catholics of the Counter Reformation, the presence of Mary in heaven did not detract from the theocentric nature of paradise. The Mother of God reigned as an essential part of the divine center.[29]

In art and theology, the presence of Mary as Queen of Heaven made a strong statement for the Catholic perspective. Since the Protestant reformers did not venerate Mary or any other saint, the Virgin's inclusion in heaven promoted the Catholic point of view while challenging those who attempted to devalue the Blessed Mother. Protestants, even in the seventeenth century, however, could not totally eliminate the feminine from heaven. The British poet Giles Fletcher (1585–1623) described the divine center of the other world in feminine terms – without referring to Mary. In the many stanzas of his *Christ's Victory in Heaven* (1610), Fletcher personified God's gentleness and love as Lady Mercy. Like the Catholic Virgin, Lady Mercy possessed unsurpassed beauty: "Ros'd all in lively crimson are thy cheeks...and on thine eyelids, waiting thee beside, ten thousand graces sit...So fair thou art that all would thee behold." The lady thus acclaimed also displayed motherly, nurturing qualities. Fletcher extolled her breasts as "those snowy mountlets, through which do creep the milky rivers." Lady Mercy gave her breasts

> To weary travellers, in heat of day,
> To quench their fiery thirst, and to allay
> With dropping nectar floods, the fury of their way.

Pl. 32.   Jean Fouquet, *The Blessed Virgin and the Trinity*. 15th century. *Le livre d'heures d'Etienne Chevalier*, Musée Condé, Chantilly

The poet humanized the divine center by adding a maternal element. The God of heaven was not distant and unattainable, but as accessible as a mother's breast to a baby.[30]

The French bishop Francis de Sales (1567–1622) shared the seventeenth-century interest in making heaven human and accessible without de-emphasizing the divine dimension. His sermons endowed the human-divine relationship with a new emotional quality reminiscent of mysticism. On All Saints' Day of 1617, he told the nuns of Annecy that the blessed not only see God, "but also hear him talk and themselves talk to him. This is one of their main sources of bliss." Heavenly life involves a constant conversation between the blessed and the deity as the saint declares his or her everlasting tender love for God. "You will always be with me, and I will always be with you," de Sales imagined the soul saying; "I will never withdraw from you even a little. From now on, you will entirely belong to me, and I will entirely belong to you. You are all mine, and I will be all thine." Like lover to beloved, like the nun to Christ, the saints dedicate their total attention and love to God. Nothing can come between that intimacy.[31]

According to de Sales, God responds in turn by revealing all divine mysteries – those of biblical history as well as those of the saint's individual biography. By bringing the blessed to comprehend "the incomparable work of the incarnation in which God made himself human, and the human was made divine," God permits them to participate in the sacred mystery. "There, our Lord will reveal to them great secrets," de Sales reported; "he will speak to them of his suffering and of what else he has done for them. He will tell them: In such a time I have suffered this for you. He will explain to them the mystery of his incarnation, salvation, and redemption, saying: I was waiting for you so long, running after you when you were stubborn, and with a gentle violence I forced you to receive my grace." For de Sales, the individual life of the saint holds importance, even in heaven, since each life is a part of sacred history. Jesus is the saint's invisible guide throughout his or her lifetime. "I gave you at such a moment such an impulse and such an inspiration," de Sales predicted Jesus would say. "I used such a person to draw you to myself." Now everything can be revealed. No secrets remain unspoken between lover and beloved, between saint and God.[32]

Jesus as the soul's gentle companion in heaven also allows the deceased to meet their friends – if only as a gift "secondary" to the beatific vision. True friends, for de Sales, will remain friends in eternity. Augustine's teaching that individual friendships are absorbed into a general community of love was forgotten. The bishop must have thought of his numerous female correspondents and friends when he insisted that "the friendships that were good already in this life will continue in eternity. We will love particular individuals [more than others]." Who dared assume that the classical spiritual marriage between the bishop and the abbess of Annecy, Jeanne de Chantal, would not end in a heavenly reunion? While Protestants demanded a this-worldly ethic, de Sales (who had been prince bishop of Calvinist Geneva) struggled to maintain the Catholic focus on the other world. By describing an intimate heaven, he increased the attractiveness of paradise. Heaven still was thoroughly theocentric, but de Sales banished the cold abstractness of the scholastic empyrean from his preaching and writing.[33]

Francis de Sales shared with many Catholic contemporaries a theocentric outlook colored by a theological optimism. The soul, rather than being doomed due to its inclination toward sin, is actually destined for heaven. In his love of us and with foreknowledge of our individual merits, God has already decided about our eternal fate in everlasting glory. This concept, called "predestination to glory," attracted the notice of the French bishop. "I find this doctrine of yours all the more pleasing," wrote de Sales to a Jesuit author, "because I myself have always felt that it is the truest, the most attractive, and the one that is most worthy of the divine grace and mercy." Such a doctrine eminently suited the practical concerns of the preacher and spiritual director. By emphasizing a confident and gentle spirituality, de Sales could more easily introduce religious ideals to lay people. French Catholic thought, from the pen of de Sales and like-minded writers, focused on what "seemed to be the most comforting, the most pleasing, and, with one word, the most human."[34]

Courage, discipline, perseverance and "a kind of Renaissance optimism about the human condition and the value of the human endeavor" became the hallmarks of the Catholic reform mentality. According to the influential philosopher Justus Lipsius (1547–1606), the human soul is noble and almost divine because it retains "some vestiges of its [heavenly] origin and is not without certain bright sparks of the pure fiery nature from whence it came forth." For Lipsius, our main care should be to subject our entire existence "to right reason and God" and thus be in harmony with the universe. This philosophy reflected ancient Stoic thought which encouraged humankind to live in harmony with nature. In his *Treatise on the Love of God* (1616), de Sales quoted extensively the ancient slave-philosopher Epictetus. Greatly admiring this Stoic thinker, de Sales recommended him as a model to his readers. De Sales's and Lipsius's interpretation of Stoic philosophy emphasized the positive role of nature and humanity. Christian revelation acted as the little extra help needed in order to enhance and perfect an already fundamentally good world.[35]

Although most Catholic reformers focused their attention on the splendor of the empyrean heaven, not all neglected the earth entirely. Unlike scholastic authors, who had no real use for a renewed earth,

Antonino Polti felt that perhaps God could utilize a restored earth. Nature, like the human character, could be improved and made useful by God. With the optimistic perspective of a Catholic reformer, Polti suggested that the earth might eventually serve as a basement or lower level of heaven. After the Last Judgment, the earth will be "cleansed and glorified" and connected to the higher spheres. Following Savonarola's *Triumph of the Cross* (1497), he speculated that the new earth will be inhabited by the children who died unbaptized. There they will live, be happy, and glorify God forever. As a Christian humanist, Polti could not relegate the innocent children to hell or a location very much like the place of torment. The earth, while not good enough for the blessed, would provide a suitable eternal home for some souls.[36]

The Catholic reformers of the period before and after the Council of Trent preached a theocentric heaven with the same vigor as Luther and Calvin. They differed from the Protestant reformers in their insistence that Mary comprised one part of that divine center. Continuing to maintain much of the scholastic description of the other world, reformers like Polti and de Sales struggled to personalize the heavenly empyrean. Medieval mystical visions of the heavenly relationship between Christ and the soul had set a precedent for their portrayal of an intimate paradise. The saints focused on the divine not because of its awe and power, but because they felt an unrestrained love for God. The optimistic theology of the reformers, with its Stoic roots, enabled them to speak in a positive manner of the saints' love for God and of God's love for the saints. Even the earth, accepted as a good part of creation, claimed a place in God's scheme for everlasting life. The hopeful attitude about the possibility of all Catholics joining the heavenly hosts encouraged the revitalization of the church following the challenges of the Reformation. Heaven, like the church, was open and accessible to all. Catholic writers continued to emphasize the divine center, but increasingly spoke of the relationship between soul and God in warm and human terms. While heaven was softened and humanized by the renewed earth for the Protestant reformers, the Catholic reformers accomplished this through an emotional and intimate language.

The Pious and Ascetic Middle Class

When the French philosopher Blaise Pascal died in 1662, his family discovered a slip of parchment sewn into his garment. On the paper, Pascal described a mystical experience which had separated him from the dry speculations of philosophy and brought him closer to the God of the

Bible. This meant, as he wrote on the parchment, "the world forgotten, and everything except God" (*oublie du monde et de tout, hormis de Dieu*). With varying degrees of intensity, many Christians of the seventeenth and eighteenth century had similiar experiences. Many French Catholics, inspired by Pascal and Jansenism, challenged the optimistic spirituality of de Sales. In English Puritanism, Richard Baxter asserted the primacy of God in heaven with new vigor. German Lutherans under Philipp Jakob Spener and Anglicans under the Wesley brothers felt the call to renounce earthly frivolities and embrace a rigorous Christian life. What has been termed "the pious middle class" of Catholics and Protestants in the New and Old Worlds turned to the contemplation of the divine and began to view the world of business with reservation.[37]

The philosophy of Puritans, Pietists, Methodists, and Catholic Jansenists stood in sharp contrast to the optimistic Stoicism of baroque philosophers like Justus Lipsius. The new ascetics did not believe in the natural goodness of human nature. For them, the human being was fundamentally sinful, not almost perfect as some baroque philosophers had maintained. Since the world is corrupt and will soon pass away, they claimed, God alone counts. While Catholic Jansenists discovered their view in Augustine, Protestants relied on the traditional doctrine of original sin as explained by Luther and Calvin. From this perspective, humankind badly needed salvation. God the Savior, rather than God the Creator, served as the focus of devotional literature and spirituality.[38]

Life, therefore, must not be celebrated in art or in conspicuous waste and display. Frugality and ascetic restraint separated the other-worldly Christians from the opulence of baroque society. Hard work became the standard Puritan advice – leading to the successful Protestant ethic. Catholics still preferred retirement to the monastery. The same spirit generated the two options. As Max Weber pointed out, disciplined work implied no less ascetic restraint than the celibate life of a priest or nun. The ascetic attitude was so universal that an Anglican bishop exclaimed, "I do not see why monasteries might not agree well enough with re-formed devotion."[39]

The new attitude did not grow in a vacuum, but was fuelled (if not caused) by what historians have termed the crisis of the seventeenth century. A period of stagnation, depression, and poverty succeeded the prosperity of the sixteenth century. Long-term economic depression, characterized as much by a series of bad harvests as by problems in trade, shook England and the Continent. Accompanied and aggravated by growing social tensions, these difficulties frequently erupted into local disturbances and sometimes grew into civil wars. The Thirty Years War in Germany (1618–48), Cromwell's civil war in England (1642–6), the Turkish advance upon Vienna (1683), and Louis XIV's endless wars against Spain, Holland, and the German Palatinate (1667–97) left thousands dead and even more homeless. In this era of crisis, Christians severely questioned baroque optimism, forming new attitudes. "The belief in progress, so dominant in the sixteenth century, was obviously broken in the seventeenth," summarizes one historian; "now, in a new era, confidence and hope gave way to anxiety and fear."[40]

What the pious middle class probably feared most was neither war nor poverty, but unbelief and laxity in Christian practice. Throughout Britain, the tension between the Puritan way of life and the (real or alleged) laxity of others resulted in numerous local conflicts and led to emigration to America. In France, the developing new class of physicians, lawyers, civil servants, businessmen and merchants involved with capitalistic enterprise lost its traditional, unquestioned adherence to the Catholic faith. Rationalism and skepticism emerged, leading to anticlerical sentiment or even outright hostility toward the church. As the Age of Reason advanced upon them, the pious found themselves in an alien world from which they fled to God.[41]

The simple monastery at Port-Royal-des-Champs – the headquarters of the Jansenist movement – provided an impressive contrast to the nearby château of Versailles where the Sun King celebrated his reign. The two styles of life aptly summarize the gap which existed between those Europeans who exploited life in the world and those who rejected its snares. Like the Puritans, the Jansenists placed a strong emphasis on original sin. The human being was intrinsically corrupt and weak. Reason could be no certain guide in things pertaining to salvation. Here only divine grace could help, grace which God bestowed upon the few elect. Only the elect were so overwhelmed by his gifts that they could not resist. For the Jansenists, grace suppressed or destroyed their own selfish will and replaced it with the divine impulse. That impulse separated the chosen few from the others – the lukewarm, the reprobate, and the dwellers of Versailles. For the Catholic Jansenists, as for other Protestant world-renouncing communities, the elect excelled in the harshness of their ascetic life and rigorous morality. Divine grace elevated them far above the world, bringing them close to God, whom they would eventually enjoy in eternal solitude.

Although the monastery at Port-Royal served as the center for Jansenism, the character of the movement can be better seen in the spiritual struggles of Mme. de Sévigné (1626–96). Widowed at an early age, Marie de Sévigné spent her life in a country house in Brittany, surrounded by relatives and often visited by friends and admirers. While her noble descent made her an unlikely candidate for the stern ways of the Jansenists, her reading and the death of her husband led her to embrace a scrupulous form of spirituality. Her esteem for Port-Royal and her love of books by Pascal, the Jansenist Arnauld, and Augustine are well known.

Her private chapel did not include any statue of a saint, because she wanted "to avoid any jealousy" and give God the exclusive honor due to him. The chapel did include, though, a picture of the Blessed Virgin, a crucifix, and an inscription that must have pleased the Jansenists: "To God alone honor and glory" (*Soli Deo honor et gloria*).[42]

While it was easy to dedicate the chapel to God alone, it was more difficult to do the same with the heart. Preoccupied with her daughter Françoise-Marguérite, Mme. de Sévigné flooded her with letters – letters which became classical French literature. A Jansenist friend scolded her for such idolatrous attention to her daughter. "This kind of idolatry," he insisted, "is as dangerous as any other." Mme. de Sévigné at least tried to share her heart between her daughter and God. "Let me love you," she wrote to her daughter, "until God Himself takes some of my heart away from you in order to place himself there. It is to Him alone that I will yield this place." She sometimes felt unable to relate to God properly because "I found myself so completely occupied and filled by yourself, with a heart incapable of any other thought." She barred herself from receiving communion when such intense feelings interfered, commenting that she must pull herself away at least "a little" (*un peu*) from her daughter in order to be worthy of the sacrament. Mme. de Sévigné's striving underscored the Jansenist demand that good Christians should leave the world, including their family. If they did not disentangle themselves from the world, then they would die with it. The world was not to be transformed, it was to be forgotten. Eventually the body would rot away and the material universe would perish. For the saved, there would then be nothing but the human soul and God celebrating their union in eternal solitude.[43]

One of Mme. de Sévigné's favorite authors was the French Jansenist Pierre Nicole (1625–95). He helped Pascal prepare his famous *Lettres provinciales* against the Jesuits, and is especially known for the numerous volumes of his *Essais de Morale*. Nicole's heaven was as God-centered as that of Francis de Sales, but free of any emotional qualities. "*God alone* will be the possession of the elect," wrote Nicole; "he alone will be their bliss... This will be the essence of their beatitude, and they will consider everything else only in relation to this essential good." The motto "God alone" summarizes succinctly Nicole's beliefs. The blessed will have no desire for anything else besides God. Their souls' "capacity to love, desire and enjoy will be so exhausted that it will be impossible for them to love and desire anything besides God." For Nicole, the communion of the blessed with each other is so unimportant that he speaks of heavenly existence as *solitude eternelle avec Dieu seul*: "The human being is created to live in an eternal solitude with God alone. The community of the blessed will in no way restrict their individual solitude, because no one will ever divert them from their total devotion to God, who is their only good, and because the view of creatures will be nothing else but an extension of the vision of God." Having God as their partner, the blessed will show no interest in angels or other creatures. Even Mary's presence will be of no concern. God alone will be the focus of the redeemed; he alone suffices.[44]

Characteristically, Nicole did not provide any further description of the eternal relationship between God and saint. We are not told what heavenly solitude might include. From Nicole's perspective there could be no intimate or sentimental relationship between the saint and the divine. The silent solitude of a hermit replaced de Sales's friendly con-versations with Jesus. Reunions with family and friends found no place in heaven. The presence of God so fully overshadowed human relation-ships that nothing distracted the saint from the beatific vision. Radically different from earth, heavenly life meant total separation from anything human or natural.

Pious Protestant writings paralleled the Jansenist assertion that God should be the sole focus of the Christian life. "It is grown a controversy," Richard Baxter (1615–91) reported in a letter of 1665, "whether a contemplative or an active life be the more excellent." Baxter, although not excluding the necessity of an active life, preferred the retirement of "an abstracted communion with God." In a conscious departure from Calvinist tradition, he wanted to be "none of those that . . . draw men to venture too boldly into the world, under pretence of seeing [God in his creatures] or of serving God." While retiring to a monastery was not an option for the Puritan Baxter, a mental state of disengagement must be accomplished. "It is your calling to forsake this world and mind the other," wrote John Howe (1630–1706), Cromwell's domestic chaplain; "make haste then to quit yourselves of your entanglement, of all earthly dispositions and affections." As the lures of urban society, the rewards of business, and the temptations of cosmopolitan culture threatened the theocentric spirituality of Protestantism, the Puritan desire to cling to the divine intensified.[45]

Even in the New World, the temptations were manifold. The American poet Richard Steere (1643–1721) echoed the Puritan sus-picion of the wealth of human life. "Such who condemn the free and cheerful use of earth's enjoyments, do it for this cause," he wrote; "all temporary honours, riches, pleasures are vain, uncertain, short, and transitory, and in comparison of heavenly joys they are not worthy of the least esteem, but rather to be scornfully despised." Over and over again in their meditations, in their sermons and on their gravestones the Puritans warned against misplaced affection for this world. Death itself, with its rot and putrefaction, symbolized the fleeting character of earthly glories. Only God was permanent, true, and worthy of love. Only medita-tion on the delights of heaven released the soul from the mire of earthly concerns. "Tis true those souls who often contemplate the heav'nly glories of eternal bliss, are above earthly pleasures lifted up," stressed Steere, "while their blest souls aspire to heav'nly joys with sweet desire they do forget the earth." The ascetic reformers set their sights on heaven even while on earth.[46]

The devout meditations of Puritans and other ascetic reformers anticipated a spiritual rather than a material heavenly reality. Heaven for the pious could never be a replica of the existing world. The old Reformation doctrine about the renewed world as a place of life everlasting was abandoned. Even those who predicted a fruitful earth during the millennium returned the righteous to their proper heavenly existence after the end of time. The other life, either immediately after death or after the millennium, freed the saints from the world; it did not continue their existence there. "It is evident," argued John Howe, "that the Creator of this lower world never intended it to be the perpetual dwelling-place of its inhabitants." How could the tiny, insignificant earth provide enough space for the blessed? For Howe, the saint was "a candidate for a better state in a nobler region." We can identify that region as the familiar empyrean heaven of scholastic teaching.[47]

The English philosopher Thomas Browne (1605–82) assumed that God would eventually destroy the whole world. What remained would be an empty space filled with the presence of God. "To place [heaven] in the empyrean or beyond the tenth sphere," he mused, "is to forget the world's destruction; for when this sensible world shall be destroyed, all shall then be as it is now there, an empyrean heaven...To ask where heaven is, is to demand where the presence of God is, or where we have the glory of that happy vision." In other words, at the Last Judgment God will annihilate the world without replacing it with a new one. In life everlasting, God serves as sufficient "space" or environment for the blessed.[48]

Richard Baxter in his *Saints' Everlasting Rest* (1649) provided the classic Puritan statement of the ascetic and God-centered attitude. Again and again he insisted that God, and God alone, should be the focus of eternal life: "The knowledge of God and his Christ, a delightful complacency in that mutual love, an everlasting rejoicing in the fruition of our God, a perpetual singing of his high praises; this is a heaven for a saint, a spiritual rest, suitable to a spiritual nature. Then, dear friends, we shall live in our own element." Although Baxter, caught up in the religious politics of Cromwellian England, had a difficult time cultivating a life of contemplation, he stressed the importance of other-wordliness. Focusing on God in this life and in the next meant rejecting worldly concerns. Spiritual rest suitable to the saints' spiritual nature entailed total commitment to the divine.[49]

Baxter commented on the human side of heaven, but never without giving his thoughts a decidedly theocentric turn. In *The Saints' Everlasting Rest* he presented his readers with a long list of forty-four people whom they could expect to meet in the hereafter. The reformers figured prominently: Luther, Zwingli, Calvin, Beza, Bullinger, and Bradford. In heaven the blessed would meet "all the saints of all ages whose faces in the flesh we never saw." Baxter, however, refrained from constructing a Ciceronian patriotic other world such as his contemporary Andrew Marvell (1621–78) imagined. Marvell – John Milton's assistant and Cromwell's court poet – placed Moses, Joshua, David, and the Lord Protector side by side in heaven. Social joys, for Baxter, were at best secondary, if not entirely irrelevant. "All the glory of the blessed is comprised in their enjoyment of God," Baxter asserted, "and if there be any mediate joys there, they are but drops from this." There would be a community of saints but all their bliss would derive from God, not from social life.[50]

In less theological but more graphic terms Joseph Hall (1574–1656), an Anglican bishop with Puritan leanings, argued the same idea. "When we casually meet with a brother or a son before some great prince," he reflected, "we forbear the ceremonies of our mutual respects, as being wholly taken up with the awful regard of a greater presence." Applied to life everlasting this meant that "when we meet before the glorious throne of the God of Heaven, all the respects of our former earthly relations must utterly cease and be swallowed up of that beatifical presence, divine love, and infinitely blessed fruition of the Almighty!" In the presence of God any meeting with a fellow saint becomes "casual" and all social relationships must fade. "I shall neither have need, nor use of inquiring after my kindred according to the flesh," the bishop wrote in 1651. While Baxter refrained from employing such vivid language, Hall explained with dramatic explicitness that "nature has no place in glory; here is no respect of blood; none of marriage: this grosser acquaintance and pleasure is for the paradise of Turks, not the heaven of Christians." Celestial glory transcends and virtually eliminates everything that belongs to social life. Nature and humanity receive no place in glory. Heaven is the kingdom of God.[51]

Only the eternal praise of God merits a place in glory. The beatific vision for the Puritan reformers did not mean silent meditation. Whereas the Jansenist Nicole preferred the silence of monastic contemplation, theocentric Protestants favored heavenly worship. Drawing from the liturgy contained in the book of Revelation, Baxter created a heavenly life filled with song and praise. During the Middle Ages divine praise in the other world was considered an angelic task, and Luther and Calvin had shown little interest in the subject. Baxter rediscovered the Augustinian emphasis on everlasting praise. He can also be credited with giving the blessed an important and independent role in celestial worship, transcending that of merely being an appendix to the superior angelic choirs. "O blessed employment," proclaimed Baxter, echoing the biblical text, "to stand before the throne of God and the Lamb, and to sound forth for ever: Thou art worthy, O Lord, to receive glory and honor and power." Over countless pages Baxter celebrated the important role the saints will have in worshipping God with song and chant. Their melodious never-ending liturgy of praise contrasts sharply with the terrifying "shrieks and cries" of the damned. Harp and song are for glorifying God; they have no place in hell.[52]

According to Baxter (known for his love of music), earthly congregational singing prepares us for the next life. "The Lord by his merciful providence and his grace," he wrote in the preface to his own book of poetry, "tunes up our dull and drooping souls to such joyful praises, as may prepare us for his everlasting praise in heaven." Singing not only prepares Christians for the next world; it also provides a foretaste of everlasting joys. "The liveliest emblem of heaven that I know upon earth is when the people of God . . . join together both in heart and voice in the cheerful and melodious singing of his praises." Baxter warned his readers not to misconstrue the joys of singing. Congregational music does not belong to carnal pleasures in which we enjoy ourselves rather than the divine. Praising God with a "deep sense of His excellency and bounty" prevents us from "sticking in the carnal delight" of singing. In his defense of congregational singing Baxter emphasized the spiritual quality of music. "Harmony and melody," he argued, "are so high a pleasure of the sense, that they are nearest to rational delights, if not participating of them," and therefore "exceedingly fitted to elevate the mind and affections to God." Whoever spurned praising God in this life would be unfit for the heavenly choir. "A swine is fitter for a lecture of philosophy," Baxter remarked sarcastically, "or an ass to build a city or govern a kingdom; or a dead corpse to feast at thy table, than thou art for this work of heavenly praise." The Puritan divine did not mince his words.[53]

Baxter was not the only Calvinist to view congregational singing as a foretaste and anticipation of our heavenly duties. John Cotton (1584–1652), in his preface to the 1640 New England *Whole Booke of Psalmes*, explained that we must sing "until he [the Lord] take us from hence, and wipe away all our tears, and bid us enter into our master's joy to sing eternal hallelujahs." In a similar vein William Law (1686–1761) urged believers to meditate on a page of Revelation "till your imagination has carried you above the clouds, till it has placed you amongst those heavenly beings and made you long to bear a part in their eternal music." *The Saints' Everlasting Rest*, Law's *Serious Call to a Devout and Holy Life* (1728) and other devotional literature made its readers appreciate the praise of God as the Christian's everlasting duty in this world and the next.[54]

Music and singing in heaven did not exist for the pleasure of the saints; it occurred for the worship of God. A similar theocentric emphasis prevailed in the discussion of the superior knowledge which the saints would acquire in the next life. "We shall know in a moment all that is to be known," asserted Baxter. Even the most complex theological or scientific problems will be understood easily as well as immediately. "The poorest Christian is presently there a more perfect divine than any[one] is here," summarized Baxter. Heavenly knowledge came instantaneously. There would no longer be any struggle, frustration, or slow progress in the educational process. Those whom God had elected to join him in heaven immediately would receive the ability to perceive and understand the divine will and the condition of humankind. "God shall create us all Doctors in a minute," John Donne (1572–1631) noted. Not only did life radically change upon entering heaven, but instantaneous knowledge placed the saints in a category which no earth-bound creature could even begin to understand.[55]

Known for their love of learning and writing, Puritan ministers revelled in the thought of finally being able to have all riddles and perplexities resolved. In heaven they would know not simply many things, but everything. Increase Mather (1639–1723) in colonial America echoed Baxter's vision of unlimited knowledge. When the soul of a just man comes to heaven, he mused, "he will gain more knowledge in one day and without being at any labor for it than he could arrive unto in this world by a thousand years' hard study." Death for the righteous signals the end of their struggles to grow in spiritual and earthly wisdom. In heaven God grants them, in a twinkling of an eye, perfect knowledge.[56]

To acquire superior knowledge and to engage in intellectual activities did not contradict the quietness of eternal rest. The saints' rest, according to Baxter, was "not the rest of a stone which ceaseth from all motion when it attains the center," but "containeth a sweet and constant action of all the powers of the soul and body..." The concluding part of the sentence is particularly important: "...in this fruition of God." Knowledge was not for the entertainment or superficial happiness of the saints. Heavenly knowledge was one more way in which God commanded the attention of the blessed. The Creator "advanceth our sense, and enlargeth our capacity...and fills up with himself all that capacity." The employment of the glorified body in this context was defined as "to stand before the throne of God and the Lamb, and to praise him for ever and ever." All heavenly knowledge and action had God as its source, its meaning, and its center.[57]

Although Baxter's work seems to have declined in appeal during the first half of the eighteenth century, it became popular again when rediscovered by John Wesley (1703–91) and reprinted in an abridged form in the 1750s. The founder of Methodism shared Baxter's preference for a theocentric lifestyle. "Deliver me, O God," Wesley prayed, "from too intense an application to even necessary business." To this he added, "I know how this dissipates my thoughts from the one end of all my business." How to keep the mind focused on godly concerns plagued the ascetic reformers. "Do I think of God first and last?" was a question posed in the self-examination recommended by Wesley as a daily exercise. It was not, however, the founder of Methodism who recreated Baxter's heaven in a new literary guise. It was one of his students, James Hervey (1714–58), whose *Meditations among the Tombs* (1746) appealed to the new Methodist emotionality and became one of the most widely read devotional works of its time.[58]

The *Meditations among the Tombs* suggest a pessimistic attitude toward life and human nature. In the text Hervey describes his strolls through the graveyard of Kilkhampton, a village in Cornwall, England. Walking from one monument to the next and reading the epitaphs, his thoughts turn to pensive and romantic reflections. He muses on the fate of the interred: their trying deathbed scenes, their lamenting friends, their ascent to heaven, and their eternal bliss. Seeing the epitaph of a young man who died shortly before his wedding inspires a thought on the vanity of this life. "Go, disappointed virgin!" Hervey addresses the mourning bride in his *Meditations*. "Go, mourn the uncertainty of all created bliss! Teach thy soul to aspire after a sure and immutable felicity! For the once gay and gallant Fidelio sleeps in other embraces, even in the icy arms of death! Forgetful, eternally forgetful of the world – and thee." Hervey and other ascetic reformers of his kind all warned their readers incessantly of placing confidence and trust in the things of this world – business, riches, family, friends. By continually holding up the image of the naked skull or the rotting corpse they vividly presented to Christians the vanity of the world. Death with its "icy arms" never failed to cut short the enjoyment of the living. For Hervey, pursuing eternal life meant psychological detachment from intense earthly relationships. Since no human relationships continue for eternity, those preparing for heaven should distance themselves from fleeting worldly illusions. Human love is not eternal.[59]

The total otherness of eternal life left no room for promises of meeting again or heavenly reunions. The "sure and immutable felicity," according to Hervey, must be found with God, not with a human partner. The somewhat distant and pale patriarchal figures of the Bible – the formulaic Abraham, Isaac, and Jacob – and perhaps one's own personal religious teacher were the only people the author envisioned meeting in the afterlife. Hervey, committed to a theocentric attitude, refrained from describing the reunion of instructor and instructed in the other world. Heaven existed not for exchanging sweet memories and renewing old friendships, but for the eternal praise of God. "The saints," explained Hervey, "always rejoice amidst the smiles of heaven; their harps are perpetually tuned; the triumphs admit of no interruption."[60]

No interruption! Hervey insisted on the unchanging nature and immobility of life everlasting. "The wheel [of fortune] never turns: All is steadfast and immovable beyond the grave. Whether we are then seated on the throne, or stretched on the rack, a seal will be set on our condition, by the hand of everlasting mercy, or inflexible justice." While the world changes with passing fashions, the divine is immovable and stable. Like Baxter and Nicole, Hervey did not intend to conquer the world. Impressed and displeased with its instability and transitoriness, he told Christians to retire from the world and elevate their spirit to that stability which only heaven can give. Nothing could be depended upon on earth; only in heaven would perfection exist.[61]

The theocentric afterlife of the pious and ascetic middle class took the God-centered heaven of the Protestant and Catholic reformers to the extreme. Whereas Luther allowed a purified earth to provide a playful diversion for the saints, the Puritans denied the earth an everlasting existence. There may be a this-worldly millennial kingdom of Christ, but they held that when the final time arrived, the earth along with all worldly affairs would vanish. The emotional and intimate heaven of Francis de Sales lost favor among Catholics who rejected his notion that the divine could be so accessible to humanity. Divine majesty should not be underestimated. Likewise, pious Catholics steered away from Polti's Mary-centered paradise. A female presence only weakened the unity of God the Father, the Son, and the Holy Spirit. During the seventeenth century, many theologians successfully insisted on a distant, majestic God as the sole focus of eternal life.

Theocentric Heaven

By the middle of the seventeenth century the notion of the theocentric heaven had spread throughout western Christianity. It motivated the Jesuits of Neuburg in Bavaria to remove Peter Paul Rubens's (1577–1640) large Last Judgment painting from its place above the altar of their church (Pl. 33). With its luscious female bodies and its intimation of reunited lovers, it looked like a forgotten survivor of the outlawed Renaissance art. It had to be replaced by a less offensive piece more in tune with reformed Catholic sentiments. The sensuality of Rubens's art, which celebrated the flesh and the passions of the world, contradicted every value the reformers sought to instill. By the time Hervey published his *Meditations* in 1746 he could rely on a traditional, time-honored view of the other world preached by many Protestants and Catholics for two centuries.[62]

Even as the religious enthusiasm of the pious middle class weakened, many continued to uphold a heaven where psalm-singing saints spent an eternity resting in the vision of the divine. The Catholic hierarchy condemned Jansenism as a heresy, Puritan zeal weakened, and dreary tombstone meditations slowly fell out of fashion. But in spite of significant cultural and religious changes, the articulation of a God-centered heaven continued throughout the eighteenth century and into the nineteenth. Even those who took no great interest in religious matters assumed a God-dominated heaven. Even in the nineteenth century, when both religious and literary communities presented creative alternatives, the traditional image still could not be ignored. All alternatives argued against the theocentric view. What was its continual attraction?

If we eliminate the diverse and unique elements which mark the heaven of Luther, Calvin, Polti, de Sales, Nicole, and Baxter, and concentrate on what they share in common, a theocentric model emerges. According to this model, heaven is for God, and the eternal life of the saints revolves around a divine center. The saints may be involved in an everlasting liturgy of praise, they may meditate in solitude, or they may be caught up in an intimate relation with the divine. Worldly activities earn no place in heaven. At the end of time the earth either is destroyed or plays a minor role in everlasting life. Heaven is fundamentally a religious place – a center of worship, of divine revelation, and pious conversations with sacred characters.

The theocentric model presents heaven as the opposite of earth. Death marks a radical difference between this life and the next. Life on earth is superficial, constantly changing, and full of disappointment. Nothing earthly can be depended upon because at any point such support may be lost. Humanity – weak, prone to sin, given to extravagance and arrogance – dominates worldly existence. Even the positive aspects of worldly life – family, friends, work, the arts – have limits. Only God should be counted on never to change, to be an endless source of love, and to survive throughout eternity. While good Christians might achieve a sense of the fullness of God on earth through their religious activities, family commitments, or personal meditation, this can only give a taste of what waits for them after death. At one's personal death or at the death of history at the end of the world, a radically new life commences.

Heavenly life is not a perfected version of life on earth. The theocentric model asserts that eternal life has little in common with everyday earthly activities. Heavenly existence means a life free not only from the pains of earth but from everything earthly. Not only do sorrow, illness, death, and labor cease, but friends, family, change, and human creativity are utterly unimportant. On earth, humanity dominates the

Pl. 33.   Peter Paul Rubens, *The Last Judgment.* 1615–17. Alte Pinakothek, Munich

affairs of government, family, and even church. In heaven, God dominates. On earth, change, growth, and decay make everything impermanent. Since only the perfect exists in heaven, there is no need for
change. On earth, work, struggle for knowledge, and family commitments
draw our attention away from God. In heaven, the saints are free from

179

labor. Since they receive immediate wisdom, God's elect are even spared the troubles of research and study. Families also never interfere with divine meditations. Death serves as an absolute divider between the realm of the imperfect and the realm of the perfect.

The theocentric model provides a simple, direct, and theologically uncontroversial perspective of heaven. Who would challenge the belief that an eternal solitude with God alone must be the most desired goal for the true Christian? How could anything rival an uncompromised relationship with the divine? By subscribing to a theocentric model, the question of what the saints *do* for eternity falls by the wayside. The saints do not have to *do* anything, they merely experience the fullness of their being by existing with God. A theocentric heaven also eliminates the possible extravagances caused by human imagination. If paradise is radically separated from earth, then the artist or the poet has only a limited set of images available through which to depict everlasting life. Not every Christian, however, was satisfied with such a sparse picture of eternity.

CHAPTER SEVEN

Swedenborg and the Emergence
of a Modern Heaven

"Today's churchman knows almost nothing about heaven, hell, or his own life after death," complained Emanuel Swedenborg in 1758. "To prevent so negative an attitude. . . it has been made possible for me to be right with angels and to talk to them person to person. I have also been allowed," summarized the Swedish visionary, "to see what heaven is like." Realizing that many of the readers of his book *Heaven and Hell* might question the sanity of such assertions, Swedenborg reassured them that "to forestall any claim that this is delusion or hallucination, I have been allowed to see them [the angels] while I was fully awake, that is, while I was with all my physical senses and in a state of clear perception." With the publication of Swedenborg's visions of heaven during the mid-eighteenth century, a vigorous alternative to an ascetic, theocentric heaven first appeared.[1]

At first glance, Emanuel Swedenborg seems an unlikely candidate to present a radical realignment of the Christian concept of heaven. Born into a wealthy family in 1688, he refused to follow his father, a bishop of the Swedish state church, into the ministry. Instead, Swedenborg pursued the life of an engineer, mathematician, and scientist. In his early years he travelled throughout Europe, reading the writings of natural philosophers like Newton, and publishing treatises on almost every aspect of scientific inquiry. Not content with merely writing about science, Swedenborg dabbled in economic and political theory, producing pamphlets such as *Modest Thoughts on the Fall and Rise of Swedish Money* (1722). At the age of thirty-five, he turned down a professorship in mathematics at the University of Uppsala to become a member of the Swedish Board of Mines. For the next twenty-five years, he led the life of a Swedish official, helping to regulate the profitable Swedish mining industry. During this period, he may be compared with the more famous Sir Isaac Newton (1642–1727) who also wrote extensively on natural philosophy, never married, eventually took a government job as master of the English mint, and like Swedenborg lived long past his eightieth year.

We must not assume that the men who created what we now refer to as the Scientific Revolution restricted themselves only to the exploration of the natural world, never venturing into more arcane areas. In his later years, Newton wrote extensively on alchemy, theology, and sacred chronology, although he published very little in this area. Swedenborg, on the other hand, published his philosophical insights in the first of three volumes of the work *Opera Philosophica et Mineralia* (1734). Nothing in this early work aroused controversy, but after its publication Swedenborg took more frequent leaves of absence from his position at the Board of Mines to travel throughout Europe, preparing scientific writings, and reflecting on religion and philosophy. Between 1744 and 1745, Swedenborg recorded in his journal of dreams his spiritual crisis, which included a vision of something "holy" and "indescribable." Whatever this presence was, it shook him, threw him to the ground, and forced him to pray.[2]

Swedenborg increasingly devoted his time to biblical exegesis and the analysis of the symbolism of his own dreams. Retiring from the Royal Board of Mines in 1747 at the age of fifty-nine, he concentrated his efforts on deciphering the religious implications of his dreams and the messages from spiritual beings which came more and more frequently. A year later he would write: "For almost three years, that is, for thirty-three months, I have now been in such a state that my mind, having been withdrawn from corporeal things, could be among societies of spiritual and celestial beings and yet I have been like any other man in the company of men without any difference." Swedenborg, who once prided himself on his astute observation of the natural world, now chronicled "the world of spirits" and "the heaven of angels." By his death in 1772, Swedenborg had produced sixteen published books based on his visions (including *Arcana Coelestia*, which numbered eight volumes), several manuscripts on biblical exegesis ("The Word Explained," also spanning eight volumes), and a private spiritual diary which now fills five volumes.[3]

During his life, Swedenborg's religious outlook captivated only a few followers. Although those followers later developed his teachings into the "Church of the New Jerusalem," Swedenborgianism never flourished as a religion. It did, however, fascinate a diverse group of philosophers, writers, and artists in the nineteenth century. Swedenborg's popular reputation as a mystic, whose heavenly conversations provided a useful philosophical system for writers like Emerson and food for ridicule by the more skeptical Kant, underplays his place in the long history of Christian constructions of heaven. It also denies Swedenborgian contributions to the development of the thoroughly anthropocentric view of heaven which flourished in the nineteenth century and is still held by many people today.[4]

Swedenborg's visions of heaven contrasted sharply with the ascetic, theocentric heaven of the Protestant and Catholic reformers. At almost every turn, he offered readers a vigorous alternative to the traditional heaven articulated by medieval theologians and refined by post-Reformation thinkers. Although we can detect elements of Swedenborg's heaven in the paradise of Renaissance artists, their views contained little supporting theological framework. While the Renaissance heaven might astonish us with its sensuality and vividness, its artistic originators and religious proponents only presented fragments of their heavenly visions. Swedenborg's writings provided both a vital challenge to the theocentric heavenly tradition and a sharpening of certain background themes dimly heard throughout Christian history.

The accentuation of those background themes into a fully articulated heavenly theology marks the beginning of a modern view of heaven. With the publication of Swedenborg's writings in the mid-eighteenth century, a major shift occurred in the perception of heavenly life. Hints of this shift were also evident in the more conventional theology of the period, indicating a slow realignment of images of the other world. While the majority of Christians during that time took little notice of the Swedish visionary, the cultural climate supported the general perspective of his views. This perspective on heaven, which we term "modern," has four characteristics: First, only a thin veil divides heaven from earth. For the righteous, heavenly life begins immediately after death. Concepts of purgatory or sleeping in the grave until the general resurrection are either denied or minimized. Secondly, rather than viewing heaven as the structural opposite of life on earth, it is seen as a continuation and fulfillment of material existence. Heaven possesses a material character which gives it a sensuous quality. Delighting the senses, once perceived as a frivolous pastime, becomes a major aspect of eternal life. Thirdly, although heaven continues to be described as a place of "eternal rest," the saints are increasingly shown engaged in activities, experiencing spiritual progress, and joyfully occupying themselves in a dynamic, motion-filled environment. The journey to God does not end with admittance to heaven but continues eternally. Spiritual development is therefore endless. Finally, a focus on human love expressed in communal and familial concerns slowly replaces the primacy of divine love experienced in the beatific vision. Social relationships, including the love between man and woman, are seen as fundamental to heavenly life and not in conflict with divine purpose. God is loved not only directly but also through the love and charity shown to others in heaven.

This modern notion of heaven surfaced in the eighteenth century with the writings of Swedenborg, peaked in the nineteenth and early twentieth centuries, and faded by the mid-twentieth. In chapters eight and nine we will elaborate on two concepts introduced here: the continuation of earthly love in heaven and the possibility of spiritual progress after death. These two themes in particular structured the understanding of heaven in the nineteenth and early twentieth centuries. It is the modern heaven, so vividly experienced by Swedenborg, which eventually loses its power of persuasion in the late twentieth century. The degree of our incredulity at his visions reflects how far we are from finding comfort in such heavenly hopes.

The Immediacy of Life after Death

The rejection of the Catholic concept of purgatory posed a lasting problem for Protestant theologians. An intermediate place between life on earth and life in heaven no longer smoothed the passage from one realm to the other. For Protestants, if the soul is not purified of earthly sins, what happens to it and where does it go after death? Likewise, what happens to the souls between the time of death and the Last Judgment? During the sixteenth century, two basic Protestant schools of thought attempted to answer these questions. For the Anabapists and some Lutherans the soul sleeps – free from pain but also free from consciousness. For the followers of Calvin the soul rests, but fully aware of being in the presence of the divine. In 1534 Calvin hoped to clarify his ideas about the rest of the dead while simultaneously refuting sectarian claims. He directed *Psychopannychia: or, the Refutation of the Error Entertained by Some Unskillful Persons, Who Ignorantly Imagine that in the Interval between Death and Judgment the Soul Sleeps* against the Anabaptists, and by extension those Lutherans who believed that the soul sleeps in the grave until the Final Judgment.[5]

After someone dies, insisted Calvin, the soul rests but does not sleep. "By 'rest' we understand, not sloth, or lethargy, or anything like the drowsiness of ebriety which they attribute to the soul," countered Calvin, "but tranquillity of conscience and security, which always accompanies faith but is never complete in all its parts till after death." Rest meant peace, not sleep. Although the dead cannot experience full bliss because they lack a spiritual body, the saints can experience the glory of their salvation. Those whom God has not saved suffer in hell. There can be no alternative to heaven and hell. Immediately after death the soul enters either glorious life in heaven or punishment in hell.[6]

In the seventeenth and eighteenth centuries, the question of what type of life the virtuous dead could expect in heaven prior to the Last Judgment was much debated in theological circles. Those who predicted the coming millennium and the end of human history tried to find their own answer. For the British theologian Thomas Burnet (1635–1715), there can be no individual judgment until the final judgment at the end of time. Until then all who die will find "peace and rest and comfort of mind promised in the Gospel." The state of death, for both the good and the evil, "is a state of quiet, of silence, and of inaction, or cessation from action...we have no more commerce with the external world, than we have in a state of sleep." Burnet, who elaborated a sacred history containing a dramatically established millennial period, maintained that the soul must wait until God winds the world down to an end before experiencing heaven or hell. Those who believed in the eventual establishment of a millennial kingdom on earth showed little concern for the fate of the soul immediately after death.[7]

Against those who insisted that the dead rest until the Last Judgment were those who emphasized the soul's immediate entry into heaven or hell. In general, these Protestant thinkers continued the traditional Catholic devaluation of the Last Judgment and millennial age, while rejecting the notion of purgatory. Expanding on Calvin's insistence that the soul does not sleep but participates in the divine, they used the promise of heaven and the threat of hell to motivate their parishioners and readers to a life of Christian virtue. The virtuous Christian did not need to worry about sleeping in the tomb until the Last Judgment, or to ponder the distance between earth and the far-away empyrean heaven. Heaven was close at hand and only the brief darkness of death separated us from it.

In 1707 the well-known hymnist, educator, and Nonconformist preacher Isaac Watts (1674–1748) wrote that "death like a narrow sea divides this heavenly land from ours." In his hymn, "A Prospect of Heaven Makes Death Easy", heaven is as close as any place one can reach by crossing a sea:

> There is a land of pure delight
> Where saints immortal reign;
> Infinite day excludes the night,
> And pleasures banish pain.
>
> There everlasting spring abides,
> And never-withering flowers;
> Death like a narrow sea divides
> This heavenly land from ours.

Watts, who chose freely from the contending theologies of his day, wrote detailed theological treatises as well as popular hymns and catechisms. Although he understood his writing as compatible with the Reformed tradition, he enjoyed his communications not only with American Puritans such as Cotton Mather and Jonathan Edwards, but also with English Anglican bishops and Methodists. His reflections on education, perhaps more than his other writings, illustrate his openness to Enlightenment views, particularly those of John Locke. Watts insisted in both his poetry and his theological writings that the good soul does not fall asleep but "begin[s] a heaven or a hell immediately after death."[8]

During the eighteenth century, the immediacy of the joys of heaven or the fires of hell was a viable theological option. Emanuel Swedenborg, however, described a much more radical connection between the world of the dead and the world of the living. While Isaac Watts poetically recalled the narrow sea which divides heaven and earth, Swedenborg insisted that he actually *crossed* that sea and experienced life on the other shore. On the basis of his very participation in the life of the angels, Swedenborg rejected the notion that a large spatial, temporal, or even metaphysical gap exists between this world and the world of the dead. For thirteen years, Swedenborg explained in his preface to *Heaven and Hell*, he had been allowed to see life in the other world. Now, he told his readers, he intended to dispel their ignorance and disbelief with evidence of what he had seen and heard.[9]

At death, according to Swedenborg, no radical change takes place in either the personality or the lifestyle of the individual. The soul enters the spirit world and lives in society, has feelings and thoughts, and functions just as it did on earth. The spirit world, while not heaven *per se*, serves as a middle ground between heaven and earth. Life there is so similar to earthly existence that some dead do not realize that they are dead. "Man after death is as much a man as he was before," Swedenborg explained, "so much so as to be unaware that he is not still in the former world." In the other world all senses and functions continue, "for he has sight, hearing and speech as in the former world; he walks, runs, and sits, as in the former world; he lies down, sleeps, and awakes, as in the former world; he eats and drinks as in the former world; he enjoys marriage delights as in the former world. In a word, he is a man in each and every respect." Life for the dead continues as always. Only an extremely narrow sea separates the living from the dead. "So the one life continues into the other," reflected Swedenborg, "and death is only a crossing."[10]

Swedenborg's discussion of the eternal nature of the human character radically changed the way the soul would be represented in burial places. Traditionally, medieval artists had depicted the soul as a naked child of no discernable sex. Before assuming its glorified body, the soul was not contiguous with the body but fundamentally different. Only after the reception of the spiritual body at the end of time would the saint resemble a human being. Sculptor John Flaxman (1755–1826), however, presented a new artistic interpretation of the soul. In 1784, influenced by the writings of Swedenborg, Flaxman joined a newly formed Swedenborgian group in London. That same year, he designed a funeral memorial for Sarah Morley with decidedly Swedenborgian elements (Pl. 34).[11]

Sarah Morley had died giving birth while travelling to England from

Pl. 34. John Flaxman, *The Sea Shall Give up the Dead.* Sarah Morley Memorial, 1784.
Gloucester Cathedral, England

India. The child and the mother were buried at sea, but Flaxman sculpted a memorial for them at Gloucester Cathedral. In the memorial, three angels greet the dead mother and child as they rise out of the waves. There is no evidence that this is a Last Judgment scene where the soul has received its body. The legend adapted from the book of Revelation, "The sea shall give up the dead" (Rev. 20:13), is not used as a reference to the Last Judgment as indicated by the original biblical context; instead, it is used as an allusion to the burial at sea. For the iconography Flaxman does not rely on traditional readings of Revelation but takes his inspiration from the gospel of Luke, where angels are said to escort the dead to the other world (Luke 16:22). Using a Swedenborgian theme he portrays the dead pair as in full possession of their human characteristics. They enter the realm of the angels not as disembodied souls but as spirits with the capacity of sensual experience. While Swedenborg's theological explanation of the soul's life after death may not have pleased all Christians in the eighteenth and nineteenth century, Flaxman's Swedenborgian-inspired art would become standard in funerary sculpture and design. The dead would be portrayed at their graves as they were when they died.

Swedenborg described in vivid detail the life of the dead in the spirit world. There men and women could no longer hide their inner natures, but lived in communities of people of similar character. Folly, greed, theological error, and all the other human frailties could not be disguised, but appeared clearer than they might on earth. When the famous Martin Luther entered the spirit world he received a house just like his earthly home at Eisleben. There "he erected a sort of throne, somewhat elevated, where he sat." Students came to him and he placed those most sympathetic to his views closest to the throne and those who challenged him farther away. Eventually Luther contacted the visiting Swedenborg and discovered that a new revelation replaced his earthly reforms. "At this," recalled the visionary, "he became very angry and railed." Through his conversations with Swedenborg, however, Luther became persuaded of his errors and even laughed at his former teachings. At death even the great reformer Luther faced a life not different from his earthly existence. He did not achieve immediate bliss or eternal damnation for his arrogance and false beliefs. In the Swedenborgian spirit world, he was slowly educated in heavenly matters. Only then could he move into a higher state of spiritual being.[12]

Spirits moved into heaven by perfecting their psychological and spiritual outlook. They were not punished or purged in the spirit world but instead they associated with others of a similar level of development until they were ready for the higher state of heaven. On achieving that state, they became angels. One of the angels' duties was to teach the spirits how to discover their higher natures. The angels first took the spirits to cities, gardens, parks, and "splendid places" and delighted their outer senses. Then, by urging the spirits to examine their own lives, the angels encouraged the shift of attention from the external loveliness of heaven to more important inward concerns. Finally, for those who responded properly to these two steps, the angels taught the spirits "as befits [their] own intrinsic character and ability to receive." Those who received such teaching discovered the paths in the spirit world which led into heaven. Those who at an earlier stage failed to move beyond the external to the internal did not receive angelic instruction, and thus could not see the paths to heaven but only to hell. Nothing but their own character and refusal to become spiritually alive condemned them to hell. Swedenborg radically departed from the orthodox Christian belief in an individual and final judgment. The spirit, not God, ultimately decided where to spend eternity.[13]

Heaven was not a distinct space but an environment perceived only by the spiritually aware. Swedenborg insisted that all angels were once living people. Moreover, angels were not asexual beings but sexually differentiated humans who, through their own spiritual development in the afterlife, evolved into the almost divine state of angelhood (Pl. 35). The angels in heaven reflected the narrow gap between the worlds of earth and heaven. "On the basis of all my experience, covering to date many years," Swedenborg wrote, "I can insist that angels are complete people in form. They do have faces, eyes, ears, chests, arms, hands, and feet. . . . In short, nothing proper to man whatever is missing." In contrast with the Platonic philosophers of his day, Swedenborg argued that the angels are "not formless minds, not ethereal gases, but people to a T." Although "not clothed with a material body" they experience everything which they did on earth. Angels see, hear, feel and think, only to a much higher and more refined level. Life in the spirit world and life in heaven continue the positive and eternal aspects of life on earth.[14]

Swedenborg developed the notion of the continuity between life and afterlife to a high degree. By travelling back and forth between the world of the spirits and this world he dramatized the close proximity of the two realms. Since the personality continues unchanged after death, there is no radical remaking of the human character. Eating, drinking, "marriage delights," parks, and cities remain in the other world. Both the spirit world and the heavens depicted by Swedenborg emphasize not the discontinuity between the living and the dead, but the maintenance of earthly character, institutions, and sensibilities. While assenting to Calvin's notion that something happens immediately after death, Swedenborg rejected the millennial, Anabaptist, and Lutheran notions that the soul sleeps between death and the Last Judgment. Swedenborg detailed an afterlife which echoed the popular sentiments summarized by Isaac Watts: only a narrow sea divides heavenly life from our own.

Pl. 35.   Female and male angel. Engraving by William Sharp after
Benjamin West. 1779. Jacob Duché, *Discourses on Various Subjects*
(London: Phillips, 1779), I, frontispiece

The Material Character of Heaven

"I once saw three spirits newly arrived from the world, who were wandering about, observing and inquiring," reports Swedenborg. They were surprised to have real bodies of flesh and bones (which they thought to lie in their graves) and to find themselves in a material environment. "To free themselves of all doubt...they now and again inspected and touched themselves and others. Moreover, they felt objects." Eventually "by a thousand proofs," they convinced themselves that the spirit world does not radically differ from the earth. Swedenborg's anecdote dramatizes a conviction he shared with other theologians of the seventeenth and eighteenth centuries: that the beyond is recognizable, tangible, and material. This belief rested on the appreciation of the material world in general. Swedenborg accepted, as did many other theologians of this period, that God gave the material world as a gift to humankind. Rather than being a source of temptation, nature was perceived as being intrinsically good. The material quality of paradise described in theological writings and created in the arts in no way diminished heaven's sacred nature. Heaven, while being pure spirit, could still have sensual characteristics. Flowers could be touched and smelled, food could be eaten and bodily pleasures could be enjoyed.[15]

In the heaven visited by Swedenborg, the angels maintained societies similar to earthly ones, only more perfect in form (Pl. 36 and Pl. 37). These societies contained cities with "avenues, streets, and squares."

Pl. 36.   Swedenborg, *Cities in the Spirit World* (original drawing). 18th century. Emanuel Swedenborg, *The Spiritual Diary* (1889; New York: Swedenborg Foundation, 1978), IV, 364

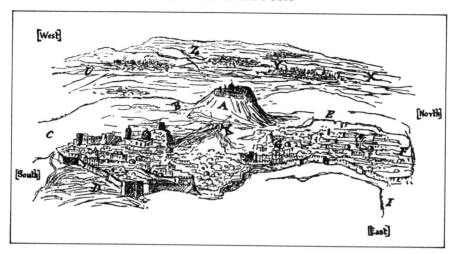

Pl. 37. Swedenborg, *Cities in the Spirit World* (modern interpretation). Emanuel Swedenborg, *The Spiritual Diary* (1889; New York: Swedenborg Foundation, 1978), IV, 365

There the angels lived in houses, "like the dwellings on earth which we call homes, except that they are more beautiful. They have rooms, suites, and bedrooms, all in abundance. They have courtyards, and are surrounded by gardens, flower beds, and lawns." The environment in which the angels lived reflected their inner state and level of spiritual development. The angels of the lowest heaven dwelt in "regions that look like rocky crags," the angels of the spiritual heaven resided in areas "that look like hills," and the angels of the highest, celestial, heaven lived for the most part in the higher regions that look like mountains rising from the earth." For Swedenborg the world of heaven was sensual — it could be seen, touched, smelled, tasted, and had spatial qualities.[16]

In order to understand how Swedenborg justified a material heaven radically different from ascetic, theocentric notions, we must first understand his "law of correspondence." In our casual, everyday existence we respond to the world as if things are comprised only of their appearance and have no connection to us as perceivers. A tree or a plant possesses "treeness" or "plantness" independently of our perception. Our psychological or moral state cannot alter the appearance of the plant or tree because a tree is just a tree; it has no deeper dimension. For Swedenborg, however, "nature was created simply to clothe the spiritual." There existed in the material world a far deeper dimension than a quick glance might reveal. Underneath the appearances was a spiritual reality. Matter was not alienated or separated from spirit, but essentially one with it.

"The whole natural world corresponds to the spiritual world," reiterated Swedenborg, "not just the natural world in general, but actually in details." For each element of the natural, material world there was a corresponding spiritual counterpart. "Heaven is yoked with earth by means of correspondences" summarized Swedenborg. Heaven might be sacred and spiritual although looking very fleshy and material, because everything on earth derived its life and essence from the spiritual world of heaven. Swedenborg's highly developed sense of analogy enabled him to see higher realities in common things, and thus to build a bridge from the earthly world to the realm of the divine.[17]

Everything which appears in heaven – from plants, to the clothing of angels, to the types of cities – has a direct connection to the psychospiritual level of the angelic person who perceives them. For instance, to Swedenborg two angels appeared at a distance to be small children. But upon closer inspection they were actually fully grown adults. Since their level of highly prized spiritual innocence was well developed, they looked like infants. To other angels "involved in intelligence, there appear gardens and parks full of every kind of tree and flower...[the angels] gather flowers, make wreaths, and adorn little children with them." Likewise, the spiritually underdeveloped may appear as animals. "Some, when explored by the angels," wrote Swedenborg in his *Spiritual Diary*, "appear as cats." Cats manage to exist in the heavens even though they are the expressions of those people who have "listened to the sermons, but have given no heed whatever to the things that were preached." Normally souls who "did not imbibe any knowledge of truth and good" would be uncomfortable in the lofty atmosphere of heaven. Cats, however, "are able to be in the sphere of the divine without being tortured." This was how Baron Stjerncrona, the husband of one of Swedenborg's female friends, appeared in the other world.[18]

The sensual world of heaven directly reflects the spiritual state of its inhabitants. Everything which exists in the other world represents the "affection" of some spirit or angel. Thus heavenly, spiritual themes are not left as purely abstract, theoretical ideas. They are clothed and invested with sensual existence and thus look very much like the forms found in the natural world of earth. Angels in heaven perceive things by their senses but "with far more clarity, crispness, and vividness." Matter, rather than being condemned as secondary and derivative of the divine, actually serves as the means by which the divine can be expressed.[19]

Heaven by no means exists merely as an Epicurean dream filled with joys and riches. Unless spirits recognize that heaven is a *state* of love and not merely a place, they will not be able to appreciate its full beauty. At one point in his other-worldly travels, Swedenborg's angel guide brought him to a beautiful rose garden surrounded by olive, orange, and citron trees. There sat several spirits wailing and weeping. When asked why they cried, one replied, "It is now the seventh day since we came into this paradise. When we entered, our minds seemed as though elevated into heaven and admitted to the inmost enjoyment of its joys. But after three days this happiness began to grow dull and to be diminished in our minds and become imperceptible, and so to become null." The fear that they had lost the delights of eternal life caused their sorrow. The angels reassured them that their anxiety was only ignorance of the true nature of heavenly life. External joys are shallow without the corresponding internal joys. The internal values of charity, love, wisdom, and truth — which issue from the divine – make the external delights eternally joyful.[20]

Consequently, Swedenborg rejected those earthly religious systems which questioned the worth of the material world and asked Christians to live an ascetic life. His ethics permitted an honest man or woman on earth to acquire wealth and "be splendidly housed in keeping with [their] status." As long as Christians think seriously about God and live justly and honestly within their community, they are preparing for heaven. "The rich enter heaven as easily as the poor," explained Swedenborg. One is not automatically accepted into heaven because one has lived in poverty. Quite skeptical of the ascetic world-renouncers of his day who sought only to meditate on God, Swedenborg revealed that "in the other life they are of mournful character; they avoid others who are not like themselves. They are resentful when they do not receive happiness beyond the lot of others, believing that they have earned it. Nor do they care about other people; they avoid the duties of charity, which are the means to a bond with heaven." Heaven is not the antithesis of earth, but rather the distilled essence of the true and beautiful found in earthly existence. Heaven continues the meaningful activities and character-istics of earth because it functions as the *source* of that goodness.[21]

The idea that heaven possesses a material, sensual character and continues the goodness found on earth appeared in other seventeenth- and eighteenth-century writings. Swedenborg was not alone in de-scribing a heavenly world filled with earthly pleasures. Beginning in the seventeenth century, a this-worldly optimism overtook much of Europe. Rediscovering Stoic philosophy, many Protestants and Catholics alike insisted that the world was fundamentally good and that one could learn how to live in harmony with a beautiful and ordered nature. The ancient concept of "nature" was slightly Christianized into "creation," but the message remained the same. Even human nature, although wounded by sin, retained its nobility which could be renewed through biblical revelation and human reason. Catholics and Protestants, who rejected the opulence and sensuality of baroque society and condemned the humanistic leanings of philosophical thought, often found themselves a persecuted minority. Their theocentric, ascetic heaven sharply con-flicted with the materialistic heaven of some of their contemporaries.

Rather than stand in fear and trembling in the hands of an angry God, some Protestant and Catholic theologians and artists rejected the theocentric heaven of the reformers and proclaimed the mercy of God and the magnificence of humankind. Swedenborg's visions make more sense when viewed as an expression of the optimistic spirit of his age.

In the first few years of the seventeenth century a Lutheran pastor, Philipp Nicolai (1556–1608), became quite well known for his speculation on life in heaven. A prolific writer and poet, his hymns are still known and sung in Germany. His two books on heaven, *The Mirror of Joy in Life Everlasting* (1599) and *Theory of Eternal Life* (1606), move far beyond the teachings of Martin Luther, although they quote the reformer extensively. Nicolai radically broke with earlier Lutheran interpretations which insisted that the heavenly "mansions" spoken about in Scripture did not imply literal "cities, village, houses, and cottages" but should be taken as "flowery words and pleasant parables." When Nicolai left his small Westphalian parish and became the pastor of a Lutheran community in the cosmopolitan port city of Hamburg, his speculations on heaven assumed a vivid character.[22]

Following Lutheran tradition, Nicolai ignored the question of what the soul does immediately after death. For him, heavenly life commences at the end of the world when God establishes the redeemed on a renewed earth. According to Nicolai, at the end of time the material structure of the earth will remain largely intact. Continents, landscapes, and cities will flourish, and the climate will be much more pleasant than in overcast Germany. Only the sea will no longer exist, thus enabling greater ease of communication and travel. In this renewed heavenly earth, each individual will live in the nation to which he or she belongs by birth, language, or culture. Aliens who reside in foreign countries will be restored to their original homeland. Since all the nations now live in peace and harmony, travel will become an important pastime. Foreign languages will be readily understood, just as the audience at Pentecost understood the apostle's sermon even though they spoke different languages. Nicolai mused about the joys of returning home from such heavenly visits – recounting adventures, showing off souvenirs, and even presenting maps and engravings of distant places. The geographical and sensual immediacy of Nicolai's writings is far removed from the cautious, tempered worldliness of Luther's teachings. His openness to the world and his delight in creation, as well as his fondness of travelling (although he never travelled himself), reflect the optimistic spirit of the seventeenth century, which embraced life as basically good and looked forward to a renewed world at the end of time.[23]

A Catholic version of similar ideas appeared a generation later in the works of a Capuchin friar, Martin of Cochem (1634–1712). Friar Martin, one of the most prolific authors of German baroque Catholicism,

Pl. 38.   G. Köler, *The Heavenly Jerusalem.* 1630. Johann Mattäus Meyfart, *Von dem himmlischen Jerusalem* (Nuremberg: Endters, 1633), I, detail of frontispiece

published numerous editions of his explanation of the Mass in Latin for priests and in the vernacular for the laity. His prayer books, lives of the saints, and meditations on the life of Christ were devotional bestsellers reissued into the nineteenth and twentieth centuries. In 1680 he appended to his *Large Life of Christ* a series of meditations, "On the Four Last Things: Death, Judgment, Hell, and the Kingdom of Heaven." While we can attribute part of Nicolai's "naturalism" to his placement of heaven on a renewed earth, following Catholic belief the righteous enter Martin of Cochem's heaven immediately after death. Yet the similarity in the degree of sensuality of the two theologians' heavens is striking.

"The first thing we have to realize," Martin warned, "is that heaven is not something spiritual as some suppose, but something corporeal, made of some kind of matter and having form and substance." Departing from traditional scholastic theology, he insisted that heaven cannot be empty. "What joys," the friar asked, "could the saints' five senses have, if in heaven nothing could be seen except for a huge, immense space?" Consequently, God fills heaven with "a real river, real trees, real fruit, and real flowers that please our vision, taste, smell, and touch in un-surpassable ways." The blessed thus spend their days strolling "about the heavenly flower-gardens and the heavenly meadows and fields, behold-ing and plucking those pleasant little flowers and all kinds of noble little plants." The mansions in heaven are also real. The palace of Christ dominates the heavenly city, followed in diminishing splendor by the palace of the Virgin Mary, the twelve palaces of the apostles, and finally the palaces and mansions of the other saints.[24]

The sensuality of Martin of Cochem's heaven is perhaps most

dramatically expressed through the architecture and interior ornamentation of German baroque and rococo churches. During the period between 1650 and 1780, Italian ceiling design combined with indigenous art styles to produce a flurry of richly decorated churches in southern Germany, Austria, Bohemia, and Switzerland. These churches display the characteristically baroque appreciation of the sensual, dramatic, and pictorial. They gather their inspiration not only from theological treatises but from the opulence of Versailles, the theatricality of court drama, and the seventeenth-century fascination with the transitoriness of earthly life. Through ceiling frescos, stucco work, and carved sculpture, the churches embody the Counter-Reformation assertion of the tangible quality of religion. As part of a missionary effort to regain the commitments of the people, the Catholic church triumphantly proclaimed the glories of heaven. Heaven and earth, spirit and matter, were joined in the baroque church.

In the Swabian pilgrimage church of Steinhausen (1728–33), designed by Dominikus Zimmermann and decorated by his brother Johann Baptist, a heavenly scene dominates the ceiling (Pl. 39). Mary and the saints whirl upwards as if caught by a gust of wind. The roundness of the clouds, the lush colors of their clothes, and fullness of their bodies provide a rich example of a sensual heaven. This heaven rests on symbolic representations of the four continents, each displaying with pride its bountiful wealth. The Garden of Eden, depicted at the back of the church, symbolically balances a cultivated garden in the front. No snake mars the beauty and hopefulness of the Garden. The Zimmermann brothers freely called upon nature, in either its wild state or its domesticated beauty, to symbolize salvation. Throughout the church, cherubs frolic amid squirrels, spiders, flowers, and birds. For the pilgrim to Steinhausen, heaven reflects the fullness of both the natural and the cultivated world.[25]

Speculation on the material character of heaven was not confined to Swedenborgians, Lutherans, and Catholics. In Zurich, Reformed minister Johann Caspar Lavater (1741–1801) wrote a work on heaven entitled *Prospects of Eternity*, the four volumes of which appeared between 1768 and 1778. Although Lavater knew and felt encouraged by Swedenborg's work, he seems to have developed his interest in the spiritual world independently. Lavater, better known in his day than Swedenborg, corresponded with Moses Mendelsohn, Goethe, and the spouse of the Russian Czar. *Prospects of Eternity* consists of a series of "letters" written to his friend J.G. Zimmermann, a physician to British royalty in Hannover and a recent widower. According to Lavater, the blessed will not only occupy a renewed earth at the end of time, but will be able to move about the infinite worlds of the universe.[26]

In the same manner that Nicolai predicted that the saints would travel

Pl. 39. Johann Baptist Zimmermann, *Mary in the glory of Heaven*. 1733. Ceiling fresco of Wallfahrtskirche Steinhausen, Germany

throughout the earth, Lavater described "pleasure travels to other places of both heaven and earth." The earth, however, as the place where Christ lived, provides "the natural climate of the blessed." There the saints will spend their time in a variety of occupations, including constructing buildings and creating paradisal gardens. Since it is not unworthy of the saints to live in heavenly palaces, why "should it be unworthy of us to erect houses for living, halls for meetings, and mansions for pleasure, and to ornament these or change them in accordance with our purposes or pleasures?" God will not merely provide everything for the saints; they themselves will transform the earth into paradise. "Why should it be unsound to assume," Lavater queried, "that it will be left to our own wisdom and discretion to make, plant, water, and decorate such

198

paradises?" Lavater's heaven was distinctly sensual: "We will have bodies, live in corporeal worlds, will have to deal with material, sensual objects, and form one or more societies." Even within the Reformed tradition, voices could be heard which foresaw a heaven of earthly delights.[27]

Swedenborg's heaven, filled with houses and parks, has its counterpart in the heavens pictured by many conventional Catholic and Protestant theologians and artists. While Aquinas's medieval heaven, devoid of plants and animals, may have been the standard for Catholic theology, the church still permitted a variety of depictions of the other life – especially when these promised to be useful for Counter Reformation concerns. The sensuality of the Renaissance heaven survived the Reformation and the attacks of the Jansenists and other Catholic reformers. Likewise, a diversity existed in Protestant theology. Pietists, Puritans, Methodists, and others who preferred an ascetic, theocentric theology created a powerful model of paradise as an ethereal world filled with psalm-singing or silent contemplation. While this heaven functioned as the normative description for many Protestants until the nineteenth century, writers like Nicolai and Lavater promoted other perspectives. Swedenborg's visions of a material afterlife, however, is unique in its scope and richness of detail.

Matter in Motion

Swedenborg not only rejected abstract notions of heaven, he defied the traditional preference for stasis over motion, sameness over variety, and contemplation over activity. If there exists an "odd, dry precision to his descriptions of Heaven that suggests the engineer far more than the mystic," then his preference for a dynamic, motion-filled heaven suggests Swedenborg the scientist, fascinated with a mechanistic universe and the organic growth of the body. For him there could be no fundamental division between the natural world of matter in motion and the spiritual world. If movement served as the basis for the natural world, then movement must be intrinsic to the source of the natural world, the divine world of heaven.[28]

By denying the possibility of either a personal judgment at death or a Last Judgment at the end of time, Swedenborg challenged the long-standing Christian belief in static heavenly conditions. From his perspective, the idea that God judged the soul fundamentally good and worthy of heaven or fundamentally bad and destined for hell (or in need of a few years of purging) underestimated the goodness of God and the

(3) **celestial heaven**	paradise restored, inhabitants male and female "celestial" angels
(2) **spiritual heaven**	civilized society idealized, inhabitants male and female "spiritual" angels
(1) **natural heaven**	life very similar to earthly existence, inhabitants male and female "natural" angels
spirit world	door to heaven and hell, inhabitants male and female spirits
earth	our world

Fig. 6.   The spiritual universe of Swedenborg

capabilities of humankind. Men and women were free agents who could choose good or evil, even after death. In the beyond it would be up to the individual, and not to God, to decide which type of eternity he or she wanted to experience. God did not save souls merely to place them on a heavenly hierarchical ladder where they could never move closer to the divine center. It would be up to the spirit, transformed eventually into an angel, to seek higher and higher realms of being. If the spirit rejected the possibility of full spiritual life, then he or she would drift farther down into the abyss of hell. No final sentence by God decided the fate of the soul.

The angels in heaven, according to Swedenborg, live in communities with those of a similar state of psycho-spiritual development. Although each community is unique, and some angels do not even live in communities, Swedenborg discovered that heavenly life divides into three worlds (Fig. 6). The angels of each of these realms do not socialize with one another because of their different degrees of spiritual awareness. In the natural heaven, the lowest of the three levels, the angels' "understanding is raised but little above what it was while they were in the world." Given the poverty of their spiritual capacities, these angels "sometimes suffer hard times," although obedience to the divine prevents distress. In the spiritual kingdom, the middle level, angels demonstrate the love between themselves in a form of Christian charity. Wise officials administer laws and "in cases of doubt, they are enlightened by the Lord." Angels in the spiritual heaven have a clergy and worship in elegant churches made of stone. Those angels who "are especially involved in the light of wisdom" sit in front of the preaching clergy, those "in lesser light" to the right and left, and "newcomers sit near the door." Sometimes hypocrites enter into their communities, "but they cannot stay around very long, because they begin to feel pain inside, to feel tortured, to turn blue in the face, and almost to die."[29]

In the celestial kingdom, the highest heaven, the angels develop their spiritual propensities most fully. We might suspect that in this exalted realm the angels would wear more elegant clothes, their houses would be more spectacular, and their churches more refined. However, the angels in the highest heaven are naked. "The angels are naked," Swedenborg explained, "because nakedness corresponds to innocence." Real innocence, for Swedenborg, was wisdom, and it physically manifested itself as "a very beautiful child, very much alive, and naked." In a similar manner, there are no churches in the celestial kingdom, only wooden "houses of God" of no grandeur. Since the angels in that kingdom focus their love on God, and not in charity to one another, they need no clergy. Every angel can spontaneously preach to his or her fellow angels. There is no angelic government in the highest heaven; all direction and guidance comes from God.[30]

The life of the African nations, according to Swedenborg, most closely resembles life in the celestial kingdom. When Africans die they form communities and live much the same way they did on earth. Africans "think interiorly" and actively follow their religion and its laws out of love, while Europeans (representatives of the spiritual kingdom) are merely born into their religion and follow its doctrine only because of its authority. In heaven, the highest angelic communities bear the characteristics which Swedenborg associated with African societies – naked, primitive, anarchic, and spontaneous. Male angels grow long beards and use a primitive script unintelligible to others. While many angels enjoy a life in a courtly, luxurious setting, they are not as highly developed as the angels of the celestial sphere. Unfortunately, Swedenborg – perhaps because of his own state of spiritual development – only permits us to see sporadic glimpses of life in this highest heaven.[31]

Swedenborg detested the artifice and hypocrisy of contemporary Christians. He insisted that in heaven one's exterior appearance and abode corresponds to one's innermost feelings. As the angels experience "more inward states of joy" they "arrive at a state of peace to the very core...a state of innocence that touches their very inmost capacity for feeling." Spiritual maturation meant the process of growth into a state of innocence. "People in heaven progress steadily toward the springtime of life," summarized Swedenborg, "and the more thousands of years they live, the more pleasant and happy the springtime. This goes on forever, with the increase keeping pace with the growth and level of their love, charity, and faith." Just as Adam and Eve in paradise felt no shame in their nakedness and lived a life of simple harmony with nature, so do the angels of the highest sphere of heaven.[32]

In Swedenborg's concept of spiritual progress, the soul does not become more sophisticated as it progresses, but more childlike. The highest heaven is not an idealized eighteenth-century society but a paradise restored. Heavenly progress entails moving from the civilized state of law, government, religion, and architecture to the simple state of the noble savage. Like many Enlightenment thinkers, Swedenborg rejected the earlier baroque preoccupation with artifice, artistic illusion, superfluous extravagance, and idle entertainment. Swedenborg's vision of heaven harmonizes well with certain ideas of the philosopher and social critic Jean-Jacques Rousseau (1712–78). In a variety of works published during this same period, Rousseau also rejected much of European culture. Rousseau extolled the simplicity of rural life, condemned the hypocrisy and deceit of so-called civilization, and encouraged readers to live in accordance with the basic goodness of their human natures. In contrast to Rousseau, however, Swedenborg recognized that few could attain the perfection of their natural state of innocence and simplicity. Nothing was intrinsically wrong with the riches of civilization experienced on earth or in heaven, as long as charity, love, faith, and wisdom ruled. The problem of an artificial society was not culture itself, but the falseness, selfishness, and ruthlessness covered up by superficial beauty.

The movement toward spiritual perfection neither followed a straight, upward path nor occurred in the same manner for all angels. While the angels could not move permanently into another kingdom or community until they were spiritually prepared, they could experience vacillation within their own state. Sometimes the angels felt an intense love and at other times a milder variety. "When they are at the peak of love," wrote Swedenborg, "they are in the light and warmth of their life, surrounded by radiance and delight. When they are at the bottom of the scale, they are in shade and cold, or in a shrouded and unpleasant state." Rather than presuming that the angels must make steady progress in their spirituality, Swedenborg acknowledged that the love of the angels changed daily like "light and shade, warmth and cold, or morning, noon, evening, and night in the world, showing an unfailing variety during the year." If angels only experienced the continued growth of their spiritual state then boredom would eventually occur. For Swedenborg, anything pleasant would deteriorate gradually if experienced forever, without respite. Swedenborg revealed yet other examples of spiritual vacillation. The angels, he felt, were still stained with an amount of egoism and vanity; it was only through fighting against these attitudes that they could steel their spiritual strength. And finally, the "perception and awareness of what is good is made more delicate by fluctuations between things pleasant and unpleasant."[33]

Swedenborg valued variety in motion and continual movement toward the divine. From his perspective, heavenly perfection would have necessitated the cessation of spiritual progress. To expect consistency in heaven overlooked the diverse character of the natural order which reflected the spiritual order. Since no soul experienced heaven or hell in the same way as any other, and one's visual appearance reflected one's inner state, then "no person, spirit, or angel exists anywhere who is exactly like another, even in his facial features." Angels in heaven constantly changed their spiritual state which, in turn, changed their clothes, their faces, and their position in the heavenly kingdoms. Nothing in heaven ever remained the same.[34]

Angels changed and developed in heaven not because of their appreciation of the beatific vision but because of their own activities. Swedenborg denied the popular belief that heaven is a place of ease where the saved are served by others. He rejected the New Testament idea that heavenly joy consists solely in praising and glorifying the Lord. For Swedenborg, only the active life of service and charity refines one's spiritual being. Eternal rest and contemplation "would not be an active life, but an idle one, in which they [the angels] would grow torpid." The Lord does not need praise and celebration, but prefers the angels to love and do acts of charity for one another. Since everything which the angels need is given to them, every activity in which they engage is performed out of love and not from a sense of duty or requirement.[35]

The angels in heaven busied themselves with a variety of charitable activities. It was up to the more highly developed souls to teach and instruct the newly arrived. Angels encouraged newcomers to separate themselves from evil influences in the spirit world, revealed to the worthy the depths of the inner world, and finally introduced the best prepared into heaven. This instruction continued in the spiritual heaven through sermons preached by the angelic clergy. In heaven, young maidens embroidered flowers on white linen which they used or gave to others. Other women, who loved children while in the world, took care of babies in heaven. Although the women were not the natural mothers, they devoted their lives to these young charges as if they were. Some angels were sent to earth to watch over and guard living people. Angels who had loved justice and the common good while on earth found themselves involved in "civic concerns" in heaven. Each task performed by an angel corresponded to his or her inner state and was performed out of love, not obligation. If the angels refused or could not provide some function for the community then they were "thrown out of heaven because their nature is different." For Swedenborg, fulfilling a useful function in the heavenly society meant displaying divine love. To refuse to act meant to reject the common good and prefer the less spiritual – to work for one's own sake.[36]

As we have seen, the question of what the saints actually do in heaven has troubled theologians since the early Church Fathers. Scholastic thought, which emphasized the beatific vision, rejected the notion that movement and progress are essential to heavenly bliss. Thomas Aquinas held that at the end of time, when the righteous fully inhabit the empyrean heaven, the universe will stand still. Movement, for Aquinas, indicated a continual cycle of growth and decay. Perfection meant the replacement of motion with eternal stasis. The blessed in heaven, relegated to their specific level in the heavenly hierarchy, feel no desire to experience anything other than the vision of God. Contemplation, based on the unsurpassable knowledge of God, replaces the active life. There can be no progress or increase in happiness in this perfect world.

While some medieval writers and Renaissance artists tried to soften the views of Aquinas, only the reworking of Christianity accomplished by the Protestant Reformation provided the theoretical foundation to challenge the lack of heavenly movement and the superiority of divine contemplation. Swedenborg's prediction of heavenly progress, while much fuller than that of any of his contemporaries, was by no means unique. Eighteenth-century Protestant theologians felt fairly comfortable in describing an action-filled heaven where the soul would experience an eternal increase of happiness and knowledge. Christians increasingly found progress and activity to be essential to the experience of life itself and therefore of eternal life.

To understand the origins of progress in heaven we return again to Calvin and the question of what happens to the righteous soul between death and the Last Judgment. Having established that the soul is awake and not asleep, Calvin argued in *Psychopannychia* that at death the soul does not immediately achieve perfect union with God. While at death God frees the soul from its cumbersome body and the "warfare of this world," the soul still lacks its spiritual body. Only after the Last Judgment, when the soul unites with its spiritual body and accomplishes full union with God, can happiness be perfect. Calling on classical philosophy, Calvin explained that since the soul lacks something it cannot be at perfect rest: "Though there is no impatience in their desire, their rest is not yet full and perfect, since he is said to rest who is where he desires to be; and the measure of desire has no end till it has arrived where it was tending." For Calvin desire is something dynamic; it keeps the soul in motion, "on the run" (*in cursu*) toward the divine. "Their desire is always moving onward till the glory of God is complete, and this completion awaits the judgment day." Calvin opened up the possibility that, at least until the soul is united with the spiritual body, it progresses in blessedness. In the intermediate period – between death and the Last

Judgment – the possibility of progress exists because one does not achieve full glorification upon arrival in the other world.[37]

That some type of progress exists in heaven was of only minimal concern for Calvin. His major purpose in *Psychopannychia* was to counter the Anabaptist theory of soul-sleeping by asserting its scriptural errancy. Heaven, for Calvin, "is nothing else than that union with God by which they are fully in God, are filled by God, in their turn cleave to God, completely possess God – in short, are 'one with God.' " Heaven is union with the divine, not the process of achieving that union. In this Calvin did not differ from Aquinas or from other theocentric perspectives on heaven. Once the saint is united with the divine after the Last Judgment, all progress stops. For Calvin, God chooses those who will dwell with him in heaven even before their birth. He condemned the idea of purgatory as unscriptural and superstitious. God gives the saints a type of heavenly progression (which involves no purging) as a free gift, like grace, to increase their glory and blessedness. Since the righteous dead have already achieved sainthood, there could be no further purification. Calvin would have had no patience with Swedenborg's scheme of everlasting saintly progress, activity, and service.[38]

Two hundred years after Calvin, however, philosophers and theologians influenced by Enlightenment views of progress and activity were less concerned with the end result of the movement toward God and more with the movement itself. While Calvin might have originated the idea of progress in heaven, it was theologians influenced by Enlightenment notions of earthly progress who changed heaven from a place of rest to a center of activity. From Diderot to Benjamin Franklin and Hume, Enlightenment thinkers extolled the life of action, this-worldly accomplishments, and human initiative. "All over the West," writes historian Peter Gay, "in London as in Philadelphia, philosophers joined articulate businessmen in commending ceaseless activity and preached the postponement of immediate gratification for the sake of some higher and more enduring satisfaction." We are no longer passive captives to the vicissitudes of nature or the punishments of a meddlesome God. The rationalists asserted the capabilities of humankind: through the active life of either the *philosophe* or the merchant, personal and societal change could be accomplished.[39]

While historians debate whether or not the *philosophes* first invented the notion of "progress," most agree that intrinsic to the Enlightenment mentality was the belief that only rational activity helped individuals and civilizations progress. Optimism and hope, tempered by what Gay terms "open-eyed pessimism," fuelled the eighteenth-century perception that discoveries in science and the dynamics of human nature indicated an evolving future of increasing progress. For Condorcet (1743–94), who wove a vision of a progressive future on the eve of the French Revolution, the infinite improvement of the human mind and the prolongation of physical life on earth made even heaven seem irrelevant.[40]

During the eighteenth century, discussions of the possibility of progress and activity in the afterlife appeared more frequently in Britain than on the Continent. The religious pluralism and comparative freedom of British society encouraged a variety of perspectives to emerge. In 1703 William Assheton, the rector of Beckenham in Kent and chaplain to the Duke of Ormond, wrote a short tract against those schoolmen who believed that heavenly life consisted "in bare speculation, gazing upon each other, and admiring each other's perfections." With the enthusiasm of a member of the growing British middle class, Assheton asserted that there would certainly be action as well as contemplation in heaven. "Now we are not in the least to suspect, when such multitudes of active beings are met together," he surmised, "that they will be idle; but will incessantly be employed, in mutual giving or receiving commands from each other." Since heaven is God's kingdom it will have "laws and statutes and governors and subjects, and those of different ranks, orders, and degrees." There will be no jealousy among the ruling or the ruled. While Assheton declined to describe the type of employment enjoyed by the saints, he appeared convinced that heavenly life includes service and obedience. Swedenborg, who made London his second home and published many of his works there, would have been sympathetic to such assumptions.[41]

Assheton's insistence on the establishment of a heavenly hierarchy, reflecting the rigid British class structure, eliminated the possibility of movement upward to a higher level of heavenly life. In 1711 Joseph Addison, ignoring the disorienting possibility of altering one's heavenly social position, discussed in some detail the individual's growth in heaven. Addison was not a cleric but an essayist, poet, and statesman. His widely read essays in the *Tatler*, *Spectator* and *Guardian* echoed common sentiments of the London educated classes. Addison rejected the changeless character of sainthood and preferred to argue that the soul progresses perpetually. Only a brute arrives at a point of perfection that is unsurpassable. Life on earth remains too short for people to subdue their passions fully, establish their soul in virtue, and gain their full measure of knowledge. Why would God grant his creatures talents, capacities, and wisdom only to dispense with them so quickly? No, Addison elaborated, God presents us with only the "rudiments of existence here, and afterwards [we will] be transplanted into a more friendly climate, where they may spread and flourish to all eternity." To illustrate how the soul progresses toward the divine without ever reaching the glory of God, Addison concluded his essay with a mathematical analogy of two lines "that may draw nearer to another for all eternity, without a possibility of touching."[42]

While the theocentric heaven of reformed and Puritan circles in Britain continued to set orthodox standards, writers like Assheton and Addison constructed heavens more appealing to "common sense." Without losing his popular standing within the British Noncomformist community, Isaac Watts also believed he presented a commonsense heaven when he filled the afterlife with saintly action, multiple worlds, and endless possibilities. In a funeral sermon delivered in 1722 entitled "Death and Heaven; or the Last Enemy Conquered, and Separate Spirits Made Perfect," Watts described a heaven which stands between the theocentric heaven of Calvin and the anthropocentric heaven of the nineteenth century. Published the same year, the sermon had been through four editions by 1737, and sixteen by 1818; it was translated into German in 1727. Watts's sermon assumed that God still garnered the attention of the saints and directed their activity while acknowledging their enduring human needs. The popularity of Watts, and his acceptance by a variety of Protestant factions, made his view an important step in the creation of a progressive, service-oriented heaven.

Isaac Watts, an author of hymns and catechisms as well as a teacher and minister of an independent church in London, prepared him to make "pleasing speculations which are agreeable to the word of God, and to the nature and reason of things, and which have often given my thoughts a sacred entertainment." Although never denying the depravity of human nature, he softened Calvinist beliefs and even questioned the doctrine of the Trinity. For the biographer Arthur Paul Davis, "Watts was a product of the rationalistic spirit of the eighteenth century as well as of the believing spirit of the seventeenth." Like Swedenborg, Watts combined a deep-seated spirituality with a feeling for the character and hopes of an increasingly pragmatic Christian community.[43]

Departing from the other-worldly asceticism typical of many Nonconformists, Watts asserted that God gave the world a great variety of riches and pleasures. Since the earth reflected the glories of heaven, it was only reasonable to imagine that an even more diverse environment existed in heaven. Likewise, the Creator endowed men and women with differing turns of genius and manner of thoughts, and so "why should not every pious mind or spirit carry to heaven with it so much of that turn and manner, as is natural and innocent?" Personality characteristics, those aspects which made an individual an individual, continued in the afterlife. Everyone in heaven was "perfect and free from sinful defects," but each soul might "be exceedingly different in degree according to the different capacity of spirits." For Watts, this diversity of personality types helped explain the existence of a heavenly hierarchy. Just as some creatures on earth were at a higher level than others, so heavenly beings assumed stations suited to their personalities.[44]

Calvinists considered that only the earth was a place of activity and labor; heaven was for contemplation and rest. Watts rejected this view. Christians accustomed to expressing their faith through an active life would not be satisfied with a passive beatific vision. "When angels are so variously and delightfully employed in service for God, in his several known and unknown worlds," reflected Watts, "we cannot suppose the spirits of just men shall be eternally confined to a sedentary state of inactive contemplation." Although contemplation "indeed is a noble pleasure," the very sight of the divine "will awaken and animate all the active and sprightly powers of the soul." Watts concluded that rather than being confined to eternal meditation, the soul will "set all the springs of love and zeal at work in the most illustrious instances of unknown and glorious duty." Since no weariness connected with work can exist in heaven, the saints all desire to join in the work of God. "Those spirits who have tasted unknown delight and satisfaction in many long seasons of devotion, and in a thousand painful services for their blessed Lord on earth," Watts reminded us, "can hardly bear the thoughts of paying no active duties, doing no work at all for him in heaven, where business is all over delight, and labour is all enjoyment." Active Christians, who have followed the Protestant preference for this-worldly spirituality, will not be satisfied with an eternity of meditation but will serve God "perhaps as priests in his temple, and as kings, or viceroys, in his wide dominions." Watts surrounded himself with pious men and women noted for their business acumen and philanthropy; none of them would appreciate a heaven of idle contemplation.[45]

Watts added the notion of "service" to what the saints do in heaven. Going beyond the concept of activity described by Baxter, he insisted that the saints will be given real tasks to perform. They will often be engaged "millions at once, in social worship," and sometimes individuals will be caught up in the beatific vision with "their intellectual powers . . . almost lost in sweet amazement." Eternal singing and everlasting meditation, however, could satisfy neither God nor the saints. Like Swedenborg, Watts portrayed heaven as a continuation of the good service performed by Christians on earth. His examples include the reporting of the "faithful execution of some divine commission" and ruling "over inferior ranks of happy spirits" or over "whole provinces of intelligent beings in lower regions." Serving God meant not only praise but also ruling as governors over the worlds and ranks which comprise the heavenly cosmos.[46]

Unlike Swedenborg, Watts does not give us a complete picture of these heavenly kingdoms. We do not know, for instance, whether the kings successfully reign forever over the less saintly. We do know that God restricts no soul – king or subject – to one type of service. "Among the pleasures and engagements of the upper world," Watts explained, "there shall be always something new and entertaining." "Perpetual change" assured that a "rotation of businesses and joys shall succeed one another through the ages of eternity." Such change occurs because at death the soul does not become perfect in an absolute sense. For Watts, only God is absolutely perfect. When compared to God, the saint wallows in imperfection. The blessed in heaven appear as perfect beings only when compared to Christians still on earth below. So from an earthly perspective the saints look perfect, but from God's vantage-point there is room for improvement. Consequently, Watts could describe how the soul acquires new knowledge and experiences increasingly refined joy forever.[47]

Souls accomplish this progress through interaction with one another and through the teaching of Christ himself. Is it not possible, Watts asked, that "our Lord Jesus Christ himself be the everlasting teacher of his church? May he not at solemn seasons summon all heaven to hear him publish some new and surprising discoveries?" Watts doubted whether the saints learn in heaven merely from "contemplation of Christ's person." "Is Jesus forever silent?" he queried rhetorically. The saints also converse with each other when they are not involved in service or worship. According to Watts, they are "most delightfully engaged in recounting to each other the wondrous steps of providence, wisdom and mercy." Saints explore "planetary worlds besides that which we inhabit," and they share their "millions of new discoveries of divine power" with their fellow spirits. "When a blessed spirit has dwelt in heaven a thousand years," he summarized, "and conversed with God and Christ, angels and fellow-spirits...shall it know nothing more of the nature and wondrous properties of God than it knew the first moment of its arrival there?" Education, so crucial to Watts's religious outlook, could not be neglected in eternal life.[48]

In his essay, Isaac Watts set forth patterns of heavenly activity which began in the eighteenth century and came to flourish in the nineteenth and early twentieth century. Heaven was a place of continuous variety and change. Writing against soul-sleeping and endless contemplation, Watts portrayed a dynamic, human-oriented heaven. The motionless perfection of the scholastic hereafter made sense only if heaven housed God and the angels. For human happiness to take place, constant growth in knowledge and joy was essential.

For the popular Isaac Watts and the lesser known Emanuel Swedenborg, heaven contained variety, movement, service, and change. Heaven existed for people. The saints still worshipped God, but they also served him as rulers, messengers, and teachers. Swedenborg's angels served each other in true Christian charity. Used to service on earth, those in heaven continued their lives of action free from strain or boredom. Contemplation and meditation, although certainly still part of paradise, was only one dimension. For the pragmatic Watts, Christ chose the more direct method of preaching to his saints rather than mystifying them through the beatific vision. In a typically Protestant fashion, Christ spread his message in heaven by way of the sermon. As hearing the sermon, rather than looking at the elevated host during mass, became the central concern, the visual experience of the divine lost its prevalence. The beatific vision, as articulated by Aquinas and repeated by Catholic theologians, required passive and motionless saints. For many eighteenth-century Protestants, who placed great value in the active life, such total concentration could neither be imagined nor desired.

This is not to say that Watts's heaven was not still strongly theocentric. While he departed from Baxter's *Saints' Everlasting Rest*, he maintained God's primacy. God commanded the attention of the saints and controlled their activities. Variety existed in the other world because God created a heaven and earth filled with "millions of inhabitants" all of whom "proclaim the skill of an Almighty Maker." God permitted the saints to carry their human natures and needs into the divine world, but he remained the controlling force. Unlike with Swedenborg, the saints were not transformed into angels. Heaven was God's world. Even though Watts mentioned that lectures to the younger spirits might be given by those of a more exalted station, Christ himself, and not the angels, functioned as the supreme authority in the beyond.[49]

While Watts showed similarity to Swedenborg in his portrayal of heavenly progress, activity, and service, he maintained an orthodox, theocentric perspective on the controlling nature of God. Swedenborg, on the other hand, though recognizing the all-powerful divine element, allowed the saints more control over their heavenly destinies. It was the spirits themselves, and not God, who had the free will to choose between heaven and hell. God did not sit in judgment over the dead, as the orthodox Watts insisted. Rather, God permitted the personalities and inclinations of the dead to work themselves out – either upward into heaven or downward into hell. Heavenly decisions for Swedenborg were made not by the divine, but by the human. While God created the possibility of progress, men and women were responsible for perfecting their higher spiritual natures.

Society, Friendship, and Love

Swedenborg's visions presented a strongly human-centered heaven. The close proximity of heaven to earth, the continuation of human personality into the next world, the enjoyment of a material, paradisal existence, and the possibility of eternal activity and progress all reflect an anthropocentric view of heaven. The concept of a saintly community in heaven has a long tradition in Christian history, originating in the book of Revelation. Christians acknowledged their belief in the "communion of saints" each time they recited the Apostles' Creed. However, what began during the Renaissance and more clearly in the seventeenth and eighteenth centuries was the recognition that heavenly happiness did not hinge on the vision of God but on the social interaction of the saints. No longer did the saints merely dance with the angels outside the celestial gates; they now enjoyed each other's company in the full sight of the divine.

The Lutheran Philipp Nicolai was one of the first post-Renaissance theologians to feel comfortable discussing the social aspect of eternal life and the probable reunion of righteous family members. He reassured his Westphalian congregation, after a plague claimed thirteen hundred lives, that families would meet in heaven. As early as 1599 he reminded his flock that "parents and children, husband and wife, bridegroom and bride, brother and sister, relatives and neighbors" all separated by the plague would meet again. In the new creation following the end of time, the reunited would love one another "with an ardent, cordial love which is a thousand times stronger, and embrace more friendly than can be thought of in this world." "Love and friendship," he argued, "are not the least part of our intelligent and immortal souls that were redeemed and beatified by Christ." For Nicolai, who imagined a heaven on a renewed earth where travellers delighted in recounting their journeys, families and friends seemed necessary for everlasting happiness.[50]

Nicolai made sure, however, that his statement on reunions in heaven was not misunderstood. There would be no sexual life in paradise. The next world would not be "the Elysian field, or field of worldly delights" made up by poets. Heavenly love involved "no sinful concupiscence, no lascivious lust, and no Epicurean pig's desire." For all his rhetoric of human love in the next world, Nicolai explicitly excluded the sexual dimension from interpersonal relationships. Sexuality would only detract the attention from the divine center; human libido must be focused on God alone. Consequently, images of sexual intimacy were reserved for describing the mutual love of God and the blessed.[51]

From a different direction, the English philosopher Henry More (1614–87) arrived at a similar conclusion. A Cambridge professor of theology noted for his Platonizing prose and poetry, More wrote a lengthy treatise on *The Immortality of the Soul* (1659) which also offered speculations about life in the other world. Life in heaven was primarily a life of study and philosophical debate by "aerial genii" (spirits) devoid of their bodies. Although More's Platonic bias would prevent him from giving too much attention to the body, he could not help treasuring something similar to bodily activities. So at times the souls "sing and play and dance together, reaping the lawful pleasures of the very animal life, in a far higher degree than we are capable of in this world." Like Nicolai, however, More told his readers to keep in mind that "the sweet motions of the spirits in the passions of love" have nothing to do with the "shameful sense of lust" demanded by our "terrestrial body." Apparently he referred to a higher, spiritualized sexuality.[52]

More was caught in the dilemma which plagued those who ventured to discuss the social relationships in heaven. In one particularly ambiguous passage, More first explained that in heaven "there be neither lust, nor difference of sex amongst them." Heavenly activities will comprise "the kindest commotion of mind [and] will never be anything else but an exercise of intellectual love, whose object is virtue and beauty." Here we see the philosopher at his Platonizing best. "Yet it is not improbable," he continued, "that there are some general strictures of discrimination of this beauty into masculine and feminine." To have beauty, yet not to have sexual differences, now appeared to be inconceivable. More completed his thought by going beyond the need for ideal beauty in the other world, and toward a theme he held in common with Renaissance writers and Swedenborg. "It is very harsh to concede," he admitted, "that Aeneas should meet with his lover Dido in the other world in any other form than that of a woman." While the corporeal nature of sexuality prevented its existence in the other world, neither the Lutheran theologian nor the Cambridge Platonist was willing to deny totally the existence of families, social pleasures, and love in the next life.[53]

The notion of sentimental love in heaven, revealed in a minor way in the writings of Nicolai and More, reached a greater height in those of Jean-Jacques Rousseau. Rousseau expressed the romantic wish for an eternal union with one's beloved both in his famous *Confessions* (1782) and in the novel *Julie ou la nouvelle Héloïse* (1759). In the *Confessions*, he described the "greatest, the most powerful, the most irrepressible of all my needs." These needs were not physical or intellectual, but were "entirely in my heart." For Rousseau, this "was the need of a companionship as intimate as was possible." Rousseau broke with the Platonic tradition that saw male-to-male friendship as the greatest form of companionship, and confided that he needed a woman and not a male friend. "This singular want was such that the most intimate corporeal union had been unable to satisfy it," he recalled; "I should have wanted two souls in the same body; without that I was always conscious of a void." Rousseau echoed the feelings of his contemporary Swedenborg and the later Romantic movement of the nineteenth century.[54]

Although written during the "age of reason," Rousseau's *Julie ou la nouvelle Héloïse*, "triumphantly embodies the qualities of romantic love

— it is intuitive, obsessive, passionate, lifelong, and extending to eternity." Due to parental pressures the heroine, Julie, leads a loveless life with her cold husband, Wolmar. At the same time she maintains her love for her tutor, Saint-Preux. In spite of Julie's dedication to her family and willingness to accept a marriage without passion, she never doubts that heaven will permit the eventual reunion with Saint-Preux. In a letter her lover reads after her death she announces, "no, I do not leave you – I go to await you." Death does not mean the end of love; it means its beginning. Julie writes to Saint-Preux that she "purchased at the price of my life the right to love you forever without sin, and to tell you so one more time." Julie, and through her Rousseau, rejects the Protestant minister's claim that in heaven the glory of God is the only object of contemplation with all else forgotten. On the contrary, heaven for Julie is a modern heaven, a place where human love fully blossoms.[55]

By the 1770s Zurich minister Johann Caspar Lavater assumed, as did his fellow countryman Rousseau, that true friends would meet in heaven. He assured the recently widowed Zimmermann that we would have many friends in heaven including: "Adam, Enoch, Noah, Abraham, Elijah, Peter, James, John, Paul, Timothy, Stephen, Cornelius, Mary, Mary Magdalene – my own friends, male and female – oh! – my friends in Hessen, yourself, H..p, G...p, Pf...and Mi...and S..., and my beloved spouse and my children." Lavater easily moved from mentioning our future relationships with biblical characters to his personal friends and family. Although he gave no details on how friends and families would relate to one another, he predicted that loving relationships would have a role in heavenly life.[56]

The meeting of friends and family in heaven occurred frequently in the literature of the eighteenth century. In 1753 the German Protestant author Christoph Martin Wieland imagined scenes in the other world where naked men and women met in picturesque open-air settings, enjoying nature, playing music, and making love. In 1767 the British theologian and social critic Richard Price described the recognition of friends in heaven with much more reserve. Elizabeth Rowe (1674–1737), a close friend of Issac Watts, pictured in her poetry and prose a heaven where "fair spirits in melodious concert join, /And sweetly warble their heroic loves./For love makes half their heaven, and kindles here/New flames, and ardent life in ev'ry breast." Even the skeptical Diderot (1713–87) ventured to write in 1759 to his friend Sophie Volland that perhaps lovers who ask to be buried side by side are not so foolish. "Maybe there is in them a rest of heat and of life," mused Diderot, "which they enjoy in their own way at the bottom of the cold urn wherein their ashes are contained." In the eighteenth century the Cult of Reason was mitigated and made bearable by the Cult of Friendship.[57]

Prior to the late 1700s, Catholic theologians, in contrast to their

Protestant counterparts, ignored the issue of families reuniting in heaven and preferred to emphasize a diffused, generalized friendship. They took as their model the idealized relationships of seventeenth-century European court life for which Versailles was to become the symbol. French theologian François Arnoux (c. 1600), for instance, could not hide his admiration of the royal court in his *Marvels of the Otherworld* (1614). This book reflects a spirit versed in scholastic theology and untouched by the stern spirit of Jansenism and similar movements developing in his days. Locating heaven in the empyrean of scholastic orthodoxy, Arnoux submitted to Aquinas's rejection of eating and drinking in heaven. In spite of this, Arnoux envisioned a sensual heaven which the blessed could enjoy apart from the vision of God. Lush parks and gardens produced the sweet smells of flowers, fruit, and herbs. Roses and carnations in particular delighted the saints. Although no one ate of the heavenly produce, they could enjoy the sense of smell. [58]

The luxurious gardens of paradise, for Arnoux, provided the background for a rich life of leisure in the heavenly court. The blessed made up the citizenry of a heavenly kingdom where pleasure could be endlessly pursued. In the heavenly kingdom, Arnoux explained, "God is the king, the archangels are the pages, the Virgin Mary is the quee, the holy virgins are her ladies-in-waiting and chamber maids, the cherub angels are the dukes, the seraphim the courts. . . and the saints the nobility. . . all the blessed together, however, are the citizens and inhabitants of this glorious kingdom." Untroubled by rival nobility, rising merchant classes, or unruly peasants, heavenly society was comprised not of friends and family but of a queen and ladies-in-waiting. [59]

Although Christ and his family occupied the highest echelon of divine royalty, Arnoux permitted all the blessed to participate in his courtly life. "My Paradise is the Escorial of the angels," Arnoux had Christ explain, "the Louvre of the blessed." There is "nothing greater in this world than being every day near the king. . . and to live with him in the Louvre," added the theologian, echoing contemporary fascination with the royal residence in Paris. As for leisure activities: "There people talk of nothing but pastimes. . . laughter never ceases." While Arnoux did not present his readers with details of the courtly life, two generations later Friar Martin of Cochem provided a fuller account. [60]

Martin described how in heaven the blessed "visit each other, converse with one another, walk about the other's mansion, one participating in the other's bliss." Although the purpose of this was to incite "the other to more praise and glorification of God," the saints obviously enjoyed this social interaction. Each of them had a particular "preference and love" for those who helped him or her to arrive in heaven. With these special patrons the saints shared many of their joys. "For this reason," Friar Martin wrote, "they will meet more often than others, will engage

ET·VITAM AETERNAM AMEN

Pl. 40.   Nicolas de Mathonier, *Life Everlasting*. 1611. N. de Mathonier, *XII articuli fidei apostolicae* (Paris: Mathonier, 1611), pl. 12

in pleasant conversation, and, walking about the heavenly gardens, they will tell one another what their lives were like on earth, and in what wonderful ways the good God has preserved them from damnation." Thus the saints cultivated friendships, were interested in pleasing one another, and led a social life.[61]

In Martin of Cochem's book the saints were no longer caught up entirely in the beatific vision. Happiness occurred not only by experiencing the divine center but also by enjoying the pleasures of social interaction. "They will also play music together," the friar wrote, "and sing psalms, dance and frolick, stroll and amuse themselves, inventing every day another pastime." In Friar Martin's commentary, heavenly music, performed only for divine worship in reformists' treatises, delighted the saints as well as God. Martin returns us to the Renaissance paradise where angels serenade the saints.[62]

Friar Martin described how the Easter season was celebrated in heaven – as if he himself had witnessed it. There was a feast of fifty days, ending with Pentecost. After the coronation of Christ as King, the heavenly masses were entertained with some engaging theater performed by the angels. The angels "presented so lively and so beautifully embellished [a play] with many characters, parables, and graceful scenes, that the entire

215

heaven was amused in an unspeakable way." As with many earthly baroque pageants, the "performance did not end before the next day." After "the choir of the archangels had again paid homage, another comedy about the life or passion of Christ was performed...thus every day until Pentecost another joyful feast was held." Friar Martin wrote in the golden age of baroque theater and pageantry. German and French Jesuit drama, playwrights Molière and Corneille, and Versailles pageants all flourished. Martin combined a sumptuous festival at Versailles with a Jersuit comedy staged at a school in Paris or Munich to produce his theatrical vision of the other world. Heaven resembled European cultural and court life – ornamental, literary, and filled with witty conversation and spectacle.[63]

The playful, theatrical heaven described by Arnoux and Martin of Cochem reached its height in the rococo churches of southern Germany. We again return to the pilgrimage church of Steinhausen. In the central ceiling fresco, Johann Baptist Zimmermann presents the communion of saints, not merely focusing their attention on Mary and the divine light but speaking with one another (Pl. 39). The fresco's verticality and circular motion invite the pilgrim to rise up and join the heavenly court. Angels, playing reed and stringed instruments, serenade the entire gathering. In the rear of the church, a drum-playing cherub joins two pipers. Their music charms not only the divine characters but all who are transported to paradise. The church itself serves as a symbol of the total church – both on earth and in heaven. The Zimmermann brothers, quite familiar with courtly life, freely decorated each column with imperial crowns, thus encouraging the pilgrims to experience the church as the heavenly palace of divine royalty.[64]

The royal leisure of heaven was not merely an extension of French, German, and Austrian court life but also recalled Catholic peasant culture. To the horror of both Protestant and Catholic reformers, much of rural Europe clung to its medieval, pre-industrial outlook and rejected the time-oriented civilization of the eighteenth century. Prior to the reforms of Empress Maria Theresa, one area of Lower Bavaria had no fewer than 204 religious holidays when work was forbidden. While reformers hoped to encourage Bavarian peasants to choose a life of industry and pull themselves out of their economic misery, the peasants refused to give up their religious processions, emotional devotions, and countless holidays. The peasants recognized the precariousness of life, and that appeasement of the divine royalty in heaven appeared to have more effect on the crops than advice from an absolutist state. Consequently, although well-manicured gardens, clever conversation, and well-staged theatrical performance had little in common with peasant life, the average pilgrim to Steinhausen understood the meaning of an eternity of music, dance, and social interaction.[65]

By the mid-eighteenth century, heavenly society for many Europeans included the luxuries of city life – good music, conversation, pleasant walks in gardens, theater – and the possibility of reunions with family, friends, and notable religious figures. While Protestants like Issac Watts painted a busy social life based on service, Catholic writers noted the pleasures of a refined, leisured society. These humanistic heavens, however, pale when compared to the elaborate social world of the Swedenborgian afterlife. While Swedenborg's depictions of kingdoms, cities, and societies far exceed those of others writers, it is his portrayal of marriage and sex in heaven which completely separates his visions from those of his contemporaries.

For most Christian theologians, to postulate the continued existence of marriage in heaven was to contradict the words of Jesus. When the Sadducees asked him to whom a woman married to seven brothers in succession would be married at the resurrection, Jesus replied that at the resurrection men and women do not marry but are like the angels in heaven. As quite often was the case, the meaning was ambiguous for eighteenth-century readers. Did Jesus mean that at death people become sexless, bodiless creatures like the ethereal angels? Or did he mean that those already married may continue in that state, but no new marriages will occur? Or did he have a very unique understanding of both marriage and angels? It was this last possibility which Swedenborg hoped to clarify in his writings on love in heaven.

For Swedenborg, all social and spiritual relationships rested on the cultivation of love. While other eighteenth-century theologians also preached the gospel of love – love of God for his people, charitable love for one's neighbors, filial piety of children to their parents – Swedenborg was unique in promoting the love of a man and a woman as the foundation of all other love. "Marriage love," he wrote in *The Apocalypse Explained*, "is the fundamental love of all the loves of heaven." While on earth marriages might be arranged and created for financial or social gain, true marriage symbolized the love of God for the church and was based on mutual love and faith. "Love is man's life," summarized Swedenborg, "and hence is the man himself." Thus, love must continue after death if the afterlife held anything meaningful for either human or divine existence.[66]

Love for Swedenborg was not merely an abstract, spiritual state. The bond between married couples best expressed the meaning of love. Men and women were not whole personalities in themselves, but each lacked something provided by the other. Their personalities and fundamental natures, according to Swedenborg, were radically different from one another. A man "thinks on the basis of reason, a woman on the basis of affection." Men have harder faces, harsher voices, stronger bodies, and bearded chins, while women are more beautiful, smoother, have gentler

217

voices, and softer bodies. Neither man nor woman could be satisfied without the other. A man, unless united with the "beauty and grace" of a woman, is "stern, austere, dry, and unlovely; nor is he wise save for himself alone, and then he is stupid." Once connected to his spiritual mate, "he becomes agreeable, pleasant, animated, and lovely, and thus wise." Without marriage in heaven, all those who died in infancy or childhood, along with all who lived unmated on earth would be doomed to forgo the highest form of human happiness and pass their eternal lives in lonely imperfection. Without marriage, one could not experience the fullness of heavenly existence.[67]

Swedenborg defined marriage as "the conjuction of two married partners into one flesh by the union of souls and minds." In order to reconcile his radical views of heavenly marriage with the Bible, he resorted to allegory and the creation of new theological definitions. By insisting that marriage in heaven was not like marriage on earth, he bowed to the biblical restriction of marriage (i.e., earthly marriages) to this life. Heavenly marriages, on the other hand, were unique. "There are spiritual weddings in the heavens," he informed his readers, "not called weddings but bondings of minds." Earthly marriages might be pleasing, but heavenly bondings were of a more intense nature. "I have seen and talked with such [couples]," Swedenborg reported, "and they said that they have one life, and are...like the two hemispheres of the brain enclosed in one membrane." For Swedenborg it was quite clear that the woman who had been successively married to seven husbands would belong to that partner to whom she was "truly" married. True love was essentially unique and could happen only once in a lifetime. Romantic love, of which Jesus and the Sadducees were unaware, must last forever.[68]

Consequently, when a husband and wife met in the spirit world immediately after death they might or might not continue as a couple in the higher spheres of heaven. If one of them was not of a "spiritual" nature and destined for heaven, then a new partner would eventually be found for the more spiritual. Thus, after a temporary period in the spirit world where natural husbands and wives would meet again, couples might split and reunite with others more suited to their psycho-spiritual level of development. Those who led celibate lives on earth and preferred to continue in their celibacy would be relegated to the "side of heaven" so that their unnatural state would not "infest the sphere of conjugial love, which is the sphere of heaven." Swedenborg himself, who was unmarried on earth, expected to be united with Countess Elizabeth Gyllenborg-Stjerncrona, whose husband apparently chose to reside in hell. Countess Gyllenborg's writing and publishing — she was the author of two devotional volumes on the Blessed Virgin — may have made her congenial to Swedenborg.[69]

Once an appropriate spiritual partner was found in heaven, a wedding took place. Swedenborg described one such wedding in *Conjugial Love*. The celebration took place in "the house of the nuptials" and the visitors were asked to put on garments which shone like flaming light. Golden candlesticks, silver lamps, and tables with bread and crystal cups decorated the house. Six female virgins then entered the room followed by the bride and groom holding hands. Wearing a radiant purple robe, a shining linen tunic, and a miter, the groom sat to the left of the bride. Following the custom of the ancient Aaronic priesthood, he also had a gold and diamond ephod engraved with a young eagle, "the nuptial badge of that society of heaven." The bride "was clothed with a scarlet mantle, and under that an embroidered gown reaching from the neck to the feet. Below the breast was a golden girdle, and on her head a crown of gold set with rubies."[70]

Once seated, the bridegroom placed a gold ring on his bride's finger and draped her with bracelets and a necklace of large pearls. Fastening the jewels on her wrists and neck he said, "Accept these pledges." As she took the pledges, he kissed her and said, "Now thou art mine," and called her his wife. After the blessing from a higher heaven, in the form of an aromatic fragrance which filled the room, the guests ate the bread and drank the wine. Since during the marriage ceremony the bridegroom and bride represented the Lord and the church, no ministering priest needed to preside over the ritual. Finally, "the husband and his wife arose, and the six virgins, holding in their hands the silver lamps now lighted, followed them as far as the threshold, when the married pair entered the bridal chamber and the door was shut."[71]

From the wedding onward, the couple would have only love and friendship for each other, "for when love meets love, it meets itself and causes it to recognize itself and at once conjoins their souls and then their minds...from day to day this grows into conjunction until they are no more two but as though one." To distinguish this heavenly love from the merely conjugal love experienced in earthly marriages, Swedenborg used the term "conjugial." After death, since "the male is a male and the female a female" and both are inclined to "conjuction," it only followed that the partners would enjoy sexual intercourse with one another. "That the intercourse is then more delightful and blessed," wrote Swedenborg, "is because, when that love becomes a love of the spirit, it becomes more interior and purer and therefore more perceptible." Conjugial love, heavenly love, was chaste, pure, and holy, and therefore sexual intercourse could be nothing other than a divine pleasure.[72]

Since the heavenly couple "returns to the flower and joys of the age when marriage love begins to exalt the life with new delights," the enjoyment of conjugial love is quite intense. The angels, we are told by Swedenborg, "declare that they are in continual potency, that after the acts there is never any weariness, still less any sadness, but eagerness of life and cheerfulness of mind." The married pair, just as they did on earth, "pass the night in each other's bosoms as if they were created into one...[the] effects are never so closed as to be lacking when they have desire, since without these their love would be like the channel of a fountain stopped up". In heaven this channel is continually open, "caus[ing] continuance and conjunction that they may become one flesh; for the vital of the husband adds itself to the vital of the wife and binds together." The "delights of the effects" are so extraordinary that they "cannot be described in the expressions of any language in the natural world, nor be thought of in any except spiritual ideas, and that even these do not exhaust them." Not only will such feelings exist in heaven, but they will be "multiplied with continued increase to eternity."[73]

The angelic pairs spend the night in each other's arms, and as one Swedenborgian author summarizes, "the wife receives the virile semination of the husband." According to later Swedenborgian theologians, these texts mean what they say – that there exists the equivalent of erotic love and sexual intimacy in heaven. This becomes particularly clear when Swedenborg recalls a series of conversations between a group of young men and their angelic guides who introduce them to a particular heavenly sphere. The novitiates question their angel tutors about the existence of the "ultimate delights" of married love in heaven. After some discussion the exasperated angels reply:

> And what is the life of that love if not from a vein of potency? If this fails, does not the love fail and grow cold? and is not that vigour the very measure, degree, and basis of the love? is it not its beginning, its foundation, and its completion? It is a universal law, that primes exist, subsist, and persist from ultimates. So is it also with this love. Therefore, unless there were ultimate delights, there would not be any delights of conjugial love.

Angelic coupling surpasses that granted on earth because earthly experiences are merely dim reflections of heavenly realities. Consequently, only the residents of heaven – the angels – are granted the privilege of "blessed intercourse." Those in hell, who cannot experience anything holy or spiritual, are thus confined to unchaste lust which cannot contain any joy or fulfillment. The novitiates are reassured that the angels, and not the earthly theologians, teach the true spiritual meaning of the Bible and of heavenly lovemaking.[74]

The novitiates, still confused, ask the angels if offspring are born from these heavenly unions. If no babies are born in heaven, why have sexual intercourse? From the novitiates' earthly perspective marriage must involve reproduction. The angels explain that there are no natural offspring but only spiritual offspring. Love and wisdom are born from the marriage relationship. The husband and wife only become "more united in the marriage of good and truth." Therefore, Swedenborg revealingly commented, "it is that angels do not become sad after the delights, as some do on earth, but cheerful."[75]

Heavenly marriage is for tender affection, love, and sensual pleasure – not for producing offspring. When infant deaths bring children to heaven, they are given over to women who want to care for them, not to their natural mothers (Pl. 41). It is a woman's psycho-spiritual state which enables her to rear children properly. Likewise, fathers, although concerned for the well-being of their heavenly children, teach them that in heaven children belong to the Lord, who is father of all. Children who die do not automatically go to the higher spheres of heaven but are raised as they would be on earth. They must learn how to distinguish what is good and true and to exercise their free will. Only an adult, who has had the opportunity of choosing innocence over self-pride, can eventually become an angel. Swedenborg, unlike later writers in the nineteenth century, admired the adult more than the child and acquired innocence more than its natural equivalent. The essential, and hence eternal, relationship between the sexes is not based on reproduction and family life, but on an adult responsibility to provide mutual spiritual companionship.

Spiritual companionship of the courtly type envisioned by Catholic artists and theologians, or of the romantic type portrayed by Swedenborg, comprised an important aspect of heavenly existence. The relationships of the saints could no longer account for a minor, secondary happiness but instead formed an increasingly central role in their heavenly activities. Divine love, although still of primary concern, did not have to be experienced in an unmediated way. The saints could feel the love of God through the love they felt for each other. Likewise, they could express their love of God not only in prayer and contemplation, but through their relationships with the other saints. For those theologians like Swedenborg who rejected the concept of a jealous God demanding the total attention of the saints, heaven could easily provide a rich environment for the enjoyment of human love and friendship.

Changes in the social texture of western Europe encouraged the notion that heaven contained an abundance of delightful and spiritually fulfilling relations. The rise of the city as a place not only for commerce but also for entertainment and asserting one's social position encouraged a realignment of the meaning of the heavenly Jerusalem. As early as the mid-sixteenth century, cities built permanent theaters, tennis courts, and opera houses to provide new forms of social pleasure for their citizens. For the leisured classes of seventeenth-century Paris, promenading under shady elms in the newly constructed Cours la Reine laid out by Marie de Médici provided occasion for conversation, people-watching, picking up news, and observing new fashions. In England, masquerade balls,

Pl. 41.   Reginald Knowles, *Children in the Other World*. 1938. Eric A. Sutton, *The Happy Isles: The Story of Swedenborg* (London: Dent, 1938), 131

races, card-playing, and drinking in coffee houses were acceptable social pastimes. By the end of the eighteenth century, clubs, salons, societies and academies, cafés, and public gardens all provided places for enjoying the company of like-minded souls. While all these environments also promoted the more serious discussion of business, marital matches, science, and politics, they were established primarily as places for pleasure.[76]

Although the pursuit of pleasure in human companionship accelerated during the seventeenth and eighteenth centuries, Swedenborg's views of the eventual union of male and female in heaven would become more popular in the nineteenth century. For many eighteenth-century Europeans, marriage still served primarily to establish social and economic bonds between families. For this, offspring were important. Swedenborg, however, confined the practical role of reproduction to earthly marriage while allowing affection, sexuality, and spiritual companionship to continue in the next world. Love, not reproduction, was the true and eternal nature of marriage which survived after death. Like Plato's myth of male and female as incomplete beings searching for their missing halves, the visions of the Swedish seer set the stage for the romantic understanding of love.

This is not to say that Swedenborg revealed a heavenly life of equality for man and woman. On the one hand, Swedenborg emphasized there is "no dominance in marriages in heaven." The husband and wife both want "to intend and think like the other – that is, with sharing, and reciprocally." On the other hand, when we look at the wedding which Swedenborg attended in heaven, we see marriage still being understood as a man's financial and social transaction. The groom "buys" his wife by giving her expensive gifts of gold and pearls. She acknowledges his purchase in silence by taking the booty. "Now thou art mine," the groom proclaims.[77]

For Swedenborg, the symbolism of the marriage ceremony followed traditional Christian patterns by presenting the male as a symbol of the Lord and the bride as embodying the church. After the wedding the husband represents wisdom, but the wife only stands for the love of his wisdom. Only through the wisdom of her husband does she participate in divine love. Swedenborg did not break with the opinion of Genesis that Eve was born from Adam. "That the feminine is from the masculine," he explained, "or that woman was taken out of man, is evident from [the] words in Genesis." Women and men both need each other, but while the man is "born into the affection of knowing, understanding, and being wise," the woman is destined for "the love of conjoining herself with the affection in the male." The equality between married couples which Swedenborg reported in heaven does not transcend traditional gender ideology.[78]

Modern Heaven

On one of his journeys into the heavens, Swedenborg met a group of newly arrived souls who anxiously awaited their life of eternal glory. They had "firmly persuaded themselves that heavenly joy and eternal happiness consist in a perpetual glorification of God. . . called a perpetual sabbath." An angel sent the newcomers to a temple gate where they met a contingent of priests who told them they were at the entrance to "a magnificent and most spacious temple which is in heaven." In this temple, God was glorified by the angels with prayers and praises to eternity. Before the newcomers could enter, they had to prepare themselves by praying, singing, and listening to sermons for three days and three nights. "Take great care," Swedenborg heard the priests say, "that, within yourselves, you think of nothing and, with your companions speak of nothing but what is holy, pious and religious."[79]

The newcomers entered a temple where guards were posted to make sure that no one left before the three days were up. When the newcomers looked around the temple they noticed that many of the worshippers were "sleeping, and those who were awake, perpetually yawning." There was delirium in the eyes of others arising from "perpetual abstraction." "In a word," Swedenborg explained, they were "oppressed in breast and weary in spirit from disgust." After pleading with the priests to end their preaching, the temple worshippers rushed to the doors, broke them open, and drove away the guards. The astonished priests ran after the congregation calling, "Celebrate the festival! Glorify God! Sanctify yourselves!" But these words fell on deaf ears because the people were dulled from their "suspension of mental activity and their detention from their domestic and forensic affairs." The desperate priests seized the people by their arms and clothes, urging them back into the temple. But the people cried, "Let us alone. . . we feel as though our body were in a swoon."

Finally, four men appeared wearing bright clothes and wearing miters. On earth they had been bishops, but now they were angels. They called the priests together and chided them:

> We saw you from heaven with these sheep, and saw how you feed them. You feed them to insanity. You do not know what is meant by the glorification of God. It means bringing forth the fruits of love, that is, doing the work of one's employment faithfully, sincerely, and diligently, this being the effect of love to God and of love to the neighbour. Moreover, it is the bond of society and it is good. It is by this that God is glorified, and not then by worship at set times.

The priests and the people had died thinking that heaven was an eternal sabbath, but when they were exposed to the reality of that thought the people found it unbearable. The priests, the angels explained, could conduct such worship because it was a part of their calling. Swedenborg's vision resembled the thoughts of the Reformed minister Johann Caspar Lavater, who predicted that in heaven "we cannot be blessed without having occupations. To have an occupation means to have a calling, an office, a special, particular task to do." The people who ran away from the temple had assumed that at death one's calling ceased and that heavenly life meant eternal worship.[80]

Protestant and Catholic reformers – Methodists, Jansenists, Puritans, pietists – while creating the concept of a divine "calling," did assume that it ended at death. The supreme calling was eternal worship and not eternal service in an earth-like environment. John Wesley, although asserting the importance of the unique calling of each person to serve in the world, insisted that heavenly life was fully devoted to God. In 1776 he recalled a "much applauded wit who has lately left the body," who did not relish "sitting upon a cloud all day long, and singing praise to God." "We may believe him," reassured Wesley, "and there is no danger of his being put to that trouble." There would be no trouble, however, for those truly chosen, to "cease not day and night, but continually sing, Holy, holy, holy, Lord God of Sabaoth." While humankind's earthly calling might be the love of God through service to others, in heaven it was the direct love of God. "And to crown all," reflected Wesley, "there will be a deep, an intimate, an uninterrupted union with God; a constant communion with the Father and his Son Jesus Christ, through the Spirit." This would be the essential part of heaven, to "see God, to know God, to love God. We shall then know both His nature, and His works of creation and providence, and of redemption." Wesley and Swedenborg, both living in late eighteenth-century Europe and spending much of their time in cosmopolitan London, presented radically different views of life in heaven.[81]

Wesley's theocentric heaven devalued anything which interfered with the soul's knowledge of God. For the theocentric reformers like Baxter, Nicole, and Wesley, the senses distracted the earthly worshipper from higher thoughts and thus had little place in a heaven based on knowledge and contemplation. Knowledge of God came directly through the spirit, unmediated by sensual, physical experience. The intellectual pleasures of supreme knowledge far exceeded the vain and inconsequential sentiments of the senses. Heaven for the seventeenth- and eighteenth-century reformers was fundamentally spiritual because there the pure spirit of God resided. For the saints to participate in heaven they must relinquish their material natures, earthly callings, and social interactions. A purely spiritual reality, heaven must remain the opposite of earth.

Swedenborg rejected the mind/body dualism imposed by Descartes, the pessimism of Pascal, who held that sexual love epitomized human vanity, and the theocentric fascination of Wesley. His was an emerging modern heaven, which extended and perfected the perceived changeless qualities of earthly existence. While religious worship had value, human "sheep" should not be "fed to insanity." Real worship in heaven meant to "bring forth the fruits of love" through useful work. Work bound all people together into a society which was the basis of both earthly and heavenly life. For Swedenborg, as for later writers who described a modern heaven, love, work, and society were the basis of heavenly pleasures.

A representative of the Enlightenment, Swedenborg insisted that humankind was fundamentally good and, given proper education in a wholesome environment, would freely progress toward the good. Free will continued after death, and God relinquished the right to judge. Only the individual decided his or her own eternal fate. For Swedenborg, the senses, rather than restricting and polluting, permitted the increasing accumulation of knowledge. God sent his love through the senses and that love produced knowledge and wisdom. From this love the saints of Swedenborg's heaven continued to serve each other, engaged in useful activities, and thus grew in perfection.

Swedenborg's heaven also reflected the elegant and courtly life of baroque Europe. Although the highest heaven was the home of the simple and pure, the heavenly societies Swedenborg most often described were variations on the rich life of nobility. Princes with purple robes, tabernacles of gold, groves of palm trees, and laurels were reminiscent not only of the splendor of Solomon but also of court life in a variety of European capitals. Swedenborg, whose family was eventually ennobled and who conversed with Swedish royalty, felt comfortable with an aristocratic way of life. As long as one's internal values were not debased, a sensual life of luxury filled with strolls in well-tended gardens, refined entertainments, and witty conversation could be enjoyed. Missing from this baroque splendor, however, was a serving class. Unlike the German rococo church paintings, where accommodating cherubs bring flowers and fresh fruits to the heavenly courtiers, Swedenborg reported that the angels serve each other. Hell, not heaven, was founded on alienating power relationships.

If we can perceive elements of Enlightenment and baroque culture in Swedenborg's heaven, we must also recognize the beginnings of Romanticism in his portrayal of heavenly love. Swedenborg in the late eighteenth century described what would be a common idealization of the love relationship in the nineteenth century. Men and women possess complementary natures which fit together like the pieces of a puzzle. Without finding one's true mate one can never be a whole person. That union not only creates mutual companionship, it also permits the "ultimate delights" experienced in sexual intercourse. The merging of man and woman during lovemaking is a part of the joys of heaven. While Swedenborg would condemn lust as quickly as any reformer, his openness to sexuality was unique in religious writing. That the sexually active couple could also – indeed must – be married to one another was unusual at least for secular writing. Swedenborg challenged both the common opinion of the eighteenth century that wives were for social status and mistresses for enjoyment, and the religious perspective that sex was an appetite caused by Adam's sin. The addition of human love and marriage to heaven, so well developed by Swedenborg, continued to appear in the modern heaven of the nineteenth and twentieth centuries.

CHAPTER EIGHT

Love in the Heavenly Realm

By the mid-nineteenth century, Swedenborg's complaint that Christians knew almost nothing about heaven could no longer be taken seriously. A flurry of publications, from the musings of poets to the deliberations of theologians, presented the reader with an attractive and well-described paradise. In the United States alone, over fifty books on heaven were published between 1830 and 1875. This number excludes fictional works such as Elizabeth Stuart Phelp's novel *The Gates Ajar*, which sold 180,000 copies in America and Britain before the century's end. Even painters and engravers sought to portray life in heaven. From theological and fictional accounts the modern heaven comes clearly into focus: a heaven near at hand, material, full of activity and progress, and based on social relationships.

Although historians fail to agree on the nature or timing of what Lawrence Stone calls the "affective revoluion," most would acknowledge that during the nineteenth century sex, love, and family were accorded more attention in literature, the arts, and the realities of everyday life. Family life, traditionally understood as serving economic and reproductive needs, now was judged by its ability to foster love and affection. The extended family, which tried to negotiate for the best financial and political match for its children, gave way to the nuclear family based on emotional ties. The key ingredient for this shift in mentality was the influx of romantic love into the institution of the family. Romantic love, earlier reserved for the medieval knight or the Renaissance courtier and his lady, gained a place in the middle-class domestic setting. Marriage ceased to be merely a means to legitimate procreation; it assumed the more crucial task of preserving love between men and women. Families nursed that love and saw that children learned the subtleties of affection and sentiment.[1]

Without losing belief in an all-powerful God, nineteenth-century Christians increasingly accorded to romantic love the attention once reserved for the soul's love for the divine. The idealization of human love reached such proportions that by the end of the nineteenth century, few Christians would deny that the family served as the foundation of heavenly life. The true Christian merely moved from one loving home to another. Meeting one's departed family in heaven became a more pressing concern than union with God. Although Swedenborg and other writers had promoted similar ideas during the eighteenth century, romantic love and sentimental domestic life in heaven became embedded in the fabric of middle-class sensibilities only during the nineteenth century. Industrialization, urbanization, the rise of mass culture, and Christian evangelism all contributed to the creation of a readership ready to associate together the notions of family love and heavenly life.

Although nineteenth-century theologians, writers, and artists asserted the importance of loving social relations in heaven, not all described the role of love in the same way. As we will see, Romantic poets and artists portrayed heaven as a place for the eternal union of lover and beloved. They developed ideas familiar to Renaissance artists and ignored by religious reformers from the sixteenth to the eighteenth century. Unconfined by theological restrictions or conventional morality, they had little to say in favor of marriage and family life. The love which existed in heaven was "true love" which recognized no institutional barriers. Theologians and sentimental novelists, on the other hand, believed that a love freed from responsibility and social order easily degenerated into passion and lust. Human love in heaven included not only the romantic attachment of man and woman but also the love of family members. They focused on the family, not the couple, as the source of heavenly love. Explaining how marriage continued in heaven in spite of the New Testament denial, comprised an important element in their theological discussions. Novelists, particularly those writing in America, filled out the picture constructed by ministerial writers. Their sensuous heavens remind us of Swedenborg, but their domestic emphasis moves the attention from the uniting couple to the reuniting family.

Pre-Romantic Precursors: Milton and Swedenborg

The romantic understanding of love in the heavenly realm arose from a belief that human affection is eternal. This idea, as indicated in the last chapter, surfaced in seventeenth- and eighteenth-century theology and literature. Swedenborg's description of married life in heaven echoed the writings of John Milton, Henry More, and Jean-Jacques Rousseau. The Puritan celebration of marital love, the Enlightenment idea of humanism, and the rise of popular sentimental fiction all encouraged the development of the concept that human love was not merely an earthly phenomenon. Let us return, then, to the last decades of the seventeenth century, when a blind John Milton (1608–74) published his literary masterpiece *Paradise Lost* (1667). Milton established in *Paradise Lost* a perspective on the respectability of love in heaven which Swedenborg developed in the eighteenth century. By the mid-nineteenth century, heavenly love appeared not only in the works of the Romantic poets but also in the writings of a wide spectrum of theologians, sentimental poets, and popular authors.

In *Paradise Lost* Milton presented to the reader two perfect worlds: the heaven of God and the paradise of the newly created human couple. Milton's heaven reflected the sparkling environment portrayed in Revelation and the celestial incandescence of the scholastic heavenly empyrean. Heaven provided the setting for the worship of God by the angels. Since the heaven of *Paradise Lost* existed prior to the creation of the earth, humankind, or the concept of death, there were no saints to take attention away from the divine. Nothing human marred the perfection of God's home. Heaven, as described by Milton, was the theocentric heaven of the Puritans.[2]

Separated from the heavenly kingdom by "worlds and worlds" and a "vast Ethereal Sky" was the earthly paradise of Adam and Eve. Milton described Eden as a garden filled with sweet-smelling flowers, luscious fruit trees, and soft green lawns all watered by a fountain. Since paradise served as the home for humanity, the poet gave it an intimacy and warmth missing from the heaven of God and the angels. While the empyrean heaven provided the stage for the battle between the good and evil angels, most of the poem's action took place in the Garden of Eden.[3]

Milton's angelic heaven and earthly paradise reflect, to a certain degree, images found in Renaissance paintings of the Last Judgment. Fra Angelico placed in his painting of the Last Judgement both a theocentric heaven and a human-oriented paradise for the blessed. Refreshing fountains appeared in the paradise gardens of Bosch, Bouts, and Bellegambe. The Renaissance tradition bound together the images of the celestial city and the paradise garden. Milton, however, went beyond the Renaissance painters and made the connection between heaven and paradise much stronger. Heaven was not only the realm of God and the angels, full of light and magnificence; it also provided the source for earthly existence. "What if Earth/Be but the shadow of Heav'n," Milton's angel Raphael rhetorically asks Adam, "and things therein/Each to other like, more than on Earth is thought?" While maintaining the spatial distance between heaven and earth, Milton revealed that the pleasures of heaven were not unlike the pleasures of the newly created paradise. The angels of heaven were familiar with the joys – including those of love – known to Adam and Eve. They joined with each other in song and dance ("that God's own ear/Listens delighted") and enjoyed the growth of heaven: "on flow'rs repos'd, and with fresh flow'rets crown'd,/They eat, they drink, and in communion sweet/Quaff immortality and joy." Angels not involved in divine worship set up camp by "living Streams among the Trees of Life" where they slept "fann'd with cool Winds." Like the angels, Adam and Eve also rested on "the soft downy Bank damaskt with flow'rs," eating fruits and watching the animals' graceful play. Thus Milton's description of angelic life acknowledged that the pastoral paradise of Adam and Eve had its counterpart in heaven. Heaven was not solely the scholastic empyrean.[4]

While the idealized sensual environment of the angels and the first couple recall biblical texts, Milton's depiction of paradisal lovemaking was unprecedented. Soon after her arrival in Eden, Eve prepared her nuptial bed with flowers, garlands, and sweet-smelling herbs. The couple then entered the bridal bower hand-in-hand, and neither "Adam from his fair Spouse, nor Eve the Rites/Mysterious of connubial Love refus'd." Adam later told Raphael that "here passion first I felt,/Commotion strange." Milton explained to his readers that their lovemaking was pure and innocent, as true wedded love should be. In paradise no adulterous lust, no "loveless, joyless, unindear'd/Casual fruition" marred the perfect beauty of conjugal love.[5]

Milton introduced in *Paradise Lost* the idea that sexual intercourse, conducted in the same manner as on earth, made up an essential ingredient in the perfect society prevailing before the Fall. While Augustine imagined that the first couple might have (but had not) had intercourse in Eden, Milton described in full detail their intimate pleasures. The love felt between Adam and Eve did not solely symbolize the divine love of God for humankind. Adam and Eve participated in a spiritual and physical love resulting from their conversation and companionship – not with God, but with each other. Their relationship produced mutual cheer, joy, relaxation, and affection. For Milton, Edenic love was devoid of the twin evils of self-love and lust, yet full of "conjugal Caresses." In the original, perfect world created by God, man and woman freely experienced love, a love that served as the foundation of their divine marriage.[6]

Adam, who eventually wondered about the intensity of his feelings for Eve, asked his angel instructor about the nature of love. Raphael reassured Adam that his love for Eve was justified, for "in loving thou dost well, in passion not,/Wherein true Love consists not; Love refines / The thoughts, and heart enlarges, hath his seat/ In Reason, and is judicious, is the scale / By which to heav'nly Love thou may'st ascend." Martial love, rather than being an outlet of animal passions or a means of procreation, was transformed into a redemptive act. Sexual delight and conjugal friendship preceded the Fall and therefore we might suspect that paradise regained – the Christian heaven – might also include the joys of human love.[7]

Milton, though, did not speculate on the existence of love in eternal life. Since he upheld the mortalist position that the entire human being is nonexistent until the general Resurrection, the soul could not meet her beloved immediately after death. Lovemaking, however, does exist in heaven. In *Paradise Lost* Milton described how the angels in heaven experience a form of love not unlike that of Adam and Eve. Confused over how love leads to heaven, Adam inquired about the working of celestial love. He asked Raphael not *if* angels love, but *how* they love – "by looks only , or do they mix/Irradiance, virtual or immediate touch?" Raphael smiled "with a smile that glow'd Celestial rosy red, Lov'es proper hue," but only had a moment to answer:

> Let it suffice thee that thou know'st
> Us happy, and without Love no happiness.
> Whatever pure thou in the body enjoy'st
> (And pure thou wert created) we enjoy
> In eminence, and obstacle find none
> Of membrane, joint, or limb, exclusive bars:
> Easier than Air with Air, if Spirits embrace,
> Total they mix, Union of Pure with Pure
> Desiring; nor restrain'd conveyance need
> As Flesh to mix with Flesh, or Soul with Soul.

An enthusiastic Edward Le Comte calls this a "superhuman, polymorphous, bisexual coitus that accomplishes mixing soul with soul in love supreme." Raphael described a union which surpassed that experienced by Adam and Eve, since the human pair were restricted by the corporeal nature of their bodies. Adam could not imagine that the joys he shared with Eve were not in some way felt by the more divine beings, the angels. Heaven and earthly paradise connected through the mutual perception of love.[8]

In his youthful travels to Oxford, Swedenborg probably read Milton's poetry and prose. Many of Milton's ideas described in *Paradise Lost* are elaborated in his heaven. Swedenborg took Milton's two perfect worlds of heaven and paradise and combined them into one heavenly realm as the scene of the afterlife. The heaven of the angels was humanized and the paradise of Adam and Eve made divine. Likewise, Swedenborg fully humanized Milton's semi-human angels. The angels did not only eat, play, and make love like humans; in Swedenborg's writings they actually *were* former humans. Although Adam and Eve did not remain in the garden long enough to develop elaborate work activities, Milton did have them busily labor in the garden – fertilizing the plants and trimming the overgrowth. "Man hath his daily work of body or mind/Appointed," Adam explained, "which declares his Dignity." Milton did not approve of idleness in Eden, and Swedenborg rejected eternal inactivity in heaven. *Paradise Lost*, like the discovered heaven of Swedenborg, was full of growth, complexity, change, and love.[9]

The unhappily married Milton and the unmarried Swedenborg both insisted that in a perfect world companionship and sexual relations were essential for happiness. Such relationships were not merely symbols of the soul's love of God, but were intrinsic to human nature. Both writers exploited the Genesis story of the primordial unity of male and female and their eventual reunion through marriage when "the two shall become one flesh" (Gen. 2:24). While Swedenborg went as far as to describe actual marriage ceremonies in heaven, thus institutionalizing the love of the reunited souls, Milton assumed Adam and Eve were married by divine plan. Both authors presented conjugal love in a perfect world as free from lust, guilt or, as Swedenborg reported, "sadness." It was only after the Fall, according to Milton, that Adam and Eve's "amorous play" produced a "grosser sleep/Bred of unkindly fumes." Love in Swedenborg's heaven did not reflect the short-lived love of Milton's Adam and Eve, but the endless love of the angels: "Total they mix, Union of Pure with Pure."[10]

We must not, however, overlook the fact that Milton's Adam and Eve had eventually to leave paradise because of their intense love for one another. Eve did not trick or seduce Adam into eating the apple, but he freely ate from it because of his love for her. Adam realized that once Eve had eaten the forbidden fruit her disobedience would merit her death. "Our State cannot be sever'd," he lamented, "we are one,/One Flesh; to lose thee were to lose myself." Adam's sin, as Irving Singer explains, "consists not in obedience to the woman, but in putting his love of her before his love of God, in giving the link of nature priority over submission to God's commandment." Adam and Eve were deluded into thinking that their love of each other was fuller than the love of God.[11]

Milton, firmly rooted in theocentric Protestantism, rejected the idea that human love might exceed and replace the love of God. Along with other seventeenth- and eighteenth-century writers, Milton placed God in control of heaven. Because the inclusion of human love in heaven, however, set him apart from theocentric reformers such as Baxter and Wesley, we must see Milton as a transitional figure in the development of an anthropocentric heaven. *Paradise Lost*, with its reflections in Swedenborg's writings, set the *precedence* for the romantic understanding of heavenly life. From these early writings we see glimmers of what comprised the nineteenth-century perspective on heavenly love.

Heaven as a Union of Lovers

The precursors of the romantic perspective on heaven still insisted that God controlled the heavens and the earth. Human love in heaven was held in check by the assumption that knowing and loving God was the final goal of human existence. Such views were common both in the medieval scholastic views of theologians such as Aquinas and in the writings of Catholic and Protestant theocentric reformers. The promotion of a romantic ideology of love, beginning in the seventeenth and eighteenth centuries, slowly shifted the focus of interest from divine love to human love. Milton and Swedenborg contributed to this realignment by helping to articulate an all-encompassing mythology of love. Mythology in this sense does not mean a lie or false premise but a guiding principle which gives fundamental meaning to the social order.

The myth of love, which structured the romantic heaven, assumed that in a perfect world (such as Milton's paradise or Swedenborg's heaven) male and female are drawn together in sweet conversation, friendship, and conjugal bliss. Man and woman, rather than being distinct and whole human characters, are basically fragments of a once primordial whole. The Judeo-Christian tradition supported this perspective by describing how God pulled Eve out of the side of Adam. Male and female thus seek to unite so that the two separated souls become one. From the classical tradition Plato's *Symposium* was used, in which the playwright Aristophanes recalled how men and women, once unified whole beings, were tragically separated. Love is the yearning for that half of ourselves we are missing. Although Plato disagreed, and upheld the notion that we seek unity with the idea of goodness and not wholeness with our lost opposite, Aristophanes' tale triumphed. Thus the love between the sexes was not a secondary result of the Fall which mandated human death and the need to reproduce – it preceded the curse of God. Once God forced humanity to leave the perfect world, however, such love was no longer possible. After the Fall, no one could experience love in the way that God intended. Consequently, it was only in a setting totally free from sin that the fullness of love could once again occur. Although Milton refused to speculate about the restoration of the love experienced in paradise, romantic writers boldly declared that after death the righteous regain perfect love in heaven.[12]

Echoes of this myth occurred throughout the nineteenth century in the thought of obscure literary figures as well as more popular ones. The writings, etchings, and paintings of William Blake (1757–1827), now very familiar, were initially shared among only the few London patrons of the unknown visionary and artist. Blake's creative expressions reveal a deep understanding of heavenly love. We can credit part of this understanding to Blake's involvement with Swedenborgianism.

In 1789, Blake and his wife Catherine attended the General Conference of the newly founded Church of the New Jerusalem, entering their names in the minutes book. Blake owned and annotated at least three of Swedenborg's books and probably read two others. Much of Swedenborgian philosophy appealed to Blake – its concern with the inner, spiritual dimension of life, its rejection of the doctrine of predestination, its condemnation of slavery. On the other hand, the development of Swedenborg's visions into an organized religion moved Blake to leave the new church sometime during the years 1790–91. In *The Marriage of Heaven and Hell* (1790–93), he parodied Swedenborg's "Memorable Relations" with his "memorable fancies" and accused the Swedish visionary of subscribing to "all the old falsehoods." By the beginning of the nineteenth century, however, Blake showed more interest in utilizing Swedenborgian concepts in his writings and art. In 1809 Blake wrote in his *Descriptive Catalogue* that one of his paintings, now lost, was taken from the visions of Swedenborg. "The works of this visionary," Blake commented, "are well worthy the attention of Painters and Poets; they are foundations for grand things." During the later part of his life, Swedenborgian thought colored much of Blake's poetry and art, but never to the extent that he lost his unique vision of the universe. Blake maintained his own mystical outlook expressed in a poetry which exceeded Swedenborg in its clarity and brilliance.[13]

Sometime during the early years of the nineteenth century, Blake began a series of drawings and watercolors which eventually culminated in a large tempera painting of the Last Judgment. Although the painting is now lost, several drawings and manuscript notes clarify Blake's understanding of the establishment of the kingdom of heaven. The *Last Judgment*, like all of Blake's art and poetry, combined traditional Christian images with a uniquely Blakean theology. Although we can never be certain how Blake envisioned life in heaven to be, certain basic themes do reappear in his art and commentaries. For Blake, the Last Judgment was not a final, historical event for which Christians waited in dread and fear. In the universal judgment, "all those are Cast away who trouble Religion with Questions concerning Good & Evil or Eating of the Tree of those Knowledges or Reasonings which hinder the Vision of God turning all into a Consuming fire." Blake separated those who had not understood from those who had – those who accepted Blake's understanding of art, vision, morality, and society. Eternal truths and ideals would replace the temporary and finite material of creation. "The World of Imagination," which Blake saw as existing simultaneously in the world and beyond it, "is the World of Eternity; it is the divine bosom into which we shall all go after the death of the Vegetated body." Our world, a "Vegetable Glass of Nature," reflected the Platonic eternal world made up of "permanent Realities of Every Thing." We would be incorrect to think that this exchange of Temporal for Eternal would occur only once, at the end of time. For Blake, the divine judgment was repeatable as well as intensely individual. "Whenever any Individual Rejects Error & Embraces Truth," he wrote, "a Last Judgment passes upon that Individual."[14]

Blake warned that the Last Judgment "is not Fable or Allegory, but

Vision . . . [which] is a Representation of what Eternally Exists, Really &
Unchangeably." What he presented in his art, according to his own
notebook, was one of his "Stupendous Visions." The engravings show
Blake's vision of error being burned up – not judged and being damned,
but being purged. As with Michelangelo's Last Judgment, no vengeful
Christ angrily condemns the evil to hell and sends the elect to paradisal
bliss. Christ, whom Blake sees as different from the cruel Father God, sits
in contemplation among the souls, who reflect either torment or release.
Those doomed are those who in their inner essence are fools or knaves
and too weak to "Reject Error" either through the "Advice of a Friend
or by the Immediate Inspiration of God." Once the hypocrisy and self-
righteousness of earthly existence are destroyed, the only thing left for
these souls is their own wickedness. Blake portrays them in their crippled
state: hands bound and chained, bodies twisted, grasping couples unable
to join each other fully.[15]

On the left side, however, Blake includes countless couples who are
successfully reunited (Pl. 42). In the 1806 engraving, they meet with
hugs and kisses. Blake draws only their heads, arms and shoulders,
emphasizing their intimacies. One female soul descends to meet a male
and their embrace forms a long line of body. Another couple cradle two
embracing children in their outstretched arms. The images appear over
and over again in the engravings. A pair in the 1808 engraving stand
with thighs pressed tightly together; the woman caresses the man's head
and the man places his hand on her buttocks (Pl. 44). It is only when the
resurrected move closer to the upper half of the engraving, nearer the
throne of Christ, that they turn their attention to the divine center.
Even here Blake allows them to stand close to one another, arms upraised
to greet Christ.

In a letter dated 1808, Blake presented a rather orthodox interpretation of the Last Judgment engraving completed for the Countess of
Egremont (Pl. 43). The blessed have burst the bounds of their graves and
are experiencing the birth of immortality. "Parents & Children, Wives
& Husbands embrace & arise together & in exulting attitudes of great joy
tell each other that the New Jerusalem is ready to descend upon Earth."
Rising into the air, the couples embrace and shout "to the Lamb who
cometh in the Clouds in power & great Glory." Here a cautious Blake
provided a conventional explanation of the Last Judgment which would
not offend current theological sensibilities.[16]

In the privacy of his notebook Blake gave a more radical interpretation. At the sound of the trumpet, a "Youthful couple are awaked by
their Children; an Aged patriarch is awaked by his aged wife. He is
Albion our Ancestor, Patriarch of the Atlantic Continent." The aged
woman is "Britannica the Wife of Albion; Jerusalem is their daughter."
From the green fields of the blessed come "various Joyful companies

Pl. 42. William Blake, *The Last Judgment*, detail. 1806. Stirling Maxwell Collection, Pollock House, Glasgow, Scotland

[who] embrace & ascend to meet Eternity." As with Swedenborg, the couples are not merely couples but representations of more complex ideas: the "Powers in Man," the "Greek Learned & Wise," the "Children of Abraham." Blake pointed to one couple and, in exquisite prose, explained that there, a "Female descends to meet her Lover or Husband representative of that Love calld Friendship which Looks for no

237

Pl. 43. William Blake, *Vision of the Last Judgment*. 1808. Petworth House, Sussex, England.

other heaven than their Beloved & in him Sees all reflected as in a Glass of Eternal Diamond."[17]

Human couples united in loving caresses represented the highest ideal for Blake. The embracing pairs served as a means for the viewer to connect the lofty principles of love and friendship with the earthly

Pl. 44. William Blake, *Vision of the Last Judgment*, detail. 1808. Petworth House, Sussex, England

feelings of sentiment and affection. Although the souls "in Paradise...
have no Corporeal & Mortal Body," they lost neither their love nor their
passion. Once they ventured into the realm of the eternal, they shed
what was impermanent – the corporeal, earthly body. Blake did not
believe they gave up their passion, which he saw as the foundation for
intellect and love. "Men are admitted into Heaven not because they
have Curbed & governd their Passions or have No Passions," as a misguided Christian might profess, "but because they have Cultivated
Their Understandings." Blake insisted that "the Treasures of Heaven are
not Negations of Passion but Realities of Intellect from which All the
Passions Emanate Uncurbed in their Eternal Glory." He condemned
those who denied their own passion and crushed the passion of others.[18]

Blake, like Swedenborg, was indebted to Milton for this view of
heavenly love. His engraving of Adam and Eve's "endearments"
experienced in the Garden of Eden clearly illustrates the Miltonian
concept of perfect love (Pl. 45). Naked and muscular, Adam and Eve
gently kiss under the nuptial bower. The couple is free from constraint
or embarrassment. Their love is the pefect love of paradise, and Satan
can only watch with jealous longing. Like Milton and Swedenborg,
Blake understood true love as distinct from carnal, corporeal, "Vegeta-
tive" lust which flourished in the temporal and finite sphere. Friendship
and love were like a "Glass of Eternal Diamond" and acceptable in the
heavenly sphere.

Blake emphasized that his *Last Judgment* was not fable or allegory, but
"Vision or Imagination" which "is a Representation of what Eternally
Exists, Really & Unchangeably." Couples uniting after death were complex, multivocal symbols for Blake. At one level they represented characters in an elaborate Blakean drama, to which he alluded in his notebook.
On a more general level Blake used uniting males and females to represent the union of the body and soul at the Resurrection. This is clearly
shown in Blake's designs for "The Grave," an 1808 poem by Robert
Blair. The designs, engraved by Louis Schiavonetti, achieved more
notoriety than most of Blake's art. In *The Reunion of the Soul and Body*,
Blake has a semi-naked man with outstretched arms reaching toward a
descending woman (Pl. 46). She puts her arms around him and their eyes
meet in a close gaze. The accompanying text explains that "the Body
springs from the grave, the Soul descends from an opening cloud; they
rush together with inconceivable energy; they meet, never again to
part!" The position of their two bodies reminds us of the couples in the
Last Judgment engravings.[19]

Since Blake's drawings are not merely allegorical but reflect the fullness of symbolic language, their literal meaning also illustrates the
eternal and true. Couples meeting after death do not only exemplify the
eternal character of love or the eventual union of soul and body. Real

Pl. 45. William Blake, *Satan Watching the Endearments of Adam and Eve*. 1808.
Museum of Fine Arts, Boston

Pl. 46. William Blake, *The Reunion of the Soul and the Body.* 1808. Engraving after Blake by Louis Schiavonetti. Robert Blair, *The Grave* (London: Gomek, 1808)

families meet after death. In another illustration for "The Grave," Blake straightforwardly showed the *Meeting of a Family in Heaven* (Pl. 47). The husband embraces his wife in what one modern critic terms a "clearly physical and connubial" manner. Through their light clothes the lines of their bodies are sensually delineated. As in the engraving of the soul meeting the body, the eyes of the couple are strikingly linked. The children also embrace, and a son raises his hands in excitement. The family is framed by a pair of angels who look on in reverence. Their touching wing-tips form a Gothic arch over the sacred scene. Blake included this drawing even though the poem does not describe a family meeting in heaven. Likewise, the *Last Judgment* etching in "The Grave" includes couples meeting, even in the clouds surrounding the throne of Christ (Pl. 48). Although Blair's poem notes "the great promis'd day of restitution," no meeting couples are mentioned. Such unions were a part of Blake's world of images, if not that of the now forgotten poet whose work Blake illustrated.[20]

The bodies in Blake's Last Judgment drawings and the engravings for

Pl. 47.   William Blake, *The Meeting of a Family in Heaven*. 1808. Engraving after Blake by Louis Schiavonetti. Robert Blair, *The Grave* (London: Gomek, 1808)

"The Grave" show great similarity in design. As with all of Blake's art, the body is presented in all its human glory. There exists a power and elegance in the loving couples which move the viewer beyond the sentimental into what Blake considered the eternal nature of things. The intense gaze which Blake gave to his reunited body and soul, as well as to the meeting husband and wife, were also used in his Adam and Eve series. These couples reflect mystical union – of the primordial man and woman, of body and soul, or of lover and beloved. Unlike the medieval mystics' hope for a heavenly union with God, Blake's drawings engage us on a more human level. Blake still retains the image of union, but he directs our attention to the eternal in the human character, not toward a Christian God. It is the angels who look at the couple; the divine is out-side the intense interaction between man and woman. The human con-centrates on the human, and the sacred blesses the connection while watching with awe. Even the devil is excluded when, in paradisal love, the couple turns their attention toward one another.

Blake's continual use of the reunion motif in his portrayal of heaven

Pl. 48. William Blake, *The Day of Judgment*. 1808. Engraving after Blake by Louis Schiavonetti. Robert Blair, *The Grave* (London: Gomek, 1808)

and the Last Judgment exemplifies the tendency in the nineteenth century to reject the theocentric heaven of the seventeenth- and eighteenth-century reformers. We have noted already Blake's disregard for the text of Blair's poem "The Grave." Sometime around 1820 Blake painted an interpretation of a longer text on death written by the minister James Hervey. Hervey's *Meditations among the Tombs* had become one of the most popular graveyard meditations of mid-eighteenth century Britain. Its assertion of the futility of worldly vanities and its warning of the unexpected approach of death set it firmly in the ascetic, pessimistic tradition of Protestant and Catholic reformers. Hervey's text repeatedly describes how those fully involved with life – the bride just before marriage, the mother giving birth, the working husband – will be met with a death that will seal them off from such earthly joys. Even the righteous must only look to God for their focus in eternity.

Blake rejected this pessimism. In his painting, *Epitome of James Hervey's Meditations among the Tombs*, he places the black-robed cleric – Hervey – in front of a vision of swirling bodies (Pl. 49). There Hervey learns the true story of life after death. In Blake's vision, those who have died while participating in some life event are permitted to continue that activity in the next world: the bride meets the groom, the mother meets the baby, the husband meets the wife. Rather than being cut off from social relations and forced to fix their vision on God, the souls are shown meeting their lost loved ones. Whereas Hervey intended to show the futility of investing too much attention in earthly sensibilities because one's proper goal is God, Blake depicted a modern heaven where social relations are given highest priority. Blake rejected both the notion that death is destructive and that life after death necessitates the discontinuity of earthly activities. Like Swedenborg, Blake assumed that whatever on earth contained true spiritual meaning continues after death.

Blake expressed in his art the salient characteristics of the romantic notion of heavenly love. Poets and philosophers of the romantic era hoped to "synthesize antinomies, to experience life in terms of polarities that are to be resolved in a higher unity." Through art, literature, and philosophy, the unity of opposites – subject and object, life and death, male and female, good and evil, glowing enthusiasm and cool restraint – could be established. Heaven became the ultimate fusion of opposing principles. The antagonisms of life and death were resolved in a heavenly existence which was not quite an earthly life. Male and female, both as abstractions and as real people, achieved unity and understanding beyond death. Whatever had separated the loving couple on earth vanished so that love could be experienced at its highest level. Love, understood as the pursuit of the whole, could not be satisfied on earth but only in the perfect world of heaven.[21]

Blake's perspective that death must not be feared because love continued in the next life became a common theme in the poetry and prose of German Romanticism. Although condemned as pornography when Friedrich Schlegel (1771–1829) first published it in 1799, *Lucinde* served as the handbook for the establishment of the religion of love. In this combination of fiction and essay, Schlegel set forth his belief (later repudiated) that human love can replace divine love as the source of

Pl. 49. William Blake, *Epitome of Hervey's "Meditations among the Tombs."* C. 1820–25.
Tate Gallery, London

ultimate good. In *Lucinde*, writes Irving Singer, "human love becomes autonomous, religious within itself and no longer seeking for the sanction of any established creed." Love, culminating in sexual intercourse, becomes the new sacrament. It is through love, Schlegel argues, that "human nature returns to its original state of divinity." While Milton condemned Adam and Eve for their preference of human love to divine love, Schlegel presented human love as itself something divine.[22]

The intensity of the love of Julius and Lucinde, rather than being challenged, was extolled. In spite of the success of his earthly love, Julius muses about the enhancement and perfection of love after death. What has begun here on earth must never end. Julius perceives his relationship with Lucinde as a "timeless union and conjunction of our spirits, not simply for what we call this world or the world beyond death, but for the one, true, indivisible, nameless, unending world, for our whole eternal life and being." While Irving Singer terms this belief "love-death," what Schlegel and other German Romantics were expressing was actually "love-death-love." Schlegel did not understand death as the final end or the beginning of an abstract, mystical merging. The Christian heaven was refined into a home for reunited lovers.[23]

In 1794, an impressionable young German poet-philosopher met a twelve-year-old girl and immediately fell deeply in love with her. They were engaged, but the girl Sophie contracted tuberculosis and died three years later. In utter agony the poet, who called himself Novalis (1772–1801), penned a series of "Hymns to the Night" giving voice to his unfulfilled love. "The Song of the Dead," also written during his grief for Sophie, included Novalis's speculations on life after death. In a place where "No wounds can be seen,/No tears are to be wiped away," a collection of children, heroes, giants, gracious women, and sincere masters sit united in a circle and discuss their fate. "Now, for us, to love means life," the people declare, "As intimately as the elements / Are mixing the raging waters of our being,/ Heart with heart." In heaven they converse in

> *Sweet talk of whispered wishes:*
> *This is all we hear,*
> *And we gaze into blessed eyes forever,*
> *And taste nothing but mouth and kiss.*
> *Whatever we touch*
> *Is transformed into the hot fruits of balsam –*
> *Into soft, tender breasts,*
> *Victims of bold desire.*

Although Novalis tells us the dead are "deeply touched by holy favor/ And absorbed in blissful contemplation," he is more eager to describe the "active" joys of our "future companions." In the other world "the desire to cling to the beloved/ Ever grows and blossoms:"

> *The desire to meet him intimately.*
> *To be one with him,*
> *Not to restrain his thirst,*
> *To consume each other.*
> *To be nourished by one another,*
> *By nothing else.*

The world for Novalis was pale; the earthbound mind "borrowed light." Only at death could true release and unification occur. Shortly after writing this poem Novalis, too, died of tuberculosis at the age of twenty-nine.[24]

Novalis's poem only vaguely refers to God, and the bliss of afterlife was not reserved for saints but for lovers. "The Song of the Dead" shows remarkable similarity to an earlier poem by Friedrich Schiller. Schiller followed the Renaissance tradition of connecting heaven with Elysium and the Isles of the Blest. Sorrow, mourning, weariness, and woe were over once one entered "the feast of Elysium." Schiller revealed that it was here that the lover and the beloved embraced "soft reposing in these verdant places;/ Balmy gales, caressing, round them play." Here love triumphed over death: "Here love finds the crown on earth denied her,/ And, death's threatening arm no more beside her,/ Keeps an endless wedding holiday!"[25]

The work of Johann Wolfgang von Goethe (1749–1832) may be used to summarize the German Romantic conception of heavenly love. In *The Sorrows of Young Werther* (1774), Goethe's youthful hero, racked with love for Charlotte, predicts that only death will restore harmony to his soul. Only after death can he join his beloved. "I go to my Father, to your Father," Werther cries in agony; "I will bring my sorrows before Him, and He will give me comfort til you come. Then will I fly to meet you. I will hold you, and remain with you in eternal embrace, in the sight of the Infinite." This conviction, that "we shall exist; we shall see each other again," encourages his eventual suicide. Goethe's tragic Werther has convinced himself that in the next world husband Albert will have no claims on Charlotte. Death does not merely free Werther from the pain of an unrequited passion, it assures him an eternity of love.[26]

Goethe's use of the meeting-again theme as a motivating factor in Werther's suicide echoed Rousseau's use of the same motif in *Julie ou la nouvelle Héloïse*. A mature Goethe later expanded the simple wish of lovers to enjoy eternal love into a symbolic statement on the meaning of eternity. In *Faust II* (published only after Goethe's death in 1832), the reunited pair is not the loyal lover and beloved but rather the seducer Faust and his friend Gretchen. Gretchen, who has murdered her illegitimate child and faces execution, has been saved by divine intervention. Her love for Faust and not her piety allows her to be taken up into heaven. When the time comes for the devil to collect Faust's soul, angels descend and their boyish beauty distracts the lustful Mephisto. Thus they steal the soul of Faust and fly up to the highest heaven. There a group of women penitents, including the transformed Gretchen, plead with the Divine Mother to accept the soul of Faust. As the shroud covering Faust's soul drops off, we see a youthful and radiant character ready to be taught by the once girlish Gretchen. In the final chorus Goethe enigmatically explains:

> *Everything transient*
> *Is but a symbol*
> *The unattainable*
> *Here is realized;*
> *The indescribable*
> *Here is accomplished;*
> *The Eternal Feminine*
> *Draws us upward.*[27]

In *Faust II* Goethe goes beyond the meeting-again motif found in *Werther*. After their death Faust and Gretchen cease to be individuals. Faust says nothing throughout the final scene and Gretchen is referred to as *Una Poenitentium*. The pair now represent philosophical concepts: the Eternal Masculine reflected in the striving, self-assertion, and amoral individualism of Faust, and the Eternal Feminine symbolized by the love, self-sacrifice, and perfect beauty of Gretchen. These two principles have been united in a perfect world. Goethe rejected any notion of morality which would have condemned the pair; he reworked traditional Christian images to suit his perspective. The patriarchal Christian God becomes a glorious matriarch. The baroque image of the Assumption of Mary into a masculine heaven is transformed into the assumption of Faust into a feminine other world. Salvation comes to the world not through the Christian avoidance of sin but through the striving and love symbolized by Faust and Gretchen.[28]

The British Romantic poets also presented heaven as the place where troubled earthly lovers find final satisfaction, although without the philosophical speculations contained in *Faust II*. In 1868–9 Robert Browning (1812–89) ventured in *The Ring and the Book* to portray the saving experience of love and the reunion of the beloved in heaven. At the tender age of thirteen, Pompilia is married by her money-hungry foster parents to an old Italian count. The count gives Pompilia a noble name, a palace, and "no end of pleasant things," but she sees him as he is: "hook-nosed and yellow in a bush of beard." Pompilia unfortunately has no choice but to marry, and Browning carefully pens, "Count Guido, take your lawful wife: 'Until death part you!'" The marriage is understandably unhappy, and Pompilia eventually falls in love with a Catholic priest whom she sees from a distance. Her desperate state eventually leads to a meeting with the priest, the birth of his child, and discovery by an enraged Guido who mortally stabs Pompilia. As she dies Pompilia recounts her tale, noting that it will not be her husband she will meet in the next world: "Tis there they neither marry nor are given/ In marriage but are as the angels: right." Marriage on earth, which neither she nor her priest lover could truly experience, is a "counterfeit,/ Mere imitation of the inimitable." Marriage is for earth, and love is for heaven. "In heaven we have the real and true and sure," Pompilia reminds us.[29]

In a more jocular vein, Lord Byron (1788–1824) playfully explained in his poem "To Miss E.P." (1806) that earthly marriage bonds will be broken so that all can enjoy the true love of heaven. Although "women are angels," Byron agreed with the common wisdom that "wedlock's the devil." "'Tis surely enough upon earth to be vex'd," he reflected, "With wives who eternal confusion are spreading." If the saints had wives, these would, "as in life, aim at absolute sway," and thus "All Heaven would ring with the conjugal uproar." But in heaven, where the Scriptures say no one is given in marriage, "The only expedient is general divorce,/ To prevent universal disturbance and riot." For the rakish Byron, marriage was a burdensome institution fettered by family responsibility, financial strains, and sexual monotony. Love, however, far transcended the restrictions of married life. At death the societal pressures which ruined marriage vanished. Love remained, and women who might have been shrews in marriage became heavenly angels.

> But though husband and wife shall at length
>   be disjoin'd
> Yet woman and man ne'er were meant to
>   dissever;
> Our chains once dissolved and our hearts
>   unconfined
> We'll love without bonds, but we'll love
>   you for ever.
>
> Though souls are denied you by fools and
>   by rakes,
> Should you own it yourselves, I would
>   even then doubt you;
> Your nature so much of celestial partakes,
> The Garden of Eden would wither
>   without you.

In a more serious moment, Byron described in "If that High World" (1815) that lovers in eternity sought "To hold each heart the heart that shares;/ With them the immortal waters drink,/ And soul in soul grow deathless theirs!" Heaven was a heaven of lovers.[30]

The American poet Emily Dickinson (1830–86) preferred earthly celibacy to the pain of either conventional marriage or the endless loves of a Byronic existence. Dickinson refused marital martyrdom and chose instead to lead a single life in her Massachusetts home, having little contact with the outside world. Like many Romantic poets of the nineteenth century, she too believed that a life empty of love would be finally filled in heaven. Experts on the work of the enigmatic Dickinson tell us that sometime during the late 1850s and early 1860s she fell in love with a "Master" whom she then somehow lost. This love comprised a second birth for Dickinson and her love for "Master" became the focus of much of her later poetry. The love of the unknown "Master" saved Dickinson from a life of emptiness and meaninglessness and gave her the hope that at death she would join him. Although they were currently separated, like "faces on two Decks, look back, Bound to opposing land," at death this parting would end:

> And so when all the time had leaked,
> Without external sound
> Each bound the Other's Crucifix –
> We gave no other Bond –
>
> Sufficient troth, that we shall rise –
> Deposed – at length, the Grave –
> To that new Marriage,
> Justified – through Calvaries of Love.[31]

Early in her life, Dickinson rejected the heavenly images of her Calvinist family and society. Their theocentric heaven reflected the reformist perspective on life after death. Dickinson could never feel at home in a paradise where "it's Sunday – all the time" and she ridiculed the popular concept of heaven as a resting-place: It "will take so many beds. There's you & me & Vinnie & the 'other house.' & the Israelites & those Hittite folks, it does appear confused to me!" As an independent woman who refused to bow to the dictates of Calvinist concepts of regeneration, she assumed that hers was a different heaven where "Ransomed folks – won't laugh at me–"; a heavenly Eden not as lonesome "as New England used to be!" What Dickinson imagined instead was the romantic heaven we have seen in Blake, Novalis, and Browning. Her earthly isolation and unrequited love, from her viewpoint, redeemed her. Heavenly love and spiritual union with her beloved was the hope of that salvation.[32]

Levi St. Armand speculates that for the poet "the experience of death entails the loss of physical virginity as well as of spiritual naiveté, and the hour of Emily Dickinson's resurrection is also the dawn of her celestial wedding day." Dickinson portrayed herself as a child fumbling at prayer, but who at the midnight hour of death passed "Unto the East, and Victory." Entrance into the other world was not a birth into childhood innocence, but just the opposite. "A Wife – at Daybreak I shall be –" predicted Dickinson. In eternity she saw the face of her beloved melting into the face of Christ.

> The "Life that is" will then have been
> A thing I never knew –·
> As Paradise fictitious
> Until the Realm of you –
>
> The "Life that is to be," to me
> A Residence too plain
> Unless in my Redeemer's Face
> I recognize your own –

Dickinson imagined a heaven where there was no distinction between divine and human love. In heaven one experienced the unity of the sacred and the profane without slighting either.[33]

Dickinson's poetry reminds us of the mystical language found in Blake's writings and art. Like Blake, Dickinson created a world of symbols whose meaning perhaps only she will ever fully understand. These symbols made up a poetic "church," complete with a sacred theology and a set of rituals. While this "church" drew from traditional Christian images, it essentially expressed the romantic vision – a world-view dependent on the magic power of language, the yearning for mystical union and the primacy of love. Dickinson's heaven was not the domesticated one of families reuniting, but a paradise comprised of two merging souls. As the parted lovers gazed into each other's eyes their mystical vision occurred. In lyrics resembling Blake's description of love which "looks for no other heaven than the Beloved" and in him sees "all reflected as in a Glass of eternal Diamond," Dickinson wrote of this vision:

> These Fleshless Lovers met –
> A Heaven in a Gaze –
> A Heaven of Heavens – the Privilege
> Of one another's Eyes –[34]

Dickinson shared with Blake a subtlety of expression which allows the reader to imagine the heavenly details of "the privilege of one another's eyes." The British Pre-Raphaelite painter and poet Dante Gabriel Rossetti (1828–82) drew this heavenly vision rather more clearly for his readers. As a young man of nineteen in 1847, Rossetti began the poem "The Blessed Damozel," which he revised until its final version of 1870. In the year the poem was begun, Rossetti bought for ten shillings William Blake's original notebook containing Blake's personal comments on his Last Judgment engravings. Rossetti's brother William later edited Blake's writings and helped prepare his biography.

A painting of the *Blessed Damozel*, started in 1873, was finished by Rossetti in 1879 (Pl. 50). He took as his subject in both poem and painting a theme developed by Blake — the reunion of lovers in heaven. Rossetti, however, found more allure in their *anticipated* reunion. "The blessed damozel," he tells us, "leaned out/ From the gold bar of Heaven," awaiting the arrival of her lover. Rather than being a place of eternal joy, heaven acted as a "gold bar" to keep her from her lover below. Rossetti postulates that "her bosom must have made/ The bar she leaned on warm." This blessed maiden did not possess the aerial spirituality of a medieval saint but the sensuous humanity of one of the elect in a Renaissance heaven. She had hair "yellow like ripe corn" and eyes "deeper than the depth/ Of waters stilled at even." It was she who prayed for his swift arrival, who taught him "The songs I sing here" and who would "take his hand and go with him/ To the deep wells of light."[35]

The loneliness of the Blessed Damozel contrasts with the activities of those who have already been reunited.

> *Around her, lovers, newly met*
> *'Mid deathless love's acclaims,*
> *Spoke evermore among themselves*
> *Their heart-remembered names.*

In the lowest layer of Rosssetti's painting, actually separated by the frame, the earthly lover lies staring upward into the distance. Above him are three female angels who appear to be holding up the gold bar of heaven. The Blessed Damozel, comprising the next level, displays the characteristic Rossettian full red lips, long neck, and lush hair. But it is a contingent of lovers who form the highest part of the canvas. Grouped above the head of the Blessed Damozel, the pairs kiss, hug, and gaze lovingly into one another's eyes (Pl. 51). Rossetti gives the uniting lovers similar clothes, hair coloring, and facial expressions. In the poem it is the earth-bound lover, and not the Blessed Damozel, who defines the meaning of these embraces:

> *Alas! we two, we two, thou say'st!*
> *Yea, one wast thou with me*
> *That once of old. But shall God lift*
> *To endless unity*
> *The soul whose likeness with thy soul*
> *Was but its love for thee?*

The Blessed Damozel weeps in the last stanza of the poem. She cries because she has not been made whole in heaven; because the other "half" of her soul still remains on earth. It is not God who renders her complete, but a man.[36]

Pl. 50. Dante Gabriel Rossetti, *The Blessed Damozel*. 1879. Fogg Art Museum, Harvard University

In "The Blessed Damozel" Rossetti created a Godhead which is not a Trinity but a quaternity. This sacred quaternity is not a distant entity but comprises aspects of the divine encountered by the couple. God the Father is basically a deep well of light in which the couple "bathe." In another stanza, the couple lie together in the shadow of "that living mystic tree," where the Holy Spirit as a dove also rests. "Every leaf that His plumes touch," Rossetti mused, "Saith His Name audibly." The

Pl. 51.   Dante Gabriel Rossetti, *Lovers, newly met.* 1876. Detail of sketch for background of *The Blessed Damozel.* Fogg Art Museum, Harvard University

figure of Mary in the poem is not merely the mother of Christ, but a sacred person in her own right. Sitting in a sacred grove attended by five handmaidens, she and the women fashion robes of golden thread for the newly arrived souls. As the celestial mother she rounds out the masculine Trinity. Mary not only provides the clothes for her heavenly children; she understands their romantic inclinations. "He [the lover] shall fear, haply, and be dumb," the Blessed Damozel muses, thinking of her lover's arrival. But with Mary's help she will dissipate his fear:

> Then will I [blessed damozel] lay my cheek
> To his, and tell about our love,
> Not once abashed or weak:
> And the dear Mother will approve
> My pride, and let me speak.

It is Mary who will "bring us, hand in hand," to a Christ surrounded by angels, and it is the Blessed Damozel, not her lover, who speaks to Christ.

There will I ask of Christ the Lord
Thus much for him and me: –
Only to live as once on earth
With Love, – only to be,
As then awhile, for ever now
Together, I and he.

Christ makes no comment on the blessed union, and we only assume that he and the other members of the sacred quaternity approve.[37]

Rossetti's heaven is dominated by active women who, like the admired Beatrice, guide their men through the intricacies of the other world. John Byam Shaw (1872–1919) captured the prominence of celestial women in his painting of *The Blessed Damozel* (Pl. 52). A middle-aged Lady Mary sits surrounded by a choir of singing women, and at her feet her five handmaidens weave golden robes. There are no men in her heavenly hosts. In the far right side of the painting, the Blessed Damozel and her newly arrived lover watch the sacred proceedings. They gently hold hands, but he is obviously an outsider. Standing the farthest away from the sacred center, he is under the control of his female guide. Byam Shaw's painting reminds us of Goethe's *Faust II* where a masculine Faust is introduced to the Mater Gloriosa by Gretchen. In a heaven devoid of a judging, paternal God, where human love is the central focus, feminine presence assumes a leading role.

Romantic poets and painters obviously utilized "artistic license" when describing heaven. They would be the first to admit that their portraits did not coincide with any notion of theological orthodoxy. Their major concern was to present heaven as the ultimate resolution of earthly

Pl. 52.   John Byam Shaw, *The Blessed Damozel.* 1895. Guildhall Library, London, England

conflicts and contradictions. For these artists, society and its institutions set up barriers to love, and even the very nature of men and women kept them from fully merging with each other. After death, however, all obstacles must fall. The artists' accomplishment derives from illustrating the tragic separation of the lovers and intimating their eventual union.

That most of the Romantic artists and poets had little or no connection with established forms of Christianity does not mean they were free from traditional religious notions. Those writers and artists who discussed eternal life maintained a dialogue with what they understood as standard beliefs. They fully accepted the underlying Christian principle that life continued after death. Death was not a final event which sealed the fate of the righteous soul but a dramatic entrance into a more fully loving existence. Like any good Catholic, Methodist, or Anglican, Romantic artists insisted that suffering would be rewarded with an eternity of heavenly life. Salvation assumed a new meaning. Redemption now occurred not solely by the saving grace of Christ but principally through the continuing experience and growing expression of human love.

The Romantics radically split from more conventional Christians in their disregard for the necessity of a judicial, masculine deity. The heaven which they rejected was the ascetic, theocentric heaven of the reformers. From the perspective of their heavenly theology, Romantic poets and artists exploited those themes of the Renaissance and the baroque periods which sought to humanize heaven. They completed the humanizing of heaven begun in the seventeenth and eighteenth centuries. The new idea, however, was not unique to the idiosyncratic Blake, the enigmatic Dickinson, or the outlandish Rossetti. Concurrent with their radical visions of social relations were the speculations of Protestant ministers on marriage in heaven and the domesticated paradises of fiction writers. Love continued to serve as the foundation of heaven, but it changed from the self-absorbed passion of the couple to the love experienced in marriage and family life. The modern heaven, where social relations were of primary importance, was the paradise of the poet, the minister, and the pious Christian.

Love and Marriage

During the nineteenth century, Protestant ministers had available to them a variety of sources which supported the possibility that love and family continued after death. The influential German theologian Friedrich Schleiermacher (1768–1834) defended the religion of love found in much Romantic literature. In 1800 he wrote a series of fictional letters supporting the ideas voiced by Schlegel in *Lucinde*. Similar views appeared in his more widely read *On Religion: Speeches to its Cultured Despisers* (1799). In one particularly revealing passage, Schleiermacher argued that although Adam's paradise before Eve's arrival was beautiful, Adam could not fully experience God because he had no "world." Only with the creation of Eve, love, and community could Adam see and hear God. Desiring and achieving love "forthwith becomes religion," wrote the theologian. Like the Romantic poets who perceived lovers as incomplete beings searching for each other, Schleiermacher assumed that "he loves most tenderly the person whom he believes combines all he lacks of a complete manhood." While Schleiermacher rejected the notion that human love continued in heaven, he firmly connected romantic love to the religious impulse.[38]

Protestant and Catholic clergy in Europe and America may not have been conversant with the subtleties of Schleiermacher's thought or willing to accept the insights of Romantic literature, but they were aware of the growing regard for love and family life among their parishioners. Nineteenth-century preaching modified the theocentric traditions of Calvinists and Jansenists by emphasizing the positive qualities of human nature, the sacred character of family life, and the importance of Christian community. In countless treatises, writers stressed that in heaven our memories persist and therefore we will recognize our friends and families. The issue of "heavenly recognition," no longer relegated to a few brief comments as it had been in most eighteenth-century writings, became a viable topic of theological discourse.

Prior to the mid-nineteenth century, American ministers schooled in Calvinist theology showed little interest in describing the social relationships of heaven. From their theocentric perspective, a husband "would be so enraptured with the Lord Jesus that [his wife] might be at his side for ages before he would think of looking at her!" By 1877, the Presbyterian Robert Patterson (1832–1911) easily rejected that opinion and insisted that "to most Christians...such a view is very chilling." Armed with biblical texts as proof he concluded that in "heaven reunited friends shall quickly know of the presence of each other, and with joy commune about what God the Lord has done for them." For Patterson, the dead would recognize each other by "tone of voice, or a quick lighting up of the face with an old familiar smile."[39]

Catholic theologians voiced similar sentiments. Reunited friends, according to the French Jesuit François-René Blot (1825–?), would remember their past "with a freshness and brilliancy that we shall never before have known." Elie Méric (1838–1905), professor of moral theology at the Sorbonne, explained that "in spite of the unjust and gloomy rigorism of the Jansenists...[we hold] the sure hope of recognizing

and loving after death those we have known and loved during life."
Wilhelm Schneider (1847–1909), the Catholic bishop of the north
German diocese of Paderborn, stressed the meeting-again motif in a
book reissued frequently throughout the nineteenth and early twentieth
centuries. While outward and visible unions stopped at death, inward
and spiritual bonds continued in the other world. "We do not picture
heaven as the abode of hermits living in seclusion," he preached. Everlasting life would "not exclude the joys of friendship and the delight of
reunion." Following scholastic tradition, Schneider predicted that at
the end of the world the renewed earth would be devoid of animals and
plants, but the redeemed who lived in the new Jerusalem would "feel
love, a love in which the dispositions will harmonize and experience the
most intense pleasure." The bishop of Paderborn, who shared little
in common theologically with the American Presbyterian Edward Kirk
(1802–74), might have fully agreed with Kirk's assertion that in heaven
"*the affections will have the supreme place*" (italics his).[40]

If friends met each other in heaven, what about husbands and wives?
How did nineteenth-century ministers cope with the New Testament
negation of marriage in the afterlife? The arguments employed by the
clergy to justify heavenly love and marriage illuminate their ambiguous
attitudes toward love, sexuality, and friendship. The clergy tried to walk
the thin boundary between acknowledging that marriages survive after
death and upholding that "in the resurrection they neither marry, nor are
given in marriage, but are as the angels of God in heaven." (Matt. 22:30;
King James Version). In order to do this, they constructed new interpretations for both the scriptural passage and the meaning of marriage.

During the 1840s, under the direction of John W. Nevin, a shift
away from Calvinism occurred in the German Reformed seminary at
Mercersburg, Pennsylvania. Departing from the Reformed orthodoxy,
Nevin and his associates rejected revivalism, challenged the prevailing
views of the Eucharist, and called for a re-evaluation of the meaning
of Christian history and community. One of the popularizers of the
Mercersburg theology, Henry Harbaugh (1817–67), also wrote extensively on heaven. *The Sainted Dead* (1848), *Heavenly Recognition*
(1851), and *The Heavenly Home* (1853) all were attempts to present his
view that "heaven is a place, and not merely a state; it has locality, and is
material." For Harbaugh, sexual intercourse between husband and wife
serves to populate the world. Where death does not exist, there can be
no need for intercourse. However, "this does not, in the least, intimate
that the affections begotten, and the friendships formed in this relation,
shall not be renewed and continue in the heavenly social life."
Consequently, although marriage "in its earthly sense, comes to an end
in death, the relation in its mystical and spiritual sense continues, and its
affections, beautiful and holy on earth, are made perfect and permanent

in heaven." By associating the term "marriage" with sexual intercourse leading to reproduction, Harbaugh acknowledged the New Testament view while not denying the eternal nature of love.[41]

In 1847, the Presbyterian John Kerr expressed that same ambiguity in *Future Recognition; or The Blessedness of Those 'Who Die in the Lord'*. Part of married life is "pure and heavenly" and this survives after death. For Kerr, wanting to unite with "the objects of our love" is a universal human trait and "springs from an indestructible affection of our nature." But unlike parental love or the love of a friend, married love includes the problematic matter of sexual intercourse. "Marriage in this world," another Presbyterian postulated in 1854, "is the ordinance God hath appointed to repair the ravages of death: but in heaven there will be no death, so there is no such compensatory institution as marriage...to counterbalance the effects of dissolution." Kerr put it more bluntly: "As there shall be no more death, neither will marriage, instituted to supply the waste of mortality, be any longer necessary, and of course have no place." Sexual intercourse belongs to the "animal and the earthly" and has nothing to do with eternal love. "Sensual pleasures," Kerr concluded, "shall not attach to our perfect and renovated nature."[42]

Victorian prudery did not keep sensuality out of heaven. Protestant clergy strove to be true to the Bible and at the same time to uphold the merits of married love. If they equated marriage with mating – an idea that they might otherwise vigorously deny – then heavenly marriage could be denied without threatening eternal love. Evoking the "no-sex" rule did not mean that the saints in heaven lacked bodies or that they refrained from touching. Samuel Phillips (1823–92) wrote in 1859 that the babe "that withered in your arms like a frost-stricken flower in winter" in heaven "will come forth clad in redemption robes, to embrace you there." He also described how the members of the Christian household would "walk hand in hand" on the "banks of the river of life." In heaven, the Presbyterian Robert Patterson explained, the "merely sensual and corporeal in love and friendship" would pass away, but "amid the perfectly refined spiritualities of heaven soul will answer to soul, and quickly clasp each other in the bonds of eternal love." There would be no "marrying nor giving in marriage," the Unitarian Francis Greenwood (1797–1843) summarized, yet the "ties and affections of earth will not be forgotten, and in spirit the twain will be one."[43]

The Catholic bishop Wilhelm Schneider concurred. He predicted that not only would husband and wife joyfully meet in heaven, but God would bless their union. "The bond," he stated in his lengthy treatise *Meeting Again in the Other Life*, "once concluded at the altar will be renewed and ratified before the almighty God and in the presence of the entire court of heaven. Once it was God who had blessed the union through his priest's hands; now he blesses it himself with all the inhabitants of heaven acting as witnesses to this sublime act." Sensual love, of the lustful and selfish kind, of course found no place in heaven. Marital love in heaven, freed from "inordinate passion," would be "ardent and tender." Celestial love was "too pure and holy to resemble any form of earthly love, unless, indeed, the ideal love of a betrothed couple before marriage may be regarded as its foreshadowing." Schneider assured his readers that "spiritual union will...continue in the other world...[and] result in the purest and most delightful interchange of mental and spiritual advantages."[44]

As a Catholic priest skeptical of the passions of sexual intercourse, Schneider preferred to assure that the married couple would live in heaven in virginal love. Marital feelings would endure, but intercourse itself belonged to the realm of earth. Given his purified version of marital love, Schneider provided his own answer to the Sadducean question about marriage in heaven. Marriage on earth could not bear the strain of a love divided among several people. Earthly polygamy entailed too much passion, too much jealousy, too much confusion. In heaven, however, such weaknesses would disappear. Bishop Schneider, who found heavenly polygyny more acceptable than the Sadducean example of possible polyandry, explained that the man who had seven wives would in heaven "love each individually as if she had been his only wife and will possess them all collectively in inseparable spiritual union." In heaven, Schneider felt, "all the blessed, who have been bound by mutual ties on earth, will belong to each other in a special manner."[45]

As if to temper his daring statement, Schneider tried to color it with traditional scholastic views on the heavenly hierarchy. In doing so he revealed how Catholic thought had changed since Aquinas. Although each of the women was equally close to their husband because of the marriage bond, some might gain more of his love than others in heaven. The wife "adorned with the greatest degree of holiness," who occupied the highest "rank in glory," would "desire and enjoy his [the husband's] love most perfectly." For Schneider, saintliness on earth not only achieved a fuller vision of God (as taught by the old-style scholasticism), it also gained for the redeemed a greater share of human love after death. Thus the bishop retained the Catholic preference for the beatific vision, heavenly hierarchy, and virginal affection while infusing it with the romantic notion of the eternal nature of love.[46]

The argument that pure love flourishes in heaven actually left room for a sexual life there. If intercourse between husband and wife could be "chaste," and productive only of love, then there should be no reason why it could not continue in the afterlife. The most prominent proponent of this theory was the chaplain to the queen of England, Charles Kingsley (1819–75), perhaps the most influential Anglican priest in Victorian Britain. His love letters to his wife, her diaries, and his private drawings expose a man with an active sexual imagination which, by public Victorian standards, would have been considered obscene. For Kingsley, heaven was everlasting conjugal union; "those thrilling writhings," he wrote before he married, "are but dim shadows of a union which shall be perfect."[47]

Even in his published letters, carefully edited by his wife Fanny, Kingsley did not shirk from asserting that sexual love continued. Following Protestant tradition, he saw the married state as "the highest state . . . through and in which men can know most of God, and work most for God." Marriage, "spiritual and timeless" as well as "pure and mysterious," was an eternal union that "once solemnized" could not be transferred to anyone else or destroyed by death. Kingsley cited Milton's description of angelic love to support his commitment to the heavenly continuation of married love. His wife Fanny appeared to uphold his views. "Beloved!" she mused to Charles, "if she [Eve] shrank not, why sh'd I? If Holy Eden was the Scene of Marriage & Married Love, why should I fear to leap into your arms to realize one of Eden's blessings or taste an Enjoyment wh[ich] *must* be pure if it was *tasted there!*" Marriage, prefigured by a Miltonian paradise, entailed love, friendship, and sexual enjoyment. For Kingsley, to limit marriage to reproduction thus confining it to earthly existence was "an old Jewish error" propagated by "Popish casuists." His own marriage was so intrinsic to his being that, "if immortality is to include in my case identity of person, I shall feel to her [Fanny] for ever what I feel now."[48]

Seen in the light of his private drawings and unpublished letters, Kingsley's feelings for his wife reveal the erotic side of heavenly love. Fanny preserved in her diary Charles's sketch of himself and Fanny as a couple in angelic embrace, recalling the classical figures of Amor and Psyche (Pl. 53). In another drawing, two naked children kiss on a pillow with the caption, "of such is the kingdom of heaven" (Pl. 54). The sketches illustrate Kingsley's conviction that marital enjoyment "will be more confirmed when we are one, & in Heaven, our love will be without oscillation, even at the same glorious full tide of delight." Kingsley rejected any notion that sexual passion should be limited to the male. Writing to Fanny in 1843, he rhetorically queried: "Do I expect to marry an *angel*, passionless, unsympathizing? – No! My wife must be a woman – subject to like passions with myself!" The mutual sexual enjoyment of husband and wife, far from being merely an unfortunate result of original sin, would survive in heaven. "*There*," Kingsley insisted, "we shall be in each other's arms forever – without a sigh or a cross."[49]

Faced with the scriptural denial of marrying in heaven, Kingsley made an attempt to ridicule it. "I am so well and really married on earth," he disclosed in a letter which Fanny published, "that I should be exceedingly sorry to be married again in heaven." It was not that

Pl. 53.   Charles Kingsley, *Charles and Fanny as Amor and Psyche*. C. 1840. Banderole reads: "She is not dead but sleepeth" (Luke 8:52). By permission of Angela Covey-Crump, Ely, England

marriage did not exist after death, it was that *marrying* did not exist. Marriage, which for Fanny and Charles meant the solemnizing of romantic love, made a permanent mark on the soul which could never be erased. Thus, according to Kingsley, the scriptural passage had nothing to do with his wife and himself. "All I can say is," Kingsley concluded, "if I do not love my wife, body and soul, as well there as I do here, then there is neither resurrection of my body or of my soul, but of some other, and I shall not be I." Kingsley refused to devalue earthly bliss. "No!" he exclaimed, "I enhance it when I make it the sacrament of a higher union...all expressions of love here are but dim shadows of a union which shall be perfect, if we will but work here, so as to work out our salvation!" Given this attitude of her court chaplain, it is no wonder that Queen Victoria had herself buried dressed in her bridal veil.[50]

The sexual character of Charles and Fanny Kingsley's heaven is not

Pl. 54. Charles Kingsley, *Of such is the kingdom of heaven.* 19th century. Manuscript Add 41, 296, fol. 3 verso, The British Library. By permission of Angela Covey-Crump

essentially different from the more modest sentiments voiced by many nineteenth-century ministers. Love, sanctified through the bond of marriage, survived death. In America and Britain, pious writers and theologians increasingly combined the images of sexual and religious ecstasy to produce a spiritualized eroticism and an erotic spirituality. "As long as it is performed within the hallowed terrain that religious doctrine and secular authority have mapped out for it," writes Peter Gay, "sexual activity is sacred activity." Earthly love, controlled and spiritualized through the institution of marriage, achieved its highest reward by being admitted into heaven. Both Protestant and Catholic clergy, in effect, refused to let the Romantic poets have a monopoly on love. For those committed to institutional Christianity, heavenly affection meant not the prolongation of love decided on by the passions and whims of sensual sinners, but the pure married love of the saved.[51]

Life in the Heavenly Home

By the second half of the nineteeth century, the romantic spirit was no longer confined to the pens of the literary or clerical establishment.

264

Women fiction writers in Britain and the United States produced visions of heaven readily accepted by the reading public. For them, heavenly love comprised not only love and marriage but also family life. Under the impact of Swedenborg and spiritualism, the limited vision of the artist or theologian expanded into a whole system of heavenly activities. Heaven for Swedenborg was not based on eternal family life, but rather on eternal "couplehood." Victorian novelists, indebted to Swedenborg for vivid descriptions of the other world, expanded this basic unit to the family. While the love of the couple continued to be important, the essential love was the love experienced within the family. Consequently, spiritualists revealed that not only did husband and wife meet in heaven, but also brothers and sisters, parents and children, and other relatives. Once families existed in heaven, homes, schools, pets, and suburbs quickly followed. Novelists who described such settings did not do so purely to entertain their readers. Their writings harmonized with spiritualist accounts, as well as the mainstream clerical belief that families would meet again in heaven.

The cornerstone of the literary push to domesticate heaven was the 1868 novel *The Gates Ajar* by Elizabeth Stuart Phelps (1844–1911). Quickly becoming a bestseller for its twenty-four-year-old author, the book earned an extraordinary $20,000 in one month alone. Before the end of the nineteenth century it had sold 80,000 copies in the United States and 100,000 in England, during which time only Harriet Beecher Stowe's famous *Uncle Tom's Cabin* sold more copies. Scholars attribute the great success of the novel to a variety of reasons: the devastation of the American Civil War, a rise in women's role in challenging Calvinist orthodoxy, and the Victorian fascination with death. The novel made available to the public a notion known to both theologians and readers of literature for a long time – that love continued in heaven.[52]

The storyline is a simple one. A New England woman, Mary, has to confront the death of her brother Roy in the Civil War. Conventional religious advice and consolation does not give her the comfort she seeks. During this time, her Aunt Winifred, a young widow, comes to help the grieving Mary. Conversations between Aunt Winifred, Mary, and a variety of skeptics, make up the bulk of the book. Aunt Winifred is always portrayed as loving, supportive, and most of all, intelligent. She easily defeats the men who challenge her perceptions of eternity. Aunt Winifred's view of heaven is not the product merely of women's intuition. The reader is shown Aunt Winifred's careful reading of Scripture, theological treatises, and literary sources. Elizabeth Stuart Phelps, the daughter and granddaughter of notable Calvinist ministers, used her book as a pulpit to promote her own theological understanding of the afterlife. At the end of the book Aunt Winifred dies – teaching Mary and the reader how the proper vision of heaven permits an easy death.

In order to establish a heaven based on domestic love, Phelps first dispelled the allegedly prevailing idea of heaven as a place for eternal worship. Deacon Quirk and Dr. Bland are quickly put in their place as representatives of the absurd notion that heaven consists of "something about adoration, and the harpers harping with their harps." Aunt Winifred's premise is that heaven is for happiness and few of us would be happy for an eternity of "study[ing] the character of God." The heaven of the book of Revelation presents "*pictures* of the truth" and must be taken symbolically.[53]

The theocentric heaven which Phelps held up to ridicule was a vanishing image by the time of *The Gates Ajar*. Phelps created a false enemy with which to do battle. At best, the ministers of this period would have supported James MacDonald (1812–76), who wrote in 1855 that since there is mutual recognition in heaven it *cannot* be "a place of isolated existence, where each individual is absorbed in a contemplation which destroys all consciousness of the presence of fellow-worshippers." While ministers like Samuel Phillips still paid tribute to the idea that "the Lamb on the throne...will absorb all interest," their major concern was to show how "there is a living union between the Christian's home on earth, and his home in heaven." Phelps must have realized that theological and literary opinion on the social nature of heaven supported her convictions. In denying that reality, and forcing an antiquated theocentric heaven on the male ministerial establishment, she took credit for popularizing already credible beliefs. *The Gates Ajar* did not invent a new heaven, but gave currency to ideas already found in Swedenborg, Blake, Goethe, and countless minor Christian theologians.[54]

Love of God, for Phelps, centered not on worship but on social relations. "Would it be *like* [God] to create such beautiful and unselfish loves," Aunt Winifred asks, "just for our threescore years and ten of earth? Would it be like Him to suffer two souls to grow together here, so that the day of separation is pain, and then wrench them apart for all eternity?" Obviously not. "Christianity", explained Henry Harbaugh in 1851, "in its very essence, identifies itself with the social law and life of our nature, and makes them eternal, by making itself eternal in them." "In the Scriptures," the *Encyclopædia of the Presbyterian Church* concurred, "heaven is always presented as a social state." No amount of harping with harps, for many American clergymen, could compensate for the lack of a society of love. They could only agree with Phelps in believing that "to love and to be separated is misery, and heaven is joy."[55]

The unique quality of *The Gates Ajar* lies in Phelps's description of a heavenly society consisting of Victorian families and celebrities all living in a picturesque natural setting. Little children have their gingersnaps, budding musicians their pianos, mechanics their inventions. Everything is cared for. Aunt Winifred expects, as she puts it, "to have my beautiful home, and my husband and [child] as I had them here; with many differences and great ones, but mine just the same." In the 1883 sequel to *The Gates Ajar*, called *Beyond the Gates*, Phelps took us to one of these heavenly homes:

> We stopped before a small and quiet house built of curiously inlaid woods . . . So exquisite was the carving and coloring, that on a larger scale the effect might have interfered with the solidity of the building, but so modest were the proportions of this charming house, that its dignity was only enhanced by its delicacy. It was shielded by trees, some familiar to me, others strange. There were flowers – not too many; birds; and I noticed a fine dog sunning himself upon the steps.

Phelps rejected the idea that heaven is made of heavenly mansions, and preferred the Victorian cottage as her resting-place.[56]

Another late-Victorian writer, Agnes Pratt, favored the idea of heavenly mansions. In her short story "The City Beyond," which appeared in the popular *Godey's Magazine*, her dead heroine owns a heavenly house reminiscent of the Queen Anne style of architecture popular in her day: "Never had our beautiful home looked more lovely in the glowing sunlight. Its window panes were spotless, its towers and fanciful spires glistened and sparkled." These homes are not located in cities or villages but

Pl. 55. Frederika Bodmer, *Crossing the River*. C. 1880. Automatic drawing. Society for Psychical Research, London

carefully placed in picturesque surroundings. Heaven has mountains, oceans, and rivers which wind "quietly in and out, in sinuous curves." Pratt's paradise recalls the heaven of *The Gates Ajar*, which contains "forests so thick that it shuts out the world, and you walk like one in a sanctuary." Houses blend in with this natural environment, and nature is tamed and fully suitable to human life.[57]

No "true" Victorian home was complete without children. Both ministers and fiction writers stressed that "the kingdom of the redeemed ...is made up, in so great a degree, of little children." Sentimental poetry from ladies' magazines reiterated this idea by portraying babies as "fresh from skies divinely bland" or "a seraph chord astray from heaven." Such tender natures could only be trained in the rarified atmosphere of heaven. Even Father Blot assures the mother of a dead daughter that "God has assumed the care of bringing her up. He has educated her Himself." Epitaphs on children's gravestones affirmed the popular conviction that a child's natural place was in heaven, since earthly life could be too harsh for the delicate child:

> *Sadie was too sweet a bud*
> *To blossom in this sinful world*
> *So God has taken her above*
> *To dwell with his immortal love.*
> *Safe in the arms of Jesus*
> *Safe in his gentle breast*
> *There by his love overshadowed*
> *Sweetly my soul shall rest.*

> SADIE ROCHE (1867–1875)[58]

The children would not, however, be left uneducated. Presbyterian George Cheever (1807–1890) postulated that "there must be a nursery, an infant school in heaven, a peculiar training of these buds and blossoms of immortal being." Cheever, evangelical pastor of the Church of the Puritans in New York City and graduate of Andover Seminary, was echoing feelings once voiced only by Swedenborgians. In George Wood's (1799–1870) novel, *Future Life or Scenes in Another World*, St. Perpetua educates a child named Persis until she is old enough to marry. Dead parents, according to James Wood in his essay "Household Religion," are only temporarily removed from the family. When they are free from "every indication of infirmity and decay" they will eventually gather "their once happy children, of all ages, from the buoyant youth to tender infancy" around them. Parents and other concerned adults continued their child-rearing activities in heaven. In a century when many argued for universal education, these ideas carried conviction.[59]

A heavenly society made up of family and friends appeared not only in Protestant writing. François-René Blot's *In Heaven We Know Our*

Own was heralded by Catholics as their *The Gates Ajar*. By quoting patristic sources and the lives of the saints, and borrowing extensively from the eighteenth-century Dominican Ansaldi, Blot arrived at the same conclusion as many Protestants. In his chapter "Relations Know Each Other; or, The Family in Heaven," he told his readers that "if enjoying the society of your relations is a consolation...then you may indulge in [this consolation] without fear, without scruple, and without imperfection." Just as Christ met his mother in heaven, so should we meet our mothers. "Oh! how pleasant it is to love on earth as they love in heaven," he rhapsodized with Francis de Sales, "and to learn mutually to cherish one another in this world as we shall do throughout eternity in the next!"[60]

Catholic acknowledgement of the domestic aspect of heaven increased during the later part of the nineteenth century as Catholic leaders gave more attention to the home and family. In an encyclical letter dated 28 December 1878, Pope Leo XIII expressed the hope that "each family would truly present a likeness of the heavenly home." Catholic hymns petition the Holy Family to "lead us safe through every danger/ Till we meet in heaven above." In 1889 the *Sacred Heart Review*, a popular American Catholic magazine, quoted Cardinal Manning's prediction that in heaven not only would we know all the saints, including those "who are not yet born," but that "fathers and mothers, children who are gone before you, you will meet them in the kingdom of God...they will meet once more in perfect identity, perfect recognition." The Jansenist theocentric heaven of eternal contemplation found no place in American Catholic theology, where family life served as the bulwark against encroaching modernization and secularization. For the late nineteenth-century Catholic, as well as the Protestant, placing the family in heaven sanctified and legitimized the Victorian home which was increasingly coming under attack by socialists, feminists, and labor reformers.[61]

The division between the earthly and heavenly spheres had become weak. The dead, Elizabeth Stuart Phelps explained, are "near you." In 1834 the Unitarian William Channing (1780–1842) asked if it was "at all inconsistent with our knowledge of nature to suppose that those in heaven...may have spiritual senses, organs, by which they may discern the remote as clearly as we do the near?..may not they...survey our earth as distinctly as when it was their abode?" Although Phelps has Aunt Winifred deny that she is a Swedenborgian, it is clear that her sympathies are with the Swedish visionary. Following Swedenborg, Phelps attempted to convince her readers that angels – which link heaven and earth – are actually dead Christians. Spiritualism, which also emphasized the connection between the family on earth and the family in heaven, further narrowed the gap between the living and the dead. "If angels can come, why should our dear ones desert us?" queried the spiritualist George Hepworth (1833–1902) in *They Met in Heaven*. As Americans and Britons became increasingly preoccupied with spiritualist concerns, his answer became a common one: "In very truth, the other world floods this world with its beauty, and the departed are near to us, very much nearer than we dare to think."[62]

It is important to emphasize that Phelps's heaven, and the heaven of many Catholic and Protestant theologians, is made up not only of nuclear families, but relatives, friends, and famous people. Their heaven is a large extended family, not sets of pairs who find bliss in the gaze of the beloved. There is no room for the type of intense, exclusive love we saw in Blake or Emily Dickinson. Although she was versed in Swedenborg's vision of heaven, Phelps had little use for his mystical understanding of the union of husband and wife. She also steered away from the tight mother-child bonds exploited in sentimental poetry. In *The Gates Ajar*, and in the sequels, Phelps centered most of her story around relatives and friends meeting in heaven. She left the more controversial romantic relationships, with their inevitable push for intimacy, for the end of her stories. Phelps carefully followed the lead of theologians like Francis Greenwood, who wrote in 1831 that "particular affection for those with whom we have been particularly connected, is not inconsistent with a kind and generous affection for many friends, for all the good from all ages and all countries of the world, to whom the better country will be the great and final meeting place."[63]

We should not be surprised, then, that Phelps visualized Civil War soldiers meeting Abraham Lincoln in heaven. Edward Kirk in *Heaven our Home* looked forward to meeting "the elite of God's empire. . .Isaiah, Paul, John, Gabriel, Mary, Bunyan, Fénelon, Pascal, [and] Harriet Newell" – the last one being a missionary's wife who died, in 1812, on the isle of Mauritius. "You shall there hold fellowship with the fathers of a thousand generations," Samuel Phillips predicted in 1865, "with the patriarchs, and prophets, and apostles, and martyrs, and reformers, and the innumerable company of angels." He echoed James MacDonald, who urged his readers to presume "that there will be felt an ardent desire to form acquaintance with the most remarkable personages," including Adam, Enoch, Elijah, Abraham, Paul, Peter, and John.[64]

Such theological speculation made it possible for Victorian visionaries like the Methodist Rebecca Springer (1832–1904) to visit a grand auditorium in heaven where on one day "Martin Luther is to talk. . . supplemented by a talk from John Wesley," or for Phelps's heroine, Mary, in *Beyond the Gates* to hear a symphony by Beethoven with a light-show by Raphael. "Was I not in a world," Mary queried, "where Loyola, and Jeanne d'Arc, or Luther, or Arthur, could be asked questions?" While eighteenth- and early nineteenth-century writers often included lists of people whom they would meet in heaven, Victorian authors took the opportunity to rid heaven of sectarian disputes. Ecumenical conversations linked Protestant to Catholic; family member to famous person.[65]

In one aspect, however, Phelps sided with Swedenborg and the Romantic poets against the more institutionally oriented ministers. Earthly marriages, she predicted, would not *necessarily* continue in heaven. Quite frequently, "the marriages of earth had no historic effect upon the ties of Heaven" because an imperfect world restricted the free expression of love. In *Beyond the Gates*, Mary eventually meets her true love who, though once married to another, now claims her as his "soul of my immortal soul." In true Swedenborgian style, Christ blesses the union and "by His blessing lifts our human love into so divine a thing that this seems the only life in which it could have breathed." For Phelps, marriage bonds – like institutional religion – were not eternal. As a higher reality, heaven also claimed a higher authority.[66]

Agnes Pratt also rejected the institutional framework of marriage. In "The City Beyond" a widower discovers that his second wife is his true soul mate with whom he will live for eternity. In another part of the story, Pratt's heroine marries in heaven her long-lost love who on earth had married another. Going one step beyond Phelps, she explains in a manner reminiscent of Swedenborg and Kingsley that since one is rejuvenated physically after death the sexual aspect of marriage survives. "Marriage – physical marriage – I find to be an existing custom here...I do not believe that as God leads us on toward perfection He would deny us the sweetest and, if rightly used, the purest means of happiness He has yet granted us." Although Pratt tried to avoid controversy by thinly disguising her heaven as an afterlife on Mars, her point is clear: In heaven it is still love which triumphs over the institutionalized relationships of marriage and family.[67]

We must not think, however, that meeting a long-lost lover, or parent, or Beethoven, is the culmination of our heavenly experience. "Yes, my child," Aunt Winifred muses, "clinging human loves, stifled longings, cries for rest, forgotten hopes shall have their answer...These things have their pleasant place. But, through eternity, there will be always something beyond and dearer than the dearest of them. God himself will be first, naturally and of necessity, without strain or struggle, *first*." For Phelps, the God of heaven was not an awe-inspiring God of "abstract Grandeur," but a "living Presence, dear and real." Rejecting the distant Calvinist God, she chose instead to talk to Jesus "as a man talketh with his friend." Like Blake, Goethe, and Rossetti before her, Phelps replaced God the judging Father with a figure who related more easily to the human condition. Christ "knows exactly what we are," Aunt Winifred reflects, "for he has been one of us." Participating in our humanity through the Incarnation, Christ has also "hoped and feared and craved, not the less humanly, but only more intensely." When the visionary Rebecca Springer met Jesus in heaven, she clung closely to him and addressed him as "My Savior – my King!" He gently stroked her hair and added: "Yes, and Elder Brother and Friend."[68]

The heaven of *The Gates Ajar* is a social heaven. Christianity, for Phelps and her ministerial supporters, is a social religion based on concepts of morality. Even God assumes social – and thus human – characteristics. By focusing on the human character of Christ, the divine becomes domesticated so that it can "socialize" with its human children. God becomes a friend, an elder brother. Elizabeth Stuart Phelps does not rid herself of God; she emphasizes the human nature of Christ so that God can be brought closer to earth and thus be more responsive to everyday cares and needs. The fatherlike God of the theocentric system, who demanded the total attention of his saints, has been replaced by the mothering God who serves her children.

Changes in the religious fiber of both Protestantism and Catholicism during the nineteenth century prepared the way for the integration of love, marriage, and family into the domesticated heaven. Both clerical and popular writers presented the home as the nursery for good Christians and citizens. Humility, charity, piety, and forbearance – "true" Christian virtues – were nurtured in the family setting. For Protestants, family worship, the display of religious articles such as Bibles and wax crosses, and the reading of religious literature all contributed to the establishment of a Christian home. Late nineteenth-century Catholics promoted family prayers where individual devotions would once have sufficed. As the world shook with theological debates, sectarian splintering, and rapid secularization, the Victorians held up the home as a religious refuge.

It was the home, and not the church, which writers described as the "antitype" of heaven. For Protestants, and eventually also for Catholics, a "good" home was the closest thing to paradise on earth. Since home reflected heaven, heavenly activities resembled domestic activities – and not ecclesiastical worship. The type of divine worship found in the book of Revelation had little in common with nineteenth-century family life. Worship was still used as a model for heaven, but it had to be *family* worship. Robert Patterson in 1877 employed the same rhetoric for describing heaven as for describing family prayer: "It [heaven] is the final meeting of the children of God, as members of the human family who are separated during the day, and scattered abroad in pursuit of their respective employments, assemble in the evening in their common habitation." By 1900 the United Bretheren bishop Job Mills could ask his readers if "of late you have begun to look forward to another family gathering and a better family worship. It will come one day" – in heaven. Just as the father assembled his children and servants at the end of the day for prayer, hymns, and a little preaching, God the Father would assemble families in the prayerful environment of heaven.[69]

Heaven could thus still be called an "eternal Sabbath," but it was a Victorian domestic sabbath, not a Puritan sabbath of private contemplation. While some historians regard the loosening of sabbath restriction as evidence of secularization, we must also note the attempts by the Victorians sanctify their everyday life. Not only the church is holy, they said, but everything has the possibility of being holy. In a perfect world there should be no distinction between sacred and profane, for all is sacred. Like Aunt Winifred's "week-day holiness," true religion must exist at all times and in all places. Consequently, every action – from admiring nature's handiwork to creating a piece of art – can be an act of divine worship. This, rather than an ecclesiastical liturgy, serves as the model for an eternal sabbath in heaven.[70]

When we set this into a family context, the rationale becomes even clearer. Increasingly, Victorian women writers, and eventually ministers, saw the sabbath as a time for family activities – not merely for private devotions. On Sunday, when the whole family comes together, the household experiences the harmony and happiness which reflects celestial joy. If this is the case, and the home is a taste of heaven, then why spend much of this precious time in church? Influential authors like Catharine Sedgwick (1789–1867) pushed to limit Sunday church to only a few hours so that the family might spend time going for walks, discussing pious topics, and playing games. Since the family is so revered, she argued, almost by definition whatever it does together is sacred. Heaven is not a dull sermon in a cold church, but father telling stories and mother cheerfully singing popular hymns. We should not be surprised, then, when Elizabeth Stuart Phelps introduced the piano, the most popular of parlor accoutrements, into heaven.[71]

The Triumph of Human Love

The heavenly society of Elizabeth Stuart Phelps frequently irritated other writers. Mark Twain (1835–1910) called her other world "a mean little ten-cent heaven about the size of Rhode Island." Agnes Repplier (1855–1950) exclaimed, "Boston tea-drinkers, here is your Paradise at last!" The Catholic Maurice Egan (1852–1924) in one of his novels poked fun at an Episcopal minister who thought "heaven was in some way an annex to England...an afternoon tea among the angels, under stained-glass windows." Ralph Waldo Emerson (1803–82), in an essay on Swedenborg, reminded his readers that "God is the bridegroom of the soul. Heaven is not the pairing of two, but the communion of all souls." More recently, the literary historian Ann Douglas christened the domesticated Victorian heaven a "celestial retirement village."[72]

What these writers rejected was what one nineteenth-century critic called the "annexation of Heaven." Earthly pleasures had been projected into the celestial sphere. A British Anglican dean put it succinctly: "So these pious ladies desired to go to heaven, not as St. Paul did, 'who desired to depart and be with Christ,' but to be with their 'John' and their 'Roy' amids all the old amusements of earth and senses. Such degrading views of eternity are worthy rather of a Red Indian's expectation, than of a Christian's." The modern heaven of the nineteenth century was not theocentric but the fulfillment of promises first made in the Renaissance.[73]

The modern heaven, which began in the late seventeenth century and flourished in the nineteenth, contained three variations on the meaning of heavenly love. In romantic writing, heavenly love centered on the couple. As a distant observer, God looked on to the lovers' paradise but did not become actively involved. Experiencing the beloved rather than God was the primary focus of the poets' heaven. Salvation came through romantic love, not through grace, the church, or ethical codes. In the poets' heaven, not only was God of little importance; other people were also superfluous. Society became a stumbling block, restraining the urges of the couple for unity. Marriage and family belonged to the institutions of the earth which must pass away so that real love could flourish eternally. Such an antisocial attitude survived within the poetic imagination but had difficulty taking root among those with vested interests in the social order.

In the second variation, heavenly love depended on the institution of marriage. The charismatic love of the poets became routinized in the family-based heaven of middle-class Christians. Romantic love continued in heaven but was ordered and refined by the institutions of church, marriage, and family. For the Protestant and Catholic clergy, only properly married couples could experience heavenly love. Heavenly love for the reunited couple was a purified version of their earthly marriage. Even the exuberance of sexual intercourse could be imagined as long as it occurred between duly married husbands and wives. The Victorian clergy accepted romantic love in heaven, but rejected the romantic tendency to place that love above God or social order. Pure love, which endured after death, was subservient to church and society.

The third variation of heavenly love fluctuated between the radically antisocial love of the Romantics and the institutionalized love preferred by the clergy. Fiction writers insisted that it was not the ordered love of marriage which survived after death, but the love experienced in the domestic setting. The domesticated version of heavenly love held the attention of European and American Christians because it allowed for the combination of romantic love, family life, and Christian values. At the same time writers like Elizabeth Stuart Phelps totally rejected the *clerical* attempt to define both religious sentiment and heavenly activities. Phelps's heaven achieved prominence because it drew its strength from the individualistic trends of Romantic poets and artists, the social conventions of women, and the religious sentiments of the pious middle class.

What Romantic poets, Christian clergy, and pious writers all held in common was the belief that the eternal in the human character would be the substance of heavenly existence. While some notion of the divine might be present, the main purpose of heaven was to cultivate human love. Heaven was not earth transformed; it was earth stripped of the non-essentials. Celestial love could be experienced in the gaze of the beloved, the embrace of a lost child, or the construction of heavenly cottages. For these writers, there was no difference between divine and "pure" human love. Heavenly love, like Christ himself, revealed the essential union of human and divine. The weak barrier between heaven and earth permitted both the imagination of a heaven which was a perfected earth, and the hope that earth would imitate heavenly conditions. The nineteenth-century heaven was not merely the projection of societal hopes up into the skies. It was an attempt to make sacred those aspects of existence which seemed ultimately relevant in the lives of everyday people. Love, marriage, children, family, friends, social relations – these were the institutions which held fundamental significance in nineteenth-century society. Although threatened, this world *was* fundamentally good. Whether it was the desire for mystical union with the beloved or a home in a celestial suburb, these writers took seriously the Christian promise of everlasting *life*.

CHAPTER NINE

Eternal Motion: Progress in the Other World

"Growth is the law of life," wrote the Methodist Leslie Weatherhead (1893–1976) in 1936; "it is inconceivable to believe that the life after death is a life without continuous growth and progress." To support his position, Weatherhead quoted at length a poem by Longfellow about his dead daughter growing up in paradise under the heavenly tutelage of Christ. Although Longfellow had penned the poem in 1848, Weatherhead confidently included it in his book *After Death*. Popular assumptions concerning the continuation of progress and growth in heaven changed little between the time of Longfellow and Weatherhead. For both, death served merely as a brief pause in the eternal growth of the soul. There could be nothing inherent in the act of dying which caused instantaneous perfection. Death was a thin veil, holding no power of its own. Only the continuous development of the soul in heaven would accomplish spiritual perfection.[1]

Leslie Weatherhead in *After Death* cited four characteristics in Longfellow's poem which resonated with his own views: the existence of heavenly recognition, reunion, growth, and progress. The recognition and reunion of family and friends in paradise, one element of the modern view of heaven, continued well into the twentieth century. Running parallel to the insistence that love survives death was the belief that service, activity, and progress make up the employments of the saints in heaven. Like the belief in the eternal nature of human love, the notion of eternal progress developed in the eighteenth century and flourished in the nineteenth. By *After Death*'s publication in 1936 most academic theologians had abandoned the argument, but many ministers and their parishioners still maintained its validity.

Following the lead of eighteenth-century preachers such as Isaac Watts, Protestant ministers in Britain and America depicted a busy heaven where the virtuous soul continued Christian service. They emphasized that the other world, while free from toil and trouble, was not free from work and service. Certain theologians went as far as to assert that in the next life the unrighteous dead actively worked at their own salvation. Spiritualists in America and Europe, too, enthusiastically portrayed a vigorous and progressive life in the the other world. Their rich and colorful descriptions went beyond the Protestant approval of heavenly growth and the Catholic skepticism of all but the beatific vision. The theocentric heaven of rest and eternal worship continued most explictly in Protestant popular hymnody. Catholic clergy, reared in neoscholastic theology, also preferred the static heaven of Aquinas. Such perspectives, however, had limited appeal: late nineteenth-century Christians, for the most part, imagined a heaven of growth and activity.

Kinetic Revolution in Heaven

While concepts of heavenly progress appeared as early as the writings of Origen (c. 185–254), mainstream western Christianity emerging out of those of Augustine and Aquinas rejected the possibility that the saints change their states in heaven. The time both prior to creation and after human history is changeless and eternal. By the end of the seventeenth century, however, the growth of scientific knowledge had presented western philosophers with a model of progress. "I feel that restless activity is an essential part of the happiness of creatures," explained Gottfried Wilhelm Leibniz (1646–1716); happiness "never consists in perfect possession...there must be a continuous and uninterrupted progress toward ever greater good." If happiness on earth required progress, why not assume that heavenly happiness also demanded growth and development? The saints, Leibniz speculated, "will always have reason to multiply their bliss infinitely," not because they move toward union with God, but since "without the continuous experience of something new and without progress there can be no thinking and therefore no pleasure." If heaven contained human happiness, then by definition it must allow for the continual movement and growth of the soul.[2]

Philosophical speculation on the development of the soul after death argued that due to the shortness of human life the soul needs more than just a lifetime to pursue the highest good. Immanuel Kant (1724–1804) presented immortality as a postulate of pure practical reason. His practical philosophy insisted on a realistic assessment of our moral being. The Enlightenment dream of putting everything under the firm control of reason is an illusion. But although we are imperfect beings, we aspire to perfection. Since saintliness or holiness demands complete "fitness of the will to the moral law," and that this perfection cannot be accomplished within a lifetime, then one must presuppose "an infinitely enduring existence and personality." Kant held that according to the principles of practical reason, "it is necessary to assume such a practical progress as the real object of our will." The personality continues to improve itself after death because the soul, like the living person, struggles to conform to the moral law. Thus one "may hope for a further uninterrupted continuance of this progress, however long his existence may last, even beyond this life." Since only God, as the highest good, possesses moral perfection, the soul must progress endlessly toward the good. For immortality to exist, eternal progress is necessary.[3]

Following the Reign of Terror after the French Revolution, and the Napoleonic Wars, many Europeans lost their optimism in the progressive movement of society. The promises of the Enlightenment seemed lost in political intrigues and social ills. By the 1830s, however, the Englishmen John Stuart Mill (1806–73) and Thomas Carlyle (1795–1881) had succeeded in reviving the notion that, in spite of periodic setbacks, the moral and intellectual condition of humanity was steadily improving. In America, a "kinetic revolution" captured the imagination of the New England Transcendentalists. Thinkers like Ralph Waldo Emerson (1803–82) were obsessed with the symbols of motion: rivers, tides, travel, burning flames, birth, and nurtured growth. "Not in his goals but in his transition man is great," wrote Emerson to a friend, "and the truest state of mind rested in becomes false." Motion and transition came from a divine imperative and illustrated the difference between good and evil: "God invents, God advances. The world, the flesh, & the devil sit & rot." For the Transcendentalists, "the most salient characteristic of religious reality was that it moved."[4]

For many in Europe and America, the availability of material goods and the news of scientific discoveries provided assurance that the nineteenth century stood as the pinnacle of western civilization. Even those skeptical of the outcome of industrialization, such as Emerson, warned: "When a man rests he stinks." By the end of the century, Darwin's theory of evolution (1859), popularized by social philosophers such as Herbert Spencer (1820–1903), supplied the scientific structure needed to explain the inevitability of human progress. Both the Gospel of Success, which legitimized the material goals of western capitalists, and the Social Gospel, which criticized American industrial society, utilized the common belief that action surpassed inaction, change was better than stability, and improvement necessitates growth. By the late nineteenth century, the careful arguments of philosophers such as Leibniz and Kant, the reasoned speculations of Watts, and the mystical visions of Swedenborg were replaced by the enthusiastic testimonies of ministers, writers, and spiritualists.[5]

In 1857 the popular Baptist preacher Charles Spurgeon (1834–1892) cautioned that "the idea of heaven as a place of rest will just suit some indolent professors." Idleness, for Spurgeon, existed as one of humanity's worst sins, almost as evil as drunkenness. "It is an abominable thing," he sermonized, "to let the grass grow up to your knees and do nothing towards making it into hay." The Victorian disdain for the idle, the unemployed, and the shiftless did not merely extend to those on earth but included those in the afterlife. Heaven, as the divine summary of the goodness of earthly life, must be a place of work. "A true idea of heaven," Spurgeon preached from London's Metropolitan Tabernacle, "is that it is A PLACE OF UNINTERRUPTED SERVICE. It is a land where they serve God day and night in his temple, and never know weariness, and never require to slumber." Work was not a curse, nor was it merely a painful means to moral health and redeeming grace. Labor was a blessing, a privilege, a glory, a delight. "Do you know, dear friends," Spurgeon asked, "the deliciousness of work?" Just as the theologians could not imagine a heaven without families, so an eternity of idle worship seemed incomprehensible.[6]

In 1892, on the other side of the Atlantic, an equally popular preacher, Thomas DeWitt Talmage (1832–1902), echoed the same sentiments from the Brooklyn Tabernacle. Instead of a place of rest, heaven is "the busiest place in the universe." Taking his proof from Revelation 8:1 ("there was silence in heaven for what seemed half an hour"), Talmage concluded that "this is the only time heaven ever stopped." For the rest of eternity heaven is, and will be, an eventful place filled with action, noise, and service. "The celestial programme is so crowded with spectacle," Talmage insisted, "that it can afford only one recess in all eternity." Since that half hour happened back in New Testament times, heaven has become even busier because of the addition of new generations of saints. "Heaven has more on hand," Talmage reported, "more of rapture, more of knowledge, more of intercommunication, more of worship." Not only will it be filled with the songs of great choruses and grand marches, but it will echo with the sounds of children: "Heaven is full of children. They are in the vast majority. No child on earth that amounts to anything can be kept quiet half an hour, how are you going to keep five hundred million of them quiet half an hour?" For Talmage, heaven is neither a sleepy suburb nor a worship-filled church, but a "great metropolis" filled not merely with streets, but with "boulevards of gold and amber and sapphire."[7]

While we can credit part of Talmage's vision of heaven to his theatrical preaching style, more conventional Protestant sources also assumed that heavenly life left little time for leisurely prayer. In 1874 the Presbyterian Robert M. Patterson (1832–1911) explained that heaven contained not "holy idleness" but served as the place where "each soul does. . .the work for which it has been exquisitely adapted and carefully trained by the life of Christian discipline on earth." The Encyclopaedia of the Presbyterian Church (1884) mused that if heaven was "a state of

inaction" we should as soon think that it was also "a nursery of vice."
Levi Gilbert (1852–1917) argued that "enforced idleness is one of the
worst forms of punishment known" and so heaven could not possibly be
"celestial lubberland – a paradise of tramps." Even the Episcopalian
Reginald Heber Howe (1846–1924) noted that a heaven of "singing
unending psalms" would be "unsatisfactory and repellent." In an action-
filled heaven, service to God and to each other cured the saints of any
remnants of idleness.[8]

Late nineteenth-century statements on active heavenly life drew from
earlier, more philosophical works. In 1836 the Scottish philosopher Isaac
Taylor (1787–1865) published *Physical Theory of Another Life*, and his
ideas became well accepted during the nineteenth century. For Taylor,
the only way to discuss life after death was by the "rule of analogy." This
life functions as an "initiatory course" for heaven and thus trains us for
the employments of the future. At death we perceive the "consciousness
of life" with more intensity and so "the sentiments we have cherished,
and the affections that have settled down upon the mind, and which
constitute its character. . . will make up the continuity of our consciousness, and compel us to confess ourselves the same." Neither the experience of death nor the judgment of God radically alters the character of
the soul. What death does do is to make the human character – good or
evil – sharper, more vivid, more intense. The life after death is actually
more heightened than that before.[9]

Taylor's rule of analogy set up a correspondence between the earthly
activities of people and their future heavenly employments. Although he
admitted that there are certain passive values – pious resignation to the
inscrutable divine will, calm fortitude, acceptance of suffering – which
prepare us for an eternity of "reverential submission," Taylor preferred to describe the continuation of the active values. He rejected
the notion that after death we have no more use for the "active excellence of courage," the "spirit of enterprise" or the "stirring sentiment of
ambition." If Christ calls us to glory and virtue and the "manly and
vigorous discharge of our parts" during life, then why would he prefer
other values after our deaths? No, Taylor concluded, "the future life shall
actually call into exercise a bold energy, and intrepidity, and ambition
too; – an ambition not selfish or vain, but loyal." When we think of
heaven as the next stage of life then it only follows that we will utilize the
skills learned on earth. All the "versatility, the sagacity, the calculation
of chances, the patience and assiduity, the promptitude and facility"
which we have developed to manage our earthly affairs will find scope in
heaven. God will not permit his creatures to "stand aloof" and be "idle
spectators of omnipotence."[10]

Taylor vigorously opposed those who assumed that the "vast and
intricate machinery of the universe, and the profound scheme of God's

government, are now soon to reach a resting place." Such were "frivolous notions" that presented heaven as a place where the souls recall their life of labor, sing anthems of praise, and exist in "inert repose" for eternity. The righteous souls lead lives of service in heaven. Taylor claimed that such service might involve "encounters with powerful and crafty opponents" which would force the saints to employ all their intelligence and resources. Some saints will be rulers, since God does not need to rule by his immediate presence. Although Taylor stopped short of giving the details of heavenly service, he insisted that the different duties of the saints will necessitate both rule and charity. "They [noble hearts] shall find millions needing to be governed, taught, rescued, and led forward, from a worse to a better, or from a lower to a higher stage of life." Heavenly activity, translated into heavenly service, becomes the means whereby souls progress and thus reach higher stages of spiritual development.[11]

Isaac Taylor's beliefs concerning heavenly service found their way into the writings of many British and American Protestants. The German Reformed minister Henry Harbaugh cited Taylor, Isaac Watts, and Longfellow's poem "Resignation" in his work, *The Heavenly Home* (1853). Harbaugh believed that heaven allows no distinction between "acts of devotion and ordinary employments." All the actions of the saints will be a form of worship, so that "nothing will be secular there. Not only the exercises of stated seasons, but celestial employments and pastimes will be worship. The ordinary flow of heavenly life will be one constant scene of worship." When the Presbyterian David Gregg (1846–1919) felt that his readers might accuse him of "secularizing heaven," he countered with a similar argument. Among "the consecrated people of God" there is no such thing as sacred and secular. "Shoemaking is as sacred as preaching," Gregg wrote in *The Heaven-Life* (1895). Were not the activities of Jesus Christ in the carpenter shop of Nazareth full of sanctity? Consequently, we should assume that in heaven the saints work. They have vocations as many and varied as their personalities and skills.[12]

Although the saints perform various types of service, most ministers only hesitantly explored the details of heavenly work. In 1834 the Unitarian William Ellery Channing (1780–1842) preached on Easter Sunday that the faithful, who now live with the resurrected Christ, are active, efficient joint workers with him. He refrained, though, from describing what type of ministry this might entail. Channing only speculated that "in the progress of their endless being, they may have the care of other worlds." Horatius Bonar (1808–89), a minister of the Free Church of Scotland, argued in 1854 that heavenly service replicates Christian service on earth. Bonar predicted that paradise will include household, citizen, spousal, kingly, and priestly service. He found a scriptural basis for this in the New Testament affirmation that "Christ has made us kings and priests unto God" (Rev. 1:6). The Episcopalian Charles Strong (1850–1915) suggested that heavenly kinghood entails guidance of the soul by other souls. Strong believed heavenly priesthood to be synonymous with service and sympathy. Carrying the theme of heavenly service into the twentieth century, the Union Theological Seminary professor William Adams Brown (1865–1943) wrote in 1912 that "it is as true of the life to come as of the life that now is, that, if it is to be Christian, it must be a life of service." Although ministers spoke only in vague terms about what saints actually *do* to prevent idleness, they enthusiastically agreed that service takes precedence over rest.[13]

Some clergy ventured more explicit discussions of heavenly work. William Clarke Ulyat (1823–1905) spent many years as a Baptist pastor in New York and for twenty years edited the *Princeton Press*. In 1901 he wrote *The First Years of the Life of the Redeemed After Death* which he subtitled, "A new unfolding in theology and in the Christian life and destiny here and hereafter." Ulyat, who confessed his affection for the writings of Elizabeth Stuart Phelps and Swedenborg, explained that heaven is "the busiest of places." Some saints rule over mansions which God has given them. Others are politicians, "but not after their earthly tactics." Partnerships are formed for cooperative work. Specifically, the saints are engaged in "bearing messages, teaching, art work, singing and playing on instruments, conversation and public discourse, philosophic, scientific and theological study, and exercises of creative art." Those with an interest in helping people act as nurses, teachers, and guides to aid those spiritually less prepared. Heaven is "a place of constructive grandeur," Ulyat concluded; "practically it is a workshop."[14]

Ulyat clearly described the activities of the saints as "work." David Gregg, pastor of a Presbyterian church in Brooklyn, New York, insisted that the angels also work. Angels "blow the trumpets of judgement; they pour out the vials of wrath; they roll the wheels of providence; they hurl thunder-bolts." While some might think that such activities are not really "work," Gregg reminded his readers that heaven is "alive with the perpetual hum of industry." Avoiding any suggestion of heavenly leisure, Ulyat and Gregg defined all celestial occupations as work – work free from stress, pain, or alienation. "Theirs is work," Gregg summarized poetically, "but it is work as free from care and toil and fatigue as is the wing-stroke of the jubilant lark when it soars into the sunlight of a fresh, clear day, and spontaneously and for self-relief, pours out its thrilling carol." No longer ruled by the laws of production, heavenly work becomes a means of self-expression, charitable service, and obedience to the will of God.[15]

Heaven is a working city where each of the residents have "their spheres and their appointments and their daily avocations." Comparing heaven to a city on earth, Ulyat noted its "immense activity" which leaves "no place for idlers." Since Christ worked, so will the saints. "Heaven will be a busy hive, a center of industry," Ulyat observed; "productive energy will characterize its inhabitants. There will be no sluggards in the camp, no drones in the hive." Andover Seminary professor Austin Phelps (1820–90), the father of Elizabeth Stuart Phelps, also assumed that in heaven the saints will be busy with their tireless activities of benevolence. Phelps imagined the saints as "ministers of God" or "swift messengers" who reign with Christ as kings and priests. The biblical references to "Sabbatic worship" with its implications of meditation and rest are surely symbolic. "The heavenly choir," he explained in 1882, "must be an emblem, rather than a literal picture." And of what is it an emblem? "Of the gladness, of the spontaneity, of the purity, and of the dignity, of untiring and diversified *service*."[16]

We must not assume that the idea of activity and work in heaven was only the belief of big-city ministers who let their imaginations run wild. Sophisticated theologians in the latter part of the century debated the question of salvation after death and arrived at similar conclusions. In 1836 Isaac Taylor had already speculated that the soul enters heaven in much the same state as it leaves earth. Any more drastic change would mean the annihilation of one being and the creation of a different one. After death the soul slowly realigns itself to more heavenly concerns. Taylor's ideas were developed more fully by the German theologian Isaac A. Dorner of Berlin (1809–84). In 1880 Dorner published his *System of Christian Doctrine*, in which he presented the controversial possibility that souls have a second chance after death to attain salvation. What separated Taylor and Dorner from others who argued that eventually "even the devils would be saved" was the concept that such salvation comes not through purifying torment over many years but through the efforts of the dead in the other world.[17]

During the 1880s Newman Smyth (1843–1925) popularized Dorner's ideas in America. Smyth, minister of a large Congregationalist church in New Haven, Connecticut, spent time studying biology at Yale. His support of Dorner's views on "future probation" harmonized well with the liberal Protestant preference for a caring God. Such a God would offer a chance for salvation to all who worked at improving their spiritual state. Like Isaac Taylor, Dorner revealed that there is no "instantaneous vision of God" at death. In clarifying this claim, Newman Smyth explained that "the final determination of character, which is an ethical process, cannot be dependent upon any physical process like the change of death." During a period of time before the Last Judgment, believers will grow spiritually and be invigorated through their proximity to Christ. Unbelievers will remain "under training which aims at decision for Christ." For Dorner and those who upheld his perspective, "all who had not come to a final decision [for Christ] in this life and all who do not shut themselves against it will be saved." Dorner also assured his readers that even after heavenly salvation "the blessed will never be in want of an arena of satisfying activity."[18]

"Is conversion after death possible?" queried the influential Lutheran professor Hermann Cremer (1834–1903). Are the "remote heathen nations" or those unduly influenced by national customs, position in life, or family traditions doomed to eternal death? What about those "born amid squalor and ignorance such as exist in the great cities of Christendom?" asked the Presbyterian professor E.D. Morris (1825–1915). The possibility of salvation will be offered to all humanity, he wrote in 1887. Only after resisting this offer will the soul be placed "beyond the range of spiritual recovery." Just as Christian missionaries sought to present the Gospel throughout the world, some of the souls in heaven will preach Christian truths to unbelievers. In a more purified existence after death people will be able to choose good over evil easily.[19]

Hermann Cremer, a German like Dorner, argued that people hear the Gospel in the intermediate state – variously termed "paradise" or "Hades." Between the time of death and the Last Judgment the soul lives in a place for growth and development, free from the temptations and trials of earthly existence. Nineteenth-century theologians differed in their appraisal of how difficult achieving salvation after death would be. They also disputed whether or not the vast majority of souls would eventually be saved. In England, Frederick Maurice, E.H. Plumtre, and Frederick Farrar broadened the debate by introducing the possibility that not only do souls in the intermediate state struggle to improve their condition, but the living on earth can help through their prayers. The introduction of prayers for the dead brought the discussion of the intermediate state close to the Catholic belief in purgatory, and accompanied other attempts to infuse Anglicanism with Catholic rituals.[20]

Protestant ministers, however, did not need German systematic theology or the Anglican rediscovery of purgatory to assert that spiritual progress continued after death. For them progress figured as a natural law. In 1847 Presbyterian John Kerr also believed that death does not stop the advancement of the human character. In heaven, the soul evolves in "benevolence, curiosity, self-love, the desire of honour, and indeed, most of our noble and generous affections." Although their founder John Wesley preached the possibility of earthly sanctification, nineteenth-century Methodists believed in heavenly spiritual growth. Writing in 1853, Methodist Jeremiah Dodsworth remarked that even after the Last Judgment the saints will advance to "higher and still higher degrees of perfection," providing them with increases of happiness, "world without end." "In the new state we live and grow in power and character," lectured the Methodist bishop Randolph S. Foster (1820–1903); there we "have opened to us employments suitable to advance and perfect us in noble manhood." After a long period, during which we are thoroughly prepared, we shall move into the third heaven which the bishop was reluctant to describe. "There is no more reason for thinking that the work of perfecting can be brought about suddenly by the disrupting hand of Death," summarized the Anglican Arthur Chambers (died 1918), "than there is for supposing that the cracking of the shell will make the newly-hatched chick a fullgrown fowl." Spiritual maturity, not accomplished on earth, can be attained in heaven. The undeveloped soul — unless it is totally depraved — is not punished but allowed to improve in the refined heavenly atmosphere.[21]

Spiritual improvement occurs in heaven because the saints grow in the knowledge of God and the world. Heavenly education forms the basis for saintly progress. According to Charles Strong the intricacies of nature, human psychology, and intimate relationships, as well as the knowledge of Christ and God, will be available for our study. Quoting an unacknowledged source, he described how heaven will invite our research "not only [of] our earth but [of] the system to which it belongs, and the systems which lie beyond." Scientific exploration, both a lay and a professional occupation in the nineteenth century, continues in paradise. Education and study is a part of the saints' work.[22]

Since the labors and difficulties of study will vanish in heaven, the saint will have continual bliss learning about the entire universe. According to Henry Harbaugh, nothing in the universe which the saints study ever duplicates itself. "Before the eternally advancing spirit, the vast universe of interesting wonders will continue to pass," Harbaugh wrote in *The Heavenly Home*, "inasmuch as these successive revelations will inspire the adoration and praise of the saints, their songs will be never the same — everyone will be a 'new song!'" Knowledge, not necessarily only of God but also of the wonders of creation, motivates eternal praise. According to Robert Patterson, instruction from Christ and the other saints as well as freedom from "bodily trammels" enables the saints to develop mental powers "which in contrast leave us but as babblers in the divine life and in all knowledge." The saints not only busy themselves with acts of service; they engage in a variety of intellectual pursuits.[23]

The heavenly search for knowledge, primarily an individual activity, might be fine for the lone scientist or theologian but it lacked a social dimension. Protestant ministers, whose support of family life in heaven underlined their commitment to heavenly societies, never overlooked the communal aspects of progress. Personal progress in heaven brought about the improvement not only of the saint, but of the whole heavenly society. Following the liberal conviction that individual education brought about societal progress, William Ellery Channing saw heaven as a "world of stupendous plans and efforts for its own improvement. I think of it as a society passing through successive stages of development, virtue, knowledge, power, by the energy of its own members." Reflecting the emphasis on Christian social responsibility during the early twentieth century, William Adams Brown echoed Channing's sentiments. In heaven, "as well as here, we shall be members of a society that is ever facing new problems, ever calling for new consecration," the professor wrote. "There too, as well as here, we may be sure, there will be lessons to be taught as well as learned, help to be given as well as received, experiences to be shared as well as enjoyed." The beatific vision, an ecstatic experience of individuals, made little sense in a liberal Protestant world which stressed the communal dimension of religion and social responsibility. The community of saints, who freely interacted with one another to improve themselves and their heavenly society, comprised the realm of paradise.[24]

The love and concern expressed when one saint taught another glued heavenly society together. The saints, according to Henry Harbaugh, would not be "left to their own resources" in heaven but would be aided in their growth by "superior, or more advanced spirits." The "older sons of immortality" would teach the younger. "Thus the saints would continue the exercise of their prophetic office in Heaven, being instructors of each other, as well as being kings and priests unto God." God directed this instruction, but unlike in Watts's writing, heavenly residents conducted most of the preaching and teaching. God receded farther into the background of heaven.[25]

Children, however, still had the privilege of receiving Christ's teaching. Since they arrived in heaven both physically and spiritually undeveloped, God assured their growth and development. Theirs was the most obvious case of progress in heaven. Ministers comforted grieving parents by predicting that their dead babies would gain training unknown on earth. "What a sight must it be, that of the spirit of a babe, an infant, a prattling child," mused the Presbyterian evangelical George Cheever (1807–90), "growing up in heaven, opening, developing, in the image of Jesus, perhaps beneath the guardianship and teaching of other angels – an employment how ecstatic, how divine!" Cheever, otherwise a proponent of the Calvinism of Jonathan Edwards, insisted that there "must be a nursery, an infant school in heaven" and that the training of the "buds and blossoms of immortal beings" may be a scene of greater rapture than any of the infinite wonders of redemption. Heaven, Cheever wrote in 1853, "might be conceived as one vast ecstatic holy school of youthful happy spirits." While Cheever stood far apart from later liberal Protestants who would open paradise to the unregenerate, the heathens, and the sinful, both assumed that education and not instantaneous sainthood occurred in heaven.[26]

During the nineteenth century, service and education replaced worship as the primary activity of the Protestant heaven. It should not be surprising that service and education, hallmarks of nineteenth-century Protestantism, came also to be the main occupations of the saints in the other life. Striving, struggling, and refining one's life were not merely earthly efforts which led to heaven. Ministers and theologians expected heaven, as the ultimate goal, to be closely tied to the good Christian's existence on earth. Leading a life of honest work, attempting to perfect one's mental and spiritual capabilites, raising a family, and enjoying the varieties of God's blessings were the "eternals" which tied earth together with heaven. For the true Christian, to move from one sphere to the other never entailed a radical break. Christians continued to perfect themselves after death through their charitable activities and through learning. While ministers avoided giving specific details on what types of education or service the saints performed, the basic assumption was that heavenly growth and progress depended on those activities.

Nineteenth-century ministers did not find it contradictory to support the notion that heaven was a place of rest *and* activity. Rest, for them, meant activity free from strain, fatigue, or alienation. They did not say that in heaven the saints alternated between periods of rest and activity. Rather the ministers equated rest *with* activity. Work was worship and celestial progress was God's eternal gift. In a similar manner, David Gregg clarified that the biblical symbol of the "many mansions" referred to homes crowded with employments, fellowship, and pleasures. "A home is a busy place," he elaborated; "the whole man and the whole woman find play there." A home, for this Victorian minister, was not a place of amusement, diversion, or sport – one meaning of the word "play." In this context, to "play" meant to be actively engaged or employed. In heaven, as at home, the total person would be actively and fully involved.[27]

Persisting Theocentric Traditions

By the mid-nineteenth century, the static, theocentric heaven of the reformers was favored by only a handful of Protestant writers. Baxter's *Saints' Everlasting Rest*, perhaps the best example of this ascetic spirit, was still widely reprinted and quoted. Although reluctant to cite it explicitly as the "authority" with which their writings argued, nineteenth-century ministers obviously felt its considerable theological power. A few Protestant works, such as James Kimball's (1812–85) *Heaven*, also described a heaven where "the all-comprehending characteristic of the occupations of the heavenly world is praise. They rest not day and night, saying: Holy, Holy, Holy." He maintained that at death everything radically changes, and that friendship and fellowship with Christ will be such that we will not require human consolation. This survival of an older tradition, by its publication in 1857, was the minority viewpoint. Liberals and conservatives still debated the nature of hell, but they agreed on the nature of life in heaven.[28]

On a more popular and probably more influential level, Protestant hymnody frequently presented a theocentric, changeless heaven. Translations of Abelard's medieval Catholic hymn O quanta qualia appeared in many Protestant hymnbooks, insisting that heaven is a place where "those endless sabbaths the blessed ones see" and that "where no trouble distraction can bring / Safely the anthems of Sion shall sing." The popular hymn Jerusalem, with its frequently quoted stanza "Where congregations ne'er break up,/ And Sabbaths have no end," is based on a Latin hymn from the eighth century. Likewise, in a typical American hymnal from 1880, anthems on heaven include theocentric texts from Peter Damiani (1002–72) and Bernard of Cluny (c. 1150). In spite of American Protestantism's vigorous rejection of Catholic values and beliefs, poetry written by medieval theologians was accepted into the canon of Protestant hymns. Images of endless praise in a jewelled celestial city continued from New Testament times, through the Middle Ages, and into American hymn books. Even Isaac Watts himself, whose hymns were sung throughout the nineteenth century, described a different heaven in his hymns from that in his prose. While an action-filled heaven occurs in his prose, the heaven of his verse is almost exclusively a place for theocentric praise.[29]

Although Protestant hymns sung at Sunday services presented a last glimpse of a God-oriented heaven, they were continuously being undermined by other hymns picturing heaven as home and describing heavenly reunions. Sentimental lyrics, such as those by William Cowper (1731–1800), describe how "the parent finds his long-lost child/ Brothers on brothers gaze." Longfellow's "Resignation," set to music by Charles Gounod, revealed that "she is not dead, the child of our affection,/ But gone unto that school/ Where she no longer needs our poor protection,/ And Christ himself doth rule." Revivalist Dwight L. Moody (1837–99), who teamed up with the hymnist Ira David Sankey (1840–1908) and attracted vast crowds during the 1870s, 1880s, and 1890s, frequently utilized the image of heaven as home. Unlike the writing of ministers who saw the home as a place of activity and work, Victorian hymnody tended to picture it as a place of rest and comfort. The heavenly home of the hymns was not filled with religious instruction, Christian service, and everyday activites. Rest, repose, white robes, and eternal praise – and the occasional meeting with mother – comprised the heavenly home for weary souls.[30]

Although nineteenth-century hymns (especially those sung in evangelical circles) described *earthly* Christian service and work, hymnists exempted heaven from such activity. At death the soul becomes free from the toils and troubles of the world and rests safely in the arms of the Savior. These hymns kept alive the theocentric tradition of the Reformation. While ministers and theologians could alter their understanding of heaven to fit changing social conditions, hymns tended to reflect older perspectives. Sung in a church environment, hymns depicting heavenly liturgy made sense. Just as earthly congregations praised the Lord through song, so would heavenly congregations. Life in a religious community reflected life in heaven. Likewise, hymns which described intimate relationships with Christ in the other world worked well in religious revivals. Making a personal commitment to Jesus while on earth would lead to an intense alliance with him in paradise. Calling on the sinner to turn away from the world, the revivalist preacher promised a future life of everlasting worship.

American and British Protestants kept alive through hymnody the heavenly characteristics of repose and eternal praise. Catholic theologians attempted to maintain the scholastic vision of a changeless heaven through their religious writings. In an 1854 publication, *Terre et ciel*, the French philosopher Jean Reynaud (1806–1863) imagined a Catholic priest rejecting the idea of heavenly progress and any activity in the beyond. "As for activity," objects the conservative priest, "I must admit that we do not share your enthusiasm. The storm that moves the modern times does not move us. The love of life, and the hope for future peace suffices us." As a progressive philosopher, Reynaud emphatically rejected this opinion and thereby provoked the anger not only of his fictitious priestly interloctor but also of the French episcopate. What the bishops and their advisors found especially unacceptable was Reynaud's doctrine of the potential of the dead to influence their fate through meritorious behavior in the other world. Quoting John 9:4 ("We must work...while it is day; night comes, when no one can work") an episcopal synod at Périgneux (1857) condemned Reynaud's teaching. Shortly after his death, the book was placed on the Roman *Index of Forbidden Books*.[31]

While Reynaud's case received little attention even in Catholic theology, Neoscholastic authors often criticized their Protestant enemies for similar errors. In 1870 the American Jesuit F.J. Boudreaux (1821–94) specifically challenged the Protestant view of heaven for allowing human happiness to come exclusively from interaction between souls. Protestants, he believed, neglected the beatific vision. The joys of heaven consisted "essentially in the vision, love, and enjoyment of God himself." He did, however, insist that the beatific vision did not render the saints "motionless and inactive as a statue." Since humankind is active by nature, and since the entrance into heaven perfects one's nature, then "it follows that in heaven we shall be far more active than we can possibly be here below." Intellect, love, memory, and the senses persist in heaven. Citing Thomas Aquinas, Boudreaux discussed how the saints' heightened agility will permit them to move "with the rapidity of thought to the most distant parts of God's universe." Likewise, without giving any details about the nature of celestial activity, French priest Elie Méric insisted that "no, we shall not be condemned, as several rationalists of the present day pretend, to remain motionless in a contemplation without end." God will reward the saints with glorified bodies to accomplish "a wise, well-ordered activity...by which we adhere to all that is true, beautiful, and good." Although activity and motion exist in the other world, they do not improve the spiritual makeup of the blessed.[32]

Wilhelm Schneider, a Catholic bishop in Germany, had little sympathy for the notion that progress should exist forever. "A progress that never reaches its goals," he wrote in *The Other Life*, "can never give contentment. We cannot really love truth if we are always in search of it and never intend to find it." Straightforward heavenly progress was not a viable option, but heavenly activity did hold merit. Eternal rest in heaven "involves the fullest possible activity of all mental faculties," Schneider explained. The constant influx of knowledge and love of God in heaven prevents the saints from suffering weariness or confusion. "This," Schneider summarized, "is the secret of constant motion in rest, or progress after the goal is reached."[33]

Schneider's moving back and forth between the acceptance of activity and the need for rest underlines the struggle between the traditional preference for eternal contemplation and the modern preference for activity. On the one hand, Schneider reported that an eternity of mirth and amusement would bring about boredom and that only a habit of regular work would make time pass quickly. On the other hand, he related a story about a monk named Peter who wondered how a creative spirit could survive an eternity of perpetual happiness in heaven. Listening to the birds sing, the monk fell into a deep sleep and woke up a thousand years later. Everything in the monastery had changed, but Peter never realized he had even slept. "At last the light dawned upon Brother Peter," Schneider recounted, "and he realized that a thousand years in God's sight are but as yesterday, and no longer doubted the possibility of enduring eternal happiness in heaven."[34]

Other Catholic teachers showed no vacillation in rejecting the idea of the eternal enhancement of the saints. Engelbert Krebs (1881–1950), professor of dogmatic theology at the University of Freiburg in Germany, totally condemned such beliefs. In a frequently republished 1917 treatise, he explicitly denied any spiritual progress or new discoveries in heaven. When the soul achieves blessedness it enjoys the "instant imprint of the divine essence." At that point, the saint possesses the highest life and eternal rest. Any thought that the soul may be able to expand its pleasures is merely transferring "ideals of earthly life into the blessedness of the life beyond." If the saints are made perfect in eternal life, why do they need to move, progress, or do anything but enjoy the beatific vision?[35]

The Catholic view of heavenly activity without progress must be seen in the context of the doctrine of purgatory. Purgatory purifies souls that are stained by sin and guilt. Unfit for the beatific vision, they must be prepared through a long and painful process of purification and refinement. Through the mercy of Christ and the petitions of the living – not through their own effort – the souls' time of suffering can be shortened and progress ensured. Once in heaven the saints experience the beatific vision without the need to move up the sacred ladder. In heaven, "each one will be perfectly contented, entirely satisfied. No one will envy another, no one would exchange with another. Everyone in Heaven is in the right place, in perfect order, in just equality with the others." Saints recognize and love family members but this interaction does not entail spiritual growth. Love is eternal, it does not grow or change. "At death," explained the Jesuit Christian Pesch (1835–1925), "the state of pilgrimage or time of making merit or demerit ends."[36]

While the doctrine of purgatory and traditional Catholic descriptions of heaven denied the need for the saints to improve their state there, papal views on progress further prolonged the scholastic heaven. Throughout the nineteenth century, as Catholicism lost its hold over the political centers of Europe, the Roman hierarchy issued condemnations of various trends in western society. Among those trends decried as departures from the true faith was the assumption that progress is inevitable and constructive – both in social life and in religious ideas. In 1864 Pope Pius IX dismissed the idea that "divine revelation is imperfect and therefore subject to a continual and indefinite progress" as an "error of our time." Again, in 1907 in order to curb liberal Catholics, Pope Pius X explicitly condemned the idea that the laws of evolution apply to "dogma, Church, worship, the Books we revere as sacred, even faith itself." Pius X rejected the notion that "in a living religion everything is subject to change, and must in fact be changed." These papal messages, aimed specifically at those who hoped to modify religious teachings to conform to changes in modern society, reasserted the Catholic preference for tradition, authority, and the eternal nature of truth. To assert that the saint slowly progressed toward God in heaven far overestimated the power of evolution. Since the Catholic hierarchy rejected those who tampered with religious truths on the less-than-perfect earth, it would never recognize the possibility of change in the perfect sphere of God's heaven. Heaven, like the Church, was eternal and unchanging. It would only be with the decline of Neoscholastic theology during the latter part of the twentieth century, and the rise of openness to Protestant and modern thought, that Catholics would modify the static heaven of the beatific vision.[37]

Spiritualism: A Thick Description of Heaven

By the end of the century, opposing groups in Britain and America were pulling the discussion of life after death in two directions. On the one hand, scientific skepticism and philosophical speculation fuelled the tendency, begun during the Enlightenment, to analyze the meaning of "immortality" rather than the theological term "heaven." The debate in philosophical circles focused not on whether heaven exists, but on whether or not the soul can survive death. At the Harvard Divinity School, the annual Ingersoll lectures provided a platform for discussing immortality. In 1898, William James (1842–1910) entirely avoided the question of the Last Judgment and proposed instead that "for my own part, then, so far as logic goes, I am willing that every leaf that ever grew in this world's forests and rustled in the breeze should become immortal." Thinkers such as William James and Josiah Royce (1855–1916) felt no impulse to create a heaven constructed out of biblical or traditional Christian images. Although they still supported the possibility of immortality, they used logical rather than theological premises to prove the soul did not die. The literature on immortality, which proliferated at the turn of the century, presented clever arguments based on reason but lacked even the most subdued descriptions of eternal life given by theologians.[38]

While philosophers remained confined in their analysis of immortality by reason, and theologians by biblical and sectarian restraints, a new movement sought to open up the afterlife to scientific inquiry. Spiritualists and religious visionaries meticulously detailed life in heaven by way of their own personal experiences. Life after death did not have to be merely believed, but could be proved through the senses. Their writings comprise a "thick description" of the nature and activities of other-worldly societies. In their portraits we find a heavenly culture containing families, social institutions, work patterns, artistic expressions, and value systems. Although each account of the afterlife contains a unique plot, series of characters, and heavenly landscape, a common set of values and beliefs structures this rich literature. The fluidity between life and afterlife, the concern of the dead for the living, the ability of the soul to progress intellectually and spiritually, and the elimination of a dramatic Last Judgment were ideas shared not only by spiritualists and visionaries, but also by many Protestant ministers. With a few exceptions, the other world of spiritualism did not radically differ from the heaven of most nineteenth-century Protestants – in spite of the antagonism felt by each group for the other. Protestant ministers preached an active, progressive heaven filled with service and spiritual growth. The literature of spiritualists began with those assumptions and went one step further to provide the colorful details which they insisted proved the existence of eternal life for all.[39]

Modern spiritualism began in the mid-nineteenth century when mysterious knockings were heard in the home of an upstate New York family. The Fox family interpreted the tappings to be the voices of the dead trying to communicate with the living. In the years following the initial 1848 tappings, countless mediums in America and Europe arranged séances or meetings between the spirits and their living relatives. Mediums assembled the messages and published them in books. Most séance transcripts, however, fall short of providing an interesting view of heavenly culture. Mediums and families questioned the spirits with the intent to prove they had contacted a specific person. Proof of a successful heavenly communication was determined not by the spirit's profound messages but by the quantity of specific (and often trivial) details he or she could remember from the past life. Such details assured the audience that the medium had actually contacted a particular dead person. If the spirit bypassed the séance and medium and spoke directly to a receptive person through telepathy, a clearer picture of heavenly activities resulted. Spiritualist descriptions of the afterlife continued well into the twentieth century, showing little deviation over a hundred-year period. Although American and European society was transformed between 1840 and 1940, the other world remained remarkably stable.

The published reports on spirit communications form a literary genre which can be compared favorably to Protestant visionary narratives and popular fiction in its ability to provide details of heavenly culture. Spiritualists and visionaries assembled their image of heaven from the information personally conveyed to them through dreams, trances, mystical visions, or in séances. Writers such as Elizabeth Stuart Phelps, Mrs. Oliphant (1828–97), and Agnes Pratt acknowledged that their portraits of heaven came from their imagination, but their descriptions closely resemble spiritualist statements. While Elizabeth Stuart Phelps drew heavily from her father Austin Phelps's theological library, all her writings show the influence of Swedenborg and spiritualism. As an advocate of women's rights, she might have been impressed by the influence women held within the spiritualist movement and the egalitarian quality of the spiritualist heaven. Agnes Pratt, in her short story "The City Beyond," combined spiritualist beliefs such as heavenly vegetarianism with more traditional Christian images. In spite of their Protestant associations, fiction and visionary writers painted – in the style of the spiritualists – a vibrant heaven full of drama and activity.

In 1898, Eliza Bisbee Duffey (died 1898) summarized the relationship between spiritualism and her perception of the Christian heaven. "It is the mission of spiritualism, with its direct communication with the inhabitants of both the higher and the lower spheres," she wrote, "to revise these [theocentric] conceptions of the future, and bring them more in harmony with reason and common-sense, justice, and mercy; to recognize the law of progress as the law of the spiritual as well as of the material universe, and to set the star of hope in the zenith of even the deepest hell." In spite of over a hundred years of Protestant discussion of a progressive heaven, Duffey criticized the Christian "old theology" as painting a heaven "of harps and crowns, idleness, palm-bearing, and perpetual psalm-singing" and a hell of "physical torture."[40]

Spiritualists knew that this could not be our eternal fate. Their communication with the dead gave them "back the fragments of their broken faith, now cemented beyond any possibility of breakage by the strength of their new knowledge and *certainty*." Spiritualists felt that they showed modern society not merely how to talk to the dead, but how to renew their trust in the eternal nature of life. Spiritualism, according to Gladys Osborne Leonard, gave people "back their lost faith, their hope for Eternity and reunion with those they love." In spite of ridicule and condemnation by more orthodox Christians, spiritualists maintained that their beliefs only served to uphold true religious sentiments. They, and not orthodox Christians, fought against the materialism which denied the existence of our spiritual being. "We want to get something that will beat materialism," reasoned the spiritualist and novelist Arthur Conan Doyle (1859–1930); "we want a religion that you can prove." For spiritualists, conversations with the dead strengthened their confidence in a just God who offered an eternity of spiritual growth and well-being to all people.[41]

The epitaph to spiritualists Catharine (died 1893) and Levi Smith at Laurel Hill Cemetery in Philadelphia succinctly sums up this conviction: "Life is eternal; Death is merely a change of conditions." The division between life on earth and in the other world for the spiritualist is nonexistent. "There is no death," reflected another commemorative tablet, "There are no dead." The movement through the veil into the spirit world happens so smoothly that the dead often are unaware that they have even died. After meeting an angel, Mrs. Oliphant's character "Little Pilgrim" wonders, "Perhaps I have died too." James Hyslop,

Columbia professor and secretary of the American Society for Psychical Research, wrote in 1918 that according to the mediums he worked with, "some spirits do not know they are dead." Dying, although a dramatic event for friends and family, merely permits the soul to be freed of certain earthly limitations. Memory, personality, fears, strengths, and character flaws accompany the soul through the veil. Even a type of body, an astral body, remains with the spirit after death.[42]

Following the path of Swedenborg, spiritualists rejected the Christian concept of the Last Judgment and stressed the loving capacity of God. Rather than condemning souls to eternal torment, God permits them to develop their spiritual capabilities in a temptation-free world. Instead of speaking of "heaven" – a term laden with Christian conceptions – many spiritualists adopted more neutral terms such as "otherworld," "afterlife," "summer land." The Anglican priest and spiritualist G. Vale Owen (1869–1931) described how all souls come into the next world, including those who want to "progress through the lower spheres into the higher." The coarseness transferred from earth "gradually gives place to more rare conditions," he wrote in 1913, "and the higher you go the more sublimated is the environment." God has created a basically good humanity which, after being freed from the debilitating environment of an earthly existence, progresses in knowledge, creativity, and love. Although each person possesses a set of higher powers, they cannot be exercised until released from the limitations of disease and decay. "This is the one desire of the spirit," reflected the medium William Stainton Moses (1839–92): "More progress! More knowledge! More love! 'till the dross is purged away, and the soul soars higher and yet higher towards the Supreme." Just as evolution dictates the gradual improvement of the earthly species, spiritualists held that a similar law exists in the next life. After death, the soul slowly refines itself, throwing off those character traits and errors of judgment natural to the lower states.[43]

Initially the soul may not be prepared for the delights of spiritual living. Those who on earth sank to sub-human levels – drunkards, seducers, murderers – languish in regions reminiscent of Dante's hell. "These lower planes are *darker*," reported Gladys Osborne Leonard in 1931; they consist of "dark gloomy rocks forming caverns and crevices, pools of dark water, and [convey] an overwhelming feeling of loneliness." If the less refined were to enter the higher levels of heaven immediately, according to John Oxenham (1852–1941), "they'd simply hate it. They've got to be trained up to it bit by bit, and that takes time." While spirits who reach higher levels of existence help those less developed to re-evaluate their lives, no one can force them to choose a more spiritual existence. Ultimately, "one must find the road by oneself and no other spirit can do that for one."[44]

At death, the spirit joins those other spirits who share a similar outlook and level of spiritual development. For most of them, this means the creation of a society which reflects their continuing attachments to earth. During this stage of development, the spirit feels hunger and wants food. When they speak through mediums about their lives, they describe their houses, their clothing, and even the type of cigars they smoke. At this early stage, spirit minds are full of the memory of earthly life so that it "shut[s] out all realization of death or a spiritual world in its proper form." Spirits who communicate to mediums at this stage often delude and trick the earthbound because of their low level of spiritual development. The Swedish politician Erik Palmstierna (1877–1959) described the same phenomenon in Christian terms: "When Christ speaks of mansions, it means stages of spiritual development of each spirit, who is ready to enter the first mansion. Those mansions do not receive bad souls who listened to evil. They remain near earth." Spirits who fixate on earthly things, according to novelist Elizabeth Stuart Phelps, in many cases "simply lack the spiritual momentum to get away from it [the earth]." The souls hover aimlessly over the earth, incapable of progressing upward.[45]

In order to progress, the spirit works toward its own improvement and aids in the improvement of others. Heavenly evolution does not merely happen; the soul must work. "Life here is a constant occupation," Palmstierna related, "spirit life is full of activity and everyone has a special work to do." The soul pursues this purposeful activity in three different ways: through the expansion of his or her knowledge, by developing creative talents, and by demonstrating an increased capacity to give love and emotional support. Work in the spiritualist heaven is a combination of education and service. If the spirit is not mired among the gloomy rocks of self-pity and error, then it must actively engage in deepening its intellectual and emotional capabilities. Rest, contemplation, prayer, and religious rituals have no place in an afterlife geared toward activity, growth, service, and work.[46]

Spirits, of course, work without ever feeling the exhaustion, frustration, or boredom of earthly toil. "There was no manifestation of corroding care," Eliza Duffey reported, "no complaint of weariness, no apparent desire to shirk their appointed tasks. Each worked as though it were not only a duty but a pleasure to be thus employed." Spiritualists noted that on earth people frequently felt forced into their jobs and although "conscious of his or her ability to do something else far better. . .did not get the chance." John Oxenham in *Out of the Body* especially sympathized with "the black-coated workers. . .Civil Servants" who after their deaths in World War II could pursue more interesting careers. "This war has been a mighty release to them," he wrote; "it gives many of them the chance of fulfilling their highest selves and becoming whole men." The alienation of the worker, and particularly the manual laborer, vanishes in heaven. Leisuretime activities, intellectual exercises, and interaction with others all form one meaningful type of "work." Rather than emphasize the limitless opportunities for enjoyable pastimes, spiritualists envisioned a non-alienating, work-based society.[47]

Spirits spend most of their time working on intellectual and creative matters. Educational institutions proliferate in the spiritualist heaven. Schools train budding scientists to invent and discover – first by using instruments and later merely by exercising their own will. In *Beyond the Gates*, Elizabeth Stuart Phelps noted that a great many souls "seemed to be students, thronging what we should call below colleges, seminaries, or schools of art, or music, or sciences." Libraries, according to Eliza Duffey, take over the roles of temples and contain "not a shrine, nor an altar of any kind, but innumerable volumes arranged on shelves which extended from floor to ceiling." John Oxenham noted how "every thought – and word – and deed, of every man, woman, and child since time began" as well as "every book ever published, from the mud tablets of ancient days, to the latest thriller published today" is catalogued and made available to heavenly readers. Mrs. Oliphant's "Little Pilgrim" discovered a heavenly archive where a "historian" worked upon a "great history...to show what was the meaning of the Father in everything that had happened, and how each event came in its right place." Knowledge of the ways of God and the universe does not come to the dead immediately, but through slow, careful work. Heaven is the perfect place for education – the student never tires, the teacher possesses excellent insight and patience, and the study lasts forever.[48]

Heavenly education benefits the living as well as promoting the spiritual progress of the dead. In *Heaven Revised* (1898), spirits whisper into the mind of an earthly orator the words which will eventually captivate his audience. Likewise, in *Lowlands of Heaven* (1922), Vale Owen related that musical conservatories in heaven are "devoted to the study of the best methods of conveying musical inspiration to those who had a talent for composition on earth." The inspiration of earthly scientists also frequently originate in the discoveries of the spirit world. John Oxenham, whose spiritualist revelations first appeared in *The Methodist Recorder*, wrote that "doctors, scientists, especially scientific chemists, psychologists, farmers and so on, had open to them here [in the other world] enormous fields of discovery reaching far beyond their highest dreams." Their greatest hope after making their heavenly discoveries is to "impart it to those still toiling in the dark below." For the spiritualists, the dead played a far greater role in the lives of the living than traditional Protestantism permitted. Reversing the Catholic notion that the living help the dead escape purgatory through their prayers, spiritualists insisted that the dead serve as the source of spontaneous inspiration, intuitive moral guidance, and scientific achievement. The dead, moreover, have more power than the Catholic saints who can only ask God or Christ to help their devotees. "We spirits have an enormous work," explained Erik Palmstierna in *Horizons of Immortality*, "as it is for us to manage man on earth."[49]

In order to progress, the souls work at occupations which engage their creative as well as intellectual faculties. From the spiritualists' perspective, no one willingly works as a coal miner or a civil servant. Teachers, preachers, physicians, artists, musicians, even lawyers – "who make the natural and spiritual laws of the universe their especial study" – develop the inventive sides of their professions. Likewise, "politics, finance, money, have no place here." Those occupations, like coal mining and governmental bureaucracy, deal with earthly matters, while music, teaching, and art have elements of creativity indicative of their "higher" origins. Musical conservatories train souls in composition, performance, singing, and ecclesiastical music. Symphony performances include color and fragrance as well as sound. In 1869 Henry Horn conveyed to his readers the existence of two heavenly theaters, one producing earthly dramas and the other for original heavenly plays. Spiritualists, who saw art, music, and theater on earth limited to leisuretime activities for a special few, took hope that in the other world they would be raised to the level of meaningful employment. Souls do not just enjoy the arts in a superficial way; they pursue them with earnestness and thoroughness. People who never had the opportunity to develop their artistic talents find the world's greatest artists to guide them and an eternity to study their craft.[50]

While institutions educate some souls and provide opportunities for their creativity to flourish, moving the soul beyond earthly cares depends on emotional, not merely intellectual, development. The refinement of interpersonal relationships through the heightened expression of affection, support, and love serves as a barometer of the soul's progress. In Eliza Duffey's narrative of heaven, men who gave their earthly lives over to intellectual, scientific, and business pursuits and never "cultivated the affections" end up in a land of "perpetual ice and snow" in the other world. Although the spirit guides, who accompany newly arrived souls on their journeys, explain and interpret the function of heavenly society, they focus primarily on integrating the soul into an emotionally refined atmosphere. Spiritualists explained how goodness, charity, affection, courage, and selflessness are innately human characteristics but are often ignored in the unhealthy environment of earthly life. Spirits must learn about their inborn emotional strengths, just as they discover their intellectual and creative talents.[51]

A sign of accomplishing this refinement of love and compassion is the willingness of the spirit to travel to the lower realms of heaven and aid the emotionally disabled. Although the men in *Out of the Body* greatly help one another to progress through a perfected form of male bonding, most spiritualists perceived this missionary activity as natural to women. A woman "with a noble purpose in her heart" can safely walk unguarded through the lower regions, "saved by her own purity and nobility." When women attend heavenly college to study science they add the "genius of motherhood" to their mechanical inventions. In *Heaven Revised*, a wife whose moral development places her in a higher sphere journeys to visit her less fortunate husband. Sitting down beside him, she speaks "kindly to him, trying to arouse the better feelings of his heart, not by reproof or moralizing, but by bringing happier emotions uppermost." When faced with the possibility that little progress is being made in spite of the uplifting conversations, the dutiful wife admits, "What a prolonged task it promised to be! However, here we are not limited by time, but have all eternity in which to work." Patience, selflessness, love, compassion – these virtues needed to be learned by both men and women.[52]

If interpersonal relations fail to cultivate emotional sensitivity, other-worldly hospitals and prisons serve to heal and rehabilitate sick souls. *Strange Visitors* (1869) describes a prison composed of "polished seashells so transparent that you could see through it the forms of the inmates." Since "idleness is the mother of crime," heavenly prisoners produce "articles of curious workmanship." Through beautiful surroundings and creative work, the inmates not only learn how to become industrious but also develop their "love of harmony." An 1898 account of heaven includes a "sanitarium for sectarians" where an "aqua-botanical marvel" made of both a tree and a fountain helps reinvigorate souls. The hospital in *Beyond the Gates*, like the prison, is made of "translucent material that had the massiveness of marble, with the delicacy of thin agate illuminated from within." Residents of the hospital lack physical ills, but feel "sick at heart" since their "spiritual being was diseased through inaction." "*They*," Phelps emphasized, "are the invalids of Heaven. They are put under treatment and slowly cured." Even in prisons, sana-toriums, and hospitals, where one might expect to find inactivity and rest, spiritualists warned that the souls are busy.[53]

Amusement and recreation also purifies the soul. Heavenly amuse-ment parks contain "elegantly-formed sleds on galvanic runners which glide over the ground with swiftness most exhilarating to the senses." The author of *Through the Mists* (1898) saw special lounges "composed of various aromatic mosses, soft as air, each one designed to produce its own peculiar effect magnetically." Sports also develop the heavenly character. While John Oxenham denied the availability of spectator sports, he acknowledged the existence of tennis, rugby, soccer, cricket, boating, and "athletics of all kinds." In contrast to more pietistic opinions, his heavenly vision revealed that "there is a great deal of dancing. We have some fine halls. Dancing, you know, has always been one of the favourite forms of Worship." As with all such amusements, heavenly sports are active, participatory endeavors. No passive "watching" is allowed.[54]

Even pets exist in the other world. Not only do they play and give pleasure to the souls, but they encourage loving sensitivity. Gladys Osborne Leonard wrote in My Life in Two Worlds that "when an animal that you have loved and who has loved you" dies, it goes to the third sphere where somebody takes care of it until you arrive. In Love after Death (1944), Shaw Desmond insisted that often a pet "is the first to greet us on the Other Side of death and that their ghosts are often with us here on earth as we move about our daily work and play." Pets, sports, and amusement parks all keep the soul busy while at the same time developing its emotional sophistication.[55]

The environment of heaven is designed to encourage the intellectual, creative, and emotional growth of its residents. Whether they dwell with like-minded souls in an icy land of business and self-interest or inhabit the higher realms of harmony and beauty, the spirits are involved in some type of activity and work. Heaven is not a "celestial retirement village" where the residents merely spend their time visiting one another and playing cards. Following the New Testament, heaven is a city:

> Though they [the cities] were thronged with people intent on various duties, not an atom of debris, nor even dust, was visible anywhere. There seemed to be vast business houses of many kinds, though I saw nothing resembling our large mercantile establishments. There were many colleges and schools; many book and music stores and publishing houses; several large manufactories where, I learned, were spun the fine silken threads of manifold colors which were so extensively used in the weaving of the draperies I have already mentioned. There were art rooms, picture galleries, libraries, many lecture halls, and vast auditoriums.

This description of heaven by the visionary Rebecca Springer underlines the urban nature of the spiritualist heaven. The image of a city captured the feeling of active productivity which spiritualists assumed was the true nature of the other world.[56]

Although they might admit that rural life on earth uplifted and purified the spirit, in a perfect heavenly world urban evils were eliminated and the positive character of the city was allowed to shine. "The width and shining cleanliness of the streets," wrote Elizabeth Stuart Phelps, "the beauty and glittering material of the houses, the frequent presence of libraries, museums, public gardens, signs of attention to the wants of animals, and places of shelter for travelers" reassured her that she beheld a city much more advanced and benevolent than the cities on the earth below. Spiritualists placed a high value not only on the refinement of affections — which perhaps could be more easily cultivated in a rural environment — but also on intellectual and creative endeavors, which demanded the educational resources of a city. For them, motion, activity, and progress were hallmarks of urban life. Along with many Progressive Era reformers, they placed their hopes for a renewed society in city life. Heavenly residents might live in a suburb, but spiritualists and writers assumed that their homes would be within walking distance to the city's educational and cultural facilities.[57]

Spiritualists conveyed movement and motion not only through the abstract concepts of intellectual, creative, and emotional progress but also through the types of technology developed in the other world. Spirits travel in heaven either by utilizing special machines or through the mere exertion of their will. In *Through the Mists*, the author reported seeing special flying chariots drawn by "four steeds of transparent creamy whiteness, gifted with the speed of the winds of a hurricane." Elizabeth Stuart Phelps imagined that those spirits who have not mastered the art of walking on water travel on "a great and beautiful shell, not unlike a nautilus." More common, however, were accounts of movement coming instantaneously, purely through the will to move. If one wants to walk, according to the spirit of Sir William Barrett, one can walk; "on the other hand, if I have been busily engaged on other work, I can project myself in the twinkling of an eye as it is called." Likewise, in *Death-Bed Visions* (1937), angels do not need wings; they materialize when one desires their company. Motion, unimpeded by the physical limitation of space and time, has no boundaries. Once the mind or the will desires to move, it moves.[58]

Will and intention replaced material resources as the basis of technology. In order to create the special amber or violet fabrics with "shadow designs of birds and curious animals," the heavenly manufacturer in *Strange Visitors* photographs the drawings onto the cloth "by the will." Sir William Barrett explained to his wife that in heaven he wears a suit, not a white robe, because he feels more comfortable in it. Although he acknowledged that he could have made the suit himself, a tailor whose thoughts are more skilled at producing suits made it for him. "I am not clever or skilled in the production of suits," explained Barrett, "but others are, and they cannot do my work. Each one to his own trade for a certain time." What defines the craft is not the quality of the materials, but the "rightness" of the craftsman's mind. Matter no longer limits technology, lifestyles, or movement but is subject to the power of the will.[59]

Most spiritualist texts concentrated on describing the everyday life of the other world but some ventured to discuss what exists in the higher spheres. Although souls actively pursue their enlightenment without the direct intervention of God, spiritualists assumed that the direction of spiritual progress is toward the Divine. In the highest spheres, the spirit nears the Divine – referred to as "the Great One," "the Omnipotent," "the great and incomprehensible God." This abstract divinity shows great love and compassion for creation but does not interfere with earthly or heavenly progress. Dennis Bradley in *Towards the Stars* called God the "inspiration of the universe," but he avoided describing God's activities *in* the universe. Souls approach God; God does not approach the souls. Spiritual matter is "ever changing, yet ever re-creating and refining, mounting higher and higher," declared Henry Horn, "from the earthly to the spiritual, from the spiritual to the celestial, on – on – till [it] finally reaches Deity – himself!" God, whose powerful will creates and supports the universe, stands at the end of the path of spiritual perfection. When one evolves to this point the spirit "passes into in-tuitive existence and there knowledge is of no service. Life becomes a life of intuition entirely." Evolving to this point is a slow process, and the spirit author of *Towards the Stars* (1924) admitted that after two thousand years of development he had not yet reached that stage. Spirits progress toward the divine, but the distance separating the two is so wide that progression, in effect, never ends.[60]

For the most part, orthodox Christian theologians rejected the heaven described by nineteenth- and early twentieth-century spiritualists, fic-tion writers, and Protestant visionaries. "Such illusive drivel and profane trifling," wrote the Catholic bishop John Vaughan (1853–1925), "only disgusts and sickens one." The Presbyterian minister Robert Patterson assured his readers that the spiritualists were silly people who predicted that grandmother had knitting-needles in heaven and busily plied her "vocation in a land where there are no cold feet to need stockings!" Christian clergy, while often voicing similar views, refused to acknowl-edge the validity of spiritualist conclusions. Even Swedenborgians con-demned spiritualists as fakes. If everyone could see into the next life, then what was special about Emanuel Swedenborg?[61]

Ministers and theologians, who felt threatened by the popularity of spiritualism in the nineteenth century, were justified in emphasizing the differences between spiritualism and Christianity. Spiritualists, in contrast with novelists like Elizabeth Stuart Phelps and visionaries such as Rebecca Springer, either ignored the existence of Christ or, like William Stainton Moses, presented him as "the great social reformer" who teaches "liberty without license." Even Anglican priest Vale Owen, who maintained that the "Christ sphere" of heaven is the highest one, defined Christ as "the perfect Son of Humankind" whose nature is a blend of "the male and female virtues in duly equal parts." The Christ event, so central to Christian theology, held little interest for spirit-ualists. They preferred the reality of communicating directly with heaven rather than having to believe in doctrines centuries old. The idiosyncratic and unsystematic character of spiritualist beliefs made them vulnerable to attack both from Christian believers and from those who rejected their "scientific" proof of the afterlife.[62]

The antagonism between spiritualists and many Christians should not cloud the similarities between Protestant views of heaven and the spiritualist other world. Vale Owen and William Stainton Moses were Anglican priests who left their parishes only because they felt called to full-time spiritualist activities. Both spiritualists and orthodox Protestants used heavenly images to support a particular lifestyle and set of beliefs. The existence of certain heavenly conditions – for instance vegetarianism or women's rights – for the spiritualists proved the need for such social reform on earth. Protestants condemned idleness on earth, not merely because it stood in the way of progress, but because it failed to prepare one for a busy, active life of service in heaven. The earth-heaven connection was circular: we may know what heaven is like if we know what is truly good on earth, and we know what is truly good on earth by following in the patterns laid down in heaven. The proliferation of treatises, articles, fictional accounts, visionary epics, and poetry concerning heaven accompanied a more concerted effort, especially by evangelical Protestants, to reform personal and social behavior. Heavenly culture during the nineteenth century reflected the common assumption that ordered change through education, creativity, and refined sentiments would lead to self-improvement and thus societal progress.

Spiritualist accounts of the other world, with their curious mixtures of pianos and pets, will-driven technologies, and fantastic environments, provided the reader with both the banalities of everyday life and the adventures of exotic, far-away places. The heaven of the spiritualists, although as remarkable as science fiction and as exciting as travelogues, still contained the simple niceties valued by middle-class Anglo-American culture. Pets, clean streets, well-endowed libraries, and non-threatening cities survived and flourished in the other world. Spiritualists not only reassured the public that life after death existed; they reassured them that *their* life continued in eternity.

Anthropocentric Heaven

Protestants and spiritualists preached from their pulpits and articulated in their books and visionary literature an anthropocentric heaven. God, although immensely "Christian" and caring, fades into the background. Christ, when spoken of at all, functions as a teacher and friend. He enters the heavenly environment only long enough to greet newly arrived souls and ascertain their willingness to live a spiritual life. Most of the action in heaven surrounds the saints themselves who work, make discoveries, study the nature of God and humanity, and live with their friends and family. Departing from the Calvinist view that God determines the fate of the living and the dead, liberal theologians even postulated that salvation can occur after death in the intermediate state. Every chance possible is given to humanity. With a positive view of human potential and a God whose charity is endless, late nineteenth- and early twentieth-century theology constructed a heaven where the saints cannot help but grow in goodness.

The theocentric heaven of reformed spirituality, while surviving in Catholicism and certain hymns, no longer captured the imagination of Protestant theologians and writers. A motion-oriented other world replaced a "God-alone" heaven with endless worship. Saintly service – to God and to others – superseded prayer as the primary activity of the other world. Preaching and teaching were substituted for contemplation and the beatific vision. Knowledge came to the saints not in a twinkling of God's eye, but gradually through their own efforts to improve their spiritual condition. In the anthropocentric heaven, where all attention was directed toward the saints – and not to God – motion, variety, and endless diversity supplied the keys to eternal happiness. Even those less spiritually prepared, who under a theocentric system would not have been permitted to sully the refined paradisal environment, worked toward their betterment in the more supportive atmosphere of heaven.

Protestant writers in Britain and America appreciated the concepts of activity and motion, endowing them not only with metaphysical value but also moral worth. Evangelical ministers as early as 1835 had already absorbed many of the Enlightenment attitudes concerning equality, the rights of man, and optimistic hopes for the future. Ministers and industrialists alike supported a gospel of work which condemned idleness as a sin against the divine progress of humankind. Such forces were particularly strong in Britain and America, where national achievement became evidence of these nations' divine election for a special mission. God's choice of the Anglo-American world as the guardian of Christianity necessitated the active involvement of all citizens in creating a model society. For liberal Protestant theologians, post-millennial beliefs that the thousand good years before the Second Coming would come about through the efforts of humankind fuelled the notion that the world was moving toward a happy destiny. It was Darwinism, exclaimed the theologian John Fiske in 1884, "which has placed Humanity upon a higher pinnacle than ever." Although conservative Protestants condemned the idea of human evolution from the ape, they hailed progress and the activities that achieved it. On the question of spiritual growth in heaven both evangelicals and liberals agreed.[63]

Historian Walter Houghton, in his classic *The Victorian Frame of Mind*, postulated that the Victorians promoted work as a remedy for the doubt and ennui which the middle class experienced in their lives. When faced with political unrest, social change, and religious doubt the Victorians girded their loins with anti-intellectualism and embraced a relentless work ethic. Houghton explained that Victorians welcomed the "possibility of by-passing the difficulties of belief by finding the essence of religion or the purpose of life in the pursuit of a creative task, suited to one's own nature and socially valuable." If this is the case, then we might suspect that the Victorians preferred a service-filled heaven not only because it legitimated their work ethic, but because it freed them from certain sticky theological problems.[64]

A theocentric, ascetic heaven depends on a strong understanding of the nature and purpose of God. Once heaven becomes the stage of human activity, and God recedes into the background, belief in that God is less crucial. If heavenly activity means eternal work – even if it is in the service of God – then anxious doubters can be comforted that their agnosticism will not be a central problem. Even if they may not believe in God, they do believe in work and progress. By emphasizing activity over contemplation, theologians avoided explaining the more complicated eschatological issues of the Last Judgment, spiritual body, and beatific vision. Such topics could be left to seminary textbooks. Ministers and spiritualists provided a motion-filled, anthropocentric heaven where overt religious expression was kept to a minimum. The souls could continue their earthly occupations without pondering over the larger issues of the nature of God, sectarian controversies, or the purpose of life.

In 1933, while holding a chair in systematic theology at Union Theological Seminary in New York City, the Scottish theologian John Baillie (1886–1960) published an influential book entitled *And the Life Everlasting*. By the thirties, the experience of a world war, an international depression, and the rise of fascism were threatening western commitment to the inevitability of progress. Protestant neo-orthodoxy challenged the liberals' optimistic doctrine of human nature, rejected their faith in historical progress, and reasserted the centrality of Christ. Baillie easily saw through the nineteenth-century preoccupation with motion, work, growth, and progress. He rightly attributed the conception that immortality entails endless progress to Kant, and pointed out that busyness, the strenuous life, and service had entered heaven during the past few generations. The tendency toward anthropomorphism had fooled people into thinking that their spirits would continue in evolutionary progress forever.

In spite of his insightful criticism, Baillie could not totally reject the notion that eternity entailed activity and motion. "There will thus be plenty of room for adventure, and even for social service, in the heavenly life," Baillie explained, "though it will be adventure and service of a different kind." The alternative to assuming that heaven is either pure repose or pure striving is to realize that fruition — the full experience of heaven — is essentially an activity. While earlier theologians emphasized progressive attainment in heaven, Baillie presented the position that heavenly existence is an end in itself. "Instead of development toward *fruition*," he explained, "there will be development *in* fruition." Baillie still rejected the image of repose and eternal psalm-singing, but he also disapproved of the frenetic activities associated with valuing movement for the sake of progress. Twentieth-century theologians would not be satisfied with either the modern heaven of the nineteenth century or the liturgical images of the theocentric heaven.[65]

CHAPTER TEN

Heaven in Contemporary Christianity

In a Gallup poll published in 1982, 71 per cent of the American public answered "yes" to the question: Do you think there is a heaven where people who have led good lives are eternally rewarded? This figure was only one per cent less than in 1952, and showed a small increase since 1965. Those who believed in heaven outnumbered those who believed in reincarnation by more than three to one. When the pollsters, however, tried to ascertain what one actually *does* in heaven, the polls revealed that the images of the modern heaven, in existence since the eighteenth century, had greatly faded. While 54 per cent of those polled assumed that they would be in the presence of God or Jesus Christ in heaven or an afterlife, only 19 per cent believed that people would have responsibilities there. Less than half assumed that they would see their friends, relatives, or spouses. Although one third believed they would grow spiritually, only 18 per cent thought that they would grow intellectually. Notwithstanding the paucity of concrete ideas of what the afterlife had in store for them, however, only 5 per cent of those polled thought that eternity would be boring.[1]

While Christians still accept heaven as an article of faith, their vigor in defining the nature of eternal life has much diminished. In spite of the current revival of religious interest in America and Europe, the desire to discuss the details of heavenly existence remains a low priority. What appears in popular culture, the writings of educated clergy, and the speculations of academic philosophers, is either a reassertion of the images of the modern heaven or a reduced, truncated doctrine that serves as a compromise between the traditional affirmation of heaven and total denial.

The modern heaven, articulated in Swedenborg's visions and elaborated by nineteenth-century Americans and Europeans, continues to be believed in our generation. Many Christians hope for reunion with their loved ones after death and express their wishes in popular magazines, newspaper in-memoriams, epitaphs, and funerary sculpture. The popularity of books about near-death experiences, such as Raymond Moody's *Life after Life*, underscores the continuing interest in first-hand accounts of the other world. For the most part, ideas about what happens after death are only popular sentiments and are not integrated into Protestant and Catholic theological systems. A major exception to this generalization is the role of the afterlife in the theology of The Church of Jesus Christ of Latter-day Saints. The feelings of many Christians who hope to meet their family in heaven and the well-articulated doctrines of the Latter-day Saints (Mormons) provide the clearest examples of the continuation of a modern heaven into the late twentieth century.[2]

While many Christians maintain a commitment to a reduced and less picturesque modern heaven, twentieth-century theologians reject almost entirely the descriptions of earlier generations of ministers, scholars, and visionaries. At best, the modern heaven is portrayed as a symbolic, imaginative representation of the unknowable. At worst, the images of an anthropocentric heaven are ridiculed as unenlightened fantasy or criticized as human constructs that rob heaven of its God-centeredness. From Fundamentalists to post-Christian radicals, theologians have deserted a human-oriented afterlife and have returned to the God-oriented heaven of the reformers. While we can see the beginning of this transformation in the writings of Kant and Schleiermacher, a full-scale retreat from the modern heaven has come only in the twentieth century. For some of the most prominent Protestant and Catholic theologians of this century, heavenly life – if heaven exists at all – cannot be described by reason, revelation, or poetic imagination.

Consequently, there exists a sharp division between two types of contemporary Christians. One type feels comfortable with a detailed afterlife in the style of either the modern heaven (continuation of family, work, progress) or the theocentric heaven (beatific vision, heavenly light, robed angels singing eternal praise). For these Christians, near-death experiences, the fictional accounts of popular writers like C.S. Lewis, or the visions of sectarian religious leaders like Mormon Joseph Smith provide the basis for discourse on heavenly existence. Life after death continues what is considered to be the best of this life – worship, loving relationships, spiritual insight. To the other type belong those who either reject our ability ever to know what comes after death or deny the possibility that eternal "life" exists at all. These Christians are dubious about the images used to describe heaven and prefer to rely on abstractions which do not depend on visions, revelations, or poetic images. The division between maximal description and minimal description, between popular and philosophical perceptions, between image and abstraction, and between hope and skepticism structures the contemporary discussion.[3]

Modern Heaven: A Wish . . .

In 1983 *U.S. Catholic*, a popular American religious periodical, published an article on what their readers believed about the afterlife. Although the 283 respondents to the survey hardly comprise a statistically significant cross-section of American Catholics, their comments document the continuation of popular nineteenth-century images. Catholics, for instance, want to "hug God" when they arrive in heaven. They expect to meet their family, even "our first baby who died and that I have never seen," and they hope for an environment of natural beauty and unlimited creativity. Although one reader complained that "to picture heaven as a sort of super vacation resort is childish," most respondents felt comfortable in describing heaven variously as a place where lots of baseball is played, an isloated spot in the country, or a region filled with whatever pleases each person. The author of an earlier article, "Heaven: Will It Be Boring?" (1975), calls purgatory a "Continuing Education Center" and heaven a place where the souls are called "not to eternal rest but to eternal activity – eternal social concern." The respondents to the *U.S. Catholic* survey echo the hopes of earlier generations: God will be a personal character willing to be hugged, individuals will retain their personalities, families will reunite, and earthly activities will continue.[4]

By far the most persuasive element of the modern heaven for many contemporary Christians is the hope of meeting the family again. Countless "in memoriam" sections of newspapers throughout Europe and America reflect the belief that families parted by death will be reunited. From the *Holborn and City Guardian* in England, where Danny hopes to meet his sister-in-law; to the *Frankfurter Allgemeine Zeitung* in West Germany, where the belief in meeting again gives a family consolation in their pain; to the *Columbus Dispatch* in the United States, where a widow writes "when my work on this earth is done / We will again be united as one"; the assumption throughout is the same: death cannot permanently separate loved ones.[5]

Even in standardized American lawn cemeteries, where the size and shape of burial monuments are closely regulated, families voice their assumptions about meeting again after death. Simple epitaphs such as "together again" or "always together" are included on the grave-markers of husbands and wives. Etchings of robed couples holding hands and facing the rising sun frequently are the only symbolic representations on markers which must be flat so that lawn mowers can easily cut the cemetery grass (Pl. 57). In European cemeteries, on the other hand, where families are permitted more freedom in expressing their sentiments in sculpture and epitaphs, more explicit statements on meeting again can

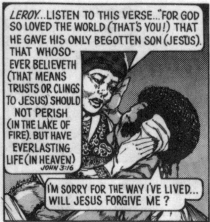

Pl. 56. *"I'll See You in Heaven, Honey!"* Comic strip, 1977. Jack T. Chick, *Soul Story* (Chino, CA: Chick, 1977)

be found. An epitaph in the cemetery of Drumcliffe, Ireland, goes so far as to substitute the vision of the human partner's face for the traditional vision of God.

> *Dear Robert – If heaven be as some aver*
> *recapturing the joys that were,*
> *those lost dear raptures that we knew,*
> *then I shall sit again with you*
> *within a quiet, sunfilled place*
> *and watch the glory of your face,*
> *and talk through all eternity*

Pl. 57.   Grave marker with couple: waiting for reunion. Forest Lawn Cemetery,
Los Angeles, CA, 1950s

of this and that of you and me.
From your ever loving wife Pat. August 1978.

On a popular level, such reflections recall Blake's discussion of friend-ship which "looks for no other heaven than the beloved," or Emily Dickinson's conviction that the "Life that is to be" will be "a Residence too plain/ Unless in my Redeemer's Face / I recognize your own." While epitaphs voicing the eternal nature of love radically have declined in popularity since the 1930s, they do still occur.

In spite of the stark character of contemporary American cemeteries, funerary sculpture frequently commemorates the family. At Forest Lawn Cemetery in Los Angeles, idealized family groups are placed among the bronze statues of American heroes and marble copies of well-known re-ligious sculptures (Pl. 58). The family statues, some bought as memorials and others constructed by the cemetery company, have parents dressed in Grecian robes with naked babies. Although never explicitly stated, the message is quite clear: the family, broken by death, will be reunited in an idealized setting in the next world. In the same manner as Victorian garden cemeteries, which the 1917 Builder's Creed condemned as "un-sightly stoneyards full of inartistic symbols and depressing customs," Forest Lawn reassures families that their love will continue after death.

For some twentieth-century notables, as for the Romantic poets, the eternal nature of love had little to do with conventional marriage. In Highgate Cemetery, London, at the tomb of Mabel Veronica Batten and Radclyffe Hall, the complicated nature of heavenly love becomes clear. Mabel Veronica Batten was the lover of Radclyffe Hall, author of the classic lesbian novel, *The Well of Loneliness*. Batten died in 1916, and when Hall died in 1943 her body was laid in the same tomb. That same

311

Pl. 58. The ideal family – here and hereafter. Forest Lawn Cemetery, Los Angeles, CA, 1980s

year, Una Troubridge, Radclyffe's lover after Batten's death, placed a plaque on the tomb: "And if God choose I shall but love thee better after Death – Una." Troubridge, who died in 1963, was buried in Rome and not at Highgate. Although it might be regrettable that Troubridge is not in the same tomb as her lover, the plaque makes clear that she assumed their love affair would continue after death. For many in the twentieth century, it is love and not official relationships which survive death.[6]

Expressions of the eternal nature of love and the hope for heavenly reunion persist in contemporary Christianity. Such sentiments, however, are not situated within a theological structure. Hoping to meet one's family after death is a wish and not a theological argument. While most

Christian clergy would not deny that wish, contemporary theologians are not interested in articulating the motif of meeting again in theological terms. The motifs of the modern heaven – eternal progress, love, and fluidity between earth and the other world – while acknowledged by pastors in their funeral sermons, are not fundamental to contemporary Christianity. Priests and pastors might tell families that they will meet their loved ones in heaven as a means of consolation, but contemporary thought does not support that belief as it did in the nineteenth century. There is no longer a strong theological commitment to the modern heaven.

. . . and a Theology

The major exception to this caveat is the teaching of The Church of Jesus Christ of Latter-day Saints, whose members are frequently referred to as the Mormons. The modern perspective on heaven – emphasizing the nearness and similarity of the other world to our own and arguing for the eternal nature of love, family, progress, and work – finds its greatest proponent in Latter-day Saint (LDS) understanding of the afterlife. While most contemporary Christian groups neglect afterlife beliefs, what happens to people after they die is crucial to LDS teachings and rituals. Heavenly theology is the result not of mere speculation, but of revelation given to past and present church leaders. Although the number of Latter-day Saints certainly cannot compare with the worldwide membership of the Roman Catholic church or many Protestant denominations, its rapid growth and the level of commitment it demands from its members make it an integral part of the contemporary Christian world.[7]

According to Latter-day Saint belief, Jesus established a church on earth called the Church of Jesus Christ whose members are called Saints. After Jesus' resurrection, he visited the people of the Americas and established his church there as well. Once Jesus had left the earth, persecution, the death of the early church leaders, and the evil character of the people caused the Church of Jesus Christ to be taken from the earth, resulting in a period called the "Great Apostasy." The Savior, however, promised that he would restore his church. In 1820 Joseph Smith (1805–44), a young man from upstate New York, received a vision from God and Jesus Christ telling him not to join any of the existing Christian churches since the true church was not yet on earth. Over the next decade, Joseph Smith received a series of revelations which marked him as the first prophet of the restored church, The Church of Jesus Christ of Latter-day Saints. The ancient golden plates which Joseph Smith discovered and translated, known as the Book of Mormon, set forth LDS sacred history and beliefs. The Bible, the Book of Mormon, and further revelations given by God to Joseph Smith and later prophets comprise their teachings and beliefs. The Latter-day Saints believe that God is a real person with a tangible body of flesh and bones, that all people existed in a premortal life as spirit children of God, and that a lay priesthood should provide spiritual leadership. They deny the existence of original sin, and they believe that family relations can be made eternal.

Latter-day Saints reject the notion that death destroys either the personality or the soul. "Actually there is no such thing as the dead," wrote Theodore M. Burton (born 1907) in 1977, "unless one refers to the mortal body, which returns again to the earth. The spirit lives on, and in the resurrection all of us will be made alive again as each body and spirit unite to form an immortal whole." Life on this earth is merely one act in a long drama spanning several worlds and existences. Before being born to earthly parents, people live as spirit children with their Heavenly Mother and Father. In order to be tested and to receive the "ordinances" (sacred rites and ceremonies that are necessary for eternal progression), spirit children enter into earthly bodies and are born into this world. Everything which occurred in "premortal" existence is forgotten at birth so that the new person may freely choose the proper religion and path of life.[8]

At death, the soul leaves the body and enters the spirit world where a new stage of life begins. The spirit world is not heaven but only another place where the soul develops until the resurrection. Following Brigham Young (1801–77), who insisted that the spirit world was contiguous with the earth, apostle Ezra Taft Benson assured the Saints in 1971 that "sometimes the veil between this life and the life beyond becomes very thin. Our loved ones who have passed on are not far from us." Tendencies and predispositions developed on earth continue in the spirit world. Those who have led an evil life are separated from the righteous, live with like-minded spirits, and experience the torments originating from guilt, fear, failure, lustful desires, and enslavement of their wills to Satan. The righteous, particularly those who have followed the teachings of the LDS church, find themselves in a paradise which contains lakes, forests, brilliant flowers, and remarkable buildings. There is no death, no confusion, and no suffering. Family members meet and greet each other. Spirits, according to the authors of *The Life Beyond* (1986), are "free to think and act with a renewed capacity and with the vigor and enthusiasms which characterized one in his prime." Babies and children who have died immediately become adults, although they can revert to their earlier stages in order to be recognized by new entrants into the spirit realm.[9]

Since there is no judgment at death, evil spirits and those ignorant of the truth are not condemned to eternal suffering. They are given the chance in the spirit world to exercise their free will and decide whether or not to believe in the LDS revelation. Departed Latter-day Saints help those unfamiliar with LDS principles and teach – to whatever extent they can – those who were unbelievers on earth. Church president Wilford Woodruff (1807–98) reported that in one of his visions he saw the prophet Joseph Smith at the door of the temple in heaven, but Smith refused to speak with him because he was in a hurry. Several other "brethren who held high positions on earth" also rushed by. Finally, Woodruff asked the prophet why he was in such a hurry. "I (Woodruff) have been in a hurry all my life; but I expected my hurry would be over when I got into the kingdom of heaven, if I ever did." Smith replied that here there is "so much work. . . to be done, and we need to be in a hurry in order to accomplish it." Latter-day Saints who have been active members in the LDS society continue to teach, do missionary work, and guide other members in the spirit world.[10]

The family, crucial for the promotion of the gospel on earth, continues to be an important teaching institution in the spirit world. Husbands and wives assume the responsibility to "search out their own progenitors and teach them the gospel." It is partly through their selfless service in the spirit world that the Saints progress and are made perfect. Not only do the activities of the Saints continue there, but the church organization itself is maintained. According to some contemporary LDS writers, whatever must be accomplished in the spirit world is under the direction of the LDS priesthood and the priesthood is under the direction of the church presidency. Consequently, emphasized the authors of *The Life Beyond*, "we do not speak of such things as harps, and clouds, and angels with wings. We speak of servants of God, each faithfully laboring according to assignment, each standing in his own office, laboring in his own calling." Work and spiritual progress are an integral part of life after death. While paradise, where the righteous live, is free from cares and sorrows of earthly existence, "it is not a place of idleness; it is the spirit's Sabbath." Just as the earthly sabbath is a time not only of prayer but also of service – visiting the sick, doing genealogical work, sharing time with family – activities in the spirit world include both religious deeds and thoughts.[11]

Although the Saints in the spirit world spend most of their time teaching other spirits, on special occasions they may also seek to help those still on earth. In her book *Angel Children*, which underwent its sixth printing in 1983, Mary V. Hill described the comforting contact that she received from her dead son. In 1971 Stephen Hill, the fifth child of Mary and Keith Hill and barely four months old, died of a congenital heart defect. To help others understand the meaning of child death, Mary Hill wrote a short book on the Latter-day Saint perspective on infant mortality. Quoting extensively from earlier LDS works, Mary Hill discussed how infants become full-grown adults in the spirit world but during the millennium return to being babies. In the spirit world, Stephen would work as an adult teaching the gospel but, if Mary lived a righteous life, she would be able to rear her child during the thousand years before the final resurrection. Mary's loss would be over when she met her grown son in the spirit world and could enjoy mothering him during the millennium.

While her faith was helpful during the crisis, it was not until she went into labor with her next child that she realized her inner resistance: "My mind said aloud that it was alright that Heavenly Father called Stephen into the spirit world, but my subconscious grieved and mourned." She feared that the baby about to be born would also die. Shortly after her new son's birth, as she lay in the recovery room, she saw Stephen, "not with my physical eyes, but in a manner very real to me." Stephen had become a young man, dressed in softly draped white clothes. "His hair was sandy colored," she recalled, "with a soft wave in it, and his jaw square and muscular." Stephen showed great love, compassion, and sympathy for his mother, telling her, "well, Mother, now you have your baby, and there's no more need to grieve for me. We'll have *our* time in the resurrection, and now I'm free to do my work in the spirit world." From Mary Hill's perspective, God had allowed Stephen to come to reassure his mother and show her that "somehow my grief prevented him from being truly free to do his work in the spirit world." Stephen had his duties to perform in the spirit world and one of them was to comfort his earthly mother. The experience of Mary Hill is not an isolated incident, but part of a long tradition in LDS history of spirits contacting earthly relatives and friends. [12]

The world of the spirits and the world of the living are linked together not only by love. A much tighter bond unites the two spheres. According to LDS teachings, the ministering Saints in the next world can teach and preach, but they cannot administer earthly ordinances which are crucial for continued spiritual progress. For each being who has heard the gospel in the spirit world and is willing to accept LDS beliefs, a specific action must be accomplished on earth. Without vicarious rituals, such as marriages or baptisms, converted souls will be limited in their spiritual growth. Members are asked to do the historical footwork needed to learn the names and dates of ancestors who died, and to submit their names so the appropriate ordinances may be performed in Mormon temples. Genealogical research and rituals performed for the dead comprise a major aspect of church life. Remembering the dead is not merely a pious sentiment, but an integral part of the religious activities of church members. "It takes as much work and effort to save a dead person," writes Theodore Burton, "as it does to save a living person." [13]

The performance of ordinances on earth for those who cannot perform them in the spirit world enables the dead to look forward to the next stages of eternity. The Latter-day Saints believe in the Second Coming of Christ when Jesus will usher in his thousand-year reign on earth. This will be accomplished by great physical transformations of the planet. Valleys will be raised, mountains levelled, and the continents will be joined together. The wicked will be destroyed and will have to wait in the spirit world until the end of the millennium when they will be resurrected, judged, and assigned to a place in eternity. The righteous, both members of the church and others who have lived virtuous lives, will be resurrected and their spirits will join their renewed bodies. They then will live on an earth transformed into a Garden of Eden with a perfect climate. Satan will be bound and have no power to tempt the people, who will live in peace and harmony together. Children will be born, grow up, marry, advance to old age, and pass through the equivalent of death – but without pain or disease.

The millennium will be a time of tremendous activity and busyness. On a practical level, "crops will be planted, harvested, and eaten; industries will be expanded, cities built, and education fostered." The work being conducted for the benefit of the dead will be finished during the millennium. During this time, temples will be built in order to conduct the ordinances. Marriages will be arranged and "sealed" in the temple for those who were either single on earth or died young. New genealogical information will be assembled and corrections will be made to any faulty research compiled earlier. During the millennium, all the virtuous who have been resurrected will be converted to the church, requiring that missionary activity continue with great vigor. "It can well be said," concluded Gordon T. Allred, "that the resurrection and millennium, among other things, will be a fine time for the genealogist and temple worker – the finale and crescendo to the whole symphony of vicarious work."[14]

All this activity – on earth, in the spirit world, and in the millennium – enables those who so choose to experience the highest order of perfection and thus to become gods. After the thousand-year reign of Christ on earth and a short period when Satan will be permitted to tempt the righteous ("a little season"), the final judgment will take place. All who have ever lived will be reunited with their bodies and assigned either to one of three stages of glory or to an endless hell. The renewed earth – a sea of glass mingled with fire – will be inhabited by those who merit the highest heaven, the celestial glory. Like the lower two divisions of heaven, the celestial glory will be divided into various levels or degrees. Only those who experience the highest degree of the celestial glory will achieve "exaltation" and become like gods. Those who merit exaltation have not merely succeeded in "going to heaven" or "living in the presence of God"; they have accomplished the higher challenge of personal perfection and godhood. All knowledge, truth, virtue, power, and wisdom may be possessed by those who have reached the highest heaven and become gods. Through exaltation the Saint will display for all eternity the powers and dominion of a god.[15]

Exaltation occurs only if the individual has moved through the appropriate stages of belief and ritual and has led a righteous life. Among the ritual actions which the Saint must accomplish in order to be permitted to enter the highest degree of heaven is to be married for "time and all eternity." LDS theology delineates two distinct types of marriage rites. Marriage performed by civil and most religious authorities joins couples together "until death do us part." At death, the married couple have no rights or responsibilities toward each other; nothing binds them together eternally. A second type of marriage (the one necessary for exaltation) is marriage which endures eternally. This is a special marriage which must be performed in a temple. According to LDS theology only those worthy may enter the temple, and so the couple must be Latter-day Saints in good standing. During this wedding ceremony, the couple kneels at the altar in the temple where they are joined together for time and all eternity under the direction of the priesthood. This marriage ceremony is called "sealing." Any children born after this special marriage are automatically sealed to their parents. Children born prior to their parents' temple marriage may later be sealed to them in a similar ceremony. It is this sealing power of the "New and Everlasting Covenant of Marriage" which enables the family to exist for eternity in heaven. Without the sealing, nothing keeps the families together after death.

For the members of the church, eternal marriage does not contradict Jesus' reflection that in the resurrection there is no marriage. They take this New Testament passage to refer to those people who were married only for their lives on earth. People who married merely according to the laws of the world will serve as ministering angels to those married for eternity. Single people can only become angels in heaven, never gods. "There is marrying and giving of marriage in heaven," insisted Theodore Burton, "only for those who are willing to accept and live the fullness of God's law." The biblical woman who had been married to seven husbands would find herself married to none of them in heaven – as Jesus stated. Only what is joined by God, through the LDS priesthood, can exist forever.[16]

The family not only serves as the basic unit of life on earth , but is the foundation of the celestial heaven (Pl. 59). Couples who have been married in the temple for all eternity, and who meet the other requirements for celestial glory, are not only able to join their families after death, but can also increase those families. One of the distinct privileges of those in the celestial glory is the power of eternal procrea-

Pl. 59.   Lee G. Richards, *Family Reunion in the Other World*. 1949. Celestial room of
Idaho Falls temple.

tion. "Exalted beings," summarized Duane Crowther, "will enjoy the
power of procreation and will continue the process of bearing children
which they began on earth during mortality." While the details of this
eternal reproduction are not known, it is suspected that the residents of
the celestial heaven reproduce "after the same manner that we are here"
but without sorrow, pain, or distress. Since the Latter-day Saints believe
that God has a body and is not spirit, it makes sense that the gods
reproduce in a human manner. A woman achieves her sense of godhood
by participating in her husband's eternal priesthood. Because of this, she
is permitted to "bear the souls of men, to people other worlds" and to
"reign for ever and ever as the queen mother of. . .numerous and still
increasing offspring." Those women who have been unable to reproduce
on earth, but have been faithful and received the proper ordinances, will
make up for the temporary lack of offspring by mothering countless spirit
children.[17]

The offspring of exalted husbands and wives are the "spirit children" who eventually enter bodies and populate other worlds. "Just as men were first born as spirit children to their Eternal Father and His companion," Crowther clarified, "the children born to resurrected beings are spirit beings and must be sent in their turn to another earth to pass through the trials of mortality and obtain a physical body." Thus, while the residents of the celestial heaven have achieved full perfection in knowledge, power, and glory, they constantly progress through their eternal reproduction. The essential activity of eternal life of the highest order is to be like God – to populate and rule over countless worlds inhabited by spirit children who have assumed bodies. God does not only grow by learning new laws and discovering new facts, but "His never-ending joy and glory is in the immortality and eternal life of His children, and the increase of His dominion is His progression throughout eternity." This is the aim of human progression on earth, in the spirit world, and in the millennium. "The secret of the ages has been made known – God is an exalted man," exclaimed the authors of *The Life Beyond*; "let none in the household of faith be guilty of reducing these exalted verities to myth or metaphor."[18]

The understanding of life after death in the LDS church is the clearest example of the continuation of the modern heaven into the twentieth century. Since the church rejects the dualism between spirit and matter and insists that "spirit" is only refined and purified matter, a fluidity exists between the two spheres. The belief that the spirit world is on or near the earth emphasizes the closeness of the two worlds. Reports of visits of the spirits to earth or of LDS members to the spirit world make the dividing veil even thinner. The notion of the family – both on earth and in the spirit world – is a controlling theme which dominates the LDS outlook. Collecting historical data on ancestors, to be used for vicarious baptisms and sealings, serves as an everyday reminder that the dead need the help of the living. The two worlds are bound together. Even the notion that human beings have the possibility of becoming gods reduces the distinction between the human and divine realms. God, the angels, and the spirits were all at one time human creatures subject to the vicissitudes of life on earth or in another world. Like the heaven of many nineteenth-century writers, the LDS spirit world remains precariously close to our own.

What continues in the spirit world is not the lives of individuals but the life of the church. Unlike earlier visionaries – novelists, spiritualists, ministers – who described many secular occupations in the other world, the activities of those in the LDS spirit world are entirely religious. Diverging from other Christians, Latter-day Saints place more importance on individual personalities in the continuation of the structure and authority of the church. Not only does a general concern for service and teaching continue, but also the specific rules (e.g., ordinances) and hierarchy (e.g., priesthood) of the church. If writers in the eighteenth and nineteenth centuries tended to eliminate denominational differences n heaven, then LDS teachings promote the reverse. Like the people on earth, the spirits in the other world need specific church ordinances in order to progress spiritually. The LDS afterlife is distinctively sectarian.

In the same manner, the continuation of the family is determined by religious considerations. While other defenders of the survival of love, marriage, and family life after death assume that all who love will be reunited regardless of religious belief, the church plays a much stronger role in LDS family reunions. It is not love by itself which merits eternal life, or even love expressed by devoted Christians, but love sanctioned and made everlasting by the special temple ordinances of the church. Without the specific involvement of the LDS church, no family can hope to be reunited for eternity. They might meet again in the spirit world, but unless the couple and children are sealed together they cannot survive as a family. So, while love, marriage, and family life are essential to the LDS understanding of the afterlife, they will not achieve anything everlasting in their own right. The key to eternal marriage and ever-lasting love comes through the specific beliefs and activities of the church, not through the human institutions of marriage and family.

Likewise, other advocates of the modern heaven would reject the notion that heavenly love between couples results in birth. Latter-day Saints hold this as a critical part of their theology because it explains how we arrived on the earth. Over and over again in LDS literature the emphasis is not on the celestial family's eternal love but on its ability to reproduce. It is not only the continuation of human love which is im-portant from the LDS perspective; it is the reproduction of spirit beings. The establishment of an eternal patriarchal order based on rule and re-production is a stark divergence from much of the nineteenth-century heavenly literature which predicted the continuation of intimate, couple-based family life.[19]

While LDS theologians would probably reject the idea that their beliefs have much in common with liberal Protestantism, they do share a confidence in post-mortem salvation with many late nineteenth-century theologians. Both would agree that earthly life, although of great significance in the plan of salvation, is not the final step. Consequently, life in the spirit world will be busy. Latter-day Saints believe they will progress through selfless service, and that non-Saints will grow in knowledge of the truth of the gospel. Growth and progress will continue during the millennium through preaching and administration of the temple ordinances. While even nineteenth-century spiritualists were reluctant to predict that spiritual growth in the other world could eventually end with human deification, LDS theology took spiritual progress after death to its logical conclusion. The possibility of people evolving into gods is a Latter-day Saint tenet. Even after the person becomes a god and experiences perfect power, knowledge, and righteousness, eternal reproduction allows for continual growth.

In the nineteenth century, the Latter-day Saints bent to the will of the United States government and stopped the practice of polygamy. Recent revelations have changed the earlier prohibition of blacks from receiving the priesthood. There has been, however, no alteration of the LDS understanding of the afterlife since its articulation by Joseph Smith. If anything, the Latter-day Saints in the twentieth century have become even bolder in their assertion of the importance of their heavenly theology. The number of books on eternal life increases yearly, Mormon information centers throughout the world dramatize the drama of salvation for the non-believing public, and contemporary LDS writers feel comfortable in quoting extensively from nineteenth-century visionary accounts. In the light of what they perceive as a Christian world which has given up belief in heaven, many Latter-day Saints feel even more of a responsibility to define the meaning of death and eternal life.

The Decline of the Modern Heaven

The modern heaven – exemplified by the visions of Swedenborg, the writings of Elizabeth Stuart Phelps, and Mormon theology – has become the minority perspective during the twentieth century. Rich and detailed accounts of the afterlife, accepted in the nineteenth century, are labelled as absurd, crude, materialistic, or sheer nonsense. "No reasonable person can hold such a belief any longer," stated a Dominican prior in 1981. For theologians concerned about the accessibility of the Christian message in a world of science and technology, the emphasis on the eternal nature of earthly institutions such as marriage and work weakens the seriousness of the promise of life after death. "The more detailed pictures of life after death are," explained Renée Haynes, "the less acceptable they seem to be." Rather than allowing for the continuation of what they consider to be infantile and materialistic concepts of heaven, many twentieth-century theologians and philosophers call for the rejection of irrational and/or unbiblical elements. Heavenly tradition must be adjusted, pruned, and carefully purged. "When dealing with the human situation after death," the Roman Congregation for the Doctrine of the Faith warned in 1979, "one must especially beware of arbitrary imaginative representations: excess of this kind is a major cause of the difficulties that Christian faith often encounters." Many modern theologians thus reduce afterlife beliefs to a minimum in the hope of developing a more rational, and hence a more acceptable and believable heaven.[20]

The criticism of the modern heaven accompanied the challenges to traditional Christianity by philosophical skepticism and science. Since the philosophy of René Descartes (1596–1650), critical thinkers have shied away from making statements about heavenly life. In 1645, the princess of Bohemia, a friend of Descartes, wrote to him about a book which she was reading on the state of the soul after death. The princess asked the philosopher what he thought about Sir Kenelm Digby's speculations on the soul's superior knowledge in the other world. "As for the state of the soul after this life," Descartes wrote back, "I am not as well informed as Monsieur Digby. Leaving aside what faith tells us, I agree that by natural reason alone we can make favourable conjectures and indulge in fine hopes, but we cannot have any certainty." Descartes distinguished between "what faith tells us" and what could be affirmed by reason. He wanted "clear and distinct ideas" whose truth could be perceived by any rational being on immediate inspection. Life after death was a fact, but according to Descartes one could not form any clear idea of its nature. Although the French philosopher refrained from using reason in order to criticize or modify traditional religious teaching, this was eventually to become unavoidable.[21]

One century after Descartes, the German philosopher Immanuel Kant (1724–1804) criticized the modern heaven by launching an attack against Swedenborg. With great enthusiasm Kant studied certain "paranormal" events connected with the Swedish visionary. He corresponded with people who knew him, wrote to the mystic himself (without ever receiving an answer), and bought the eight heavy tomes of the *Heavenly Arcana*. In the end, however, Kant decided that Swedenborg's visions were the delusions of a misguided mind. Here two intellects, two worlds clashed: the religious enthusiast completely immersed in the realm of the transcendent and the Enlightenment rationalist whose entire work was critical, often to the point of destruction. It was Kant's perspective and not Swedenborg's which would shape twentieth-century theological speculation.

While Swedenborg perceived an ever-expanding religious universe, Kant recognized only three ideas capable of surviving the test of reason: freedom, God, and immortality. For him, Swedenborg's visions failed to convey any real knowledge of the next world. As speculations "consisting of nothing but air," they had "applicable weight only in the scale of hope." We have no knowledge of the spirit world, "because for this purpose no data can be found in the whole of our sensations." Since our reason depends upon data transmitted through the senses, we have no way of knowing what goes on after death. Convinced that his own study "exhausts all philosophical knowledge" about the spirits of the deceased, Kant left no room for visions and dreams. "In the future, perhaps," he speculated, "many things may be thought about [this subject], but never more known." Death for Kant was a gap that the senses cannot bridge. "Human reason was not given strong enough wings to part clouds so high above us," he summarized poetically, "clouds which withhold from our eyes the secrets of the other world." Although he may have gone through periods of doubt, Kant did not deny the existence of the eternal nature of the soul. Immortality could be postulated, but the details of the soul's survival lay hidden from reason. Kant thus recommended a healthy skepticism toward all alleged communications from the other side, as well as restraint in all assertions about life after death. Human knowledge concerning immortality was minimal.[22]

Although at times Kant went beyond the realms of reason and mused about the possible nature of life after death, it was his skepticism which made a long-lasting impact. The founding father of Protestant liberalism, Friedrich Schleiermacher (1768–1834), continued Kant's suspicion of descriptions of heaven. "We cannot really make a picture of it," he declared; "to such a task our sensuous imagination is unequal." Since we have no experience of the future state, we cannot have any real, conceptual knowledge of that state. In *The Christian Faith*, Schleiermacher hinted that belief in Christ is possible even though one might consider Jesus' sayings on the afterlife as "all figurative, and not to be interpreted strictly. . .[since] he nowhere claims personal survival." The consequences of acting on this proposition, however, would be "a complete transformation of Christianity" – a transformation Schleiermacher hoped to avoid. After several pages of discussion of whether the soul achieves perfection immediately at death or slowly develops in heaven, Schleiermacher ended on a negative note. "We really can solve neither problem," he confessed, "and we therefore always remain uncertain how the state which is the Church's highest consummation can be gained or possessed in this form by individual personalities emerging into immortality." Schleiermacher refused to accept either the reformers' heaven of instantaneous perfection or the modern heaven's image of eternal progress. Heavenly blessedness could be achieved, but Schleiermacher was uncertain as to how this occurred after death.[23]

Privately, Schleiermacher admitted an even greater skepticism about the existence of any type of life after death. In a moving letter of consolation, sent to a nineteen-year-old widow (whom he later married), he felt unable to give assurance about a post-mortem reunion of lovers:

Dear Jetty, what can I say to you? Certainty beyond this life is not given to us. Please don't misunderstand me: I am speaking of certainty for an imagination which wants to have everything in graphic clearness. Otherwise this is the greatest certainty — and nothing would be certain, if not this — that there is no death, no perishing of the spirit. The individual life, however, does not essentially belong to the spirit, it is only an appearance. In which way this appearance is repeated, we do not know; we can form no conception of it, we can form only poetic visions.

Later, at the grave of Nathanael — the son of Jetty and himself — he reaffirmed his doubts. "To someone who is very much used to intellectual rigor and stringency, these images [conventional concepts of an afterlife] imply thousands of unanswered questions, and thus lose much of their consolatory force." Even faced with the reality of death, Schleiermacher could not escape his doubt.[24]

Schleiermacher was among a growing number of intellectuals who presented critical views at a time when other theologians and popular writers were producing increasingly detailed versions of heavenly life. In 1841 the radical theologian David Friedrich Strauss (1808–74) reported that the Kantian view was typical of the "educated believer." The modern mind, Strauss announced, "leaves, without showing particular emotion, the complete inventory of ecclesiastical eschatology to be burnt at the stake of criticism, content with rescuing for itself the mere survival of death." Other philosophers like David Hume, Hegel, and Ludwig Feuerbach rejected afterlife beliefs altogether. They were joined by the political theorists Marx and Lenin, as well as the founder of psychoanalysis, Sigmund Freud. Heavenly beliefs, these critics insisted, were superstitious wishful thinking which diverted attention from earthly misery. While Descartes and Kant rejected descriptions of the other world on grounds of reason, nineteenth-century social scientists pointed out the dubious origins and aims of many of the images characterizing heaven. Voices of caution, restraint, doubt, and criticism accompanied the bold assertions and unbridled speculation of the Victorian period.[25]

Although Kant's philosophy made a tremendous impact on theologians, the influence of modern science reached even further. In the last three centuries science has become increasingly independent of religion and has established its authority in all areas of discourse. Now the astronomer no longer looks for the empyrean heaven where God supposedly resides, and the biologist no longer assumes that the human personality is located in an immaterial entity called the soul. For modern science, the mind is a function of the brain rather than an independent, spiritual entity. There is no soul to survive physical death. When the body dies, and with it the brain, the mind and its personality also vanish. This "monistic" or non-dualistic position is implied in the entire range of disciplines dealing with the human being: biology, medicine, psychology, and psychiatry. Charles Darwin (1809–82), originally at home with Victorian Christianity, described in a moving passage of his autobiography how gnawing doubts gradually led him to reject two basic

Christian convictions: the existence of God, and immortality. German biologist Ernst Haeckel (1834–1919) felt compelled to include in his best-selling *Riddle of the Universe* (1899) a chapter on physical death as the real termination of life. In the United States, the philosopher Corliss Lamont (born 1902) concluded, from a rational and scientific view-point, that immortality is an illusion. Although individual scientists may hold their own religious beliefs on the fate of the soul, such are private opinions which should not interfere with scientific discourse. The intellectual climate created by thinkers like Kant, Feuerbach, Lenin, and numerous scientists such as Darwin provided a harsh climate for the nurturing of religious claims concerning the afterlife in heaven.[26]

The Symbolist Compromise

"Belief in eternal life," the German Jesuit Karl Rahner reported in 1979, "has grown weaker in the consciousness of modern people." Even more alarming for Rahner is the fact that some of these people are Christians. "There are Christians," he explained, "who are sure of the existence of God...but who do not think it necessary to show any great interest in the question of eternal life." Even believers are affected by the scientific world-view and the doubt which it inspires. In West Germany, only 56 per cent of all Catholics believe in some kind of life after death; the percentage of Protestants is a meager 35 per cent. "There is a doubting Thomas in all of us," declared Lutheran Hans Schwarz (born 1939). While the "doubting Thomas" in the average Christian may be in-consequential, the skepticism found among academic theologians has a strong impact on the shape of contemporary Christianity. The training which the clergy receives involves reading and discussing the writings of Tillich, Bultmann, Rahner, Niebuhr, and Barth, as well as liberation and process theology. Even those who would deny being "doubting Thomases" – fundamentalists for example – rely on the insights of previous generations to shape their outlook on life after death. Faced, then, with the challenges of the social and natural sciences and the doubts of fellow Christians, how do twentieth-century theologians explain the meaning of heaven?[27]

In 1913 the French Nobel prize winner Roger Martin du Gard (1881–1958) wrote a long novel which attempted to articulate the struggle which modern people have with traditional beliefs and the compromises they make in order to maintain a viable religious outlook. The protagonist of the novel *Jean Barois* struggles with questions of faith throughout his lifetime as a scientist, teacher, and journalist. As his doubts threaten his adherence to Catholicism, a priest (who is also a biochemist) fortifies his faith by offering him the "symbolist compromise." For the priest, theology is fundamentally a system of symbols which requires a level of spiritual awareness in order to be understood. The meaning of Christianity is not located on the surface of theological language to be easily read, but lies deep within traditional religious images. To unlock the meaning of those symbols, although a difficult task, is the mark of true spiritual understanding. Martin du Gard recalls St. Paul's own confession that "when I was a child, I spoke like a child, I thought like a child, I reasoned like a child; when I became a man, I gave up childish ways" (I Cor. 13:11). St. Paul's words legitimize the quest for new, mature forms of Christian thought. Therefore Jean accepts the symbolist faith.[28]

The attenuated faith of Jean Barois, however, does not last long. It serves instead to smooth his passage to full, militant atheism. In his old age, Barois, disillusioned with free thought, again meets a priest and is again offered the symbolist compromise. The priest, who confesses to be a regular and not unsympathetic reader of rationalist literature, gains the trust of Barois. Finally, Barois as an old man yields to Christianity as a convert. Yet he is still not free of doubts. Speaking of death, he asks how one can picture human consciousness without a material basis. "It is not important to have a precise idea of the future life," the priest replies; "what counts is that the future life itself is a certainty!" As far as Martin du Gard is concerned, no more can be claimed.[29]

The symbolist compromise becomes the inevitable and almost natural form of Christian belief in a rationalist age. The compromise occurs between two opposing forces: a supernatural Christianity of images, doctrines, and rituals, and a scientific world-view which equates reality with everyday life. The symbolist, rather than rejecting either religion or the contemporary world, argues that there are dimensions of reality which cannot be approached in any other way than by symbols. Symbols, which can be any type of religious language, connect transcendent reality with daily experience. To mistake the symbol for the reality which stands behind it is, in St. Paul's words, to speak, think, and reason like a child, since only a child would mistake a picture of a flower for the flower itself. Consequently, if traditional images of heaven – from the beatific vision to eternal family life – no longer convey the reality of eternal life, then the problem must lie in religious language. Symbolists urge Christians to re-evaluate the language they use to describe heaven and to move beyond the surface and toward the "meaning" of the symbol.

Symbolic readings of afterlife beliefs are prominent in the work of Reinhold Niebuhr (1892–1970) and Paul Tillich (1886–1965), both of whom were influenced by European philosophy. "The biblical symbols cannot be taken literally," explained Niebuhr, "because it is not possible for finite minds to comprehend that which transcends and fulfills history...The symbols which point toward the consummation from within the temporal flux cannot be exact in the scientific sense of the word." He therefore recommended that one should "maintain a decent measure of restraint in expressing the Christian hope." Since the symbols of post-mortem life are elusive, Niebuhr refused to elucidate their meaning. When publicly challenged to make a definitive pronouncement as "to what extent there stands behind 'eschatological' symbols a *reality*," Niebuhr preferred to remain silent. To a friend he confided, "I do not believe in individual immortality." "Perhaps there was some kind of life after death," explains Niebuhr's biographer, "but since that life was totally beyond our experience, he would not count on it." By sweeping away the images of heaven, Niebuhr was left with a realistic but barren perspective on the afterlife.[30]

Like Niebuhr, Paul Tillich avoided any open denial of life after death. "Symbols such as life after death, immortality, reincarnation, heaven," however, are "dangerously inadequate" since their dramatic quality promotes naive literalism. The language used in describing eternal life is symbolic and must not be taken as the thing itself. Heaven for Tillich was a symbol and not a description of a locality. This was not to say, however, that the symbol should be ignored because it was a mystery which could not be penetrated or a purely poetic device which need not be taken seriously. Although Tillich condemned the "neurotic consequences of the literalistic distortion" of symbols of eternal life, and explained that it was hardly necessary to refer to "heaven" at all, he did recognize the importance of the promise of eternal life. While he would deny that one can ever fully get behind the symbol to its "nonmetaphorical" sense, he was willing to discuss the "concept" – the theological meaning of the symbolic imagery. In doing so, Tillich used what he termed "negative metaphorical language" – a language which tends to leave the reader with a series of paradoxes, contradictions, and descriptions of what eternal life is not. Such problems in conceptualization did not appear to bother Tillich, who might have suggested that the very ambiguity of the concepts makes the use of images and symbols necessary.[31]

Eternal Life (the conceptualization of the symbol of heaven) includes the fulfillment both of history and of the individual. Time and eternity – frequently symbolized as earth and heaven – were not understood by Tillich as radically separated realms. The future end of time and the present moment were viewed as being connected. Both time and eternity, present and future, impinge on one another. Consequently, the ever-present end ("end" meaning aim or goal as well as termination) "elevates the positive content of history into eternity at the same time that it excludes the negative from participation in it." Eternal life does not stand apart from history, but rather it is the final liberation of the positive side of existence. The symbol of the Last Judgment thus may be understood as the separation of the positive in existence from the negative. This does not occur at some point in the future, but because the future and the present exist in the "eternal now" there is a continual transition from the temporal to the eternal, with the vanishing of the negative permitting the liberation of the positive. "Eternal life," Tillich ventured, "means that the joy of today has a dimension which gives it transtemporal meaning." In other words, eternity is a quality sometimes experienced in the present life; it has nothing to do with the life hereafter. Consequently, the eternal is not a future state of things; it is always present in the human individual as well as in everything which has being.[32]

But what of the individual? Is there some type of survival after death? Tillich asked his readers to accept only the barest of descriptions and numerous paradoxes. In his influential book, *The Courage to Be* (1952), he seemed to reject any claims of human immortality. His suggestion that Plato's doctrine of immortality is only a symbol for Socrates' courage to accept his own death may be a hint that the Resurrection of Jesus can be given a similar reading. In his later *Systematic Theology*, Tillich presented more speculative ideas as well as numerous paradoxes. When he addressed the issue of the existence of a self-conscious self in Eternal Life, he admitted that the only meaningful answer is in the form of two negative statements. Since Eternal Life is life, and not undifferentiated identity, the self-conscious self cannot be excluded. In Eternal Life there exists the complete integration and balance between the polar structures of being, including participation and individualization. The persistence of "individual centers" does not contradict their rest in an all-encompassing divine center. Somehow Eternal Life includes the "unambiguous and non-fragmentary life of love," although Tillich did not explain what that means. When speaking of Eternal Life with regard to the end of history, Tillich described it as without morality, culture, and religion – all of which are the result of independent human enterprise or estrangement. Tillich insisted that any fuller description of the self-conscious self in Eternal Life cannot be given. Tillich's second negative statement went on to contradict the first. With equal strength he asserted that the self's participation in that Eternal Life cannot be "the endless continuation of a particular stream of consciousness in memory and anticipation." Since eternity transcends temporality, Eternal Life must mean the end of the experienced character of self-consciousness. There can be no continuation of "old or new physical particles" which continue a temporal life. Again, anything which went beyond this conceptualization, according to Tillich, would not be theology but poetic imagination.[33]

Although we might feel uncomfortable with Tillich's contradictory assertions, as in all his theology he found meaning in the uniting of two paradoxical and conflicting notions. The very term "eternal life" contains the paradox of which he spoke. The understanding of "eternal" excludes the notion of time. At the same time the concept of "life" implies some form of consciousness which exists within the temporal. Consequently, "we need two polar assertions above which lies the truth." Those assertions cannot be expressed either positively or directly, hence our frustration as readers of Tillich's theology. The paradox teaches that "eternity is neither timeless identity nor permanent change, as the latter occurs in the temporal process. Time and change are present in the depth of Eternal Life, but they are contained within the eternal unity of the Divine Life."[34]

Paul Tillich could not accept any of the standard Christian views on heaven, life after death, or immortality. For him there was no beatific vision, meeting family members, hugging Jesus, or angelic choir of eternal praise. Tillich's colleague Nels F.S. Ferré seemed surprised to discover that Tillich "did not believe in the Christian God who raises the dead and who works personally in human history." John Hick, in *Death and Eternal Life* (1976), was disappointed that Tillich left his readers to "suffer in silence" with a set of unresolved contradictions. What Tillich did do, as an influential twentieth-century theologian, was to challenge all the images of heaven which had accumulated over two thousand years of Christian history. He asked other theologians to move toward an abstract, philosophical understanding of Eternal Life. In view of the Eternal, all believers should find the courage to overcome the fundamental anxiety and finite nature of human existence. The Eternal *did* exist for Tillich, but not as a place or state after death or the end of time. Just as God was not a being besides other beings, but the foundation of all being, so Eternal Life functioned not as a separate reality, but as the non-estranged, essential part of our experience. It should surprise no one conversant with Tillich's preference for existentialism, psychoanalysis, and socialism that he showed little interest in the other-worldly individualism of heaven.[35]

A no less radical but somewhat less cryptic attempt to decipher the symbol of heaven can be found in the thought of Rudolf Bultmann (1884–1976), an influential German New Testament scholar. Bultmann and his followers preferred to speak of myth rather than of symbol. A myth, according to this view, is an ancient mode of representing the human as divine and the divine as human. God or gods walk on earth, influence the course of events, and live as we live, although normally in far-away parts of the universe. While gods are humanized, men and women are sometimes deified, endowed with divine power and supernatural immortality. Heaven, understood in the mythological sense, is a place where human individuals receive divine characteristics, especially immortality and omniscience. In order to decode the biblical myth of resurrection and eternal life, thus making it relevant, Bultmann insisted that we have to keep the two spheres — the human and the divine — separated.

The two realms, however, *can* meet when the creature grasps the divine in faith and trust. Although the human being cannot become immortal, it can be a "new creature," living a new and authentic life under the grace of God. Through the Resurrection, we are not given another life beyond death but rather the present existence is given a new quality. In a letter written in 1973, Bultmann related what he thought about heaven:

> Heaven, in existential terms, refers to a transcendent reality of which we can only speak once we realize that our individual existence cannot find its authenticity in this world. Once we realize this, we lose our anxiety about the future. We also become independent of all ideologies which, although they are constantly changing, wish to project a new future in a definitive blue-print. We are also free of the desire to subject others to our will. We accept them in their otherness, meeting them in trust and love. We are also free from anxiety in the face of the tragedy of fate, because we can see our fate as open to the future — mysterious and incomprehensible as that fate may seem at the moment.

According to Bultmann, this demythologized understanding of heavenly or eternal life is nothing invented by himself, nor is it simply inspired by existentialist philosophy. It is the teaching of John's gospel in the New Testament.[36]

Asked about the individual's post-mortem future, Bultmann gave a "minimalist" answer. For the modern mind, he argued, the concept of a "translation to a heavenly world of light, in which the self is destined to receive a celestial vesture, a spiritual body," is "not merely incomprehensible by any rational process" but totally "meaningless." While dismissing all images of the world beyond, the life beyond, or a resurrection as wishful thinking, he nevertheless retained an element of hope. In a letter addressed to a theologian he explained:

> It is true that, as you are writing yourself, nonmythological discourse omits any reference to 'something after death' and that one can speak only about the historical dimension of human life. . .on this side of death. This should not lead, however, to the exclusion of hope as a structural element of faith. To put in all brevity and distinctness what merits thorough theological reflection: we must hope for our death to be the end of nothingness ("death swallowed up in victory"), indeed, paradoxically: hope for death being resurrection itself (in John, crucifixion means glorification). In the resurrection belief, the paradox of faith is most radically expressed. However, we cannot give visual graphicness to the eternity which is given us in death or

resurrection, for an endless succession of time would immediately come to mind. Strictly speaking, there is not a beyond *after* death, but only a beyond *above* death. For God is not a God of the dead, but of the living.

From this highly ambiguous affirmation of an empty hope there is only a small step to renouncing the traditional Christian doctrine. In a published letter addressed to his former student, the philosopher Hans Jonas, Bultmann admitted not to claim personal immortality for himself. As with Tillich, the interpretation of heaven can reach a point where it is unclear whether anything really exists other than the symbol, the image, or the myth.[37]

The symbolist interpretation of heaven, as seen in Niebuhr, Tillich, and Bultmann, includes three main ideas. First and perhaps most importantly, symbolists ask that the traditional images of heaven be "broken" in order to reveal their inner meaning. To assume the literal truth of the image is to mistake the symbol for the reality and thus to distort the meaning of eternal life. Second, the interpretation of the symbols produces a set of abstract, philosophical, and often paradoxical concepts which the symbolists admit are only tentative possibilites. The very abstract quality of the concepts makes it possible to question the existence of heaven altogether or to plead agnosticism. Finally, the symbolists tend to reject the notion that eternal life is purely an other-worldly phenomenon. This third notion, that the Christian hope lies not in the distant future but in the "eternal now," has been more fully deve-loped by a diverse group of theologians who reject the other-worldly im-plications of heaven. Eschatological symbols, they argue, are essential, but their meaning has been distorted by historical trends which have confined the Christian promise to a future after death.

Realized Eschatology: Heaven on Earth

There is a long tradition in Christian history which acknowledges that glimpses of heaven can be experienced on earth: in the quiet of meditation, the beauty of the cathedral, the drama of the Mass, or the fellowship of Christian community. Friedrich Schleiermacher, when confronted with death, found consolation not in the expectation of a future life but in the experience of the divine in the present. Schleier-macher maintained that the Christian should strive to increase those glimpses of heaven on earth, rather than becoming preoccupied with life after death. "In the state of pious emotion," he reminded his readers, "the soul is rather absorbed in the present moment than directed toward the future." Hope, the expectation of something else, would destroy the completeness and harmony of the religious feeling. Schleiermacher summarized his creed by saying that "in the midst of finitude to be one with the Infinite and in every moment to be eternal is the immortality of religion." The problem of life after death, for him, was insignificant because it was remote from the inner life and immediate religious feelings. Christians should not bother themselves with speculations about the other world, but instead concentrate on the world they occupied now. "Be not troubled for the future [after death], nor weep for things which pass, but take heed lest you lose yourself," Schleiermacher warned his fellow Christians, "and weep if you are swept along in the stream of time without carrying heaven within you" – that is, in every moment of *this* life. Preoccupation with the character of heaven, which Schleiermacher saw everywhere in nineteenth-century Europe, robbed Christians of experiencing the fullness of God in the present.[38]

The conviction that Christian speculation on the other world is a debility rather than a blessing was more clearly articulated in the liberal Protestantism of the early twentieth century. Walter Rauschenbusch (1861–1918), the celebrated American theologian of the Social Gospel movement, advocated a radical new course in Christian teaching and practice. Rather than focusing attention on the perfection of the individual with the hope of attaining heaven after death, Rauschenbusch insisted that Christians should concern themselves with the society in which they lived. For Rauschenbusch and other activists in the Social Gospel movement, the Kingdom of God was not an idealized life in heaven but a reality which should be accomplished on earth. In spite of the problems of industrialization and urbanization, which could easily cause many to despair, Rauschenbusch insisted in *Christianity and the Social Crisis* (1907) that the possibility of social, economic, and religious improvement could mark the beginning of the "great day of the Lord for which the ages waited." Perfection should not be an individual goal accomplished after life but a social goal achieved on this earth. Heaven was not a reality after death but the symbol of a perfected world here and now.[39]

To argue his case for the coming of the Kingdom of God on earth, Rauschenbusch preached a return to the original, unadulterated teachings of the New Testament. Jesus did not teach the postponement of social justice until after death, but rather that the Kingdom of God – "a fellowship of righteousness" – must be brought about in this world. From Rauschenbusch's view, the Greek idea of the individual soul's flight into eternal life had weakened, if not supplanted, the original hope for an earthly Kingdom of God. As the notion of a heaven of redeemed souls came to dominate Christian teaching, Christianity lost much of its social potency. Caught up in their privatized pursuit of salvation, Christians felt little concern for working with God to bring about a world which guaranteed to all people their highest and most free development. He encouraged people to move beyond the privatized images and to discover the "real" meaning of heaven as a collective and this-worldly expression of hope.[40]

For advocates of the Social Gospel, although belief in life after death cannot be completely dispensed, it should have no more than a modest place at the periphery of Christian doctrine. The true meaning of the coming of the Kingdom of God has to do with this world, not the next. Concerned about our present society and how to eradicate its misery, social activists have no time for speculation about the beyond. "The Christian Church in the past has taught us to do our work with our eyes fixed on another world and a life to come," wrote Rauschenbusch in 1912, "but the business before us is concerned with refashioning this present world, making this earth clean and sweet and habitable." In the simplest terms, heaven can and must be created on earth. The Social Gospel in America and religious socialism in Europe asked for nothing less than the rejection of a privatized, individualized afterlife in exchange for a regenerated social order on earth. The other-worldly orientation of previous generations of Christians had to be eliminated not because it contradicted reason or science, but because it ignored the fundamentally social concerns of the New Testament.[41]

While there was never a powerful socialist movement in the United States, the Social Gospel idea took root in the Protestant churches and sharpened their social consciousness. Asked, in 1961, to name the most outstanding achievement of the church during the past fifty years, half the American students of major divinity schools replied, "preaching the social gospel." The young Protestant theologians supported disarmament, racial integration, abolishment of capital punishment, and wished for "a decent place to live" for all Americans. The enthusiasm for social and political causes is paired with a striking – though not surprising – disinterest in questions concerning the hereafter. Only 29 per cent of those questioned believed "there is a real heaven and hell," and not more than 2 per cent considered belief in human immortality "a major tenet." Attracted to practical Christianity, the divinity students, whose age averaged twenty-five years, had little interest in the subtleties of traditional doctrine.[42]

The Social Gospel movement and religious socialism were early twentieth-century attempts to argue that God's goal for humankind is nothing less than total liberation within the world. Sin, both social and individual, obscures that goal. By the late twentieth century, black theologians, feminist theologians, theologians of hope, and Latin American liberation theologians are voicing similar themes. Yes, they concur, Christianity is an eschatological religion based on hope and promises of the future. That hope and future, however, do not lie in correct beliefs which will secure heaven for the individual, but in right actions which will establish a just society for all generations. When Rosemary Radford Ruether (born 1936) asked in *Sexism and God-Talk* (1983) what would happen to the "me" after death, she concluded that, "it is not our calling to be concerned about the eternal meaning of our lives, and religion should not make this the focus of its message." Finite beings should concentrate on concerns they can influence. "Our responsibility," she explained, "is to use our temporal life span to create a just and good community for our generation and for our children...Our agnosticism about what this [everlasting life] means is then the expression of our faith, our trust that Holy Wisdom will give transcendent meaning to our work, which is bounded by space and time." Thus the biblical images of heaven and the millennium are not ends in themselves, but point to possibilities which can be accomplished on earth.[43]

Liberal Protestants and Catholics attempt to acknowledge the full biblical richness of heavenly descriptions while at the same time supporting the skeptical mind which strives to defend its integrity. Since liberals have no wish to trade tradition for reason or reason for tradition, they propose a compromise between naive acceptance and outright rejection. In order to establish a middle ground between the biblical heritage and the rationalistic mind, some invoke notions of "myth" and "symbol." Others argue that to speak of a future eternity at all deflects concern for the problems of this world. Heaven should be seen as an image of what life on earth can be like. This middle ground – between acceptance and rejection – has some properties of a no man's land between the trenches of opposed armies. Neither skeptics nor believers in an image-filled heaven, liberal theologians easily become estranged from both the believing and the non-believing world.

Theocentric Minimalism

On the one hand skeptics reject liberal theological compromises as fancy footwork designed to give confidence to believers by overwhelming them with philosophical doublespeak; on the other, however, conservative Christians point out that liberals have sold their faith for dubious accommodation to the modern world. Conservative Christians thus also reject the liberal view, replacing it with either a reiteration of the modern heaven or a variation of the reformed heaven which we will call "theocentric minimalism." If one excludes the duplication of traditional accounts of heaven – from the Catholic's beatific vision described by saints to the heavenly journeys of Protestants – a surprising similarity

appears between a diverse group of contemporary theologies. Fundamentalists, Catholic followers of Karl Rahner, and Protestant followers
of Karl Barth reject the symbolist compromise but, for a variety of
reasons, are left with an equally meager picture of heaven. While
accommodations to the modern world may no longer be a controlling
factor, the very seriousness with which they take religious claims
radically limits their heavenly descriptions.

With its emphasis on the revealed, supernatural nature of the Bible
and Christian doctrine, fundamentalism represents the most conservative school within Protestant thought, if not in modern Christianity.
The movement has its origins in the latter half of the nineteenth
century, when conservative American Protestants realigned to fight both
secular atheists and liberal thinkers within the church. They rejected
the Darwinian theory of evolution as much as the Social Gospel's
emphasis on building the Kingdom of God through political effort. The
Bible, as fundamentalists see it, does not lend itself to manipulation and
interpretation, but should be accepted as it stands, as the Word of
God. Liberals who doubt this — as historical criticism generally does —
are on their way to atheism (Pl. 60).

Fundamentalists base their religious views exclusively on the Bible,
their divinely inspired and inerrant authority. Their theology follows a
method developed in the nineteenth century and is sometimes referred to
as deriving from the British philosopher Francis Bacon (1561–1626). For
Bacon there was no rational proof for revelation; it must simply be
accepted on divine authority. Although rejected by the Enlightenment,
this view seemed viable again in an age of science, an age which had
great respect for "facts." Just as scientists rely on empirical data which are
to be ordered and brought into a system, so must theologians take the
Bible as their raw material. Fundamentalist theologian Charles Baker
compares the "many facts" contained in the Bible with "certain facts
about electricity and magnetism"; these have been known for thousands
of years, but only modern science has enabled us to use them to our
advantage. "The Bible," he wrote, "reveals many facts about God, man,
sin, and a host of other things." Theology's task consists of "assembling,
classifying, and drawing conclusions from these facts," and putting them
to our best use. While this method allows for some flexibility in commentary, the biblical data are never questioned. For fundamentalists,
eternal life is a fact.[44]

Fundamentalists thus see heaven, the new earth, and the new Jerusalem as real, literal places, and define eternity as never-ending time.
They rely on the Scriptures for information concerning the details, while
admitting that the biblical text is often rather vague about these matters.
"There's really very little said [in Scripture] about the nature of the new
heaven and the new earth," admits best-selling author Hal Lindsey. Is

Pl. 60. *The Descent of the Modernists.* Cartoon, 1924. William J. Bryan, *Seven Questions in Dispute* (New York: Revell, 1924)

the new Jerusalem, for instance, really a cube, as the text of Revelation seems to imply, or must we visualize it in pyramidal form? Will this immense city be located on earth, which will make the earth look rather odd, or can we think of it in terms of a satellite circling around our planet? Since the book of Revelation does not give an answer, theology, fundamentalists believe, should refrain from too much speculation. From this perspective, even the widely publicized near-death visions of the 1970s cannot tell us any more about heaven than we already know from biblical sources. When resuscitated heart-patients report their visions of meeting friends and angels, and travelling to a golden city in order to meet a being of light, this may be a hallucination or a satanic delusion. On the other hand, if what some people experience during a comatose state is a genuine glimpse of heaven, then it confirms the Bible without adding to its revelation. By limiting the source of their knowledge to the Bible, the fundamentalists also present a minimal picture of the afterlife.[45]

Contrary to popular understanding, fundamentalists do not claim to know what heaven and eternal life are really like. They also do not take the Bible "literally," or refuse to interpret biblical images. One of the most radical conservative theologians to "deliteralize" Scripture and to reject the science-fiction-like view of the modern heaven was Cyrus Scofield (1843–1921). An early fundamentalist leader and editor of the best-selling *Scofield Reference Bible*, Scofield stressed the limits of our

337

knowledge of things eternal. For him, the biblical message merely implied that the saint in heaven will be "a perfect being in a perfect environment." Commenting on the heavenly mansions of the New Testament, he demanded that we recognize our ignorance of their design. "We are not to suppose," he insisted, "that heaven is a place full of brown stone houses. That would be a very crude and fleshly conception of it. I don't know what glorified architecture is like." Like later fundamentalists, Scofield had no patience with the speculations of ministers and novelists who imagined a perfected earthly world in heaven.[46]

A 1975 article in the *Moody Monthly* repeated Scofield's position but in a more poetic, fictional manner. In heaven, Jesus says to a new arrival: "Don't look for precisely what My servants said in the Bible about heaven...I was limited in what I could reveal to them, limited to what their eyes had seen and their language could express." Jesus explains himself with the help of parables and similes: "How would the Eskimo describe a pineapple to others in his village, even if he were transported to Hawaii and then returned? Sweet and juicy blubber." Even fundamentalists, who take seriously the images and events in the Bible, assume that glimpses into the other world are rare and limited.[47]

The reason for the absence of a more detailed revelation concerning the final state is not that God wants us to live with a mystery, but that such knowledge is superfluous. From the fundamentalist perspective, the Bible tells us only what we have to know. In the "dispensationalist" school of fundamentalism we learn that God deals differently with humanity at different periods of history. God establishes each dispensation or period of history for a specific reason. The most common fundamentalist system distinguishes seven dispensations. The first dispensation was one of innocence when Adam and Eve were in paradise. Our present period is the sixth – the time of grace between the lives of the twelve apostles and the "rapture." During the present dispensation, Christ creates for himself a spiritual body, the Christian Church. The last dispensation is the millennium, the thousand-year reign of Christ on earth. It is important to realize that what happens after the millennium – eternal life – is outside the dispensationalist scheme.[48]

As our current dispensation draws near its end, human history will develop into a great apocalyptic drama. Starting with the re-establishment of a Jewish state in Palestine, its suffering from military aggression, and a great "falling away and apostasy" from Christianity, the drama will culminate in the "rapture" (Pl. 61). This is the central saving act of the future when God will suddenly and dramatically snatch away all true believers. "You'll be riding along in an automobile," Jerry Falwell (born 1933) imagined; "when the trumpet sounds you and the other born-again believers in that automobile will be instantly caught away – you will disappear, leaving behind only your clothes...That unsaved

Pl. 61.   Charles Anderson, *The Rapture*. 1974

person or persons in the automobile will suddenly be startled to find the car moving along without a driver, and the car suddenly somewhere crashes." While there is controversy over whether or not those caught up in the rapture would also participate in the ensuing thousand-year reign of Christ on earth, their immortality is affirmed. Whoever died a true Christian or is found to be one at the hour of the rapture, will be resurrected or transformed, never again to die.[49]

Since the events leading up to the rapture are a part of this dispensation, they are of great interest to fundamentalists. Hal Lindsey's *The Late Great Planet Earth* makes all these events contemporary. The drama, violence, and action of the last days provide an impressive narrative which has captured the attention of over eighteen million readers. The interest in the last days, however, is not matched by an interest in eternal life. Dispensationalist theory considers *eternal life* to be outside of the dispensational scheme altogether and so to have nothing to do with the drama of the days before the end of history (Fig. 7). According to Scofield, each dispensation involves a particular test of obedience to which God subjects his human creatures. In the present dispensation, for instance, the point of testing is acceptance or rejection of Christ; at the end of the millennium, this test is once more repeated when "Satan shall be loosed out of his prison" for a short period of time. In eternity, after the thousand-year reign, there will be no more testing.

339

God's dispensational stewardship ends with the termination of the millennium. The eternal state has little to do with our present dispensation; it is not even contiguous with it, since the millennial kingdom comes between the two. "It is of much greater importance for us to be correctly informed about our present dispensation" than about other ones, explains Charles F. Baker in A *Dispensational Theology*.[50]

No more testing means no more drama – and nothing to report. Heaven, in dispensationalist thought, does not belong to the main subjects of theological inquiry. Theology must concern itself with the structured subordination of the human to the divine, rather than the unstructured relationship between God and his co-regents after the end of history. It is to history that God's "great plan of salvation," and the "faith once for all delivered to the saints" are related. When William Biederwolf (1867–1939) departed from standard fundamentalist practice in actually writing about heaven, he accused himself of "somewhat unusual beliefs," warning his readers that his teachings were "in no way essential to the great plan of salvation." While feeling that his contribution might be reassuring and comforting to mourners, Biederwolf admitted to delving into the unknown and irrelevant. Both the dramatic days before the thousand-year reign of Christ and the new reign itself were richly portrayed because they could be deduced from the Bible. Beyond that, eternity was unknown.[51]

But what happens to good Christians who die before the rapture, the millennium, and the end of time? The Bible, as one author carefully pointed out, is not spatially oriented toward the "above" or "beyond"; it is concerned with *time* – the past and the future. For the time being, it is sufficent to know that those who died in the true faith are "at home with the Lord awaiting their resurrection in due order." The righteous soul at death goes immediately to live with God in a place sometimes called "paradise." Although presses might publish an edited version of Rebecca Springer's visionary account *Intra Muros* (retited *Within the Gates*), more recent fundamentalist writing on heaven assumes a decidedly theocentric stance. In speaking about heaven, fundamentalists underplay the graphic nature of its human dimension in order to emphasize the divine center. "The most important thing" about the eternal abode of the blessed, according to Hal Lindsey, is "that God will be there in person, and we'll see Him face-to-face." We will also have "face-to-face" fellowship with Christ and experience "the unfathomable dimensions of the love of a perfect Father toward His much beloved children." Fundamentalist writers, in spite of their rich rhetoric, attempt a return to the reformed theocentric heaven of Luther and Calvin. "It's exciting," Lindsey mused, "to think about kneeling at God's feet one minute and sitting beside His throne the next! There's no chance of eternity being boring with that kind of challenge alternating with adoring service." In view of

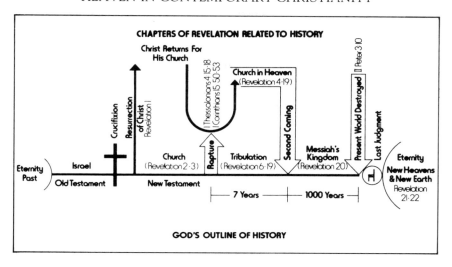

Fig. 7. *God's Outline of History.* Fundamentalist diagram, 1973. Hal Lindsey, *There's a New World Coming*, rev. ed. (Eugene, OR: Harvest House, 1984), 8

this close union with the divine, musing about social life in heaven is really a secondary, if not irrelevant, concern.[52]

The return to a theocentric heaven becomes even more vivid when fundamentalists consider the question of whether marriage and family exist in heaven. Conservative Christians of the nineteenth century certainly assumed that the family is an eternal institution blessed by God, but some fundamentalists reject this postulate. In *Seeing the Invisible: What Happens After You Die?* (1977), Anne Sandberg argues that the family experienced in heaven is the family of God, not the human family. She explains that after the death of a loved one a curious truth occurs: "After even so short a span as a year's time, they have forgotten the excruciating pain of the separation." As time passes, "even the memory of that loved one becomes dim and almost fades." Consequently, we should not regret that human relationships are not perpetuated in heaven. Natural love, according to Sandberg, is inadequate and so the Lord provides a higher and better relationship in heaven – the spiritual family of God. Don Baker in *Heaven* (1983) is even more explicit. In heaven there is no gender, sex, or marriage. We will know each other, but "earthly husband and wife will not be husband and wife in Heaven; parent and child will not be parent and child in Heaven." We might regret this now, but once in heaven such ties will be "totally eclipsed by the glory of a new relationship there."[53]

For the most part, fundamentalism has remained an American phenomenon. European born-again Christians rely heavily on translations of American writers on the rapture and the millennium. In the course of the twentieth century, however, European Catholics and Protestants have faced similar problems of how to understand biblical Christianity in a modern society. While for many European theologians, liberalism (on the Protestant side) and modernism (the Catholic equivalent) have held attraction, others have found them unconvincing. Like conservative American Christians, they were dissatisfied with liberal vagueness, its excessive concessions to the skeptical mind, and its lack of interest in the church as a believing community. A new theology was called for, one that would be sensitive to twentieth-century concerns while remaining loyal to the Protestant heritage and Catholic dogma respectively. A new orthodoxy was needed, which avoided the literal and uneducated belief of Protestant pietists and the equally unenlightened traditionalism of Catholic neoscholastics. European conservative theology, although sharing the American concern for a theocentric piety, developed along different lines.

Among the many who attempted to work out such a new teaching, two have been most successful: the Reformed theologian Karl Barth (1886–1968) in Switzerland and the German Jesuit Karl Rahner (1904–84). Both thinkers agreed with the liberal school that we have just *one* life which begins at birth and ends at death. With that existence being "our real and only life," explained Barth, there can be "no question of the continuation into an indefinite future of a somewhat altered life." Thus, after death there is no "further extension in time of acts and experiences following one upon another in a series arising from some neutral substantial entity [the soul] which impels itself forward through ever fresh epochs, and is forever engaging in some fresh activity within these constantly changing sections of time." Death, according to Rahner, cannot be understood as a simple change of horses on a continuing journey. In a 1980 interview, he explained (without the jargon for which he was famous) that "with death it's all over. Life is past, and it won't come again. It won't be given one for a second time." Rahner, the active Jesuit, was actually glad to be able to escape from the continuous struggle of life, from the eternal return of ever the same. He wanted to rest.[54]

While this sounds like a complete acceptance of the modern scientific view, it is only part of the story. The scientific account of death leaves out what is most important for neo-orthodoxy – the encounter with God. At death, life comes to a final halt, but this is a halt before God. Eternal life, for Barth, is "our manifestation with Him, with Jesus Christ who was raised again from the dead, in the glory of not only the judgment but also the grace of God." Rahner rejected the view that heaven is a family reunion or an everlasting banquet as crude and mistaken. Such concepts degrade the immediate vision of God "to being a nice occupation besides others." Responsible theology, he emphasized, must stress that "the absolute deity will precipitate in unveiled nakedness into our narrow creatureliness." For both Barth and Rahner, the great error of theology was to soften the theocentric heaven of the reformers with anthropocentric notions.[55]

In the situation of death, we lose much of what constituted our earthly life. "The angels of death will evacuate the rooms of our spirit of all the useless trash that we call our biography; only the true essence of our free acts will remain with us," explained Rahner. We have to accept "an immense silent emptiness...as our true essence." This emptiness, however, "is filled with that mystery which we call God, is filled with his pure light and his love which takes away but also restores everything. Although the divine mystery remains undifferentiated, there also appears the face of Jesus, the blessed one, looking at us." For Rahner, eternal life consists in our emptiness being filled in timeless eternity with the light of the divine presence under the gaze of the Savior. This is a theocentric heaven free of even the praise and music of earlier traditions.[56]

Rahner's view of heaven is admirably, although unknowingly, represented in a large fresco in the Catholic church of Maria Regina Martyrum in West Berlin (Pl. 62). Built and decorated in 1963, it serves as both a parish church and a place to commemorate victims of the Nazi era. The wall behind the altar is taken to give a glimpse of the other world. We can distinguish a frame of dark patches of color through which breaks the light of eternity. The deity, represented by an eye and a crowned lamb that stands for Christ, holds the center. A sickle reminds the beholder that death serves as the only way to bring us into immediate contact with that center. Death, in Rahner's theology, brings "the essence of our free acts" as harvest into the eternal light.[57]

Maria Regina Martyrum, built in the international style with straight lines, carefully omits all non-functional, ornamental elements. Nothing is placed on the walls or ceilings, and no stained-glass windows give color to the light. Its interior is a perfect auditorium, complete with loudspeakers. The almost invisible crucifix on the altar, a small statue of the Madonna, and the fresco – empty patches of color with no faces or figures – do not detract the churchgoer's attention from the sermon. The ritual of the Mass as celebrated in such an environment has been pared down to its essential elements and is unceremonial. The priest's address is delivered as straightforward instruction. Catering for the mind rather than for the heart, he indulges in abstract reasoning. What the congregation is taught – on everlasting life for example – is as abstract as the painting behind the altar. Christians are shown not to be dazzled by the images of heaven; instead, they should focus on the immediacy of their spiritual predicament. The representation of the beyond, whether in art or in theological texts, must never be concrete and specific. Any

Pl. 62.   Georg Meistermann, *Apocalypse*. 1963. Maria Regina Martyrum, West Berlin, Germany

directness must be avoided. This church building, strongly reminiscent of International Style architecture, reflects the world-view of theologians like Karl Rahner who insist that all but the essential will be eliminated after death.

While Rahner sees the mind emptied of the "trash" of its biography, Karl Barth gives a somewhat more human account. Although there is no new life in heaven, Barth predicts that we will as least have our past lives – not just some remains. Our biographies, moreover, will not only be conserved, but also elucidated in the light of God. We will see the "reverse side which God sees although it is as yet hidden from us." At that time we finally understand how our own suffering – "our tears, death, sorrow, crying, and pain" – relates to the "decree of God fulfilled in Jesus Christ." We will come to a comprehensive understanding of ourselves before God, and God's dealing with us through Christ. "Often I have tried to imagine this for myself," reports Barth. He imagines that during our own lifetime our life is mysterious; hidden as if it was under a veil. At death, however, "this veil will be removed, and our whole life, from the crib to the grave, will be seen in the light and in its unity with the life of Christ, in the splendor of Christ's mercy, of his grace and of his power."[58]

In heaven, Barth hopes to speak to others and clarify his understanding of their theology. He expects to meet the liberal Schleiermacher and to debate with him many issues "for, let us say, a couple of centuries. 'There in that light I shall discern, what here on earth I dimly saw' – along with so many other things. I can imagine that this will be a very serious matter for both sides, but also that we will both laugh very heartily at ourselves." We should not, however, read too much into this fine example of Barth's humor. Meeting and fellowship with others can in no way constitute another life comparable to the present one. The conversation, therefore, can only be about the past and must be about religious matters. The mystery of God and the "hidden links of Providence" are the only possible objects that can enter our minds in an eternity which is outside time as we know it.[59]

Neo-orthodoxy, whether Protestant or Catholic, is consistent in its theocentric emphasis. It is this insistence on the divine center that unites all conservative theologians. "We have said very little about eternal life which is concrete and specific," concluded the British theologian Michael Perry of his own presentation of heaven. "All the same," he added, "I believe we have said what matters; that is, that it is a life in which God has the prime part." Fundamentalists, Barthians, and the disciples of Rahner can all agree with their British colleague. The conservative point of view, theocentric minimalism, rejects all efforts to distract the saints from their primary focus on God. It differs from the Reformed theocentric view of the seventeenth and eighteenth centuries by eliminating even the possibility of life existing in heaven. The images used in Reformed theocentric art – the circles of heavenly bodies praising the divine center – are gone. Even the harps and eternal singing, which the proponents of the modern heaven ridiculed, no longer appear. Theocentric minimalists, from American fundamentalists to European neo-orthodox theologians, have pared away any image which stands between the soul and the divine center. Conservatives present theocentric minimalism, probably the most widely accepted orthodox version of heaven in twentieth-century theology, as the way to save the Christian heaven from liberal disintegration.[60]

Theology without Promise

Conservatives react against liberal Christianity's compromises by reasserting a theocentric heaven. Still other theologians refuse any efforts to mediate between supernatural religion and the materialistic world by totally rejecting the concept of heaven. A view as surprising and radical as this required the particular intellectual climate of the 1960s in order to be openly stated and made public. Throughout that decade, the need for radical change in social and political consciousness was voiced in Europe and America. Popular movements for peace in Vietnam and Northern Ireland, the redefining of female roles, the Civil Rights movement, and the student riots in Paris and other European cities signalled a change in the order of western society. Religion did not remain unaffected. For the Catholic church, the Second Vatican Council with its *aggiornamento* or "opening to the world" brought the greatest change seen in centuries, and Protestantism was shocked by the radical teachings of some of its theologians. Christians were recommended to be "honest to God" and revise their often outdated beliefs (Bishop John A.T. Robinson). They should live without a bad conscience in the "secular city" (Harvey Cox). More radical writers declared the "death of God." According to William Hamilton (born 1924), one of the "death of God" theologians, "America is the place that has travelled furthest along the road from the cloister to the world that Luther and the Reformation had mapped out. We are the most profane, the most banal, the most utterly worldly of places." In the secular society, theology itself became tinged with secularism. Its links to traditional belief and the established churches became weak, if not abandoned altogether.[61]

It was only logical that belief in heaven should be rejected by radical secular theology. On the afternoon of 4 May 1961, a large crowd filled the Andover chapel of the Harvard Divinity School in Cambridge, Massachusetts, to listen to the annual "Ingersoll Lecture on the Immortality of Man." The audience witnessed the birth of a theology without heaven. The lecturer, the philosopher and religious historian Hans Jonas (born 1903), declared that "the modern temper is uncongenial to the idea of immortality." He could not respond to the wish of the founder of these lectures to elucidate the perplexing issue of life after death. Instead, he preferred to "throw some light on the present state of our mortal condition." To be eternally remembered by God or, mythically speaking, to be inscribed into the heavenly Book of Life, was all Jonas could offer to his audience. We will have no individual, conscious life after death. The existentialism of Sartre and Heidegger, "this extreme offspring of the modern temper or distemper," has no room for immortality. "And we," the lecturer continued, "whether of its doctrine or not, share enough of its spirit to have taken our lonely stand in time between the twofold nothing of before and after."[62]

A year later, the Chicago philosopher Charles Hartshorne (born 1897), a famous defender of the existence of God, repeated his earlier disbelief in life after death. In 1968, Gordon Kaufman, professor of theology at the Harvard Divinity School, did the same. In 1977, the French Dominican friar and psychoanalyst Jacques Pohier joined the growing list of secular and radical theologians. Within several years, a number of major theologians had ceased to believe in an afterlife.

Inspired by the writings of Hartshorne and an earlier Anglo-American philosopher, Alfred North Whitehead (1861–1947), a group of theologians began to develop a new system of thought, now known as "process theology," which radically challenges the existence of heaven. Although there have been attempts to reconcile this philosophy with more traditional notions of an afterlife, the process school presents detailed arguments against immortality.[63]

"Can you imagine anything more idiotic than the Christian idea of heaven?" Whitehead once asked; "what kind of deity is it that would be capable of creating angels and men to sing his praises day and night to all eternity?" Not only is the concept of God, depicted as an Oriental despot in need of entertainment, mistaken; the underlying idea of the human person or soul which survives death is also misleading. In the philosophy of Whitehead and Hartshorne, there is no place for the survival of persons, because there are no persons. This is not to say that individuals do not exist. To refer to a person as a substance which persists in essentially unchanged fashion from birth to death, however, is a meaningless abstraction. Whitehead redefines the human being not as a static entity but as a summary of a series of events or occasions. Process and change take priority over the persisting features attributed to substances. As a concrete entity, the individual is a momentary reality, and change is understood as the successive creation of a new entity, rather than a superficial process affecting some static substance.[64]

For process philosophy, everything is in flux and substances do not actually exist. This general rule is used to criticize the traditional idea of the immortal soul. Traditional metaphysics took the human soul to be immortal because it was something that persisted through time, something simple that could not dissolve into its components when the body died. From the perspective of process theology, however, we are temporary units of a fragile kind which change and perish easily. In fact, like any other aggregate of events, the person is caught up in the process of "perpetual perishing." At any new moment, the specific constellation of events that constitutes a person slips away into the past and thus perishes. In the next moment, a new being is there. It has inherited many traits of its predecessor, but it is not simply a replica. It is in a way something new. At death, the entire series of events comes to a halt. There can be no survival of anything like a substantial person, because a substantial being never existed.

What happens to us as perishing events? If we are events, clearly even a past event cannot become completely nonexistent. An event that took place is still an event; it cannot be undone. Here Whitehead and Hartshorne introduce the notion of God: past events are somehow "recorded" and "remembered," and the recording agent can be called God. In the divine mind and memory, no past event can ever be lost.

Here everything is stored up forever and never cast out. Here every event retains forever its original vividness, freshness, and immediacy. And it is here, too, that human biographies are eternally remembered. The Whitehead-Hartshorne approach does not imply that our biographies come into existence only at death, but that each perishing event or moment is immediately recorded. "Death is the last page of the book of one's life," summarized Hartshorne in 1962, "as birth is the first page." After the last chapter is completed – "Death writes 'The End' upon the last page" – nothing further happens to the book. There is no further addition, nor is anything blotted out. Yet, the book of life does not remain as unused as do most books in our libraries. "We write our book of life. . .for the one adequate Reader," for God.[65]

Process thought not only rejects the traditional static view of the human person, but also the notion of an unchangeable God who reigns somewhere above the world in everlasting immobility. God himself is subject to change. He is the Cosmic Consciousness into which every past event is incorporated. It would be wrong, however, to reduce God to an accountant who does nothing but keep track of otherwise perishing events. God also responds. "We can interpret 'heaven,'" according to Hartshorne, "as the conception which God forms of our actual being, a conception which we partly determine by our free decisions, but which is more than all our decisions and experiences, since it is the synthesis of God's participating responses to these experiences." At every moment, God notes and responds. At every moment, he is enriched. God is an involved reader.[66]

This doctrine of everlasting existence in the divine mind gives God absolute priority. In this sense, process theology fulfills one important requirement of the Christian creed. Everything happens for God and his glory; every person and event has abiding value only in the divine. We have to realize, however, that we are finite, perishable beings. If we asked to survive eternally with individual consciousness and endless life, we would ask to be like God or even to replace him. Process theology realizes that this is what some people actually want, but this wish must be abandoned. "Of course the immortality of the past in God does not give people everything they may happen to want," acknowledged Hartshorne. "We have been enjoying a spouse, a son or daughter, a friend, and our capacity for such enjoyment is not exhausted. So we may find it pleasant to think of continuing the relationship after death. However, if we know anything at all about the human condition it is that things do not always go as we might wish." As Freud observed, the world is not a kindergarten. We have to be realistic and realize that we are fundamentally mortal beings.[67]

In spite of process theology's emphasis on God's glory, its belief in a rather insubstantial life after death departs from traditional Christian teaching. For Hartshorne, the idea inspired by St. Paul, "that our chief concern should be over what happens after death," is for him "a dubious side of the New Testament." Traditional Christianity, according to this view, has promised too much by promoting unrealistic expectations. Hartshorne's wish is that our culture should return, after a long detour, "to the original Jewish insight that only two things matter, creaturely life between birth and death, and the unborn and undying life in God." Elsewhere, Hartshorne speaks of the process view not so much as a return to a forgotten element of western culture, but as something to be learnt from an encounter with Buddhism. "Buddhism," he reflected, "stood almost alone on the side of truth for two thousand years until the West, first in Hume and Peirce, and then more radically in Whitehead, finally saw the light." Theology no longer uses philosophy in order to understand or develop its traditional teaching, but philosophy looks for a different religious world-view to answer the inadequacies found inside Christianity.[68]

What Happened to Heaven?

Christian theology, as understood in the eighteenth and nineteenth centuries, was based on a heaven which included the following characteristics: (1) Describability: life after death continues the present existence and must therefore share its concrete, describable features; it cannot be totally different. (2) New experiences: as a real life, the new existence must involve a continuing succession both of time and of new experiences in time. Life must always go on, it cannot simply stand still as if it were frozen. (3) Self-consciousness: eternal life is not something that happens, as it were, from the outside to some immortal substance. Whatever survives death – the "person" or the soul – must be a self-conscious individual with the will to participate actively in a new existence. (4) Relatedness to God: Christian doctrine expected a stronger and more explicit relationship of the individual to the deity in heaven than is possible in the present life. God must be present to the blessed in an overwhelming way.

Those contemporary Christians who maintain the modern perspective on heaven continue to see life after death as fulfilling these categories. Twentieth-century religious visions, near-death experiences, imaginative literature or poetry, and spiritualist accounts continue to describe the existence of life in the other world. Life after death is still life and so a mother's voice may still be recognized, a heavenly field will blossom with flowers, a warm and loving God will greet each new arrival. The dead continue to be tested, to learn, and to develop their spiritual potential. The growth of the soul after death, especially in Latter-day Saint theology, requires the self-conscious spirit to make choices and to participate actively in the various levels of after-death experience.

Contemporary versions of the modern heaven assume that the personality and individuality of the righteous soul persist in the afterlife. At the same time, the contemporary modern heaven is decidedly more theocentric than its Victorian ancestor. In the Gallup survey with which we began this chapter, only 8 per cent of those polled assumed they would enjoy material comforts in life after death, while 54 per cent believed that they would be in the presence of God or Jesus Christ. Even though Christians expect to meet their families, they accept that the primary focus of heaven will be the divine. In a time when it is easy not to believe in heaven, those who choose to continue in this belief insist that communion with God is basic to eternal life.

Twentieth-century theologies have successively questioned the qualities of describability, new experiences, and self-consciousness. They reject the modern heaven of Swedenborg, the Victorians, and the Mormons, and promote a minimalist, theocentric eternal life. Fundamentalists insist that the Bible reveals very little about the future state, and the liberal school regards such knowlege as essentially unattainable. The limitations inherent in our experience – due either to limited biblical revelation or to reason – do not allow for any graphic distinctness in theological language. We may form symbols or tell myths (liberal school), or consider visions (fundamentalists), but these cannot be translated into clear, concrete, real information. Only abstractions and possibilities can be used to create a vague idea of what life after death might be like. While liberal and conservative Christians may argue endlessly about the reality of the devil and hell, they agree on the indescribability of heaven. The concept of "describability" must therefore be dropped from the list of the characteristics of eternal life.

Neo-orthodox theology, while emphasizing the unique relationship with the divine, denies the second quality, the possibility of having new experiences after death. Death marks a radical change in the existence of the human being. Although we will retain our self-consciousness and memory in heaven, there will not be another life. No new experiences, no continual succession of time, and no new relationships will mar our relationship with the divine. Karl Barth predicted that we will be able to talk only about the past, about earthly existence, which can be better understood but certainly not expanded. In other words, there will be eternal life or eternal consciousness, but not everlasting, continuous living.

Secular theology, going one step further, denies the continuing self-consciousness of the individual. Paul Tillich began this process by arguing that it is not the individual soul which is immortal – this is a symbol of something else – but the spirit or the essence of being: not the essence of the *human* being but the essence of all being. Eternity is not spoken of in terms of souls, but in terms of abstractions. Process theology continues that trend, denying that anything can remain fixed and eternal. Every thing and every person is caught up in the process of perpetual perishing. When the numerous and manifold series of events which combined to constitute a person separate again, then it is only the memory of the past that remains. Heaven has become empty of human beings. What continues is God alone with his unfailing memory of past events.

While both modern and minimalist heavenly theologies place God in heaven, their diverse understanding of the divine underlines the separation of the two perspectives. The difference between the LDS concept of God as a perfected being made of matter, and the understanding of Tillich that God is the "Ultimate Concern," cannot be over-estimated. The Catholic who responds in a poll that he wishes to go to heaven and "hug God" has little in common with the process theologian who sees God as the growing Cosmic Consciousness. Christians still associate God with the afterlife, but the great variety of concepts of God which exist in the contemporary Christian world erases the possibility of a common notion of heaven. Perhaps the only thing which all might agree on is that much of heaven is a mystery of which little can be asserted with confidence.

"Ah! where the image with such warmth was rife, /A shade alone is left," wrote the German poet Schiller in memory of the gods of Greece who were no longer believed but survived as poetic beings. The history of heaven has a similar ending. It ends with the view that God has given us just one life, the life we lead between birth and death, and that we should struggle to make the best of that life. Minimalist views of heaven accompany the overall culture with its pervasive rational and technological qualities. Western culture, according to sociologist Max Weber, has been brought about through a process of rationalization and intellectualization. As European and American culture has become increasingly rational, religion has also stressed and developed its intellectual dimension. The denial of individual life after death agrees with the very substance of contemporary ideology which rejects the supernatural and insists that the true concern of humanity is life on earth.[69]

While liberal and secular theologians teach reduced and truncated versions of the afterlife in the attempt to compromise between traditional affirmation and critical denial, fundamentalists and neo-orthodox thinkers produce a similiar compromise against their will. Fundamentalism which fights against modern secular trends cannot help but be influenced by its enemy. Although fundamentalists would discard the suggestion that heaven no longer is an active part of their belief system, eternal life has become an unknown place or a state of vague identity. Conservative Christians confront rationalized religion with a heightened sense of faith, religious feeling, and community, but they do not return to the rich heavenly images of previous generations. The drama of the future is decidedly this-worldly; it occurs during the period before and during the millennium, not in a heavenly world.

With the notable exception of the Latter-day Saints, the Swedenborgians, and some spiritualists, few western Christians have not been influenced by a skeptical perspective on life after death. Nor does real or alleged empirical evidence generally dispel skepticism. Accounts of near-death experiences relate glimpses of what lies beyond death, but present no long-term narratives. "I've Been to Heaven and Back," boasts the headline of the *Weekly World News*, although only a bright light and mother's voice comprise heaven. Near-death experiences, in effect, describe the gate of heaven and not the interior. Likewise, while nineteenth-century spiritualists were eager to provide descriptions of what dead relatives were doing in heaven, twentieth-century psychic research concentrates on questions of "survival" and avoids association with non-scientific methods of inquiry. Life after death, for many Christians, means existing only in the memory of their families and of God. Scientific, philosophical, and theological skepticism has nullified the modern heaven and replaced it with teachings that are minimalist, meager, and dry.[70]

Paradise Found:
Themes and Variations

Milton's poem *Paradise Lost*, though offering a promise of redemption, actually closes with the expulsion from the Garden to Eden. His friend Thomas Ellwood (1639–1713), who read the manuscript, handed it back to the author with the remark, "Thou hast said much here of Paradise Lost, but what hast thou to say of Paradise Found?" The poet gave no answer, but sat some time in a muse.

The History of Life of Thomas Ellwood
(London, 1714)

How have Christians visualized life everlasting? After reading, researching, and struggling with endless heavenly speculations, can we arrive at any convincing conclusions? Without underestimating the diversity, richness, and complexity of centuries of thought, certain patterns do emerge. Two major images dominate theology, pious literature, art, and popular ideas. Some Christians expect to spend heavenly life in "eternal solitude with God alone." Others cannot conceive of blessedness without being reunited with friends, spouse, children, or relatives. Using convenient theological jargon we have termed these views theocentric – "centering in God," and anthropocentric – "focusing on the human." Although social and religious expectations combine and balance in various ways to produce a variety of heavens, a certain emphasis on the divine or a clear preference for the human appears in each heaven. These two concepts do not depend on the level of sophistication of those presenting the image (theologians versus lay people), or time frame (early versus contemporary), or theological preference (Protestant versus Catholic). Rather, we have found that throughout Christian history anthropocentric and theocentric models emerge, become prominent, and weaken.

Each of the two views takes on a variety of historical forms and has its own history. In the case of the *theocentric model* we can point to:

(1) **The New Testament** view, characterized by a clear, uncompromising, "charismatic" fixation on God. As a charismatic leader, Jesus called his followers out of their kin and family relationships and sought

to focus their minds on God. No longer defined by ordinary social relationships, Christians are "children of God" – in this world and the next. Heavenly liturgies, spiritualized bodies, and angelic, non-married lifestyles comprise eternal life.

(2) In the **early Augustine** the theocentric model was reaffirmed but also redefined in terms of the monastic lifestyle and Neoplatonic philosophy. In a different cultural climate, the original charismatic inspiration gave way to more intellectual, philosophical concerns that focus on "God and the soul." The "flight in solitude to the Solitary" emphasized the privatized nature of heaven. Even the community of psalm-singing saints takes a second place to the individual's relationship with God.

(3) **Medieval scholasticism** again redefined the view of the other life. While Augustine's "beatific vision" of God was reaffirmed, its intellectual quality stressed, and all earthly concern denied, the schoolmen also speculated on heaven as a locality. God and the soul meet in the empyrean: a transcendent, light-filled place outside of, but enveloping, the universe. The fruition of the divine light provides the highest bliss human creatures can attain. The scholastic vision reaches out through the centuries, not so much in dry treatises but in the brilliance of the Gothic cathedral and the magnificence of Dante's *Paradiso.*

(4) **Medieval mystics** like Mechthild of Magdeburg envisioned a more intimate blessed union with Christ. While scholastic theology only assumed different degrees in the intensity of the beatific vision, the mystics added a higher kind of reward. The Lord grants heavenly lovemaking to the purest of his virgins. Intimate union transcends the intellectual joys of the vision of God. Christ in heaven meets the soul as friend, companion, and lover. The theocentric heaven is not merely God dazzling the saints with his majesty; it can also be the place where the soul is caressed as a lover.

(5) **Protestant reformers** rejected scholasticism as unbiblical, and mysticism as visionary fancy. In their critical attitude they were joined by the promoters of the Catholic reform who also found little in medieval thought relevant to their pastoral concerns. Protestants, and to a lesser extent Catholics, revived the charismatic zeal of the New Testament at the expense of the intellectualism inherited from the early Augustine and scholasticism. The most extreme version of the God-centered heaven could be found in Jansenism and Puritanism. As elected and transformed people, true Christians enjoy praising the Lord more than anything else – in this world and the next.

(6) Much of **contemporary theology** reiterates the theocentric heaven. Eternal life will concern God; this is all we know. Theologians of the most diverse backgrounds, from Catholic liberals to conservative

Protestants, present a heaven of minimal description. At times, the human presence in heaven becomes so weak that it almost disappears and nothing of ourselves continues after death. In a century marked by two world wars, people look to God alone to exist eternally. Whatever may happen to the human being, God abides.

The theocentric model presupposes a distinct view of the relationship between God and the human creature. The inequality of the two is emphasized, with God being absolutely superior. He claims complete surrender: emotional, intellectual, even physical. Unless guided by the divine will alone, human beings are lost. Once autonomy is surrendered, however, one can be assured of everlasting life. This attitude appeals to those who accord a lower priority to social commitments than to spiritual values. The theocentric heaven is preferred by people who, for various reasons, seek distance from "the world." Religious enthusiasts and charismatic leaders; philosophers inspired by some form of Platonism; members of celibate groups who want to lead the unmarried life of the angles even here on earth; reformers who discover the power of a demanding God and find themselves in an alien and often hostile world: these Christians find rest in an eternity filled with the divine. Conversely, the theocentric view has little appeal for others who prefer the settled, "normal" life of family, work, and business. The world, with all its compromises and lack of true religious heroism, constantly threatens a full commitment to Christian ideals.

Those who would not readily follow the injunction to "seek first the Kingdom of God" (Matt. 6:33) or subscribe to Teresa of Avila's dictum that "God alone suffices" are unlikely to speak of heaven in theocentric terms. They ask whether human integrity is really possible when God claims complete, undivided attention. Why would a world be created at all if the divine intended everlasting life to leave no room for non-religious concerns? Since Christians do not generally accept a theology out of tune with their world-view, a different afterlife has to be envisioned. The resulting *anthropocentric* description of heaven is equally well represented in the history of western Christianity:

(1) **Irenaeus of Lyons** in second-century France focused his attention not on life everlasting proper, but on its initial phase, a thousand-year period when the saints will inhabit the renewed earth. During the millennium, the martyrs will be compensated for whatever was denied them in their earlier life. An existence unmolested by enemies, enjoying the goodness of God's creation and producing numerous children throughout a long life, overshadows the eternity that will follow.

(2) **Augustine** in his later years came to abandon the Neoplatonic notion of an abstract, theocentric heaven characteristic of his early theology. His view of the afterlife involved meeting friends and enjoying the physical beauty of glorified yet sexually differentiated bodies. As a

bishop and pastor more involved with the world, he incorporated the theme of heavenly reunion into his teaching. This originally Greek motif was mediated to the West through the work of the Roman philosopher and statesman Cicero.

(3) **In the Middle Ages** we find one version of the anthropocentric afterlife in the popular theological manual, the *Elucidation*. Christians will spend eternity on a renewed earth which is paradise restored. The image of heaven as a city which includes a royal court strengthened the social dimension of the afterlife. While the meeting-again motif was not very prominent, some poets dreamed about being eternally united to the lady whom they adored in courtly love.

(4) **In the Renaissance** the Ciceronian hope of heavenly reunion assumed center stage. The separation of God's own heaven from an earthly paradise enabled theologians, humanists, and artists to humanize the other world. Here men and women meet, play, kiss, and caress in a pastoral environment. The Golden Age and the Elysian Fields of classical mythology filtered into Christian concepts of the afterlife. Before the Renaissance, anthropocentric heavens had never been so fully human and attractive.

(5) **The eighteenth century** ushered in the modern heaven with its emphasis on the nearness of the next world to this one, its material character, and its acceptance of human love and progress. The starkness of the reformers' theocentric heaven fuelled the development of a human-oriented afterlife. The writings of Swedenborg provided a vivid alternative to both Enlightenment skepticism and the religious enthusiasm of Puritan and Jansenist reformers.

(6) **With the nineteenth century** came the apex of the anthropocentric heaven. A wide variety of preachers, theologians, poets, and popular writers depicted heaven as a social community where the saints meet their relatives and friends. The union of God and the soul after death gave way to the union of the lover and the beloved. Ideas of productive work, spiritual development, and technological progress contributed to the completeness of the other-worldly society. This type of heaven continues in Latter-day Saint theology, contemporary popular culture, and in the glimpses of the afterlife in near-death experiences.

The anthropocentric view of heaven presupposes a value system fundamentally different from that of the theocentric model. In general, the world is looked upon more optimistically. Social life, marriage, sexuality, and work are divinely instituted and eternal. God permits them to be enjoyed by men and women in both worlds. Ideas of eternal life are modelled not on the enthusiastic worship of religious charismatics, but on an idealized life of leisure, service, and spiritual growth. The divine is no longer experienced solely in ecstasy, extraordinary events, and heroic commitment, but in the calm course of everyday life.

Moreover, the loneliness of the ascetic world-renouncer is considered a deficient mode of existence, not a preparation for eternity. Since the natural world, personal relationships, and work itself are sacred, they must continue in some form in the next life. The anthropocentric system of values is related to a socially-established Christianity. Its distinctive view of heaven appeals to Christians who do not feel separated or alienated from the world: to Irenaeus, head of a Christian merchant community; to the later Augustine who had settled into his role as the bishop of a state church; to lovers affected by the various surges of sentiment between the Renaissance period and the present day; in sum, to all who are convinced of the ultimate harmony of the human and the divine.

Although the two models often co-exist, one of them can generally be considered the dominant view for a given time and place. But the leading position, whether occupied by the theocentric or the anthropocentric view, cannot be firmly established in the long run. Whenever the theocentric model is given its full expression, a softening of its uncompromising quality is called for. Since human love and longing cannot be utterly suppressed, even the most rigorous theocentric theology retains a human element. The anthropocentric alternative receives a fair hearing. Likewise, when the human dimension threatens to weaken or supplant the divine, the pendulum again swings to the other side. Like human passion, the love of God can never be suppressed or forgotten. Even the most human-centered views of the afterlife endow heaven with divine presence. A basic tension occurs at the heart of the Christian mentality – a tension foreshadowed in its founder's injunction to love both God and neighbor.

Despite the vacillation between the two directions, no simple repetition of images occurs. Shifting models does not mean the mere restoration of the opposite. Whatever traditional elements are reused or revitalized, the result is a unique formulation. Traditional concepts and concerns lead to ever new and characteristic configurations colored by the general cultural and social climate. We would be wrong in defining the history of heaven as the alternation between human wishful thinking and biblical truth. This suggestion overlooks the pervasive role of needs, wishes, and creativity in the construction of all theologies. We also would be incorrect to assume that changing notions of eternity are responses to the challenge of "heresy." While some types of Christian doctrine may change under pressure of what is or is not considered orthodox, changes in the images of heaven do not respond to that pressure. Views of life everlasting may be presented with polemic and enthusiasm, but the history of heaven is remarkably free of doctrinal debates, heresy trials, and formal definitions. The common patterns of the history of doctrine – progressive evolution, response to heresy, defection from truth, return to the pure teaching – are of little help in understanding the beyond.

The history of heaven, moreover, cannot be presented as a simple alternation between theocentric and anthropocentric models. In the twentieth century certain Christian thinkers refuse to see heaven as focused on either God or humankind. Some writers recommend that we turn away from discussing life after death and concentrate on life before death. For them, the Christian message has little to do with heavenly speculation. Others reduce "life everlasting" and "heaven" to symbols that do not lend themselves to investigation and conceptualization. Still others become so preoccupied with the thousand-year reign before eternity that everlasting life remains an afterthought. Here we have something quite new and unprecedented in the history of Christianity: the discontinuity with traditional belief is greater than the continuity. Are we witnessing the emergence of a post-Christian theology, one whose relationship with classical afterlife affirmations is vague and ultimately irrelevant? Or have the social developments and scientific discoveries of the past century robbed heaven of any believable images for even the most devoted Christian? Christians – presumably most Christians – will continue to believe in some form of an afterlife. We cannot look back and evaluate the history of heaven like one would an ancient civilization or the biography of someone who died. As new ideas about life everlasting emerge in the future, earlier views will be reassessed in fresh ways.

NOTES

ABBREVIATIONS

AE	Emanuel Swedenborg, *The Apocalypse Explained*
CL	Emanuel Swedenborg, *Conjugial Love*
CR	*Corpus Reformatorum*
CSEL	*Corpus Scriptorum Ecclesiasticorum Latinorum*
HA	Emanuel Swedenborg, *Heavenly Arcana*
HH	Emanuel Swedenborg, *Heaven and Hell*
J	*The Complete Poems of Emily Dickinson*, ed. Thomas H. Johnson
LDS	The Church of Jesus Christ of Latter-day Saints ("Mormons")
PG	Jacques-Paul Migne, ed., *Patrologiae cursus completus. Series graeca*
PL	Jacques-Paul Migne, ed., *Patrologiae cursus completus. Series latina*
SC	*Sources chrétiennes*
SD	Emanuel Swedenborg, *The Spiritual Diary*
Sth	Thomas Aquinas, *Summa theologica*
TCR	Emanuel Swedenborg, *The True Christian Religion*
WA	*D. Martin Luthers Werke. Kritische Gesamtausgabe* ("Weimarer Ausgabe")
WA Br	*D. Martin Luthers Werke. Briefwechsel* ("Weimarer Ausgabe")
WA TR	*D. Martin Luthers Werke. Tischreden* ("Weimarer Ausgabe")

CHAPTER ONE

1. Ancestor-worship and the condition of the dead in the ancient Semitic and biblical worlds are surveyed in: Klaas Spronk, *Beatific Afterlife in Acient Israel and in the Ancient Near East* (Kevelaer: Butzon & Bercker, 1986); Herbert C. Brichto, "Kin, Cult, Land and Afterlife – A Biblical Complex," *Hebrew Union College Annual* 44(1973), 1–54; Oswald Loretz, "Vom kanaanäischen Totenkult zur jüdischen Patriarchen – und Elternehrung," *Jahrbuch für Anthropologie und Religionsgeschichte* 3(1978), 149–204; Jack N. Lightstone, "The Dead in Late Antique Judaism," *Cahiers de recherches en sciences de la religion* 6(1985), 51–79; George C. Heider, *The Cult of Molek* (Sheffield: JSOT Press, 1985); Akio Tsukimoto, *Untersuchungen zur Totenpflege (kispum) im alten Mesopotamien* (Kevelaer: Butzon & Bercker, 1985). For the veneration of a deceased mother, see the case of Assyrian prince Assurbanipal: Simo Parpola, *Letters from Assyrian Scholars to the Kings Esarhaddon and Assurbanipal* (Kevelaer: Butzon & Bercker, 1970), 106.

2. Robert Cooley, "Gathered to His People: A Study of a Dothan Family Tomb," Morris Inch *et al.*, eds., *The Living and Active Word of God: Studies in Honor of Samuel J. Schultz* (Winona Lake, IN: Eisenbrauns, 1983), 47–58.

3. "Goes to; gathered to," Gen. 15:15; 25:8. For the deceased as "god," see 1 Sam. 28:13; the term rendered "ghostly form" by the New English Bible is *elohim*, i.e. "god." Ps. 16:3 calls the dead the "gods [lit. "holy ones"] who are in the earth"; Spronk, *Beatific Afterlife*, 249.

4. Isa. 14:4–21.

5. 1 Sam. 28. The "digging of a hole" is inferred from similar ancient accounts; see e.g. Homer, *Odyssey*, 11:25ff.; and Jürgen Ebach and Udo Rüterswörden, "Unterweltsbeschwörung im Alten Testament," *Ugarit-Forschung* 9(1977), 57–70; 12(1980), 205–20; Heider, *Cult of Molek*, 249f.

6. On the Yahweh-alone movement, see Bernhard Lang, *Monotheism and the Prophetic Minority* (Sheffield: Almond, 1983), 13–59.

7. Henri Hubert and Marcel Mauss, "Théorie générale de la magie," *Année sociologique* 7 (1902/3), 1–149, at 19.

8. Hezekiah's reform document seems to be Exod. 20:23–23:19, the so-called covenant code; see Rainer Albertz, "Die Religionsgeschichte Israels in vorexilischer Zeit," Erich Lessing, ed., *Die Bibel: Das Alte Testament* (Munich: Bertelsmann, 1987), 287–360, at 342. The rule of giving the first-born is in Exod. 22:29, cf. Jacob Milgrom, "First-born," *The Interpreter's Dictionary of the Bible. Supplementary Volume* (Nashville, TN: Abingdon, 1976), 337–38. "You shall be," Exod. 22:31.

9. "Josiah got rid," 2 Kings 23:24 (New English Bible). For the possibility of identifying the "household gods" (teraphim) as ancestors, see Spronk, *Beatific Afterlife*, 40–41 and 50; Tsukimoto, *Untersuchungen zur Totenpflege*, 104f., and Hedwige Rouillard and J. Tropper, "*Trpym*, rituels de guérison et culte des ancêtres," *Vetus Testamentum* 37(1987), 340–61. The measures taken by King Josiah are echoed in Lev. 19:31; 20:6.27; Deut. 18:11. The toleration of funerary offerings is presupposed in Deut. 26:14 and Tobit 4:17, cf. Brichto, "Kin, Cult, Land," 28f. and Lightstone, "The Dead in Late Antique Judaism," 66ff.

10. Matt. 23:27. Cf. Num. 19:11–16; Jer. 8:1f.

11. Job 14:21; also Isa. 63:16, a passage which makes Yahweh the only "father" of Israel while asserting that "Abraham does not know us nor Israel [i.e. patriarch Jacob] acknowledge us"; Spronk, *Beatific Afterlife*,255.

12. "A land of," Job 10:22; "the house wherein," Gilgamesh, tablet 7 in James B. Pritchard, ed., *Ancient Near Eastern Texts Relating to the Old Testament*, 3rd ed. (Princeton: Princeton Univ. Press, 1969), 87 (107 and 509 for further Mesopotamian texts); place free from trials, Job 3:17–19.

13. "Who will praise," Sir. 17:22f., elaborating Pss. 6:5; 88:10ff.; not sing the Lord's song, Ps. 137:4; "for they are," Ps. 88:6.

14. "You are the," Deut. 14:1 with parallel in Lev. 19:28. Rule for priests, Lev. 21:11.

15. For the veneration of patriarchs etc., see Loretz, "Vom kanaanäischen Totenkult"; Lightstone, "The Dead in Late Antique Judaism," and Joachim Jeremias, *Heiligengräber in Jesu Umwelt* (Göttingen: Vandenhoeck & Ruprecht, 1958). "Vindicated their race," 4 Macc. 17:10 in James H. Charlesworth, ed., *The Old Testament Pseudepigrapha* (Garden City, NY: Doubleday, 1983/85), II, 562; "wealth remains in," Sir. 44:11f.

16. Job 42:10.

17. Mary Boyce, *A History of Zoroastrianism* (Leiden: Brill, 1975), I, 236, 245f.; Boyce, "On the Antiquity of Zoroastrian Apocalyptic," *Bulletin of the School of Oriental and African Studies* 47(1984), 57–75.

18. Ezek. 37:1–14 (without v. 12b.13, which is a gloss) as explained in Bernhard Lang, "Street Theater, Raising the Dead, and the Zoroastrian Connection in Ezekiel's Prophecy," Johan Lust, ed., *Ezekiel and His Book* (Leuven: Leuven Univ. Press, 1986), 297–316. Zoroastrian funerary customs: Boyce, *History of Zoroastrianism*, I, 325–30.

19. For another exilic resurrection prophecy, see Isa. 26:19 and Gerhard F. Hasel, "Resurrection in the Theology of Old Testament Apocalyptic," *Zeitschrift für die alttestamentliche Wissenschaft* 92(1980), 267–84.

20. "Of those who," Dan. 12:2; "it was from," 2 Macc. 7:11.

21. 1 Enoch 10:10; 25:6 (in *Old Testament Pseudepigrapha*, I, 18.26) on the basis of Gen. 5. The eschatology of the book of Enoch is discussed in Bernhard Lang, "No Sex in Heaven: The Logic of Procreation, Death, and Eternal Life in the Judaeo-Christian Tradition," André Caquot et al., eds., *Mélanges bibliques et orientaux en l'honneur de M. Mathias Delcor* (Neukirchen: Neukirchener Verlag, 1985), 237–53, esp. 238f.

22. Ps. 73:3, 4, 23–5 (New English Bible).

23. "But God will," Ps. 49:15 as explained by Harold H. Rowley, *The Faith of Israel* (London: SCM Press, 1956), 171–5; "all who inhabit," riddle," Ps. 49:1.4.

24. The Hebrew word rendered "to receive, to take" is a technical term for heavenly assumption in Ps. 49:15; 73:24 as well as in Gen. 5:24 (Enoch); 2 Kings 2:3.5.9 (Elijah).

25. Andrew B. Davidson, *The Theology of the Old Testament* (Edinburgh: Clark, 1904), 439.

26. Our explanation of Greek eschatology is based on: Paul Capelle, "Elysium und die Inseln der Seligen," *Archiv für Religionswissenschaft* 25(1927), 245–64 and 26(1928), 17–40; Larry J. Alderink, *Creation and Salvation in Ancient Orphism* (Chico, CA: Scholars Press, 1981); Dietrich Roloff, *Gottähnlichkeit, Vergöttlichung*

und *Erhöhung zum seligen Leben* (Berlin: de Gruyter, 1970); Ioan P. Culianu, *Psychanodia, I: A Survey of the Evidence Concerning the Ascension of the Soul* (Leiden: Brill, 1983); Anthony T. Edwards, "Achilles in the Underworld," *Greek, Roman, and Byzantine Studies* 26(1985), 215–27; Holger Thesleff, "Notes on the Paradise Myth in Ancient Greece," *Temenos* 22(1986), 129–39. On Jewish interest in Greek ideas, see T. Francis Glasson, *Greek Influence in Jewish Eschatology* (London: SPCK, 1961).

27. The Greek relief is in Martin P. Nilsson, *Geschichte der griechischen Religion*, 2nd ed. (Munich: Beck, 1961), II, plate 4,1. On the Virgil miniature, see Thomas B. Stevenson, *Miniature Decoration in the Vatican Virgil* (Tübingen: Wasmuth, 1983), 72; Virgil, *Aeneid*, 6:642–4 [*The Aeneid*, trans. Robert Fitzgerald (New York; Vintage, 1984), 182].

28. This seems to have been the Orphic idea: Alderink, *Creation and Salvation*, 93. Cf. Plato, *Phaedrus*, 246E-249D, and *The Republic*, 614A–621D (Er's other-world journey); Cicero, *Scipio's Dream*; Paul's paradise in the third heaven (2 Cor. 12:2f.).

29. Philo, *On the Giants*: "a higher existence," 15. On asexuality, see the asexual "idea of man" which precedes the creation of material, sexual persons: Philo, *On Creation*, 134.

30. Harry A. Wolfson, *Philo*, 4th ed. (Cambridge, MA: Harvard Univ. Press, 1968), I, 403f.; Philo, *On Dreams*: "some, longing for," 1:139.

31. Testament of Job: angels, chariot, 52 (*Old Testament Pseudepigrapha*, I, 867f.).

32. Hans C. Cavallin, *Life after Death* (Lund: Gleerup, 1974); Cavallin, "Leben nach dem Tode im Spätjudentum and im frühen Christentum," Wolfgang Haase, ed., *Aufstieg und Niedergang der römischen Welt*, 2nd ser. (Berlin: de Gruyter, 1979), XIX/1, 240–345.

33. Josephus, *Jewish Antiquities*: "the soul perishes," 18:16; *The Fathers according to Rabbi Nathan*: "use vessels of," A 5 in George W.E. Nickelsburg et al., eds., *Faith and Piety in Early Judaism. Texts and Documents* (Philadelphia: Fortress Press, 1983), 32; "let us eat," 1 Cor. 15:32. All ancient sources dealing with the Sadducees are discussed in Jean Le Moyne, *Les Sadducéens* (Paris: Gabalda, 1972).

34. "A day in," Ps. 84:10.

35. For a convenient summary of Pharisaic teachings, see Jacob Neusner, *Judaism in the Beginning of Christianity* (London: SPCK, 1984), 26f.

36. Josephus, *Jewish War*: "the soul of," 2:163, taken to refer to resurrection; "born and bred," Acts 23:6ff. (New English Bible).

37. All quotations from Josephus, *Jewish War*, 2:154f.

CHAPTER TWO

1. Mishnah, *Nedarim*: half-shekel, 2:4; Talmud Yerushalmi, *Shabbat*: "hate the Torah," 16:15d. The Galilean attitude is discussed in Sean Freyne, *Galilee from Alexander the Great to Hadrian* (Wilmington, DL: Glazier, 1980), 315, 277f.

2. For the "holy man" in Palestinian Judaism, see Sean Freyne, "Galilean Religion of the First Century CE against Its Social Background," *Proceedings of the Irish Biblical Association* 5(1981), 98–114; Morton Smith, *Jesus the Magician* (London: Gollancz, 1978), 81–152, and Geza Vermes, *Jesus the Jew*, 2nd ed. (London: SCM Press, 1983), 58–82.

3. Luke 20:34–6. The words "of a place in the age to come and" are omitted because it is believed that Jesus did not speak of an "age to come." The terminology of the two ages is not used in the parallel reports of Matthew and Mark (Matt. 22:23–33; Mark 12:18–27), it is also hardly attested before 70 CE, see Dale C. Allison, *The End of the Ages Has Come* (Philadelphia: Fortress Press, 1985), 107.

4. Josephus tells us an anecdote which implies that the first husband will be the legitimate one in the beyond. A widow, who married several times after her first husband's death, was told by this husband in a dream that he would claim her back. Two days after this dream, she died and could thus join him. Josephus, *Jewish War*, 2:114–16.

5. For marital fertility after death, in the divine kingdom on earth, see 1 Enoch 10 (James H. Charlesworth, ed., *The Old Testament Pseudepigrapha* Garden City, NY: Doubleday, 1983), I, 17–19) and Talmud, b*Shabbat* 30b. In the latter source a rabbi who flourished around 90 CE is reported to have suggested that in the messianic kingdom women will give birth to another child every single day! "Sons of God," Gen. 6:1–4.

6. "Moses in the," Luke 20:37f. God of the living, Deut. 5:26 and God of Abraham, Exod. 3:15 with the two passages taken to refer to the same incident.

7. That the patriarchs live with God appears occasionally in texts and is presupposed in the cult of the patriarchal tombs, see 4 Macc. 16:25 [*The Old Testament Pseudepigrapha*, II, 562] and Jack N. Lightstone, "The Dead in Late Antique Judaism," *Cahiers de recherches en*

sciences de la religion 6(1985), 51–79, at 63. For other attempts to understand the reasoning, see John J. Kilgallen. "The Sadducees and the Resurrection from the Dead," *Biblica* 67 (1986), 478–95 and Otto Schwankl, *Die Sadduzäerfrage (Mk 12,18–27 parr)* (Frankfurt: Athenäum, 1987). How ancient rabbinic theology wrestled with "proving" resurrection from Scripture is discussed in Jacob Neusner, *What is Midrash?* (Philadelphia: Fortress Press, 1987), 95–101.

8. "Carried by the," Luke 16:22.

9. The doctrine of a spiritual (rather than bodily) "resurrection from Sheol into heaven" seems to have been developed in certain Jewish circles and specifically applied to martyrs, see Klaus Berger, *Die Auferstehung des Propheten und Erhöhung des Menschensohnes* (Göttingen: Vandenhoeck & Ruprecht, 1976) and Ulrich Kellermann, *Auferstanden in den Himmel* (Stuttgart: Kath. Bibelwerk, 1979).

10. Luke 16:19–31.

11. The problem of the authenticity of Luke 16:19ff. is discussed by Walter Schmithals, *Das Evangelium des Lukas* (Zurich: Theologischer Verlag, 1980), 171. For ancient parallels, see Hugo Gressmann, "Vom reichen Mann und armen Lazarus," *Abhandlungen der Berliner Akademie der Wissenschaften*, philos.-hist. Klasse 1918, no.7 (Berlin: Akademie-Verlag, 1918); Isidore Lévy, *La légende de Pythagore: de Grèce en Palestine* (Paris: Campion, 1927), 310–12. An Egyptian parallel is "Setne and Si-Osire," Miriam Lichtheim, *Ancient Egyptian Literature* (Berkeley: Univ. of California Press, 1980), III, 138–42. Jacques Dupont, *Etudes sur les évangiles synoptiques* (Leuven: Peeters, 1985), 1066–75 is right in rejecting the common assumption that Jesus (or Luke) here refers to an "intermediary state" between death and Last Judgment.

12. Luke: Elijah and Moses, 9:28–36; "today," 23:43. "There are many," John 14:2. The precise meaning of John 14:2 is not clear. While earlier commentators thought of "a hospitable heavenly palace with many chambers," recent authors think of no rooms at all, but of a "state" – that of permanent communion with God, see Günther Fischer, *Die himmlischen Wohnungen. Untersuchungen zu Joh 14.2f.* (Bern: Lang, 1975) and James McCaffrey, "John 14:2–3," Proceedings of the Irish Biblical Association 6(1982), 58–80.

13. Luke: "follow me," 9:59f. "Kill the body," Matt. 10:28. There is much debate about the precise meaning of the "kingdom of God" in Jesus' original preaching, see Bruce J. Chilton, ed., *The Kingdom of God in the Teaching of Jesus* (London: SPCK, 1984). According to

Chilton, "Jesus was impelled to preach by his certainty that God would reveal himself powerfully; the kingdom announcement affirmed vividly but simply that God was acting and would act in strength on behalf of his people" (23). He goes on to explain that the term does not imply any particular location in space or time. Luke 23:42f. seems to involve Jesus' rejection of a futuristic and this-worldly understanding of the kingdom – "today" the repenting thief will be in paradise.

14. 1 Thess. 4:15 seems to echo an authentic saying of Jesus.

15. Ernst Troeltsch, *The Social Teaching of the Christian Churches*, trans. O. Wyon (London: Allen & Unwin, 1931), 50.

16. Abba, Mark 14:36, "all things have," Matt. 11:27.

17. "Come to me," Matt. 11:28f. For the disruption of families and the ideal of itinerant existence, see Gerd Theissen, *Sociology of Early Palestinian Christianity*, trans. John Bowden (Philadelphia: Fortress Press, 1978).

18. James G. Dunn, *Unity and Diversity in the New Testament* (London: SCM Press, 1977): "was characterized by," 186. Max Weber, *On Charisma and Institution Building*, ed. S.N. Eisenstadt (Chicago: Univ. of Chicago Press, 1968), 21f. For Jesus as a charismatic leader, see Michael N. Ebertz, *Das Charisma des Gekreuzigten: Zur Soziologie der Jesusbewegung* (Tübingen: Mohr, 1987), 53–110.

19. Matt. 10:35. There is complete silence in the gospels concerning the marital status of Jesus. No wife accompanied him in his (short) public career, or stayed at home as the wives of his disciples were expected to do. Ancient Jewish sources report that Moses freely decided to terminate cohabitation with his wife after he had received his call from God. A rabbi of the late first century CE is reported to have remained unmarried altogether in order to devote his life to biblical study. Any reconstruction based on such parallels must of course remain conjectural, see Vermes, *Jesus the Jew*, 99–102.

20. On Jesus and his family, see Luke 2:41–51; 8:19–21; Ernest Renan, *The Life of Jesus*, introd. Charles Gore (London: Dent, 1927), 52f.; Dupont, *Etudes sur les évangiles synoptiques*, 131–45. Ferdinand Mount, *The Subversive Family* (London: Cape, 1982) shows that similar hostility toward settled family life can be found in such diverse figures as Plato, Jesus, Marx, Lenin, and Hitler.

21. Luke 18:29. On the new Passover ritual, see Gillian Feeley-Harnik, *The Lord's Table: Eucharist and Passover in Early Christianity* (Philadelphia: Univ. of Pennsylvania Press,

1981), 144.

22. On early Christian enthusiasm, see James D.G. Dunn, *Jesus and the Spirit: A Study of the Religious and Charismatic Experience of Jesus* (London: SCM Press, 1975). For theoretical perspectives on ecstatic worship and the participation of women, see Ioan M. Lewis, *Ecstatic Religion* (Harmondsworth: Penguin, 1971) and Mary Douglas, *Natural Symbols*, revised ed. (Harmondsworth: Penguin, 1973), 93–112.

23. "What I am writing," 1 Cor. 14:37. On the Pauline communities in Asia Minor, see Wayne A. Meeks, *The First Urban Christians: The Social World of the Apostle Paul* (New Haven: Yale Univ. Press, 1983), 43; on Paul's authority, Bengt Holmberg, *Paul and Power* (Philadelphia: Fortress Press, 1980).

24. "The unmarried man," 1 Cor. 7:32f.; "finances," 2 Cor. 11:7–9.

25. Dunn, *Jesus*, 194.

26. "Caught up," 2 Cor. 12:2. The "third heaven" may actually be a lower level, but Paul also claims to have been in "Paradise" (2 Cor. 12:3), i.e. in God's throne room, possibly located at the seventh level; see James D. Tabor, *Things Unutterable: Paul's Ascent to Paradise* (Lanham, MD: Univ. Press of America, 1986), 119. For Paul's attitude to ancestor worship, see 1 Cor. 10:14–22 where the "idols" seem to refer to symbols in ancestral shrines; the issue is discussed in Charles A. Kennedy, "The Cult of the Dead in Corinth," John H. Marks et al., eds., *Love and Death in the Ancient Near East* (Guilford, CT: Four Quarters, 1987), 227–36. Death as "sleep," 1 Cor. 15:6, 20 and 1 Thess. 4:1f.

27. Spiritual body, 1 Cor. 15:44.

28. "In a twinkling," 1 Cor. 15:52; "meeting the Lord," 1 Thess. 4:17. In 1 Thess. 4:16f. the eternal abode of the faithful is certainly heaven rather than the earth, see the parallel case of Enoch (Gen. 5:24) and Joseph Plevnik, "The taking Up of the Faithful and the Resurrection of the Dead in 1 Thess. 4:13–18," *Catholic Biblical Quarterly* 46(1984), 274–83. The opposite argument is given by Traugott Holtz, *Der erste Brief an die Thessalonicher* (Zurich: Benziger, 1986), 204.

29. Hans Conzelmann, *Der erste Brief an die Korinther*, 2nd ed. (Göttingen: Vandenhoeck & Ruprecht, 1981): messianic rulership a present reality, 330 n. 63 and 336; life-giving spirit, 1 Cor. 15:45; "I live no," Gal. 2:20. It was nothing special in the New Testament world to be possessed by someone who died, see Smith, *Jesus the Magician*, 33–6.

30. "Though our outer," 2 Cor. 4:16; "he who has," 2 Cor. 5:5 (cf. 1:22).

31. Tent or garment, 2 Cor. 5:1–5 with comments by Joseph Osei-Bonsu, "Does 2 Cor 5:1–10 Teach the Reception of the Resurrection Body at the Moment of Death?" *Journal for the Study of the New Testament* 28(1986), 81–101. For Paul's ignorance of the legendary reports on an empty tomb of Jesus, see Rudolf Bultmann, *Theology of the New Testament*, trans. K. Grobel (London: SCM Press, 1952), I, 45 and Hans Grass, *Ostergeschehen und Osterberichte*, 3rd ed. (Göttingen: Vandenhoeck & Ruprecht, 1964), 146–73. A different opinion is favored by Murray J. Harris, *Raised Immortal: Resurrection and Immortality in the New Testament* (London: Marshall, Morgan & Scott, 1983), 40f.

32. Destroying stomach and food, 1 Cor. 6:13f. Wilhelm Bousset, *Kyrios Christos*, trans. John E. Steely (Nashville, TN: Abingdon, 1970): "the fine celestial," 176f. According to Bultmann, *Theology of the New Testament*, I, 198, "spirit" is the substance and "body" the form of the resurrected person. Harris, *Raised Immortal*, hesitates between defining the spiritual body as a physical body "animated and guided by the spirit" (120) and as a body "with the characteristics of the divine Spirit" (257, n. 19).

33. "The desires of," Gal. 5:17; virtues and vices and their "spiritual" context are discussed in Gal. 5:16–25; 6:7f.; Rom. 8:1–17; "deeds of the," Rom. 8:13; "the proper act," Gerhard Kittel and Gerhard Friedrich, eds., *Theological Dictionary of the New Testament*, abridged ed. (Grand Rapids, MI: Eerdmans, 1985), 890.

34. Mary Douglas, *Natural Symbols*, 17, 195f.; Douglas, "Social Preconditions of Enthusiasm and Heterodoxy," *Proceedings of the 1969 Annual Spring Meeting of the American Ethnological Society* (Seattle: American Ethnological Society, 1969), 69–80.

35. Rom. 6:1–4; 8:14–15. A baptismal context of Rom. 8:15 is assumed by Meeks, *The First Urban Christians*, 152.

36. Charisma, 1 Cor. 12; J. Christiaan Beker, *Paul the Apostle* (Edinburgh: Clark, 1980): "exhibition before the," 280; "common good; edification," 1 Cor. 12:7; 14:12; celibacy, 1 Cor. 7:7.

37. Adela Y. Collins, "Insiders and Outsiders in the Book of Revelation," *To See Ourselves as Others See Us: Christians, Jews, "Others" in Late Antiquity*, Jacob Neusner et al., eds. (Chico, CA: Scholars Press, 1985), 187–218, esp. 216, and David E. Aune, *Prophecy in Early Christianity* (Grand Rapids, MI: Eerdmans, 1983), 197 offer their views on the author of the book of Revelation. His celibacy is implied in

Rev. 14:4.

38. One martyr, Rev. 2:13. On the Roman imperial cult and John's fight against accommodation see S.F.R. Price, *Rituals and Power: The Roman Imperial Cult in Asia Minor* (Cambridge: Cambridge Univ. Press, 1986); Collins, "Insiders," 215; Collins, *Crisis and Catharsis: The Power of the Apocalypse* (Philadelphia: Westminster Press, 1984). Collins refutes the traditional view that John responded to a massive Roman persecution. The alleged persecution under emperor Domitian never existed. In first-century Asia Minor, Christians were sometimes accused and brought to trial by hostile neighbors, but never actually persecuted.

39. Rev.: "come up here," 4:1; divine throne room, 4:2–5:2.

40. Another, probably contemporary Jewish apocalypse has its visionary see God "sitting on the throne of his glory surrounded by the angels *and the righteous ones*," 1 Enoch 60:2 [*The Old Testament Pseudepigrapha*, I, 40]. The priestly identity of the "elders" can be suggested on the basis of 1 Chron. 24:4. Rev.: "a Lamb that," 5:6; "a high number," 7:9; half an hour, 8:1.

41. Rev. 7:14–17.

42. Rev.: souls under altar, 6:9–11; resurrected prophets, 11:3–13.

43. Lucetta Mowry, "Revelation 4–5 and Early Christian Liturgical Usage," *Journal of Biblical Literature* 71(1952), 75–84. Cf. also David E. Aune, "The Influence of Roman Imperial Cult on the Apocalypse of John," *Biblical Research* 28(1983), 5–26.

44. Invitation to service, Rev. 4:1.

45. Two phases, Rev. 19:11–20:6 and 20:7–22:5. Thousand years: this is the standard reading of Rev. 20:1–6. The passage may imply, however, that the reign of the martyrs with Christ is heavenly rather than terrestrial, see Michel Gourgues, "The Thousand-Year Reign (Rev. 20:1–6): Terrestrial or Celestial?," *Catholic Biblical Quarterly* 47(1985), 676–81. "The camp of," Rev. 20:9.

46. Rev.: city of God, 21:10–22:5; "river of life; trees; cure for pagans," 22:2. Sanctuary, 1 Kings 6:20.

47. Josephus, *Jewish War*: "unapproachable; invisible," 5:219.

48. 1 Cor. 15:50.

CHAPTER THREE

1. William H.C. Frend, *Town and Country in the Early Christian Centuries* (London: Variorum Reprints, 1980), first paper, 34; Per Beskow, "Mission, Trade, and Emigration in the Second Century," *Svensk Exegetisk Årsbok* 35(1970), 104–14.

2. On the social and cultural situation in Lyons, see Pierre Wuilleumier, *Lyon, métropole des Gaules* (Paris: Les Belles Lettres, 1953), 54; Moses I. Finley, *The Ancient Economy* (London: Chatto & Windus, 1975), 59; C.P. Jones, "A Syrian in Lyons," *American Journal of Classical Philology* 99 (1978), 336–53; William H. C. Frend, *Martyrdom and Persecution in the Early Church* (Oxford: Blackwell, 1965), 4f.

3. The persecution report is in Eusebius, *Ecclesiastical History*, 5:1–2 (in J.P. Migne, *Patrologia Graeca* 20:407–36, to be abbreviated *PG*); Irenaean authorship is suggested by Pierre Nautin, *Lettres et écrivains chrétiens des IIe et IIIe siècles* (Paris: Cerf, 1961), 54–9.

4. For the influence of 2 and 4 Macc. on this persecution report, see Frend, *Martyrdom and Persecution*, 19f. "That they might," Hebr. 11:35; 4 Macc. 18:17 [in James H. Charlesworth, ed., *The Old Testament Pseudepigrapha* (Garden City, NY: Doubleday, 1985), II, 564] refers to Ezek. 37; "it was from," 2 Macc. 7:11.

5. Eusebius, *Ecclesiastical History*, 5:1, 62–3 (*PG* 20:433/4).

6. *Martyrdom of Polycarp*, 14 (in *Sources chrétiennes* 10:229, to be abbreviated *SC*).

7. Irenaeus, *Against the Heresies*: "the Latins are," 5:30, 3; "the world enjoys," 4:30, 3 (*SC* 153:380ff.; 100/2:778f.).

8. Irenaeus, *Heresies*: reputation, 1:25, 3; unauthorized meetings, 3:3, 2 (*PG* 7:682, 849). For the interpretation, see Gérard Vallée, "Theological and Non-theological Motives in Irenaeus's Refutation of the Gnostics," E.P. Sanders, ed., *Jewish and Christian Self-Definition* (London: SCM Press, 1980), I, 174–85.

9. Irenaeus, *Heresies*, 4:30, 3 (*SC* 100/2: 780f.).

10. Irenaeus, *Heresies*, 5:32, 1 (*SC* 153: 396–99).

11. From the 1985 field notes of Johannes Niggemeier, Paderborn, Germany. The feelings of the peasants quoted are the very stuff of millenarian movements in Brazil, see Maria Isaura Pereira de Queiroz, *Images messianiques du Brézil* (Cuernavaca, Mexico: Centro Intercultural de Documentación, 1972).

12. Irenaeus, *Heresies*: "nothing is," 5:35, 2; "wax stronger," 5:35, 1 (*SC* 153:450, 438f.).

13. Eusebius, *Ecclesiastical History*, 3:28 (*PG* 20:375f.).

14. Irenaeus, *Heresies*: Kingdom of God, 5:36, 3 [Armenian version]; "subsequently bestow," 5:36,3 [quoting 1 Cor. 2:9]; "communion with," 5:35,1 (*SC* 153: 462f., 464f., 438f.).

15. Augustine, *Confessions*: "it was a sweet," 3:1; "a savage and," 3:3; "was brought down," 3:6 [cf. Prov. 9:18]; (in J.P. Migne, *Patrologia Latina* 32:683, 685, 688, to be abbreviated *PL*). The translation used is Augustine, *Confessions*, trans. Rex Warner (New York: New American Library, 1963).

16. Augustine, *Confessions*, 8:12 (*PL* 32:762). The biblical text is Rom. 13:13f.

17. Augustine, *Confessions*, 9:10 (*PL* 32: 773/5). On heavenly trance journeys as anticipating the soul's ascent after death, see Alan F. Segal, "Heavenly Ascent in Hellenistic Judaism, Early Christianity, and their Environment," Wolfgang Haase, ed., *Aufstieg und Niedergang der römischen Welt*, 2nd series (Berlin: de Gruyter, 1980), XXIII, 1333–94, esp. 1341.

18. Paul Henry, "Die Vision zu Ostia," Carl Andresen, ed., *Zum Augustinus-Gespräch der Gegenwart* (Darmstadt: Wiss. Buchgesellschaft, 1962), 201–70, at 268.

19. Augustine, *Confessions*, 9:10 (*PL* 32: 775).

20. Plotinus, *Enneads*, 1:6, 4–7.

21. Plotinus, *Enneads*, 6:9. This is the last sentence of the *Enneads* in the trans. of A. H. Armstrong, *Plotinus* (New York: Collier Books, 1962), 148.

22. Corpus Hermeticum, *Poimandres*, 24ff. in C.K. Barrett, *The New Testament Background. Selected Documents* (New York: Harper & Row, 1961), 87.

23. Augustine, *Confessions*: "step by step," 7:17; "a kind of," 10:40 (*PL* 32:745.807). On the ascent of the soul in Augustine, see Frederick van Fleteren, "Augustine's Ascent of the Soul in Book VII of the Confessions," *Augustinian Studies* 5 (1974), 29–72, and Vernon J. Bourke, "Augustine of Hippo: The Approach of the Soul to God," E. Rozanne Elder, ed., *The Spirituality of Western Christendom* (Kalamazoo, MI: Cistercian Publications, 1976), 1–12.

24. Abbot Allois in the *Verba Seniorum*: "unless a man," 11:5 (*PL* 73:934); A. Wilmart, "Le receuil latin des apophtegmes," *Revue bénédictine* 34 (1922), 185–98: "as far as I am," 196.

25. Augustine, *Confessions*: "may your scriptures," 11:2 (*PL* 32:810); *Holy Virginity*: "let all conjugal," 13 (*PL* 40:401/2). On angel-like virginity as an ascetic ideal that anticipates heaven, see Ton H.C. van Ejik, "Marriage and Virginity, Death and Immortality," *Epektasis: Mélanges patristiques Jean Daniélou* (Paris: Beauchesne, 1972), 209–35; Ugo Bianchi, "The Religio-historical relevance of Lk. 20:34–36," R. van den Broek et al., eds., *Studies in*

Gnosticism and Hellenistic Religions (Leiden: Brill, 1981), 31–7, and Peter Brown, "The Notion of Virginity in the Early Church," Bernard McGinn et al., eds., *Christian Spirituality: Origins to the Twelfth Century* (New York: Crossroad, 1985), 427–43.

26. Augustine, *On Faith and the Creed*, 10:24 (*PL* 40:195/6); Margaret R. Miles, *Augustine on the Body* (Missoula, MT: Scholars Press, 1979): "began his career," 99.

27. Augustine, *Confessions*: "fellow citizens," 9:13; "whoever knows you," 5:4 (*PL* 32:780. 708).

28. Augustine, *City of God*: "we shall have," 22:30, 4; "there we shall," 22:30, 5; "he shall be," 22:30, 1 (*PL* 41:803. 804. 802); *Sermon*: "what will I," 243:9 (*PL* 38:1147). The translations of the *City of God* used are Philip Schaff, ed., *A Select Library of Nicene and Post-Nicene Fathers*, (1887; rprt. Grand Rapids, MI: Eerdmans, 1982), II and Augustine, *The City of God against the Pagans*, trans. William M. Green (Cambridge, MA: Harvard Univ. Press, 1972), VII.

29. Augustine, *Letters*: "you should not grieve," 92:1 (*PL* 33:318); *Literal Commentary on Genesis*: "see each other," 8:25 (*PL* 34:391).

30. Robert Garland, *The Greek Way of Death* (London: Duckworth, 1985), 66. Socrates, according to Plato's *Apology*, 41A–C, was looking forward to meeting famous people like Orpheus, Musaeus, Hesiod, Homer, etc. on the other side.

31. Pierre Courcelle, "La postérité chrétienne du *Songe de Scipion*," *Revue des études latines* 36(1958), 205–34, esp. 207–13; Ambrose, *On the Decease of His Brother Satyrus*: meeting again, 2:135 (*Corpus Scriptorum Ecclesiasticorum Latinorum* [CSEL] 73:324, echoing Cicero, *On Old Age*, 84); *On Theodosius*: "when he receives," 40 (CSEL 73:392).

32. *Vision of Paul*, also called the *Apocalypse of Paul*, 46–51 [Edgar Hennecke and Wilhelm Schneemelcher, eds., *New Testament Apocrypha*, trans. R. McL. Wilson (Philadelphia: Westminster Press, 1965), II, 790–95]; for Augustine's knowledge of the *Vision of Paul*, see *PL* 35:1885 and Bertold Altaner, *Kleine patristische Schriften* (Berlin: Akademie-Verlag, 1967), 210f. Augustine, *The Predestination of the Saints*: "why do we," 28 (*PL* 44:931), quoting Cyprian, *On Mortality*, 26 (*Corpus Christianorum Series Latina* 3A:31).

33. Augustine, *Retractations*, 1:17 (*PL* 32: 613).

34. Augustine, *Sermon*: "take away death," 155:15; "our faith, instructed," 241:7 (*PL* 38:849.1137); *Retractations*: "the substance of,"

1:17 (*PL* 32:613). Eating and drinking in heaven are discussed in *City of God*, 13:22 and *Letter* 102:6 (*PL* 41:395; 33:372). On seeing God with bodily eyes, see *City of God*, 22:29,6 (*PL* 41:801), dated to c. 426. Earlier, in *Letter* 92 of 408 (*PL* 33:318f.), Augustine had excluded the vision of God with the eyes of the body, see F.J. Thonnard, "La vision de Dieu," *Oeuvres de Saint Augustin*, ed. Etudes Augustiniennes (Paris: Desclée de Brouwer, 1960), XXXVII, 853–7; and Margaret Miles, "Vision: The Eye of the Body and the Eye of the Mind in St. Augustine's *De Trinitate* and *Confessions*," *Journal of Religion* 63 (1983), 125–42. On Augustine's changing view on the "flesh," see François Altermath, *Du corps psychique au corps spirituel; Interprétation du 1 Cor. 15.35–49 par les auteurs chrétiens des quatre premiers siècles* (Tübingen: Mohr, 1977), 234f.

35. Augustine, *City of God*, 13:20, repeated in *Sermon* 242:8 (*PL* 41:393; 38:1142).

36. Augustine, *City of God*: "where there is; overgrown and," 22:19,2; "shall be of," 22:20, 3 (*PL* 41:781.783).

37. Augustine, *City of God*, 22:19,3 (*PL* 41:782). According to an ancient belief, those who died a violent death retained their wounds in the other world: see A. Hilhorst, "The Wounds of the Risen Jesus," *Estudios Bíblicos* 41(1983), 165–7.

38. Augustine, *City of God*: "need is bound," 22:24,4; "both sexes will," 22:17 [trans. W.M. Green] (*PL* 41:791.778).

39. The distinction between love and lust is explained in *On the Christian Doctrine*, 3:10 (*PL* 34:72): "I call love (*caritas*) the activity of the soul that aims at enjoying God for His own sake as well as oneself and one's neighbor with reference to God. Lust (*cupiditas*), on the other hand, aims at enjoying oneself and one's neighbor and any object whatsoever without reference to God."

40. Augustine, *On the Christian Doctrine*: "all of us, who; when you enjoy," 1:32–3 (*PL* 34:32f.), cf. Philem. 20 (Vulgate), "Yeah, brother, may I enjoy thee in the Lord!"

41. Irving Singer, *The Nature of Love*, 2nd ed. (Chicago: Univ. of Chicago Press, 1984), I, 346.

42. Augustine, *On the Trinity*: "how much love," 8:8 (PL 42:959). For Augustine's concept of love, see Miles, "Vision," 137f.; Johannes van Bavel, "The Double Face of Love in Augustine," *Louvain Studies* 12(1987), 116–30, and R. Canning, "The Unity of Love for God and Neighbor," *Augustiniana* 37(1987), 38–121.

43. Augustine, *Commentary on 1 John*: "we should not," 8:5; "our love must," 6:4 (*PL* 35:2038.2021).

44. Augustine, *Sermon*: "friends, household, children," 80:7; Cicero, *On Friendship*: "always unite two," 20.

45. Augustine, *On the Psalms*: "in this sojourning," 55:9; *Letters*: "better known to," 92:2; *Sermon*: "most of the," 306:9; "I alone am," 249:2 (*PL* 36:652; 33:318; 38:1401 and 1162).

46. Augustine, *On the Psalms*: "the hearts of," 44:33; *Letters*: "the better known; for none will," 92:2 (*PL* 36:514; 33:318). On Augustine's notion of universalized love, see John Burnaby, *Amor Dei: A Study of the Religion of St. Augustine* (London: Hodder & Stoughton, 1938), 248f.

47. Augustine, *Letters*, 238:13 (*PL* 33:1043).

48. Peter Brown, *Augustine of Hippo* (London: Faber & Faber, 1967): "far more open," 324; and Brown, *Augustine on Sexuality* (Berkeley: Centre for Hermeneutical Studies in Hellenistic and Modern Culture, 1983), 30f. Augustine, *On Continence*: "according to each," 8; *Sermon*: "conjugal embraces," 159:2; *City of God*: "original good," 22:24,1 (*PL* 40:362; 38:868; 41:788).

49. Augustine, *City of God*, 20:9 (*PL* 41:672/5); William H.C. Frend, *The Donatist Church*, 2nd ed. (Oxford: Clarendon Press, 1970), 233.

50. Augustine, *City of God*: "in some wonderful," 22:24,2 (*PL* 41:789); *Letters*: kings must serve, 93:3 (*PL* 33:325) dating from 408. For a theoretical discussion of the spirit/matter relationship, see Mary Douglas, "Social Preconditions of Enthusiasm and Heterodoxy," *Proceedings of the 1969 Annual Spring Meeting of the American Ethnological Society* (Seattle: American Ethnological Society, 1969), 69–80.

51. Albrecht Dihle, *The Theory of the Will in Classical Antiquity* (Berkeley: Univ. of California Press, 1982), 130f. According to Dihle, Augustine is "the inventor of our modern notion of will" as a psychological concept (144).

CHAPTER FOUR

1. Otfrid of Weissenburg, *Book of the Gospel*, 5:23, 273–7, trans. in Hartmut Kugler, *Die Vorstellung der Stadt in der Literatur des deutschen Mittelalters* (Munich: Artemis, 1986), 85. On the symbolic meaning of various flowers, see Augustine, *Sermons*, 304 (PL 38:1396); on the paradisal quality of sweet-smelling herbs and flowers, see Jean-Pierre Albert, "Le légendaire médiéval des aromates: longévité et immortalité," Comité d'anthropologie et d'ethnologie

françaises, ed., *Le corps humain* (Paris: Comité des travaux historiques et scientifiques, 1985), 37–48.

2. The *Elucidation* is edited by Yves Lefèvre, *L'elucidarium et les lucidaires* (Paris: de Boccard, 1954); for information on this work, see Georg Steer, "Lucidarius," *Die deutsche Literatur des Mittelalters. Verfasserlexikon*, 2nd ed. (Berlin: de Gruyter, 1985), V, 939–47. *Elucidation*: "the punishment for," 3:78 in Lefèvre, *L'elucidarium*, 462f. For monastery gardens, see *PL* 185:569ff. and Albertus Magnus, *On Plants*, 7:1,14 in B. *Alberti Magni opera omnia*, ed. Auguste Borgnet (Paris: Vives, 1890–99), X, 294; trans. in Hermann Fischer, *Mittelalterliche Pflanzenkunde* (1929; rprt. Hildesheim: Olms, 1967), 171ff.

3. *Elucidation*: "they will be," 3:81; "as a thirsty," 3:107 (Lefèvre, *L'elucidarium*, 464 and 470).

4. *Le registre d'inquisition de Jacques Fournier*, trans. Jean Duvernoi (Paris: Mouton, 1978): "beautiful groves with," III, 775. Otto of Freising, *The Two Cities: A Chronicle of Universal History to the Year 1146 AD*, trans. Charles C. Mierow (New York: Columbia Univ. Press, 1928), 508 (8:33); William of Auvergne, *On the Universe*, I, 2,39 and 48 in *Guilelmi Alverni opera omnia* (Paris: Pralard, 1674), I, 742, 752.

5. On the religious implications of the urban revival, see Barbara H. Rosenwein and Lester K. Little, "Social Meaning in the Monastic and Mendicant Spiritualities," *Past and Present* 63(1974), 4–32 and C. Warren Hollister, *Medieval Europe*, 5th ed. (New York: Wiley, 1982), 155.

6. On the urban preaching of the friars, see David L. d'Avray, "Sermons to the Upper Bourgeoisie by a Thirteenth-Century Franciscan," Derek Baker, ed., *The Church in Town and Countryside* (Oxford: Blackwell, 1979), 187–99 with Latin sermon text in d'Avray, *The Preaching of the Friars* (Oxford: Clarendon Press, 1985), 260–71; Rosenwein and Little, "Social Meaning," 29–32; Lester K. Little, *Religious Poverty and the Profit Economy in Medieval Europe* (Ithaca, NY: Cornell Univ. Press, 1978), 197–217.

7. The idea of the heavenly city or palace can be found before the eleventh and twelfth centuries, but fairly infrequently, according to Jacqueline Amat, *Songes et visions: L'au-delà dans la littérature latine tardive* (Paris: Etudes Augustiniennes, 1985), 397f.

8. Damien Sicard, *La liturgie de la mort dans l'église latine* (Münster: Aschendorff, 1978): "may the angels," 215–20. The shift from

paradise garden to paradise city is documented and discussed by Kugler, *Die Vorstellung der Stadt*, 84–8 and 121–31. The following are sources for the "urban heaven" in the high Middle Ages: Peter Damiani, "The Joys of Paradise" (*PL* 145:980–83) in *The Song of S. Peter Damiani*, ed. and trans. Stephen A. Hurlbut (Washington: St. Albans Press, 1928) [for Damiani, terms like *urbanus, urbanitas* – the urban way of behavior – have a negative meaning, see *PL* 144:270, 925; 145:454, 730]; Abelard, "O quanta qualia sunt illa sabbata" (*PL* 178:1786f.) in *Medieval Song: An Anthology*, trans. James J. Wilhelm (London: Allen & Unwin, 1972), 45f.; *Psalterium decem cordarum abbatis Joachim* (1527; rprt. Frankfurt: Minerva, 1965), 280f.; *Godeschalcus und Visio Godeschalci*, ed. Erwin Assmann (Neumünster: Wachholtz, 1979), 134f.,190f., 56f., 59f.

9. Giacomino of Verona, "The Heavenly Jerusalem," 61–8 in Esther I. May, *The De Jerusalem celesti and the De Babylonia infernali of Fra Giacomino da Verona* (Florence: Le Monnier, 1930), 75. Trans. from Joseph Tusiani, *The Age of Dante* (New York: Baroque Press, 1974), 137.

10. *Acta Sanctorum*, rev. ed. by Jean Carnandet (Paris: Palmé, 1866), vol. 7 of May, 168. See the brief remarks of Peter Dinzelbacher, *Vision und Visionsliteratur im Mittelalter* (Stuttgart: Hiersemann, 1981), 109.

11. David Herlihy, ed., *The History of Feudalism* (New York: Harper & Row, 1970), 198f.; Alfred Haverkamp, "Die Städte im Herrschafts- und Sozialgefüge Reichsitaliens," Friedrich Vittinghoff, ed., *Stadt und Herrschaft* (Munich: R. Oldenburg, 1982), 149–245, esp. 197 (castles), 227ff. (*contado*).

12. Peter Dinzelbacher, "Reflexionen irdischer Sozialstrukturen in mittelalterlichen Jenseitsschilderungen," *Archiv für Kulturgeschichte* 61(1979), 16–34, and "Klassen und Hierarchien im Jenseits," *Miscellanea Mediaevalia* 12(1979), 20–40, comments on the heavenly groups or "choirs" and the absence of kinship networks in medieval heavens. See also Ian Bishop, "Relatives at the Court of Heaven: Contrasted Treatments of an Idea in *Piers Plowman* and *Pearl*," Myra Stokes et al., eds., *Medieval Literature and Antiquities* (Cambridge: Brewer, 1987), 111–18. The middle-English poem "Pearl" can be found in Mary V. Hillmann, *The Pearl* (Notre Dame, IN: Univ. of Notre Dame Press, 1967); we use Schotter's translation of the controversial passage *Pearl*, 603ff.: Anne H. Schotter, "The Paradox of Equality and Hierarchy in *Pearl*," *Renascence* 33 (1981), 172–9 with reference to Matt. 20:1–15, the Parable of

the Vineyard Laborers.

13. William Langland (c. 1332–76), *Piers Plowman*, B 12:203–5, trans. Schotter, "The Paradox of Equality," 175.

14. Herrad of Hohenbourg, *Hortus Deliciarum. Reconstruction*, ed. Rosalie Green et al. (London: Warburg Institute, 1979), 447 – text of *Elucidation* 3:79 with marginal gloss 1; *Purity*, 114–16, trans. Schotter, "The Paradox of Equality," 176; *On god ureisun of ure lefdi* [A good orison of Our Lady], 34 and 51 in *Old English Homilies and Homiletic Treatises of the Twelfth and Thirteenth Centuries. First Series*, trans. Richard Morris (London: Trübner, 1868), 192; Hildegard of Bingen, *Scivias*: "clad in garments," 3:3 (in *Corpus Christianorum. Continuatio Mediaevalis* 43:371).

15. Giacomino da Verona, "The Heavenly Jerusalem," 119–20 in May, *The De Jerusalem*, 77 and trans. in Tusiani, *The Age of Dante*, 139. Reinhold Hammerstein, *Die Musik der Engel* (Munich: Francke, 1962), 34 with n. 48 traces the motif of the saints' heavenly singing in medieval sources. The French poem dating from c. 1300 is *La court de paradis*, ed. Eva Vilamo-Pentti (Annales Academiae Scientiarum Fennicae, series B, 79/1; Helsinki: Suomalainen Tiedeakatemia, 1953).

16. The hymn *Urbs Hierusalem beata*, which uses motifs of Rev. 21:18f., may be found in Clemens Blume, *Die Hymnen des Thesaurus Hymnologicus H.A. Daniels* (Leipzig: Reisland, 1908), no. 102. For Rev. 21:2ff. as liturgical reading connected with the dedication of a church see Michel Andrieu, *Le pontifical romain au moyen-âge* (Vatican City: Biblioteca Apostolica, 1938), I, 193; II, 439. The church building as replicating the heavenly Jerusalem is discussed in: Hans Sedlmayr, *Die Entstehung der Kathedrale* (Graz: Akademische Druck- und Verlagsanstalt, 1976), esp. 95–164; Otto von Simson, *The Gothic Cathedral*, 2nd ed. (New York: Harper & Row, 1962), 8–11, 227, etc.; Laurence H. Stookey, "The Gothic Cathedral as Heavenly Jerusalem," *Gesta* 8 (1969), 35–41; and Marco Rossi and Alessandro Rovetta, "Indagini sullo spazio ecclesiale immagine della Gerusalemme celeste," M.L. Gatti Perer, ed., *La dimora di Dio con gli uomini [Ap, 21:3]: Immagini della Gerusalemme celeste dal III al XIV secolo* (Milan: Università Cattolica, 1983), 77–115.

17. William Durandus, *Rationale divinorum officiorum* (Lyons: Fradin, 1521), fol. xl verso (book 4, sect. "De accessu sacerdotis"). Hammerstein, *Die Musik der Engel*, devotes an entire chapter to the medieval merging of the earthly and heavenly liturgies (30–52).

18. Suger in Erwin Panofski, ed., *Abbot Suger on the Abbey Church of St. Denis*, 2nd ed. (Princeton, NJ: Princeton Univ. Press, 1979), 65.

19. Some examples of allegorical readings are quoted in Barbara Nolan, *The Gothic Visionary Perspective* (Princeton: Princeton Univ. Press, 1977), 13–29. Claude Carozzi, "Structure et fonction de la vision de Tnugdal," André Vauchez, ed., *Faire croire* (Rome: Ecole Française de Rome, 1981), 223–34 argues that Tnugdal's vision of 1149 insists on the literal, corporeal nature of other-worldly places like paradise and other heavenly realms in which the various categories of the blessed live.

20. Cosmas, *Christian Topography* 7:67 and 5:184f. (SC 197:126f.; 159:280f.). A translation is Cosmas Indicopleustes, *The Christian Topography*, trans. J.W. McCrindle (London: Hakluyt Society, 1897).

21. Augustine, *Literal Commentary on Genesis*, 2:9–10; cf. *Enchiridion*, 9(PL 34:270–72; 40: 235f.). The irrelevance of cosmological views was expressed earlier by Lactantius, *Divine Institutes*, 3:3 (PL 6:354–6).

22. For summaries of the various levels of heaven, see Honorius Augustodunensis, *De imagine mundi*, 1:138–40 (PL 172:146) and Albertus, *Summa de creaturis*, 3:10 in *B. Alberti Magni opera omnia*, XXXIV, 415–20. The empyrean is referred to in the *Glossa* (the medieval textbook on the Bible) and in Peter Lombard's widely used *Sentences* (PL 113:68; 192:656). Secondary sources include: Bruno Nardi, *Saggi di filosofia dantesca*, 2nd ed. (Florence: La Nuova Italia, 1967), 167–214; Gregor Maurach, *Coelum empyreum: Versuch einer Begriffsgeschichte* (Wiesbaden: Steiner, 1968); Thomas Litt, *Les corps célestes dans l'univers de Saint Thomas d'Aquin* (Leuven: Publications universitaires, 1963), 255–61.

23. John Ruusbroec, *Spiritual Espousals*, 2:50 in *The Spiritual Espousals and Other Works*, trans. James A. Wiseman (New York: Paulist Press, 1985), 111.

24. Aquinas, *Commentary on the Sentences*, II, 14:1,2, comments on the quintessence. Alexander of Hales, *Summa theologica* (Quaracchi: Collegium S. Bonaventurae, 1928), II, 328.

25. Aquinas, *Summa theologica*, Suppl. 84:2, to be abbreviated *Sth*; the translation consulted is *The Summa theologica of Saint Thomas Aquinas*, trans. Fathers of the English Dominican Province (London: Encyclopaedia Britannica, 1952). Alexander, *Summa theologica*, IV, 288f.

26. On the medieval metaphysics of light see James McEvoy, "The Metaphysics of Light in

the Middle Ages," *Philosophical Studies [Dublin]* 26(1979), 126–45 and Hans Sedl-mayr, "Das Licht in seinen künstlerischen Manifestationen," *Studium Generale* 13(1960), 313–24. See also 1 John 1:5 – "God is light and in him is no darkness at all." One red gem, the "carbuncle," was considered an independent source of light, see Marbod of Rennes (1035–1123), *Book of Gems* (PL 171:1754) and Albertus Magnus, *On Minerals*, 2:2. According to Albertus, "when it is really of good quality, [carbuncle] shines in the dark like a live [burning] coal, and I myself have seen such a one"; Albertus Magnus, *Book of Minerals*, trans. Dorothy Wyckoff (Oxford: Clarendon Press, 1967), 77f.

27. Aquinas, *Sth*, Suppl. 91:3; Albertus, *Commentary on the Sentences*, 4:44,31 in *B. Alberti Magni opera omnia*, XXX, 584.

28. Aquinas, *Sth*, Suppl.: luminosity restored, 91:3 [cf. Isa. 30:26]; elements infused with light, "the excess of," 91:4; light in hell, 97:4. Dante, *Inferno*, 5:28; Otto of Freising, *The Two Cities*, 490 (8:25).

29. Aquinas, *Sth*, Suppl.: plants, animals, 91:5; heavenly bodies, 91:2. See Litt, *Les corps célestes*, 242–54; Edward Grant, "Medieval and Renaissance Scholastic Conceptions of the Influence of the Celestial Region on the Ter-restrial," *Journal of Medieval and Renaissance Studies* 17(1987), 1–23.

30. Dante, *Paradiso*: ciel ch'è, 30:39; Beatrice smiles, 31:91–3; "within its depthless," 33:115–17. The translation used is Dante Alighieri, *The Divine Comedy. Vol. III: Paradise*, trans. Mark Musa (Harmondsworth: Penguin, 1986). Dante, *Letter to Can Grande*: "when the Source," 33 in Charles A. Dinsmore, *Aids to the Study of Dante* (Boston: Houghton Mifflin, 1903), 286. For Dante's view of light see Joseph A. Mazzeo, "Light Metaphysics, Dante's Con-vivio, and the Letter to Can Grande della Scala," *Traditio* 14(1958), 191–229, and Patrick Boyde, *Dante: Philomythes and Philosopher* (Cambridge: Cambridge Univ. Press, 1981), 207–14.

31. Wiltrud Mersmann, *Rosenfenster und Himmelskreise* (Mittenwald: Mäander, 1982), 95f. and esp. 87–91 for Italian "rose windows" (Assisi, Orvieto, Siena, etc.). The various meanings given the rose window are also discussed by Robert Suckale, "Thesen zum Bedeutungswandel der gotischen Fensterrose," Karl Clausberg et al., eds., *Bauwerk und Bildwerk im Hochmittelalter* (Giessen: Anabas-Verlag, 1981), 259–94. Suger in Panofski, *Abbot Suger*, 101.

32. Suger: "brighten the minds," in Panofski, *Abbot Suger*, 47f. Suger's theology is discussed in von Simson, *The Gothic Cathedral*, 50–55; Panofski, *Abbot Suger*, 18–24; and Georges Duby, *The Age of the Cathedrals*, trans. E. Levieux and B. Thompson (Chicago: Univ. of Chicago Press, 1981), 99f., 147f.

33. For the intellectual situation of the thir-teenth century see Norman F. Cantor, *Medieval History*, 2nd ed. (New York: Macmillan, 1969), 464f. and Tina Stiefel, *The Intellectual Revolu-tion in Twelfth-Century Europe* (London: Croom Helm, 1985), 102–6.

34. Aquinas, *Sth*: "to ponder an," II II 181:3; cf.180:3. On special rewards in the hereafter, see Aquinas, *Sth*, Suppl. 96:7 and 11. In medie-val iconography, the special reward or "aureole" (little crown) is represented by a crown worn by virgins, martyrs, and teachers: Edwin Hall and Horst Uhr, "Aureola super auream: Crowns and Related Symbols of Special Distinction for Saints," *The Art Bulletin* 67(1985), 567–603.

35. Aquinas, *Sth*: cessation of active life, II II 181:4; Aquinas, *Summa contra gentiles*: "intel-lectual cognition is," 3:53. For "sight" as the noblest of our senses see Augustine, *On the Trinity*, 11:1; Alain de Lille (PL 42:985; 210:521f.); Anfinn Stigen, "On the Alleged Primacy of Sight – with some remarks on Theoria and Praxis – in Aristotle," *Symbolae Osloenses* 37(1961), 15–44.

36. Aquinas, *Sth*, I II 1–5.

37. Aquinas, *Summa contra gentiles*: "every agent acts," 3:2–3 [after Aristotle, *Nicomachean Ethics*, 1049a]; to know God, 3:25. *Sth*: "not depend on," I II 3:3. For a statement that "all our natural knowledge is based on the perception of the senses," see I 12:12.

38. Aquinas, *Sth*: "a perfect union," Suppl. 96:1; "love results from," I II 27:2; "the ultimate and," I II 3:5; many activities, I II 3:2; *Summa contra gentiles*: "nothing that is," 3:62.

39. Aquinas, *Sth*: illumination, I 12:5 (with reference to Rev. 21:23); the blessed cannot, Suppl. 92:3. The idea of illumination seems to be derived from Islamic theology, see Miguel Asin Palacios, *Islam and the Divine Comedy*, trans. H. Sutherland (1926; rprt. London: F. Cass, 1968), 161–3.

40. Aquinas, *Sth*: "the more love," I 12:6; "all the blessed," I 62:9; no more merit, I 62:9 and II II 26:13. For the happiness of the unbaptized see Aquinas, *Quaestio disputata de malo* 5:3, and W.R. Connor, "Natural Beatitude and the Future Life," *Theological Studies* 11(1950), 221–39.

41. Dante, *Paradiso*: "but tell me," 3:64–6; "e 'n la," 3:85. On beatific immobility see Carl J. Peter, *Participated Eternity in the Vision of*

God. *A Study of the Opinion of Thomas Aquinas* (Rome: Gregorian Univ. Press, 1964), 35, 254f.

42. Aquinas, *Sth*: types of vision, II II 175:3; "God can in," Suppl. 92:2.

43. Aquinas, *Sth*, Suppl. 93:1. The "ridiculous theories" are discussed in Jorge Aguadé, "Wer isst und trinkt, muss auch Notdurft verrichten: Ein Beitrag zur jüdisch-christlichen Polemik gegen den Islam," *Welt des Orients* 10(1979), 61–72. The idea that sweet-smelling sweat will replace the excrements in heaven is still listed by Christians in the seventeenth century among the "absurdities" of Islamic theology, see Hugo Grotius, *On the Truth of the Christian Religion* (1627), 6:10 in *Opera omnia theologica* (Amsterdam: Blaeu, 1679), III, 93.

44. Aquinas, *Sth* I II 4:8. Aristotle, *Nicomachean Ethics*, 9:1169B in *The Complete Works of Aristotle*, ed. Jonathan Barnes (Princeton, NJ: Princeton Univ. Press, 1984), II, 1848. A recent commentator speculates that according to Aquinas already existing friendships would continue but somehow be absorbed into the beatific vision, while no new relationships could be formed: see William J. Hoye, *Actualitas omnium actuum. Man's Beatific Vision of God as Apprehended by Thomas Aquinas* (Meisenheim: Hain, 1975), 174, n. 41.

45. Aquinas, *Sth*, Suppl. 81:4, distances himself from the sensuous heaven of the "Jews and Saracenes [Muslims] and certain heretics called Chiliasts." This theme is common in medieval Christian polemic against Islam, see Aquinas, *Commentary on the Sentences* IV 44:1,3 (end), and William of Auvergne, *On the Universe*, I 2:34 in *Guilelmi Alverni opera omnia*, I, 738f.

46. Giles of Rome [Aegidius Romanus], *Quodlibeta*, 6:25 in Hermann J. Weber, *Die Lehre von der Auferstehung der Toten in den Haupttraktaten der scholastischen Theologie* (Freiburg: Herder, 1973), 260f. n. 500.

47. Bonaventure, *Sentences*, III 31:3,2 in Hinrich Stoevesandt, *Die letzten Dinge in der Theologie Bonaventuras* (Zurich: EVZ-Verlag, 1969), 265.

48. Hugh of Saint-Victor, *PL* 177:563.

49. Jacques Le Goff in Jerôme Dumoulin et al., eds., *The Historian between the Ethnologist and the Futurologist* (Paris: Mouton, 1973), 209. For the new twelfth-century view of love see two essays by Peter Dinzelbacher: "Sozial- und Mentalitätsgeschichte der Liebe im Mittelalter," Ulrich Müller, ed., *Minne ist ein swaerez spil* (Göppingen: Kümmerle, 1986), 75–110, and "Pour une histoire de l'amour au moyen âge," *Le moyen âge* 153(1987), 223–40.

50. Andreas Capellanus, *On Love*, ed. and

trans. P.G. Walsh (London: Duckworth, 1982), 113 and 115; Betsy Bowden, "The Art of Courtly Copulation," *Medievalia et humanistica* 9(1979), 67–85, at 78.

51. For a Celtic parallel, see the eighth-century CE *Voyage of Bran* with an other world called the "land of women," the free love-making and beds of which are mentioned. One passage reads: "A beautiful game, most delightful, they play sitting at the luxurious wine, men and gentle women under a bush, without sin, without crime." Kuno Meyer, *The Voyage of Brán Son of Febal to the Land of the Living* (London: Nutt, 1895), I, 20 (no. 41; cf. nos. 30 and 62).

52. *Aucassin and Nicolette*, trans. Francis W. Bourdillon (London: Folio Society, 1947), 20f. Giacomino da Lentini, "Io m'agio posto in core a Dio servire" in Ernest F. Langley, *The Poetry of Giacomino da Lentino* (Cambridge, MA: Harvard Univ. Press, 1915), 73 (Italian) and Tusiani, *The Age of Dante*, 24 (trans.).

53. Guido Guinizelli, "Al cor gentil" in Bernard O'Donoghue, *The Courtly Love Tradition* (Manchester: Manchester Univ. Press, 1982), 265.

54. Arnaut Daniel, "Lo ferm voler" in Alan R. Press, ed., *Anthology of Troubadour Lyric Poetry*, 2nd ed. (Edinburgh: Edinburgh Univ. Press, 1981), 191. For placing the "lady" next to God see Arnaut, "Ans que'l cim," *Les Poésies d' Arnaut Daniel*, ed. René Lavaud (1910; rprt. Geneva: Slatkine, 1973), 96ff.

55. Dante, *La Vita Nuova*, trans. B. Reynolds (Harmondsworth: Penguin, 1969), 99; Boccaccio, *Life of Dante* (earlier version), 86 in *Tutte le opere di Giovanni Boccaccio*, ed. Vittore Branca (Verona: Mondadori, 1974), III, 458 and *The Early Lives of Dante*, trans. Philip H. Wicksteed (London: De la More Press, 1904), 40.

56. Jordan of Saxony, letter 13 in Berthold Altaner, *Die Briefe Jordans von Sachsen* (Leipzig: Harrassowitz, 1925), 17(Latin) and Simon Tugwell, ed., *Early Dominicans* (New York: Paulist Press, 1982), 403 (English). The passage alludes to Ps. 60:9.

57. L.T. Tospsfield, *Troubadours and Love* (Cambridge: Cambridge Univ. Press, 1975), 195.

58. Petrarch, *Canzoniere*: "holy and unsullied," no. 302; "veggia il mio," no. 349. Petrarch's praise of Arnaut Daniel is included in *Trionfi d'Amore*, 4:40ff.

59. Jill Tilden, "Spiritual Conflict in Petrarch's *Canzoniere*," Fritz Schalk, ed., *Petrarca 1304–1374: Beiträge zu Werk und Wirkung* (Frankfurt: Klostermann, 1975), 287–319: "humanist

confidence," 319. Petrarch, *The Secret Book:* "she has detached," 3rd dialogue in *Petrarch's Secret or the Soul's Conflict with Passion,* trans. William H. Draper (London: Chatto & Windus, 1911), 124. For Petrarch's spiritual struggle see also Irving Singer, *The Nature of Love* (Chicago: Univ. of Chicago Press, 1984), II, 130–41.

60. Jacques de Vitry, *Life of Mary of Oignies,* preface, in *Acta Sanctorum,* vol. 5 of June, 548b. Dinzelbacher, *Vision und Visionsliteratur,* 226–51 comments on the feminization, emotionalization, and individualization of the visionary experience in the thirteenth century.

61. Mechthild, *The Flowing Light of the Godhead,* 7:57. In the absence of an adequate English translation we relied on the modern German version: Mechthild von Magdeburg, *Das fliessende Licht der Gottheit,* trans. Margot Schmidt (Einsiedeln: Benziger, 1955).

62. Mechthild, *Flowing Light,* 3:1. The structure of Mechthild's heaven is discussed in Petrus W. Tax, "Die grosse Himmelsschau Mechtilds von Magdeburg und ihre Höllenvision," *Zeitschrift für deutsches Altertum* 108 (1979), 112–37. That the saints will fill the "empty spaces" is a common medieval view, see for example Otto of Freising, *The Two Cities,* 505–8 (8:31–2).

63. Mechthild, *Flowing Light,* 4:24, with reference to Rev. 2:10.

64. Mechthild, *Flowing Light,* 3:1.

65. Mechthild, *Flowing Light:* "beautiful youth; the beloved goes," 1:44. The courtly connections of 1:44 are explored in Elizabeth Wainwright-de Kadt, "Courtly Literature and Mysticism," *Acta Germanica* 12(1980), 41–60.

66. Mechthild, *Flowing Light,* 1:44.

67. Mechthild, *Flowing Light,* 3:1; cf. Tax, "Die grosse Himmelsschau," 124f.

68. Andreas Capellanus, *On Love,* 470f.

69. For education and intellectual life in the Helfta convent see Caroline Walker Bynum, *Jesus as Mother: Studies in the Spirituality of the High Middle Ages* (Berkeley, CA: Univ. of California Press, 1982), 176. Gertrude, *Herald:* "a handsome youth," 2:1; friendship, 2:3; "you are the delicate," 3:65; "I am so closely," 3:5 (SC 143:230, 236, 266, 26); *Mass, Celebrated by the Lord Himself:* sang a song, 14 (SC 331: 304).

70. Gertrude, *Herald:* "the Lord took," 4:14; "I cannot be," 3:8 (SC 255:162; 143:34); *Spiritual Exercises:* "when I love," 3:276–8 (SC 127:114). In *Mass,* 5 (SC 331:29ff.), Gertrude is placed upon a throne right next to Christ and clothed in royal purple.

71. Phyllis B. Roberts, "Stephen Langton's Sermo de Virginibus," Julius Kirshner et al.,

eds., *Women of the Medieval World* (Oxford: Blackwell, 1985), 103–18, at 117.

72. Gertrude, *Spiritual Exercises:* "in conjugal," 3:166f. (SC 127:104). *Breviarium Romanum,* pars aestiva (Mechelen: Dessain, 1903): "the Virgin Mary; today, the Virgin," 605f.; both texts can be found in most medieval antiphonaries, e.g. that of Bamberg of the twelfth and that of Rheinau of the thirteenth century, see *Corpus Antiphonalium Officii,* ed. René-Jean Héobert (Rome: Herder: 1963–8), III, nos. 3707 and 3105.

73. Gertrude, *Spiritual Exercises:* "in a kiss; we beseech Thee," 3:174f. (SC 127:104). On belonging to a group see Bynum, *Jesus as Mother,* 82–109. For "roles" of religious experience see Hjalmar Sundén, *Religionspsychologie,* trans. H. Reller (Stuttgart: Calwer Verlag, 1982), 33–49 and Johan Unger, *On Religious Experience* (Uppsala: Almqvist & Wiksell, 1976), 9–32.

74. Gertrude, *Herald:* "Jesus, the Spouse," 5:10, 3; she heard Jesus, 5:27, 9; reposing in the arms, 5:32, 2(SC 331:146, 220f., 257).

75. Gertrude's preference of women is evident in the way she speaks about the post-mortem fate of men associated with her convent. When the men die she describes their deaths in an unemotional, detached manner. See Gertrude, *Herald,* 5:11–15 (SC 331:148–68). For Bernard's identification of the human soul as the spouse of the Song of Songs and the heavenly setting of their meeting see Bernard, *Sermons on the Song of Songs,* 52:2 in *The Works of Bernard of Clairvaux* (Kalamazoo, MI: Cistercian Publications, 1979), IV, 50f. The *coelum Trinitatis* is discussed in Albertus Magnus, *Summa de creaturis,* 3:10 (see above, n. 22).

76. Caroline W. Bynum, "...And Woman His Humanity: Female Imagery in the Religious Writing of the Later Middle Ages," C.W. Bynum et al., eds., *Gender and Religion* (Boston: Beacon Press, 1986), 257–88, at 272 on the basis of PL 197:336. For twentieth-century nuns dressed as brides, see Eve Arnold, *The Unretouched Woman* (New York: Knopf, 1976), 136–45.

77. *The Anchoresses' Rule* (c. 1200): "O Lady, St. Mary," in *The Ancrene Riwle,* trans. M.B. Salu (London: Burns & Oates, 1955), 15f. *Sawles warde* [Soul's Ward]: "the beauty of," in *Old English Homilies.* First Series, 260; this text forms part of a series that aims at extolling female virgintiy, see Albert C. Baugh, ed., *A Literary History of England,* 2nd ed. (London: Routledge & Kegan Paul, 1967), 123–6. For further sermonic material addressing nuns, see Alain de Lille (1120–1202) in PL 210:194f.

and Stephen Langton, *Sermo de virginibus*, in Roberts, "Stephen Langton's Sermo."

78. William L. Moran, "The Ancient Near Eastern Background of the Love of God in Deuteronomy," *Catholic Biblical Quarterly* 25 (1963), 77–87.

79. Otto of Freising, *The Two Cities*: Jerusalem not on earth, not of stones, 492 (8:25); no golden streets, 495 (8:25); "refreshed and affected; these things are," 508 (8:33).

CHAPTER FIVE

1. *Dialogo facetissimo et ridiculosissimo* in Angelo Beolco il Ruzante, *I Dialoghi*, ed. Giorgio Padoan (Padua: Antenore, 1981), 92–5. The *Dialogo* was first recited in public in 1529.

2. For the new appreciation of "the world" and the married state see Denys Hay, *The Italian Renaissance in Its Historical Background* (Cambridge: Cambridge Univ. Press, 1979), 130; Clarissa W. Atkinson, "Precious Balsam in a Fragile Glass: The Ideology of Virginity in the Later Middle Ages," *Journal of Family History* 8(1983), 131–43; and especially Charles Trinkaus, *In Our Image and Likeness: Humanity and Divinity in Italian Humanist Thought* (London: Constable, 1970), II, 674–82.

3. Walter Rüegg et al., "Cicero im Mittelalter und Humanismus," *Lexikon des Mittelalters* (Munich: Artemis, 1983), III, 2063–77: *aetas aristoteliana/ciceroniana*, 2063. For Renaissance theology we rely on Trinkaus, *In Our Image and Likeness*.

4. *The Painter's Manual of Dionysius of Fourna*, trans. Paul Hetherington (London: Sagittarius Press, 1974), 50. This eighteenth-century manual echoes medieval tradition as can be seen in the Last-Judgment-paradise illumination in *Manuscrit grec 74*, fol. 93 (Bibliothèque Nationale, Paris), an eleventh-century gospel written in Constantinople: *Evangiles avec peintures byzantines du XIe siècle*, ed. Bibliothèque Nationale (Paris: Berthaud, 1908), I, pl. 81.

5. On Abbot Desiderius see Leo of Ostia, "The Chronicle of Monte Cassino," 3:27 in Elizabeth G. Holt, ed., *A Documentary History of Art* (Garden City, NY: Doubleday, 1957), I, 13.

6. Our interpretation differs slightly from that of Otto Lehmann-Brockhaus, *Abruzzen und Molise, Kunst und Geschichte* (Munich: Prestel, 1983), 395–7.

7. *Elucidation*, 3:78 in Yves Lefèvre, *L'elucidarium et les lucidaires* (Paris: de Boccard, 1954),

463. For the palm of victory, see Rev. 7:9 and Jacobus a Voragine, *Legenda aurea*, ed. Th. Graesse, 3rd ed. (1890; Osnabrück: O. Zeller, 1965), 505 (no. 119). The story of the knight is in "St. Patrick's Purgatory" in the *Legenda aurea*, 215f. (no. 50).

8. Savonarola, *The Compendium of Revelations* in *Apocalyptic Spirituality*, trans. Bernard McGinn (New York: Paulist Press, 1979), 247.

9. Savonarola, *The Compendium*: Mary's throne in Paradise, 247; ladder, 260f. The presence of the divine in Paradise can also be seen in the "adoration of the Lamb" scene in Jan van Eyck's Ghent Altarpiece of 1432.

10. Charles de Tolnay, "Two Drawings after a Lost Triptych by Hieronymus Bosch," *Record of the Art Museum. Princeton University* 20 (1961), 43–8.

11. Hesiod, *Works and Days*, 111 and 168–73. See Harry Levin, *The Myth of the Golden Age in the Renaissance* (London: Faber & Faber, 1970) and Elizabeth Armstrong, *Ronsard and the Age of Gold* (Cambridge: Cambridge Univ. Press, 1968).

12. Virgil, *Aeneid*, 6:673–5 in *The Aeneid*, trans. Robert Fitzgerald (New York: Vintage, 1984), 183. For the fountain, see Ps. 36:9, "with thee is the fountain of life." *Roman de la Rose*, 1595–1599 in Guillaume de Lorris and Jean de Meun, *The Romance of the Rose*, trans. Charles Dahlberg (Princeton: Princeton Univ. Press, 1971), 52. Claudio Tolomei, letter of 26 July 1543, trans. in Elisabeth B. MacDougall et al., *Fons Sapientiae: Renaissance Garden Fountains* (Dumbarton Oaks Colloquium on the History of Landscape Architecture, 1977; Washington, DC: Stinehour Press, 1978), 5f.

The immediate inspiration for Bosch's tents seems to have come from his reading of the twelfth-century *Vision of Tundal* which he read in a Dutch version. There the protagonist saw in paradise "many tents of purple and white silken drapes, with gold and silver and silk fashioned in wondrous costliness." The precious materials of God's biblical tent-sanctuary (Exod. 26:1) are transferred to human dwellings in Paradise. D. Bax, *Hieronymus Bosch: His Picture-Writing Deciphered*, trans. M.A. Bax-Botha (Rotterdam: Balkema, 1979), 362.

13. Vittore Branca, *Boccaccio* (New York: New York University Press, 1976), 129 (*Epistola consolatoria a Piano de' Rossi*); Giovanni Boccaccio, *The Decameron*, trans. G.H. McWilliam (Harmondsworth: Penguin, 1972), 233 (introduction to 3rd day).

14. John Pope-Hennessy, *A Sienese Codex of the Divine Comedy* (London: Phaidon Press, 1947).

15. That angelic music is not only for God's entertainment, but also for "enhancing the delights of the blessed," was a Renaissance idea expressed, for instance, by musician Johannes Tinctoris (1435–1511) in *Complexus effectuum musices* (after 1475), to be found in *Opera theoretica*, ed. Albert Seay (Rome: American Institute of Musicology, 1975), II, 168. Tinctoris quotes Virgil's *Aeneid* 6:643–6 to support his opinion.

16. The Renaissance influence of *Scipio's Dream* is discussed in Pierre Courcelle, "La postérité chrétienne du *Songe de Scipion*," *Revue des études latines* 36(1958), 205–34, at 229ff. and Dominic Baker-Smith, "Juan Vivès and the *Somnium Scipionis*," R.R. Bolgar, ed., *Classical Influences on European Culture AD 1500–1700* (Cambridge: Cambridge Univ. Press, 1976), 239–44. For the numerous copies of *Scipio's Dream* and *On Old Age* in Italian libraries, see Berthold L. Ullman and Philip A. Stadter, *The Public Library of Renaissance Florence* (Padua: Antenore, 1972) and Elisabeth Pellegrin, *La bibliothéque des Visconti et des Sforza, ducs de Milan, au XVe siécle* (Paris: CNRS, 1955).

17. Petrarch, *Familiarum rerum libri*, 2:1 in Francesco Petrarca, *Le Familiari*, ed. Vittorio Rossi (Florence: Sansoni, 1933), I, 58. Erasmus, *Familiar Colloquies*, section entitled "Convivium religiosum," in *Desiderii Erasmi opera omnia*, ed. Joannes Clericus (1703; rprt. Meisenheim: Hain, 1961), I, 682.

18. Tibullus, *Elegies* II 3:70–74 and I 3:57–66 [in *Catullus, Tibullus and Pervigilium Veneris*, trans. F.W. Cornish et al. (Cambridge, MA: Harvard Univ. Press, 1962), 267 and 209]. *La Métamorphose d'Ovide figurée* (Lyons, 1557) has the following poem which is reproduced as frontispiece in Levin, *The Myth of the Golden Age in the Renaissance*: "L'amour n'estoit suget au blasonneur,/Ains pouvoit on de s'amie estre aymé,/Hanté, baisé, sans creindre deshonneur:/ Dont à bon droit l'aage d'or fut nommé." (Love was not a matter for evil tongues. Thus one could be loved by one's friend, be visited and kissed without fear of dishonor: wherefore this was with good reason called the Golden Age.)

19. Francesco Colonna, *Hypnertomachia*, English trans. (London: Waterson, 1592), 93–4. Written in 1467, the novel was first printed in 1499.

20. Ronsard, "O pucelle plus tendre," 1550: "Et baisant nous mourrons./ Tous deux morts en mesme heure/Voirrons le lac frangueux,/Et l'obscure demeure/De Pluton l'outrageux,/Et les champs ordonnez/Aux amans fortunez." "Plus estroit que la vigne à l'ormeau," 1578: "Là,

morts de trop aimer, sous les branches myrtines/ Nous voirrons tous les jours/Les anciens Heros aupres des Heroines/Ne parler que d'amours." Pierre de Ronsard, *Oeuvres complètes*, ed. Gustave Cohen (Paris: Gallimard, 1950), II, 702 and I, 295. Both poems are based on an earlier Latin poem by Joannes Secundus (1511–1536): see F.A. Wright, *The Love Poems of Joannes Secundus* (London: Routledge, 1930), 40–43; Ronsard, however, has also read Tibullus, see Andrée Thill, "Tibull au miroir de Ronsard," *Bulletin de l'Association G. Budé* (1979), 188–98 and R.E. Hallowell, *Ronsard and the Conventional Roman Elegy* (Urbana, IL: Illinois Univ. Press, 1954), 109f., 121–28.

21. Marot, "Lamentation for Mme Louise of Savoy" in Thomas P. Harrison, ed., *The Pastoral Elegy*, trans. Harry J. Leon (1939; rprt. New York: Octagon Books, 1968), 142f.

22. Valla, *On Pleasure*: "the bells of," 3:25, 2; "as for me," 3:25, 17; "will clasp you," 3:25, 21 in Lorenzo Valla, *On Pleasure – De voluptate*, trans. A. Kent Hieatt and Maristella Lorch (New York: Abaris Books, 1977), 307, 313, and 315.

23. Valla, *On Pleasure*: "that thrills you," 3:25, 11 in Laurentius Valla, *Opera omnia* (Turin: Bottega d'Erasmo, 1962), I, 990 [as a translation of the attenuated 2nd ed. of Valla's book, the Hieatt/Lorch ed. omits the passage]; "without error," 3:24, 17; "does not inflame," 3:23, 6; play with angels, etc., 3:24, 13 (Hieatt/Lorch ed., 305, 295, 301f.).

24. Emma Spina Barelli, "Note iconografiche in margine alla Cantoria di Donatello," *Storia dell'arte* 15/16 (1972), 283–91.

25. "From the 1420s to the 1450s, painters, as they had not done in more than a thousand years, devoted themselves to rendering landscape, the careful depiction of trees, flowers, plants, and cloud-filled skies." James Beck, *Italian Renaissance Painting* (New York: Harper & Row, 1981), 4f.; see also Bernard Berenson, *The Italian Painters of the Renaissance* (London: Phaidon Press, 1968), II, 13. Herbert A. Stützer, *Malerei der italienischen Renaissance* (Cologne: Du Mont, 1979), 92.

26. John Pope-Hennessy, *Giovanni di Paolo 1403–1483* (London: Chatto & Windus, 1937), 136.

27. Pope-Hennessy, *Giovanni di Paolo*, 135. The later version of Giovanni's *Paradise* (c. 1463/83) is in the Pinacoteca of Siena, Italy.

28. Francis Silvester, "Life of the Blessed Osanna," *Acta Sanctorum*, rev. ed. by Jean Carnandet (Paris: Palmé, 1867), vol. 4 of June, 557–601: meeting St. Paul, God, Aquinas, 573 (no. 71); meeting Dominic, 574 (no. 72);

Columba's embrace, 574 (no. 73); death of Columba, 577 (no. 89).

29. Erasmus, *Colloquia familiaria*, section on "The Apotheosis of that Incomparable Worthy, John Reuchlin," in *Desiderii Erasmi opera omnia*, I, 689–692.

30. Celso Maffei, *Delitiosa explicatio de sensibilibus deliciis paradisi* (Verona: Lucas Antonius Florentinus, 1504), no pagination.

31. The sermons referred to are by Pseudo-Augustine [Ambrosius Autpertus] and Bernard of Clairvaux (*PL* 39:2134; 183: 416]; the latter imagines how the Blessed Virgin is received into heaven with "joyful embraces" and with "kisses ...from the mouth of Him who sits at the right hand of the Father."

32. On Celso Maffei, see D. Nicola Widlocher, *La congregazione dei canonici regolari lateranensi* (Gubbio: Scuola Tipografica Oderisi, 1929), 335–9.

33. Ernest T. DeWald, *Italian Painting 1200–1600* (New York: Holt, Rinehart & Winston, 1961), 317f.

34. *Elucidation*, 3:81 in Lefèvre, *L'elucidarium*, 464. On the added loincloths, see Götz Kraft, *Studien zur Erzähltechnik des Luca Signorelli* (Diss. Munich; Munich: Salzer, 1980), 153. Leo Steinberg, *The Sexuality of Christ in Renaissance Art and in Modern Oblivion* (New York: Pantheon, 1984), comments on the meaning of nakedness in Renaissance art.

35. Bartolomeo Facio, *The Happiness of Life*, quoted by Trinkaus, *In Our Image and Likeness*, I, 225. Aquinas, *Sth*, Suppl. 81:4.

36. Aquinas, *Sth*, Suppl. 84:2. For love of travelling see Valla, *On Pleasure* 3:25, 6 (Valla, *On Pleasure – De voluptate*, 309), and Jacob Burckhardt, *The Civilization of the Renaissance in Italy* (New York: Harper & Row, 1929), 279–82.

CHAPTER SIX

1. *Imitation of Christ*: "Quando memorabor Domine tui solius?" 3:48 in *Thomae Hemerken a Kempis opera omnia*, ed. Michael J. Pohl (Freiburg: Herder, 1904), II, 231.

2. Altman K. Swihart, *Luther and the Lutheran Church* (London: P. Owen, 1961), 64; Luther, *WA Br*: "does not sufficiently," 1:90; and *WA TR*: "we are beggars," 5, no. 5677. Luther's works are contained in *D. Martin Luthers Werke. Kritische Gesamtausgabe* ("Weimarer Ausgabe"; Weimar: Böhlau, 1883ff.), to be referred to as *WA*. A subset of *WA* contains Luther's letters ("Briefwechsel"), referred to as *WA Br* and Luther's table talks ("Tischreden"),

referred to as *WA TR*. The English edition used is *Luther's Works*, ed. Jaroslav Pelikan et al. (St. Louis and Philadelphia: Augsburg Press and Fortress Press, 1955ff.).

3. Calvin, *Institutes*: "our very being," 1:1 (*CR* 30:31); *CR*: "there is no part," 77:471 [quoting 1 Cor. 10:13]; "that nothing worse," 34:9/10. Calvin's and other reformers' works are collected in the *Corpus Reformatorum*, referred to as *CR*. We have cited the *Institutes* (*CR* 30) separately. The English edition quoted is *Institutes of the Christian Religion*, trans. Ford L. Battles, 8th ed. (Philadelphia: Westminster Press, 1977). Calvin's views on the afterlife are studied by Heinrich Quistorp, *Calvin's Doctrine of the Last Things*, trans. H. Knight (London: Lutterworth, 1965) and David E. Holwerda, "Eschatolgoy and History: A Look at Calvin's Eschatological Vision," Donald K. McKim, ed., *Readings in Calvin's Theology* (Grand Rapids, MI: Baker, 1984), 311–42.

4. Luther, *WA TR* 3, no. 3901 with reference to John 14:8; Melanchthon, *CR*: "let us rejoice," 11:731.

5. Calvin, *CR*: "wholly intent," 33:190; *Institutes*: "He will reveal; give himself to," 3:25,10 (*CR* 30:741f.); *CR*: "our glory will," 83:331f.

6. Melanchthon, *Apology of the Augsburg Confession*, art. 17 (*CR* 27:583). Council of Florence (1439), *Laetentur caeli*: "yet according to" [text in Heinrich Denzinger et al., eds., *Enchiridion symbolorum*, 32nd ed. (Freiburg: Herder, 1963), no. 1305]; Calvin, *Institutes*: biblical landowner, 3:18,3 (*CR* 30:605f.) with reference to Matt. 20:1–16.

7. Luther, *WA*: "will be equal," 12:266; "close to God," reported by Johannes Mathesius, *Leychpredigten* (Nuremberg: Johann vom Berg, 1559), part I, 6th sermon on 1 Cor. 15 (no pagination). Augustine's view is best expressed in his *Sermon 87* in which he comments on Matt. 20:1–16: "That denarius [which all the workers receive irrespective of their actual work] is eternal life, and in eternal life all are equal" (*PL* 38:533). Standard reformation discussions of the issue include: Luther, *WA* 36:635f. and 32:538; Calvin, *Institutes*, 3:25,10 (*CR* 30:742). Gerhard (1582–1637) also states that the "essential beatitude" is the same for all the blessed: Johannes Gerhard, *Loci theologici* (Leipzig: Hinrichs, 1875), IX, 387–95 and 417.

8. Luther, *WA* 32:371.

9. Luther, *WA*: "to rule an," 11:252; "God has placed," 16:353.

10. Calvin, *CR* 60:328.

11. Luther, *WA TR* 1, no. 1149. While Luther rejected the Copernican system (*WA TR* 4, no. 4638), Calvin never mentioned it,

see Christopher B. Kaiser, "Calvin, Copernicus, and Castellio," *Calvin Theological Journal* 21(1986), 5–31. The new astronomy does not necessarily pose theological problems, because the empyrean can be located outside a heliocentric universe, see Jürgen Hübner, *Die Theologie Johannes Keplers zwischen Orthodoxie und Naturwissenschaft* (Tübingen: Mohr, 1975), 188 and 288f.

12. Luther, *WA*: "all heaven [sky]," 14:72; "play with heaven [sky]," 36:660. Since the German *Himmel* denotes both sky and heaven, the text here is ambiguous.

13. Luther, *WA TR*: "the flowers, leaves; you must not think; ants, bugs," 2, no. 2652b; *WA*: "was stronger than," 42:46; Elbe river, 36:599.

14. Luther, *WA TR*: "lots of apples," 2, no. 2584; *WA TR*: "cheerful speculation," 2, no. 2507, also *WA Br* 5:377 and *WA* 37:159; *WA Br*: "a pretty, beautiful and," 5:377; *WA*: milk and solid food, 5:602, with reference to 1 Cor. 3:1f.; 13:11.

15. Luther, *WA*: "forget about eating," 36:660; "will be delightful," 36:595.

16. Calvin discusses the location of paradise in *CR* 74:788 with reference to Matt. 5:5; *Institutes*: "dross and other; in the very," 3:25,11 (*CR* 30:743); *CR*: perfection of animals and plants, 77:153. The English reformer John Bradford (1510–1555) challenged Aquinas on the non-existence of animals and plants and the movements of the heavenly bodies in the new creation. When Paul in Rom. 8 referred to "the renovation of the world and of all things," Bradford argued that "it hath some shew or probability that these things [animals, plants] shall be renewed to eternity for the glory of God's children." Bradford, "The Restoration of All Things," *The Writings of John Bradford*, ed. Aubrey Townsend (Cambridge: Cambridge Univ. Press, 1848), I, 359, paraphrasing Martin Bucer, *Metaphrases et ennarationes perpetuae epistolarum D. Pauli apostoli* (Strasbourg: Rihel, 1536), 344f.

17. Calvin, *CR*: "as the world," 77:547 (see also Luther, *WA* 36:595 and 634).

18. Luther, *WA*: no households, 36:634; *WA Br*: "shortly see," 5:241; *WA*: "if my wife," 36:659; Calvin, *CR*: "will be torn," 73:675. On the family and authority, see Steven Ozment, *When Fathers Ruled: Family Life in Reformation Europe* (Cambridge, MA: Harvard Univ. Press, 1983).

19. Cicero's *On Old Age* as school text, see Calvin, *CR* 38:78f., R.R. Bolgar, *The Classical Heritage and Its Beneficiaries* (Cambridge: Cambridge Univ. Press, 1954), 351–7 and M.L. Clarke, *Classical Education in Britain 1500–*

1900 (Cambridge; Cambridge Univ. Press, 1959), 12. Melanchthon, *CR*: "in the heavenly," 9:822.

The text of Zwingli is worth quoting in full: "After that you may expect to see the communion and fellowship of all the saints and sages and believers and the steadfast and the brave and the good who have ever lived since the world began. You will see the two Adams, the redeemed and the Redeemer, Abel, Enoch, Noah, Abraham, Isaac, Jacob, Judah, Moses, Joshua, Gideon, Samuel, Phinehas, Elijah, Elisha, Isaiah and the Virgin Mother of God of whom he prophesied, David, Hezekiah, Josiah, the Baptist, Peter, Paul; Hercules too and Theseus, Socrates, Aristides, Antigonus, Numa, Camillus, the Catos and Scipios; Louis the Pious and your predecessors the Louis, Philips, Pepins, and all your ancestors who have departed this life in faith." Zwingli, *Exposition of the Faith* in Geoffrey W. Bromiley, ed., *Zwingli and Bullinger* (London: SCM Press, 1953), 275f. with comments by Rudolf Pfister, *Die Seligkeit erwählter Heiden bei Zwingli* (Zollikon: Evangelischer Verlag, 1952), 88. The text was first written in 1531 for the king, but it was published with modifications by Bullinger in 1536. Bullinger omitted all references to the French king's ancestors. Zwingli seems to have derived the combination of the "Catos and Scipios" from his favorite classical author Seneca, *Consolation to Marcia*, 25:2, who in turn relies on Cicero. Luther, *WA*: criticizes Zwingli, 54:143f.; *WA TR*: hope for Cicero, 3, no. 2412b and 4, no. 3925.

20. Calvin, *CR* 33:227; Georg Loesche, *Johannes Mathesius* (Gotha: Perthes, 1895), II: Mathesius's knowledge of *On Old Age*, 147; Mathesius, *Leychpredigten*, part I: *Scipio's Dream*, 9th sermon on 1 Cor. 15; Alexander, Scipio, etc., 6th sermon on 1 Cor. 15; Johannes Mathesius, *Ausgewählte Werke*, ed. Georg Loesche (Prague: Tempsky, 1896), I: meeting again, 5. 19. 40f. 86f. 90; Melanchthon, "Funeral Oration," *CR* 11:733.

21. *Oeuvres complètes du Cardinal de Bérulle* (1644; rprt. Monsoult: Maison d'Institution de l'Oratoire, 1960), 171f.; *The Complete Works of St. Teresa of Jesus*, trans. E.A. Peers (London: Sheed & Ward, 1946), III, 288.

22. *Catechism of the Council of Trent for Parish Priests*, trans. J.A. McHugh and C.J. Callan, 9th ed. (New York: Wagner, 1945), 136. For the theocentric nature of post-Tridentine Catholic eschatology, see Philipp Schäfer, *Eschatologie: Trient und Gegenreformation* (Freiburg: Herder, 1984), 67–73.

23. Louys Richeôme, *Catechisme royal* (Lyon:

J. Pilehotte, 1607): "qui d'un bon clin," 215.
24. Antonino Polti, *Della felicità suprema del cielo* (Perugia: G.B. Rastelli, 1575), 187f. On the author (d. after 1596), who is also known as Antonio di Collemancio, see Jacques Quétif and Jacques Echard, *Scriptores ordinis praedicatorum recensiti* (1719/23; rprt. New York: Burt Franklin, n.d.), II/1, 317.
25. Polti, *Della felicità*: "the most serene," 207; "exalted above all," 215. Polti, *Della belleza corporale e spirituale della B. Vergine* (Perugia, 1590), referred to in Quétif and Echard, *Scriptores*, II/1, 317. Other Dominican writers on Mary's beauty were Richard of St. Laurent (13th cent.), *On the Praise of the Blessed Virgin Mary*, 5:2 [in *B. Alberti Magni opera omnia*, ed. S.C.A. Borgnet (Paris: Vives, 1896), XXXVI, 279–319] and Antoninus Pierozzi of Florence (1389–1458), *Summa theologica*, IV 15:10.
26. Polti, *Della felicità*: "to see your face," 214, with reference to Gen. 33:10. The crown of Mary is the *aureola* or "little crown" of scholastic theology, representing the special heavenly reward the Virgin receives for her virginity. It also has regal connotations. As the foremost of the saints, Mary is considered the Queen of Heaven. She shares the royal status of her son, like the *spouses* of medieval and early-modern queens. French queens, for instance, were crowned until 1610 and sometimes compared to the Blessed Virgin. On Mary as queen, see Michael O'Carroll, "Queen of Angels," *Ephemerides Mariologicae* 34(1984), 221–37; Edwin Hall and Horst Uhr, "Aureola super auream: Crowns and Related Symbols of Special Distinction for Saints," *The Art Bulletin* 67 (1985), 567–603, esp. 575; Claire R. Sherman, "The Queen in Charles V's Coronation Book," *Viator* 8(1977), 255–97, esp. 269, 293; Marina Warner, *Alone of All Her Sex: The Myth and the Cult of the Virgin Mary* (New York: Knopf, 1976), 81–117. Savonarola describes an (imaginary) crown presented to Mary, see *Apocalyptic Spirituality*, trans. Bernard McGinn (New York: Paulist Press, 1979), 242–6.
27. For the *Salve Regina* and the *Ave Maria* as late-medieval texts that were in 1568 incorporated into the Roman Breviary, see *Lexikon für Theologie und Kirche*, 2nd ed. (Freiburg: Herder, 1957–67), I, 1141 and IX, 281f. For the custom of praying to Mary at the hour of death, see Petrus Canisius, *De Maria virgine incomparabili et Dei genitrice sacrosancta* (Ingolstadt: D. Sartorius, 1577), 618–21 and 735. The function of Mary in Last Judgment iconography is discussed in Luther, *WA* 51:128 and Philippe Ariès, *The Hour of Our Death*, trans.

H. Weaver (Harmondsworth: Penguin, 1983), 101f. and 108f.
28. For the Council of Trent's (1545–1563) ruling about art, see Elizabeth G. Holt, ed., *A Documentary History of Art*, 2nd ed. (Princeton, NJ: Princeton Univ. Press, 1982), II, 65 and Paolo Prodi, "Ricerche sulla teoria delle arte figurative nella riforma cattolica," *Archivio italiano per la storia della pietà* 4(1965), 121–212, at 198. Counter-Reformation art promoted Marian iconography according to Emile Mâle, *L'art religieux de la fin du XVIe siècle, du XVIIe siècle, et du XVIIIe siècle* (Paris: A. Colin, 1951), 29–48. Mary as the "woman" of Rev. 12:1 appears as early as the eighth century: see Ambrosius Autpertus in *Corpus Christianorum, Continuatio mediaevalis* (Turnhout: Brepols, 1975), 27:443f. and Georg Kretschmar, *Die Offenbarung des Johannes* (Stuttgart: Calwer Verlag, 1985), 131–3.
29. On the status of Mary in heaven, see Bonaventure, *Soliloquy*, 4:26 in *The Works of Bonaventure*, trans. J. de Vinck (Paterson, NJ: St. Anthony Guild, 1966), III, 125; Savonarola, *The Compendium of Revelations* (1495) in *Apocalyptic Spirituality*, 256; and Canisius, *De Maria virgine*, 272. A late-medieval *Te Deum* adaptation with the angels singing "Holy, holy, holy, Mary Virgin Mother of God" is translated in [Pseudo-] Bonaventure, *The Mirror of the Blessed Virgin Mary and the Psalter of Our Lady*, trans. Sr. Mary Emmanuel (St. Louis, MO: Herder, 1932), 294f.
30. Giles Fletcher, *Christ's Victory in Heaven* (1610), from nos. 46, 50, and 52 in Giles and Phineas Fletcher, *Poetical Works*, ed. Frederick S. Boas (Cambridge: Cambridge Univ. Press, 1908), I, 29f.
31. De Sales, *Oeuvres*, 9:117, refering to Song of Songs 2:16. De Sales's work is quoted from *Oeuvres de Saint François de Sales. Edition complète* (Annecy: Niérat et al., 1892–1964).
32. De Sales, *Oeuvres* 9:117f.
33. De Sales, *Oeuvres*: "une certaine gloire accidentelle qu'ils reçoivent en la conversation qu'ils ont par ensemble" [a certain secondary glory which they receive through the interaction with each other], 10:239; "the friendships," 10:240.
34. De Sales, *Oeuvres*: "I find this," 18:273; Henri Bremond, *Histoire littéraire du sentiment religieux en France* (1923; rprt. Paris: A. Colin, 1967): "seemed to be," I, 11.
35. Marvin O'Connell, *The Counter-Reformation* (New York: Harper & Row, 1974): "a kind of," 111; Justus Lipsius, *De constantia* (Antwerp: Oficina Plantiniana, 1605): "some vestiges," 7; "right reason," 46; de Sales,

Oeuvres: Epictetus, 4:36. 81f.148. On the influence of Stoic philosophy in the early seventeenth century, see Antoine Adam, *Sur le problème religieux dans la première moitié du XVIIe siècle* (Oxford: Clarendon Press, 1959).

36. Polti, *Della felicità:* "terra purgata, e fatta gloriosa," 180; here he also discusses earth as "limbo" for the unbaptized children with reference to Girolamo Savonarola, *The Triumph of the Cross,* trans. John Procter (London: Sands, 1901), 122f.

37. Pascal, "Le mémorial" (1654) in *Oeuvres de Blaise Pascal,* ed. Léon Brunschvicg (Paris: Hachette, 1904), XII, 4.

38. For seventeenth-century "pessimism," see Adam, *Le problème religieux.*

39. Max Weber, *The Protestant Ethic and the Spirit of Capitalism,* trans. T. Parsons (New York: Scribner, 1958); Bramhall, *A Just Vindication of the Church of England* (1654) in *The Works of John Bramhall* (Oxford: John H. Parker, 1842): "I do not see," I, 120.

40. Hartmut Lehmann, *Das Zeitalter des Absolutismus* (Stuttgart: Kohlhammer, 1980), 111. Lehmann gives a good summary of the seventeenth-century crisis.

41. On the pious middle class in Germany, Britain, and France, see Hartmut Lehmann, "The Cultural Importance of the Pious Middle Classes in Seventeenth-Century Protestant Society," Kaspar von Greyerz, ed., *Religion and Society in Early Modern Europe* (London: Allen & Unwin, 1984), 33–41; Avihu Zakai, "The Gospel of Reformation: The Origins of the Great Puritan Migration," *Journal of Ecclesiastical History* 37(1986), 584–602; Bernhard Groethuysen, *Die Entstehung der bürgerlichen Welt- und Lebensanschauung in Frankreich* (Frankfurt: Suhrkamp, 1978).

42. Madame de Sévigné, *Correspondence,* ed. Roger Duchêne (Paris: Gallimard, 1972–78): "to avoid any," II, 1035; "Soli Deo," 1057f. On Mme de Sévigné's religion, see Henri Busson, *La religion des classiques, 1660–1685* (Paris: Presses universitaires de France, 1948), 5–23, and Eva Avigdor, *Madame de Sévigné* (Paris: Nizet, 1974), 127–43.

43. Mme. de Sévigné, *Correspondence:* "this kind," I, 238; "let me love; I found myself," I, 723 (see also 741); "un peu," III, 572. For the religious devaluation of attachment to family, see Jean-Louis Flandrin, *Families in Former Times: Kinship. Household, and Sexuality* (Cambridge: Cambridge Univ. Press, 1979), 160. For the anti-reformist ideology implied in Jansenism, see Gérard Ferreyrolles, *Pascal et la raison politique* (Paris: Presses universitaires de France, 1984), 25.

44. Pierre Nicole, "Des quatre dernières fins de l'homme," *Essais de Morale* (Paris: G. Desprez, 1733): "God alone," IV, 247; "capacity to love," IV, 255, reprinted in *Essais de Morale* (Geneva: Slatkine, 1971), I, 373 and 375. Nicole, "Traité de la préparation à la mort," *Essais de Morale:* "the human being," V, 348f. (rprt. I, 506).

45. Baxter's letter of June 14,1665 is printed in *The Works of the Honourable Robert Boyle* (London: W. Johnston, 1772), VI, 518f.; Howe, "The Blessedness of the Righteous," *The Works of John Howe* (London: The Religious Tract Society, 1862–3), I, 376.

46. Steere, "Earth Felicities, Heaven's Allowances," Harrison T. Meserole, ed., *American Poetry of the Seventeenth Century* (University Park: Pennsylvania State Univ. Press, 1985), 258. Although pointing out the limits of the Puritan attitude to his contemporaries, Steere aptly summarizes the prevailing mentality. For contemplation and meditation on the glory of heaven, see Charles E. Hambrick-Stowe, *The Practice of Piety: Puritan Devotional Disciplines in Seventeenth-Century New England* (Chapel Hill, NC: Univ. of North Carolina Press, 1982), 278–87; Frank L. Huntley, *Bishop Joseph Hall, 1574–1656* (Cambridge: D.S. Brewer, 1979), 71–90.

47. Howe, "A Discourse Relating to the Expectation of Future Blessedness," *The Works of John Howe,* VI, 3. In early seventeenth-century Protestant theology, belief in a "new earth" virtually disappeared. While for Arthur Dent (d. 1607) the new earth was still a reality for the use of the angels and the blessed, later Puritans had no real use for the concept. According to Hezekiah Holland, the "new earth" refers to the glorified human bodies, but James Durham took it to be something God will create not for human use, but solely "for his own glory." Arthur Dent, *The Ruine of Rome* (London: N. Okes, 1631), 379f.; Hezekiah Holland, *An Exposition…upon the Revelation* (London: G. Calvers, 1650), 168; James Durham, *A Commentarie upon the Book of the Revelation* (London: Company of Stationers, 1658), 755. On the annihilation of the physical universe in continental theology, see Erhard Kunz, *Protestantische Eschatologie: Von der Reformation bis zur Aufklärung* (Freiburg: Herder, 1980), 62–4. On the development of such ideas in America, see James West Davidson, *The Logic of Millennial Thought* (New Haven: Yale Univ. Press, 1977), 81–121.

48. Thomas Browne, *Religio Medici,* ed. L.C. Martin (Oxford: Clarendon Press, 1964), 47. Similar views can be found in Johann Gerhard

(1582–1637), the founder of Lutheran systematic theology in Germany, and in the French philosopher Malebranche (1638–1715), see Gerhard, *Loci theologici*, IX, 157.323; *Oeuvres de Malebranche*, ed. André Robinet (Paris: J. Vrin, 1976), XII/XIII, 399–403.

49. Richard Baxter, *The Saints' Everlasting Rest* (London: T. Underhill & F. Tyton, 1649), 98. This is the first edition of the often-reprinted work.

50. Baxter, *The Saints' Everlasting Rest*: Luther, Zwingli etc., 84f. (the list includes 12 biblical and 32 non-biblical names); "all the saints," 86; "all the glory," 24. Marvell, "A Poem upon the Death of O[liver] C[romwell]," *The Poems and Letters of Andrew Marvell*, ed. H.M. Margoliouth, 3rd. ed. (Oxford: Clarendon Press, 1971), I, 136f. Seventeenth-century theologians often distinguish between the "primary" glory of the blessed which consists in the vision of God, and the "secondary" or "accidental" glory which may consist in the enjoyment of the company of other saints, see Gerhard, *Loci theologici*, IX, 352f. and de Sales, *Oeuvres*, 10:239.

51. *The Works of Joseph Hall* (Oxford: Talboys, 1837): "when we casually," VIII, 262 (from *Susurrium cum Deo*, 1651); "nature has no," VI, 197.

52. On the medieval concept of angelic music, see Reinhold Hammerstein, *Die Musik der Engel* (Munich: Francke, 1962). Baxter, *The Saints' Everlasting Rest*: "o blessed employment," 30 [with reference to Rev. 4:11]; "shrieks and cries," 325. N.I. Matar, "Heavenly Joy at the Torments of the Damned in Restoration Writings," *Notes and Queries* 231(1986), 466–7 is wrong in attributing to Baxter the view that the blessed hear and take pleasure in the cries of the damned.

53. Baxter, *Poetical Fragments* (London: T. Snowden, 1681): "the Lord," preface; *The Saints' Everlasting Rest*: "liveliest emblem; deep sense of," 680; "sticking in the," 682; "a swine is," 273. *A Christian Directory*, 2nd ed. (London: R. White, 1678), part 3: "harmony and melody," 166f. For the Puritan love of singing, see Hambrick-Stowe, *The Practice of Piety*, 111–16; Horton Davies, *Worship and Theology in England* (Princeton, NJ: Princeton Univ. Press, 1965–75), II, 268–85; Percy A. Scholes, *The Puritans and Music in England and New England* (London: Oxford Univ. Press, 1934), 253–74.

54. *The Bay Psalm Book: A Facsimile Reprint of the First Edition of 1640* (Chicago: Univ. of Chicago Press, 1956), end of preface. The unsigned preface is by John Cotton, according to

Zoltan Haraszti, *The Enigma of the Bay Psalm Book* (Chicago: Univ. of Chicago Press, 1956), 19–27. William Law, *A Serious Call to a Devout and Holy Life – The Spirit of Love*, ed. Paul G. Stanwood (New York: Paulist Press, 1978): "till your imagination," 223 with reference to Rev. 7:9–12. Singing in heaven, of course, was not unknown to Catholics, see de Sales, *Oeuvres*, 9:49: "Everything is created because of adoration. When God created the angels and humankind, he did so in order that they shall praise him in eternity, up there in heaven."

55. Baxter, *The Saints' Everlasting Rest*: "we shall know," 763; "the poorest Christian," 103. *The Sermons of John Donne*, ed. George R. Potter et al. (Berkeley: Univ. of California Press, 1962), IV, 128.

56. Increase Mather, *Meditations on the Glory of the Heavenly World* (Boston: Eliot, 1711), 81.

57. Baxter, *The Saints' Everlasting Rest*: "not the rest," 28; "advanceth our sense; to stand before," 29.

58. For the renewed interest in Baxter's work in the eighteenth century, see Frederick J. Powicke, "Story and Significance of the Rev. Richard Baxter's *Saints' Everlasting Rest*," *Bulletin of the John Rylands Library Manchester* 5(1918/20), 445–79. John and Charles Wesley, *Selected Writings and Hymns*, ed. Frank Whaling (New York: Paulist Press, 1981): "deliver me," 80 (prayer dating from 1733); "do I think," 82. James Hervey's *Meditations and Contemplations* (London: Bourne & Evans, 1811) were first published in 1746 and reached a 25th edition in 1791 according to *Dictionary of National Biography* (London: Smith, Elder & Co., 1891), XXVI, 282–4. Contemporary graveyard poetry includes Edward Young, *Night Thoughts* (1742/5) and Robert Blair, *The Grave* (1743).

59. Hervey, *Meditations*, 15. Hervey's attitude toward the world is aptly summarized in the following story from the *Meditations*: "Not long ago I happened to spy a thoughtless jay. The poor bird was idly busied in dressing his pretty plumes, or hopping carelessly from spray to spray. A sportsman coming by, observes the feathered rover. Immediately he lifts the tube, and levels his blow. Swifter than a whirlwind flies the leaden death; and, in a moment, lays the silly creature breathless on the ground. Such, such may be the fate of the man who has a fair occasion of obtaining grace today, and wantonly postpones the improvement of it till tomorrow. He may be cut off in the midst of his folly, and ruined for ever, while he is dreaming of being wise hereafter."(3)

60. Hervey, *Meditations*: Abraham etc., 36f.; "the saints always," 59.
61. Hervey, *Meditations*, 59.
62. Joseph Braun, *Die Kirchenbauten der deutschen Jesuiten* (Freiburg: Herder, 1908), 187f. discusses the 1653 removal of the Rubens painting. On the Renaissance character of the painting, see Reinhard Liess, *Die Kunst des Rubens* (Braunschweig: Waisenhaus, 1977), 359–69.

CHAPTER SEVEN

1. Emanuel Swedenborg, *Heaven and Hell*, trans. George F. Dole, 2nd ed. (New York: Swedenborg Foundation, 1979), nos. 1 and 74. To be referred to as *HH*.
2. For a discussion of Newton's non-scientific or mathematical writings see Richard S. Westfall, *Never at Rest: A Biography of Isaac Newton* (Cambridge: Cambridge Univ. Press, 1980). Cyriel Odhner Sigstedt, *The Swedenborg Epic: The Life and Works of Emanuel Swedenborg* (London: Swedenborg Society, 1981), 94, 185; Swedenborg, *Journal of Dreams*, trans. J.J.G. Wilkinson (New York: Swedenborg Foundation, 1977), nos. 51 and 52.
3. Swedenborg, *The Spiritual Diary* (London: Swedenborg Society, 1977), no. 1166. To be referred to as *SD*. "World of spirits" and "heaven of angels" are included in the subtitle of *Arcana Coelestia*, first published 1749/56.
4. On Swedenborg's impact on eighteenth- and nineteenth-century thought, see Marguerite Block "Swedenborg and the Romantic Movement," *The New Christianity* (Winter 1938), 3–7, although this includes no references to the works she cites as having Swedenborgian influence. Michael Heinrichs, *Emanuel Swedenborg in Deutschland* (Frankfurt: Lang, 1979) and Karl-Erik Sjödén, *Swedenborg en France* (Stockholm: Almqvist & Wiksell, 1985) are more critical discussions of Swedenborg's contintental influence. Block's earlier work, *The New Church in the New World: A Study of Swedenborgianism in America* (New York: Holt, 1932), mentions that nineteenth-century Americans like Emerson and Henry James read Swedenborg, but she only briefly discusses Swedenborgian connections to Transcendentalism (158f.) and Fourierism (155f.). On Emerson's views on Swedenborg (in *Nature* and *Representative Men*) see Kenneth W. Cameron, *Emerson's Transcendentalism and British Swedenborgianism* (Hartford: Transcendental Books, 1984); Anne C. Rose, *Transcendentalism as a Social Movement, 1830–1850* (New Haven: Yale Univ. Press, 1981), 164–74;

and Russell M. and Clare R. Goldfarb, *Spiritualism and Nineteenth Century Letters* (Rutherford, NJ: Fairleigh Dickinson Univ. Press, 1978), 66–7 (Henry James, Sr.), 53–5 (Emerson), 56 (Bronson Alcott).

Kant published his reaction to Swedenborg in *Dreams of a Spirit-Seer Illustrated by Dreams of Metaphysics* in 1766. He negated Swedenborg's ability to see beyond reason and the catogories of space and time. "The big work of this author," he wrote, "comprises eight volumes quarto full of nonsense" (trans. Emanuel F. Goerwitz, ed. Frank Sewall [London: Sonnenschein, 1900], 100). On the other hand there is some evidence that Kant originally suspected some truth in the reports about Swedenborg. On April 8, 1766 he admitted to Moses Mendelssohn that "my own mind was in a state of paradox...I can't help suspecting that there was some truth in the stories mentioned, and the same applies to the principles of reason concerning them, regardless of the absurdity of the former and the incomprehensible character of the concepts, and all the concoctions surrounding them, which render them valueless." Kant, *Dreams of a Spirit-Seer*, trans. John Manolesco (New York: Vantage Press, 1969), 155f.
5. For the idea that the soul sleeps upon death or is actually annihilated (until resurrection day), see Norman T. Burns, *Christian Mortalism from Tyndale to Milton* (Cambridge, MA: Harvard Univ. Press, 1972); Bryan W. Ball, *A Great Expectation: Eschatological Thought in English Protestantism to 1660* (Leiden: E.J. Brill, 1975), 244–6; George H. Williams, "Socinianism and Deism," *Historical Reflections* 2(1975), 265–90; Philippe Ariès, "Une conception ancienne de l'au-delà," *Death in the Middle Ages*, ed. Herman Braet and Werner Verbeke (Leuven: Leuven Univ. Press, 1983), 78–87.
6. Calvin, *Psychopannychia* (CR 33:188) in *Tracts and Treatises in Defense of the Reformed Faith* (Grand Rapids, MI: Eerdmans, 1958), 432. This tract was written in 1534 but not published until 1542. On Calvin's view that souls do not sleep after death, see Harro Höpfl, *The Christian Polity of John Calvin* (Cambridge: Cambridge Univ. Press, 1982), 224–6.
7. Thomas Burnet, *A Treatise Concerning the State of Departed Souls Before, and at, and after the Resurrection* (London: Bettesworth & Hitch, 1733): "peace and rest," 56; "in a state," 119. On British millenarian revivals, see Paul Christianson, *Reformers and Babylon: English Apocalyptic Visions from the Reformation to the Eve of the Civil War* (Toronto: Univ. of Toronto Press, 1978) and Peter Toon, ed., *Puritans, the*

Millennium, and the Future of Israel: Puritan Eschatology 1600 to 1660 (Cambridge: Clarke, 1970).

8. "A Prospect of Heaven Makes Death Easy" (1707) in Arthur M. Eastman et al., eds., *The Norton Anthology of Poetry* (New York: Norton, 1970), 427. According to John Dahle, in *Library of Christian Hymns* (Minneapolis: Augsburg, 1928), II, this is one of the first hymns written by Watts. "It has been related that he wrote this hymn at the age of 21 while enjoying the splendid view over the Isle of Wight from Southampton...A statue of the author has been raised upon the place where the hymn was written. It is turned so as to face the beautiful island upon the other side of 'this narrow sea'." (815f.) Isaac Watts, *The World to Come* (Romsey: Sharp, 1816), 4.

9. Swedenborg, *HH*, no. 1.

10. Emanuel Swedenborg, *The True Christian Religion* (1771, New York: Swedenborg Foundation, 1972), no. 792. To be referred to as *TCR*. Swedenborg, *HH*: "so the one," no. 493.

11. Examples of a child (*homunculus*) symbolizing the soul may be found on the tympanum depicting the Last Judgment at Bourges, Reims, and Paris cathedrals. On the evolution of the artistic representation of the soul and the Flaxman contribution, see H.W. Janson, "Thorvaldsen and England," *Bertel Thorvaldsen* (Cologne: Museen der Stadt Köln, 1977), 109–12, and the same author's "Psyche in Stone: Images of the Soul," *Chrysalis: Journal of the Swedenborg Foundation* (special issue, winter 1985), 31–44. Flaxman's Swedenborgian connections are discussed in David Irwin, *John Flaxman 1755–1826* (London: Studio Vista, 1979), 116–18, and his friendship with William Blake at p. 8.

12. Swedenborg, *TCR*, no. 796.

13. Swedenborg, *HH*: "splendid places," no. 495; "as befits," no. 513. The idea that personality continued after death is hinted at in the writings of Sir Kenelm Digby (1603–1665), who de-emphasized divine judgment. In *Two Treatises...of the Immortality of Reasonable Soules* (Paris: Blaizot, 1644) he wrote that "if a man die in a disorderly affection to anything as to his chief good, he eternally remains, by the necessity of his own nature, in the same affection: and there is no imparity that, to eternal sin, there should be imposed eternal punishment."(445)

14. Swedenborg, *HH*: "on the basis; not clothed with," no. 75; "not formless minds," no. 77.

15. Swedenborg, *The Delights of Wisdom Concerning Conjugial Love* (London: Sweden-

borg Society, 1978), no. 44[1]; to be cited as *CL*.

16. Swedenborg, *HH*: "avenues; like the dwellings," no. 184; "regions that look; live for the," no. 188.

17. Swedenborg, *HH*: "nature was created," no. 102; "The whole natural," no. 89; "Heaven is yoked," no. 112.

18. Swedenborg, *CL*: angels appearing as children, no. 137; *HH*: "involved in intelligence," no. 176; *SD*: "some, when explored...tortured," no. 5899.

19. Swedenborg, *HH*, no. 175.

20. Swedenborg, *CL*, no. 8.

21. Swedenborg, *HH*: "be splendidly housed," no. 358; "the rich enter," no. 357; "in the other life," no. 360.

22. Christophorus Irenaeus, *Spiegel des ewigen Lebens* (Ursel: N. Henricus, 1582): "cities, villages; flowery words," ch. 10 (no pagination). This work provided the model for Nicolai's *Freudenspiegel des ewigen Lebens* (1599; Soest: Mocker & Jahn, 1963): see Martin Lindström, *Philipp Nicolais Verständnis des Christentums* (Gütersloh: Bertelsmann, 1939), 30ff.

23. Philipp Nicolai, "Theoria vitae aeternae," *Erster Theil aller teutschen Schrifften*, ed. Georg Dedeken (Hamburg: Herings, 1617), with separate pagination for "Theoria," 343–74. The lack of a sea on the renewed earth is biblical, cf. Rev. 21:1.

24. Martin of Cochem, *Das grosse Leben Christi* (Mariazell: Holtzmayr, 1753), appendix: "the first thing," 165–6; "what joys could," 167; "a real river; about the heavenly," 170; Christ's palace, 169.

25. On the Zimmermann brothers and Steinhausen see Hermann and Anna Bauer, *Johann Baptist und Dominikus Zimmermann* (Regensburg: Pustet, 1985), 54–7 and 176–89. Peter Hawel analyzes the baroque church as an image or symbol of heaven on the basis of sermons delivered at church dedications and jubilees: *Der spätbarocke Kirchenbau und seine theologische Bedeutung* (Würzburg: Echter, 1987), 331–50. We would like to thank Chris Mooney for pointing out the importance of the church at Steinhausen for our research. He provided us with invaluable information on its artistic composition and its role in reflecting the heavenly court.

26. For Lavater's knowledge of Swedenborg's work, see Alfred Action, *The Letters and Memorials of Emanuel Swedenborg* (Bryn Athyn: Swedenborg Scientific Association, 1955), II, 641–3, and Ernst Benz, "Swedenborg und Lavater," *Zeitschrift für Kirchengeschichte* 57(1938), 153–216. Benz speculates that Lava-

ter was largely inspired by Swedenborg whom he tried to contact in vain in order to have Swedenborg's opinion on his books. He also asked for information about a dead friend (155f.). Lavater seems to have avoided acknowledging his indebtedness to Swedenborg because of Kant's critique in *Dreams of a Spirit Seer*.

27. Johann Caspar Lavater, *Aussichten in die Ewigkeit in Briefen an J.G. Zimmermann*, 2nd ed. (Hamburg: Buchhändlergesellschaft, 1773): "pleasure travels to," III, 99; "the natural climate," I, 125; "should it be unworthy," III, 96; "why should it be unsound," III, 97; "we will have," III, 93.

28. Clarke Garrett, "Swedenborg and the Mystical Enlightenment in Late Eighteenth-Century England," *Journal of the History of Ideas* 45(1984), 67–81, at 68. For a discussion of Swedenborg's scientific outlook, see Sigstedt, *The Swedenborg Epic*, 107–17 ("The Universe a Mechanism") and 149–59 ("The Search for the Soul").

29. Swedenborg, *The Apocalypse Explained*, 11th ed. (New York: Swedenborg Foundation, 1976) (to be abbreviated AE): "understanding is raised," no. 834; *The Divine Love and Wisdom* (New York: Swedenborg Foundation, 1976): "sometimes suffer hard," no. 253; *Heavenly Arcana* (London: Swedenborg Society, 1967): obedience, no. 9812 (to be cited HA); *HH*: "in cases of," no. 215; "are especially involved," no. 223; "but they cannot," no. 48.

30. Swedenborg, *HH*: "The angels are," no. 280; "a very beautiful," no. 341; "houses of God," no. 223; preaching, no. 225.

31. Swedenborg, *SD*: "think interiorly," no. 5518; beards, nos. 5126–7 and 5131; writing, 5579; *HH*: no government, no. 214. For Swedenborg's opinion on Africa, see J.D. Odhner, "Reflections on Africa," *The New Philosophy* 81(1978), 255–70. Swedenborg's idea of the black race's religious nobility has helped create the African state of Liberia and substantial Swedenborgian communities in several parts of Africa: see Morton D. Paley, "A New Heaven is Begun," *Blake* 13(1979), 64–91, at 83ff., and Kurt Hutten, *Seher, Grübler, Enthusiasten*, 12th ed. (Stuttgart: Quell, 1982), 580f.

32. Swedenborg, *HH*: "more inward states," no. 412; "people in heaven," no. 414.

33. Swedenborg, *HH*: "when they are... during the year," no. 155; "perception and awareness," no. 158.

34. Swedenborg, *HH*, no. 405.

35. Swedenborg, *HA*, no. 454.

36. Swedenborg, *SD*: young maidens, no.

5661; mothers, no. 5668 (and *HH*, no. 332); *HH*: angels sent to earth, no. 391; "civic concerns," no. 393; "are thrown out," no. 64.

37. Calvin, *Psychopannychia*, 435 (*CR* 33: 190f.).

38. Calvin, *Psychopannychia*, 463 (*CR* 33: 211).

39. Peter Gay, *The Enlightenment: An Interpretation* (New York: Knopf, 1969), II, 45.

40. Gay, *The Enlightenment*, II, 105. The classic discussion of eighteenth-century concepts of progress is Carl L. Becker, *The Heavenly City of the Eighteenth-Century Philosophers* (New Haven: Yale University Press, 1932), 119–68. The argument for the Christian origins of the concept of progress is contained in Ernest Lee Tuveson, *Millennium and Utopia: A Study in the Background of the Idea of Progress* (1949; New York: Harper Torchbooks, 1964). A good summary of the debate is W. Warren Wagar, "Modern Views of the Origins of the Idea of Progress," *Journal of the History of Ideas* 28(1967), 55–70. The last chapter of Antoine-Nicolas de Condorcet, *Sketch for a Historical Picture of the Progress of the Human Mind*, trans. J. Barraclough (1793; London: Weidenfeld & Nicolson, 1955) is entitled "The Tenth State: The Future Progress of the Human Mind" (173).

41. William Assheton, *A Vindication of the Immortality of the Soul and a Future State* (London, 1703), 57–60.

An early author to argue heavenly progress was Hugh McCaughwell (1575–1626), an Irish Franciscan friar who taught in Rome. In his notes on the work of the medieval theologian Duns Scotus he wrote, in tantalizing brevity, that "the saints will not have all the secondary perfections [automatically], and therefore by way of their own creativity will be able to procure them, according to their free will." He also suggested that thereby "the secondary beatitude [the one based on other creatures] can grow indefinitely." John Duns Scotus, *Opera omnia* (Lyons 1639; rprt. Hildesheim: Olms, 1968), X, 605 and XI/1, 296.

The earliest discussion of progress in heaven in English appears to be in a book by "a country gentleman," *The Future State: or, A Discourse Attempting Some Display of the Souls' Happiness in Regard to that Eternally Progressive Knowledge, or Eternal Increase of Knowledge, and the Consequences of it, which Is Amongst the Blessed in Heaven* (London: Greenwood, 1683). He defends the idea that there will be activity in the hereafter because man is essentially an active being. Activity, however, is referred to only in intellectual terms. The author does imagine that people will travel from one heavenly country to the next studying the customs, manners, laws, and institutions under which the saints live (36f.). Isaac Watts commented approvingly on this work in a footnote to his 1722 sermon "Death and Heaven; or the Last Enemy Conquered, and Separate Spirits Made Perfect" (416; see below, n. 43). *The Future State* became quite popular in the eighteenth century; there exist several German editions (1729 and after), and a French translation printed in Amsterdam in 1700.

42. Joseph Addison in *Spectator* no. 111, July 7, 1711 in Donald F. Bond, ed., *The Spectator* (Oxford: Clarendon Press, 1965), I, 456–9. Swedenborg may have read this text on one of his early stays in Britain, see editor's note on *SD* no. 5565.

43. Isaac Watts, *Death and Heaven; or the Last Enemy Conquered, and Separate Spirits Made Perfect; With an Account of the Rich Variety of their Employments and Pleasures,* Discourse II, "The Happiness of Separate Spirits" in Watts, *Works* (London: Longman, Hurst, Rees, Orme & Brown, 1812), II, 374–442, at 386; Arthur Paul Davis, *Isaac Watts: His Life and Works* (New York: Dryden Press, 1943), 109.

44. Watts, *Works*, II: "why should not," 386; "perfect and free," 395.

45. Watts, *Works* II, 398–9.

46. Watts, *Works* II, 402–3. Although never at the same level of detail as Watts, the American Puritan Cotton Mather (1663–1728) voiced similar concerns. He wrote in *Coelestinus* (Boston: Kneeland for Belknap, 1723) that "the blessed God will go on to show wonders unto His raised ones, in the employments that shall be assigned unto them. It is among the Songs of the Redeemed, Rev. 5:10: *Thou hast made us unto our God, kings and priests, and we shall reign over the earth.* Our Lord will make his raised ones to be the teachers and the rulers of the nations, while the long, long, long day of judgment shall be going on." (149f.)

47. Watts, *Works* II, 404.

48. Watts, *Works* II: "our Lord Jesus...of saints above," 400f.; "most delightfully engaged," 402; "planetary worlds besides," 403; "when a blessed," 407. While Watts infers that the saints will grow in knowledge of their heavenly world as well as of God, Cotton Mather comments more traditionally in *Coelestinus* that "a glorious Christ illuminating of thy mind in the heavenly world will make the discoveries of God unto thee. But the knowledge of God will be eternally progressive. T'wil be impossible for a finite being to take in all at once. Nothing less than eternity can take in all that is to be found in an infinite God. Thy knowledge of God will ever be proceeding with new and fresh discoveries. By what means, besides a more immediate irradiation, the discoveries of God will then be carried on; 'tis as yet unknown to us. What will be the intuition of God, what will be the revelation from God, who can say?" (145)

49. Watts, *Works* II, 387.

50. Nicolai, *Freudenspiegel*: "parents and children; with an ardent," 92; "Theoria": "love and friendship," 399.

51. Nicolai, *Freudenspiegel*: "the Elysian field," 312; "no sinful concupiscence," 92.

52. Henry More, *The Immortality of the Soul* (London: Morden, 1659): "aerial genii," 413; "sing and play...terrestrial body," 420.

53. More, *The Immortality of the Soul*, 413.

54. *The Confessions of Jean-Jacques Rousseau* (New York: The Modern Library, n.d.), 428 [book 9].

55. Jean H. Hagstrum, *Sex and Sensibility: Ideal and Erotic Love from Milton to Mozart* (Chicago: Univ. of Chicago Press, 1980), 234. Jean-Jacques Rousseau, *La Nouvelle Héloïse. Julie, or the New Eloise. Letters of Two Lovers, Inhabitants of a Small Town at the Foot of the Alps,* trans. and abridged by Judith H. McDowell (University Park, PA: Pennsylvania State Univ. Press, 1968), 407. The debate between Julie and the Protestant minister is missing from the abridged ed. but it occurs in the 1769 English translation: Jean-Jacques Rousseau, *Eloisa; or, Series of Original Letters* (London: Becket & DeHondt, 1769), IV, 199f.

56. Lavater, *Aussichten in die Ewigkeit*, III, 64.

57. Christoph Martin Wieland, *Briefe von Verstorbenen an hinterlassene Freunde* (Zurich: Orell, 1753), 100f.; Richard Price, *Four Dissertations* (London: Cadell, 1777), 321f.; Elizabeth Rowe, "On Heaven," in Hoxie N. Fairchild, *Religious Trends in English Poetry* (New York: Columbia Univ. Press, 1939), I, 138; Denis Diderot, *Correspondence,* ed. Georges Roth (Paris: Ed. de Minuit, 1956), II, 284 [letter of Oct. 15, 1759].

58. François Arnaux, *Merveilles de l'autre monde* (Lyons: Rigaud, 1614). The Bibliothèque Nationale catalogues the name as "Arnoulx"; some editions of the book have Arnoux. The issue of smell is discussed in Vol. II, chap. 19. His acceptance of the saints' ability to appreciate the sense of smell in heaven comes from Aquinas, *Commentary on the Sentences,* IV, 44, 3:1 (end).

59. Arnaux, *Merveilles*, II, 33f.

60. Arnaux, *Merveilles*, II: "my Paradise," 41; "nothing greater," 53f.; "there people talk," 42.

61. Martin of Cochem, *Das grosse Leben Christi*, appendix: "visit each other," 174; "preference and love...damnation," 180.

62. Martin of Cochem, *Das grosse Leben Christi*, appendix, 180.

63. Martin of Cochem, *Das grosse Leben Christi*, part II, 580. Baroque theater, court pageants, and Jesuit drama of the late seventeenth century are discussed in Margarete Baur-Heinhold, *Theater des Barock* (Munich: Callwey, 1966), 9–32, and Heinz Kindermann, *Theatergeschichte Europas*, 2nd ed. (Salzburg: O. Müller, 1972), IV, 55–65.

64. A discussion of the baroque church as a symbol of the total church is included in Karsten Harries, *The Bavarian Rococo Church: Between Faith and Aestheticism* (New Haven: Yale Univ. Press, 1983), 176–95.

65. Harries, *The Bavarian Rococo Church*, 200–3.

66. Swedenborg, *AE*, no. 993; *CL*: "love is man's," no. 36.

67. Swedenborg, *HH*: "thinks on the," no. 368; *CL*: "beauty and grace...thus wise," no. 56.

68. Swedenborg, *CL*: "the conjunction of," no. 156F; *HH*: "there are spiritual," no. 382B; *AE*: "I have seen," no. 1004. The divine revelation or illumination concerning the true meaning of Matt. 22:23f. is referred to in *CL* 44[10].

69. Swedenborg, *CL*, no. 54. Swedenborg's friendship with Countess Gyllenborg-Stjerncrona is described in R.L. Tafel, *Documents Concerning the Life and Character of Emanuel Swedenborg* (London: Swedenborg Society, 1875), I, 699f.

70. Swedenborg, *CL*, no. 20.

71. Swedenborg, *CL*, nos. 20 and 21.

72. Swedenborg, *CL*: "for when love," no. 44; "the male is...perceptible," no. 51.

73. Swedenborg, *AE*: "returns to the flower," no. 1000; "declare that they...eternity," no. 992.

74. Hugo L. Odhner, *The Spiritual World* (Bryn Athyn, PA: Academy Publications, 1968), 260; Swedenborg, *CL*, no. 44.

75. Swedenborg, *CL*, no. 44.

76. The development of the city as a center of leisure is recounted in Mark Girouard, *Cities and People: A Social and Architectural History* (New Haven: Yale Univ. Press, 1985), 181–210.

77. Swedenborg, *HH*: "no dominance in," no. 369; *CL*: heavenly wedding, no. 20.

78. Swedenborg, *CL*, nos. 32–3. On the symbolism of Christian marriages, see Kenneth Stevenson, *Nuptial Blessing: A Study of Christian Marriage Rites* (New York: Oxford Univ. Press, 1983).

79. Swedenborg's anti-theocentric story of priests and the people is from, *CL*, no. 9.

80. Lavater, *Aussichten in die Ewigkeit*, III, 93.

81. *The Works of the Rev. John Wesley*, 11th ed. (London: John Mason, 1856): "much applauded wit," VI, 307; "and to crown," VI, 278; "see God, to," XIII, 29. Wesley was well aware of the writings of Swedenborg and commented on them several times: in 1770, "His waking dreams are so wild, so far remote both from Scripture and common sense, that one might as easily swallow the stories of 'Tom Thumb,' or 'Jack the Giant-Killer' " (III, 368) and in 1779, "His ideas of heaven are low, groveling, just suiting a Mahometan paradise" (IV, 142). Wesley's longest analysis of Swedenborg is his 1782 "Thoughts on the Writings of Baron Swedenborg" (XIII, 401–22). Although Wesley quotes the visionary extensively he insists that "it would be tedious to point out the particular oddities and absurdities in the preceding account. It may suffice to remark in general, that is contains nothing sublime, nothing worthy the dignity of the subject." (XIII, 417).

CHAPTER EIGHT

1. Lawrence Stone, *The Family, Sex and Marriage in England, 1500–1800* (New York: Harper & Row, 1977) and Edward Shorter, *The Making of the Modern Family* (New York: Basic Books, 1975) are the major historical studies for the evolution of "affective individualism." Recently, however, historians have challenged the findings of Stone and Shorter, see esp. Alan Macfarlane's review of Stone in *History and Theory* 18 (1979), 103–26 and Macfarlane, *Marriage and Love in England: Modes of Reproduction 1300–1840* (Oxford: Blackwell, 1986). Macfarlane rejects Stone's emergence of "affective individualism" during the late seventeenth century, arguing that it must date back at least to the Middle Ages. No one doubts, however, that the romantic attitude to love dominated the nineteenth century.

2. On Miton's portrayal of heaven, see Roland Mushat Frye, *Milton's Imagery and the Visual Arts* (Princeton: Princeton Univ. Press, 1978), 189–205; John R. Knott, *Milton's Pastoral Vision* (Chicago: Univ. of Chicago Press, 1971), 62–87, and Michael Murrin, "The Language of Milton's Heaven," *Modern Philology* 74 (1976/

7), 350–65. Milton's understanding of death is perceptively discussed in Julia J. Smith, "Milton and Death," *Durham University Journal* 79 (1986/7), 15–22.

3. John Milton, *Paradise Lost*, V, 267–8.

4. Milton, *Paradise Lost*: "What if earth" V, 574–6; "that God's own ear," V, 626–7; "on flow'rs," V, 636–8; "living Streams," V, 652–7; "the soft downy," IV, 334.

5. Milton, *Paradise Lost*: sweet-smelling herbs, IV, 709; "Adam from his," IV, 742–3; "here passion," VIII, 530–31; "loveless, joyless," IV, 766–7.

6. Milton, *Paradise Lost*, VIII, 56. The idea of Edenic love as devoid of self-love and lust is described in Jean H. Hagstrum, *Sex and Sensibility: Ideal and Erotic Love from Milton to Mozart* (Chicago: Univ. of Chicago Press, 1980), 24–49 ("Milton and the Ideal of Heterosexual Friendship"). On prelapsarian sexuality, see James Grantham Turner, *One Flesh: Paradisal Marriage and Sexual Relations in the Age of Milton* (Oxford: Clarendon Press, 1987), esp. pp. 40–52 on the origins of the concept in Augustine; Michael Müller, *Die Lehre des Hl. Augustinus von der Paradiesehe und ihre Auswirkung in der Sexualethik* (Regensburg: Pustet, 1954); Peter Lindenbaum, "Lovemaking in Milton's Paradise," James D. Simmonds, ed., *Milton Studies* (Pittsburg: Univ. of Pittsburg Press, 1975), VI, 277–305, now in Lindenbaum, *Changing Landscapes: Anti-Pastoral Sentiment in the English Renaissance* (Athens, GA: Univ. of Georgia Press, 1986), 158–77.

Milton apparently developed an idea of Augustine's and commented on by other Christian theologians including Luther (Turner, 58). Augustine explained that, "although according to Scripture our first parents were not united and did not beget children before being expelled from Paradise, I do not see why there should not have been, even in Paradise, an honorable marriage bond and a conjugal bed without stain...They would have produced the fetus from their own seeds but without any irritating heat of lust and without any hardships and birth pangs." Since there would have been no sin or death, reproduction would take place only until a suitable population was reached. At a certain point, God would exchange their animal bodies for a glorified body of the angelic kind. *Literal Commentary on Genesis*, 9:1, 6 (*PL* 34:395).

7. Milton, *Paradise Lost*, VIII, 588–92.

8. Milton describes how both body and soul are dissolved at death, in order to be recreated at the resurrection in *The Christian Doctrine*, 1:13, found in *Complete Prose Works of John Milton* (New Haven: Yale Univ. Press, 1973), VI, 399–414; see Leonora Leet Brodwin, "The Dissolution of Satan in *Paradise Lost*: A Study of Milton's Heretical Eschatology," *Milton Studies* (1975), VIII, 165–207; Milton, *Paradise Lost*: "by looks only...Soul with Soul," VIII, 616–29; Edward LeComte, *Milton and Sex* (New York: Columbia Univ. Press, 1978), 93.

9. According to Hugo Lj. Odhner's paper "Swedenborg's Epic of Paradise and Its Literary Sources," Swedenborg sent a letter to Eric Benzelius in 1712 recommending Milton as worthy of reading. Odhner points out some similarities between Milton and Swedenborg but in a very uncritical manner. Pamphlet available from The General Church of the New Jerusalem, Bryn Athyn, PA. Milton, *Paradise Lost*: "Man hath his," IV, 618–19. On work in paradise, see Diana K. McColley, *Milton's Eve* (Urbana: Univ. of Illinois Press, 1983), 110–39; Anthony Lee, *The Georgic Revolution* (Princeton, NJ: Princeton Univ. Press, 1985), 316–20, and Peter Lindenbaum, *Changing Landscapes*, 151–7.

10. Milton, *Paradise Lost*: "amorous play," IX, 1045.1049–50; "Total they mix," VIII, 627.

11. Milton, *Paradise Lost*, IX, 958–9; Irving Singer, *The Nature of Love* (Chicago: Univ. of Chicago Press, 1984), II, 244.

12. Although he uses a different notion of the myth of love, Denis de Rougemont, *Love in the Western World*, trans. Montgomery Belgion (1940; rprt. Princeton: Princeton Univ. Press, 1983), 213–35, is helpful; Singer, *The Nature of Love* (Chicago: Univ. of Chicago Press, 1966), I, 49–90, provides a good introduction to the Platonic meaning of *eros*.

13. Blake, "Descriptive Catalogue" (1809) in *The Poetry and Prose of William Blake*, ed. David V. Erdman, 4th ed. (Garden City, NY: Doubleday, 1970), 537. See also the discussion in Morton D. Paley, " 'A New Heaven is Begun': Blake and Swedenborgianism," Harvey F. Bellin and Darrell Ruhl, eds., *Blake and Swedenborg: Opposition Is True Friendship* (New York: Swedenborg Foundation, 1985), 15–34, and Désirée Hirst, *Hidden Riches; Traditional Symbolism from the Renaissance to Blake* (New York: Barnes & Noble, 1964), 200–26. Blake also knew of the work of Johann Caspar Lavater, see Lavater, *Aphorisms on Man* (1788); *A Facsimile Reproduction of William Blake's Copy*, introd. by R.J. Shroyer (Delmar, NY: Scholars' Facsimiles & Reprints, 1980). While this book does not comment on heaven, we suspect that Blake might have learned of Lavater's views from Henry Fuseli [Johann Heinrich Füssli] – a friend of both men and

translator of *Aphorisms*.

14. Blake, "Vision of the Last Judgment," *William Blake's Writings*, ed. G. E. Bentley (Oxford: Oxford Univ. Press, 1978), II: "all those are Cast," 1007; "The World of Imagination; Vegetable Glass," 1010; "Whenever any Individual," 1021f.

15. Blake, *Writings*, II: "is not Fable," 1007; "Stupendous Visions," 1008; "Reject Error," 1023. The non-judgmental Christ of Blake is discussed in David Bindman, "Apocalypse and Last Judgment," *Blake as an Artist* (Oxford: Phaidon, 1977), 163–71 esp. at 167, and that of Michelangelo in Leo Steinberg, "Michelangelo's Last Judgment as Merciful Heresy," *Art in America* 63 (Nov.–Dec., 1975), 49–63, and John W. Dixon, "The Christology of Michelangelo: The Sistine Chapel," *Journal of the American Academy of Religion* 55(1987), 503–33.

16. Letter of Blake to Ozias Humphry (2nd draft, Febr. 1808) published in *The Letters of William Blake*, ed. Geoffrey Keynes, 3rd ed. (Oxford: Clarendon Press, 1980), 134 (no. 110).

17. Blake, *Writings*, II: "a Youthful couple," 1016; "Powers in Man," 1017; "A Female descends," 1018. The influence of Swedenborg on Blake's portrayal of the Last Judgment is completely overlooked in Albert S. Roe, "A Drawing of the Last Judgment," *Huntington Library Quarterly* 21 (1957), 37–55.

18. Blake, *Writings*, II: "in Paradise," 1025; "Men are admitted; the Treasures of," 1024.

19. Blake, *Writings*, II: "Vision or Imagination", 1007. Blake: "the Body springs," in the rprt. part of Robert N. Essick and Morton D. Paley, *Robert Blair's The Grave* (London: Scholar Press, 1982), 35. Blake was a friend of sculptor John Flaxman, a Swedenborgian. According to S. Foster Damon, ed., *Blair's Grave. A Prophetic Book* (Providence, RI: Brown Univ. Press, 1963), n.p., Flaxman may have suggested that Blake be commissioned to do the drawings for "The Grave."

20. Essick and Paley, *Robert Blair's The Grave*: "clearly physical and," 57; Blair: "Great promis'd day," in the rprt. section of *Robert Blair's The Grave*, 28.

21. Raymond Immerwahr, "The Word 'Romantisch' and its History," Siegbert Prawer, ed., *The Romantic Period in Germany* (New York: Schocken, 1970), 34–63, at 34.

22. Singer, *The Nature of Love*, II, 385; Friedrich Schlegel, *Lucinde and the Fragments*, trans. Peter Firchow (Minneapolis: Univ. of Minnesota Press, 1971), 113.

23. Schlegel, *Lucinde*, 48; Singer, *The Nature*

of *Love*, II, 434.

24. Novalis, "Lied der Toten," in *Schriften*, ed. Paul Kluckhon and Richard Samuel, 3rd. ed. (Stuttgart: Kohlhammer, 1977) I, 350–55: "No wounds can," stanza 4; children, heroes, giants, stanza 3; "Now for us," stanza 7; "sweet talk of," stanza 8; "deeply touched," stanza 5; "future companions," stanza 14; "the desire to," stanza 9; "borrowed light," stanza 15. A brief summary of Novalis and German Romanticism is contained in Robert M. Wernaer, *Romanticism and the Romantic School in Germany* (New York: Haskell House, 1966), 76–82; 208–29. Novalis appears to have known the work of Lavater, Boehme, and perhaps Swedenborg, see Jacques Roos, *Aspects littéraires du mysticisme philosophique et l'influence de Boehme et de Swedenborg* (Strasbourg: P.-H. Heitz, 1952), 231–7.

25. Friedrich Schiller, "Elysium," John Boening, ed., *The Reception of Classical German Literature in England, 1760–1860* (New York: Garland Publishing, 1977), X, 388.

26. Johann Wolfgang von Goethe, *The Sorrows of Young Werther*, trans. Victor Lange (New York: Holt, Rinehart & Winston, 1949), 121. The background of the meeting-again motif in Goethe is discussed in Eudo C. Mason, "Wir sehen uns wieder! Zu einem Leitmotiv des Dichtens und Denkens im 18. Jahrhundert," *Literaturwissenschaftliches Jahrbuch*, New Series 5 (1964), 79–109. Goethe's knowledge of Swedenborg's works is discussed in Michael Heinrichs, *Emanuel Swedenborg in Deutschland* (Frankfurt: P.D. Lang, 1979), 174–205.

27. Goethe's use of Rousseau's *Nouvelle Héloïse* as model for *Werther* is discussed in Carl Hammer, *Goethe and Rousseau* (Lexington: Univ. Press of Kentucky, 1973), 65–70. The translation of the last verse of *Faust II* is from Eudo C. Mason, *Goethe's Faust: Its Genesis and Purport* (Berkeley: Univ. of California Press, 1977), 359. Helpful notes on the last sections of *Faust II* are by editor Cyrus Hamlin in *Faust: A Tragedy*, trans. Walter Arndt (New York: W.W. Norton, 1979), 344f.

28. Jacob Steiner discusses the Eternal Masculine and the Eternal Feminine in *Faust II* but notes only the juxtaposition, not the union: "Die letzte Szene von Goethes Faust," *Etudes germaniques* 38 (1983), 147–55. A more congenial reading of Faust is offered by Gottlieb C.L. Schuchard, "The Last Scene in Goethe's Faust," *Publications of the Modern Language Association* 64 (1949), 417–44. We would like to thank Jane Brown for directing us to this part of *Faust* and helping us interpret its meaning.

29. *The Ring and the Book*, part 7: "Pompilia":

"No end of," line 554; "hooknosed and," line 369; "Count Guido, take," lines 582–3; "'Tis there they," line 1827; "counterfeit, Mere," lines 1824–5; "in heaven we," line 1826. "Pompilia" is printed in *The Complete Works of Robert Browning*, ed. Charlotte Porter and Helen A. Clarke (New York: Sproul, 1898), VII, 1–58.

30. "To Miss E[lizabeth] P[igot]" and "If that High World" in Lord Byron, *The Complete Poetical Works*, ed. Jerome J. McGann (Oxford: Clarendon Press, 1980/81), I, 144–6 and III, 290f.

31. *The Complete Poems of Emily Dickinson*, ed. Thomas H. Johnson (Boston: Little, Brown & Co., 1960), poem 322. Hereafter the poems will be cited only by their Johnson number (e.g. J322). Barton Levi St. Armand interpretes Dickinson's concept of heaven as "domesticated" in "Paradise Deferred: The Image of Heaven in the Work of Emily Dickinson and Elizabeth Stuart Phelps," *American Quarterly* 29 (1977), 55–78, of which a later version appears in this author's *Emily Dickinson and Her Culture* (New York: Cambridge Univ. Press, 1984), 117–51. An alternative interpretation, which assumes that Dickinson took a skeptical stance regarding heaven is Robin Riley Fast, "The One Thing Needful: Dickinson's Dilemma of Home and Heaven," *ESQ: A Journal of the American Renaissance* 27 (1981), 157–69. Joan Burbick in "Emily Dickinson and the Economics of Desire," *American Literature* 58 (1986), 361–78 mentions Dickinson's understanding of heaven as a place for reunited lovers.

32. "It's Sunday," J413; *The Letters of Emily Dickinson*, ed. Thomas H. Johnson (Cambridge: Belknap Press, 1958), II: "will take," 451–2 (#317); Dickinson: "Ransomed folks," J215.

33. Levi St. Armand, "Paradise," 70–71; Dickinson: "Unto the East," J461; "The Life that," J1260.

34. "These Fleshless Lovers," J625. The striving for unity with the beloved is also vividly portrayed in Shelley's poem "Epipsychidion" (1821). J.R. de J. Jackson, *Poetry of the Romantic Period* (London: Routledge & Kegan Paul, 1980), explains that for Shelley "the ambition to unite is in the end incompatible with life itself. Only by dying can the author and Emily become one"(217).

35. "The Blessed Damozel," *The Poetical Works of Dante Gabriel Rossetti*, ed. William M. Rossetti (London: Ellis & Elvey, 1898), 232–6: "The blessed damozel," stanza 1; "her bosom must," stanza 8; "yellow like ripe," stanza 2; "deeper than the depth," stanza 1; "The songs I," stanza 16; "take his hand," stanza 13.

The sensuousness of Dante Gabriel Rossetti's poem is easily contrasted with the poetry of his more pious sister, Christina Rossetti. In her poem "Saints and Angels," she models her description of heaven on Revelation. In spite of this, she still assumes that "You and I who parted will meet in Paradise,/Pass within and sing when the gates unclose." She later explains that "in the life to come which fades not away/Every love shall abide and every lover." *The Poetical Works of Christina Georgina Rossetti*, ed. William Michael Rossetti (London: Macmillan, 1911), 229f.

36. Rossetti, "The Blessed Damozel": "Around her, lovers," stanza 7; "Alas! we two," stanza 17. The idea of lovers in heaven may have derived from Rossetti's spiritualist connections, see Russell M. and Clare R. Goldfarb, *Spiritualism and Nineteenth-Century Letters* (Rutherford, NJ: Fairleigh Dickenson Univ. Press, 1978), 115–20. The possibility of heaven as a union of opposites, including male and female, is intimated in Wendell Stacy Johnson, "D.G. Rossetti as Painter and Poet," *Victorian Poetry* 3 (1965), 9–18. This author, however, is not concerned with the circle of lovers in the background but with the opposition of the Blessed Damozel and her lover. Ronnalie Roper Howard in *The Dark Glass: Vision and Technique in the Poetry of Dante Gabriel Rossetti* (Athens, OH: Ohio Univ. Press, 1972) calls the Blessed Damozel the "Shelleyan 'true mate' for the earthly lover, as he for her, and their desire is the communion of their whole natures" (45). The women of Rossetti's poems and paintings are studied by David Sonstroem, *Rossetti and the Fair Lady* (Middletown, CT: Wesleyan Univ. Press, 1970), 17–48. Sonstroem insists that Rossetti placed himself in his art and poetry, which is why the "Blessed Damozel" assumes a particularly sexual slant. During the time Rossetti was musing over "Blessed Damozel" his lover Lizzie Siddal was withholding her favors from him. Sonstroem explains that "in denying Gabriel 'passion of the naked kind' Lizzie was also denying him Paradise. Rossetti's strong sexual desires and his equation of earthly and heavenly love make it easy to see why he would see sexual consummation as the salvation of his spirit" (48).

37. Rossetti, "Blessed Damozel": "clothed in white," stanza 13; "that living mystic," stanza 15; "He shall fear," stanza 20; "brings us hand," stanza 21; "There will I," stanza 22.

38. Friedrich Schleiermacher, *On Religion: Speeches to its Cultured Despisers*, trans. John Oman (New York: Harper & Row, 1958), 72.

39. Robert M. Patterson, *Visions of Heaven*

for the *Life on Earth* (Philadelphia: Presbyterian Board of Publication, 1877): "would be so," 161; "to most Christians," 162; "heaven reunited friends," 178f.; "tone of voice," 178.

40. François-René Blot, *In Heaven We Know Our Own: or, Solace for the Suffering* (New York: Benziger, 1863), 74; Elie Méric, *The Blessed Will Know Each Other In Heaven* (1881; New York: Catholic Publication Society, 1888), xiv; Wilhelm Schneider, *The Other Life*, trans. Herbert Thurston (New York: Wagner, 1920): "we do not; not exclude the," 160; "feel love, a," 343; Edward Norris Kirk, *Heaven Our Home* (Boston: Rand & Avery, n.d.), 13.

41. Henry Harbaugh, *The Heavenly Home: or, The Employments and Enjoyments of the Saints in Heaven* (Philadelphia: Lindsay & Blakiston, 1853), 125. Henry Harbaugh, *The Heavenly Recognition: or, An Earnest and Scriptural Discussion of the Question, Will we Know our Friends in Heaven?* 5th ed. (Philadelphia: Lindsay & Blakiston, 1853), 247 and 250.

42. John J. Kerr, *Future Recognition: or. The Blessedness of Those 'Who Die in the Lord'* (Philadelphia: Hooker, 1847), 93 and 95; James Miller Killen, *Our Friends in Heaven: or, The Mutual Recognition of the Redeemed in Glory Demonstrated* (Philadelphia: Presbyterian Board of Publication, 1854), 152; Kerr, *Future Recognition*: "as there shall; sensual pleasures shall," 94; "animal and the," 93

43. Samuel Phillips, *The Christian Home. As it is in the Sphere of Nature and the Church* (1859; New York: Gurdon Bill, 1865), 370 and 371; Patterson, *Visions of Heaven*: "merely sensual," 191; "amid the perfectly," 179; Francis W.P. Greenwood, *Sermons of Consolation* (1842; Boston: Ticknor, 1847), 250f.

44. Wilhelm Schneider, *Das Wiedersehen im anderen Leben* (Paderborn: Schöningh, 1879): "the bond once," 117; Schneider, *The Other Life*: inordinate passion, ardent, 343; spiritual union, 161.

45. Schneider, *The Other Life*, 346.

46. Schneider, *The Other Life*, 346.

47. Susan Chitty, *The Beast and the Monk: A Life of Charles Kingsley* (London: Hodder & Stoughton, 1975), 17.

48. *Charles Kingsley: His Letters and Memories of His Life*, ed. by his wife (Leipzig: Tauchnitz, 1881): "the highest state," I, 124; "spiritual and timeless," I, 123; Fanny Grenfell's letter (otherwise unpublished) is cited in Peter Gay, *The Tender Passion* (New York: Oxford Univ. Press, 1986), 305, with implied reference to Milton, *Paradise Lost* IV, 742–3. Kingsley, *His Letters and Memories*: "an old Jewish; if immortality," II, 74.

49. From letters of Charles Kingsley to Fanny Grenfell (1843) in Gay, *Tender Passion*, 308f.

50. Kingsley, *His Letters and Memories*, II: "I am so...shall not be I," 74; "No! I enhance," 76f. For the information about the instructions Queen Victoria left for her funeral we are indebted to the archivist to the royal family at Windsor Castle. Walter L. Arnstein, "Queen Victoria and Religion," Gail Malmgreen, ed., *Religion in the Lives of English Women, 1760–1930* (London: Croom Helm, 1986), 88–128 at 104ff. and 123, comments on the queen's heavenly beliefs.

51. Gay, *Tender Passion*, 293. The role of American Christianity in legitimating ecstatic, sexual pleasure is persuasively analysed in Peter Gardella, *Innocent Ecstasy: How Christianity Gave America an Ethic of Sexual Pleasure* (New York: Oxford Univ. Press, 1985).

52. In 1964 Belknap Press of Harvard University Press reprinted Elizabeth Stuart Phelps's *The Gates Ajar*, with an introduction by Helen Sootin Smith, thus rescuing it from literary oblivion. Since then several articles have set it in social and literary context: Elmer Suderman, "Elizabeth Stuart Phelps and the Gates Ajar Novels," *Journal of Popular Culture* 3 (1969/70), 92–106; Ann Douglas, *The Feminization of American Culture* (New York: Knopf, 1977), 200–26 ("The Domestication of Death"); and the previously cited article by Barton Levi St. Armand (above, n. 31). Biographical information on Phelps and description of the publication success of *The Gates Ajar* series of novels are found in her autobiography: *Chapters from a Life* (Boston: Houghton, Mifflin & Co., 1897). A psycho-social appraisal of Phelps's life is Christine Stansell, "Elizabeth Stuart Phelps: A Study in Female Rebellion," *Massachusetts Review* 13 (1972), 239–56. A more conventional biography is Mary Angela Bennett, *Elizabeth Stuart Phelps* (Philadelphia: Univ. of Pennsylvania Press, 1939).

53. Elizabeth Stuart Phelps, *The Gates Ajar* (Boston: Fields, Osgood & Co., 1868): "something about adoration," 70; "study the character," 69; "pictures of the," 186 and a similar discussion 77ff.

54. James MacDonald, *My Father's House: or, The Heaven of the Bible*, 3rd ed. (New York: Scribner, 1856), 240; Phillips, *The Christian Home*, 367 and 368. The idea of a heaven made up of families was not unique to white Victorian America. In spite of a radically different social setting, black slave religion also described heaven as home: see Lewis V. Baldwin, "A Home in dat Rock: Afro-American Folk Sources and Slave Visions of Heaven and Hell," *Journal*

of Religious Thought 41 (1984), 38–57, and David R. Roediger, "And Die in Dixie: Funerals, Death, and Heaven in the Slave Community 1700–1865," *Massachusetts Review* 22 (1981), 163–83.

55. Phelps, *The Gates Ajar*, 74; Harbaugh, *Heavenly Recognition*, 75–6; Alfred Nevin, ed., *Encyclopædia of the Presbyterian Church* (Philadelphia: Presbyterian Publishing Co., 1884), 315; Phelps, *The Gates Ajar*, 75.

56. Phelps, *The Gates Ajar*, 140; Phelps, *Beyond the Gates* (Boston: Houghton, Mifflin & Co., 1883), 124f.

57. Agnes L. Pratt, "The City Beyond: The Story of One Who Dwells in the Next Planet," *Godey's Magazine* 137(June–July, 1898), 49–62 and 161–172, at 165; Phelps, *The Gates Ajar*, 137.

58. George Cheever, *The Powers of the World to Come: and The Church's Stewardship, as Invested with Them* (New York: Robert Carter & Bros., 1853), 247; J. Clement, "The Infant," *Godey's Lady's Book* 41(Nov., 1850), 259; Blot, *In Heaven We Know Our Own*, 88; William B. Moore and Stephen C. Davies, "Rosa is an Angel Now: Epitaphs from Crawford County, Pennsylvania. Part 2," *Western Pennsylvania Historical Magazine* 58 (1975), 185–253: "Sadie was too," 203.

59. Cheever, *Powers of the World to Come*, 250; George Wood, *Future Life: or, Scenes in Another World* (New York: Derby & Jackson, 1858) with the discussion with Persis about marriage in heaven at 78; James Wood, "Household Religion," *Home, School, and Church: The Presbyterian Education Repository* 8 (1858), 2–20, at 19.

60. "In Heaven We Will Know Our Own" (review), *Catholic World* 18 (1870), 139f.; Blot, *In Heaven We Know Our Own*, 103 and 136. Blot's book is based on Casto Innocente Ansaldi, *Della speranza e della consolazione di rivedere i cari nostri nell' altera vita* (Turin: Derossi, 1772) and the quote "Oh! how pleasant" (136) is from Francis de Sales, *Introduction to the Devout Life*, 3:19.

61. Leo XIII, "Quod apostolici muneris," J.J. Wynne, ed., *The Great Encyclical Letters of Pope Leo XIII* (New York, 1903), 30; "Hymn to the Holy Family," Francis X. Lasance, ed., *The Catholic Girl's Guide* (New York: Benziger, 1906), 414; Cardinal Manning, "In Heaven We Know Our Own," *Sacred Heart Review* (Oct. 19, 1889), 6. The late nineteenth-century Catholic move to promote the family as a bulwark against modern social trends is discussed in Colleen McDannell, *The Christian Home in Victorian America 1840–1900* (Bloomington,

IN: Indiana Univ. Press, 1986), 16.

62. Phelps, *The Gates Ajar*: "near you," 87; angels are dead Christians, 90; Swedenborg, 169–173; Channing, "The Future Life" (preached Easter, 1834), *The Works of William E. Channing* (Boston: American Unitarian Association, 1880), 363; George Hepworth, *They Met in Heaven* (New York: Dutton, 1894), 149.

63. Greenwood, *Sermons of Consolation*, 241.

64. Phelps, *The Gates Ajar*, 83; Kirk, *Heaven Our Home*, 17 [Harriet Atwood Newell, 1793–1812, accompanied her husband as a missionary to India. Newell, barely nineteen, gave birth prematurely on board their ship which had been turned away from landing by the British East Indies Company. The child died, as did Newell upon landing in Mauritius. Newell was thus the first American to die in foreign missionary service, and became the proto-martyr of the foreign missions.] Phillips, *The Christian Home*, 364; MacDonald, *My Father's House*, 246.

65. Rebecca Springer, *Intra Muros* (Elgin, IL: Cook, 1898), 87; Phelps, *Beyond the Gates*: Beethoven, Raphael, 156–68; "was I not," 182.

66. Phelps, *Beyond the Gates*: "the marriages of," 149; "soul of my," 192, "by His blessing," 194.

67. Pratt, "The City Beyond," 167.

68. Phelps, *The Gates Ajar*: "Yes, my child," 197–8; "abstract Grandeur," 196; "as a man," 201 [Exod. 33:11]; "knows exactly what... intensely," 202; Springer, *Intra Muros*, 73.

69. Patterson, *Visions of Heaven*, 185; Job S. Mills, *A Manual of Family Worship* (Dayton, OH: Funk, 1900), 54. For a discussion of Protestant family worship, see McDannell, *The Christian Home*, 77–85.

70. Phelps, *The Gates Ajar*, 145; on Protestant and Catholic forms of sabbath devotion, see McDannell, *The Christian Home*, 91–6.

71. Catharine Sedgwick, *Home*, 20th ed. (1835; Boston: Munroe, 1850), 54–66; Phelps, *The Gates Ajar*, 146.

72. *Mark Twain in Eruption*, ed. with introduction by Bernard DeVoto (New York: Harper, 1940), 247. In 1868 Mark Twain wrote a short story on heaven which eventually turned into a satire of *The Gates Ajar*. Twain had reservations about publishing it and excerpts were not printed until late 1907. The full version, *An Extract from Captain Stormfield's Visit to Heaven*, was not published until after his death. Although his burlesque is quite mild, Twain was aware of the serious attention readers gave to the *Gates Ajar* series. He mused that Captain Stormfield "is not likely to see the light for fifty years yet, and at that time I shall have been so long under

the sod that I shan't care about the results" (248). See also Robert A. Rees, "Captain Stormfield's Visit to Heaven and *The Gates Ajar*," *English Language Notes* 7(1969/70), 197–202. Agnes Replier, "Heaven in Recent Fiction," *Catholic World* 40 (1885), 843–52, at 848; Maurice Egan, *A Marriage of Reason* (Baltimore: Murphy, 1893), 8; Ralph Waldo Emerson, *Representative Men: Seven Lectures* (Boston: Houghton, Mifflin & Co., 1876), 123f. Douglas, *Feminization of American Culture*, 226.

73. "The Annexation of Heaven," *Atlantic* 53 (Jan., 1884), 135–43; *The Gates Ajar Critically Examined*, by a Dean (London: Hatchards, 1871), 45f. [quoting Phil. 1:23].

CHAPTER NINE

1. Leslie D. Weatherhead, *After Death* (New York: Abingdon, 1936), 54–6. Rev. Weatherhead's belief in the growth of the soul after death was certainly colored by his spiritualist associations. Although he was the minister of the City Temple, London (1936–60) and the president of the Methodist Conference (1955–6), he was also an active member of the Society for Psychical Research. His other books include *The Resurrection of Christ in the Light of Modern Science and Psychical Research* (1959) and *Life Begins at Death* (1969). Longfellow's poem is entitled "Resignation."

2. Examples of Origen's belief in progress after death can be found in: *On the Principal Doctrines* (*De principiis*) 2: 11, 6 (*PG* 11: 254f.); *Commentary on 1 Thessalonians* (*PG* 14: 1302) and *Homily on Numbers* 27:4, 6 (*PG* 12:784–7); see also Leonhard Atzberger, *Geschichte der christlichen Eschatologie* (Freiburg: Herder, 1896), 395–8. Leibniz, *Nouveaux Essais* II, 21, in Gottfried Wilhelm Leibniz, *Sämtliche Schriften und Briefe*, ed. Deutsche Akademie der Wissenschaften zu Berlin (Berlin: Akademie-Verlag, 1962), 6th ser., VI, 189, and Leibniz, *Confessio philosophi*, ed. Otto Saame (Frankfurt: Klostermann, 1967), 100f. The second Leibniz text on the progress of the blessed dates from 1673 but remained unpublished until 1915; for a similar statement by Leibniz, see his "Principles of Nature and of Grace" (1714) in Leibniz, *Philosophical Papers and Letters*, trans. Leroy E. Loemker (Chicago: Univ. of Chicago Press, 1956), 1043. How Protestant ideas on work filtered into British literature and thus to the educated and gentry is described in Anthony Low, *The Georgic Revolution* (Princeton: Princeton Univ. Press, 1985).

3. Kant, *Critique of Practical Reason*, trans. L. W. Beck (1788; Indianapolis, IN: Bobbs-Merrill, 1956), 127. Kant wrote in 1794 that "the idea that one day all change – and with it, time itself – will come to an end scandalizes our imagination. Nature as a whole would become motionless and as it were petrified: the last thought, the final emotion of a thinking subject would remain static and immobile without any alteration. For a being which can think of its existence and the extension thereof only within time, such a life – if it can thus be called – must appear as annihilation." Kant, *The End of All Things* in *Kants Werke*, ed. Königlich-preussische Akademie der Wissenschaften (rprt. Berlin: de Gruyter, 1968), VIII, 334.

4. The concept of a kinetic revolution occurring among the New England Transcendentalists is discussed in Catherine L. Albanese, *Corresponding Motion: Transcendental Religion and the New America* (Philadelphia: Temple Univ. Press, 1977), 56–97; Emerson to Samuel G. Ward, c. 1840, *Letters from Ralph Waldo Emerson to a Friend, 1838–1853*, ed. Charles Eliot Norton (Boston: Houghton Mifflin, 1899), 30; Ralph Waldo Emerson, *The Journals and Miscellaneous Notebooks*, ed. William H. Gilman et al. (Cambridge, MA: Belknap Press, 1969), VII: "God invents, God," 172 (9 March 1839); Albanese, *Corresponding Motion*: "the most salient," 94. In his analysis of 202 Congregational funeral sermons published in New England between 1672 and 1910 James R. Armstrong found that the term "progressive happiness" first appeared in 1771: *Trends in American Eschatology* (Diss. Boston College, 1976), 160.

5. Emerson's dictum is quoted in Albanese, *Corresponding Motion*, 64.

6. Charles Spurgeon, "Foretastes of the Heavenly Life" (1857) in *Spurgeon's Expository Encyclopedia* (Grand Rapids, MI: Baker, 1951), VIII, 424; Daniel T. Rodgers, *The Work Ethic in Industrial America 1850–1920* (Chicago: Univ. of Chicago Press, 1978), 6.

7. Thomas DeWitt Talmage, *Trumpet Blasts: or, Mountain-Top Views of Life* (Chicago: North American Publishing Co., 1892): "the busiest place; this is the only," 500; "the celestial programme," 502; "heaven has more . . . an hour," 503; "great metropolis," 506; "boulevards of gold," 507.

8. Robert M. Patterson, *Paradise: The Place and State of Saved Souls* (Philadelphia: Presbyterian Board of Publication, 1874), 159; Alfred Nevin, ed., *Encyclopædia of the Presbyterian Church* (Philadelphia: Presbyterian Publishing Co., 1884), 315; Levi Gilbert, *The Hereafter and*

Heaven (Cincinnati: Jennings & Graham, 1907): "enforced idleness," 184; "celestial lubberland," 181; Reginald Heber Howe, "An Episcopal View of Heaven," *North American Review* 157 (1893), 456–61, at 460.

9. Isaac Taylor, *Physical Theory of Another Life* (New York: Appleton, 1836): "rule of analogy; initiatory course," 160; "consciousness of life; the sentiments we," 152. A late ninteteenth-century reworking of Taylor appeared in John Haynes Holmes, *Is Death the End* (np, 1915). Holmes, a minister at the Church of the Messiah in New York City, quotes extensively from Sir Oliver Lodge, president of the British Society for Psychical Research. Holmes, using Lodge as a source, discusses the "Laws of Continuity" which allow for heaven to be "simply the next step in the evolution of the spiritual life" (295).

10. Taylor, *Physical Theory of Another Life*: "reverential submission," 162; "active excellence of," 164; "manly and vigorous...but loyal," 165; "versatility, the sagacity," 167; "stand aloof," 166.

11. Taylor, *Physical Theory of Another Life*: "vast and intricate...inert repose," 166; "encounters with powerful," 165; "they shall find," 168.

12. Henry Harbaugh, *The Heavenly Home*, 3rd ed. (Philadelphia: Lindsay & Blakiston, 1853), 329–30. Harbaugh refers to Isaac Taylor (155f., 181) and Longfellow's "Resignation" (182). He quotes (255f.) from Isaac Watts, *Death and Heaven* (*Works*, II, 406) on the impossibility of immediate knowledge in heaven: "As if a man who was born blind should be healed in an instant, and should open his eyes first against the full blaze of the noon-day sun." David Gregg, *The Heaven-Life: or, Stimulus for Two Worlds* (New York: Revell, 1895): "secularizing heaven ...preaching," 63; broad and varied, 61. To support their ideas that the saints work and that work is a legitimate heavenly activity, ministers frequently cited John 5:17, "My Father has never yet ceased his work, and I am working too."

13. Channing, "The Future Life" (1834), *The Works of William E. Channing* (Boston: American Unitarian Association, 1880), 362 and 366; for the interest in "other worlds" mentioned by Channing and Watts, see Michael J. Crowe, *The Extraterrestrial Life Debate 1750–1900: The Idea of a Plurality of Worlds* (Cambridge: Cambridge Univ. Press, 1986). Horatius Bonar, *The Eternal Day* (New York: Carter, 1854), 151–69; Charles H. Strong, *In Paradise: or, The State of the Faithful Dead* (New York: Whittaker, 1893), 85–6; William Adams

Brown, *The Christian Hope: A Study in the Doctrine of Immortality* (London: Duckworth, 1912), 170.

14. William Clarke Ulyat, *The First Years of the Life of the Redeemed After Death* (New York: The Abbey Press, 1901): "the busiest," 188; "but not after," 190; "bearing messages, teaching," 191; nurses, teachers, 109; "a place ...workshop," 191.

15. Gregg, *The Heaven-Life*: "blow the trumpets," 78; "alive with the," 58f.; "there is work," 62.

16. Gregg, *The Heaven-Life*: "their spheres," 60; Ulyat, *The First Years*: "busy hive," 191; Austin Phelps, *My Portfolio* (New York: Scribner, 1882), 278. We would like to thank Mary Grosselink De Jong for bringing the Phelps material to our attention.

17. Taylor, *Physical Theory of Another Life*, 154. Isaak August Dorner, *System der christlichen Glaubenslehre*, 2nd ed. (Berlin: Hertz, 1887), II, 947–77. Daniel P. Walker, *The Decline of Hell: Seventeenth-Century Discussions of Eternal Torment* (Chicago: Univ. of Chicago Press, 1964), 225, mentions that Jane Lead (1624–1704) and other members of the Philadelphian Society in England believed in the eventual rehabilitation of even the devil.

18. Newman Smyth, *Dorner on the Future State, Being a Translation of the Section of his System of Christian Doctrine Comprising the Doctrine of the Last Things* (New York: Scribner's Sons, 1883): "instantaneous vision of," 93; "the final determination," 102; "under training," 106; "all who had," 108; "the blessed will," 142.

19. Hermann Cremer, *Beyond the Grave*, trans. Samuel T. Lowrie (New York: Harper, 1886), 104f.; E. D. Morris, *Is there Salvation After Death? A Treatise on the Gospel in the Intermediate State* (New York: Armstrong, 1887), 32. On Protestant theologians' rejection of the importance of death, see James H. Moorhead, " 'As Though Nothing at All Had Happened': Death and Afterlife in Protestant Thought, 1840–1925," *Soundings* 67 (1984), 453–71, and James J. Farrell, *Inventing the American Way of Death 1830–1920* (Philadelphia: Temple Univ. Press, 1980), 74–98 ("Religious Liberalism and the Dying of Death"). For a brief discussion of the influence of German thought on American concepts of future probation, see William R. Hutchinson, *The Modernist Impulse in American Protestantism* (Oxford: Oxford Univ. Press 1976), 84–7.

20. Frederick D. Maurice (1805–1872) became famous when he was expelled from teaching at King's College in 1853 for his

controversial stand on hell. Edward Hayes Plumtre (1821–1891), dean of Wells, published a summary of his views in *The Spirits in Prison and Other Studies on the Life After Death*, rev. ed. (1884; New York: Whittaker, 1894). Frederick W. Farrar (1831–1903), canon of Westminster and Chaplain in Ordinary to the Queen, preached five sermons at Westminster Abbey in 1877, coming close to the universalist position but stopping short of saying that all would eventually be saved. The sermons were printed in a popular book, *Eternal Hope* (New York: Dutton, 1878). On Anglican prayers for the dead see Geoffrey Rowell, *Hell and the Victorians* (Oxford: Clarendon Press, 1974), 99–108.

21. John J. Kerr, *Future Recognition: or The Blessedness of Those "Who Die in the Lord"* (Philadelphia: Hooker, 1847), 95; Jeremiah Dodsworth, *The Better Land: or The Christian Emigrant's Guide to Heaven* (London: R. Bryant, 1853), 269–70; Randolph S. Foster, *Beyond the Grave: Being Three Lectures Before Chautauqqua Assembly in 1878* (New York: Phillips & Hunt, 1880), 147–8; Arthur Chambers, *Our Life After Death: or The Teaching of the Bible Concerning the Unseen World*, 19th ed. (1894; Philadelphia: Jacobs, 1897), 102.

22. Strong, *In Paradise*, 115.

23. Harbaugh, *The Heavenly Home*, 253; Patterson, *Paradise*, 161.

24. Channing, "The Future Life," 365f.; Brown, *The Christian Hope*, 175.

25. Harbaugh, *The Heavenly Home*, 256f.

26. George B. Cheever, *The Powers of the World to Come and The Church's Stewardship, As Invested with Them* (New York: Carter, 1853), 250f.

27. Gregg, *The Heaven-Life*, 58. For a discussion of the symbol of the home, see Colleen McDannell, *The Christian Home in Victorian America 1840–1900* (Bloomington, IN: Indiana Univ. Press, 1986), 45–51.

28. James Kimball, *Heaven* (Boston: Gould & Lincoln, 1857), 266. Heaven may include Christian friends (231), but these will be almost superfluous when compared to friendship with Christ (251). Kimball writes, "In heaven surrounding circumstances will be entirely changed. In heaven there will be neither poverty, sickness, nor ignorance, neither weakness nor pain; therefore there can be none of the works of Christ's earthly beneficence to be done" (270). This statement may have been directed against his fellow theologians who emphasized heavenly service.

29. Two versions of *O quanta qualia* may be found in Carl F. Pfatteicher, ed., *The Oxford American Hymnal* (New York: Oxford Univ. Press, 1930):#290a; Charles H. Richards, *Songs of Christian Praise* (New York: Taintor Brothers, Merrill & Co., 1880): Jerusalem, #624; Peter Damiani, #611; Bernard of Cluny, #626, #627, #628. According to Mary Grosselink De Jong, "Meeting Mother in 'that home beyond the skies' ", by 1901 more than eight million copies of Watts's *Divine Songs* had been printed (unpublished paper, 1983 Organization of American Historians Meeting, Philadelphia). We would like to thank Gene Paul Strayer for showing us this hymnbook and for his suggestions concerning Victorian hymnody.

30. J.P. Thompson et al., *Home Worship for Daily Use in the Family* (1871; New York: Armstrong, 1883), #105; Richards, *Songs of Christian Praise*, #605 ("Resignation"). On the evangelical use of the themes home, heaven, and reunion, see Sandra Sizer, *Gospel Hymns and Social Religion: The Rhetoric of Nineteenth-Century Revivalism* (Philadelphia: Temple Univ. Press 1978) and Mary Grosselink De Jong, "'I want to be like Jesus': The Self-Defining Power of Evangelical Hymnody," *Journal of the American Academy of Religion* 54 (1986), 461–93.

31. Jean Reynaud, *Terre et Ciel*, 4th ed. (1854; Paris: Furne, 1864), appendix. For the inclusion in the Index of Forbidden Books, see *Acta Sanctae Sedis* 1(1865), 433.

32. F.J. Boudreaux, *The Happiness of Heaven* (1870; Baltimore: Murphy, 1875): on the Protestant heaven, 138–40; "essentially in the," 141; "motionless and inactive," 154; "it follows that," 155; "with the rapidity," 158; Elie Méric, *The Blessed Will Know Each Other in Heaven* (1881; New York: Catholic Publication Society, 1888), 62.

33. Wilhelm Schneider, *The Other Life*, rev. and ed. Herbert Thurston (New York: Wagner, 1920): "a progress that," 296; "involves the fullest...reached," 294.

34. Schneider, *The Other Life*, 297f.

35. Engelbert Krebs, *Was Kein Auge gesehen*, 13/14th ed. (1917; Freiburg: Herder, 1940), 45f.

36. John Stoger, *The Crown of Heaven: The Supreme Object of Christian Hope*, trans. M. Nash (New York: O'Shea, 1877), 255; Christian Pesch, *Praelectiones dogmaticae*, 3rd ed. (Freiburg: Herder, 1911), IX, 278.

37. *Syllabus of the Principal Errors of Our Time*, Dec. 8, 1864 [published together with the enclyclical *Quanta cura*], no. 5; *Pascendi dominici gregis* (On the Doctrines of the Modernists) Sept. 8, 1907, no. 26. These texts can be found in Heinrich Denzinger et al., eds., *Enchi-*

ridion Symbolorum, 32nd ed. (Freiburg: Herder, 1963), nos. 2905 and 3493.

38. William James, *Human Immortality: Two Supposed Objections to the Doctrine* (Boston: Houghton, Mifflin & Co., 1898), 43; Josiah Royce's Ingersoll lecture was entitled "The Conception of Immortality" (1900). Although James does not include references to spiritualism in his Ingersoll lecture, there is evidence that he was interested in the subject. He is credited with the discovery of the famous medium "Mrs. Piper" in 1885 and bringing her to the attention of the spiritualist community. In the 1880s he talked some of his Harvard colleagues into founding the American Society for Psychical Research to infuse an element of scientific inquiry into spiritualist claims.

39. The term "thick description" is borrowed from Clifford Geertz, *The Interpretation of Cultures* (New York: Basic Books, 1973), 3–30, and refers to the ethnographer's task to report events with immediacy, specificness, and detail.

40. Eliza Bisbee Duffey, *Heaven Revised: A Narrative of Personal Experiences After the Change Called Death*, 10th ed. (1898; Manchester: "The Two Worlds" Publishing Company, 1921), 3.

41. Gladys Osborne Leonard, *My Life in Two Worlds* (London: Cassell, 1931), 298 and 4; Arthur Conan Doyle in *Liverpool Daily Post and Mercury* (July 3, 1922). This article was brought to our attention by David Owen, the grandson of G. Vale Owen, who graciously shared his extensive collection of spiritualist materials with us. Janet Oppenheim, *The Other World: Spiritualism and Psychical Research in England, 1850–1914* (Cambridge: Cambridge Univ. Press, 1985), traces the endeavor to "prove" Christianity to the beginnings of the spiritualist movement in the 1850s.

42. "There is no death, there are no dead" is inscribed on a memorial tablet placed in 1927 at the home of the Fox sisters by M.E. Cadwaller. A similar sentiment occurs in Longfellow's poem "Resignation":

There is no Death! What seems so is transition;
   This life of mortal breath
Is but a suburb of the life elysian,
   Whose portal we call Death.

Margaret Oliphant, *A Little Pilgrim in the Unseen* (London: Macmillan, 1882), 10. James H. Hyslop, *Life After Death: Problems of the Future Life and its Nature* (New York: Dutton, 1918), 248. John Haynes Holmes in *Is Death the End* (1915) mentioned a recent mediumistic communication which said that the victims of the Titanic sinking (1912) did not recognize that anything happened to them when they awoke in the next world. The medium had to tell them where they were (296).

43. G. Vale Owen, *The Life Beyond the Veil: The Lowlands of Heaven* (1922; London: Greater World Association, 1982), 100 (automatic writing of 1913); William Stainton Moses, *Spirit Teachings* (London: Spiritualist Alliances, 1924), 26.

44. Leonard, *My Life in Two Worlds*, 114; John and Erica Oxenham, *Out of the Body* (London: Psychic Book Club, c. 1944), 60; Erik Palmstierna, *Horizons of Immortality: A Quest for Reality* (London: Constable, 1937): "one must find," 173.

45. Hyslop, *Life After Death*: cigars, 277; "shut out all," 274; Palmstierna, *Horizons of Immortality*, 188; Elizabeth Stuart Phelps, *Beyond the Gates* (Boston: Houghton Mifflin & Co., 1883), 77.

46. Palmstierna, *Horizons of Immortality*, 181.

47. Duffey, *Heaven Revised*, 56; Leonard, *My Life in Two Worlds*: "conscious of his," 111; Oxenham, *Out of the Body*: "the black-coated," 88; "this war has," 90f.

48. Phelps, *Beyond the Gates*, 120; Duffey, *Heaven Revised*, 35; Oxenham, *Out of the Body*, 24f.; Oliphant, *A Little Pilgrim*, 91f.

49. Duffey, *Heaven Revised*, 56; Owen, *The Life Beyond the Veil: The Lowlands of Heaven*, 41; Oxenham, *Out of the Body*, 77; Palmstierna, *Horizons of Immortality*, 182.

50. Duffey, *Heaven Revised*: "who make the," 57; Palmstierna, *Horizons of Immortality*, "politics, finance, money," 181; musical conservatories: Owen, *The Life Beyond the Veil: The Lowlands of Heaven*, 41; Henry J. Horn, *Strange Visitors: A Series of Original Papers by the Spirits of Famous People* (New York: Carleton, 1869), 173f.

51. Duffey, *Heaven Revised*, 63.

52. Duffey, *Heaven Revised*: "with a noble," 41; Owen, *The Life Beyond the Veil: The Lowlands of Heaven*: "genius of motherhood," 81; Duffey, *Heaven Revised*: "kindly to him," 38f.

53. Horn, *Strange Visitors*, 162f.; Robert James Lees, *Through the Mists: Leaves from the Autobiography of a Soul in Paradise* (London: Rider, 1898): "sanitarium for sectarians," 131; "aqua-botanical marvel," 135; Phelps, *Beyond the Gates*, 122–3.

54. Horn, *Strange Visitors*: "elegantly-formed sleds," 167; Lees, *Through the Mists*, 73; Oxenham, *Out of the Body*, 46.

55. Leonard, *My Life in Two Worlds*, 121; Shaw Desmond, *Love after Death* (London: Rider, 1944), 157.

56. Rebecca Ruter Springer, *Intra Muros* (Elgin, IL: Cook, 1898), 112. Ann Douglas in the *Feminization of American Culture* (New York: Knopf, 1977) concludes her discussion of "The Domestication of Death" by writing: "The occupants of Phelps's heaven – engaged in good works, keeping up with earthly news, redecorating their homes, falling in love, and gratifying their various tastes – live in a celestial retirement village; they constitute a consecrated leisure society. The carefully contrived world of the dead in heaven, as in the rural cemetery, a world created in protest against the larger competitive society, in actuality served to transfer, isolate, and protect what would become the most essential ritual of that society: The chaos of productivity is eliminated in order to insure the pleasures of consumption" (226). Our research challenges this conclusion by arguing that the "chaos of productivity" was not eliminated but purified in heaven.

57. Phelps, *Beyond the Gates*, 118.

58. Lees, *Through the Mists*, 86; Phelps, *Beyond the Gates*, 110; *Personality Survives Death: Messages from William Barrett*, ed. by his wife (London: Longmans, Green & Co., 1937), 165; William Barrett, *Death-Bed Visions* (London: Methuen, 1926), 63.

59. Horn, *Strange Visitors*, 168; Barrett, *Personality Survives Death*, 23.

60. Palmstierna, *Horizons of Immortality* "Great One," 172; Moses, *Spirit Teachings*: "the Omnipotent," 15; H. Dennis Bradley, *Towards the Stars* (London: Laurie, 1924): "the great and; inspiration of," 92; "passes into the," 290; Horn, *Strange Visitors*: "ever changing, yet," 201.

61. John S. Vaughan, *Life Everlasting: or, The Delights Awaiting the Faithful Soul in Paradise* (London: Burns Oates & Washbourne, 1925), 6; Patterson, *Paradise*, 141; R. Laurence Moore, *In Search of White Crows: Spiritualism, Parapsychology, and American Culture* (New York: Oxford Univ. Press, 1977), 40–69 ("Spiritualism and the Complaint of Christian Orthodoxy"); for a similar report on the British situation, see Oppenheim, *The Other World*, 63–110.

62. Moses, *Spirit Teachings*, 149; G. Vale Owen, *The Life Beyond the Veil: The Ministry of Heaven* (1922; London: Greater World Association, 1982), 79. The "Christ sphere" is discussed by Owen in *Life Beyond the Veil: The Battalions of Heaven* (1922; London: Greater World Association, 1982), ch. 5. The understanding of the divine as essentially a unity of male and female also appears in Oxenham, *Out of the Body*, 95, where God possesses the dual nature of "Father-Motherhood."

63. Major L. Wilson, "Paradox Lost: Order and Progress in Evangelical Thought," *Church History* 44 (1975), 352–66, at 354. John Fiske, *The Destiny of Man Viewed in Light of His Origins* (Boston: Houghton Mifflin, 1884), 118.

64. Walter E. Houghton, *The Victorian Frame of Mind, 1830–1870* (New Haven: Yale Univ. Press, 1957), 256.

65. John Baillie, *And the Life Everlasting* (New York: Scribner's Sons, 1933), 281.

CHAPTER TEN

1. George Gallup with William Procter, *Adventures in Immortality* (London: Corgi Books, 1984), 172, 176, 198. A further analysis of such statistics may be found in Bradley R. Hertel, "Inconsistency of Beliefs in the Existences of Heaven and Afterlife," *Review of Religious Research* 21 (1979/80), 170–83, and Hart M. Nelson, "Life Without Afterlife: Toward Congruency of Belief Across Generations," *Journal for the Scientific Study of Religion* 20 (1981), 109–18.

2. Raymond A. Moody, *Life after Life: The Investigation of a Phenomenon – Survival of Bodily Death* (New York: Bantam, 1976). The popular interest in this subject is amply documented in Carol Zaleski, *Otherworld Journeys: Accounts of Near-Death Experience in Medieval and Modern Times* (New York: Oxford Univ. Press, 1987), and Hans Küng, *Eternal Life?* (New York: Doubleday, 1984), 10–20.

3. C.S. Lewis, *The Great Divorce* (1946; Glasgow: Collins, 1977). This book's ideas are developed in Peter J. Kreeft, *Everything You Ever Wanted to Know about Heaven* (San Francisco: Harper & Row, 1982).

4. James Breig, "Beyond the Pearly Gates: What *U.S. Catholic* Readers Believe about the Afterlife," *U.S. Catholic* 48 (May, 1983), 6–18; Josephine M. Ford, "Heaven: Will It Be Boring?" *U.S. Catholic* 40 (Nov., 1975), 16–20, at 19. More scholarly Catholic writers, who appeal to a popular audience, present similar views. After discussing statistics on heaven and the psychological form of happiness which heaven might hold, Andrew Greeley concludes that "The Kingdom of heaven is a perpetual spring festival, celebrating, as do all spring festivals, the persistence of life as life, triumphing, however painfully, over death." *Death and Beyond* (Chicago: Thomas More Press, 1976), 136. John Shea is more explicit. Heaven can be represented symbolically as the messianic banquet: "Heaven is everything a good meal (a few cocktails before, fine wine during, brandy after) is to friends." *What A Modern Catholic Believes About Heaven and*

Hell (Chicago: Thomas More Press, 1972), 87f.

5. *Holborn and City Guardian* (London) no. 5075 (18 March 1983), 38; *Frankfurter Allgemeine Zeitung* no. 284 (7 Dec. 1983), 27; *The Columbus Dispatch*, Columbus, OH (10 Sept. 1983).

6. Felix Barker, *Highgate Cemetery: Victorian Valhalla* (Salem, NH: Salem House, 1984), 41.

7. The Church of Jesus Christ of Latter-day Saints acquired its first million members in 1946. It took another sixteen years, until 1963, to gain a second million. After the sixties, however, the number of members increased sharply. In 1971 the membership had climbed to three million, in 1978 to four million, and by 1986 the membership was six million. While over four million of those members live in North America, the church's active missionary work has made converts in over ninety-five different countries. The church takes pride in explaining that every two minutes a new convert is made.

We would like to thank Harald Frome for loaning us hard-to-come-by Mormon materials and for patiently explaining to us the LDS afterlife.

8. Theodore M. Burton, *God's Greatest Gift* (Salt Lake City: Deseret Book Co., 1977), 175.

9. Ezra T. Benson in *Official Report of the Annual General Conference of the Church of Jesus Christ of Latter-day Saints* (Salt Lake City: The Church of Jesus Christ of LDS, 1971), 18. Robert L. Millet and Joseph F. McConkie, eds., *The Life Beyond* (Salt Lake City: Bookcraft, 1986), 18.

10. Wilford Woodruff as quoted in Millet and McConkie, eds., *The Life Beyond*, 64.

11. Millet and McConkie, eds., *The Life Beyond*: on the priesthood and persidency persisting in the next life, 53; "search out their," 54; "we do not...Sabbath," 64.

12. Mary V. Hill, *Angel Children* (Bountiful, UT: Horizon Publishers, 1975), 40f.

13. Burton, *God's Greatest Gift*, 237.

14. Bruce R. McConkie, *Mormon Doctrine* (Salt Lake City: Bookcraft, 1958): "crops will be," 497; Gordon T. Allred, *If a Man Die* (Salt Lake City: Bookcraft, 1964), 174.

15. Exaltation is described in *Doctrine and Covenants* section 132, especially verse 20: "Then shall they be gods, because they have no end; therefore shall they be from everlasting to everlasting, because they continue; then shall they be above all, because all things are subject unto them. Then shall they be gods, because they have all power, and the angels are subject unto them." See also Duane S. Crowther, *Life Everlasting*, (Salt Lake City: Bookcraft, 1971),

333f.

16. Burton, *God's Greatest Gift*, 20. On eternal and temporal marriages, see *Doctrine and Covenants* 132:15–19. The best scholarly discussion of the evolution of Mormon marriage practice is Lawrence Foster, *Religion and Sexuality: The Shakers, the Mormons, and the Oneida Community* (Urbana, IL: Univ. of Illinois Press, 1981), 123–80.

17. Crowther, *Life Everlasting*: "exalted beings," 339; "after the same" (citing Orson Pratt), 341; N.B. Lundwall, ed., *The Vision or The Degrees of Glory* (Salt Lake City: Bookcraft, n.d.): "bear the souls," 147; Crowther, *Life Everlasting*: "reign for ever," 339 (citing Parley P. Pratt).

18. Crowther, *Life Everlasting*: "just as men," 340; Lynn A. McKinlay, *Life Eternal* (Salt Lake City: Deseret Book Co., 1950): "his never-ending," 164; Millet and McConkie, eds., *The Life Beyond*, 143.

Like many of his nineteenth-century contemporaries, Joseph Smith believed in a plurality of worlds in the universe. The earth is not the only planet inhabited by intelligent beings: see Michael J. Crowe, *The Extraterrestrial Life Debate 1750–1900* (Cambridge: Cambridge Univ. Press, 1986), 241–6.

19. The importance of rule and reproduction is emphasized in Crowther, *Life Everlasting*, 340.

20. Paul Tillich, *Systematic Theology* (Chicago: Univ. of Chicago Press, 1963), III: absurd, 408; Karl Rahner, *Kritisches Wort* (Herder: Freiburg, 1970): crude, 189; A.R. van de Walle, *From Darkness to the Dawn: How Belief in the Afterlife Affects Living*, trans. John Bowden (1981, London: SCM Press, 1984): "infantile; materialistic; sheer nonsense; no reasonable person," 26f. Renée Haynes, "Some Christian Imagery," Arnold Toynbee et al., *Life after Death* (London: Weidenfeld & Nicolson, 1976), 132–43, at 136. *The Pope Teaches: 1979* (London: Catholic Truth Society, 1979), 334; the original document of 17 May 1979 is in *Acta Apostolicae Sedis* 71(1979), 939–43.

21. Sir Kenelm Digby, *Two Treatises...in Way of Discovery of the Immortality of Reasonable Soules* (Paris: Blaizot, 1644); René Descartes, letter to Elizabeth of Bohemia of 3 Nov. 1645 in Descartes, *Oeuvres et lettres*, ed. André Bridoux (Paris: Gallimard, 1953), 1222 and *Philosophical Letters*, trans. Anthony Kenny (Oxford: Clarendon Press, 1970), 185.

22. Immanuel Kant, *Dreams of a Spirit-Seer, Illustrated by Dreams of Metaphysics*, trans. E.F. Goerwitz (London: Sonnenschein, 1900): "consisting of nothing; applicable weight," 87; "be-

cause for this; in the future," 89; "human reason was," 121.

23. For Kant's musings on spending eternity without body or meeting others, see *Kant's gesammelte Schriften*, ed. Preussische Akademie der Wissenschaften (Berlin: Reimer, 1917), VII, 40; Felix Gross, ed., *Immanuel Kant: Sein Leben in Darstellungen von Zeitgenossen* (1912; rprt. Darmstadt: Wiss. Buchgesellschaft, 1968), 172. Friedrich Schleiermacher, *The Christian Faith*, ed. H.R. Mackintosh and J.S. Stewart (Edinburgh: Clark, 1928): "we cannot really," 705 (§ 159:2); "all figurative...of Christianity," 700f. (§ 158:2); "we really can," 720 (§ 163).

24. Schleiermacher, letter of 25 March 1807 to Henriette von Willich in *Friedrich Schleiermachers Briefwechsel mit seiner Braut*, ed. Heinrich Meisner, 2nd ed. (Gotha: Klotz, 1920), 74; Schleiermacher, *Predigten* (Berlin: Reimer, 1844), IV, 882f.

25. David Fr. Strauss, *Christliche Glaubenslehre* (Tübingen: Osiander, 1841), II, 697.

26. Charles Darwin and Thomas H. Huxley, *Autobiographies*, ed. Gavin de Beer (London: Oxford Univ. Press, 1974), 54; Ernst Haeckel, *The Riddle of the Universe*, trans. Joseph McCabe, 5th ed. (London: Watts, 1906), 67–75; Corliss Lamont, *The Illusion of Immortality*, 4th ed. (1935; New York: Ungar, 1965).

27. Karl Rahner, *Theological Investigations*, trans. Ed. Quinn (London: Darton, Longman & Todd, 1984), XIX, 169; Hans Schwarz, *Beyond the Gates of Death* (Minneapolis, MN: Augsburg, 1981), 10. The West German (1982) statistics come from Elisabeth Noelle-Neumann and Edgar Piel, eds., *Allensbacher Jahrbuch der Demoskopie 1978–1983* (München: K.G. Saur, 1983), 124. Keep in mind that being a Protestant or Catholic in Germany has nothing to do with beliefs or church attendance. It merely denotes which group receives one's church taxes. The percentage of Germans who believe in some kind of afterlife has only slightly varied over the past thirty years: 1956: 42%; 1964: 39%; 1971: 35%; 1980: 40%; 1982: 42%. The sharp difference between the number of heavenly believers in Europe and in America is discussed (unsatisfactorily) in Greeley, *Death and Beyond*, 60–65.

28. *Jean Barois*, quoted from Roger Martin du Gard, *Oeuvres complètes* (Paris: Gallimard, 1955), I, 205–559: 1 Cor. 13:11 and "symbolist compromise," 227.

29. Martin du Gard, *Oeuvres*, I, 542.

30. Reinhold Niebuhr, *The Nature and Destiny of Man* (New York: Charles Scribner's Sons, 1947), II: "the biblical symbols...Christian hope," 289; Emil Brunner in Charles W. Kegley and Robert W. Bretall, eds., *Reinhold Niebuhr: His Religious, Social, and Political Thought* (New York: Macmillan, 1956): "to what extent," 32; Richard W. Fox, *Reinhold Niebuhr: A Biography* (New York: Pantheon, 1985): "I do not...count on it," 215.

31. Paul Tillich, "Existential Analyses and Religious Symbols," Harold A. Basilius, ed., *Contemporary Problems in Religion* (Detroit: Wayne Univ. Press, 1956), 37–55: "symbols such as," 53f.; *Systematic Theology*, III: symbol not description, 418; "neurotic consequences," 419; "negative metaphorical lauguage," 401.

32. Tillich, *Systematic Theology*, III: "elevates the positive," 397; eternal now, 395; Tillich, "Existential Analyses": "eternal life means," 53f.

33. Tillich, *The Courage to Be* (New Haven: Yale Univ. Press, 1952), 168f.; Tillich, *Systematic Theology*, III: divine center, 401; "unambiguous and non-fragmentary," 402; "the endless continuation...particles," 414.

34. Tillich, *Systematic Theology*, III, 418.

35. Nels F.S. Ferré, "Tillich and the Nature of Transcendence," *Religion in Life* 35(1966), 662–73, at 663; John Hick, *Death and Eternal Life* (London: Collins, 1976), 217.

36. Bultmann's draft letter of June 1973 (unpublished); Rudolf Bultmann, "The Eschatology of the Gospel of John," *Faith and Understanding* (London: SCM Press, 1969), 165–83; Johannine texts that do not fit this reading (John 5:28f.; 6:39–40, 44, 51b–58) are attributed to an "ecclesiastical editor" who made the gospel acceptable to mainstream believers.

We thank Professor Antje Bultmann Lemke for giving permission to use her father's unpublished letters.

37. Bultmann, "Neues Testament und Mythologie," Hans W. Bartsch, ed., *Kerygma und Mythos* (Hamburg: Reich & Heidrich, 1948), 15–53: "translation to a," 21; Bultmann, letter of 23 March 1943 (unpublished) and c. 1961 in Hans Jonas, *Zwischen Nichts und Ewigkeit* (Göttingen: Vandenhoeck & Ruprecht, 1963), 66. See also Bultmann, "The Christian Hope and the Problem of Demythologizing," *Expository Times* 65(1953–4), 228–30.276–8, esp. 278; letter of 5 March 1962 in Rudolf Bultmann and J.A. Dvoráček, "Auferstehung und Leben – Kerygma und Mythos," *Communio Viatorum* 5(1962), 57–63, at 60f.

38. Schleiermacher, *On Religion: Speeches to Its Cultured Despisers*, trans. John Oman (New York: Harper & Row, 1958): "in the state," 117; "in the midst," 101; Schleiermacher, *Soliloquies*, trans. H.L. Feiss (Chicago: Open Court, 1957): "be not troubled," 23.

39. Walter Rauschenbusch, *Christianity and*

the Social Crisis (New York: Macmillan, 1907), 422.

40. Walter Rauschenbusch presents his view on Greek influence on Christian teachings in *Christianity and the Social Crisis* (New York: Macmillan, 1913), 162f. For his own eschatological speculations see *A Theology for the Social Gospel* (New York: Macmillan, 1922), 227–38; this work also discusses the "fellowship of righteousness," 133f.

41. Walter Rauschenbusch, *Christianizing the Social Order* (New York: Macmillan, 1912), 42.

42. Jhan and June Robbins, "The Surprising Beliefs of Our Future Ministers," *Redbook* 117 (Aug. 1961), 36 and 107–10.

43. Rosemary R. Ruether, *Sexism and God-Talk* (Boston: Beacon Press, 1983), 258. For this perspective, see also Gregory Baum, *Religion and Alienation: A Theological Reading of Sociology* (New York: Paulist Press, 1975), 266–94 ("Heaven as Revealed Utopia"); Monika K. Hellwig, *What Are They Saying about Death and Christian Hope* (New York: Paulist Press, 1978), 64–6; Bernard P. Prusak, "Heaven and Hell: Eschatological Symbols of Existential Protest," *Cross Currents* 24(1975), 475–91.

44. On fundamentalist "Baconianism," see Martin E. Marty, *Modern American Religion* (Chicago: Univ. of Chicago Press, 1986), I, 221f. and 232–7. Charles F. Baker, *A Dispensational Theology*, 2nd ed. (Grand Rapids, MI: Grace Bible College, 1972), 13.

45. On the temporal character of eternity, see Edward G. Kettner, "Time, Eternity, and the Intermediate State," *Concordia Journal* 12 (1986), 90–100. Hal Lindsey, *There's a New World Coming*, rev. ed. (Eugene, OR: Harvest House, 1984): "there's really," 271; cube or pyramid, 274; location on earth, 272; Baker, *Dispensational Theology*: satellite circling planet, 657. Maurice Rawlings, *Beyond Death's Door* (Nashville, TN: Nelson, 1978): some reports closely resemble Revelation, 97.

46. Cyrus I. Scofield, *Addresses on Prophecy* (New York: Gaebelein, 1910), 130.

47. Joe Bayly, "What Heaven Will Be Like," *Moody Monthly* 76(1975/6), no. 8, 25–7, at 27.

48. The basic presentation is in *The Scofield Reference Bible* (1917; rprt. New York: Oxford Univ. Press, n.d.), 5 and 1250; recent discussions include Charles C. Ryrie, *Dispensationalism Today* (Chicago: Moody Press, 1965) and Baker, *Dispensational Theology*. For the "rapture" see 1 Thess. 4:17; on the nineteenth-century Scottish origin of the doctrine, see Dave MacPherson, *The Great Rapture Hoax* (Fletcher, NC: New Puritan Library, 1983).

49. Quoted in J. Anthony Lukas, "The Rapture and the Bomb," *The New York Times Book Review* (8 June 1986), 7.

50. Hal Lindsey, *The Late Great Planet Earth* (Grand Rapids, MI: Zondervan, 1970); Ryrie, *Dispensationalism Today*, 53; Baker, *Dispensational Theology*, 5.

51. William E. Biederwolf, *The Adventure of the Hereafter* (New York: R.R. Smith, 1930), viii.

52. Calvin R. Schoonhoven, *The Wrath of Heaven* (Grand Rapids, MI: Eerdmans, 1966): not spatially oriented, 161–4; Baker, *Dispensational Theology*: "at home with," 583; Gordon Lindsay, *Paradise: Abode of the Righteous Dead* (Dallas, TX: Christ for the Nations, 1980); Rebecca Springer, *Within the Gates*, ed. Gordon Lindsay (Dallas, TX: Christ for the Nations, 1982) is a shortened version of *Intra Muros* (Elgin, IL: Cook, 1898); Lindsay, *There's a New World Coming*, "the most; the unfathomable," 273f.; "It's exciting," 278.

53. Anne Sandberg, *Seeing the Invisible* (Plainfield, NJ: Logos International, 1977), 124; Don Baker, *Heaven* (Portland, OR: Multnomah Press, 1983), 13.

54. Karl Barth, *Church Dogmatics*, trans. G.W. Bromiley (Edinburgh: Clark, 1960), III/2: "our real and," 624; Karl Rahner, *Theological Investigations*, trans. David Bourke (London: Darton, Longman & Todd, 1975), XIII: "further extension," 174. Rahner takes the image of "changing horses" from Ludwig Feuerbach, *Thoughts on Death and Immortality*, trans. J.A. Massey (Berkeley: Univ. of California Press, 1980), 19. Paul Imhof and Hubert Biallowons, eds., *Karl Rahner in Dialogue*, trans. Harvey D. Egan (New York: Crossroad, 1986): "with death it's," 238 (interview of 2 April 1980); wants to rest, 341 (interview of 29 April 1982).

55. Barth, *Letters 1961–1968*, trans. G.W. Bromiley (Grand Rapids, MI: Eerdmans, 1981): "our manifestation with," 9 (letter of 6 July 1961); Rahner, *Kritisches Wort*: crude, mistaken, 189. Rahner, "Erfahrungen eines katholischen Theologen," Karl Lehmann, ed., *Vor dem Geheimnis Gottes den Menschen verstehen* (Munich: Schnell & Steiner, 1984), 105–19: "to being a; the absolute," 118f.

56. Rahner, "Erfahrungen eines kathoischen Theologen," 118f.

57. Hilde Herrmann in *Maria Regina Martyrum* (Berlin: Morus Verlag, 1963), 19f. The wall painting is by Georg Meistermann (b. 1911). For the space behind the altar as "heaven" in modern church architecture see Rudolf Schwarz, *Vom Bau der Kirche*, 2nd ed. (Heidelberg: Schneider, 1947), 56–64.

58. Barth, *Letters*: "reverse side which," 9;

Barth, *The Faith of the Church*, trans. Gabriel Vahanian (New York: Meridian, 1958): "often I have," 166.

59. Barth, *The Theology of Schleiermacher*, trans. G.W. Bromiley (Grand Rapids, MI: Eerdmans, 1982), 277 (modified). Barth quotes a poem by C.F. Gellert which can be found in Catherine Winkworth, *Christian Singers of Germany* (Philadelphia: Lippincott, 1869), 319.

60. Michael Perry, *The Resurrection of Man* (London: Mowbrays, 1975), 113.

61. William Hamilton, "Thursday's Child: The Theologian Today and Tomorrow," *Theology Today* 20(1963/4), 487–95, at 488. For the "secular 1960s" see Sidney E. Ahlstrom, *A Religious History of the American People* (New Haven: Yale Univ. Press, 1972), 1079–96; Paul Avis, ed., *The History of Christian Theology* (Basingstroke: Marshall Pickering, 1986), I, 334–44, and Wace C. Roof and William McKinney, *American Mainline Religion* (New Brunswick: Rutgers Univ. Press, 1987), 11–39.

62. Hans Jonas, "Immortality and the Modern Temper," *Harvard Theological Review* 55 (1962), 1–20: "that the modern; throw some light," 1; "this extreme offspring...and after," 6.

63. Charles Hartshorne, *The Logic of Perfection* (La Salle, IL: Open Court, 1962), 245–262 ("Time, Death, and Everlasting Life") with subsequent popularizations in *A Natural Theology for Our Time* (La Salle, IL: Open Court, 1967) and *Omnipotence and Other Theological Mistakes* (Albany, NY: State Univ. of New York Press, 1984). Gordon D. Kaufman, *Systematic Theology: A Historicist Perspective* (New York: Charles Scribner's Sons, 1968), 467f. Jacques Pohier, *Quand je dis dieu* (Paris: Seuil, 1977). The Hartshornian "process" view is represented by Schurbert Ogden, *The Reality of God* (New York: Harper & Row, 1966), 206–30, and Norman Pittenger, *After Death: Life in God* (New York: Seabury Press, 1980).

For an attempt to reconcile the negative stance of most process theologians and philosophers with more traditional views, see John B. Cobb, "The Resurrection of the Soul," *Harvard Theological Review* 80 (1987), 213–27.

64. *Dialogues of Alfred N. Whitehead* as recorded by Lucien Price (New York: New American Library, 1956): "can you imagine,"

223f. The classical definition of person as "individual substance of a rational nature" (*definitio personae: naturae rationabilis individua substantia*) is that of Boethius, *Against Eutyches and Nestorius*, 3 in *The Theological Tracts*, trans. H.F. Stewart and E.K. Rand (London: Heinemann, 1913), 84f.

65. Hartshorne, *The Logic of Perfection*: "death is the," 250; "death writes," 253; *A Natural Theology*: "we write our," 112.

66. Hartshorne, *The Logic of Perfection*, 258.

67. Hartshorne, *Omnipotence*, 37.

68. Hartshorne, *A Natural Theology*: "that our chief," 106f.; "to the original," 110. Hartshorne, "Emptiness and Fullness in Asiatic and Western Thought," *Journal of Chinese Philosophy* 6(1979), 411–20: "Buddhism stood," 411; see also Hartshorne, "Toward a Buddhisto-Christian Religion," Kenneth K. Inada and Nolan P. Jacobson, eds., *Buddhism and American Thinkers* (Albany, NY: State Univ. of New York Press, 1984), 2–13. John Hick in "Present and Future Life," *Harvard Theological Review* 71 (1978), 1–15, combines the modern view of progress in the afterlife ("We must, then, proceed on the basis that life as we know it is part of a long person-making process which is not completed in this present life and which we can only presume to continue beyond it." 10) and reincarnation ("where Buddhism and Hinduism...teach a horizontal process or reincarnation, along the plane of earthly history, I have been outlining what might be called a vertical, or perhaps better a diagonal, series of many lives in many worlds, moving nearer to the divine heart of reality." 14).

69. Friedrich Schiller, "The Gods of Greece," after *The Poems and Ballads of Schiller*, trans. Edward B. Lytton (New York: Crowell, n.d.), 300.

70. *Weekly World News*, Los Angeles, 2 June 1987. We could like to thank Lillian Wondrack for bringing this article to our attention. Karlis Osis and Erlendur Haraldsson, *At the Hour of Death* (New York: Avon, 1977) have investigated, even cross-culturally, numerous near-death reports; their conclusion: near-death visions concern only "the initial stages of postmortem existence," but never communicate "what 'life' after death is really like – its activities, purposes, joys and sorrows, customs, social structure" (197).

AUTHOR INDEX

Abelard, Peter, 73, 80, 288
Addison, Joseph, 206
Albertus Magnus, 83
Alexander of Hales, 83
Allred, Gordon T., 317
Ambrose of Milan, 60–61
Anderson, Charles, Pl. 61
Andreas the Chaplain, 95
Angelico, Fra (Giovanni da Fiesole),
    128–33, Pls. 19–21
Aquinas, Thomas, 80, 88–93, 109, 122,
    143, 261
    no animals or plants, 84, 118, 133
    irrelevance of friends, 92–93, 140
    glorified body, 83–84, 91–92, 137
    vision of God, 89–91, 210
    immobility and movement, 84, 91, 144
    in Renaissance, 112, 118, 123, 128
Aristotle, 80, 81, 88, 89, 92, 111
Arnaut, Daniel, 96, 97
Arnoux, François, 214
Assheton, William, 206
Augustine, 48, 54–67, 69
    cosmology, 81
    friendship, 58, 64–65, 93, 165
    glorified body, 58, 61–63, 137
    merit, 151
    Middle Ages, 77, 88, 89, 97, 102,
    108–9

Bacon, Francis, 336
Baillie, John, 305
Baker, Charles, 336, 340
Baker, Don, 341
Barrett, William, 301
Barth, Karl, 344–45, 350
Batten, Mabel Veronica, 311
Bellegambe, Jean, 140–141, Pl. 26
Benson, Ezra Taft, 314

Bernard of Clairvaux, 98, 102, 103, 106
Bérulle, Pierre de, 157
Biederwolf, William, 340
Blake, William, 234–45, 252, 311, Pls.
    42–48
Blot, François-René, 258, 268–69
Boccaccio, Giovanni, 96, 122, 140
Bodmer, Frederika, Pl. 55
Bonar, Horatius, 281
Bonaventure, 93, 118
Bosch, Hieronymus, 119–22, 143, Pl. 14
Boudreaux, F.J., 289
Bouts, Dieric, 134, Pl. 135
Bradley, Dennis, 302
Brown, Willam Adams, 282, 286
Browne, Thomas, 172
Browning, Robert, 249–50
Bultmann, Rudolf, 330–32
Burnet, Thomas, 184–85
Burton, Theodore, 314, 316
Byron, George Gordon (Lord), 250–51

Calvin, John, 147–56, 184–85, 189, 208
    progress after death, 204–5
Canisius, Peter, 160, 162–63, Pl. 31
Chambers, Arthur, 285
Channing, William Ellery, 269, 281, 285
Cheever, George, 268, 286
Chick, Jack T., Pl. 56
Cicero, 16, 60–66, 155, 173
    in Renaissance, 112, 124, 125, 127,
    142, 143
Colonna, Francesco, 125–26, 130
Condorcet, 205–6
Copernicus, Nicolaus, 152
Cosmas Indicopleustes, 80, Pl. 5
Cotton, John, 174
Cranach, Lucas, Pl. 18
Cremer, Hermann, 284

Crowther, Duane, 319
Cyprian of Carthage, 61

Damiani, Peter, 73
Dante, 84–86, 98, 116
  no progress in heaven, 91
  Renaissance elaboration on, 122–23,
    140, Fig. 6, Pls. 15–17
Darwin, Charles, 325
Descartes, René, 323
Desmond, Shaw, 300
Dickinson, Emily, 251–52, 311
Diderot, 213
Digby, Kenelm, 323
Dodsworth, Jeremiah, 284
Donatello, 128
Donne, John, 175
Dorner, Isaac A., 283
Douglas, Ann, 274
Doyle, Arthur Conan, 294
Duffey, Eliza Bisbee, 294, 296, 297, 298

Egan, Maurice, 273
Emerson, Ralph Waldo, 273, 278
Erasmus of Rotterdam, 111, 123, 134, 144
Eusebius, 53

Facio, Bartolomeo, 140
Falwell, Jerry, 338
Farrar, Frederick, 284
Ferré, Nels F.S., 330
Feuerbach, Ludwig, xiii, 325
Fiske, John, 304
Flaxman, John, 186, Pl. 34
Fletcher, Giles, 163
Foster, Randolph, 284
Fouquet, Jean, 163, Pl. 32

Gallup Poll, 307
Gerardesca of Pisa, 74–77
Gertrude of Helfta, 102–7, 109
Giacomino of Verona, 74, 78
Giacomo da Lentini, 95
Gilbert, Levi, 280
Giles of Rome, 93
Giotto, 112–13, Pl. 10
Giovanni di Paolo, 122–24, 132–33, Pls.
  16–18, 22
Goethe, Johann Wolfgang von, 248–49
Gottschalk of Holstein, 73
Greenwood, Francis, 260, 270
Gregg, David, 281, 282

Guido Guinizelli of Bologna, 96
Gyllenborg-Stjerncrona, Elizabeth, 218

Haeckel, Ernst, 326
Hall, Joseph, 173
Hall, Radclyffe, 311
Harbaugh, Henry, 259, 266, 281, 285
Hartshorne, Charles, 346–49
Haynes, Renée, 322
Heemskerck, Maarten van, 157, Pl. 28
Hepworth, George, 270
Hervey, James, 176–77
Hick, John, 330
Hildegard of Bingen, 78, 107
Hill, Mary V., 315
Horn, Henry, 298, 302
Howe, John, 171–72
Howe, Reginald Heber, 280
Hugh of St. Victor, 94
Hyslop, James, 294

Irenaeus of Lyons, 48–53, 67

Jacques de Vitry, 98
James, William, 292
Jeanne de Chantal, 166
Joachim of Fiore, 73
John Ruusbroec, 82
Jonas, Hans, 332, 346
Jordan of Saxony, 96
Josephus, 19–21

Kant, Immanuel, 277–78, 305, 323–24,
  325
Kaufman, Gordon, 346
Kerr, John, 260, 284
Kimball, James, 287
Kingsley, Charles, 261–64, Pls. 53, 54
Kingsley, Fanny, 262, Pls. 53, 54
Kirk, Edward, 259, 270
Krebs, Engelbert, 290

Lamont, Corliss, 326
Langton, Stephan, 103
Lavater, Johann Caspar, 197–99, 213
Law, William, 174
Leibniz, Gottfried Wilhelm, 277
Leo XIII (pope), 269
Leonard, Gladys Osborne, 294, 295, 300
Lindsey, Hal, 337, 340, Fig. 7
Lipsius, Justus, 166, 168

Longfellow, Henry Wadsworth, 276, 281, 288
Luther, Martin, 102, 147–56, 188

MacDonald, James, 266, 270
Maffei, Celso, 136
Marot, Clement, 126
Martin du Gard, Roger, 326–27
Martin of Cochem, 196, 215–16
Marvell, Andrew, 173
Mather, Increase, 175
Mathesius, Johannes, 155–56
Mathonier, Nicolas de, Pl. 40
Maurice, Frederick, 284
Mechthild of Magdeburg, 100–106, 109, 118, 143
Meistermann, Georg, 344
Melanchthon, Philipp, 148–50, 155, 156, 162, Pl. 27
Méric, Elie, 258, 290
Meyfart, Johann, Pl. 38
Milton, John, 230–33, 353
    influence of, 262
More, Henry, 211
Morris, E.D., 284
Moses, William Stainton, 302, 303

Newton, Isaac, 181–82
Nicolai, Philipp, 195, 198, 211
Nicole, Pierre, 170–71, 173
Niebuhr, Reinhold, 327–28
Novalis, 247–48

Oliphant, Margaret (Mrs.), 293, 294
Orcagna, Nardo and Andrea di Cione, 112, Pl. 11
Osanna of Mantua, 133–34
Otfrid of Weissenburg, 70–71
Otto of Freising, 72, 84, 108
Owen, G. Vale, 295, 303
Oxenham, John, 295, 296, 297, 299

Palmstierna, Erik, 296, 298
Pascal, Blaise, 167, 170
Patterson, Robert, 258, 260, 272, 279, 285, 302
Paul, 19–20, 23, 32–37, 44–45, 150
    spiritual body, 34–36, 58
    visions, 34, 61
Perry, Michael, 345
Pesch, Christian, 291
Petrarch, 97, 98, 122, 125, 140

Phelps, Austin, 283
Phelps, Elizabeth Stuart, 228, 265–73, 282, 293, 297, 301, 322
Phillips, Samuel, 260, 266, 270
Philo of Alexandria, 17–18, 21
Pius IX (pope), 291
Pius X (pope), 291
Plato, 16, 18, 45, 210, 329
Plotinus, 56, 58
Pohier, Jacques, 346
Polti, Antonino, 158–59, 167
Polycarp of Smyrna, 49
Pratt, Agnes, 267–68, 271, 294, 393
Price, Richard, 213

Rahner, Karl, 326, 336, 342–44
Rauschenbusch, Walter, 333–34
Reynaud, Jean, 289
Richeôme, Louys, Pl. 29
Ronsard, Pierre de, 126, 130
Rossetti, Dante Gabriel, 252–56, Pls. 50, 51
Rousseau, Jean-Jacques, 202, 212–13
Rowe, Elizabeth, 213
Royce, Josiah, 292
Rubens, Peter Paul, 177, Pl. 33
Ruether, Rosemary Radford, 335
Ruzzante (Angelo Beolco), 111

Sales, Francis de, 165–66, 269
Sandberg, Anne, 341
Savonarola, 118–19, 143, 146, 156, 163, 167
Schleiermacher, Friedrich, 257–58, 324–25, 332–33, 344
Schneider, Wilhelm, 259, 260, 290
Schwarz, Hans, 326
Scofield, Cyrus, 337
Sedgwick, Catharine, 273
Sévigné, Madame de, 169–70
Shaw, John Byam, 256, Pl. 52
Signorelli, Luca, 136–38, 157, Pls. 24, 25
Smith, Joseph, 313
Smith, Levi and Catharine, 294
Smyth, Newman, 283
Springer, Rebecca, 270, 300, 302, 340
Spurgeon, Charles, 278–79
Steere, Richard, 171
Strauss, David Friedrich, 325
Strong, Charles, 282
Suger (abbot), 79, 85
Swedenborg, Emanuel, 181–84, 186–95,

198–203, 209–11, 217–27, Pls. 36, 37, 41
influence, 182, 269, 282
Kant's critique of, 323–24

Talmage, Thomas DeWitt, 279
Taylor, Isaac, 280, 283
Teresa of Avila, 157
Thomas à Kempis, 146
Thomas Aquinas, *see* Aquinas
Tibullus, 124–26
Tillich, Paul, 327–30, 350, 351
Troubridge, Una, 312
Twain, Mark, 273

Ulyat, William Clarke, 282–83

Valla, Lorenzo, 125–28, 144

Vaughan, John, 302
Victoria (queen), 261, 263
Virgil, 16, Pl. 2

Watts, Isaac, 185–86, 189, 207–10
Weatherhead, Leslie, 276
Wesley, John, 175–76, 225, 284
Whitehead, Alfred North, 347, 348, 349
Wieland, Christoph Martin, 213
William Durandus, 79
William of Auvergne, 72
Wood, George, 268
Wood, James, 268
Woodruff, Wilford, 315

Zimmerman, Johann Baptist and
Dominikus, 1971, Pl. 39
Zwingli, 155

Abraham, 26, 27, 28, 115, 176
Acta Sanctorum, 74
Acts of the Apostles, 20, 33
Adam and Eve
  in Augustine, 63, 68
  in medieval texts, 70, 72
  in Milton, 230–33, 247
  in Blake, 240–41, 243, Pl. 45
  in Schleiermacher, 258,
  See also Eden (garden of)
Aeneid (Virgil), 16
Affective revolution, 228
African societies in heaven, 201
After Death (Weatherhead), 276
Afterlife
  Greek, 60
  Iranian, 12
  ancient Israelite, 1–7
  early Judaism 7–22
  ancient Near East, 1–3
  See also Heaven
Against the Heresies (Irenaeus), 50
Allegory, 52, 79, 218, 240
Amusement parks, 299
Ancestor worship, 3, 5–8, 10, 33
Ancrene Riwle, 107
And the Life Everlasting (Baillie), 305
Angel Children (Hill), 315
Angels
  abode of, 74, 76, 80, 82, 100, 119
  crowning and robing, 137, 140, Pls. 24–26
  gender of, 128, 137
  as guides and escorts, 27, 73, 127, 188
  performing theatre, 215–16
  playing instruments, 122
  pleasures similar to saints, 230–31
  pleasures not similar to saints, 136
  in book of Revelation, 38–41, 44
  same as saints, 188–94, 200–203, 217–21, 224, 269
  singing, 79, 143, 173
  testing worthiness of soul, 98, 117
  virginal life, 26, 54, 58
  welcoming saints, 118, 128, 132, 134, 143, 188
  working, 282
  heavenly worship, 39–41, 173, 230
Angels (Swedenborgian)
  gender of, 189, Pl. 35
  societies of, 191–92, 199–201
  as teachers and preachers, 188–89, 203
  variation in appearance, 202–03
Animals, 118, 127, 153–54
  birds, 72, 120, 127, 142, 144, 267
  cats, 193–94
  dog, 267
  ermines, 119
  insects, 153
  oxen, 153
  ponies, 153
  rabbits, 119, 133
  sheep, 119, 152
  See also Pets
Antichrist, 50
Apocalypse Explained (Swedenborg), 217
Apocalypticism, Jewish, 11–14, 25–27, 29, 34
Apostles, 76, 100, 102, 107, 148, 156, 270
Arcana Coelestia (Swedenborg), 182
Asceticism
  early Christian, 54–59, 67, 68, 108
  medieval, 73, 136
  early modern, 146, 167–77
Aucassin et Nicolette, 95, 98
Axis mundi, 143

Baptism, 36–37, 45, 90
Beatific union. *See* Lovemaking
Beatific vision
  Augustine 59, 61
  Scholasticism, 89, 90, 91, 93
  medieval mysticism, 101–2, 106
  Renaissance, 116
Beauty, 107, 160
  Augustine's views on, 56, 62–63
  Henry More on, 212
Béguines, 98, 100, 102, 107
Benedictines of Cluny, 78
Beyond the Gates (Phelps), 270–71, 299
Blessed Damozel (Rossetti), 252–56, Pls.
  50–52
Blessed Virgin Mary. *See* Mary, Blessed
  Virgin
Bodily eyes, 61, 91
Body
  astral, 285. *See also* Body, spritual
  dead
    Greek attitude toward, 18
    Jesus and, 29, 32
    Jewish attitude toward, 19, 21
    Paul and, 35
    in millenium, 52
  and spirit. *See* Spirit and matter
  spiritual
    Aquinas on, 83, 91–93
    Augustine on, 58, 61, 65
    Blake on, 240–243
    Paul on, 32–35, 44
    in Renaissance, 119, 127, 134
  union with soul, 92–93, 204–5, 240,
    317, Pl. 46
Book of Life, 43, 346, 348
Books, 300
Boredom, 59, 90, 201, 307, 309, 340
Bridal bed, 95, 101, 103
Bridal chamber, 101, 103, 106
Brides of Christ, 98, 107
Bridge, 117, 118
Buddhism, 349
Byzantine influence, 115

Catechism of the Council of Trent, 157
Cathars, 72
Cathedrals
  Gloucester, 188
  Gothic, 72, 73
  as symbol of heaven, 78–80, 84, 108
  Notre Dame 98, 109, Pl. 7

Orvieto, 136–39, Pls. 24, 25
Torcello, 115, Pl. 12
Celibacy. *See* Virginity
Cemeteries, 309–12
Charisma, in early Christianity, 31–33,
  36–37, 45, 59
Chastity. *See* Virginity
Children
  abode of, 100
  numerous in heaven, 279
  heavenly fantasies of, 153
  Holy Innocents, 133
  as symbol of innocence, 193, 201
  in Mormon spirit world, 315–16
  rearing of, 203, 221, 268, 286, Pl. 41
  soul portrayed as, 115, 186, 262, Pls.
    12, 54
  spirit children, 320
  unbaptized, 90, 167
Christ's Victory in Heaven (Fletcher), 163
Christ
  resurrected body of, 61
  as bridgegroom, 98
  as friend, 165, 271–72, 303–4, 309
  as judge, 149–50, 162, Pl. 27
  as medieval Lord, 97, 98
  sacrificial Lamb, 39, 41
  spiritualist view of, 302–3
  as spouse, 102, 106
  as True Light, 85
Christian Faith (Schleiermacher), 324
Christian Topography (Cosmas
  Indicopleustes), 80
Christianity and the Social Crisis
  (Rauschenbusch), 333
Church, as symbol of heaven, 197–98,
  343–44, Pl. 62
  See also Cathedral
Church of the New Jerusalem, 182, 234
"City Beyond, The" (Pratt), 267
City, heavenly
  in book of Revelation, 38–44
  in early Christianity, 58, 60
  in Middle Ages, 73–78, 97, 108, Pl. 4
  in Renaissance, 117–18, 130–31, 142
  early modern, 189–93, 195–96,
    Pls. 35, 36, 38
  nineteenth century, 279, 282, 300–301
  in Mormon millennium, 317
  twentieth century, 336–37
City of God (Augustine), 43, 66, 68
Clarity (*claritas*), 84

Clothing
  robes, 79, 98, 137, 140, 260, 288
  suits, 301
  See also Nakedness
Columba, 134
Community of saints; 64, 91, 93, 128–33,
    173, 211, 188–89, 286
Compendium of Revelations (Savonarola),
    118
Confessions (Augustine), 54, 57, 58
Confessions (Rousseau), 213
Conjugial Love (Swedenborg), 218
Contemplation, in heaven, 89–90
Correspondence, 280
  law of, 192–93
Cosmology
  geocentric, 80–82
  heliocentric, 152, 157, Pl. 5
Courage to Be (Tillich), 329
Creed, 149, 160, 211
Crown, 39, 98, 100, 106, 137, 139, 140

Dancing, 100, 101, 125, 128, 131, 300
Daniel (book of), 13, 52
Dead
  communicating with, 2
  feeding, 8
  prayers for, 284, 297
  unaware of death, 186, 294–95
Death
  Homeric concept of, 15, 17
  importance of, 171, 176, 178
  as state of rest, 185
Death and Eternal Life (Hick), 330
Death-Bed Visions (Barrett), 301
Decameron (Boccaccio), 122
Devil. *See* Satan
Dispensationalism, 338–40
Divine Comedy (Dante), 84–85, Fig. 5
  See also Paradiso
Dominicans, 73, 88, 96, 97, 119, 126,
    128, 133, 134

Earth
  composition of, 83
  destruction of, 172
  renewed, 23, 70–72, 115, 152, 154,
    167, 195, 198, Pl. 3
Eating and drinking, 77, 92, 111, 127,
    153, 191
Eclogues (Virgil), 123
Eden (Garden of)

heaven as, 72, 73, 108, 121, 122
  lovemaking in, 231–33, 262
  Milton on, 230–33
Education, 285–86, 287, 297, 304
  institutions of, 297, 300
Elijah, 15, 29, 100
Elucidation, 71, 72, 77, 109, 118, 137
Elysian fields, 16–18, 22, Pls. 1, 2
  in Renaissance heaven, 121, 123, 125,
    126, 127, 140
Empyrean heaven, 82–88, 85, 108,
    158–59
  changes in Renaissance, 123
Encyclopaedia of the Presbyterian Church,
    266, 279
Enlightenment, 185, 202, 205, 226, 229,
    277–78, 292, 304, 323
Enoch, 15, 18, 100
Enoch (book of), 13
Epitaphs, 268, 309–12
Eschatology, realized, 20, 332–34
Essais de Morale (Nicole), 170
Essenes, 2, 19–22, 23, 24
Eucharist, 37, 69
Exaltation, 317–19
Excrement, 92, 153
Exodus (book of), 8
Exposition of the Faith (Zwingli), 155
Eyes. *See* Bodily eyes
Ezekiel, 12, 21, 39, 49, 52

Facio, Bartolomeo, 140
Factories, 300
Fall, the, 68, 84, 233
Familiar Colloquies (Erasmus), 125
Family
  in ancient world, 2–6, 7, 10, 11
  disruption of in early Christianity,
    31–37, 44, 45
  rejection of importance in heaven, 27,
    68, 153–56, 341
  See also Meeting-again motif; Worship,
    family
Fathers, role in heaven, 221
Faust II (Goethe), 248–49
Fields of the Blest. *See* Elysian fields
*First Years of the Life of the Reedemed
    After Death* (Ulyat), 282
Fletcher, Giles, 163
Flowers. *See* Plants
Flowing Light of the Godhead (Mechthild of
    Magdeburg), 100

Forest, 268. *See also* Plants
Fountain, 121, 126, 140, 143
Franciscans, 73, 74, 78, 93
Friendship
    in Aristotle, 92
    in Augustine, 64–65
    in Scholastic thought, 92–93
    See also Christ, as friend
Fundamentalism, 336–42, 351
Funerary sculpture, 188, 309–12
Future Life or Scenes in Another World
    (Wood), 268
Future probation, 283–85
Future Recognition (Kerr), 260

Garden
    Middle Ages, 70–71, 74, 76, 100–101,
        117–23
    Renaissance, 132–33,
    early modern, 193, 198–99, 214
    nineteenth century, 300
    See also Plants
Gates Ajar (Phelps), 228, 265–68
Gender, of saints, 62–63, 189, 212, Pl. 35
Gems, 39, 76, 79, 115, 118, 153, 279
Genesis (book of), 70, 112, 233
Gilgamesh epic, 9
Gnosticism, 50–51, 59
Gods
    of sky, 3–5, 10
    of dead, 1–6
Golden Age, 121, 123, 125, 140
Golden Legend (James of Voragine), 118

Happiness, 89, 140
Harp, 39, 174, 266
Heaven
    anthropocentric, 211, 303–6
        feminine center, 163, 249, 255–56,
            272
    as home, 185–86, 264–73
    levels of, 77, 100, 101, 119,
        199–202, 285, 295, Fig. 6
    location of, 80–83, 186
    material nature of, 191–198
    merit and, 83–84, 90, 113, 115, 133,
        150–51
    modern, 183–84, 245, 274, 349–50
    loss of earthly rank, 154, 158
    as Garden of Eden restored, 118, 133,
        139, 142
    rest in, 289

skepticism about, 322–26, 349–52
    See also Afterlife
theocentric
    early Christian, 31, 43, 56, 60, 63
    medieval, 78, 92–93, 94, 97
    early modern, 145–227, 195
    nineteenth century, 287–92, 304
    twentieth century, 340–42, 342–45
Heaven (Baker), 341
Heaven and Hell (Swedenborg), 181, 186
Heaven-Life (Gregg), 281
Heaven Revised (Duffey), 297, 299
Heavenly Arcana (Swedenborg), 323
Heavenly Home (Harbaugh), 259
Heavenly Recognition (Harbaugh), 259
Hell, 3, 82, 84, 128, 131, 189, 220
Herald of Divine Love (Gertrude of
    Helfta), 102
Hezekiah (king), 7, 9
Home. *See* Heaven, as home; Mansions
Horizons of Immortality (Palmstierna),
    298
Hospitals, 299
Houses. *See* Mansions
Humanism, 134, 167, 195
Hymns
    on heavenly city, 288
    on heavenly homes, 288–99
    See also Music; Singing
*Hypnerotomachia: The Strife of Love in a
    Dream* (Colonna), 125

"If That High World" (Byron), 250
Illumination, 90
Imitation of Christ (Thomas à Kempis),
    145, 156
Immortality, 18, 211, 292–93, 329
In Heaven We Know Our Own (Blot),
    268–69
Innocence, 108, 193, 201, 221
Intellect. *See* Knowledge
Intermediate state, 284, 304
Islamic heaven, polemic against, 92–93,
    140, 153, 173
Isles of the Blest. *See* Elysian fields

Jansenism, 168–71
Jean Barois (Martin du Gard), 326
Jesus, 23–32, 44. *See also* Christ
Job, 9, 11
John (First Letter of), 89
John of Patmos, 37–44, 78, 91, 142

Josiah (king), 8, 9, 10, 11, 12
Judaism, ancient, 1–22
Judgment, Last (Final). *See* Last
    Judgment
Julie ou la nouvelle Héloïse (Rousseau),
    212–13, 248

Kingdom of God the Father, 53
Kingdom of the Messiah, 34, 51–53
Kinship, 76
    See also Family
Kissing, 102–3, 106, 126, 127, 133, 136,
    236, 240, 253
Knowledge, 89–90, 175, 209, 285–86,
    344–45
    See also Education

Language, 93, 128, 195
Large Life of Christ (Martin of Cochem),
    196
Last Judgment
    in book of Revelation, 43
    Renaissance, 115, 117, 118, 128, 137
    Blake on, 235–44, Pls. 42, 43, 48
    iconography of, 230, Pls. 7, 10, 19, 27,
      33
    lack of, 189, 295
Late Great Planet Earth (Lindsey), 339
Latter-day Saints, Church of Jesus Christ
    of, 313–22
Lawns. *See* plants
Lazarus, 27–29
Lecture halls, 300
Leisure, 127, 221–23
    activities of, 297, 299–300
Libraries, 300
Life Beyond (Millet, McConkie), 314,
    320
Life of Dante (Boccaccio), 96
Light, 79–88
Literal Commentary on Genesis
    (Augustine), 81
Liturgy. *See* Worship
Love After Death (Shaw), 300
Love
    angelic, 231–32
    in Augustine, 63–65
    in Aquinas, 90–93
    courtly, 69, 94–97, 102–7, 109
    in Dante, 85
    as juridical concept, 107
    romantic, 233–57, 258, 274–75

    in Swedenborg, 217–18
Lovemaking
    medieval texts, 95
    mysticism, 101–06
    nineteenth century, 233–57
    See also Sexual intercourse
Lowlands of Heaven (Owen), 297
Lucifer. *See* Satan
Lucinde (Schlegel), 245–46
Lust, lack of, 26, 63, 109, 128, 137, 212

Maccabees (books of), 49
Man
    Swedenborg on, 217–18, 223
Manichaeism, 55
Mansions, heavenly, 29, 195, 196, 214,
    267, 296
    in Swedenborg, 192, 201
Maria Regina Martyrum (church), 343
Marriage of Heaven and Hell (Blake), 235
Marriage
    between Christ and soul, 102–7
    between humans after death, 25–27,
      53, 249–50, 260–63, 267, 274
    as earthly social institution, 31, 44, 45,
      94, 151
    Mormon, 318–19
    in Swedenborg, 217–21
Martyrdom of Polycarp, 49
Martyrs
    abode of, 71, 100, 107
    as guides, 73
    Jewish, 40, 49
    in millenium, 48–53
    in book of Revelation, 40, 44
    special rewards for, 88, 102
    displaying scars, 62, 133
Marvels of the Otherworld (Arnoux), 214
Mary, Blessed Virgin
    abode of, 74, 76, 82, 100, 163, 197,
      214, 255, Pl. 19, 32, 33
    advocate for the dead, 160, 162
    Assumption of, 103, 136
    beauty of, 160
    feminine center of heaven 255–56,
      Pl. 52
    as medieval Lady, 96
    meeting in heaven, 61, 127, 150
    model for nuns, 10
    in paradise garden, 105, 123, Pls. 12, 17
    queen of heaven, 78, 112, 160, 214,
      Pls. 9, 11, 30, 31

as symbol of soul, 103, Pl. 8
throne, 119, 144
Mendicant orders, 73
Medieval synthesis, 88
Meditations among the Tombs (Hervey),
    176, 245
Meeting-again motif
    early Christianity, 60–61
    medieval, 94–98, Pl. 99
    Renaissance, 124–142, Pl. 22
    early modern, 155–56, 165, 173, 176,
        211–13
    nineteenth century, 233–75, Pls. 42,
        43, 44, 47, 48, 51
    twentieth century, 309–13, 315–16,
        341, Pls, 56, 57, 59
    See also Family; Marriage
Meeting Again in the Other Life
    (Schneider), 260
Messiah, 34.
    See also Kingdom of the Messiah
Methodism, 175–76
Middle Ages, 69–110, 142–44
Millenarianism
    Jewish, 26
    early Christian, 41, 52–54, 66, 67
    early modern, 184–85
    twentieth century, 317, 339–40
Mirror of Joy in Life Everlasting (Nicolai),
    195
Monasticism, 57–58, 69, 70, 72, 102,
    108, 118
Monica, 55–56
Mormon Church. *See* Latter-day Saints,
    Church of Jesus Christ of
Most Ridiculous Dialogue (Ruzzante),
    111
Mothers, role in heaven, 221
Motion
    of saints, 119, 128, 143–44, 199–210
    lack of, 91, 119, 177
Museums, 300
Music
    inspiration coming from other world,
        297
    instrumental, 215, 298
    singing as praise, 57, 79, 100, 134,
        172–175, 198
    singing for enjoyment, 125–26
    stores, 300
Mystical union. *See* Beatific union
Mysticism, early Christian, 56–57;

medieval, 94–109

Nakedness
    Augustine, 63, 77
    Elucidation, 72, 77, 108, 137
    Renaissance, 117, 122–23, 125,
        137–40, 143, Pls. 13, 15, 16, 24,
        25, 26
    Swedenborg, 201–2
    Blake, 140, Pls. 42, 43, 45, 46, 48, 49
    Kingsley, 262, Pls. 53, 54
    See also Clothing
Near-death experiences, 307, 308, 337,
    352
Necromancy, 7
Neo-orthodoxy, 342–45
Neoplatonism
    influence on early Christianity, 56, 59,
        64, 65
    influence on medieval thought, 83
Netherworld, 2–17, 23, 33
New Jerusalem. *See* City, heavenly
New Testament, 24–26
Nuns, 96, 98–107
Nursery, 286

Occupations in heaven
    art, 282, 298
    civic concerns, 230
    constructing buildings and gardens,
        198–99
    education, 209
    inventing, 267
    medicine, 282, 298
    messengers, 209, 282, 283
    missionary, 315
    music, 267, 282
    nurturing children, 203
    ruling, 208, 209, 283, 286
    studying, 282
    teaching, 209, 282, 286, 304, 315
Old Testament, 1–19
    in medieval texts, 70, 100
On Continence (Augustine), 65
On Faith and the Creed (Augustine), 58,
    61
On Love (Andreas the Chaplain), 95
*On Mary the Incomparable Virgin and
    Most Holy Mother of Gold* (Canisius),
    163
On Mortality (Cyprian), 61
On Old Age (Cicero), 60, 123, 125, 155

On Pleasure (Valla), 127
On Religion (Schleiermacher), 258
On the Supreme Felicity of Heaven (Polti), 158
The Other Life (Schneider), 290
Out of the Body (Oxenham), 296, 298–99

Paradiso (Dante), 84–85, 122–123
Pardise Lost (Milton), 230–233
Passion, 240
Pearl, 77
Peter (saint), at entrance to heaven, 118
Pets, 300
Pharisees, 2, 19–22, 23, 24
Physical Theory of Another Life (Taylor), 280
Plants, 153
    carnations, 214
    flowers, 119, 132, 152, 191, 192, 193, 196, 214, 226, 267
    fruits, 119, 132, 153, 214, 266
    herbs, 214
    laurels, 226
    lawns, 192
    lilies, 71, 118
    palms, 115, 117, 118, 142, 226
    roses, 71, 118, 194
    trees, 43, 72, 76, 193, 194, 196, 267
    violets, 118
    See also Garden
Pleasing Explanation of the Sensuous Pleasures of Paradise (Maffei), 134–35
Poimandres, 57
Prisons, 299
Process philosophy, 347–49
Progress
    on earth, 204, 205
    heavenly
        early modern, 200–210
        nineteenth and twentieth centuries, 276–306, 320–22
        lack of, 289–91
Prospects of Eternity (Lavater), 197
Psalms, 14, 15, 18, 66
Psychopannychia (Calvin), 184–85, 204
Ptolemy, 80
Publishing houses, 300
Purgatory, 39, 84, 100, 118, 183, 184, 185, 205, 291, 297
Puritanism, 169, 171–75, 229
Purity, 77

Rapture, 338–39
Reformation, 145–56, 204
Reformers
    Catholic, 156–67, 177–80
    Protestant, 145–56, 171–80
Renaissance, 108, 111–44, 230
Reproduction, 318–20
    lack of in Swedenborg, 220
Resurrection
    bodily, 12, 26, 33, 49, 51
    of nation of Israel, 11–14
    Pharisees on, 21
Retractations (Augustine), 61
Revelation (book of), 23, 37–45
    use of:
        in early Christianity, 50, 52
        in medieval sources, 73, 76, 78, 91, 92
        in Renaissance, 130, 142
        in Counter-Reformation Catholicism, 162–63
        in nineteenth century, 266, 272
        in twentieth century, 336–38
Riddle of the Universe (Haeckel), 326
Ring and the Book (Browning), 249
Rituals for the dead, ancient Israelite, 3, 5, 7
    See also Ancestor worship
Rituals. *See* Worship
River of life, 43
Robes. *See* Clothing
Roman de la Rose, 121
Romans (letter to the), 55
Romanticism, 228–29
Rose window, 85, 88, Pl. 6

Sabbath, eternal, 273
Sadducean question, 25, 27, 29, 217–18, 259, 261, 318
Sadducees, 19–21, 23, 24, 25, 27, 28, 44
Saint-Denis, 79, 85
Sainted Dead, The (Harbaugh), 259
Saints' Everlasting Rest (Baxter), 172–74, 210, 287
Satan, 38, 40–41, 43, 100, 240–41, 339, Pl. 44
Saul (king), 6
Scholasticism, 80–89, 94, 189
Science in heaven, 175, 285
Scipio's Dream (Cicero), 60, 123, 155
Sealing, 318
Seeing the Invisible (Sandberg), 341

Serious Call to a Devout and Holy Life
(Law), 174
Sermons of the Song of Songs (Bernard of
Clairvaux), 98
Service. *See* Occupations
Sexism and God-Talk (Ruether), 335
Sexual intercourse
early Christianity, 26, 59, 65
Middle Ages, 95
Milton, 231–233
Swedenborg, 219–20, 226
nineteenth century, 259–60, 262–64,
271, 274
Mormon, 318–20
See also Lovemaking; Marriage;
Sadducean question
Shades, 15
Shoel, 1–18, 23, 25, 27, 28, Figs. 1, 2, 3
See also Netherworld
Ship, 119, 121, 143
Sleeping: soul sleeps until Last Judgment,
33, 183, 189
Social Gospel, 333–34, 336
Societas perfecta (perfect society), 93
Song of Songs, 98, 102, 107, 109
"Song of the Dead" (Novalis), 247–48
Sorrows of Young Werther (Goethe), 248
Soul
character of, 17–21, 32, 56–58
Christ as lover of, 101–06
iconographic expressions of, 186–88
symbolized by queen, Pls. 8, 9
union with God, 90
Spirit and matter, 34–37, 45, 59, 61–62,
66, 91–93, 192–93, 320
Spirit world (Swedenborgian), 186,
188–89, Fig. 6
Spirits
in Swedenborgian heaven, 186–89,
191, Fig. 6
low level of development, 294–296
Spiritual Exercises (Gertrude of Helfta),
106
Spiritualism, 265, 270, 292–303
Sports, 299
Stained-glass windows, 85, 88
Steinhausen, church of, 196, 198, 216
Stoic philosophy, 166, 195
Strange Visitors (Horn), 299
Suger (abbot), 79, 85
Summa against the Gentiles (Aquinas), 88
Summa theologica (Aquinas), 88, 140

Symbolism, 240, 283, 326–32, 351
Synagogue, Jewish, 78
System of Christian Doctrine (Dorner), 283
Systematic Theology (Tillich), 329

Taboos, on dead bodies, 9
Tent, 119, 121, 143
Theater, 215–16, 298
Theocentric heaven. *See* Heaven,
theocentric
Theology, radical, 345–49
Theory of Eternal Life (Nicolai), 195
They Met in Heaven (Hepworth), 270
Throne, divine, 39, 101–3, 106, 107,
123, 340, Fig. 4
Through the Mists (Lees), 299, 301
"To Miss E.P." (Byron), 250
Tomb, empty, 35
Towards the Stars (Bradley), 302
Transfiguration, 29, 83
Travel, 195, 198
Treatise on the Love of God (de Sales), 166
Tree of Life, 43
Trinity
abode of, 82, 119, 157, 163
adoration of, 100
Troubadours, 94–96, 98

Underworld. *See* Netherworld
Universe, physical, 80–82
status after Last Judgment, 152
Urbs Hierusalem beata, 78

Virginity
of angels, 54, 58
as preferred Christian state, 31, 37, 38,
58–59, 67–8, 88
in Swedenborg, 218
Virgins
special merit in heaven, 71, 100–7, 107
as spouse and lover of Christ, 100–6,
109
Vision of God. *See* Beatific Vision
Vision of Paul, 61
Vision of Piers Plowman (Langland), 77
Visions of heaven
New Testament, 29, 34, 38–39
medieval, 74, 76, 77, 98, 100–102,
106, 290
Renaissance, 118, 133–34
Swedenborg, 182
nineteenth and twentieth centuries,

234, 236, 270, 293, 300, 313, 316, 323, 352
Vita Nuova (Dante), 96

Weddings in heaven, 218–20, 223
Whole Booke of Psalmes, 174
Wisdom (book of), 17
Witch of Endor, 6
Women
  guides in other world, 299
  medieval mystics, 98–107
  in Mormon heaven, 319
  resurrected bodies, 62–63
  Swedenborg on, 217–18, 223
Work
  in modern heaven, 225, 279–87, 296

lack of in hymns, 289
in Mormon spirit world, 315
Worship
  family, 272–73
    See also Ancestor worship
  heavenly
    in book of Revelation, 39–44
    medieval, 73, 79, 101, 106
    early modern 173–75, 176–77, 224–25
    nineteenth century, 266, 289

Yahweh-alone movement, 7, 10, 18, 20

Zoroastarian beliefs, 12–13